William Faubion's

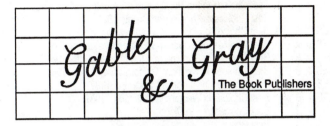

You are cordially invited
to the

BEST CHOICES
IN
NORTHERN CALIFORNIA
BAY AREA EDITION

For additional copies, write or call:
Gable & Gray, The Book Publishers
1307 West Main Street
Medford, Oregon 97501
In Oregon: 1-800-622-7753
Outside Oregon: 1-800-522-7753

Published in the U.S.A.

Gable & Gray Publishing "Best Choice Series"

Library of Congress Catalog Card Number: 86-083396
ISBN: 0-9615833-3-9   First Edition 1987

DEDICATION

This book is dedicated to these two men, the best friends and backers I have, whether by choice or by blood.

To my father, Ed Baker, whose support has been the best any father's could be; his role model is one I continually strive to emulate. And to my uncle, Stanley Baker, a fine artist and foremost antique collector and author. His critical sense and supremely well-developed taste are most remarkable.

Dec 87

Dear Bob —

Take time out of your busy life &
"smell the flowers"!

Love
Mom

III

Editor .... Carole Johnson
Associate Editor .... Jane Crawford
Associate Editor .... Stephen F. Guettermann

Author .... Tom Baker

Cover design .... Laura Kay
Cover Photography .... Tom Myers
Maps .... Impac Publications

Business Manager .... Debbie Winters
Bookkeeper .... Vicki Nelson
Secretary .... Sherrie Reynolds

FORWARD

Diversity is the watchword of California recreation and touring. Historically, geologically and culturally California offers unrivaled diversity and opportunity. The unprecedented scenery, excellent weather and cultural richness are realities that bring millions to the region every year. This magnificent land has been populated, claimed and owned by people from many nations throughout its history. They all have recognized it as a natural paradise, a place where their destinies seemed assured. At one time or another, the British, Russians, Spaniards and Mexicans claimed all or parts of this land, which was once the exclusive domain of the native Indians.

This is a land of powerful extremes and tranquility, crowds and solitude, eight lane highways coursing through metropolitan areas and wilderness trails in the High Sierra. California seemingly has a destiny of its own and we, as people, do not seem to be able to alter it, but only to experience it. That could well be its real allure. It is a never ending treasure which doles out its riches to captivate and inspire us, from gold nuggets and golden sunshine to hot springs and health spas, from fruits and vegetables to sparkling wine, from trend-setting fashions and California cuisine to cities which are a haven to free spirits, thought and expression. Perhaps we all owe a debt to California, whether or not we have ever been there. California is an adventure. Going there is like wrapping up many vacations into one.

This book, *Northern California, Bay Area Edition* includes several distinct regions. San Francisco and the Bay Area are places of discovery and cosmopolitan wonder. They offer enough in the way of food, entertainment, culture and seaside recreation to persuade the most sedate to thrill at the wonder of it all. Perhaps taking a cue from the two major rivers of the Central Valley, which flow into San Francisco and the San Francisco Bay, people and products from throughout California find their way here as well.

The rugged North Coast reminds us that Nature is still her own master and a wise one at that. Mountains step down into the sea. The trees are bigger and the wind and the coast more savage than on the Central and South coasts. Roads follow rivers which power their way through deep canyons. These wonders provide the raw materials in both substance and inspiration to artists, who create some of the most imaginative works of art to be found in the world.

The Shasta-Cascade area of Northern California is dominated by Mount Shasta, a massive 14,000 foot high mountain of volcanic origins. The rivers of the area are renown for their fishing and white water rafting. There are hundreds of square miles of mountain and forest wilderness as well as prime cross-country and downhill skiing. There are large man-made lakes at the base of the mountains which are ideal for waterskiing, houseboating, swimming, camping and fishing. Experienced guides are available from the wilderness gateway towns of Redding and Yreka who can help you design the wilderness experience for which you have been looking, be it for hunting, fishing, backpacking or rafting.

The fertile Sacramento Valley is the north part of California's Central Valley Area and extends about 150 miles north of Sacramento, the state capital. Through the valley runs the Sacramento River as well as Interstate 5, from which travelers can see one of the most important agricultural areas in the world. The valley also offers great jumping off points for the Gold Country and the High Sierra in the eastern part of the state.

In fairness to you, our adventurerous reader, this book also contains sections on Yosemite National Park and Nevada's Reno/Lake Tahoe area. These two areas draw visitors from throughout the world. Many people spend time in either or both places during a vacation which takes them to other parts of California as well.

Traveling through and learning about the "Best Choices" of the Bay Area and North California has certainly been an adventure, one I hope you will experience first hand. It never ceases to amaze me how so many different California products can find their way to the same table for the same meal from so many parts of the state. Products such as seafood, fresh water fish, steak, fruits, vegetables, breads, pastries and of course wine. To meet the people responsible for performing this juggling act has certainly been a treat. The people and this state have my thanks and admiration for allowing me to experience the sense of wonder that is uniquely California.

With so much from which to choose, you may wonder what constitutes a "Best Choice?" Among the most important variables is value. Does the customer receive an equitable return on the dollar spent? Overall quality is another basic indicator. Although the masses may patronize a given establishment, it may not be included in this book because it lacks in these important criteria. Service is also a key. This book features businesses that present a positive attitude. Pride in ownership is also considered. Invariably the best run businesses show it. Atmosphere is important. Restaurants with charm and ambiance, lodgings and shops where a certain luster presents itself are sought. Uniqueness counts as well. As you visit the establishments listed in this book, you will find that some of them are the most marvelous and the most unusual you will ever see.

Many people have helped bring this book to you. In addition to the business owners, I would also like to thank the Chambers of Commerce of just about every city mentioned herein for providing excellent advice and direction. They helped me discover people, places and things which doubtlessly would have gone unnoticed. I would also like to thank the California Office of Tourism, the State Department of Commerce and the Department of Parks and Recreation for supporting this project and making an enjoyable task even easier.

My contributions to the book include managing a dedicated team of travel writers and researching and writing about businesses in the East Bay from San Leandro south to Milpitas, as well as San Jose and parts of San Francisco. The great love of discovery, of meeting some of the finest people in the world and of writing about "Best Choices" was shared with me by others to whom I owe a special thanks.

First I would like to mention Scott Williams, who covered Los Gatos and down the coast from Santa Cruz to the Monterey Peninsula. Scott loves skiing and the outdoors. He is a double major in English and Journalism from Chico State and came to us with a background as a newspaper reporter and recreation columnist.

Nena McKinzie provided the sections on Oakland and Alameda, Crockett, San Pablo and others, as well as parts of San Francisco. Nena's exuberance was always appreciated; a byproduct of her lust for travel and adventure. With roots that go back three generations in California, her knowledge of the Golden State is most extensive.

Brian Wagner contributed the information on the lower Peninsula portions, from Redwood City south through Silicon Valley and a section of the North Coast. He hopes to get back to writing screenplays now that this book is finished. He also enjoys baseball, sixties rock, conversation and spending time with his son, Ross.

I have Duke Roberts to thank for compiling information on the Monterey Peninsula from San Mateo north to San Francisco. Duke is a consummate aesthete whose selections were always well researched. A professional musician and music teacher, Duke also enjoys racquetball, tennis, windsurfing and golf.

John McCurry pitched in with Marin County. A native Californian, he has traveled extensively throughout the Northwest. His strong background in people-related services primed him for the search and discovery needed to complete such a project.

Berkeley and part of Walnut Creek were handled by Jeff Jennings. Jeff is a professional model, one whose poise, appearance and good taste made him equal to his research tasks.

Another contributor was Lynne Paradise, who worked in Novato and portions of Marin County. Thank you, Lynne, for a great job.

My warmest appreciation goes out to our publisher, Bill Faubion, the originator of Gable & Gray's "Best Choice" series, for the countless hours he personally spent in this book's production and for offering an avenue for us to achieve our goals. In addition to Bill, there's the editorial staff: Carole Johnson the Managing Editor, and Jane Crawford and Steve Guetterman, the Associate Editors, who added polish, humor and insight to this book, and who miraculously have pulled it all together in spite of "Murphy's" having camped in their office. Thanks to their patience the computers and too-new software weren't chucked thru the plateglass windows, the book was completed, and new experts in desk top publishing have emerged.

Special kudos are in order for Tam Moore. Tam combined experience with mountains of information to write the county and city introductions and attractions listed in each section. Other wordsmithing was done by Joe Keifer, Roy Scarbrough, Liz Redler, Sherry O'Sullivan, Chris Adams, Joan Wood and Betty Pennington. Through wordplays and a sincere desire to capture the unique character of the hundreds of businesses listed herein, these writers have accomplished our top priorities: to give you information not only on "Best Choices," but, when faced with the daunting challenge of really deciding where to go, giving enough information to help you make that choice.

No matter what choices you make, we wish for you this -- enjoy!

HOW TO USE THIS BOOK

The Best Choices in Northern California, Bay Area Edition is a complete travel guide. You will find information on best businesses to patronize as well as parks, events, museums and maps to help you plan your itinerary. You can also use the book as a shopping guide. Clothing stores, gift shops, candy stores, restaurants, accommodations and many more categories are used to describe the businesses in detail so you can choose those which match your needs and desires.

This book is set up with the counties of the Bay Area and Northern California listed in alphabetical order. Each county section begins with an introduction highlighting that county's major highways and cities, topography and a smattering of history. Following the county introductions are pieces about points of interest within the county which relate to such things as attractions on public lands, state parks, museums and historic areas.

A profile of the major cities in each county is next, with information about the "Best Choices" of that city listed alphabetically by category then by name. The page on which each of these headings appear within each county section is listed in the Table of Contents. The Index in the back of the book is your easy-to-use guide for finding on what page specific attractions and businesses are listed. If you would like to have a day adventure and good food, try one of our self-guided tours listed at the end, or within, each chapter. The tours also give you a quick reference as to an outstanding feature associated with selected businesses.

As you read about the "Best Choices," you will often find the message "See special invitation in the Appendix" at the end of the copy. Turn to the back of the book to find the invitations listed city by city as they are in each chapter. The invitations are real! The merchants are inviting you to save at their establishments. Each invitation is for money off or a free gift with purchase. So, use your scissors and cut out your invitations to the "Best Choices" of the San Francisco Bay and Northern California. Remember, not every "Best Choice" was found, so if you find one you like that is not mentioned, please write to us so we can include it in a future edition.

Many of the state parks included in this book include prime attractions and facilities. In addition to the information supplied herein about the parks, helpful publications are offered by the California Department of Parks and Recreation. To get an updated list of available publications or to order them call (916) 445-6477. Phone numbers to call in regards to other attractions and points of interest are usually listed which each individual entry.

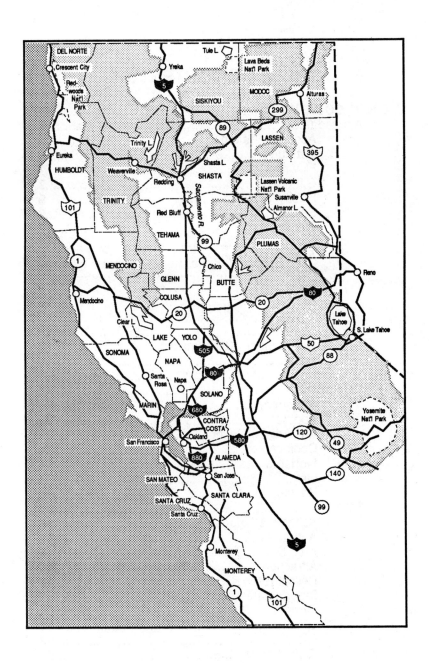

IX

TABLE OF CONTENTS

XI

XVIII

XXII

XXIII

ALAMEDA COUNTY

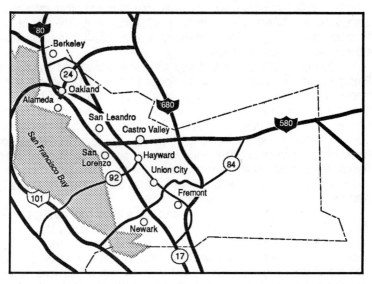

This 736 square mile East Bay county is a land of contrasts. Heavy industrial plants and shipyards near the bay are replaced inland with some seasonal grazing and agriculture. On the flat lands, from the bay shore to the foothills, some intense farming continues, most of it in competition with spreading urbanization. The county line, drawn by an act of the legislature in 1853, from parts of Contra Costa and Santa Clara counties, starts just north of Albany and heads for the hills to the east, then jogs south, taking in what were large feudal ranch holdings during the Spanish and Mexican administrations. The bay makes up Alameda's western boundary. Oakland is the most populous city in the county of about 1,200,000 residents.

Cities follow cities south along the Nimitz Freeway (state highway 17), which links Oakland to San Jose. The county line cuts through at Coyote River, north of Milpitas. The massive Berkeley Hills are a string of parks, providing panoramic views to the east and west. A series of tunnels, the oldest drilled more than fifty years ago, breech the hills east of Oakland, taking state highway 24 east to Walnut Creek. The route, now paralleled by trains of the Bay Area Rapid Transit (BART), opened small valley communities to urbanization by commuters with jobs in the cities.

Alameda County

San Lorenzo Creek, which empties into the bay near the city of the same name, provides one of two natural east-west passes through the San Jose Mountains, a continuation of the Berkeley Hills. Alameda Creek provides the southern most pass, leading state highway 84 in a winding path up Niles Canyon and on to Livermore past the pioneer Vallecitos Nuclear Center. The Livermore Valley includes walnut orchards, vineyards and other agricultural operations fitted to hot, dry summers. I-680, which climbs the hills out of Fremont, now reaches the interior valley much more quickly than either of the older roadways through the passes.

Don Luis Peralta, who soldiered with the troops at San Francisco's Presidio during the final years of the Spanish period, established a huge rancho in what is now northern Alameda County. Albany Hill was the north limit of a holding which extended south to where San Leandro Creek enters the bay. Peralta's four sons divided up the rancho. Their lands now include the cities of Oakland, Berkeley, and five smaller municipalities. The name "la Alameda" or grove of poplar trees in Spanish, refers to the country south of Peralta's Rancho San Antonio. That name was given to the county created in 1853, and was voted as the name of the city of Alameda the same year. Rancho de la Alameda was located where Fremont now stands.

Alameda County cast its lot for regionalism years ago, participating in the East Bay Municipal Utility District, popularly called "East Bay MUD" by its customers. Domestic water for the county's cities and those of much of Contra Costa County to the north, is drawn from the Tuolomne River in the Sierras, then piped to storage reservoirs which dot the hills of Alameda county providing dozens of recreation areas. East Bay MUD also pioneered regional waste water treatment as part of a program to clean up the waters of San Francisco Bay.

Eucalyptus, a tree imported from Australia by early farmers, has forested much of the hills of the East Bay. During the Spanish land grant days, there were redwood trees on the west slope; most were cut into lumber for construction of buildings in early San Francisco. Interior valleys have some California live oak and other trees hardy enough to survive prolonged dry periods each year. This country is ripe with paleontological history of a lusher time. Bones of a mammoth were discovered near Irvington and dated back 500,000 years to the time of a fresh water lake. The fossils are on display now at the University of California paleontology museum in Berkeley.

ATTRACTIONS

Sunol Regional Wilderness, in the hills south of Scotts Corner, gives a feel for what this country was like in the time of the Spanish ranchos. Cattle still graze here. Hiking trails crisscross the land and camping is permitted.

East Bay Regional Park District provides naturalists to lead weekend sorties. Ohlone Regional Wilderness, now undeveloped, lies between Sunol and Del Valley parks.

Located just south of Livermore, **Del Valle Regional Park** is part of another old rancho. Its 4,249 acres surround a 750 acre lake with fishing and boating facilities. A tour boat operates during part of the year.

The city of Berkeley's **Tilden Regional Park,** located in the hills to the east offers an 18-hole championship golf course, steam train rides, and the University of California botanical garden which specializes in the flora of Northern California displayed by geographic location. Hiking trails abound.

Regional shoreline areas are designated on the beach at Hayward, and at San Leandro Creek right in Oakland, where a fishing pier, boating and recreation areas are part of a 680-acre park.

Chabot Regional Park in the Oakland hills includes horses for rent, and interconnects with hiking paths to other parks along the ridge top. A 73-site RV and tent camp overlooks a lake. There is an 18-hole golf course. **Redwood Regional Park** is a northerly extension for backpackers and horseback riders traveling the East Bay Skyline National Trail.

Sibley Volcanic Preserve, a bit further north on the ridge-top road, features a self-guiding trail that helps you to understand some of the geologic past of these hills.

Just at the toll plaza for Dumbarton Bridge west of Fremont is **Coyote Hills Regional Park,** where the Indian shell mound is dated as 2,300 years ago. The adjacent Indian village has been reconstructed.

Historic farm equipment is assembled at **Garin Regional Park** east of Hayward. This adjoins the **Dry Creek Pioneer Park,** which also honors early settlers in the East Bay hills.

Ardenwood Regional Preserve in Fremont includes 168 acres around the Patterson mansion, an historical farming area where techniques of the 1870s are demonstrated.

Undeveloped, above the University of California stadium in Berkeley, is **Claremont Canyon Preserve**. The timbered hillsides provide a hiker's link to trails along the ridge line.

3

Mission Peak, and adjoining **Monument Peak** east of Fremont and Mission San Jose, are a natural reserve with pedestrian and horse trails affording views of the flat lands below.

The **Alameda Creek Quarries** in the Niles district of Fremont provide fishing, bird watching and hiking with access to the **Alameda Creek Regional Trail** leading east. Enter from Niles Community Park at the foot of T street.

Cull Canyon and **Don Castro** regional recreation areas east of Hayward, on tributaries of San Lorenzo Creek, provide swimming and hiking opportunities just a few minutes from urban areas.

For more information on the regional recreation attractions call East Bay Regional Parks District at 531-9300. Bus transportation is available in much of the county through AC Transit. Call 6753-3535 for information on their urban routes.

Alameda

This island, lying next to East Oakland is about six and one-half miles long, created by a tidal canal dug in 1902 to provide a deep draft harbor for Oakland. One of the oldest cities on the bay, Alameda was the retirement port for many sailors. Shrubs from many parts of the world were planted here by the sea captains who made their home on what was part of the 1820 Spanish land grant run by the Peralta family.

Developers W.W. Chipman and Gideon Aughinbaugh bought out the interest of one of Peralta's sons and developed the peninsula as a farm supplying the San Francisco residents. With about 100 people living here full time in 1853, the town was created and the name Alameda chosen by a vote of the people. Among its early residents were writers Jack London and Mark Twain. The Alaska salmon fleet once made its winter port here. Alameda Naval Air Station, completed in 1942, is home port for some of the largest aircraft carriers. Shore facilities include an aircraft rework plant. Modern water-related industries thrive here, too.

The city's 75,000 residents live in a combination of housing from modern condominiums at water side to many neighborhoods of charming Victorian homes dating from its days as home to many seafarers before the turn of the century.

4

Attractions

The **Alameda Historical Museum** at 1327 Oak Street has photographs of the city's development and other displays. The society which sponsors the museum is active in efforts to preserve the city's many Victorian homes.

Downtown Alameda is involved in a preservation of the old Main Street buildings. Webster and Park street shopping districts feature conversions of historic buildings to boutiques, restaurants and other retail ventures. The Versailles and Morton stations, now minus their railroads, also sparkle with new shops.

Alameda Municipal Golf offers a total of forty-five holes in a multiple layout complete with driving range.

An historic bay shore recreation area on the Alameda Peninsula, **Robert W. Crown State Beach** is now operated by the regional park district. A **Visitor Center at Crab Cove** provides information on creatures of the tide pools and shore from March through November. Naturalists are on duty weekends.

Lincoln Park on High Street has a monument commemorating the site of an Indian shell pile once fourteen feet high and over 400 feet across. Developers leveled it in 1908, taking the shells for road construction on Bay Farm Island. The remains of about 450 Indians were found in the mound.

The inner harbor waterfront is dotted with yacht clubs and other moorages including berths for some U.S. Coast Guard vessels based on nearby Government Island, a 100-acre island, created in 1916, by dredge spoils from work on the estuary channels. **Government Island Administration Building** features frescos from a 1930's Works Progress Administration art project depicting the history of road building.

For further information contact the **Alameda Chamber of Commerce,** City Hall room 101, 2263 Santa Clara Avenue, telephone (408) 552-0414.

Accommodations

GARRATT MANSION
900 Union Street
Alameda, CA 94501
Tel. (415) 521-4779
Hrs: check in 3:00 p.m., check out 11:00 a.m.
American Express card is accepted.

Alameda is the best kept secret in the East Bay. Garratt Mansion on the other hand, located at Union Street and Clinton, is a highly celebrated Colonial Revival residence just ten miles from Berkeley or San Francisco, and minutes from the Oakland Airport. This historical home is owned by Mr. and Mrs. Royce Gladden and has been lovingly restored.

The Garratt Mansion was constructed in 1893; there were various alterations done in 1903, and full restoration began in 1979. The interior of the home represents one of the most outstanding examples of workmanship and style of the period. Oak panelling, chandeliers, matte glazed tiles, Jacobean-style turned balusters, ornate walnut molding, faceted crystal windows accentuated with a ribbon design in cranberry glass, built-in china closets with beveled glass doors, and numerous fireplaces with their original mantles.

At the Mansion, Royce takes care of the day-to-day caretaking, and Betty creates a stress-free environment for her guests. For example, guests may eat their breakfast in bed, or in the dining room downstairs. Need privacy? Curl up with a book in one of the windowseats. Want to bike ride around the Alameda Island? Betty will provide you with bicycles for touring and advise you on the sightseeing spots.

With beaches nearby and a shopping center just three blocks away, the Garratt Mansion makes for an ideal "get away from it all" bed and breakfast in the East Bay.

Antiques

TAMMY'S ANTIQUES, 1505 Park Street, Alameda, California. You'll find Victorian furniture, silver, jewelry, paintings, hard-to-find, and one-of-a-kind items at Tammy's.

Flowers

LYN'S FLOWER SHOPPE
2524 Santa Clara Avenue
Alameda, CA 94501
Tel. (415) 522-1555
Hrs: Mon. - Sat.   9:00 a.m. - 6:00 p.m.
            Sunday   9:00 a.m. - 5:30 p.m.

Elegance and sophistication, mixed with a pinch of glittering magic, make Lyn's Flower Shoppe a fantasy land of beautiful creations.
From the traditional and classic, to the exotic and tropical, you will find a huge selection of fresh flowers assuring that your arrangements will be lovely. A full service FTD and Teleflora member, Lyn's offers unusual, stunning dried and silk arrangements. Gift baskets with beer, wine and champagne are made to order and unusual gift ideas such as award winning dolls and lovely fairies by Cindy McClure will hold you spellbound.
Complimentary gift wrapping, fresh greens and floral preservatives always accompany your flowers; just an indication of the friendly, helpful service you can count on at Lyn's Flower Shoppe, a "Best Choice" in Alameda.

Gift

ALAMEDA COFFEE AND TEA MERCHANT
2306 Central Avenue
Alameda, CA 94501
Tel. (415) 521-1521
Hrs: Mon. - Fri.   8:00 a.m. - 6:00 p.m.
            Saturday   8:00 a.m. - 5:00 p.m.
            Sunday   9:00 a.m. - 5:00 p.m.

Stopping off for a fresh cup of coffee is one thing, experiencing the Alameda Coffee and Tea Merchant shop is truly another! Showcased in a charming and adorable Victorian house that's nestled within flower-bedecked grounds; this is a shop which is a true representation of the proprietors collecting together the best that can be offered for their customers.
Richard and Peggy Williams, the owners, have gathered an impressive array of art and art gifts for your enjoyment; nearly all are handmade, and represent the best efforts of craftsmen from all over the world. You'll see Japanese Mingei craftware, jewelry, scarves, shawls, carpets and American and South American folk art.

The selections of coffee, tea and desserts are quite extensive. Lunch is served everyday between 11:00 a.m and 2:00 p.m. A large outdoor deck is provided for your outdoor dining enjoyment, and for your reading pleasure a rack with current newspapers is supplied. Lunch specialties are a variety of sandwiches and soups. Do try the Armenian. Superb!

If a chocoholic lurks within, you've come to the right place. The choice of fine chocolates and candies is selective, and includes Godiva. You will also find a wide variety of wines, crackers, coffee beans, cookbooks, stuffed animals and Crabtree & Evelyn soaps to take home for your enjoyment or as gifts for those special people in your life.

So, treat yourself the next time you're in Alameda...visit the Alameda Coffee and Tea Merchants.

THE GASLIGHT EMPORIUM
1708 Lincoln Avenue
Alameda, CA 94501
Tel. (415) 522-1900
Hrs: Tue. - Sat. 11:00 a.m. - 6:30 p.m.

Step into the past and the enchantment of gift buying from days gone by! Old fashioned gifts and antiques with charm. Owners Tom and Tommie Viers have made The Gaslight Emporium a place of learning, as well as a place to buy. A "tour" of the store will reveal rare antique display cases, cash registers and other accoutrements from stores of yesteryear.

What will you find? Handmade chocolates from antique molds, truffles made with real gold leaf, elaborate hand made Victorian candy boxes, baskets, antique gimcracks, clothing and jewelry, antique style dolls and stuffed animals, homemade jams and jellies. Many items are imported from Europe and the Orient.

The Gaslight Emporium offers classes on making authentic Christmas ornaments and decorations from the Victorian era. So, treat yourself to the experience offered...for a unique gift, or just a little something to lift your spirits and take you away from the fast pace of today's world; visit Alameda's Gaslight Emporium...a touch of yesteryear.

GREAT STUFF
1333 Park Street
Alameda, CA 94501
Tel. (415) 522-8886
Hrs: Mon. - Sat.   10:00 a.m. - 6:00 p.m.
         Thursday   till 8:00 p.m.
MasterCard, Visa and American Express are accepted.

Cheryl Heihn, the owner of Great Stuff, has done her best to fill her store with items that other shops don't have. From the silly to the strange and funny, it can all be found at Cheryl's store.

Cheryl has selected cards for every imaginable occasion, plus wrapping paper, balloons, novel pens and pencils, t-shirts, plush stuffed animals, party favors galore, gag gifts, funny TP and an "adults only" section for the adventurous.

This is a place to have fun and browse through all the Great Stuff that Cheryl stocks in this "Best Choice" store.

Hobby Shop

ALAMEDA HOBBY, 1410 Park Street, Alameda, California. A full line hobby shop featuring radio controled model planes, boats, cars and trains.

Salon

NAIL TREND/ISLAND TANNING
2329 Santa Clara Avenue
Alameda, CA 95051
Tel. (415) 522-2414
Hrs: Mon. - Sat. 9:00 a.m. - 6:00 p.m.

When you put on a pair of shorts do you find it necessary to wear sunglasses because of the glare reflecting off of your legs? Do you keep yourself from going to beaches and other similar public places because of the lack of a tan? If so, you're in luck, because problems like these can be pleasantly taken care of at Nail Trend/Island Tanning.

Cast your inhibitions away after just a few visits to the tanning booths at Nail Trend/Island Tanning. Just fifteen minutes in their private tanning rooms can equal two hours in the sun! You no longer need sticky oils or sandy towels to get a beautiful golden tan. But that's not all, Nail Trend/Island Tanning is also a full service salon for both men and women. Here you can get

9

perms, cuts, manicures, pedicures, ear piercing, cosmetic touches and much more.

This shop is quite a confidence builder. After a visit here you can look the way you've always wanted. So, make an appointment, get a nice tan and take advantage of the wonders a salon can provide. When you leave it will be with a much more positive attitude about yourself.

Textiles

FIELD'S FABRICS
1229 Park Street
Alameda, CA 94501
Tel. (415) 865-7171
Hrs: Mon. - Sat. 9:30 a.m. - 5:00 p.m.

When a hobby becomes a highly successful business, you know you're not only receiving a quality product, you're reaping the immeasurable benefits of an inspired individual who loves what they do.

Marion Fields fits into that special category. Her shop, Field's Fabrics, reflects her background in art and clothing. She stocks fabrics purchased directly from the finest mills; to provide a panorama of choices in color and design.

Field's features their own drapery and upholstery workroom. Bring a carpet sample from your home and receive expert advice to assist you in creating the look you love to live with; from authentic Victorian to crisp contemporary. There are draperies to suit your fancy; from balloon shades, Victorian swags to Levelors. A member of the staff will make an appointment to meet with you in your home to measure for the draperies, slipcovers, bedspreads, upholsters, and more.

Home is where the heart is, as well as being ones castle...Field's Fabrics can help you create an environment of color and texture to reflect your own unique personality and needs.

So, you are staying in Alameda, but have someone special back home for whom you would like to find something unique? Try the someone special gift tour. A stop at any of the restaurants listed will be a special gift to yourself.

SOMEONE SPECIAL GIFT TOUR			
a.m.	Lyn's Flower Shoppe	Best champagne basket	Ala/Gift
a.m.	Field's Fabrics	Best home decor	Ala/Tex
a.m.	Great Stuff	Best party gift/card	Ala/Gift
a.m.	Coffee and Tea Merchant	Best snack	Ala/Gift
a.m.	Gaslight Emporium	Best antique	Ala/Gift
p.m.	Lyal Nickals	Best crystal	SanL/Flor
p.m.	Horatio's	Best late lunch	SanL/Rest
p.m.	Family Hobby	Best hobby shop	SanL/Hob
For your "Best Choice" of dinner:			
p.m.	Enrico's	Best food & dance	SanL/Rest
p.m.	The Blue Dolphin	Best Bay view	SanL/Rest

Berkeley

The town, now a city of 106,000 people which blurs into the urban reach of its neighbor Oakland, was formed in May, 1866 by trustees of what was then the College of California. The flagship institution of the University of California is located here, tucked next to the hills, and its campus includes a famous art museum, several theaters, and other public attractions. About 8,000 people are on the university faculty.

The name Berkeley was proposed to honor George Berkeley, an English bishop who emigrated to American in 1728 (with the aim of starting a college) and penned a poem which opened, "Westward the course of empire takes its way...." The resulting campus has over 1,600 acres. The city around it is famed for its sometimes radical politics and a tough rent-control ordinance crafted to help students find affordable housing.

Attractions

Lawrence Radiation Laboratory located east of the University campus is where Nobel prize-winner Glenn Seaborg identified plutonium in 1941, and Ernest O. Lawrence invented the cyclotron or atom-smasher.

The **Strawberry Canyon Botanical Garden** includes over 5,000 rare varieties of rhododendrons and countless other plants growing in settings arranged by geographic area. It is located above the University's Memorial Stadium, or can be reached from Tilden Regional Park in the Berkeley Hills.

Plays are staged year around by the **Berkeley Repertory Theater** at 2025 Addison Street. For the playbill and reservations, call 841-6108.

Berkeley Marina on the bay is home for a large fleet of charter fishing boats. There is a public pier where you can fish without a license. **Aquatic Park**, next to the marina, has a salt-water lake for water skiing and model boat racing.

The **Takara Sake** plant is located at 708 Addison street. They offer tours and tasting hours from 12:00 noon to 6:00 p.m. daily. Both sake and plum wine are produced here.

For further information, contact the **Berkeley Chamber of Commerce**, 1834 University Avenue, telephone 845-1212, or the **University of California** information number, 642-5215.

Accommodations

THE BERKELEY MARINA MARRIOTT
200 Marina Boulevard
Berkeley, CA 94710
Tel. (415) 548-7920
      (800) 228-9290

Located on the beautiful Berkeley Marina overlooking the San Francisco Bay, the Berkeley Marina Marriott is conveniently located midway between San Francisco, the wine country and the East Bay. In addition to its central location, the spacious and attractive Berkeley Marina Marriott offers a variety of beautiful accommodations, a full scale restaurant and lounge and all the other amenities you expect to find in a hotel bearing the Marriott name.

With over 375 rooms, the Berkeley Marina Marriott is well equipped to handle the busiest seasons. Expansive, handsome guest rooms offer a stunning view of the bay and the San Francisco skyline, while elegant, roomy suites are available in both bi-level and living room styles; perfect for entertaining guests. All rooms feature color TV, AM/FM radio, in-room movies and alarm clocks.

Fine dining is only a few steps from your room at the Marriott's first class Bay Grille and Lounge. Here, you can dine in casual splendor surrounded by a gorgeous bay view. The Bay Grille offers a broad variety of delicious specialties, with an emphasis on fresh seafood and pasta. With several menus from which to choose , the options range from a light fare of seafood salad with fresh greens, bay shrimp and Dungeness crab, to pastas such as fettucine with tender strips of chicken in a garlic cream sauce. Other choices include grilled chicken, fish and grilled Pacific prawns with tomato salsa and Polenta. The Bay Lounge is a fine spot to relax with a glass of California premium wine or a light cocktail while enjoying the spectacular moonlit bay.

The Berkeley Marina Marriott makes an ideal location with fifteen meeting and banquet rooms to accommodate 5 to 500 people. The new Concierge Level offers the exclusivity of a private club, it boasts the Executive Lounge for business meetings and makes available such niceties as complimentary continental breakfast, a fully stocked honor bar with cocktail hors d' oevres and late night desserts. Busy executives can make use of the hotel courtesy car, which shuttles to and from the Oakland International Airport and the Berkeley BART station. Commercial limousine service is available to and from San Francisco International Airport.

Additionally, the Marina Marriott features a fitness center complete with lap pool, exercise room, sauna and jacuzzi. For a beautiful day relaxing on the bay, motor yachts and sailboats can be chartered from the Marriott's 700 foot dock.

Whatever your traveling needs may be, the Berkeley Marina Marriott will accommodate you at this "Best Choice" in Berkeley.

THE SHATTUCK HOTEL
2086 Allston
Berkeley, CA 94794
Tel. (425) 845-7300

Out of the rubble left by the 1906 earthquake rose what is still one of the best East Bay hotels, The Shattuck.

The Shattuck was the first hotel to be built after the earthquake to meet the demands of discriminating travelers. The Shattuck continues to offer elegance to today's discriminating travelers. Although remodeled, it retains a turn of the century charm with touches like antique desks, and 1900 vintage night stands in rooms accented with lace curtains and bedding. Fruit baskets and floral arrangements lend even more warmth. The new bar and grill offers a full range of tasty fish, meat and poultry entrees.

So if the tremblers of the highway get you down, free yourself from the after-shocks in comfort and style at this "Best Choice".

Apparel

ANDREA
2938 College Avenue
Berkeley, CA 94705
Tel. (415) 848-4191

Andrea's spacious, beautifully decorated boutique has pale peach walls, two enormous skylights and natural wood dressing rooms that are just an indication of owner Andrea Faber's discriminating taste. Andrea carefully chooses fabrics and styles that appeal to a wide variety of clientele.

An array of apparel and accessories in natural fibers, such as cotton and leather, can be found in this shop. Andrea carries stylish dresses, cozy sweaters and a wide variety of pants and shirts. One of the more popular items are casual leather jackets at moderate prices. A collection of hard to find accessories including a huge selection of socks and stockings, purses and travel bags, as well as belts, stunning sunglasses and fun straw and fabric hats are available to complement any outfit. After you have assembled your new look, finish it off with a pair of new earrings.

Andrea's goal is to provide a fun place to experiment with creative clothing. Her repeat customers are a sign that she has achieved this goal and become a "Best Choice" in the Bay Area.

DRESSING UP
1224 Salano Avenue
Berkeley, CA 94706
Tel. (415) 527-5540
Hrs: Mon. - Sat. 11:00 a.m. - 6:00 p.m.
Visa, MasterCard and American Express are accepted.

Since 1980, Marlene Dietrich lookalike Donna Charcowicz has been helping adventurous souls create their own fantasy clothing. Her "unique boutique" features the most elegant, eclectic mix of contemporary and vintage consignment clothing and accessories available. Indeed, the motto of Dressing Up is "if you can't find it anywhere else, you will find it here."

Contributions hail from the closets of the locally famous, the internationally renowned and everything in between. All of the clothing in the store can be bought or rented at extremely reasonable prices. Donna carries a top notch collection of antique hats, broaches, pearl necklaces, earrings and bracelets. Customer service is personal and attentive; your fantasy is taken seriously here! Stop by Dressing Up and give them the blueprint of your fantasy. They will do all they can to help you construct the look you desire.

(See special invitation in the Appendix.)

Art

ROBERT BRUCE OF BERKELEY
2910 Telegraph Avenue
Berkeley, CA 94705
Tel. (415) 845-7424
Hrs.: Mon.-Sat. 10:00 a.m.-5:00 p.m.

When you think Japanese, you think imports, right? When you think imports, you think Toyota, Honda and Datsun?
Robert Bruce of Berkeley will change that for you. Instead. you'll be walking out thinking Kosuga and Karhu--artists whose works Robert Bruce brings to you from Japan. A full seventy-five percent of the merchandise in this shop is Japanese art and crafts, some new, all of it rare. This sun-bathed showroom does justice to the art that includes hard wood chests, graceful baskets, pottery, bamboo and intricate wood block prints.
But if your taste looks more to the west, there's also California made crafts, as well as china ware from England, such as Spode and Wedgewood. New, or old, east or west, Robert Bruce has something of each.

(See special invitation in the Appendix.)

Brewery

TRIPLE ROCK BREWERY & ALEHOUSE
1920 Shattuck Avenue
Berkeley, CA 94704
Tel. (415) 843-2739
Hrs: Mon. - Sun. 11:30 a.m. - 12:00 midnight

If you peel away Berkeley's facade of superior restaurants, hotels and the university, and look beneath the surface, you will find an uncomplicated, friendly town characterized by an unpretentious concern for quality. It is fitting then, that in such a friendly, uncomplicated town one should find an establishment which serves a unique, quality beer in a friendly setting with simple but superior cuisine. The Roaring Rock Brewery is such a place.

This is Berkeley's first brewpub (a saloon which houses their own microbrewery and serves their own brews), it is the creation of brothers Reid and John Martin. Their aim was to capture the spirit of the brewery houses of the 1800's and still serve a meal worthy of their location in Berkeley's "Gourmet Ghetto;" they've accomplished both.

Reid's the brewmaster at Roaring Rock and he's achieved quite a following for his product. On any given afternoon or evening you can sample one of three English-style ales: Pinnacle Pale Ale, which is a light, American-type beer; Red Rock Ale, a heavier and hoppier brew, and Black Rock Porter, a thick beer with a higher proportion of dark roasted barley. All three brews are produced a few feet from the bar in the custom designed, glass-encased microbrewery. The gleaming, state-of-the-art equipment sits comfortably juxtaposed beside the dark, polished wood paneling and pine plank floors that give the Rock it's casual ambiance. It's an atmosphere perfectly suited to good beer and good food--the other half of this establishment's appeal.

For lunch and dinner, the tavern offers thick, spicy soups, sandwiches stuffed with fresh meats, cheeses and vegetables, and tasty homemade pizza. Try the garden sandwich: fresh vegetables and cream cheese stuffed between pieces of seeded baguette--a real treat. The black bean chili is a thick, smoky, flavorful example of the many fine soups the Roaring Rock offers.

The hearty, delicious food, the fresh, tasty brews and the friendly, service-oriented staff help to make the Roaring Rock Brewery a healthy slice of the uncomplicated, unceasing quality that is Berkeley.

Coffee

PEET'S COFFEE AND TEA
2124 Vine Street
Berkeley, CA 94709
Tel. (415) 841-0564
Hrs: Mon. - Sat.   9:00 a.m. - 6:00 p.m.
         Sunday   10:00 a.m. - 6:00 p.m.
and,

2916 Domingo Avenue   4050 Peidmont Avenue
Berkeley, CA 94705   Oakland, CA 94611
Tel. (415) 843-1434   Tel. (415) 655-3228

899 Santa Cruz Ave.   2156 Chestnut Street
Menlo Park, CA 94025   San Francisco, CA 94123
Tel. (415) 325-8989   Tel. (415) 931-8302

3419 California Street   88 Brock-Morton
San Francisco, CA 94118   Mill Valley, CA 94941

If you find the aroma of freshly roasted coffee irresistible, make your way to Peet's Coffee and Tea. Here is where your tastebuds can savor the java delights of Arabia, Colombia and Sumatra, just to name a few of the places where Peet's coffees originate. You can sample a brew, or pick up a pound or two.

And, if coffee is not your cup of tea..well there's that too. Peet's offers quite an impressive selection of fine teas from which to choose. Specialty teas like Golden Dragon Oolong, Lion Mountain Keemun and the unparalleled Yin Hao Jasmine are exquisite teas available only at Peet's.

To accompany the best of coffee and tea, Peet's selection of brewing devices ranging from tea pots to home espresso machines are also available. So, if you find yourself addicted to high quality coffee and teas, don't fret, Peet's friendly and knowledgeable staff will set you up with just the right brew and the right equipment. Your palate will love you. Two new stores, San Francisco - California Street and Mill Valley, will be open Fall of 1987.

Furniture

SLATER/MARINOFF & CO.
2956 College Avenue
Berkeley, CA 94705
Tel. (415) 548-2001
Hrs: Mon.-Sat.   10:00 a.m. - 5:30 p.m.
       Sunday   12:00 noon - 5:00 p.m.

Furniture for the whole family? You bet! Slater/Marinoff is the kind of store that caters to individuals, not just the buying public. Over the years owners Patsy Slater and Susan Marinoff have built a reputation for offering personal decorating advice, and furniture with high marks for, quality, design and function.

Decorating advice is their specialty, so customers are counseled, rather than merely sold merchandise. They take into consideration, the needs of everyone in the family by providing everything from a comfortable resting place for the hard-working adult to fashionable children's furniture that is safe and durable.

So with good advice and good selection, this is a place where you can easily slip into something more comfortable.

Gift, Sundry, Knick-knacks

THE GEM GALLERY AT BILL'S TRADING POST
2945 College Avenue
Berkeley, CA 94705
Tel. (415) 841-1615
Hrs: Mon. - Sat.   9:30 a.m. - 5:30 p.m.
      Sunday   12:00 noon - 5:00 p.m.
Visa, MasterCard and American Express are accepted.

The Gem Gallery at Bill's Trading Post is one of the most exciting stores in Berkeley! It was originally a shoe repair shop owned by Bill and Carolyn Gulley, until daughter Peggy Casey began buying and trading pottery, beadwork, leather and silver from Native Americans in the late sixties. The rest is history.

Some of the riches you'll find are precious gems, award winning, custom made jewelry, striking rainbow colored beads, quartz crystals, ivory netsukes, American fresh-water, natural pearls, amber, Mediterranean coral, masks, pyrite eggs, fossils, amythst geodes, Ashanti fertility figures and a fine collection of Native American sterling silver and turquoise jewelry. You'll be delighted by the wide selection of diamonds, rubies, emeralds, sapphire, tourmaline, peridot, garnets, topaz, lapis, malachite and much more at astonishingly reasonable prices.

Whatever you're looking for in the way of gems or unique gifts, this "Best Choice" store in Berkeley is sure to please.

MAGNUM OPUS
2905 College Avenue
Berkeley, CA 94705
Tel. (415) 843-9143
Hrs: Tue. - Sat. 11:00 a.m. - 5:30 p.m.

So exotic are some of the items, you'd believe Indiana Jones began searching for the lost ark here at Magnum Opus.

Owners Veronica and Albert Braver wanted their shop to be an eye-opening experience. So they have cultivated a network of anthropologists, Peace Corps volunteers, and other acquaintances who keep their eyes open in distant corners of the earth for unusual gifts and artwork. Take for example the Philippine eel traps, or the African tribal wedding dresses, or the bright Chinese parasols. Every inch of wall space is covered with basketry and woven curtains and lamps from scores of countries. And the show room floor is an array of sculpture and fine furniture pieces sure to make a difference in your home.

So if its something different you are looking for, try this "Best Choice". As long as its not an ark you're looking for, you won't feel you have missed the boat.

(See special invitation in Appendix.)

Pizza

ARINELL PIZZA
2109 Shattuck Avenue
Berkeley, CA 94704
Tel. (415) 841-4035
Hrs: Mon. - Thu.   11:00 a.m. - 8:30 p.m.
     Friday   11:00 a.m. - 9:30 p.m.
     Saturday   12:00 noon - 8:30 p.m.
     Sunday   12:00 p.m. - 7:30 p.m.

Walking the streets of Berkeley opens a Pandora's Box of delights. The downtown Shattuck area is jam-packed with unique coffee houses and clothing stores. You could easily spend several enjoyable hours here shopping, and people watching. To limit your "down-time" to a minimum, search out Arinell Pizza, for an on your feet meal, right in the middle of downtown Shattuck.

Ron Demirdjian, owner and New York pizza over says his secret for this worth standing in line for pizza is in his mix. He makes his dough daily; his sauce is his own blend of herbs and spices, and all cheeses are of the highest quality. Ron features both Neapolitan, thin crust, and Sicilian, deep crust, pizzas with a variety of toppings.

Arinell Pizza is easy to miss because it's so small, don't give up. Circle the block.....keep your eyes peeled, and you'll be glad you took the time to uncover this inexpensive gem of a pizza kitchen, a taste-bud landmark in downtown Shattuck.

(See special invitation in the Appendix)

ZACHARY'S CHICAGO PIZZA
1853 Solano Avenue
Berkeley, CA 94707
Tel. (415) 525-5950
Hrs: Mon. - Thur.   11:00 a.m. - 9:30 p.m.
          Fri. - Sat.   11:00 a.m. - 10:30 p.m
and, 5801 College Avenue
Oakland, CA 94618
Tel. (415) 655-6385
Hrs: Sun. - Thur.   11:00 a.m. - 10:00 p.m.
          Fri. - Sat.   11:00 a.m. - 10:30 p.m.

Here's a pizza that's guaranteed to crush your previous notions of what pizza should be; it may even ruin you for the traditional variety forever. At Zachary's, owners Robert "Zachary" Zachowski and Barbara Gabel have developed a deliciously unique version of Chicago "stuffed pizza" that's appealingly different from the "deep dish" style so popular these days.

"Stuffed pizza" is actually somewhere between pizza and quiche! Zachary developed his noteworthy rendition while touring twelve countries with Barbara. Together, they sampled various types of pizza and Zachary took copious notes on the merits of each.

This scrumptious pizza consists of a bottom layer of crust which extends up the sides of the pan and is filled with rich cheeses and a various combination of fresh meats or vegetables, another thin layer of dough covers the cheese and ingredients; the top layer of dough melts succulently into the cheese as the pie bakes, the side crusts become crispy and crunchy. It's all topped with Zachary's own mildly spicy tomato sauce for a wonderful blend of tastes and textures.

Zachary's also offers a variety of crisp, fresh salads and a more traditional thin pizza. The decor at both the College Avenue and Solano Avenue locations is clean, modern and orderly, the atmosphere is friendly and lively. The service is prompt and smiling - a direct reflection of the ownership.

Restaurant

BERKELEY THAI HOUSE
2511 Channing Way
Berkeley, CA 94704
Tel. (415) 843-7352
Hrs: Mon. - Sun. 11:00 a.m. - 9:30 p.m.

The Berkeley Thai House has a reputation it lives up to--from incredible chicken coconut soup to sauteed seafood--you're in for a treat! The restaurant sits on Channing Way, a few short steps from Telegraph Avenue. There's ample seating with an elevated outdoor deck cafe leading to more subdued and intimate dining indoors. Step inside and be greeted warmly by owner Amy Tongsuk, who alternates as hostess, server, co-chef (with husband, Peter, and his assistants) and cashier.

Amy is somewhat of a young success story, having emigrated with Peter from Thailand to San Francisco when she was 18 years old. That was nine years ago. In San Francisco she worked in a cousin's restaurant until she had saved enough to open a small restaurant with a partner. Eventually, she sold her share to the partner and moved to Berkeley to open the restaurant she's always wanted. She and Peter have been creating Thai food here ever since.

Both Amy and Peter personally supervise the kitchen. Thai noodles, coconut milk, lemon leaf and galanga (a lemony, ginger-like root) are but a few of the ingredients they import from Thailand to maintain the Tongsuk's high standard of dining quality.

The chicken coconut soup is a creamy-smooth symphony of flavors. Moist and tender pieces of chicken blend with straw mushrooms in a rich broth with green onions, chili and galanga. We also recommend the satay: juicy pork chunks marinated overnight, then skewered and grilled to succulent perfection. Or if you're really hungry, try hoa-mok--a sizzling seafood stew brimming with shrimp, scallops, crab legs and yes, coconut milk. Delicious. Wash it all down with a smooth, creamy iced coffee.

The Berkeley Thai House is one of those rare finds: a reasonably priced restaurant with excellent food, relaxed ambience, and friendly service. It's a little hard to find, but look for it. It's worth the hunt.

CASA DE EVA
2826 Telegraph Avenue
Berkeley, CA 94705
Tel. (415) 540-9092
Hrs: Mon. -Fri.   11:00 a.m. - 10:00 p.m.
      Saturday   3:00 p.m. - 10:00 p.m.

Enter Casa de Eva and step into the heart of northern Mexico. Chihuahuan cuisine is the specialty of this long established and well loved Berkeley restaurant. No one in the Bay Area does Chihuahuan cuisine quite like Casa de Eva.

Eva and Miguel Lopez began their restaurant in the early 60's. Previously they had worked in a restaurant frequented by a prominent local attorney who loved their food. When the attorney bought a local building, he invited the couple to open their own restaurant in the building and so the team opened Casa de Eva and the rest, as they say, is culinary history.

Eva and Miguel are proud of their restaurant's excellent reputation. Eva's expertise with sauces and Miguel's insistence on buying and importing only the best ingredients combine to result in Mexican dishes that are consistently innovative and delicious. The flautas, for example, are a house specialty. Corn tortillas are filled with spicy shredded beef, rolled and deep fried to a crispy perfection, topped with a dollop of sour cream and served with one of Eva' mildly-seasoned sauces. Pure heaven. Another outstanding dish is the machaca. A homemade, soft flour tortilla is wrapped around flavorfully-seasoned barbecued beef chunks. If you prefer something a bit milder, try the scrumptious quesadilla--ham and melted cheese in a soft flour or corn tortilla, topped with rich guacamole.

At Casa de Eva, the food is not only outstanding, it's also very reasonably priced.

CHOYCE'S SOUTHERN CUISINE
2725 San Pablo Avenue
Berkeley, CA 94702
Tel. (415) 848-4023
Hrs: Mon. - Sun. 9:00 a.m. - 9:00 p.m.
Visa, MasterCard and Diner's Club are accepted.
Catering is available.

For eighteen years, Choyce's has maintained bragging rights as the Berkeley spot to enjoy authentic southern cuisine. As long as James Choyce II is behind the apron turning out his many specialties, it will continue to reign supreme. The restaurant, begun by James' father, has maintained the comfortable, homey atmosphere which endeared itself to its early patrons. It's more than likely that you'll be served by James himself when you sit down to order; he supervises the small, efficient kitchen closely and gives each meal careful attention.

Take your time when ordering; there's a lot to choose from and the menu is quite varied. One of the house specialties is the New Orleans seafood gumbo; if you've never had gumbo, try Choyce's. Just a few examples of the fare James offers are: country breakfasts, smothered pork chops, ribs, chicken, smoky barbecued crab, spicy Louisiana hot links, meaty shrimp and tender chicken along with bits of celery, okra, bell peppers and onions simmered to seasoned perfection and served with rice and salad. The tender smothered steak and pork chops are also delicious and like all entree's, include soup or salad and a "Choyce of two" vegetables. Along with your meal, cool your tastebuds with a tall glass of southern style, spiced, iced tea and then satisfy your sweet tooth with Choyce's tempting peach cobbler made with fresh peaches and a moist, flaky homemade crust.

Enter the friendly, comfortable world of Choyce's Southern Cuisine and enjoy fine, filling food at this "Best Choice" restaurant in Berkeley.

FRANK'S SEAFOOD FACTORY
2337 Sacramento Street
Berkeley, CA 94702
Tel. (415) 547-7578
Hrs: Mon. - Thu. 10:00 a.m. - 7:00 p.m.
Fri. - Sat. 10:00 a.m. - 10:00 p.m.
Sunday 10:00 a.m. - 5:00 p.m.

Everybody, including MacDonald's, serves some seafood these days, but even by today's standards Frank Davis has enough fish to make your head swim.

23

Both his seafood and his hospitality come southern style. In the seafood department, that's everything from catfish to gar. The wide variety of fish entrees come breaded and deep fried. But don't let the fried part put you off. This food is not greasy. That's because the New Orleans-bred chef uses only light vegetable oil. People come from throughout the east bay to get their regular dose of Frank's gumbo. A specialty of the house, this spicy Louisiana treat is thick with succulent shrimp, crab and shell fish.

And if you know your soul food (that's soul, not sole) you know how good fresh mustard greens can be. And so does Frank, southern style.

(See special invitation in the Appendix.)

GERTIE'S CHESAPEAKE BAY CAFE
1919 Addison Street
Berkeley, CA 94704
Tel. (415) 841- CRAB

Hrs:			
Mon. - Sat.	Lunch	11:30 a.m. - 2:30 p.m.
Mon. - Thu.	Dinner	5:30 p.m. - 9:30 p.m.
Fri. - Sat.		5:30 p.m. - 11:00 p.m.
Sunday	Dinner	4:30 p.m. - 9:30 p.m.
Sunday	Brunch	10:30 a.m. - 3:00 p.m.

Take your choice: crab in soup, crab in cakes, or crab steamed in beer tossed right onto your table. In any case, by the time you 'll be ready to drive off with a bumper sticker reading, "Gertie's = Crabs."

In spite of the how it might look when Gertie's serves its fine steamed east coast blue crabs, this is upscale but reasonably priced dining with meals provided by one of the great chefs of northern California, John Shields. It's a popular lunch spot for business people and students, as well as a renown dinner house. Afternoon favorites include Maryland crab soup, Louisiana seafood gumbo, and one of the best burgers in Berkeley. A raw seafood bar is available at dinner and it includes clams, prawns and oysters. Try the crab cakes, done up Chesapeake style with backfin crab meat and old bay seasoning. They're deep-fried and served with slaw, fries and tartar sauce. Sunday brunch is an informal meal featuring favorites like Grand Marnier French toast and seafood hash.

Whether you try something new, or something a little more familiar Gertie's is fun.

(See special invitation in Appendix.)

INDIA KASHMIR
1888 Solano Avenue
Berkeley, CA 94707
Tel. (415) 525-1122
Hrs: Mon. - Sun. from 5:30 p.m.

Berkeley is known for its diverse and interesting population; with such a variety of cultures comes a fine mixture of restaurant cuisine. India Kashmir represents some of the finest Indian cuisine you will find anywhere. A cozy, romantic atmosphere and warm, friendly service contribute to this popular eatery. In the subdued hues of the subtly lit dining room you will enjoy the plentiful, sumptuous tandoori (dishes cooked in mesquite-fired, clay ovens), exotic curry creations and delicious vegetarian meals.

To begin your meal, samosas are an excellent appetizer of vegetable filled pastries with spicy choices of sauces for dipping. If you're with a large party, you'll want to order several of these popular starters. Save room for one of the premier tandoori dishes such as chicken Tikka; it's a healthy portion of boneless chicken chunks, marinated in herbs and spices then slow cooked. Another fine tandoori dish is the Seikh Kabob, ground lamb seasoned with onions, chilis, coriander, cumin, cinnamon, cloves and garlic. If it's the renowned curry you desire, you won't be disappointed with the chicken Vindaloo, a fiery dish marinated in several spices, yogurt and then braised. Bengan Bharta is a mildly spiced eggplant cooked with peas, onions and curry.

There are four basic elements to a superior meal, fine food, fine surroundings, fine service and fine friends. India Kashmir is a "Best Choice" in Berkeley for fulfilling your culinary desires.

LA MEDITERRANEE
2936 College Avenue
Berkeley, CA 94705
Tel. (415) 540-7773
Hrs: Mon. - Thu.   10:00 a.m. - 10:00 p.m.
        Fri. - Sat.   10:00 a.m. - 11:00 p.m.

Located in the Elmwood district on College Avenue in Berkeley, La Mediterranee sports a bright blue awning that graphically displays it's name and shelters the casual outdoor dining area. A very pleasant place to stop for an espresso and lunch on a sunny day, this Middle Eastern flavor cafe is also one of the best stops in town for dinner and certainly ranks at the very top of the list if you are looking for authentic and reasonably priced Greek, Lebanese, and Armenian cooking.

The third in a string of very successful restaurants in the Bay Area, this appealing cafe, whose management's motto is, "The smallest things make the biggest difference", is in every way authentic Middle East. The owners' goal is to make clients a little happier. Not only does this mean an attention to detail that results in exceptional food, but also a commitment to keeping prices reasonable. The menu offers a variety of appetizers, soups, salads, combination dinners, desserts and coffees. If you're unsure where to start, any of the combination plates will provide satisfying selections of several different delightful foods. Mediterranean Meza will give two or more people a healthy sampling of just about everything including Lule Kebab, Dolma, Hummos, Baba Ghanoush, Tabuleh and much more. Other samplings include baked chicken Pomegranate, quiche of the day, and sampling of various fillo dough specialities. One of the many great choices for a combo plate would be the Middle Eastern plate, which comes in a vegetarian style as well. Don't forget to complement your meal with a fine wine from their modestly priced wine list.

All of the La Mediterranee restaurants have been reviewed with high praise from many Bay area restaurant critics. The restaurant has also received the San Francisco Restauranteur Award from its peers signifying recognition as an outstanding San Francisco restaurant. Be sure to take the time to stop in at this "Best Choice" in dining while in Berkeley.

LARRY BLAKE'S RESTAURANT AND NIGHTCLUB
2367 Telegraph Avenue
Berkeley, CA 94704
Tel. (415) 848-0888
Hrs: Restaurant
               Mon.-Fri.   11:30 a.m. - 12:00 midnight
               Sat. -Sun.   12:00 noon - 12:00 midnight
      Bar   Mon.-Fri.   11:30 a.m. - 1:30 a.m.
               Sat.-Sun.   12:00 noon - 1:30 a.m.
Visa and MasterCard are accepted.

Some places can really give you the blues, but when it's a "Best Choice" it has to be the kind of blues that makes you boogie, such is the case with Larry Blake's.

Since 1940 jazz and rhythm and blues aficionados have snapped their fingers and tapped their toes to the tunes while enjoying the food at this restaurant and club. Expect to see the east bay's top talent here, and occasionally legendary favorites like Charlie Musselwhite.

Larry Blake's is split into two levels. At street level you'll find a clean and simple dining room accented with wood beams and hardwood floors where there's cuisine that includes juicy barbecued chicken and meaty ribs. If you can make if for weekend brunch, try the Rockefeller omelette, made from spinach, onions and smoky bacon. It's down stairs where people get down and get funky on the sawdust covered dance floor.

Either way, Larry Blake's is where it's at for filling your stomach, or your ears.

(See special invitation in Appendix.)

RISTORANTE VENEZIA
1902 University Avenue
Berkeley, CA 94704
Tel. (415) 644-3093
Hrs: Tue.- Thu.   6:00 p.m. - 10:00 p.m.
          Fri. - Sat.   5:30 p.m. - 10:30 p.m.
Visa and MasterCard are accepted.
Reservations suggested.

It may be Berkeley on the outside, but once inside the setting is a northern Italian seaside village, where you can almost hear neighbors holler across the balconies.

A laundry line hangs above the "street" giving an extra dimension to the charming illusion created by the mural depicting neighborhood bakeries and storefronts.   The feeling is carried over to the meals--authentic, unpretentious Italian fare right down to the pasta. You'll enjoy the house specialty, conchiglie con uova di pesce--roughly translated that's scallops and flying fish roe in mushroom and wine sauce over fettucine.

When returning to the street, you'll remind yourself of what was make believe, but your taste buds will know the real thing.

SHATTUCK AVENUE SPATS
1974 Shattuck Avenue
Berkeley, CA 94704
Tel. (415) 841-7225
Hrs: Mon. - Sat.   11:30 a.m. - 2:00 a.m.
          Sunday   4:00 p.m. - 2:00 a.m.

If your world seems a little hazy and you feel like being a little lazy, try a Fogcutter. That's right, a Borneo Fogcutter to be exact. That's one of many original drinks Shattuck Avenue Spats is famous for.

This restaurant and bar has become a popular Berkeley water hole for its fabulous cocktails, zesty burgers, tasty seafood, and funky decor. Try the specialty, seafood fettuccine. When you walk into the bar, you step into

27

Victorian America. Furnished with antique furniture, bric-a-brac, period paintings and poster art, this room speaks of a much younger nation. But if you feel a little wild, go ape over the back room where a continuous jungle mural surrounds you as you lounge amid lush tropical plants.

And when you are finally ready to go, you might find some of the fog in your life lifted.

(See special invitation in the Appendix.)

SPENGER'S FISH GROTTO
1919 4th Street
Berkeley, CA 94710
Tel. (415) 845-7771
Hrs: Mon. - Sat.   8:00 a.m. - 12:00 midnight

Spenger's Fish Grotto is a colorful, seafaring establishment whose century-long tradition of fine food and service has kept it at the forefront of the culinary arena. The history surrounding the Spenger family and their special restaurant is, by now, Berkeley lore.

Johann Spenger arrived here from Bavaria in 1865 and opened a country store on the site of what is now Spenger's Fish Grotto. His teenaged son, Frank, operated a small fleet of fishing boats in the San Francisco Bay. The Spengers would prepare the day's catch outdoors in huge, steaming cauldrons. The enormous response to their fresh and deliciously prepared seafood led Frank to develop Spenger's as we enjoy it today. Currently, the grotto is operated by two Spenger generations: Frank Jr., President and his son "Spanky" Spenger. They've come a long way since Johann's days: In addition to their commercial fishing operation, the Spenger's manage their own oyster beds and raise mussels in Tomales Bay!

The Spenger's have also developed a one-of-a-kind nautical decor for their restaurant and cocktail lounge. The original buildings have been preserved and enlarged; the interior walls are decorated with ancient relics from around the world. Rich, teakwood wall paneling was taken from the old Lurline and the knees, or braces, in the dining room and cocktail lounge were taken from San Francisco's old time ferryboats and schooners.

The cuisine at Spenger's has maintained the purity of the old sea. Many of the recipes on today's menu were developed by Frank's wife, Marcella; the chefs maintain her integrity in their meals, both in quality and portion. If there's an overriding rule at Spenger's, it is that no one leaves hungry.

After a long day of Berkeley touring, start with a bowl of rich, creamy Boston clam chowder. Large, meaty chunks of clam and potatoes with plenty of fresh sourdough bread. If you're still hungry, try one of the many delightful daily specials: Cajun-style catfish with spicy rice Creole or tender, breaded calamari supreme are two examples...if you can't decide what to order, pick the captain's plate. It is a hearty smattering of scallops, prawns, oysters and fish fillets that's guaranteed to tame the meanest hunger pangs. The steaks at Spenger's are choice, grilled to tender, juicy perfection at your request.

What better way to end your meal than an after dinner cocktail in Spenger's spacious lounge. It's an active room with interesting articles from Davy Jones' locker--a fitting end to a hearty meal in a historical setting.

SUSHI CALIFORNIA
2033 Martin Luther King Jr. Way
Berkeley, CA 94704
Tel. (415) 548-0737
Hrs: Mon.-Fri.   Lunch 11:45 a.m. - 2:00 p.m.
      Mon. - Sat.   Dinner 5:30 p.m. - 10:00 p.m.

Sushi fit for a shogun is what regular patrons of Sushi California have come to expect. Ryoji and Yayoi Arakaki are setting the standard for Sushi restaurants in this country with the freshest fish, expert preparation and reasonable prices.

Schooled from sushi masters in Japan, Ryoji has put his ten years of restaurant experience to work by opening his own restaurant with his wife. He has brought with him the know-how to find the best and freshest fish. With these raw materials, he offers customers delicate sushi prepared from giant clam, tender prawns, crab and mackerel. Try the California roll, a mouth-watering concoction of crab cake and avocado.

The decor is bright, cheerful and contemporary--just the right touches in a restaurant that does things just right.

(See special invitation in Appendix.)

Alameda County

This tour is sure to give you an out-of-this-country experience.....without ever having to leave our shores.

	Exotic Gift & Food Tour of Berkeley		
a.m.	Neldam's Danish Bakery	Best bakery	Oak/Bak
a.m.	Magnum Opus	Best gift from far away	Ber/Gift
a.m.	Peet's Coffee & Tea	Best morning pick-me-up	Ber/Cof
a.m.	Gem Gallery	Best gems & jewelry	Ber/Gift
	Lunch at either of these restaurants will be a treat		
p.m.	Berkeley Thai House	Best lunch	Ber/Res
p.m.	Sushi California	Best selection of sushi	Ber/Res
	Now, to continue the tour....		
p.m.	Robert Bruce	Best Japanese art	Ber/Art
p.m.	Takara Sake Plant	Best sake tour	Ber/Att
p.m.	Strawberry Canyon	Best botanical tour	Ber/Att
	For your "Best Choice" exotic dinner:		
p.m.	Indian Kashmir	Best East Indian dinner	Ber/Res
p.m.	La Mediterranee	Best Middle East dinner	Ber/Res
	For an exotic after dinner drink:		
p.m.	Shattuck Avenue Spats	Best Borneo Fogcutter	Ber/Res

Castro Valley

Antiques

MELODAN GIFTS: HOME OF LA MELODIE
2584 Castro Valley Blvd.
Castro Valley, CA 94546
Tel. (415) 538-8866
Hrs: Mon. - Sat. 10:00 am-6:00 pm

Melodan Gifts and La Melodie are the result of the creative outgrowth of three people whose fertile imaginations and artistic abilities have created a wonderful world of fantasy. Dan and Melody Richardson and their son, Denny , are inspiring examples of what courage and creativity can do, for it was Denny's blindness that became the catalyst behind La Melodie creations.

One day when Denny was enjoying a children's TV show, he asked Melody how a certain character looked. He had several toy puppets and knew their features, but none of this particular creature. So Melody sculpted the figure in clay for Denny to feel. She loved doing it and discovered a hidden talent. Soon afterwards, while pondering some delicate crystals in a shop window, she began to wonder if they could be turned into sculptures. And so Melody's first La Melodie pieces emerged.

Melody now sculpts each piece, then uses the lost wax process to create an original. She makes a mold to cast the sculpture, then applies 24-kt. gold electroplate and integrates Austrian leaded crystals into the sculpture. Thus, a grape bunch consists of the gold-plated stem with grapes of round crystals. Melody's showroom is breathtaking, a place where magic prisms send dancing rainbows through the air and gold gleams. Animals, flowers, candleholders and music boxes create a fantasy world. The crowning masterpiece is an exquisite peacock with dozens of glistening crystals in its tail. Each piece is an heirloom, signed and dated in limited editions.

As the popularity of La Melodie grew, Dan came into the partnership, and the family opened the gift shop, Melodan Gifts. As you enter Melodan, you are greeted by a large stuffed animal, Koko the Gorilla, lounging on the sofa. Antique furniture of rare quality and value displays many of the shop's pieces from around the world. Just a few of the items we loved were carved ivory figurines from China, Murro porcelains from Stratford-on-Avon, each signed and dated and depicting beautiful birds and water lilies. We marveled at Oriental geisha dolls with porcelain faces, carved jade figures, bridal doll, hand-wrapped silk flowers, ornate antique mirrors and more. People come from miles around just to purchase Melodan's jewelry such as the lovely and affordable cloisonne earings, and rings of opal, onyx and zirconium. In addition to the superlative gifts, Melody runs a full floral service and can fulfill all of your wedding requirements.

Denny's own shop is next door, where blind people can meet him and purchase stuffed animals and other materials that are helpful to them. Dreams can come true, delighting and inspiring us all.

WARREN'S ANTIQUES, 1558 A Street, Castro Valley, California. An unusual selection of antiques, especially mechanical items are offered.

Apparel

ROBIN'S NEST
20649 Rustic Drive
Castro Valley, CA 94546
Tel. (415) 538-4996
Hrs: Mon.-Fri.   10:00 a.m.-6:00 p.m.
      Sat.   10:00 a.m.-5:30 p.m.
      Sun.   12:00 p.m.-5:00 p.m.

For fashion-conscious ladies, Robin's Nest is one of the nicest places to shop in Castro Valley. The shop is filled with satin, silk, and lace lingerie so pretty your senses will seem borne on wings of fantasy. Owner Robin Walker has always had a fancy for fine lingerie, even before she opened Robin's Nest. She attends trade shows with her mother, and together they select the apparel for the shop. The pure silk lingerie is designed for sensuous comfort. There are camisole and tap-pant sets, and teddies for intimate wear, sleep, or daytime elegance. Many of these come with the most delicate and intimate Venetian laces. You can rely on Robin's expert fitting service to streamline any item to your figure's best advantage.

The dress selection features the Sterling Silver and Climax lines. The Sterling Silver is 30's and 40's modern, using Shantung rayon, cotton and satin fabrics. The Climax line is upbeat contemporary, and includes many strapless designs, and fitted skirts. Robin carries the Nina Piccalino line, which offers a more casual look in attire.

The unique charm of the boutique is enhanced with fine accessories. You'll love the fancy hosiery, beautiful beaded handbags, fluffy slippers, and potpourri-filled little Teddys near the counter. Alluring silk kimonos await your selection, and handmade Niobium and silver jewelry sparkles with quality. You can order exotic feathered masks and fanciful fans from the catalogues at Robin's Nest. Elegant, contemporary and stylish, touching and intimate, this Robin's Nest invites you.

(See special invitation in Appendix.)

PATTY QUINN, 10652 Rustic Drive, Castro Valley, California. A large selection of high qualifty women's fashions are featured at this lovely shop.

Art, Artists, Gallery

A TOUCH OF SPLENDOR
20407 Santa Maria
Castro Valley, CA 94546
Tel. (415) 881-1162
Hrs: 10:00 am - 5:00 pm Mon. - Sat.

A Touch Of Splendor is an apt name for this enchanting place. The sun streaming through the stained glass in the window creates colorful patterns all around as owner Maria Rosen's Hungarian hospitality welcomes you. She comes from a long line of Hungarian artists and carries on the family tradition in this splendid gallery, framing shop, and gift store.
You will be intrigued by her knowledge of the esthetic effects of different kinds of glass: non-glare, window, plexiglas. Custom framing and consulting are second nature to her. Whether you want to frame old or new photographs, prints or paintings, or need a shadow box for a collection of Colt 45s, spoons, or dolls, Maria can help you.
The gallery features an artful blend of media, including oil painting, lithographs, hand-colored etchings, serigraphs, and laser engravings on slate and wood. The walls are filled with the paintings of local artists, along with limited edition, signed lithos: poured, paper embossed sculpture art; and hand-colored etchings, including an early-American family scene that will catch your eye. Among the collectible prints, you'll find scenes by the masters, landscapes, wildlife paintings and art that's simply fun. You can have Maria custom-frame your selection, or buy your own matting and molding to frame it yourself.
Handmade art pieces and gifts fill the floor of this shop: pewter sculpture, stained glass boxes, Precious Moments porcelain and other figurines, lovable stuffed animals, china plates, holographic art. Once you've experienced A Touch Of Splendor, you're sure to become a trusting customer for years to come.

FROYLAND GALLERY AND FRAME CO., 20660 Redwood Road, Castro Valley, California. Orignial paintings, art classes, framing and restoration are available.

Cookies

MARY'S COOKIES
20667 Rustic Drive
Castro Valley, CA 94546
Tel. (415) 886-2797
Hrs: Mon.-Fri.   9:00 a.m. - 6:00 p.m.
      Saturday   10:00 a.m. - 6:00 p.m.
      Sunday   12:00 noon - 5:00 p.m.
      Closed last Saturday of every month

A stroll through Castro Village means that you will eventually reach the aroma zone of Mary Farris' cookie shop. The heralded "cookie queen" of Castro Valley bakes as many as 70 dozen cookies a day. She started baking cookies for customers, as well as family and friends, when she worked at a Hayward restaurant. Soon she could barely keep up with the demand. Dana August came along and urged Mary into a business partnership, knowing that her cookies were too incredible to be kept under cover. She was right.

Mary's Cookies have become an enormous success. Mary ensures that the 4" wide and 1/2" thick cookies are fresh. Choose from chocolate chip, peanut butter, coconut oatmeal, the breakfast cookie, chocolate mint, chocolate with walnut, or double chocolate--they all have spectacular taste and texture.

(See special invitation in Appendix.)

Florist

DRIED AND TIED FLOWERS AND GIFTS, 10633 Rustic Drive, Castro Valley, California. This shop carries dried and silk flowers and floral arrangements.

Gift

CRAFT PEDDLER'S
3317 Castro Valley Blvd.
Castro Valley, CA 94546
Tel. (415) 537-8778

Don't let Pearl Arhontes' petite stature fool you. She is an artist capable of completing large projects such as repainting a 7 x 12 foot carved redwood mural. The mural depicting the 1870 Hayward Volunteer Fire Department was severely deteriorated. Pearl volunteered her efforts to keep this piece of Hayward history alive and completely refurbished the mural. Her talents and energies extend to her shop. She excels in the field of Tole art and decorative painting.

Tole is the art of painting country and Early American scenes on tin, glass, ceramic, or wood. Throughout the shop you'll find spice cabinets, wine dispensers, coat racks, rocking chairs, jewelry boxes, wooden dolls, and many other charming items displaying this art. Beyond handpainted items, there are quilted ducks, fluffy woolen lambs, cuddly bears, giant stuffed mice, quilted pillows, and much more. Pearl also stocks paint supplies including: raw wood patterns and stencil patterns for Tole projects; acrylic and oils; sprays, brushes, and more than 250 books on all areas of painting and crafts.

Extensive classes in Tole, decorative painting, and canvas painting in both oils and acrylics are offered. The entire shop is a showcase for local artists and craftspeople. For those who appreciate handcrafted products, visit the Craft Peddler's. According to Pearl, "Everything here is made with tender loving care." It shows.

(See special invitation in Appendix.)

RHODES'S COUNTRY MOUSE, 20879 Redwood Road, Castro Valley, California. The perfect place to find thousands of antiques and collectibles.

THE SILVER ETCHING, 3352 Village Drive, Castro Valley, California. Wedding, anniversary gifts and etchings beautifully provided.

THINGS YOU LOVE, 3161 Castro Valley Boulevard, Castro Valley, California. You will love the gifts, imports, collectibles and antiques at this delightful store.

TOUR OF CASTRO VALLEY			
a.m.	Craft Peddlers	Best paint/art	Cas/Gift
a.m.	Melodan Gifts	Best sculpture	Cas/Gift
p.m.	Prior's Espresso	Best early lunch	Cas/Rest
p.m.	Mary's Cookies	Best pie & cookie	Cas/Cook
p.m.	Touch of Splendor	Best art gallery	Cas/Art
p.m.	Robin's Nest	Best silk	Cas/App

Restaurant

PRIOR'S ESPRESSO HOUSE
20634 Rustic Drive
Castro Valley, CA 94546
Tel. (415) 582-1410
Hrs: Mon. - Sat.   10:00 a.m. - 5:30 p.m.
     Sunday   12:00 noon - 5:00 p.m.

There's a quaint little cafe in the heart of Castro Valley...on a typical day you'll find the top section of the Dutch door swung open and the aroma of fresh ground coffee wafting through the air. It will gently pull you within to see the sunbeams dancing through the stained glass window and playing colors across the cozy tablecloths. Warmth emanates from the pecky cedar paneling and overhead beams.

Lily and her husband, Don, are there as the consummate hosts. They have provided the atmosphere and over thirty varieties of tea, and an equal number of fresh coffee beans that you can buy in bulk or have ground for you. Enjoy the Mexico Pluma, Columbia Supreme, Africa Kenya, Guatemala Antiqua, Jamaican Mountain, Hawaiian Kona, and more. Take a taste trip around the world without leaving home!

If you're just stopping in for a cup or two, Lily will fix you up with espresso, Caffe Dante, Cafe Viennese, Kaffe mit Schlag, or some excellent iced coffees like espresso a la Freddo (a tall glass of espresso over vanilla ice cream, topped with whipped cream), and espresso San Marco (a tall glass of espresso and steamed chocolate milk over chocolate ice cream, topped with whipped cream and bitter chocolate).

The sandwiches, to go with your drink, deserve rave notices. Try liver sausage, turkey pastrami, salmon mousse and ham. Lily suggests you try the terrific Salad Nicoise or the Quiche Prior. Breakfast or lunch, this is the place.

(See special invitation in Appendix.)

Fremont

The 1956 consolidation of the historic towns of Mission San Jose, Warm Springs, Centerville, Niles and Irvington produced this city named in honor of explorer John C. Fremont. At last count, the city boasted thirty shopping centers, a 325-bed hospital, and several manufacturing facilities allied with electronics firms in Santa Clara County.

Consolidation is the name of the game at Fremont, where the latest amalgam is a joint venture in auto-manufacturing between Toyota and General Motors, called the United Motor Manufacturing, Inc. When the last census was taken in 1980, 131,000 people lived in this sprawling community between the San Jose mountains and the bay. The latest population estimate now tops that census by 11,000 more residents.

Attractions

The old **Vallejo Mills** of the 1850s were located in Niles on the Rancho Arroyo de la Alameda, and the stone aqueduct that brought water to the grist stones can still be seen by driving up Niles Canyon Road.

Mission San Jose, visible to I-680 travelers, and accessible from Mission Boulevard (state highway 238), fell into disrepair before being returned to the church. This fourteenth in the chain of California missions was founded in 1779 and served as the starting point for Spanish expeditions to California's interior. The modern parish chapel now offers visitors an opportunity to inspect gardens dating back to mission days.

Olhone Burial Ground is a mile from the mission. A monument commemorates the estimated 4,000 Indian people buried here who helped build the mission and its farms.

The city's **Central Park** includes Lake Elizabeth, an 85-acre lake for sailboat and windsurfers. Rentals and classes are available year around. The park is on Civic Center Drive, off Stevenson Boulevard.

Shinn Historical Park is the showcase for three old homes. A cottage built in 1840, the main Shinn house in 1875 and another in 1876. This pioneer nurseryman's estate includes a botanical garden. It is on Peralta Boulevard. It is open from 8:00 a.m. to dusk, April through October.

The city also operates a restored 1843 adobe house put up by Don Jose Vallejo as token residence for a 17,000 acre rancho he was granted. Located on Niles Boulevard, the **Vallejo Adobe** is rented by the city for group parties and weddings.

For further information, the **Fremont Chamber of Commerce** may be contacted at 39501 Paseo Padre Parkway, or by calling 657-1355.

Alameda County

Accommodations

LORD BRADLEY'S INN
43344 Mission Boulevard
Fremont, CA 94539
Tel. (415) 490-0520

Next door to the Mission San Jose is Lord Bradley's Bed and Breakfast Inn; presenting a unique lodging for travelers and Northern California's residents. Keith and Anne Medeiros provide family-style hospitality in an old-world atmosphere.

Keith is a retired schoolteacher and master carpenter. He created the Inn from two turn-of-the-century buildings; the former Washington Township Hotel and Brown's Barber Shop.

Anne's influence is felt in the impeccable decorating of the predominantly English Victorian interior. Precious collectibles, gathered by them on their worldwide sojourns adorn the intimate rooms. In the Commons Room are abundant books and magazines; placed there for your reading enjoyment. Curl up on the Victorian sofa, complemented by the peach-colored wallpaper and intricate lace curtains, and relax in comfort.

Each bedroom is named after a member of the family. There are eight in all: Lady Anne's, Lady Shaunna's, Lady Whitney's, Sir Todd's, Lady Christina's, Sir Douglas', Lady Violet's and Sir Keith's. Each suite has its own special motif. The Lady Anne room features framed antique Valentines, a print from a Charles Dickens story, Hummel figurines, a marvelous old ceramic water pitcher, a stunning French armoire and fancy country-style flowered wallpaper.

The outdoor patio is a world unto itself...a beautiful red brick deck invites you to partake of your Continental breakfast in the open air and watch the hummingbirds sipping from the burgeoning fuscias. Olive trees line the driveway and a profusion of flowers define, with bursts of color, this outdoor scene.

Lord Bradley's, where all your comforts are met with the tradition accorded royalty.

MARGOT'S CONTINENTAL LODGING
41600 Vargas Road
Fremont, CA 94539
Tel. (415) 657-8862

Rolling hills, eucalyptus groves, lolling cows, and a gentle winding drive up Vargas road prepare you for a peaceful stay at Margot's Continental

Lodging. Nestled in the Mission San Jose Hills, just a short distance from the bustling city of Fremont, this California chateau is an ultimate treat for those who seek a respite and old-world charm. Innkeepers Nick and Margot Kover know how to make you comfortable.

Your own spirits will be immediately enlivened once you set foot on the remarkable grounds. You'll find six acres of hillside, a warm hot tub that has an exalted view of Mission Peak, a rustic octagon gazebo (great for wedding parties), and lovely manicured gardens of roses, geraniums, grape vines, iridescent chrysanthemums, and lush moss. There is a separate secluded enclave where you can sit, relax and enjoy the view of a Italian fountain, cypresses and olive trees. If such extravagant grounds are meant to please, they certainly do.

The gallery entrance (featuring many of Margot's own paintings) is the spacious causeway to the three lodging suites. You'll find an antique coat rack, thick oriental carpets, travel brochures, and finely-crafted walking canes (a Nick Kover hobby). The family room is designed for relaxation with a T.V., fireplace, and comfortable armchairs and sofa. The living room has a Victorian feel with a grand old English gas lamp hanging from the ceiling's center. A huge Karastan rug exudes warmth throughout the room, and a corner secretary contains many of Margot's special treasures: porcelain dancing ladies dating from pre-WWII.

The consummate hostess, Margot will always have fresh coffee ready for you even if you are an early riser. Soon to follow is a terrific country breakfast: fresh orange juice, quiche, apple pancakes, baked goodies , and assorted surprises. Elegant and sweet, the hospitality stems from a deep European tradition to make Margot's Continental Lodging a "Best Choice" for your stay in Mission San Jose.

Alameda County

THE RESIDENCE INN

5400 Farwell Place
Fremont, CA 94536
Tel. (415) 794-5900
and,
2000 Windward Way
San Mateo, CA 94404
Tel. (415) 574-4700
and,
750 Lakeway
Sunnyvale, CA 94086
Tel. (408) 720-1000

2761 S Bascom Avenue
Campbell, CA 95008
Tel. (408) 559-1551

854 El Camino Real West
Mountain View, CA 94040
Tel. (415) 940-1300

1080 Stewart Drive
Sunnyvale, CA 94086
Tel. (408) 720-8893

A new, modern and unique abode for travelers is being experienced as Residence Inns emerge across this country. Conceptually thought of as a friendly neighborhood, The Residence Inn provides every possible home-like comfort available. The suites have fully-equipped kitchens with an ice maker, pots and pans, cutlery, coffee maker, toaster, popcorn popper, and place settings. Some of the suites include the added touch of a wood-burning fireplace. A living room area is complete with satellite television, full wardrobe closet and a separate bath.

The Penthouse suite has about double the space of the regular suite, the same amenities, plus a beautiful two-story floor plan with kitchen and living area on the first floor and private loft above. Beds and full baths on both floors, a dining table that seats four, vaulted ceiling, a wood-burning fireplace, and phones on both levels.

The Residence Inn features a large communal living room, which is located across from the reception desk. It's there you can enjoy the numerous current magazines and newspapers placed at your disposal. Continental breakfast is served each morning and the staff's dedication to hospitality and service is unsurpassed. They will aid with your grocery shopping, laundry service, VCR and tape rental, and supply the airport shuttle. Recreational facilities include heated pools, whirlpool spas, *Sportscourt*, and propane barbeque grills. In the summertime a complimentary barbeque dinner is served by The Residence Inn each week.

Succeeding in making your visit cordial, convenient and, wonderfully comfortable...The Residence Inn.

THUNDERBIRD INN, 5400 Mowry Avenue, Fremont, California. Full amenities including air conditioned rooms, color TV, swimming pool and a full service restauranat are provided.

40

Antiques

HIGH STREET GENERAL STORE
3765 Washington Boulevard
Fremont, CA 94538
Tel. (415) 657-1321
Hrs: Mon. - Wed. 10:00 a.m. - 6:00 p.m.
       Thur. - Sat. 10:00 a.m. - 8:00 p.m.

The High Street General Store isn't on High Street anymore. Gordon and Cindy Meyers expanded the store and moved it to Washington Boulevard...but, it's still the High Street General Store...bringing you a wide selection of farm implements, saddles, tack, feed, horse trailers and buggies!

Gordon handles the exclusive distributorship for Squire wood-burning stoves. Cindy pursues her interests with a full floral and gift shop that offers a world of beauty and antiques. Bouquets and floral arrangements for weddings are a specialty of this shop. Fresh cut flowers in artful array. Furniture, such as hutches, curio cabinets, tables and chest of drawers. High quality pieces and quite reasonably priced.

Enjoy displays of collector dolls, bisque clowns, rolling pins, stained glass artwork, hand-painted washboards, shelves, benches, wagons, and dozens of hand-crafted country gifts. There are mobiles, balloons, humorous greeting cards, gift boxes, stuffed animals, scented soaps, and lots more.

An old-fashioned general store--super services, great gifts, fun things, fresh flowers--all in a county setting. There's nothing else like the High Street General Store.

J STREET ANTIQUES
120 J Street
Fremont, CA 94536
Tel. (415) 793-0202
Hrs: Wed.-Sat. 11:00 a.m.-5:00 p.m.
      Sun.   12:00 p.m.-5:00 p.m.

Marge and her partner Mitch Darnell embody the spirit of Niles through their pioneering knowledge and workmanship. Marge got started in the antique business by selling furniture out of her garage and at antique shows and then eventually managed The Antique Emporium before moving to Niles. Her shop on J Street was once--among other things--the Niles Post Office. You would never know that now, however; it has been transformed into a showroom for some of the very best antique furniture, limited-edition prints, oriental carpets, and cute collector's Teddys too.

Alameda County

Receiving merchandise from all over the country and Europe, Marge is very knowledgeable about woods, grains, cuts and tooling. She'll show you oak tables that aren't made anymore with a quarter-sawn wood grain, and matching chairs that are in mint condition. Throughout the shop you'll find dining room tables, armoires, buffets, dressers, and elegant English old oak bars with marvelous stained glass doors.The floors are covered with thick, ornate Oriental rugs that are 100% wool and very reasonably priced. Along the walls are collector's prints that are limited-edition signed lithographs. J Street is your prestigious Greenwich Workshop dealer.

After viewing these wonderful antiques, you will know why "J" Street Antiques is one of the finest and most unique antique stores in the San Francisco bay area.

(See special invitation in appendix.)

MY FRIENDS AND I
37521 Niles Blvd.
Fremont, CA 94536
Tel. (415) 792-0118
Hrs: Mon.-Sat. 11:00 a.m.-5:00 p.m.
         Sun.   12:00 p.m.-5:00 p.m.

"Country" can mean many different things to many people, but for a wonderful feel of what country means in antiques, come to My Friends and I in the heart of the historic Niles district.

Carol Williamson and Janice Quinn are truly artists, collectors, history buffs, and preservers of country comfort. The shop is a collective of 14 women dealers, all of whom possess a given skill at creating country crafts. In addition to displaying their own creations, they display creations of other accomplished artisans. And Carol and Janice have knowledge of how every hand-crafted item was made.

As you stroll through the shop, you can examine the excellent quilts, doilies, oak mirrors, pottery, kitchen utensils, toys stuffed dolls, and a plethora of items that reflect country living to a tee. You'll even find children's items such as the Lizzy High doll line. Each wooden doll is hand painted and dressed in 19th century children's clothing. You'll love the authentic old Raggedy Anns, whether you're a doll collector or not.

My Friends and I will take you back to the warmth of 19th and early 20th century country living. Come visit and enjoy this wonderful shop. Janice, Carol, and a diversity of country-loving women open their art to you.

(See special invitation in Appendix.)

42

LES BELLES ANTIQUES
37549 Niles Boulevard
Fremont, CA 94536
Tel. (415) 794-4773
Hrs: Mon.-Fri. 1:00 p.m.-5:00 p.m.
Appraisals by appointment

Professional appraisers, Suan Perry and Norma Carey attend auctions and estate sales tracking down the most valuable and best preserved Victorian sofas and chairs. Although the shop is not huge, it has a premiere atmosphere and classic grace. Suan and Norma also have an artistic knack for re-upholstering that is outstanding.

The Staffordshire plates at Les Belles are rarities, as are the hard-paste porcelains. Some, like the handsome Peter Von Recum, date back as far as 1795. Suan and Norma feature some superb Royal Vienna hand-painted plates encrusted with gold. Sterling silver from Tiffany's, Burmese, Majolica, Ruby and Cranberry glass glimmer in their glass cases. The oriental items include 19th century Chinese cameo vases and intricate Netsuke ivory carvings. The flowing Victorian mirrors, any of which would be a grand showpiece, are fabulous. There is also a lovely jewelry case displaying precious Art Deco, Art Noveau and Victorian treasures. You'll love the Baccarat cut glass

and the Steuben and Tiffany chintz stemware. The displays of pink slag, mother of pearl, miniature portraits on ivory, and satin and cameo glass are worth admiration.

These two knowledgeable ladies at Les Belles Antiques are worth traveling many miles to meet.

(See special invitation in Appendix.)

RED ROSE ANTIQUES
37683 Niles Boulevard
Fremont, CA 94536
Tel. (415) 792-7965
Hrs: Mon. - Sun. 10:00 a.m. - 6:00 p.m.

Half the fun in antique collecting is in the hunt. Collectors and browsers from all over the Bay Area have long enjoyed coming to Red Rose Antiques. Maybe it's because owners, Barbara and LeRoy Cunha are true connoisseurs of yesterday's treasures. They spend untold hours scouring garage sales, barns, flea markets, antique shows...anywhere and everywhere to come up with the unusual and prized in vintage goodies.

43

The first thing you'll notice as you enter this cozy emporium is the welcoming aroma of fresh-roasted coffee beans. Barbara grinds them to order and she's very knowledgeable about the specialty blends like: Amoretto decaf, Columbian supreme, Antigua, Nut Cream, Grand Marnier, Viennese, and French roast.

Be sure to note Barbara and LeRoy's unusual selection of vintage hats--everything from the Roaring Twenties to the Sibilant Sixties. Record collectors can enjoy a whole trunk full of 78's, while a delightful array of kitchen collectibles perch in their own nook here, along with racks of magazine classics and vintage comic books.

Throughout the shop you'll enjoy the clocks, mid-century chests of drawers, mirrors, crank telephones, framed prints of numerous persuasions, beautifully restored curio cabinets, and a great deal more--all reasonably priced.

Afterwards, take a stroll through the back patio to get a feel for their special love...country primitives. Here you'll find old plows, blacksmith tools, an ice saw, wood burning stoves, Conestoga wheels, tin advertising signs, beer barrels, carts, even a vintage bathtub or two from the Twenties!

Barbara and LeRoy are happy to personally assist you in tracking down your individual wants. They'll call you once they find the item that fits your description. The Red Rose Antiques is a "Best Choice" for great collectibles and owners who are very accommodating.

S & H ANTIQUES
130 "J" Street
Fremont, CA 94536
Tel. (415) 792-7792
Hrs: Wed. - Sun. 12:00 pm - 4:00 pm

Niles has a history that is extremely interesting and at times can become an enigma. Was the last continental spike really driven at Promontory or was it here at Niles? Is the present day Niles Station building the erstwhile hotel in which Charlie Chaplin lodged? If you would like to speak to someone who has bountiful answers, and you want to see some of the most splendid art glass available, then look up Shirley Filgate at S & H Antiques. For many years now this lady has been a fountain of information. A lady whose reputation for high quality antiques is unsurpassed. At S & H choice pieces can often be purchased for far less than at the exclusive antique shows and from dealers elsewhere. Shirley has a eagle eye for great finds at the auctions and estate sales.

Look around this lovely emporium and you'll detect a glimmer from the cabinets and shelves. This is the iridescent sheen of her Tiffany, Loetz,

Steuben and carnival glass. Walk over and feel the intricate *au natural* etched Galle patterns and the silky satin glass. Then scan about and enjoy the adorably painted Mary Gregory, lustrous Lalique and Venetian glass. See the Cambridge, Pearpoint, Webb, and Baccarat. If you gravitate toward porcelain, Shirley is likely to have some nice Lenox and R. S. Prussian to look over. You'll see some beautiful camphor perfume bottles from the 30's, a full showcase of flow blue, Wedgewood bisque, and several shelves of primitives.

There's a lovely selection of fine linens, plus I was quite taken by the sterling silver spoons, candelabra, compacts, hair brushes and more. Shirley also has the collector of Oriental antiques at heart. Enjoy lots of ornate ivory carvings, Satsuma, cloisonne, high quality hand-painted porcelain vases and plates, snuff bottles, and Chinese apparel.

Shirley caters to a sophisticated taste. She specializes in English Victorian and French periods. The tables, cabinets and other pieces would lend grace to any home.

There's more.sheet music, pottery, Hummels, depression glass, mantle clocks.you can spend the day roaming at S & H Antiques feasting your eyes on Shirley's wonderful wares.

Three excellent meals and shops full of treasured finds makes this a popular tour with collectors.

ANTIQUE TOUR OF FREMONT			
a.m.	Lord Bradley Inn	Best breakfast	Fre/Acc
a.m.	Red Rose Antiques	Best farmstead	Fre/Ant
a.m.	My Friends and I	Best dolls	Fre/Ant
a.m.	Bite and Browse	Best Old West	Fre/Ant
a.m.	Les Belles Antiques	Best Victorian	Fre/Ant
p.m.	Pearl's Cafe	Best lunch	Fre/Rest
p.m.	S & H Antiques	Best glass	Fre /Ant
p.m.	High General Store	Best general store	Fre/Ant
p.m.	J Street Antiques	Best Oriental rug	Fre/Ant
p.m.	Massimo's	Best Italian dinner	Fre/Rest

Art

FREMONT ART ASSOCIATION STUDIO GALLERY, 37659 Niles Boulevard, Fremont, California. You will find original paintings galore at this gallery.

OHLONE ARTS
43319 Mission Boulevard
Fremont, CA 94538
Tel. (415) 657-2977
Hrs: Mon. - Sat. 10:00 a.m. - 5:30 p.m.

What does fine picture framing, watercolor art, and a Texas cowboy have in common? The answer is Roy Coker, the owner of Ohlone Arts...across the street from the Mission San Jose.

The pictures on the bulletin board chronicle his life as a cowboy, WW II glider pilot, auto dealer, Real Estate broker, and now, art gallery owner. Since 1977 he has run this gallery and art supply store.

A ten year, ranking member of the Professional Picture Framer's Association; Roy brings all his skills to bear on the craftsmanship and taste necessary to construct and devise the correct mat and frame to enhance your art object.

The gallery portion of Ohlone Arts places its emphasis on watercolors. It primarily features local artists, such as Evangeline Johnson and her interpretation of soft, glowing still life portraitures that capture and encapsulate the tones and shapes of California. Hal Booth's paintings stress the local scenes, including the Mission itself, Mission Valley, farm life, and rural landscapes. Ted Harpainter ranges wide in his renditions of ghost towns, ferryboats and views of the coast and bay.

The lithograph section is varied, high-quality, and suitable for framing. Thumb through the racks and you'll notice an well balanced selection of American and European masters. Original oil paintings are displayed on the walls...ask Roy, he'll be glad to assist you with your selection.

Attraction

MISSION SAN JOSE
43300 Mission Boulevard
Fremont, CA 94539
Tel. (415) 657-1797
Hrs: Mon. - Sun. 10:00 a.m. - 5:00 p.m.

Founded in 1797 by Padre Fermin Francisco de Lasuen, the successor to California's first padre, Father Junipero Serra; this is the fourteenth of twenty-one missions established along the California coastline.

The site chosen was inhabited for generations by the Ohlone Indians. The Indians were brought into a new way of life, with the padres, and learned how to plow, cultivate, irrigate, reap and store the product of their labors; tanning of leathers, making rope, adobe bricks, and a host of other husbandry skills.

The Mission prospered into a thriving community; but in 1834 the Mexican government secularized all the Mission lands and they were divided into ranchos. At the end of the Mexican War, in 1848, Alta California, which included the Mission lands, was ceded to the United States. The Gold Rush added to the influx of pioneer families, such as the Livermore, Peralta and Alviso's, and turned San Jose into a booming provision center. In 1858 the United States government returned a small portion of the Mission lands to the Catholic Church.

A devastating earthquake, in 1868, ruined the original adobe church and outbuildings. Subsequently, the church site was cleared and a Gothic wooden church built above the original tile floors. In 1982, after extensive archaeological excavations and much planning, the wooden church was moved to a new site and a complete reproduction of the original church was built with interiors, richly decorated, that follow the historic inventories of the 1830s.

The Mission has retained many of the key objects that were prominent in the days when such heroic figures as Kit Carson, Jedediah Smith and John C. Fremont came to visit. There are beautiful, ornate vestments as worn by the priests at religious ceremonies, and all four Mission bells. Today the old timbers and rawhide thongs demonstrate the practicality of the padres who, having no iron nails for building, substituted leather laces. The overhang of the roof features 12,000 hazelwood branches, carefully lashed with rawhide. Following a tour of the church and museum, guests may choose to walk through the fascinating old cemetery.

The gift store at the Mission San Jose features a large selection of religious items; crucifixes, hand-painted clay sculptures, statutes, original oils, lithos, greeting cards and wonderful weaved tapestries. The ladies who tend the shop are conversant with interesting and little known personal stories about the people and Mission-times; and will share those stories once prompted.

The past lives on at Mission San Jose. There are plans for the reconstruction of the living quarters and further restoration of the surviving church wing. The Mission bells continue to toll, pealing forth memories of California's rich history and abundant future.

Antiques

BITE AND BROWSE
37725 Niles Boulevard
Fremont, CA 94536
Tel. (415) 796-4537
Hrs: Mon. - Sat. 10:00 a.m. - 5:00 p.m.
      Sunday   11:00 a.m. - 5:00 p.m.

Come in and have a bite, enjoy some freshly made sweets and a cup of coffee. There is plenty to see in this neatly arranged collective. You will know Bite and Browse among the store fronts on Niles Boulevard from the Charlie Chaplin collection in the front part of the store. For years, people have been coming in with Chaplin items for owner Beverly Wredberg to add to her collection. Now it is a veritable museum. She has books, lighters, original movie posters, an oil painting, t-shirts, a ceramic mask and much more - a fascinating display. She'll take you into the back room and run old Charlie Chaplin movies for you, some filmed in Niles. This charming collection is a must to see.

Bite and Browse offers merchandise from more than twenty-five exhibitors. It began as a means for aspiring dealers to have a place in which to sell. Through Beverly and husband Will's direction, it has become a favorite stop for antiquers in Niles. It is ideal for the beginning collector because prices are very reasonable, the advanced collector will find good buys also. There is a 19th century French writing desk fit for a mansion, rare pendulum clocks, a Queen Anne table and some wonderfully restored Victorian chairs among the items that were of advanced value.

THE CHEESE TASTER
43367 Mission Boulevard
Fremont, CA 94538
Tel. (415) 656-5480
Hrs: Mon. - Fri.   9:00 a.m. - 5:00 p.m.
      Saturday   9:30 a.m. - 5:30 p.m.
      Sunday   11:00 a.m. - 4:00 p.m.

As you descend the steps of Mission San Jose, your eyes scan the boulevard to the left; you'll notice a curious sign, in bold letters, that proclaims The Cheese Taster. A quaint, little white building with a big, open window that somehow naturally beckons you across the street and thru the front door. When you enter you will pleasantly discover much more than the sign would have led you to expect. You'll discover a deli-deluxe.

Judy Miller, the owner, is behind the counter. She'll introduce you to a sampling of the gourmet cheeses. Try the Kasseri (Greek), it's delicious; or the St. Andre that is known for its buttery texture and goes well with breakfast or as a dessert. If you love exotic cheese spreads, Judy suggests tasting the creme de Neufchatel in chocolate, wild berries, and certainly the French-style garden vegetables.

For one of the most superb potpourris of fresh, signature salads, feast your eye's on the display in the front cooler. Although too numerous to sample them all, try the antipasto--special cheeses, pepperoni, salami, artichokes, olives, carrots and celery bathed in a homemade Italian vinaigrette.

But, don't stop there...Judy's also a sandwich whiz and will gladly fix you a sandwich you aren't likely to forget. The tender, moist, aged roast beef is simply delicious. Select from turkey, ham, salami, and much more. Enjoy your lunch at the tables inside and chat with Judy. She'll share her knowledge about the nearby hiking trails through the Mission Valley and what the progress is on the Mission's restoration project.

If you like, ask for a sack lunch, and enjoy it on the trail or at the close-by picnic tables. The Cheese Taster, an adventure in a deli-deluxe.

MISSION DELICATESSEN
155 Anza Street
Fremont, CA 94539
Tel. (415) 657-8062
Hrs: Mon. - Fri.   11:00 a.m. - 7:00 p.m.
      Saturday   11:00 a.m. - 5:00 p.m.

Owner Mary Chamberlin brings extensive training and abundant experience to Mission Delicatessen. Mary has studied at such well known

Alameda County

European schools as Cordon Bleu and La Verenne, she also travels round the world each year searching for new recipe ideas.

Only the finest butter, vinegar, cheese, olive oils, wines and natural ingredients go into the foods. All soups, salads, terrines and pates are entirely homemade. Thirty great sandwiches with familiar names such as, BLT, Proscuitto, roast beef and egg salad come with the finest condiments. Choice of bread is baker's dozen. Try the turkey Imperial - hot open faced on an English muffin with layers of turkey breast, apple salad, melted cheese, pineapple and cranberry; Moron's Ecstasy - dark rye with turkey, roast beef and ham stacked high, then two kinds of cheese, cucumber, tomatoes, sour cream and horseradish or many other unique creations. Luncheon items with choices such as omelettes, quiche, ravioli, taco salad, super burritos and chicken enchiladas are more tempting choices. Save room for dessert with choices ranging from New York cheesecake to moist, tasty date bars.

Be sure to visit Mary and delight in her culinary expertise at your "Best Choice" - Mission Delicatessen.

(See special invitation in the Appendix.)

Entertainment

HOT ROD CAFE
39148 State Street
Fremont, CA 94538
Tel. (415) 793-5491
Hrs: Mon. - Fri.   5:00 p.m. - 2:00 a.m.
          Sat. - Sun.   7:00 p.m. - 2:00 a.m.

So you're revved up and ready to go, or maybe you've been spinning your wheels. Whatever the case, the Hot Rod Cafe will give you just the lift you're seeking. It's ingenious. In tune with current trends, it has stupendous effects and a super-friendly staff. These are just some of the reasons so many people come here. You can mingle among the homogeneous crowd of enthusiasts, some come because it's an "in" place to be seen, others simply mingle and meet, or relax and partake of the stimulating surroundings and expertly-mixed libations.

The decor is striking, blending elements of art deco, 50's nostalgia and modern effects. On one wall is an impeccably-painted mural of classic cars parked on the beach. Beside the dance floor sits a gleaming hot rod roadstar with chromium trim and engine. There are old gas pumps stationed at various locations, an electric guitar mounted on one wall and a figure of Mighty Mouse on another. Most amazing are the large gas-filled multi-colored globes that shoot crackling light inside like an electrical storm. Neon lights in stripes above the bar and on pillars add further energy and life. The speaker system is above the dance floor and provides heightened sensations with blinking beacons, strobes, stage lights of various bright colors, and--most incredible-- the cyclops. The cyclops is a unique fixture with numerous lights and whirls, cascading its rays to the music. The classic Cadillac bar features an old-time movie marquee with four tv's for video viewing. Marvel at the miniature space shuttle hanging from the ceiling, the striped umbrellas, and parachuting clowns.

For a break during your dancing spree, visit the video arcade where you can play pinball machines and electronic games. There are hot and cold *hor d'oevres*, and plenty of special events that will bring you back night after night. So, if you've tired of running down the same old strip, and gotta find a new place that's completely hip, here you are--the Hot Rod Cafe.

Florist

FREMONT FLOWER PAVILLION, 43377 Mission Boulevard, Fremont, California. A wide selection of flowers, cards, gifts and chocolate await your delight.

Gift

THE GIFT CONNECTION
3129 Walnut Ave.
Fremont, CA 94538
Tel. (415) 794-8445
Hrs: Mon.-Fri.   10:00 a.m.-8:00 p.m.
         Saturday   10:00 a.m.-6:00 p.m.

As its name implies, The Gift Connection has that special gift for that special someone for whom you are shopping. Owner Naomi Seuferer has a personable, helpful manner that makes you feel perfectly at ease as you stroll about the store. You will notice what a wonderful miniaturist she is when you see the displayed refrigerator magnets. One magnet was a country basket containing a bottle of Brer Rabbit molasses, catsup, a bundle of daisies, and a canvas sack stamped "Idaho Potatoes." The white lace around it made it a very dainty creation. You will also notice the great bear display Naomi keeps at the front counter. There are bears dressed as doctors, firemen, nurses, patients, and Yuppy businessmen (toting genuine leather briefcases). All of the costumes are handstiched, with an eye for detail, realism, candor and color.

There is an impressive display of items by some of California's most talented creators. On the back wall are Robert Sexton's lithos, all limited editions that are signed and dated. Also impressive is the greeting card collection. Naomi was a greeting card salesperson, and her selection reflects her expertise. Naomi's choices in Vandor masks are greatly admired, too. In addition, you'll find a large selection of specific gifts for men and women from embossed brass button covers, shaving mugs, and money clips, to gold mesh purses, compacts, and cigarette cases. Naomi offers a shopping service for people on the go. The tremendously generous selection of gifts at the Gift Connection never seems to end.

(See special invitation in Appendix.)

JB'S GIFTS, 39146 Fremont Hub, Fremont, California. In this delightful shop you will find gifts, keys and engraving services.

NOOKS 'N' CRANNIES
3964 Washington Blvd.
Fremont, CA 94539
Tel. (415) 657-5028
Hrs: Tues.-Wed.   10:00 a.m.-6:00 p.m.
       Thur.-Fri.   10:00 a.m.-7:00 p.m.
       Saturday   10:00 a.m.-6:00 p.m.

Standing at the intersection of Washington and Fremont, one can sense what it was like when this was the bustling center of the Irvington Township. Horse and buggy once strutted along where autos now whiz by. Many of the original old buildings still stand, most of them refurbished, giving the district a distinct atmosphere--a fun place to browse. And, no gift shop in Irvington teases you back to those pioneer days so much as Nooks "N" Crannies. Mary Gutierrez, with the help of her husband Patrick, have created a special spirit of country art in this shop. They have always been avid collectors of Americana, and you'll see this in the blend of authentic period pieces with hand-made country crafts.

The porcelain and wooden geese and ducks that are hand-crafted by local artisans appear so real that they seem to quack, honk, and wiggle their tails right in front of you. Bear huggers will find Mary's selection irresistible. She carries the Steiff line from Germany, which is the Cadillac of bear makers since the early 1900's. The North American line features favorites among character bear collectors. You'll meet Scarlet O'Beara, Anna Bearlova, Dr. Killbear and more. A marvelous selection of bisque carousel horses is displayed in the front window. Each, with its unique design, is mounted on a polished brass or wooden stand and some have music boxes. There are also plenty of hand-sewn quilted pillows, wooden baskets, primitives, bunnies and pigs dressed in a country array of chintz, hand-painted spice racks and paper towel holders and porcelain clowns with intricately painted faces.

(See special invitation in Appendix.)

Glass

STAINED GLASS OVERLAY DESIGN STUDIO
3255 Walnut Avenue
Fremont, CA 94538
Tel. (415) 790-5715
Hrs: Mon. - Thur. 9:00 a.m. - 6:00 p.m.
     Friday   9:00 a.m. - 5:00 p.m.
     Saturday   10:30 a.m. - 4:30 p.m.

It is not just the stunning effects you get with stained glass overlay that impresses. It is the versatility in patterns, virtually unlimited, and the economy of price as compared with cut stained glass. The process of stained glass overlay constitutes a breakthrough (no pun intended) in design possibilities. It has greater strength than a cut-glass panel because it is all one sheet of glass...rather than individually cut pieces. The overlay process begins with a solid sheet of glass that is stained using a patented coloring system and then leaded, creating your own custom design.

The veined and textured cathedral effects you see in traditional stained glass are also possible with the overlay. The end result is a stained glass overlay panel that can only be differentiated from one of cut glass by a closely discerning eye. Stained glass overlay is perfect to add wondrous color to any window, be it skylight, sidelight, sliding glass door, hexagonal window, arch, or shower door.

Tim and Debra Sanders opened their business on Walnut Avenue and business has been brisk ever since. In addition to the overlay, the shop features exceptional etched glass, beveled glass, and hand-crafted doors and designer in-laid rugs. Tim and Debra will visit with you at your home to take the measurements and consult with you on the design. Their philosophy is that it is your design for your home...and they want to help in the creation taking full-bloom. This couple has a rich appreciation for their work and a warm approach that glows with goodwill.

If you're looking to decorate your home, or office, contact Tim and Debra Sanders. They know how to add richness to your life.

Party Articles

THE PARTY ARTS HOUSE
40919 Fremont Boulevard
Fremont, CA 94538
Tel. (415) 651-1530
Hrs: Mon. - Fri.   10:00 a.m. - 6:00 p.m.
       Saturday   10:00 a.m. - 5:00 p.m.

Put your party and wedding plan worries behind you and leave them in the hands of the professionals! Tucked away in the oldest shopping center in Fremont, in the heart of the quaint historic Irvington district, The Party Arts House has all the supplies and experienced guidance you'll need for any special occasion.

Whether it's personalized stationery, favors, etched champagne glasses or cake tops, owner Maxine Northon can match items to your specifications. The store carries rental items, such as large floral baskets, money trees, lace parasols, and a large inventory of unique centerpieces and unusually shaped cake pans.

Party supplies are virtually unlimited. You'll find balloons, trick favors, banners and piñatas. Make celebrations joyful and memorable with hats, noisemakers, confetti, streamers and poppers, and wrap the presents from a large selection of paper and ribbons. Leave your worries behind, have a ball planning the best gig you ever had, and enjoy the party!

Restaurant

THE ALPS
5200 Mowry Avenue
Fremont, CA 94538
Tel. (415) 791-1141
Hrs: Tues.-Fri.   10:00 a.m.-9:00 p.m.
       Sat.   7:30 a.m.-9:00 p.m.
       Sun.   7:30 a.m.-5:00 p.m.

When Roger Amaral first purchased The Alps, it was already a highly successful deli. He had a yearning, though, to expand it into a full restaurant. So, with the passing of time, a glass dining room was added and the menu extended to include breakfast and dinner.

You can choose for your breakfast from a selection of twenty one omelets, such as the Smoked salmon that is accompanied by onions and cream cheese, or, try the Lisbon with its diced chili peppers, mushrooms, tomatoes, cheese, and linguisa. The Bavaria breakfast is a well-known favorite, with two pieces of fresh toast layered with Bauern Schniken, ham and choice of eggs. Or, try the gourmet French toast, prepared with sliced sourdough that's been dipped in Grand Marnier and egg batter, served with hot apples, sour cream, and chopped walnuts.

For lunch you can choose from twenty two specialty sandwiches such as: The Alps, smoked Black Forest ham and Jarlsberg cheese on a croissant, or the Cabo San Lucas, with turkey, bacon, pepper cheese, and jalapeño peppers on sourdough bread.

For dinner there is veal, chicken, and steak entrees, and a delectable calamari dish. Pasta is also popular. Try the Fettucine Carbonara, fresh egg noodles with onions, bacon, and tomatoes in a rich cream sauce.

This deli cafe will take you to another continent with its chalet interior and European cuisine. Order one of the 250 beers available, sit back, and enjoy.

(See special invitation in Appendix.)

CAJUN JIM'S
39217 Fremont Hub
Fremont, CA 94538
Tel. (415) 794-0409
Hrs: Mon. - Fri.   9:00 a.m. - 9:00 p.m.
     Saturday   11:00 a.m. - 9:00 p.m.
     Sunday   11:00 a.m. - 6:00 p.m.

An easy step from the Fremont sidewalk right into downtown New Orleans. Bourbon Street atmosphere--slow moving polished-brass fans swirl eddies of air across the room and gently touch and sway the lace curtains. Scenes of Mardi Gras, a giant alligator and lush, tropical plants adorn the interior. The only thing missing is the jazz band plaintively wailing the blues.

Jim Wisinger is from Louisiana and he's brought the Cajun culture and cooking to his grateful customers. The Chef, Steve Fagrey, interprets the authentic Louisiana cuisine; spicy, but not too hot to eat.

The menu includes seafood gumbo, loaded with shrimp, crab, oysters and hot sausage blended into a superb stew; or try the chicken Jambalaya, cooked with smoked ham, hot sausage, and capped with a snappy Creole sauce, and there's always deep fried catfish; light and crispy, mildly spiced, cooked to perfection. Among the regulars the barbeque platter and Cajun Jim's sampler plate seem to be the favorites.

Save room for dessert--true Southern hospitality dictates a scrumptious savory to end your meal; there's thick-crusted pecan pie baked daily, sweet potato pie, pralines, karo-nut pie, or bread pudding. You'll think you've died and gone to heaven...for that reason, be thankful he doesn't have the jazz band. Cajun Jim's, a "Best Choice" for authentic Arcadian cuisine.

LUCIA'S FISH HOUSE
681 Mowry Avenue
Fremont, CA 94536
Tel. (415) 794-7247
Hrs: lunch: Mon. - Fri.   11:00 a.m. - 2:30 p.m.
    dinner: Mon. - Fri.   5:00 p.m. - 9:00 p.m.
               Saturday   5:00 p.m. - 10:00 p.m.
               Sunday   5:00 p.m. - 9:00 p.m.

Near Mission Boulevard and Mowry Avenue, Lucia's Fish House maintains one of the Fremont area's richest family traditions--good eating. Across the street from this area's favorite fish house, you'll note Lucia's Italian Restaurant, which serves a steady stream of regulars for breakfast, lunch and dinner. Italian-style.

Dick and Lu Lucia, the owners, and their sons, Rich and Bob possess a healthy, family work ethic and uphold the highest standards of graciousness and hospitality at both restaurants.

At Lucia's Fish House the freshest catch from the seas is offered broiled, baked, deep-fried, or charbroiled. There's salmon, halibut, sea bass and shark--to name a few. Or, try the hand-breaded, deep-fried scallops, the oysters, calamari, prawns or clam strips.

Cajun-Creole specialties draw the crowds. The alligator tail, thinly sliced, breaded and deep-fried is prized as an appetizer. Spicy, Cajun dressing sparks your salad prior to an order of authentic, blackened redfish. The pan-fried fresh fish with pecan butter sauce is superb. Jambalaya is served and prawns Creole are featured with tasty ham, sausage, chicken, and special spices 'n herbs, baked with rice and prawns in a great sauce. Complete your meal with a sampling of New Orleans bread pudding or Chantilly cream.

Once you've tasted the specialties of Lucia's Fish House you will come to know why so many positively insist on eating here.

MASSIMO'S CONTINENTAL ITALIAN CUISINE
5200 Mowry Avenue
Fremont, CA 94538
Tel. (415) 792-2000

Hrs:	lunch:	Mon. - Fri.	11:30 a.m. - 3:00 p.m.
	dinner:	Mon. - Thur.	5:00 p.m. - 10:00 p.m.
		Fri. - Sat.	5:00 p.m. - 11:00 p.m.
		Sunday	private parties only

If great grandfather Massimo were alive today, his big Italian heart would swell with pride over his namesake restaurant. Three generations of the Rinetti family take meticulous care to see that their impeccable standards in hospitality and cuisine are maintained.

Among the enticing appetizers are Escargot Maison, Scampi Allegro, and Tortellini Supreme--delicate hand-rolled ring pasta that is filled with pork and subtle spices, then capped with sun-dried tomatoes from Italy, a creme fraiche sauce and freshly-grated Parmesan. *Bellisimo!*

If you hadn't ordered your wine yet, do it now, cause this is just the preamble to what is yet to come. Your waiter will pull a cart up to the table and commence to stir and add the unique ingredients that will make up your salad. There'll be light anchovies, finely chopped garlic, sprinkles of vinegar and Worchestershire, Dijon mustard, a single drop of Tabasco, half of an egg white, olive oil and freshly chopped romaine lettuce topped with home-made croutons. *Fabuloso!*

As you await the entree, relax in an atmosphere of soft-light cascading from the hand-carved wooden chandeliers, sepia still-lifes and idyllic European scenes adorn the walls and classical-style sculptures complete the scene.

The veal scampi combines the brilliant culinary accomplishments of two of Massimo's specialties, veal and seafood--thinly cut slices of veal with large fancy prawns resting on top are sauteed with sherry, butter, shallots, a pinch of lemon and Tabasco. Equally taste-rewarding are the poultry, al a carte pastas and beef dishes.

For the very best in Continental Italian dining--Massimo's.

PAPILLON RESTAURANT FRANCAIS
37296 Mission Boulevard
Fremont, CA 94536
Tel. (415) 793-6331

Hrs:	Lunch	Mon. - Fri.	11:30 a.m. - 2:00 p.m.
	Dinner	Mon. -Thu.	5:30 p.m. - 10:00 p.m.
		Fri. - Sat.	5:30 p.m. - 10:30 p.m.
		Sunday	5:00 p.m. - 10:00 p.m.

Some great families are born into success, others can build it, still others are destined to rise to the top. Fremont is privileged to claim one of the latter variety, the Tom Foreman family, proprietors of the fabulous Papillon Restaurant Francais.

Although you will often notice the glimmer of a polished limousine in the parking lot, the atmosphere inside Papillon exudes a sincere grace that defies pomp or pretension, it is never stuffy or prudish. Tiffany glass lamps hang in the entryway of the famous garden room and a tuxedo'd maitre d' escorts you across a gleaming tiled floor. The menu offers epicurean delights to please the palate. Begin the meal, perhaps, with a rich seafood pate, a light blend of scallop, egg, salmon, sole and olive oil, chilled into a mousse. Follow with an extremely smooth and full bodied soup du jour and salad consisting of romaine lettuce, grated cheddar, shredded carrots and topped with a light Caesar dressing that has become a Papillon tradition. The Coquilles St. Jacques proves a more than worthy entree, remarkably tender and sweet, with butter and garlic sauce. Finally, a lovely chocolate mousse for dessert - a gentle chocolate swirl with whipped cream floating on a pool of raspberry sauce.

Such fine dishes are the norm, you will enjoy exploring this menu filled with magnificent surprises.

(See special invitation in the Appendix.)

This tour gives you a chance to see the outskirts of Fremont as well as enjoy some fine attractions both inside and outside the city.

Culture Tour of Fremont			
a.m.	Mission San Jose	Best mission	Fre/Att
a.m.	Ohlone Burial Ground	Best monument	Fre/Att
p.m.	Mission Deli	Best lunch	Fre/Deli
p.m.	Ohlone Arts	Best gallery	Fre/Art
p.m.	Shinn Historical Park	Best culture park	Fre/Att
p.m.	Papillon Restaurant	Best variety	Fre/Rest

PEARL'S CAFE
4096 Bay Street
Fremont, CA 94538
Tel. (415) 490-2190
Hrs: Tue. - Fri.   11:00 am - 2:30 pm
                          5:00 pm - 9:00 pm
         Saturday   5:00 pm - 9:00 pm

There is something uplifting about finding a restaurant where old-world cooking blends with a simple setting. You could hardly find a place in the far reaches of Fremont where this feeling is so implicit as at Pearl's, where owner and chef Ernst Angst and his daughter, Marcella, bring you to center stage in the arena of fine European cuisine and hospitality.

Ernst was born in Switzerland where he grew up mixing bread dough by hand and cooking meals in an alpine early-century world where modern means were meager and skills essential. At 15 he began his formal apprenticeship, spending 15 years in pastry shops and resort hotels in Zurich. Signing on as a pastry chef with a Panamanian shipping line, Ernst began an odyssey of travels that lasted years, until he settled in old historic Irvington. When he first arrived in the U.S., Ernst spoke fluent German, French and Spanish, but no English. With remarkable resourcefulness, he made his way to the Ambassador Hotel in Los Angeles and eventually to San Francisco's Mark Hopkins. Ernst describes himself as self-taught, largely due, no doubt, to his originality. Each dish is individually-prepared. We marveled as we watched him create dinner entrees in the kitchen with perfect timing, knowing when to check the sauces, open the oven door, prepare the garnishes. His movements confirmed years of knowledge and experience.

Ernst has passed this knowledge on to Marcella. Both prepare meals, Marcella most often lunch. You'll enjoy her sandwiches and fine specialties such as Quiche Maison, delicious with ham and Gruyere cheese, and served with fruit, vegetables and freshly baked bread. If you'd like a zesty experience in pasta, try the Liguine Polonaise. It boasts a meat and tomato sauce and rich liguine noodles you will truly savor. Blackout cake, pecan pie, cassata, German chocolate cake, Swiss kirsch mousse--all are heavenly.

Dinner at Pearl's is a romantic experience created by the intimately-lit room, Ernst's exquisite preparations and Marcella's charm. Specials, always highly recommended, include such Continental favorites such as Escallops de Veau and Beef Bourguignoone. Other favorites include Veal Piccata, canneloni and Emincee de Veau: minced veal sauteed in white wine, mushrooms and shallots and served in a cream sauce over homemade pasta. Ernst learned this Swiss recipe many years ago: and now he carries on that old-world knowledge and tradition in this cafe on Bay Street, preparing dishes you should surely taste for yourself.

Toys

GIFT CAROUSEL
39199A Farwell Drive
Fremont, CA 94538
Tel. (415) 794-0333
Hrs: Mon. - Thur.   10:00 a.m. - 7:00 p.m.
     Friday   10:00 a.m. - 9:00 p.m.
     Saturday   10:00 a.m. - 6:00 p.m.
     Sunday   12:00 noon - 5:00 p.m.

Even when its not Christmas time, curious little children, with widened eyes, press their noses against the window to watch the toy train go round and round. In the other window, a genuine, hand-carved carousel horse, lends a joyous spirit to the gathering. Welcome to the Gift Carousel.

Come in and browse awhile, you'll find rubber stamp art galore...an array of stuffed animals in tumbled profusion..teddy bears on parade...artist dolls with charming, hand-painted porcelain faces; dressed in ribbons 'n lace, all set for an outing. There's jesters and clowns, waiting to make you laugh...silken Christmas tree ornaments for home and gift-giving.

In the Victorian Corner you'll find charming, hand-painted tiles that depict country living, wreaths, lace and potpourri to fill your home with romance and lovely, glazed cookie jars just waiting to be taken home and filled with home-baked goodies.

For the kids there are helium balloons, buy one or a bunch...near the cash register there are music boxes, Mickey Mouse watches, the Raven line of handmade pins, porcelain earrings in Roaring 20s or Art Deco design, a cache of neatly bagged and labeled spicy teas, sweet jelly beans bursting with flavor, books for children and, boy! there's so much to see...once your selection is made, move on over and select from the hundreds of cards and unique gift wrappings available.

The Gift Carousel, a special place for kids of all ages.

(See special invitation in Appendix)

Entertain yourself as you buy for someone else as you shop and play in Fremont

Fremont Gift Shopping Tour			
a.m.	Alps Restaurant	Best breakfast	Fre/Rest
a.m.	Gift Connection	Best yuppy teddy	Fre/Gift
a.m.	Stained Glass Overlay	Best stained glass	Fre/Glass
a.m.	Gift Carousel	Best toy & dolls	Fre/Toy
p.m.	The Cheese Taster	Best sandwich	Fre/Deli
p.m.	Nooks 'N' Crannies	Best stuffed bear	Fre/Gift
Pack away your gifts then relax at any of these "Best Choice" restaurants:			
p.m.	Cajun Jim's	Best Cajun	Fre/Rest
p.m.	Lucia's Fish House	Best fish dinner	Fre/Rest
p.m.	Hot Rod Cafe	Best late nite fun	Fre/Ent

Hayward

The fourth largest city in Alameda county is astride two key transportation links. Over 95,000 people live in the community which remembers its farming heritage with an annual Zucchini Festival each August. Traffic began rolling across the low-level San Mateo toll bridge in the late 1920s, heading to and from San Francisco and the San Joaquin Valley through a community already busy with north-south traffic. Today, Bay Area Rapid Transit refines that connection with two BART stations for travel by rail on both sides of the bay.

There are about 30 square miles of land area inside the city limits, nearly that much more in tide flats and estuaries of the bay. California State University has a campus in Hayward. Retail and commercial centers dot the city named after William Hayward who opened a hotel in 1852, and remained when Guillermo Castro laid out the town site from his Rancho San Lorenzo two years latter. The town was settled by many Portuguese emigrants connected with the farming on nearby fields. A Portuguese park recalls the emigrants.

Attraction

Ardenwood Historic Farm, at 5453 Jarvis Avenue in nearby Newark, is a living history farm demonstrating agriculture from the Victorian era such as hundreds of farms practiced in early Hayward. A horse-drawn railway car is among the rides.

Chabot Community College is on a 93 acre site at 25555 Hesperian Boulevard, offering vocational and technical classes. It has a second campus in the Livermore Valley. Information on events is available by calling 786-6600.

In the city center are the **Hayward Japanese Gardens,** one of the first sites where traditional Japanese design was used with native California plantings. There is a teahouse available. Open daily. At Foothill Boulevard and San Lorenzo Creek.

Hayward Area Art Forum operates a gallery at 1015 E Street, open Wednesday through Saturday, 10:00 a.m. - 4:00 p.m. Changing exhibitions of museum-quality works are shown and a gift shop is operated by the non-profit organization.

Several historical events are promoted during the year by the **Hayward Area Historical Society.** Information can be obtained by calling 581-0223. The **Historical Museum** is located at 22701 Main Street. A second museum is operated at **McConaghy House,** 18701 Hesperian Boulevard.

For further information, contact the **Hayward Chamber of Commerce,** 22300 Foothill Boulevard, telephone 537-2424.

Accomodations

BEST WESTERN INN OF HAYWARD, 360 West A Street, Hayward, California. Enjoy your restful sleep and then indulge in a complimentary Continental breakfast. Relax after working out in the exercise room in a jacuzzi.

Antique

B STREET ANTIQUES
1025 B Street
Hayward, CA 94541
Tel. (415) 889-8549
Hrs: Mon. - Sat. 10:00 a.m. - 6:00 p.m.
     Sunday 11:00 a.m. - 4:00 p.m.

In Hayward, there is no antique dealer more respected than Herb Sexton at B Street Antiques. His large shop is central to the B Street historic mall. Other dealers up and down the street admire his honesty, and the wellspring of knowledge that is his trademark. Retired from the Army, Herb opened his store in 1982.

"Hayward is loaded with treasures," says Herb. Thus, a lot of the contents of the B Street Antiques store come from local estate sales that Herb and his wife Janice attend. Other items come from Europe, the Midwest and eastern United States. By buying wisely, Herb is able to mark quality items and rare pieces at prices you'll applaud.

The sizeable showroom is full of fun choices to bring out the kid in you. "No reproductions!" is Herb's first rule. " Everything in the store is genuinely collectable." Herb keeps a constant eye out to acquire the best for his shop: You'll find early American oak and walnut dining tables, Victrolas, bed sets, chairs and chests of drawers at B. Street Antiques. All of his items are sound investments sturdy enough to last generations, all with good finishes; many are ornately hand-carved.

You'll also find fine examples of Lalique, Royal Doulton, crystal, nautical items, depression glass, and hundreds of other items. You can never go wrong by investing in sterling silver goblets, vanity sets, and spoons. For the casual collector of the unusual, Herb offers chalk carnival figures, Coca-Cola collectables, cartoon characters and the like. You can add to your American pottery collection or glassware at B Street Antiques, and the loft at the shop is crammed with delights you'll want to explore.

B Street Antiques is worth a trip out of your way when you are near Hayward.

(See special invitation in the Appendix)

DORIS' ANTIQUES GALLERIA, 935 B Street, Hayward, California. This galleria specializes in antiques and framed prints.

HAYWARD FAIRE ANTIQUES, 926 B Street, Hayward, California. You will find thousands of items from which to choose, among them are antiques and many collectibles.

Apparel

GRANDE ILLUSIONS, 938 B Street, Hayward, California. A fine collection of men's and women's vintage and classic clothing.

Attraction

SHORELANDS CORPORATION BUILDING
21800 Hesperian Boulevard
Hayward, CA 94541
Tel. (415) 783-2856
Tours and meetings by appointment.

A walk with John Thorpe through the Shorelands Corporation office building will reveal Hayward history. The Thorpe family survives here, through pictures and artifacts, as well as the presence of John Thorpe himself, who has carried on with accomplishments worthy of a remarkable ancestry. The Thorpe family is among America's great and has been written about in numerous history books. The Shorelands office building is a part of that history. It is a turn of the century classic Victorian built originally for the Ostreloh family.

A former farmhouse, it retains the original curved leaded glass windows that were transported from Germany on a sailing ship. Rare in this day, it features the old fish scale shingle siding and incorporates beautiful scrollwork. The inside is wonderfully restored. The Shoreland offices are located on the lower level and are appointed with genuine period antiques. To this day the kitchen stove and a fireplace are the sole sources of heat. The upstairs is a loft that serves as the Shorelands Corporation board room. The main room features rough wood beams and a large antique conference table with hand carved chairs. John Thorpe's hobbies are reflected by the artifacts tastefully displayed: a large wooden sculpted eagle, moose and caribou heads, a fire alarm bell (one of twelve that went off in San Francisco during the great earthquake and fire), a beautiful statue of Venus and other fascinating relics. In the turret room, one can view old photographs from Hayward history, as well as the Thorpe family of authors, legislators, industrialists and inventors. None of them was more remarkable than John's grandfather, William Chatterly Thorpe. This man invented the first rotary tub washing machine, sawtooth key and cylinder lock. His early airplane hangs in the Smithsonian next to the one the Wright brothers flew at Kitty Hawk.

A tour of the building and grounds includes a trip to the Coach House. Here you will have the pleasure of viewing one of the finest classic car collections to be seen on the West Coast. Each vehicle is in mint condition. There is a 1912 green convertible Mercedes and a 1927 Lincoln, Isadora Duncan's 1914 Rolls Royce is splendid it its regal luster. Two Deusenbergs, a 1916 race car and a 1929 model J are also on display. The old Hispano Suiza models from Spain are extremely elegant and very rare, as only a few remain.

The upstairs director's room is available to groups for meetings as approved by Shorelands Corporation. . A trip through the Shorelands building is enlightening with all of its history, preserved beauty, splendor and heritage.

Brewery

BUFFALO BILL'S BREWERY
1082 B Street
Hayward, CA 94541
Tel. (415) 886-9823

"Buffalo" Bill Owens has rightly adopted the tag of "Buffalo" Bill, the old West's most famous scout and buffalo hunter. This pub, the beehive of B Street, is brimming with that adventuresome bent that won the West. People flock from miles around just to quaff glass after glass of his rich, whole-bodied, micro brewed beer. Generic beers just don't pack the same wallop as Bill's brew. So his customers keep coming back for more. Not that there's anything different about the ingredients...just hops, barley, yeast, and good old San Francisco Hetch Hetchy water. The consistency may vary slightly from batch to batch, but that's the way of home brew. One must realize that many consider Bill's brewmastery a throwback to medieval alchemy. He's making these suds in the back room rather than somewhere in the Rockies. If you catch him on brew day, that's Mondays, you can watch him stir the musty concoction and see it take its magical turns. Separate tanks have pipes connected to the taps out front where the bartenders ensure that your cup runneth over.

When you visit the pub, you will soon notice the buffalo head mounted above the bar. You will also notice that this icon of the plains is dressed in appropriate garb. Bill explained that its dress changes with the seasons. During the summer, for example, it sports giant yellow sunglasses and an inner tube, or around Christmas time, it wears a long white beard and Santa Claus cap. The happy environment here is a blend of bright rays beaming through the ceiling skylight, genuine oak booths and barstools, Bill's good cheer, and a selection of five great draft beers in addition to his own. So, hitch up, take a trot down B Street, tether your pony on a parking meter and partake of some of Hayward's most remarkable refreshment.

Gift

EDYTHE'S GIFT BOUTIQUE, 969 B Street, Hayward, California. At Edythe's you will find high quality gifts and many handcrafted items for your home or a friend.

GIFTS N' GREETINGS
1098 A Street
Hayward, CA 94546
Tel. (415) 581-1131
Hrs: Mon. - Sat. 9:00 a.m - 6:00 p.m.
Open Sundays during holiday season.

Whether you are looking for an important present for someone special, or simply must select a card that's super unusual, Gifts 'N Greetings is the place to go in Hayward.

There are wonderful things to squeeze and touch such as plush bears with fuzzy fur, shaggy slippers and stuffed animals. Among the latter you'll particularly enjoy the funny pigs dressed as policemen, firemen, football players and mailmen. For a light hearted gift idea be sure to see the shiny silk mobiles. There are giant lips, parrots, hearts and a clown seated on a trapeze. Character mugs by the dozen will make you laugh. Figurines are always a great gift idea. The Sandicast sculptures of animals in enchanting natural poses are collector's dreams.

The selection of books for special occasions is comprehensive, there are also photo albums with exotic flowers and unicorns on the covers, as well as fancy scrapbooks. For parties, there are pretty napkins, confetti, wrapping paper, streamers, party caps and more. Additional gift ideas for all occasions include jewelry boxes, bisque birthday girl figures, music boxes and terrific seasonal items for every holiday. There are colorful helium balloons to take home and bounce to your heart's content.

You won't find a more complete selection of cards anywhere. Beautiful Blue Mountain Arts cards with lovely verses and designs of sunsets, flowers, lakes and more are found in soft pastel shades. The Recycled friendship and congratulations cards are very popular, as is the California Dreamer series. Owner Ilene Kohler is very proud of her personal service which extends to in-house engraving and special order invitations.

Gifts 'N Greetings is an enchanting emporium filled with hundreds of unique and beautiful ideas that will suit your needs when shopping for that terrific gift or preparing for a special occasion.

Museum

HAYWARD AREA HISTORICAL SOCIETY MUSEUM
22701 Main Street
Hayward, CA 94541
Tel. (415) 581-0223
Hrs: Mon. - Fri.   11:00 a.m. - 4:00 p.m.
         Saturday   12:00 noon - 4:00 p.m.

Visitors to downtown Hayward will be happy to find a fascinating attraction just a short walk from the B Street commercial center. It is the Hayward Area Historical Society Museum and gift shop. Admission is free, donations happily accepted.

The gift shop is housed in the front of the museum and offers antiques, collectables, books, crystal bells, antique style fold-out cards, reproduction Regulator clocks, collector's plates, old costume jewelry, marvelous sculptures, pottery, collector's glass and high quality souvenirs. Near the doorway is a book carousel with a diverse selection of books on art and historical subjects such as the history of the Washington Township, Art Deco, crocheting, collecting dolls, and hard-to-find historical reference books.

The museum displays photographs, paintings, tools, utensils, photographs of all the mayors of Hayward, an elegant nineteenth century piano, a well preserved Victrola, a rare View-Graflex studio photographer's camera, a magnificent hand-carved clock and changing exhibits. Auto buffs will enjoy the superb 1912 automobile and early nineteenth century fire pumper which are restored to mint condition. The museum library has extensive resources and is open for public use. Researchers will find old maps, photos, news clippings and books on the history of Alameda County. Old high school yearbooks are available for memory collecting. The helpful museum staff will explain artifacts and Hayward history. The Society also oversees the McConaghy House and sponsors various civic events. A visit to Hayward Area Historical Society Museum will be a pleasant venture into the past.

Restaurants

A STREET CAFE, 1213 A Street, Hayward, California. A fun cafe offering Mesquite grilled cooking and California cuisine.

Alameda County

CAFE RENDEZVOUS
1060 B Street
Hayward, CA 94541
Tel. (415) 538-2300
Hrs: Mon. - Tue. 8:30 a.m. - 4:30 p.m.
Wed. - Fri. 8:30 a.m. - 9:30 p.m.
Saturday 10:00 a.m. - 9:00 p.m.

Your itinerary must include a visit to the quaint Cafe Rendezvous. The colorful awning and lovely white lace curtains in the window have the *espirit* of gay Paris. Inside are verdant ferns and spiraling vines, soft pastel stripped French wallpaper, ceiling fans, wicker chairs and clean white tables arranged to create European charm. If it's early, try the cappaccino and a sweet, flakey fresh-baked apricot croissant or cherry puff. The tortes are divine - Black Forest, mocca, chocolate rum and raspberry. Other breakfast fare consists of a choice of omelette combinations such as chicken, mushroom and Jack cheese or avocado and sour cream, or if you prefer, strawberry waffles and French toast.

The entres served at Cafe Rendezvous are European style. The Viandes are *deliceux*...and uniquely prepared. The filet mignon is served with fresh herb butter, the Rond De Gigot Aux Herbes De Provence is grilled slices of leg of lamb with herbs. The Poulet Saute Au Champagne is a favorite, and consists of sauteed chicken in champagne with mushroom sauce. For unusual seafood dishes in the French tradition, try the Saumon De Loire Grille, the Palourdes Farcies Grill which is grilled stuffed clams Melanie style, or any of the delectable specials.

While dining, sip an imported white wine such as Pomino Bianco, a zesty Pellegrini varietal, full of flavor, a Riesling, Beaujolais, or a zooming Fume Blanc as you muse and contemplate the shores of the Seine.

(See special invitation in the Appendix)

EDEN EXPRESS
799 B Street
Hayward, CA 94541
Tel. (415) 886-8765
Hrs: Mon. - Fri. 7:00 a.m. - 2:30 p.m.
Sat. - Sun. 9:00 a.m. - 3:00 p.m.
MasterCard and Visa are accepted.

A peaceful and soothing atmosphere, fresh roses on the tables, the strains of classical music filling the air, Eden Express, located near the BART station, offers a respite from the hustle and bustle of a fast moving society. A non-profit organization trains the mentally and physically disabled, the restaurant becomes even more special with the warmth and love that the staff provides.

In keeping with the railroad theme of its neighbor, exposed red brick walls are reminiscent of an old railroad roundhouse, and the terminology on the menu takes you back to yesteryear. Breakfast may include the Stoker - thick French toast capped with fresh strawberries and served with bacon or ham. Or try a Casey Jones omelette. For lunch the menu offers a good selection of tasty sandwiches such as the Whistle Stop, Zephyr and Ham Track. On Sundays, a delightful champagne brunch offers crepes, eggs Benedict and French toast.

Look for the green ruffled canvas awning and a picture of a powerful steam locomotive painted on the front window of Eden Express. Stop in for a nice meal while on your travels and hail the train of social progress.

GREEN SHUTTER RESTAURANT
22636 Main Street
Hayward, CA 94541
Tel. (415) 537-4364
Hrs: Mon.-Fri.   6:30 a.m.-3:00 p.m.
         Sat.- Sun.   8:00 a.m.-2:30 p.m.

The Green Shutter Restaurant was built in 1927 along with the Green Shutter Hotel, which still operates today. The restaurant has been a focal point and gathering place for city patrons since its inception. The VFW, Lions Club, Kiwanis, Rotary, Odd Fellows, and business and civic leaders have met in the banquet room since the twenties. When current owners, Tony and Sue Hayes, first took over the Green Shutter, they redecorated extensively and added modern necessities. Thus, some stainless steel had to replace the original wood cabinets, but plenty of the original artifacts are still intact. The counter is original and features swivel stools with hat clips on the back. Many of the original tables and chairs are still used today.

Sue and Tony's combined experience is the cornerstone of the high-quality service and preparation that continues to bring people in. The customers have come to depend on the absolute freshness of the dishes: pastries baked from scratch each day, crisp, fresh salads, and mashed potatoes and gravy. The soup du jour is so popular that people call in every day inquiring about their favorite. Breakfast at the Green Shutter will meet your fondest expectations. Tony prepares terrific omelets, and eggs the way you like them. The pan-fried potatoes and delicious date loaves served with breakfast are favorites. At lunch time, the regulars check the specials first, delighting in such plates as beef tips and rice, lasagna, teriyaki baked chicken, or pot roast. Sunday brunch is a splendid affair with some out-of-this-world plump blueberry muffins and buttermilk biscuits. One could hardly imagine a Hayward without the Green Shutter. A mainstay for decades, it has served thousands and continues a heritage of fine service and excellent meals for all to experience and enjoy.

THE HAYWARD FISHERY
22701 Foothill Boulevard
Hayward, CA 94541
Tel. (415) 537-6410
Hrs: Sun.-Thu.   11:00 a.m. - 9:30 p.m.
      Fri.-Sat.   11:00 a.m. -10:00 p.m.
Visa and MasterCard are accepted.
and,
7400 San Ramon Blvd.
Dublin, CA 94568
Opening October 1987

It all began as a fish market back in 1942 owned and operated by Eugenia and Gus Aguiar. A bait shop was soon added and so the business remained until the 1950's. In the early 50's, the business was taken over by Eugenia's son, Mel Silva, and her son-in-law, Pete Rivers. By the 70's, the owners were being persuaded by their local customers to begin serving their excellent quality seafood on the premises. The Hayward Fishery, born out of its 1942 fish market, has been an east bay landmark since its inception.

The restaurant is still a family affair owned and operated by Mary Rivers and her children, Mike, Ron and daughter Joell. All the sauces and batters are prepared fresh each morning and the fish is the actual fresh catch of the day. The Hayward Fishery is so well known throughout the Bay Area for its food and friendly atmosphere that it is a favorite gathering place of professional athletes in the region and visiting players.

Stop by either of the two Hayward Fishery locations, eat some great fish and enjoy the River's family hospitality.

(See special invitation in the Appendix.)

LOS COMPRADES
944 C Street
Hayward, CA 94541
Tel. (415)-582-1937
Hrs: Tues.-Sun. 11:00 a.m.-9:00 p.m.
      Closed Mondays

Los Compadres is one of the best Mexican restaurants in the Bay Area. Frequently mentioned in the media, Los Compadres consistently ranks at the top. It's the place to enjoy a comfortable atmosphere, prompt service, and a menu filled with superlative homemade dishes.

Los Compadres is the home of the Super Burrito, a fresh flour tortilla full of tasty rice and beans, your choice of tender spicy chicken or beef, and zesty Chile Verde. For a variety plate, the Boomers are delicious. There are three in all: the San Leandro, the San Lorenzo, and the Hayward. The San Lorenzo features a Taco, Chile Relleno, Deluxe Tostada, Enchilada, and a Burrito to boot. A good bet for an appetizer at Los Compadres is their delicious nachos, with cheese melted throughout the chips, savory beans, guacamole, and sour cream. Or try the Chile Verde, Chorizon Con Huevos, Chile Colorado. For the more daring, there's the Nopales Con Huevos which administers cactus tid-bits, seasoning, onions, tomato, and chile to your taste buds with a flair.

Los Compadres has established, through the dedication of ten family members, a well-known institution in Hayward. Ignacio and Teresa Ramirez and their children are all integrally involved in preparing these home cooked favorites. Though controversies may persist over which Mexican restaurant ranks first in Hayward, at Los Compadres you'll know it is the guest who is considered first and foremost. For lunch or dinner, Los Compadres is a winner in Hayward.

THE HAYWARD RANCH, 22877 Mission Boulevard, Hayward, California. This homey ranch-style atmosphere will make you feel relaxed while you enjoy their specialty - supreme beef dishes.

Alameda County

MANZELLA'S SEAFOOD LOFT
1275 West Winton Avenue
Hayward, CA 94545
Tel. (415) 887-6040
Hrs: Lunch Mon. - Fri. 11:00 a.m. - 4:00 p.m.
      Dinner Mon. - Thur. 5:00 p.m. - 10:00 p.m.
             Fri. - Sat. 5:00 p.m. - 11:00 p.m.

Light aircraft taxi down the runway, speed off and soar into the distance. Outside your window the San Leandro Hills loom beyond the airport on the far horizon. Mt. Diablo can be seen from your booth, and yet this seafood villa has a marine cuisine and interior setting that brings back memories of a Caribbean cruise. Located at the Hayward Airport, Manzella's since 1974 has been a favorite.

It is doubtful that Hemingway's ancient mariner knew more about fish than John Manzella. This spirited gentleman goes way back in family heritage on fishermen, fish purveyors, and restauranteurs. As a teenager during WWII he worked full-time on Fisherman's Wharf at the Fisherman's Grotto #9, and many of the other great seafood restaurants. Along the way he has become an expert at preparing seafood dishes to perfection.

When John and his wife/partner, Lola, designed The Loft, they knew exactly what they wanted. The interior incorporates lofty rustic wood beams, subtle earth tone chairs and booths, a roomy lounge, and oil paintings of seafaring vessels. The seafood is drawn from international waters, from the far reaches of Finland to the southern extremes of the Chilean Pacific.

For lunch you can start off with some scrumptious appetizers: steamed Eastern mussels, bluepoint oysters or steamed cherrystone clams Bordelaise. The Manzella's seafood salad is a favorite--a combination of their very finest shellfish. The scallops Dore are dipped in light egg batter and gently pan fried, the Calamari steak Almondine is a supreme preparation.

The menu boasts wonderful fresh fish plates and excellent specialties like broiled Malaysian shrimp, basted in garlic butter and then gently broiled. Delicious! The stuffed Mexican prawns are juicy and plump and stuffed with crab meat, shrimp and cheese. The Bouillabaisse Cioppino features fresh clams, scallops, prawns, crab meat and mussels simmered in white wine sauce. Enjoy prime rib, great steaks, chicken a la lime, and quality vintage wines. Manzella's Seafood Loft is one of our "best choices" to share with someone you love.

RUE DE MAIN, 22622 Main Street, Hayward, California. This is a classy restaurnt which features Continental French cuisine.

72

To enjoy Hayward, at its best, take the time to experience all the nuances and flavors; as shown by this full day's tour:

TOUR OF HAYWARD			
a.m.	Cafe Rendezvous	Best omelet	Hay/Rest
a.m.	Green Shutter	Best Sun. brunch	Hay/Rest
a.m.	Japanese Gardens	Best early walk	Hay/Att
a.m.	Gifts 'N Greetings	Best gift	Hay/Gift
a.m.	Shorelands Bldg	Best historic tour	Hay/Att
p.m.	Hayward Fishery	Best lunch	Hay/Rest
p.m.	Art Forum	Best gallery	Hay/Att
p.m.	Buffalo Bill's	Best brewery	Hay/Brew
Top of your tour with dinner at either of these restaurants:			
p.m.	Manzella's	Best seafood	Hay/Rest
p.m.	Los Compadres	Best Mexican	Hay/Rest

Livermore Valley

Three cities, a famous laboratory developing nuclear devices, and the Altamont Pass with its forests of windmills mark the eastern panhandle of Alameda County. Dublin, at the intersection of I-580 and I-680, didn't incorporate until 1982 and experienced phenomenal growth as the commute became easier. This community was on the miner's road from Hayward to the gold country beyond Stockton, and Jose Amador's adobe served as an Inn, christened Dublin in 1852 because many Irishmen were in the area.

Livermore has about 50,000 residents, modern community facilities and the Lawrence Livermore Laboratory. Vineyards and livestock operations nearby make this a traditional shipping point. Pleasanton, with 37,000 people living within a thirteen square-mile city, continues to grow. It is home of the Alameda County Fairgrounds. General Electric Co. made nuclear history at the Vallecitos power plant in 1957 with the first electricity generated by a boiling water reactor which later received the first reactor license in the country.

Attractions

St. Raymond's Church on State Route 21 out of Dublin was built in 1859, the **Fallon House**, up the road a mile, was built in 1850 out of redwood timbers hauled from the forest in what is now Oakland.

Livermore Valley Wineries offer tours and tasting. Some of the six wineries have been growing grapes since the 1830s. Tour literature available by writing Box 2052, Livermore, CA 94550.

Lawrence Livermore National Laboratory science education center. Programs for students and teachers in community school systems are offered in the mathematics and science fields. A summer program includes instruction here. There is a small library and picnic area. Call 432-0556 for information. Open Monday - Friday 8:30 a.m. - 4:30 p.m.

The restored old town hall in Pleasanton houses the **Amador-Livermore Valley Historical Society's Museum.** Primarily a local history collection and reference material for researchers. Wednesday through Sunday open 1:00 p.m. - 4:00 p.m.

Altamont Pass on the freeway to Tracy provides a view of the windmills developed in the past decade for the generation of electrical energy from wind power. Several different designs are visible without leaving the highway.

Newark

Accommodations

**BROOKSIDE HOTEL
AND HERITAGE RESTAURANT & LOUNGE**
5977 Mowry Avenue
Newark, CA 94560
Tel. (415) 795-7995
Hrs: Sun.-Thu.   7:00 a.m.- 9:00 p.m.
        Fri.-Sat.   7:00 a.m.- 1:00 p.m.
Visa, Mastercard, and AMEX are accepted.

The Brookside Hotel is a charming little place with a Spanish California decor complete with a clay sculptured fountain, large, ornate iron chandelier, hexagonal tiles, and copper artwork adorning the walls. Amenities of the hotel include limousine service, dry cleaning service, 2 - 225 person meeting rooms, swimming pool and exercise gym. Rooms are simply appointed with armchairs, desks, and queen beds, and the room rates are correspondingly modest.

Contrasting with the hotel's simple grace, the Brookside Cafe is in a separate more contemporary structure and is the local hot spot for dinner and entertainment on Friday and Saturday nights (comedy nights). The fare is American traditional featuring broiled steak and chicken entrees served with homemade fresh pasta - try the BBQ back ribs and terrific Fajitas served sizzling at your table. Lunches feature hearty sandwiches and seafood specials, the salads are spectacular, and breakfasts offer pancakes, omelettes, and waffles try the Belgian waffles for a taste treat.

All in all the Brookside Hotel and Cafe are an unexpected gem hidden right in the heart of the San Francisco Bay Area.

(See special invitation in the Appendix)

NEWARK HILTON, 39900 Balentine Drive, Newark, California. Exquisite accommodations, great restaurants, and live entertainment are at the Hilton in Newark!

An easy day's tour, for your family or meandering by yourself, that highlights the Newark and Irvington area:

THE LATE DAY TOUR OF NEWARK/ IRVINGTON			
p.m.	Pearl's Cafe	Best lunch	Irv/Rest
p.m.	High Street General Store	Best antique	Irv/Gift
p.m.	Nooks 'N' Crannies	Best collectable	Irv/Gift
p.m.	Party Arts House	Best party supply	Irv/Gift
p.m.	Bobby McGee's	Best entertainment	Irv/Rest

Apparel

LA MODE FASHIONS BOUTIQUE
33970 Cedar Blvd.
Newark, CA 94560
Tel. (415) 651-1314
Hrs: Mon. - Thurs.   10:30 a.m. - 8:00 p.m.
         Friday   10:30 a.m. - 9:00 p.m.
         Saturday   10:00 a.m. - 7:00 p.m.
         Sunday   10:00 a.m. - 6:00 p.m.

With an eye for elegance and her own exquisite taste in fashion, Terry Pinpin opened La Mode Boutique. A confirmed shopaholic, Terry's worldwide travels netted her an extensive wardrobe which just kept growing. After a while her friends began urging her to sell to them some of her unusual and beautiful finds. Unable to keep up with demand, Terry opened her boutique. It was an instant success.

The dynasty Collection at La Mode embodies elegance in the tradition of Crystal Carrington herself. The selection may even look familiar to you, as if taken straight from the set. These dresses, three piece suits and glorious evening gowns are designed to make you the glowing focus of any crowd during your evening on the town. You'll also find discriminating wear for the career woman such as designer suits, dresses, and jackets--all of them expressing quality in every stitch. Beyond these, you'll enjoy a diverse choice in pure silk dresses, lovely lingerie, work skirts, slacks, sweaters and mesh knits. The extensive inventory is stocked in all sizes from petite to large. And you'll appreciate Terry's taste in furs--beautifully-cut trend-setting varieties.

Once you've chosen some exciting new additions to your wardrobe, you will likely find just the shoes to match, or perhaps a lovely beaded bag, earrings bracelet or necklace to complete your purchase. Terry's astute buying assures you of quality and uniqueness in apparel, and allows her to offer everything at affordable prices.

Along with great fashions, Terry offers person consultation on your fittings. She'll be honest in helping you decide which styles, colors, patterns and cuts do you the most justice. You can count on Terry and her associates to be there making prudent recommendations. And La Mode offers alterations at no charge.

Restaurants

BOBBY MCGEE'S
5995 Mowry Avenue
Newark, CA 94560
Tel. (415) 794-7482
Visa, Mastercard, AMEX are accepted.
and,
3110 Crow Canyon Commons
San Ramon, CA 94583

Bobby McGee's is where its happening in the Newark Fremont area. The moment you step in the door, the elaborate atmosphere, complete with gas lamps, crystal chandelier, period sofa and ornate oriental carpet will transport you into the special world of Bobby McGee's.

The hostesses, waiters, and waitresses are all in costume. Little Miss Muffet, Scarlet O'Hara, and Robin Hood are some of the characters brought to life by the staff whose often witty impersonations are hilarious. The dining areas are divided into separate rooms each with its own theme in decor. A general store room, a tack room, a doll house, and even a Hawaiian room add to the unique environments in this exciting restaurant. The menu features beef, shellfish and super salads prepared to your specifications and are consistently delicious.

After dinner the fun continues in the lounge, where the staff sings a myriad of songs and games such as musical chairs are played by the young at heart. All in all if fun is what you're after, fun is what you'll find at Bobby McGee's.

EL BURRO, 3100 New Park Mall, Newark, California. Mexican food in an authentic setting.

NIJO CASTLE
39888 Balentine Drive
Newark, CA 94560
Tel.   (415) 657-6456
Hrs: Lunch   Mon.-Fri.   11:30 a.m. - 2:30 p.m.
       Dinner   Mon. - Sat.   5:00 p.m. - 9:00 p.m.
       Dinner   Sunday   5:30 p.m. - 9:00 p.m.
Visa, Mastercard, AMEX and Diner's Club are accepted.

A Japanese castle in Newark, California? Strange as it sounds, Nijo Castle Restaurant is a scaled down replica of Nijo Castle in Kyoto, Japan. The

77

architectural style represents the highest degree of refinement and richness in traditional Japan. Tiles, murals, decorative screens, and sculptures are reproductions of the same ornamentation in the original castle.

Once inside, you can choose from four separate and diverse dining areas: the formal Japanese dining room with its black lacquered tables and hanging paper lanterns; the Tatami area of paper screen enclosed private booths; the Teppan room where the seating is around a grill and your own private chef performs acrobatic magic his knives while he prepares your entree before your eyes; and of course, the Sushi bar with sushi in all its variety of shapes and tastes. The menu is extensive serving well known favorites such as tempura and beef teriyaki and lesser known delicacies such as kushikatsu - deep fried beef and onions coated with light batter on bamboo skewers.

Experience the opulence and grace of Japan in a convenient Bay Area setting, and be prepared for food that is dramatically made, delicious to the taste and graciously served.

(See special invitation in the Appendix.)

RED ROBIN
Newark Mall
Newark, CA 94560
Tel.   (415) 791-2644
Hrs: Sun. - Mon.   11:00 a.m. - 12:00 midnight
       Tue. - Sat.   11:00 a.m. - 2:00 a.m.

Red Robin presides over this spirited establishment, touting himself as "The World's Greatest Burger Maker and Most Masterful Mixologist." It would be folly to dispute his claim. He offers some twenty-eight fantastic hamburgers from which to choose, along with salads, seafood, barbeque specialties, soups, sandwiches, zesty Mexican dishes, Sweet Tweets, tantalizing appetizers and delicious exotic bar creations. Red Robin's motto is "We're here to create happy guests." He does.

Decorating the walls are posters of contemporary subjects, as well as old movie classics like *Gone With The Wind* and *Casablanca*. A carousel horse adorns one of the dining rooms, miniature palms and potted plants add to the decor while handmade lamp shades arch over tables on polished brass arms. A full bar overlooks the dining area and a video screen and arcade keep things lively.

The main attraction is the burgers, each one a gourmet delight. The one third pound banzai burger is marinated in teriyaki sauce and topped with broiled pineapple rings and melted cheddar cheese. The avocado aficionado's burger, the Whiskey River barbeque burger and durango style chili burger deluxe are just a few more.

Red Robin pledges, "We use only the freshest ingredients." This applies to the burgers and to the impressive supporting choices. Try the sensational spinach salad or the Chef's Gone Crazy salad. Other delectables include beer-battered fish n chips, Whiskey River barbecued chicken, Big Red's barbeque and dilly of a philly cheese steak sandwich. The Chimichangas will make you exclaim, "Ole!" Sweet Tweets include monster mudd pie and Mother Robin's cheesecake.

This tour is designed to keep the outdoor enthusiast well primed with good food and wonderful views:

THE HIKE & EAT TOUR OF			
NEWARK			
a.m.	La Mode Fashions	Best personal	Newa/App
a.m.	Brookside Hotel	Best late brkfst	Newa/Rest
p.m.	Coyote Hills R. Park	Best p.m. hike	Newa/Att
After the wail of Coyote Hills has left your ears, fill your stomach at one of these distinctively different restaurants:			
p.m.	Nijo castle	Best Japanese	Newa/Rest
p.m.	Red Robin	Best burger	Newa/Rest
p.m.	Bobby McGee's	Best night show	Newa/Rest

Oakland

This beautiful city on the "other" side of the bay basks in sunshine much of the year, enjoying an average daytime temperature of about 63 degrees. It is home to 340,000 people. First a major sea port, then the western terminus of transcontinental railroads, Oakland grew to become a commercial and industrial giant. The port presently ranks as the largest containerized cargo facility on the West Coast. New interest in the city brought high-rise office buildings in recent years, broadening the transportation-related economy.

Four farmers leased 460 acres from Vincente Peralta in 1849 to produce grain and hay for the miners who used this side of the bay to mount their expeditions to the gold fields. Horace W. Carpentier acquired what is now downtown Oakland in 1852, incorporated it as a town, and later moved the city limits to the waterfront. The population boomed and the growth continues.

Alameda County

The Bay Bridge, a quick five-mile auto and rail link between San Francisco and Oakland, brought the two cities into a closer relationship, but not without political pain. It took a Presidential Commission to resolve the route finally put under construction about fifty years ago. Now a complex freeway system fanning out from the Oakland terminus of the bridge speeds traffic in the East Bay and to the Oakland International Airport near Alameda.

Attractions

One of the best museums in the west, the **Oakland Museum** is located at Tenth and Oak Streets. It features California history and natural history plus extensive art exhibits and a sculpture gallery set in a Babylonian-type garden. Open Wednesday through Saturday 10:00 a.m. - 5:00 p.m. Sundays 12:00 noon - 7:00 p.m.

Victorian homes on the Bret Hart Boardwalk, Fifth Street at Jefferson. These old houses, for one block, are converted into shops and eating places.

There's a venerable **Oakland Chinatown** on Webster Street, with businesses concentrated between Seventh and Ninth Streets, including some traditional Chinese markets.

Black history is featured at **East Bay Negro Historical Society**, 5606 San Pablo Avenue. Many of the exhibits focus on California, but include other United States and Mexican events in black history. Call 658-3158 for museum hours.

The **Dunsmuir House and Gardens** at 2960 Peralta Oaks Court is a restored colonial revival mansion on a forty acre estate. Tours are available on Sundays from the first Sunday in April through the last Sunday in September.

Jack London Square, a modern development at Embarcadero West and the Oakland Estuary, celebrates the place where the author and his friends spent many hours. A sod-roofed cabin is restored, tourist attractions are nearby in **Jack London Village.**

Knowland Park and Zoo is home to around 900 animals which are on view every day of the year except Christmas. Located at Golf Links Road exit to I-580.

Once the tidewater arm of the bay, the 155 acre **Lake Merritt** is now sealed from saltwater and forms a centerpiece for the city. Jogging paths surround it, boat rentals and other attractions are available. A miniature sternwheel steamer cruises the lake daily in summer and on weekends the rest of the year.

The Coliseum complex is home for the Oakland A's baseball team and the Golden State Warriors, plus professional football and other large events.

For further information contact the **Oakland Convention and Visitors Bureau,** 1000 Broadway, Suite 200, telephone 839-9008. There is a daily update on events in the Oakland area, available by calling 839-9008.

For those who like to be on the go all day, start this tour with a brisk morning walk followed by a well-earned breakfast.

B A C K T O T H E B A S I C S T O U R			
a.m.	Lake Merritt	Best city walk	Oak/Att
a.m.	Emil Villa's Hickory Pit	Best hearty breakfast	Oak/Rest
a.m.	Crossing Gate	Best railroad car tour	Oak/Rail
a.m.	Cotton Basics	Best feel good clothing	Oak/App
a.m.	Me and Mr. C Tees	Best "sporty" clothing	Oak/App
p.m.	Mesa Cafe	Best southwest food	Oak/Res
p.m.	Fenton's Creamery	Best ice cream	Oak/Ice
p.m.	Asta Records	Best record collection	Oak/Rec
p.m.	Piedmont Springs	Best spa	Oak/Spa
For a "beyond the basics" evening meal relax in Berkeley at one of these fine restaurants:			
p.m.	Zachary's	Best Chicago style pizza	Ber/Res
p.m.	Spenger's	Best clam chowder	Ber/Res
p.m.	Ristorante	Best authentic Italian	Ber/Res
p.m.	Larry Blake's	Best night club	Ber/Res

Accommodations

CLAREMONT RESORT HOTEL
41 Tunnel Road
Oakland, CA 94623
Tel. (415) 843-3000

The regal Claremont Hotel majestically dominates Berkeley's northern foothills with Gatsbyesque elegance, redefining luxury for all those who cross its threshold. Originally styled as an English castle, the Claremont now stands as a palm lined Victorian estate backdropped by the romantic Berkeley hillside.

Spread over a sprawling twenty acres with a spectacular Bay view, the Mobil four Star getaway offers non stop activities with day and night tennis courts, an Olympic sized swimming pool and a Parcourse for invigorating workouts. For post workout relaxation, there are full sauna and whirlpool facilities. The Claremont's Pavilion Room offers palatial world class dining to rival the best. Dishes are executed with healthy flair and employ the best local vegetables, prime fowl, veal and fresh seafood. Specialty dishes include flavorful rack of lamb and crusted salmon, fresh salmon baked with Dungeness crab, sliced mushrooms and seasoned spinach in a light pastry crust topped with Hollandaise.

The Claremont Hotel represents excellence, superior service and indulgent opulence with a pronounced emphasis on catering to your needs. It is a return to the romantic splendor and genteelness of yesteryear that should not be missed.

Apparel

B.B. GEAR
4125 Piedmont Avenue
Oakland, CA 94611
Tel. (415) 658-5711
Hrs: Mon.-Sat.   11:00 a.m.-6:00 p.m.
       Sunday   12:00 noon-5:00 p.m.
Visa, Mastercard and AMEX are accepted.

The total look is what counts at b.b. Gear. At this unique shop in Oakland, owner Barbara Blumberg and her service oriented staff will gladly assist you in selecting casual or career looks. Find the labels you know and love, Adrienne Vittadini, Max Studio by Leon Max, M.A.C., K. Kit, Quess ?, Nouvelle, Basco and much more. Shopping is now fun and exciting in this high energy specialty shop for customers fifteen to sixty-five years of age.

Special attention to each customer's needs in a relaxed environment makes shopping a pleasure. Barbara's motto is, "When the customer is happy, we're thrilled!" Happy shopping and enjoy the compliments you will receive.

CAPEZIO DANCE-THEATRE SHOP
5900 College Avenue
Oakland, CA 94618
Tel. (415) 655-3608
Hrs: Mon.-Sat.   10:00 a.m.- 6:00 p.m.
         Sunday   1:00 p.m.- 5:00 p.m.
Visa, Mastercard, AMEX are accepted.

Capezio is well known by professional dancers and serious athletes as the place to go for dance and exercise togs. Only the highest quality lines are carried and the staff is helpful and knowledgeable. A real dancers paradise, Capezio, carries an extensive inventory of dance clothing and footwear by such manufacturers as Guess, Marika, Flexatard, and Danskin. Owner, Susan Spinner, is dedicated to selling only the absolute highest quality merchandise and as such carries only the best products of a particular manufacturer. All clothing is extremely well made and is available in all sizes and a dazzling array of colors. Most of the outfits are color coordinated and are therefore interchangeable for maximum flexibility and style. In the theater section, costumes and accessories are in abundance for work or fun.
It's not necessary to be a dancer or athlete to shop at Capezio, since the clothing is both well made and beautiful and will enhance everyone's wardrobe.

ME AND MR. C TEES AND SWEATS
30 Jack London Square
Oakland, CA 94607
Tel. (415)839-3118
Hrs: Mon. - Thurs.   10:30 a.m. - 6:00 p.m.
         Friday   10:30 a.m. - 9:00 p.m.
Visa, Mastercard, AMEX are accepted.

One of the joys of Oakland is strolling around Jack London Village, taking in its flower bordered walks and garden courtyards, watching the sailboats float on the Bay, and wandering through the various waterfront shops. Like some of the other Jack London Village shops, Me and Mr. C Tees & Sweats is a cut above its competition. The merchandise is of very high quality, yet the prices remain reasonable.

Me and Mr. C have every color and style you could possibly imagine in a T-Shirt or sweats. For women, they not only have designer T's and sweats, but lightweight T-shirt dresses ranging from casual to dressy. Custom lettering is available, as are heat transfers which are so much like screen printing that you will be amazed. There are also designer lines of silk screened shirts. Their line of one-of-a-kind sweats are truly incredible, and you can also find items like licensed NFL jackets by Starter.

Convenient dressing rooms may tempt you to spend hours searching through the variety of patterns and designs. Bring the kids, too, as Me and Mr. C have a large assortment of children's sizes, from six months to size fourteen youth. Whether or not you work out, this is a place to check out!

(See special invitation in the Appendix.)

COTTON BASICS
6052 College Avenue
Oakland, CA 94618
Tel. (415) 655-1710
Hrs: Mon.-Sat.   10:30 a.m. - 6:00 p.m.
          Sunday   12:00 noon - 6:00 p.m.
Visa, Mastercard, AMEX are accepted.

Fashion and comfort, the ideal ingredients for fine clothing are found perfectly blended in the clothes at Cotton Basics.

Much of the inventory is made by the owners, artists Susan Ciochetto and Karl Buhler, who have created beautiful and practical clothing using natural fiber fabrics. The store contains a good selection of t-shirts (all dyed and silkscreened by the owners), 100% cotton maternity fashions, jackets, jeans, sweats, cardigans, and scarfs attractively displayed in a clean, bright, and cheerful environment. The help is friendly and knowledgeable.

A person's apparel affects both the person and all who see them. Clothing created at Cotton Basics feel good on a person and will please the eye of all their beholders.

(See special invitation in the Appendix)

SAYS WHO?
3903 Piedmont Avenue
Oakland, CA 94611
Tel.   (415)547-5181
Hrs: Mon. - Sat.   10:00 a.m. - 6:00 p.m.
       Sunday   12:00 noon - 5:00 p.m.
and,
1626 A Union Street
San Francisco, CA 94123
Tel.   (415) 771-1746
Hrs: Mon. - Fri.   11:00 a.m. - 7:00 p.m.
       Saturday   10:00 a.m. - 6:00 p.m.
       Sunday   12:00 noon - 5:00 p.m.

Big women don't want beautiful clothes? SAYS WHO??? Say's Who? specializes in high style clothing and accessories for the large size beauty. Says Who? carries a quality selection of natural fiber clothing. Fashions come in bright, bold colors, as well as sophisticated neutrals. The service is almost miraculous and shopping is fun.

The motto at Says Who? is "Love yourself now!" So if you're a big, beautiful woman, what are you waiting for? Says Who? is the place for you.

V.B.C. CHILDREN'S CLOTHING
5902 College Avenue
Oakland, CA 94618
Tel.   (415) 652-5548
Hrs: Mon. - Sat.   10:00 a.m. - 6:00 p.m.
       Sunday   12:00 a.m. - 5:00 p.m.

What would Jackie Onassis wear if she was five years old today? A visit to V.B.C. will provide all the answers. V.B.C. stands for *vestiti bambini* in Italian, which translates as "children's clothing."

The selection at V.B.C. covers contemporary domestic resources and imports from Europe, Asia and Australia. The "look" is different and unique, yet all the clothing is practical, wearable, and certainly fashionable. Sizes range from infants to boys and girls fourteen.

V.B.C. also offers a large selection of accessories, from socks to belts, hats, gloves, children's jewelry, and novelty items. A special section of play clothes will amaze and delight you. In addition to dressing rooms, you'll find a play area for the children. The staff will lend you their expertise in putting together a total look for your very special child.

If you're a parent, take your children to V.B.C. -- they'll love it. (Psst... kids, take your parents -- they'll love it!)

Art

FOLKS' ART
4164 Piedmont Avenue
Oakland, CA 94611
Tel. (415) 653-5448
Hrs: Mon. - Sat. 11:00 a.m. - 6:00 p.m.

Artists and craftspeople from California are what Folks' Art is all about. Owners Beth Beatty, Bernice Brooke, Yae Maru and Darlene Ownbey have selected and created a broadly fascinating array of jewelry, ceramics, handblown Mt. St. Helen's glass, hand-woven wall hangings, wind chimes, photographs framed and unframed, and a potpourri of other interesting items from all over California.

Some of the more unusual things include hand-turned knitting needles and crochet hooks, natural stone beads, and handmade hapi coats by Yae. The owners of Folks' Art are committed to reflecting the finest of California's arts and crafts in their diverse inventory.

If you're looking for a special and unusual gift, whether it be jewelry, a card, or a teapot, Folks' Art is the place to find it.

(See special invitation in the Appendix.)

Bakery

LEAVEN & EARTH
5427 College Avenue
Oakland, CA 94618
Tel.   (415) 652-7969
        (415) 658-9836
Hrs: Mon. - Fri.   7:00 a.m. - 7:00 p.m.
       Saturday   7:00 a.m. - 6:00 p.m.
       Sunday   8:00 a.m. - 5:00 p.m.

Pure, fresh ingredients. Not a mix out of a box. No preservatives. Just pure, fresh ingredients, prepared with caring and forethought.   All pastry decorating is done with pure, natural products which use no dyes or food colorings.

When owners Georgia Harper, Thelma Lancaster, and Sydney Kennedy got together they wanted to create a bakery for people with special needs. If you have an allergy, health requirements, special diet, or just appreciate good quality, fresh-baked goodies. This is the place.

Fourteen kinds of bread baked daily, delicious orange, banana, carrot, chocolate almond, poppy seed, lemon and spice cakes, Danish, croissants, rolls, sticky buns and brioche. This is definitely a "Best Choice" bakery with excellent confections and friendly, considerate service--Leaven & Earth. Superb!

NELDAM'S DANISH BAKERY
3401 Telegraph Avenue
Oakland, CA 94609
Tel. (415) 658-1967
Hrs: Mon. - Fri.   7:00 a.m. - 6:00 p.m.
     Saturday   8:00 a.m. - 5:00 p.m.
     Sunday   10:00 a.m. - 3:00 p.m.

Bay Area residents have enjoyed the flavor, quality, and service of fine Danish baking at Neldam's since 1929. Neldam's offers a staggering array of baked goods made from real cream, honest-to-goodness butter, and many original recipes such as "Dream of Cream" cake. Known for their magnificent wedding cakes, Neldam's also offers popular "theme," holiday, and special occasion cakes. Christmas displays include real ginger-bread houses; Easter brings Bunny cakes and special Easter baskets with cookies.

Follow your nose to fresh coffee and your favorite baked treat, then sit down and plunge into a delectable treat. You won't want to leave without a sack full of cream cakes, cookies, eclairs, bread, rolls, Danish, and pies.

With thirty-seven employees, including eighteen bakers, the Neldam family has one of the largest retail bakeries in the entire area. Jim Lucas, also a member of the Neldam family, maintains that Old World commitment to quality and excellence, making Neldam's a real treat for the eyes, nose and tummy.

Delicatessen

CURDS & WHEY
6311 College Avenue
Oakland, CA 94618
Tel. (415) 652-6311
Hrs: Mon. - Sat. 10:00 a.m. - 6:30 p.m.
MasterCard and Visa are accepted.

If you're upwardly mobile, too busy to cook and want to impress your dinner guests, or if you simply want to impress your own taste buds, Curds & Whey fills the bill. They'll even fill your picnic basket with the very best in delicacies!

Curds & Whey takes pride in the quality of ingredients and presentations, and they are constantly adding items and changing entrees, so there are always delectable surprises in store for customers. You may choose to dine upstairs in the loft, or simply take home an order to be baked or warmed in the oven.

Holidays become memorable when accompanied by Curds & Whey's special holiday foods, such as persimmon pudding, fruit cakes, cheese balls, and at Thanksgiving, wild rice stuffing and sausages made right on the premises. So whether you need catering for a party of twelve or are dining alone, Curds & Whey can supply every need. Ms. Muffet never had it so good!

GENOVA DELICATESSEN AND RAVIOLI FACTORY
4937 Telegraph Avenue
Oakland, CA 94609
Tel. (415) 652-7401
Hrs: Mon. - Sat. 9:00 a.m. - 5:45 p.m.
Sunday 8:30 p.m. - 4:30 p.m.

Genova Delicatessen and Ravioli Factory is a classic deli with fresh salads, sandwiches, cold cuts and cheeses, salamis, breads, wines and a friendly atmosphere. Whether you are planning a picnic or stocking up your munchies for the road, this deli is the place to find any delicacy you have the urge for.

This high quality deli "manufactures" their own very special, authentic ravioli and Italian dishes. Be sure to visit and experience the fast paced, high energy atmosphere that this Italian family deli generates.

LAKESIDE DELI
3257 Lakeshore Avenue
Oakland, CA 94610
Tel. (415) 832-4374
Hrs: Mon. - Sat. 9:00 a.m. - 6:00 p.m.

"Homemade" is the word at Lakeside Deli. People drive for miles to enjoy the freshness and quality of old family recipes and good Italian cooking.

Lakeside Deli features hot fresh entrees such as ravioli, lasagne, and spaghetti all made from their own pasta and sauces. A full deli, ranging from pasta to pizza to patés to pastries, is complemented by beer and wine, freshly ground gourmet coffee, and a full espresso bar.

Family owned and operated since 1937, you'll enjoy eating in this pleasant environment with its beautiful marble floor. You can also dine outdoors if you prefer, or you can place your order "to go."

House specialty is fresh homemade ravioli, using only the finest ingredients without any preservatives. Cart them home by the box or enjoy them hot at the deli!

Furnishings

NEW ERA FURNITURE
4920 Telegraph Avenue
Oakland, CA 94609
Tel. (415) 653-3003
Hrs: Mon. - Thu.   9:00 a.m. - 8:30 p.m.
       Fri. - Sat.   9:00 a.m. - 6:00 p.m.
       Sunday   11:00 a.m. - 5:00 p.m.
Most major credit cards are accepted. Delivery is available.

Since 1965 Scott Lewis has been giving his customers what they want - - finished or unfinished furniture to suit their needs and pocketbooks. If the pride and satisfaction of owning solid wood furniture is important to you, you'll want to pay a visit to New Era Furniture.

New Era will explain to you how to finish a piece or how to match your existing colors. If you need an extra chair to go with your set at home, they can match both color and style. Their custom shop will create and design to fit your specific needs. You'll find chairs and chest beds, tables and end tables, bookcases and display cases, plus wall units, stereo cabinets, butcher block tables, and more.

New Era has a "workshop" environment. Upon entering, the pungent fragrance of wood signals your senses that this is a place of quality and craftsmanship. You'll find products here that simply aren't available at your local department store or furniture showroom. If it's wood you want, New Era Furniture is the place to find it, established 1905.

Gift

BUMBLE BEE
17 Glen Avenue
Oakland, CA 94611
Tel. (415) 420-5798
Hrs: Mon.-Sat. 10:00 a.m.-6:00 p.m.
Visa and Mastercard are accepted.

Bumble Bee owner, Pamela Tom, is special. Besides personally selecting the entire inventory of her shop, she is concerned that all the unique gifts she carries are placed in good homes. Her customers are so important to her that she carries only items she would personally own.

Filling the shop with plush toys, dried flowers, unusual frames, custom jewelry, bath soaps, sachet, handmade gifts and romantic embroideries, Pamela delights in creating the intimate, friendly atmosphere of an English country shop. Browsing is welcome and gift selection is accomplished in the unhurried pace of another era. Pamela insists that your shopping be enjoyable and offers assistance with home decorating advice and gift selection.

Shopping at Bumble Bee is an experience that shouldn't be missed by anyone who loves romantic settings and sharing wonderful treasures with that special someone in your life.

Ice Cream

FENTON'S CREAMERY
4226 Piedmont Avenue
Oakland, CA 94611
Tel. (415) 652-8006
Hrs: Mon. - Sun. 11:00 a.m. - 12:00 midnight

If you grew up in the Bay Area, chances are Fenton's Ice Creamery was high on your "treat list." Established in 1922, Fenton's is known for it's tantalizing and extensive menu of fresh ice cream delights. All ice cream is made fresh daily on the premises.

In addition to the Bay Area's best ice cream, Fenton's offers a variety of sandwiches made in the same famous tradition of quality. The favorite of many generations is the fresh crab sandwich, featuring crab straight from San

Francisco's Fisherman's Wharf. The portions at Fenton's are unbelievable -- it takes the heartiest of appetites to polish off a fabulous Fenton's creation!

Fenton's atmosphere is everything you'd expect from a bright and bustling 1922 soda fountain/creamery. The family tradition of "fresh from the dairy" refers not only to the food and ice cream but to the standards set for their employees -- cheerful, honest, and friendly.

If you're the type that believes delicious treats, huge portions, and friendly service are a thing of the past, you've got a great opportunity to prove yourself wrong at Fenton's.

Jewelers

GIVEN GOLD JEWELERS
4156 Piedmont Avenue
Oakland, CA 94611
Tel.   (415) 652-4168
Hrs: Tues. - Sat. 10:00 a.m. - 6:00 p.m.

Approximately half of the inspired jewelry on display at Given Gold is the work of master jeweler and owner Jim Foley. Jim is a goldsmith, gemologist and registered jewelry appraiser.

Chic and elegant, or casual and witty, Jim has an eye for perfection. If you have a particular design in mind, Jim can turn your idea into a timeless work of jewelry that you can cherish for a lifetime.

In addition to Jim's creations you will find unique pieces fashioned by other designers, all hand selected by Jim and Lyn Foley. Included are Seiko watches, gold and sterling bracelets, necklaces, earrings, rings, diamonds, pearls, and many fine gemstones.

Given Gold Jewelers are wedding band specialists -- not to be missed if there's a wedding in your plans. Wedding or not, Given Gold is worth a visit if you're still looking for that special gift or unique piece of jewelry you've always dreamed of owning.

GOLDEN TREASURES
6232 La Salle Avenue
Oakland, CA 94611
Tel. (415) 339-3201
Hrs: Tue. - Sat. 10:30 a.m. - 5:30 p.m.
Visa, MasterCard and AMEX are accepted.

There is a subtle elegance as you enter this jewelry store, and you find a world of experience when you consult with Cleve Oppenheimer, the owner and artisan who turns out most of the fine work on display here.

After apprenticing with a third generation jeweler, studying gemology with the Gemological Institute of America (GIA), and operating a custom jewelry store at North Lake Tahoe for ten years, Mr. Oppenheimer opened his Oakland store.

Golden Treasures offers the discriminating buyer the choice of limited edition jewelry, one of a kind designs, and the resetting of the family treasures into contemporary settings. Mr. Oppenheimer specializes in fine handmade gold jewelry with an understated, subtle elegance, and exquisite colored gemstones and diamonds.

Kitchen Articles

CALIFORNIA CUISINE
4158 Piedmont Avenue
Oakland, CA 94611
Tel. (415) 652-0928
Hrs: Mon.-Fri.   10:00 a.m. - 6:00 p.m.
          Saturday   10:00 a.m. - 5:30 p.m.
          Sunday   12:00 noon - 4:00 p.m.
Visa and Mastercard are accepted.

California Cuisine is a charming shop that offers products and services specially designed for both novices and experts of the joys of cooking and casual home entertaining.

A broad assortment of domestic and imported table linens, glass wear, baskets, gadgets, bakeware, cutlery and cookware are carried by the store. California Cuisine's complete orientation is toward making customers feel important and special. The selection of merchandise is large and displayed in an attractive courtyard setting. Most any item desired that is not on display can be special ordered with the help of the personable staff who will also gladly assist in the creation of special gift baskets and one of a kind presents. In keeping with the store's customer oriented philosophy, many cooking classes for home cooks are offered at California Cuisine. They are taught by some of the best known chefs, cooking teachers and cookbook authors in the Bay Area. At these classes, students are treated to personal instruction in both food preparation and presentation.

Sample the culinary spirit of the Bay Area at California Cuisine; you'll find it alive and, in the cooking classes, very tasty.

NAPP'S - THE KITCHEN COMPANY
3417 Lakeshore Avenue
Oakland, CA 94610
Tel.   (415) 444-7448
Hrs: Mon. - Sat.   9:00 a.m. - 5:30 p.m.
      Sunday   12:00 noon - 4:00 p.m.
Visa, Mastercard, AMEX and Diners cards are accepted.

If you cook, this is your place. Over 4,000 square feet of kitchenware, cookware, and just about everything else associated with the preparation and enjoyment of food make Napp's the place for cooks. You'll find bakeware, cookware, appliances, barbecues, cutlery, spices, coffee beans, picnic baskets, napkins, gourmet foods, and many hard-to-find specialty items in this kitchen of kitchens.

Not surprisingly, owners Patt and Dick Napp are themselves excellent cooks.   This ensures that you receive knowledgeable, enthusiastic service. More important, as cooks, they know and understand what a good cook or chef needs and wants. Patt and Dick are also "the picnic headquarters" for those mobile feasts we all love to create and experience.

If you love to cook, or if you're looking for the ideal gift for someone who loves to cook, don't miss out on this kitchen lover's dream store.

Railroad, Model

THE CROSSING GATE
6128 LaSalle Avenue
Oakland, CA 94611
Tel. (415) 339-9722
Hrs: Mon.- Sat.   10:00 a.m.-6:00 p.m.
      Thursday   10:00 a.m.-9:00 p.m.

Model railroading is not just for kids. Nowhere is that more evident than at The Crossing Gate in Oakland.

Located in the charming Montclaire District of Oakland, owner John Selby's, The Crossing Gate, has hard to find trains and accessories such as the

Alameda County

LBG German line, brass train sets, radio controlled cars and imported models both antique and contemporary. Favored by collectors of all ages, The Crossing Gate has one of the largest collections of trains, accessories and books on the West Coast.

For toy trains or serious model railroad lines, there is only The Crossing Gate in Oakland, a model railroad store for railroaders and by railroaders.

(See special invitation in the Appendix)

Records

ASTA RECORDS
5488 College Avenue
Oakland, CA 94618
Tel. (415) 654-0335
Hrs: Mon.-Thu. 11:00 a.m.- 9:00 p.m.
      Fri.-Sat.   11:00 a.m.-10:00 p.m.
      Sunday   11:00 a.m.- 7:00 p.m.

Listening to yesterday's recordings is a bridge between the past and the present. The spirit, hopes, fears, dreams, and ideals of each generation are captured in their music and passed on as a legacy to each future generation. Asta Records is a record store where the music of the past is preserved for enjoyment in the present.

A musicians and music lovers paradise, Asta Records, is the place to find original print music, Bluegrass, Gospel, Dixieland, Classical, Rock, Jazz, Reggae, etc., and the favorite, interesting, and beautiful records of our past. The owners of Asta Records are serious musicians who bring to the store a tremendous wealth of musical knowledge. Collectors can find much to enhance their collections and the store holds "swap meets" where collectors can trade with other collectors from their private collections. If a particular record is not available at the store, the staff will gladly research and find the selection if possible. The atmosphere is bright and cheerful and children are not only welcomed but encouraged; Kiddie books are provided for the childrens' amusement and parent's freedom to browse.

Asta Records in Oakland gives its customers the opportunity to enjoy the beauty produced by the artists of our past through the sensory window of recorded music.

(See special invitation in the Appendix.)

This Oakland tour will enable you to find something for everyone on your gift list, no matter the person or occasion.

GIFTS FOR EVERYONE TOUR			
a.m.	Napp's Kitchen Co.	Best hard-to-find items	Oak/Kit
a.m.	V.B.C.	Best children's clothing	Oak/App
a.m.	Capezio's	Best exercise clothing	Oak/App
a.m.	B.B. Gear	Best family apparel	Oak/App
p.m.	Genova Deli	Best homemade ravioli	Oak/Res
p.m.	Says Who?	Best full figure fashions	Oak/App
p.m.	Given Gold	Best jewelry	Oak/Jw
p.m.	Teddie's	Best party supplies	Oak/Sta
p.m.	California Cuisine	Best special gift baskets	Oak/Kit
p.m.	Greetings	Best cards and more	Oak/Sta

Restaurant

BERTOLA'S
4659 Telegraph Avenue
Oakland, CA 94609
Tel. (415) 658-8103
Hrs: Mon.-Sun. 11:30 a.m.-10:00 p.m.
Visa, Mastercard, AMEX are accepted.

Happy hour has been going on at Bertola's since 1932. Well drink prices have changed very little for over twenty-five years and is one reason that Bertola's is one of the friendliest, happiest bistros in town.

The atmosphere at this bar and restaurant can be described as uproarious, definitely casual, and genuinely fun. Bartenders are efficient, the service is quick, and the wise-cracking and reparté at the bar are entertaining and continuous. Good, old fashioned Italian dinners are served family style in the restaurant at a modest cost and with generous portions. Old linoleum floors, movie posters and photo's on the wall, red checkered tablecloths, give Bertola's the friendly feeling of a favorite neighborhood bar.

Bertola's is the type of place where you can feel comfortable going alone, since after a while everyone feels like one big happy family, and you are, therefore, no longer alone.

95

BROADWAY TERRACE, 5891 Broadway Terrace, Oakland, California. Fresh, seasonal food with a constantly changing menu.

THE DIGGERY
4212 Park Boulevard
Oakland, CA 94602
Tel. (415) 531-0224
Hrs: Mon. - Sat.   7:30 a.m. - 10:00 p.m.
        Sunday   7:30 a.m. - 9:00 p.m.
and,
DIGGERY INN
5400 Ygnacio Valley Road Unit A-13
Concord, CA 94521

Delve in to The Diggery, burrow into a cozy booth and dig in...to delicious homemade breakfasts, lunches and dinners in a relaxing and casual atmosphere.
Hearty breakfasts may include the Manzanita waffle, made with fresh whole milk, homemade butter and crispy bacon. For lunch, try a sour green burger, prepared with green chiles and sour cream, or a pasta dish covered with homemade sauce. Dinner entrees include fish, chicken and prime sirloin steak. Fresh biscuits, prepared from scratch are a specialty.
Desserts are made daily at The Diggery, and the pleasant service keeps people coming back. Stop in for a home-cooked meal...."you'll dig it!"

EMIL VILLA'S HICK'RY PIT
1982 Pleasant Valley Avenue
Oakland, CA 94611
Tel. (415) 654-0915
Hrs: Mon.-Sun. 6:00 a.m.- 9:45 p.m.
and,
San Leandro   Hayward Fremont
Santa Rosa   Walnut Creek
Concord   Campbell

Emil Villa was a well known baker around Oakland back in 1928. His original restaurant in downtown Oakland was built on his reputation for quality food, friendly service, fair prices, and his unique barbeque technique and became the talk of the town. This tradition for quality has been continued to the present day at all Emil Villa locations.
Emil Villa's Hick'ry Pit Restaurants serve breakfast, lunch, and dinner featuring traditional American fare of excellent quality and hearty

proportions. Steak and eggs for breakfast, salads and sandwiches for lunch and of course barbecued specialties for dinner. The meats are slow cooked over a wood fire just as Emil used to do and for anyone who is fond of homestyle barbecued food, Emil's is a must.

At Emil's the atmosphere is casual, the surroundings unpretentious, and the food is out of this world. Emil Villa's Hick'ry Pit is a great place to relax and enjoy some of the best food in the Bay Area.

FRENCH QUARTERS RESTAURANT
737 Buena Vista Avenue
Oakland, CA 94501
Tel. (415) 523-7555
Hrs: Mon. - Fri. 11:30 a.m. - 2:30 p.m.

Known for its fine Cajun cuisine and spirits, French Quarters features a genuine New Orleans chef, fresh food flown in three times weekly from New Orleans, and a menu that must be from the best eatery in Cajun heaven. Owners John and Alta Monroe treat their guests not only to the finest Cajun cooking but to the wonderful experience of good 'ole southern hospitality.

The menu here is seasonal, depending on the availability of fresh ingredients. All sauces and desserts are made fresh each day. Fresh gulf crab with spinach salad; Bayou St. John linguine with shrimp and crab meat in Creole sauce; fresh gulf shrimp sauteed in herbs and spices; and classic blackened Cajun fish with lemon butter sauce are just a few of the mouth-watering temptations on the list.

Dessert features some of the South's all-time favorites: pecan pie, old fashioned bread puddin' with rum sauce, mind you, Creole cream cheese cake, and Alta's famous pralines.

The atmosphere at French Quarters is lovely and gracious in the best southern tradition. A converted three-bedroom colonial house sets the stage for your dining pleasure. A grand piano played nightly, an intimate bar, and an outstanding menu complete the experience of another time, another place, and a dining memory that will remain for years to come.

(See special invitation in the Appendix.)

MESA RESTAURANT AND CAFE
3909 Grand Avenue
Oakland, CA 94610
Tel. (415) 652-5223
Hrs:
Cafe

Mon. - Thu.	11:30 a.m. - 10:00 p.m.
Friday	11:30 a.m. - 10:30 p.m.
Saturday	5:30 p.m. - 10:30 p.m.
Sunday	10:00 a.m. - 9:30 p.m.

Restaurant

Tue. - Thu.	6:00 p.m. - 9:30 p.m.
Fri. - Sat.	6:00 p.m. - 10:00 p.m.

Come to the Mesa Restaurant Cafe and you will consider it one of your all time favorites. The incredible menu changes constantly to provide an amazing variety of delectable delights.   This varied menu is the result of the inspirations of the award winning cooks.

For lunch the cafe offers charming outdoor seating and a special menu with sandwiches such as chicken breast on Fuccacia with basil aioli, marinated bean salad and shoestring potatoes or pork paillard with bitter orange marmalade and red onion relish.

Experience grilled sturgeon in banana leaves with tea sauce, wild mushrooms and greens sauteed in seasoned goose fat, fried quail eggs on toast or speared, five spice pork loin with mango salsa, just to name a few typical choices. After dinner treat yourself to cranberry walnut tart with Black Velvet ice cream or hot apple Charlotte with apricot sauce and cream. A fine selection of after dinner port wines, apertifs and special dessert wines from the full service bar are available.

The atmosphere of the cafe is dramatic with mirrored and salmon colored walls. The servers are professional and friendly. Be sure to visit the Mesa Restaurant and Cafe where the food is always fresh, creative and delicious.

SCOTT'S SEAFOOD GRILL & BAR
73 Jack London Square
Oakland, CA 94607
Tel.   (415)   444-3456
Hrs: Mon. - Thur.   11:00 a.m. - 10:00 p.m.
      Fri. - Sat.   11:00 a.m. - 11:00 p.m.
      Sunday   11:00 a.m. - 9:00 p.m.
Visa, MasterCard, Amex and Diner's Club accepted.

Scott's Seafood, located in the picturesque Jack London Waterfront, situated on the Oakland Estuary with windows overlooking the great water view. Weather permitting, enjoy your meal on the deck and watch the boats as they ply the river.

Start your meal with freshly-shucked oysters on the half shell, a crisp, garden-fresh salad, and then...a platter of scallops sauted with fresh tomato, mushrooms, and lemon butter...or, fresh salmon grilled, broiled, or poached with beurre blanc.   An Australian lobster tail?   Tonight's not the night for seafood?   A menu selection for one of their great steaks or pasta dishes will do admirably.

Scott's has a superb wine list, premium wine by the glass, and a full service bar. Jazz piano is played nightly for your dining and listening pleasure. It's easy to understand why Scott's Seafood Grill & Bar is such a crowd pleaser.

Alameda County

When you're ready to come back home from the exotic tour, try these Berkeley and Oakland area businesses for a taste of <u>real</u> America.

	Taste of Real America Tour		
a.m.	Leaven & Earth	Best bakery	Oak/Bak
a.m.	New Era Furniture	Best furniture	Oak/Fur
a.m.	Folk's Art	Best folk art	Oak/Art
a.m.	Lakeside Deli	Best morning snack	Oak/Deli
a.m.	Dressing Up	Best unique boutique	Ber/App
p.m.	Slater/Marinoff	Best interior design	Ber/Fur
	You cannot go wrong at either of these "Best Choice" lunches		
p.m.	Choyce's Restaurant	Best southern lunch	Ber/Res
p.m.	Gertie's Chesapeake Bay	Best seafood lunch	Ber/Res
p.m.	Andrea's	Best fabrics and styles	Ber/Ap
p.m.	Asta Records	Best record collection	Oak/Rec
p.m.	The Bumble Bee	Best gift	Oak/Gft
	Top your tour with drinks and/or dinner at any of these "Best Choices"		
p.m.	Scott's Grill & Bar	Best outdoor dining	Oak/Res
p.m.	French Quarters	Best Cajun cuisine	Oak/Res
p.m.	Bertola's	Best family style Italian	Oak/Res

Spa

PIEDMONT SPRINGS
3939 Piedmont Avenue
Oakland, CA 94611
Tel. (415) 652-9191
Hrs: Mon. - Sun. 11:00 a.m. - 11:00 p.m.
Hourly rentals

Taking time out of one's busy, stressful life is important to one's overall health and well being. Piedmont Springs offers such an atmosphere in the heart of a busy metropolitan area. There is no need to drive for hours to a resort, instead your time may be spent soaking in a relaxing hot tub, cleansing in a Finnish sauna or receiving relief with a therapeutic massage.

Piedmont Springs has been brilliantly engineered to accommodate your needs with outdoor, redwood hot tubs and authentic Finnish saunas. Use separately or in combination, but all in private. Piedmont Springs provides the towels and peaceful surroundings.

Therapeutic massage, in a variety of techniques, is available from one of several highly trained and experienced massage technicians.

Be sure to visit Piedmont Springs, an unquestionable "Best Choice" for relaxing.

Stationery

GREETINGS
4152 Piedmont Avenue
Oakland, CA 94611
Tel.   (415) 547-2555
Hrs: Mon. - Sat.   10:00 a.m. - 6:00 p.m.
       Sunday   11:00 a.m. - 5:00 p.m.

Looking for that perfect card? It's here. Some 120 feet of cards line this shop, featuring over 3,000 images from romantic to Ansel Adams, classic reproductions to contemporary designs.

Although cards are the specialty here, owner Lyn Foley also stocks all kind of party supplies: T-shirts, balloons, stickers, paper-by-the-pound, calendars, stuffed toys, gift candies (remember red hots?), mylar balloon bouquets, and much, much, more.

The atmosphere at "Greetings" is bright and party-like. You may start out as a "one-time buyer," but you're apt to end up as a regular customer!

TEDDIE'S DISCOUNT CARD AND PARTY
4009 Piedmont Avenue
Oakland, CA 94611
Tel.   (415) 547-4149
Hrs: Mon. - Sat. 10:00 a.m. - 6:00 p.m.

Do you constantly worry that you'll forget the punch when you throw a party? Keeping track of everything you need is enough to make anyone a party-pooper.

The party people at Teddie's are no party poopers, and they'll also keep you from becoming one. They'll even check over your party list with you to make sure you haven't forgotten anything! If it's a party item, you'll find it at Teddie's: balloons, helium balloon bouquets, toys, party favors and supplies, plush animals, a large variety of greeting cards - all at discount prices!

Don't be a party-pooper, especially at your own party! Stop in at Teddie's and enjoy the party!

(See special invitation in the Appendix.)

San Leandro

Once the home of vast cherry orchards, San Leandro now has an agricultural heritage which tends toward production of cut flowers to supply the floral needs of a large area. Squatters settled here while this was still a rancho, and rather than evict them, Jose Joaquin Estudillo sold part of his Rancho San Leandro as a town site. Many Portuguese emigrants flocked here from the Azores. About 65,000 people live in San Leandro.

Attractions

Frontier Town/Marina Park is located at the city's marina, overlooking a 21 acre lagoon. Three restaurants are located here. Sailing is popular on the sheltered lagoon.

The **Tony Lema Golf Course** is next door, and includes a driving range. The club house is at 13800 Neptune Drive.

Sixteen parks are operated elsewhere in the city, with several different facilities. A regional shoreline park is at the mouth of San Leandro Creek, with hiking trails, fishing and bird watching opportunities. For further information, contact the **San Leandro Chamber of Commerce**, 262 Davis Street, telephone 351-1481.

Florist

LYAL NICKALS
15031 Hesperian Boulevard
San Leandro, CA 94578
Tel. (415) 276-6600
Hrs: Mon. - Sat. 8:00 a.m. - 5:30 p.m.
Open Sunday November 15 - December 24

Flowers and quality gifts share the spotlight at this forty year old family business. The full service florist shop offers complete wedding decoration service, a wide selection of home floral decorations, and cut flowers for creating custom arrangements.

Marge Cacioppo presides over a staff ready to consult on any special occasion. For weddings, the service can include everything from aisle runners to outfitting the reception room. The unique Trim-a-Home department turns out festive decorations crafted to fit the decor of the room, on a year-around basis. Fresh flower arrangements are drawn from a refrigerator room stocked with dozens of varieties, all waiting for the customer's selection and the skilled hands of a Lyal Nickals arranger. The Christmas season is special here, with the gift shop placing animated scenes in the display windows.

European crystal, delicate figurines, and stylish lamps are featured in the gift shop. Collectors and window shoppers alike choose Lyal Nickals, a place of beauty and people ready to help you with a special look for your special occasion.

Hobby

FAMILY HOBBY
14288 E. 14th Street
San Leandro, CA 94578
Tel: (415) 895-1530
Hrs: Mon. - Fri.   10:00 a.m. - 7:00 p.m.
      Saturday   10:00 a.m. - 5:00 p.m.

Three generations of the Don Ellis family are likely to be on hand when you come shopping for models, craft supplies, and games in San Leandro. The store began in 1981 when Consuela Ellis sought a retail outlet for the handcrafted items she was making at home.

Now, Consuela has a wide assortment of supplies for other craft persons, and advice for fellow artists, or would-be artists just learning. There are traditional hand-craft materials, and supplies for weavers and knitters. Don specializes in models, from radio-control boats to those popular plastic model kits, from little HO-gauge trains to slot-type race cars. The couple's daughters Jaunita and Dona are buyers, and a grand-daughter, Christiana, often helps too.

This unique hobby store also features a group of games, jigsaw puzzles, and doll houses plus miniature furniture. The family touch means there's a wide selection and you will get the help from experts for making your craft project a success.

Restaurants

THE BLUE DOLPHIN
No. 30 San Leandro Marina
San Leandro, CA 94577
Tel. (415) 483-5900

Hrs:		
Mon. - Thur.	10:00 a.m. - midnight
Fri. - Sat.	10:00 a.m. - 2:00 a.m.
Sun.	10:00 a.m. - midnight

The Blue Dolphin is a "best choice" for its view of the marina and the Bay and for its incomparable food. Inside, the first thing to get your attention is the collection of character liquor bottles in the foyer. The restaurant interior is cool and refined, with gray and maroon furniture complemented by polished brass railings.

As the owner of ten fine restaurants, William Peluso has for decades been one of the great seafood purveyors of San Francisco and the East Bay. Since 1965 he has focused his attention on the Blue Dolphin. It's a family enterprise, and son Terry helps to run a tight ship.

The lunch menu will entice you with magnificent entrees. Terry suggests the fresh crab omelet or the prawns Parmigiana, both favorites for years. Another gourmet treat is the shrimp Creole d'Orleans.

Dinner becomes a culinary wonder as you watch the moon reflecting on the waves outside your window. For appetizers, try the Escargots a la Bourguignonne, oysters St. Patrick or coquille de Mer. The broiled lobster tail is served with drawn butter flamed at your table with a touch of pernod. In addition to the seafood, the Blue Dolphin serves superb beef, veal and fowl. The tournedos Rossine are filets of tenderloin with calvados sauce, pâte and mushroom caps. Prime rib, steak Dianne or chicken Blue Dolphin are more options. The desserts are renowned, especially those that burst into flame at your table: crépes Sir Raleigh, peach flambé, cherries jubilee.

Look all the way through the flames. You might spot a great blue dolphin rollicking through the waters beyond the marina on its way toward the Golden Gate.

ENRICO'S RESTAURANT of SAN LEANDRO
604 MacArthur Boulevard
San Leandro, CA 94577
Tel. (415) 562-3000
Hrs: Mon. - Thur.   6:00 a.m. - 10:00 p.m.
      Friday   6:00 a.m. - 11:00 p.m., music at 9
      Saturday   5:00 p.m. - 11:00 p.m., music at 9
      Sunday   8:00 a.m. - 10:00 p.m., music at 6

There is an atmosphere of sophistication about Enrico's; yet it is a casual elegance you will feel most comfortable with...a place for fine dining and intimate dancing.

The lunch at Enrico's has exciting selections and reasonable prices. Choose from pasta favorites like the fettuccini Enrico, with its plump prawns, scallops, mushrooms sauteed in a rich sauce and topped with bits of fresh green onion, or the Tortellini with pesto. *Magnifico!* For sandwiches you might try Enrico's version of a Club House, or the French dip that's made with prime beef.

The spacious main dining room is richly appointed in maroon and gold; a large dance floor invites your participation. Dinner entrees include Enrico's famous prime rib, Veal Marsala, flame-broiled scampi, scallops sauté supreme, and Petrale sole Meuniere. The chefs also present unforgettable specialties such as chicken breast sauté Enrico, veal Parmigiana and veal scallopini sauté Sec.

On Friday, Saturday, and Sunday nights Enrico's becomes highly energized and festive. Live, big band and swing music from the 40s and 50s is presented. Toe-tapping and invigorating. Every weeknight, between 4 to 6:00 p.m. you can join the the "Happy hour" merriment and feast on the gourmet hors d'oeuvres. If planning a banquet or reception, be sure to think of Enrico's; they have facilities to seat up to 250.

For excellently prepared cuisine, or dancing to music that will waltz you down memory lane; come in and experience all that Enrico's has to offer.

105

HORATIO'S
60 San Leandro Marina
San Leandro, CA 94577
Tel. (415) 351-5556

Hrs:	Lunch	Mon. - Fri.	11:15 a.m. - 2:30 p.m.
		Saturday	12:00 noon - 2:30 p.m.
	Dinner	Mon. - Thur.	5:30 p.m. - 9:30 p.m.
		Friday	5:30 p.m. - 10:30 p.m.
		Saturday	5:00 p.m. - 10:30 p.m.
		Sunday	5:00 p.m. - 9:30 p.m.
	Sunday Brunch		10:00 a.m. - 2:30 p.m.

Seafood, select corn-fed beef and a serene marina view give some indication of why this uniquely appointed restaurant is talked of up and down the East Bay. Life sized portraits of Admiral Nelson and his lady look upon the lobby, while the dining areas are filled with decorations from the days of sail.

There's nothing historic about the seafood here. It is fresh, daily. The house specialty is grilling fish over kiawe charcoal, a clean-burning import from Hawaii that gives a distinctive flavor. Fish, in season, present choices from salmon to Louisiana catfish. There's calmari, prawns and clams to round-out the seafood selections. For luncheon, in addition to chicken grilled over kiawe charcoal, the choice includes pasta combinations and a wide range of special sauces.

A meal at Horatio's, where they strive for quality at modest prices, includes the opportunity to choose from among some of the best known California wines. To top off the meal, your "Best Choice" could be Blum's coffee toffee pie or their now legendary burnt cream.

RED ROBIN, Bay Fair Mall, San Leandro, California. World famous hamburgers, sandwiches, BBQ and libations.

San Lorenzo

Pottery

MAINLY SECONDS POTTERY, PLANTS AND THINGS
15715 Hesperian Boulevard
San Lorenzo, CA 94580
Tel. (415) 481-1902
Hrs: Mon. - Sun. 10:00 a.m. - 6:00 p.m.
Hours are extended in the summer.

This place began as a shop offering mainly seconds. Now it is certainly a first for pottery shoppers. A shrewd and knowledgeable buyer, Michael Greenberg, started by scouting for pottery seconds which he could offer the public at incredibly low prices. Since then, the business has become so successful that Mainly Seconds has diversified and now offers the most extensive selection of top quality pottery, plus plants and many other items that make shopping here a sheer pleasure. The rustic sheetmetal building contains a virtual forest of lush, green healthy plants for home or office. Here you will also be delighted to examine the high quality, handcrafted silk flowers. The tiger lilies, orchids, snapdragons, tulips and other exotic types have a breathtaking beauty that will last for years. These, along with an equally impressive selection of dried flowers are priced far below the rest of the market.

For fantastic planters and picnic baskets, Mainly Seconds is unparalleled. The rattan, bamboo, willow and wicker seem unlimited in variety. For vases and Mexican red clay planters, Mainly Seconds is a must. Potting supplies are here too: plant food, potting moss, charcoal, sand, vermiculite, watering cans, fertilizer, garden books, chains and hangers. Michael also makes special purchases of a variety of other items such as, microwave cookware, oak towel rings, cake boxes, storage jar racks, wrought iron bird cages, apothecary jars, cookie jars and much more - all are great bargains.

Beside the main structure is a huge outdoor lot filled with thousands of pots, planters, vases and cacti. Cactus enthusiasts will find a wide selection of succulents. Ceramic vases with beautiful glazes and colors, handpainted clay planters from Mexico, Ingrid pots of all sizes and plastic planters - they are all here at this "Best Choice" shop.

Union City

Accommodations

HOLIDAY INN
32083 Alvarado-Niles Road
Union City, CA 94587
Tel. (415)   489-2200

This new Holiday Inn, known for it's luxurious amenities, has quickly become a favorite convention site, as well as a favored stop for vacationers. A brief drive from Interstate 880 at Alvarado-Niles Road, it serves as a gateway to the East Bay. A free shuttle serves the airports at San Jose, Oakland and San Fransisco.

The guest rooms are both elegant and comfortable, one may choose suites or king leisure rooms. Many of the rooms have a marvelous view of the waterway that meanders through the hotel grounds. Other amenities include a swimming pool, spa and sauna, raquetball and tennis courts and a hair salon on the premises. The fine dining and entertainment are major attractions at this Holiday Inn. In the lounge the guests can enjoy large screen TV, great appetizers and, at the bar, refreshing island drinks. For dining, there is a choice of three restaurants, all serving excellent cuisine in a pleasing ambiance.

This hotel is a true bonanza! Where else can you find a combination of excellent lodging, entertainment and gourmet food? For business or pleasure, the Holiday Inn on Alvarado-Niles Road is the "Best Choice."

(See special invitation in the Appendix.)

BUTTE COUNTY

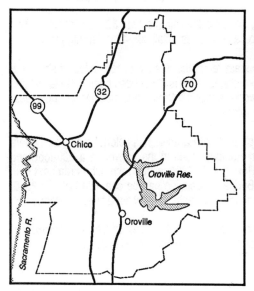

The upper, or north-eastern portion of the Sacramento Valley is included in this 1,646 square mile county with about 145,000 residents. Most people live in small cities--Chico is the largest in the county with about 27,000 residents inside city li-mits -- or on rural farms.

When the county was formed, one of California's original twenty-seven, the Sutter Buttes in the valley opposite Marysville were within the boundaries. They are now one county to the south. The Sierra foothills rising east of Oroville and Chico leave plenty of buttes within the county, although not the ones for which it was named in 1850. The Feather and American river watersheds were major mining locations in gold-rush days.

Agriculture dominates the economy. Timber from the Sierras is significant, and recreation a continued draw for visitors. The Feather River is an area of natural beauty, with waters of the huge Oroville dam creating many recreation opportunities, and Feather Falls, 640-feet from top to bottom, the sixth highest in the continental United States.

ATTRACTIONS

Feather River, accessible by Highway 70, features granite cliffs above the waters, and its middle fork is a federal wild and scenic river. Feather Falls is one of the attractions of the Plumas National Forest.

Lassen National Park, located north of the county, is reached from the south on Highway 32. Resorts and campgrounds are located along the highway as it climbs toward the park and its volcanic area with bubbling sulphur vents and a very climbable peak. Call Lassen National Forest, 257-2151, for information on campgrounds and attractions approaching the park.

Black Butte Lake, on Road 200 off Highway 32 west of Chico, has fishing and boating and two campgrounds. Call 865-4781 for information.

Lake Oroville is a state recreation area with 167 miles of shoreline. Located east of its namesake city, the lake is impounded behind the tallest and widest earthfill dam in the world. A Visitor's Center and museum are open year around. Call 534-2409 for information.

Butte Creek Canyon north of Paradise has colorful rock walls, offers swimming and floating. On Humbug Road in the canyon is a 230-foot long covered bridge at **Honey Run,** built in 1894, with a recreation area next to it. The Honey Run Covered Bridge Association can be contacted at 877-2550. Centerville Museum, on Humbug Road, features early good mining history.

For additional information, contact the **Greater Chico Chamber of Commerce,** Box 3038, Chico CA 95927. Telephone (916) 981-5556.

Chico

This historic town is home to the California State University Chico, and to businesses now moving beyond the the traditional food processing and timber manufacturing economic base of past years. Rancho Arroyo Chico, little stream in Spanish, was granted in 1844 and sold to John Bidwell in 1849. Bidwell, one of the first to cross the plains with a wagon train, was a political force in California as a congressman and general of the state militia. In 1892 he was presidential nominee for the National Prohibition Party.

Bidwell discovered gold on a Feather River bar in 1848, touching off a Butte County gold rush. Today, auto dealers have the largest piece of the action among Chico retailers, but income from farming dominates the county just as it did when Bidwell was farming his rancho long after gold played out.

Attractions

Stansbury House, 307 West Fifth, was built in 1882 and is now a museum operated by the city and a citizen group. Call 895-3848, evenings, for current operating hours.

Bidwell Park, a 2,400 acre gift to the city, contains developed areas and forests, and is next to the Bidwell Mansion, home of Chico founder John Bidwell. Park information is available at 343-4401. Open year around.

Bidwell Mansion, 525 The Esplanade, is a land mark, built about 1865. The mansion is open daily from 10:00 a.m. to 5:00 p.m.

On West Sacramento Avenue between Mechoopda Street and the railroad tracks is the **burial ground** for the local Indian tribe, still in use. An Indian mission church, where Bidwell's wife once taught, burned to the ground in 1961.

Chico Fun World, 2275 Elm Street, next to the Silver Dollar Fairgrounds, has water slides, bumper cars, swimming pool and other amusement park attractions. Call 893-0320.

For information, contact the **Greater Chico Chamber of Commerce,** Box 3038, Chico CA 95926. Telephone (916) 891-5556.

Accommodations

HOLIDAY INN
685 Manzanita
Chico, CA 95926
Tel. (916) 345-2491

Whether it's business or pleasure, overnight or a lengthy stay, the Holiday Inn in Chico is your "Best Choice" for complete accommodations.

King and executive suites with wet bars, handicapped equipped rooms, an outdoor pool, spa and fitness room supplement the 175 rooms and 3,120 square feet of meeting and banquet space. Valet laundry service and a free shuttle service to Chico Municipal Airport accentuate the professionally trained staff's determination to make your stay a pleasant one.

Chef Steven Cox, a graduate of the Culinary Institute of America in New York, oversees the catering, banquet and room services in addition to the main dining room. There's dancing, entertainment and libations in the lounge.

Antiques

TRENDS & TRADITIONS
126 W 3rd Street
Chico, CA 95928
Tel. (916) 891-5662
Hrs: Mon. - Sun.   10:00 a.m. - 5:00 p.m.
Visa and MasterCard accepted.

Are you an antique hunter? Do you travel what seems like the face of the earth looking for that special deal? If you are, you'll surely want to visit Trends & Traditions.

Owner Nancy Conn, offers high quality antique items, as well as custom made, contemporary wares. You'll think you've discovered a treasure trove as you browse through her fine inventory of merchandise. Quality pine furnishings, several brass items, porcelains, fine jewelry, wardrobe closets, trunks, one of a kind chest of drawers, an oak china buffet and Steuben martini glasses, are only a sample of what's in store for you. Not only can you shop at Trends & Traditions, but you can also enjoy a custom made work of art that's crafted according to your personal specifications. If you need restoration or refinishing work done, this shop performs that service as well.

So, there you have it, not only can you find what you're looking for, but you're liable to find that rare piece you thought you'd never see. Stop by and visit the friendly folks at Trends & Traditions, a "Best Choice" in Chico.

VOSE'S SHOPPING CENTER
P.O. Box 162 Cohasset Stage
Chico, CA 95926
Tel. (916) 342-5214
Hrs: Fri. - Tue.   10:00 a.m. - 5:00 p.m.

For those of you who are in need of a leisurely drive through beautiful mountainous country with the eventual destination being a couple hours worth of browsing through priceless treasures, then Frank and Darlene Vose have just what the doctor ordered.

Vose's Shopping Center is is quite ironical. When one thinks of shopping centers, connotations of contemporary facilities and surroundings come to mind. However, Frank and Darlene's shopping center isn't a Mecca for

for those seeking high-tech, rather it is a place for consumers of delightful, second hand merchandise and one of a kind items. The wares range from frivolous knickknacks to some of the finest imported oak chests, dressers, sewing machines and wardrobe closets you'll find anywhere. And if antique American bottles and glassware is your desire, Frank has dug up and preserved some of the rarest bottles throughout the local area, making collectors green with envy.

Probably the most precious commodity on the premises are the proprietors themselves. Frank and Darlene are the quintessential "junkies" you would hope to find while traversing narrow foothill roads. They are archaeologists, historians and barterers extraodinaire. "One man's junk is another man's treasure," is an axiom that Frank and Darlene live by. It is truly a pleasant experience to meet the Vose's and rummage through their renovated land mark grocery store.

Apparel

CORWIN & SON CLOTHIERS
130 W 3rd Street
Chico, CA 95928
Tel. (916) 342-6521
Hrs: Mon. - Sat.   9:30 a.m. - 5:30 p.m.
        Thursday   9:30 a.m. - 8:00 p.m.

When man first saw the need for clothing he could only swathe himself with available resources from his immediate surroundings. However, we've come a long way from animal skins and fig leaves. Today, after centuries of clothing evolution, we can dress in garments that are more comfortable and aesthetically pleasing. Stores like Corwin & Son Clothiers, family owned since 1921, deserve much of the credit for this needed commodity that is so too often taken for granted.

Owners Norman Corwin and son David are consistent in their efforts to provide complete service ranging from assistance in choosing an ensemble, to timely alterations. They've broken away from the traditional offering of fresh product lines, and have channeled that energy into presenting top-of-the-line clothing with quality service. A few of the clothing lines carried are the Perry Ellis line, the Alexander Julian line and the Pendelton line, a standby in tradition. For your other needs, they have a wide selection of accessories including hats, belts, shoes and much, much more.

The next time you experience the dilemma of not knowing where to shop for clothing, remember the well respected name of Corwin & Son Clothiers.

Centuries ago, without clothing you were naked. Today, without quality clothing, you may as well be.

Art

ORIENT & FLUME ART GLASS
2209 Park Avenue
Chico, CA 95928
Tel. (916) 893-0375
Hrs: Mon. - Sun. 9:00 a.m. - 5:00 p.m.

Orient & Flume, a small American art glass studio located at the foot of the Sierra Nevada mountains, has created works that can be found in such notable collections as the Metropolitan Museum, Smithsonian Museum, Chicago Art Institute, Corning Glass Museum and many other fine stores and galleries throughout the world.

Early efforts of the studio were directed towards recreating the silver-luster of such turn of the century glass studios as Tiffany, Steuben and Loetz. They have continually experimented with glass formulas, glass melting and innovative decorating techniques. In time, after fourteen years of evolution, this has led to the production of intricate, three dimensional designs encased in clear glass. Inspired by wildlife indigenous to the American landscape, Orient & Flume is proud to offer these unique works to serious collectors everywhere.

Orient & Flume offers several lines of their unique glass. The Art Glass line is the culmination of the finest in artistry, technical expertise and collectability. The Gift Glass line features a wide assortment of high quality, but inexpensive, glass items specifically designed for the gift market. Studio Glass, available in paperweights, vases and perfume bottles, has been produced since the founding of Orient & Flume in 1972. They also offer beautiful jewelry and accessory lines, all in the unmistakable workmanship of Orient & Flume. Visit this studio and obtain a collectable that will reflect your smile for years to come.

Bakery

THE UPPER CRUST
130 Main St.
Chico, CA 95928
Tel. (916) 895-3866
Hrs: Mon. - Sun.   6:30 a.m. - 7:00 p.m.

If you are seeking the aromas and tastes that only dedicated bakers can offer, The Upper Crust is highly recommended. Owner Pat Hofhenke uses trial and error to develop unique recipes and her busy bakers are diligently at work from midnight on to ensure that the eager morning crowd will have plenty of fresh baked goods.

Voted Chico's best bakery, The Upper Crust delights patrons with scrumptious pies, cakes, pastries, croissants and over fifteen varieties of bulk roasted coffee beans to enjoy with your meal or take home.

With the first bite, you will know why The Upper Crust is a "Best Choice" in Chico.

Gift

MADE IN CHICO
138 West Third Street
Chico, CA. 95928
Tel. (916) 894-7009
Hrs: Mon. - Sat. 10:00 a.m. - 5:30 p.m.
Visa and MasterCard accepted

The nature of this store reflects the philosophy and image the owner wanted to project...Made in Chico is a store which takes pride in the Chico community. People shop to buy gifts to send to their friends because they are proud of Chico and its personality, atmosphere and local talent. Customers bring out-of-towners to this store as if it were a local attraction.

In a restored 1900s store, graced with pine beams, exposed brick walls and a sixteen foot ceiling you will find Kiwi products, such as jams and dried Kiwi mixes. Locally made vinegar, olive and almond oils, as well as a variety of nuts and other gourmet condiments are featured. You will also find award-winning, locally brewed beers--Sierra Nevada Beer and Saxton Brewery.

A central feature of the shop is the Woof & Poof line of gift items. They offer a large selection of their famous covered hot water bottles, aprons, potholders, tote bags, wash mitts and more! Irregulars are available at bargain prices. Other unusual and elegant gift items include blown paper weight from Orient & Flume and wood gift items such as giant mirrored sunglasses, blackboards and salad servers from Field & Grey.

You will find at this "Best Choice" gift store a display of pride in community and finely crafted gifts.

ZUCCHINI & VINE
294 2nd Street
Chico, CA 95926
Tel. (916) 345-3551
Hrs: Mon. - Sat.   9:30 a.m. - 5:30 p.m.
        Sunday   12:00 noon - 5:00 p.m.

For those who revel in the art of gift giving, whether for yourself or others, it is always a pleasure to find a shop where the sights and scents are reminiscent of old fashioned shopping and recreational browsing.

Such a shop is Zucchini & Vine, located in the heart of downtown Chico. For the past ten years, owner Nancy Lindhal has perfected the skill of selective merchandising, and brings her crafty insights to you via her elegant general store. Zucchini & Vine has an eclectic collection of unique and beautiful gifts, cookware, gadgets, crafts, glassware, silver, doo-dads, gourmet foods and many accessories and knickknacks. But most of all, Zucchini & Vine has personality.

Described by one patron as the "Ultimate in kitchen, dining and home decorating," Zucchini & Vine is very theme oriented and sponsors several events that are anticipated with great eagerness throughout Chico. For Valentine's Day, Nancy hosts bread baking and chocolate recipe contests; for the annual Summer Sale, champagne and mellon balls are served while the store has a twenty-five percent off sale for three hours. Zucchini & Vine's slogan, "For the Art of Living Well," is suitable to say the least.

Pizza

WOODSTOCK'S PIZZA PARLOR
222 1/2 Normal Street
Chico, CA 95928
Tel. (916) 893-1500
Hrs: Sun - Thu.   11:00 a.m. - 1:00 a.m.
        Fri. - Sat.   11:00 a.m. - 2:00 a.m.

If you're striving for a higher "pizza consciousness", Woodstock's Pizza Parlor, Chico division, has a masters degree! An offspring of the parent parlor in Corvallis, Oregon, Woodstock's has "campuses" in college towns in California, all serving a scholarly product!

Sporting the traditional Woodstock color scheme of reddish orange awning and accents, the interior is dominated by cedar booths, tables, and pine benches. The old fashioned pizza dough is hand rolled and made fresh daily, with a choice of white or wheat. Tasty specials include the Vegetarian Delight, which consists of black olives, mushrooms, onion, tomatoes and green pepper, or the Upper Park, with beef, canadian style bacon, extra cheese, mushrooms, onion and green pepper. You can also choose from sixteen fresh toppings to create your own special.

The entire pizza is made in front of the customer, from hand tossing the dough to baking in the oven. Go to the head of the class....order a pizza from Woodstock's and experience a "Pie Beta Kappa"!

Restaurant

ANGELO'S SICILIAN CLAN CAFE
820 Oroville Ave
Chico, CA 95928
Tel. (916) 345-2643
Hrs: Mon. - Fri.   Lunch   11:30 a.m. - 2:00 p.m.
     Mon. - Thu.   Dinner   5:30 p.m. - 9:30 p.m.
     Fri. - Sat.   Dinner   5:30 p.m. - 10:00 p.m.

It's time for an association test. What comes to your mind when reading the following words: Sicilian...Dining...Mouth watering...Poppy State? Well, how did you do? The association should have gone something like: Delicious Italian food in California. Don't worry if you didn't do so well, just go to Angelo's Sicilian Clan Cafe for a re-examination.

Angelo's Sicilian Clan Cafe, in business since 1971, is a truly authentic Italian restaurant. All the guarded family recipes come from the owners home town in Sicily. There are over fifty dinner items to choose from including scaloppine al Tosca, Provim veal, artichoke hearts and lemon, veal scallops with fresh mushrooms, calzones and many others. Included with each dinner is a choice of antipasta, minestrone or salad. Of course, as is tradition with Italian dinners, there is a healthy selection of wines.

The ambiance of this cafe is another sign of it's authenticity, being snug and romantic. Angelo's Sicilian Clan Cafe is a restaurant of proven excellence, in as much as, once you've eaten there you'll pass your next test by associating this restaurant with the "Best Choice."

BURGER HUT
933 Nord Avenue
Chico, CA 95926
Tel.   (916) 891-1418
Hrs: Mon. - Sun.   10:00 a.m. - 9:00 p.m.

The hamburger, one of America's favorite foods, is a wondrous subject. When was it first conceived? Was it an accident? Hmmm...That's doubtful, they taste too good and come in handy far too many times for it to have been other than on purpose. Well, perhaps it was meant to remain a mystery, but that doesn't mean they can't be enjoyed. Where? At Burger Hut of course.

Burger Hut may not know the origin of the hamburger, but they certainly know everything else about them. Their patrons, ranging from farmers to attorneys, are always satisfied with the fast service and the quality of the food. Burger Hut serves a fantastic barbeque sauce, and has great pickles brought all the way from Oregon. If you want a hot dog instead of a burger, they've got those too.

Burger Hut, catering to volume and speed goes thru 150 pounds of fresh ground beef daily without loosing the quality expected by the customers. So, even though the origin of the archetypical Hamburger may elude us, it's well know that the best hamburgers originate on the grills of Burger Hut.

FREDUCCINI'S, 1020 Main Street, Chico, California. Enjoy northern Italian cuisine in the intimate, tastefully- decorated dining room of one of Chico's finest restaurants.

GASHOUSE PIZZA
1444 Park Avenue
Chico, CA 95928
Tel. (916) 345-6602
Hrs: Mon. - Sun.   5:00 p.m. - 10:00 p.m.
and,
Chico, CA, 95926
Tel.   (916) 345-3621
Hrs: Mon. - Sun.   11:30 a.m. - 10:00 p.m.

Scenario one: a group of friends are gathered for a reunion and are looking for a place to get a good pizza. Scenario two: it's Friday night and Mom and Dad are taking the kids out for dinner. The children don't want Chinese, they want pizza. Scenario three: the football team just won a game and want to celebrate. One of the team shouts "Pizza!" Guess where friends, family and football team end up? They go to Gashouse Pizza.

118

Gashouse Pizza, in business for over ten years, caters to all for the simple expedient that everyone wants a good pizza. The pizza sauce is one of the reasons for their success. It was passed to the owner from an aged Sicilian man and this, in combination with the fresh toppings, separates Gashouse's pizzas from the mass produced types. The building that houses this restaurant used to be an old gas station dating back to the 1930s. Memorabilia from several decades hangs upon the walls, attracting the interest of the patrons.

There are four types of beer on tap, as well as, six other choices of imported of domestic varieties. Here you can eat a delicious pizza, enjoy a cool draft and get an eye-full of history. Whatever the scenario, Gashouse Pizza is the perfect end result.

KAREN'S RESTAURANT
912 W 1st
Chico, CA 95928
Tel. (916) 343-4340

Hrs:	Breakfast	Tue. - Fri.	7:00 a.m. - 11:00 a.m.
		Saturday	8:00 a.m. - 11:45 a.m.
	Lunch	Tue. - Fri.	11:00 a.m. - 2:30 p.m.
		Saturday	12:00 noon - 3:00 p.m.
	Dinner	Tue. - Fri.	5:00 p.m. - 9:30 p.m.
		Sat. - Sun	5:00 p.m. - 9:00 p.m.
	Brunch	Sunday	9:00 a.m. - 2:00 p.m.

Karen's Restaurant, in business fourteen years, is located in a turn of the century Del Monte prune factory and maintains the rustic, lodge-like atmosphere.

The open kitchen, inviting observation of cooking in process, the irregularity of tables and settings, some booths, some antique oak and pine tables, some on oak flooring, some on raised carpeted areas, add to the casual warmth reflective of this small northern California town.

All of the food is prepared on the premises. While there are many subtle delights on the fairly extensive menu, the primary focus of most dishes is wholesome, simple home cooking. You will find light to heavy meals for meat and fish lovers, as well as vegetarians. Wine and beer are available.

LA SALLE'S GARDEN CAFE
229 Broadway
Chico, CA 95926
Tel. (916) 893-0226
Hrs: Mon. - Sat.   9:00 a.m. - 2:00 a.m.
      Sunday   10:00 a.m. - 2:00 a.m.

What used to be a barber/shoeshine shop is now one of the favorite gathering spots in Chico. It took a little work and a lot of visualization, but now, twelve years later, La Salle's Garden Cafe is a sight to be seen.

At La Salle's Garden Cafe the people on staff help to generate a friendly, second home atmosphere. It's open, airy and has a relaxing nature that is sure to provide for a super evening. For entertainment, there's jazz on Friday nights and dance/contemporary music on Saturdays. But wait, it's not just a bar, they also serve a terrific breakfast, lunch, brunch and dinner! La Salle's has quite a happy hour, in fact, displayed on the walls, are several Best Bar and Happy Hour awards.

La Salle's caters to all types of crowds, the only prerequisite being an ability to have fun. It used to be a great place for a haircut and shoeshine. Now, it's the great place to go after you get that haircut and shoeshine.

REDWOOD FOREST RESTAURANT
121 W 3rd Street
Chico, CA 95928
Tel. (916) 343-4315
Hrs: Mon. - Sat.   11:00 a.m. - 4:00 p.m.

It's lunch time and hunger gnaws at your belly. Looking through the on hand supplies, you note that nothing looks particularly appealing. Hmmm...Maybe it's time to go to a restaurant. But where? Fast food? No, not really in the mood for it. How about Redwood Forest Restaurant? Now, that sounds like a good idea; assuage that hunger in a first-class fashion.

At Redwood Forest Restaurant lunch is their speciality. You can choose from soups, sandwiches, quiches, chowder, enchiladas,, carrot cake and on Tuesdays chicken pot pies. They don't boast of fancy dishes that flame at your table, but instead, are proud of the simple, delicious entrees that make customers return for more.

All of this, in a restaurant with a forest like atmosphere, is ample reasoning to venture to the Redwood Forest Restaurant. Why settle for an unsavory lunch when it's possible to eat in a forest full of wonderful meals. Hansel and Gretel had the right idea, but were in the wrong neck of the woods.

RESTAURANT TOUR OF CHICO			
a.m.	Upper Crust	Best bakery	Chico/Rest
a.m.	Karen's	Best breakfast	Chico/Rest
p.m.	Burger Hut	Best hamburger	Chico/Rest
p.m.	Redwood Forest	Best specialty	Chico/Rest
p.m.	Angelo's	Best Sicilian	Chico/Rest
p.m.	Gashouse Pizza	Best Pizza	Chico/Rest
p.m.	La Salle's	Best all around	Chico/Rest

Oroville

What is now a town of 8,700 persons living in tree-shaded houses was in the winter of 1849 a tent city called Ophir, its only reason for being the gold strike in the Feather River. The name was changed in 1855 when a post office was designated and there were already Ophir and Ophirvilles on the record. Oro is Spanish for gold, a popular name in California. Enterprising mining engineers later devised canals to bring water in during dry summer months and dredges followed up the stream beds, taking millions of dollars worth of gold from here.

The $121 million Oroville Dam and Reservoir, started in 1962, is upstream, creating a 15,500 acre lake at full pool. The valley is full of olive and fruit orchards, and the town earned fame in the industry for commercial adaptation of a method for pickling olives for preservation.

Attractions

The **Butte County Courthouse** is here, and so is the memory of what was California's most populous Chinatown in the 1870s. The **Chinese Temple**, 1500 Broderick, is now a city museum.

Table Mountain, near town, is now famous for its spring wild flowers. A ghost town dubbed Oregon City was here, and several hydraulic mining spoils piles can be seen, along with deposits from some of the thirty-three mine shafts drifted into the side of the mountain.

Feather River Fish Hatchery, 5 Table Mountain Road, is a giant place, with rearing ponds for salmon and steelhead which lost their spawning grounds

121

to Oroville Dam. Underwater viewing windows let visitors see the fish, and learn about the artificial spawning process.

Pioneer Museum is on Montgomery Street, and one of the first homes, Lott House, at 1067 Montgomery Street, is open for viewing in Sank Park. For hours of operation and other information, contact the **Oroville Chamber of Commerce**, 1789 Montgomery Street, Oroville CA 95965. Telephone 533-2542.

Paradise

This sprawling community with 22,571 residents is in the hills east of Chico. It is one of fifty places in California with the name Paradise, and first showed up in the land maps done in 1879. One story goes that the name really came from the "Pair o' Dice" saloon. Wags like to point out that in gold rush days it was a short ride from Paradise to Helltown. Helltown does not survive.

The modern Paradise is a linear community, stretching from Paradise Lake in the north south for a considerable distance along the west fork of the Feather River.

Attractions

Gold Nugget Museum, on Pearson Road, is a good place to start exploring this community under the pine trees. The history of the Dogtown gold nugget and other strikes is told in the exhibits.

Tall Pines Golf Course, a public links, is at 5325 Clark Road.

For information, contact the **Paradise Economic Development Commission,** 5555 Skyway, Paradise CA 95969. Telephone 872-9642.

COLUSA COUNTY

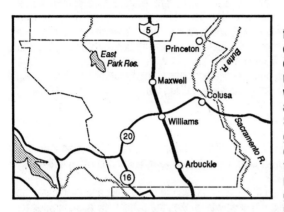

The Sacramento River is on the east, the first crest of the Coast Range mountains on the west and in between are the plains of the Sacramento Valley, green with rice and other crops which thrive on hot summers and ample irrigation water. Colusa County is 1,153 square miles devoted to agriculture, with a population of about 14,700 people and a history which reaches to settlements on the Sycamore Slough of the Sacramento long before any resident of California knew how to write.

When white settlers came to this land on the far side of the Sacramento from the Sutter Buttes, it was 1846 and over 1,000 Indians lived in thirteen dozen villages on the river's west bank far above annual levels of flooding. Today, only a few Indian people survive, their Rancheria seven and a half miles north of Colusa featuring jackpot bingo weekly. The Colus Indians gave their name to the county, formed in 1850 as one of California's original twenty-seven counties. It has been farmed from the start, a breadbasket for the gold miners who launched the state's economy.

Temperatures here are mild, a forty five degree average in January, seventy eight in July. The growing season is 268 days. The sparse rainfall, about sixteen inches a year, is augmented by coast range water flowing from the Tehama-Colusa canal. In addition to rice, the alluvial soils produce several field crops and vast acreages are in tomatoes, all machine picked. I-5, and I-505 to processing plants at Vacaville, provide rapid highway transportation for farmers and travelers. Highway 20, a scenic route over the coast range, passes from east to west through Colusa and Williams.

123

Colusa County

ATTRACTIONS

Colusa, the county seat, is on the site of the capital village for the Colusa people. Part of John Bidwell's 1845 land grant, it was purchased by Colonel Charles D. Semple who built the first house in 1851. The courthouse dates to 1861, a Greek-style brick building with columns in front and a belvedere above the roof line. Large houses shaded by trees typify the residential areas, and folks like to brag that there isn't a stop light in town. The community, laid out on a precise grid, has a population of about 4,600. An historic directory, which makes an easy walking tour guide book, is available at the **City Hall** on Market Street.

Colusa-Sacramento River State Recreation area is upstream at the edge of town, providing camping and water sports on a sixty seven acre site which is part of an old river channel. Open all year, telephone (916) 458-4927.

Williams, founded in 1876, is a creature of the railroad which came up the west side of the valley. Highway 20 makes the community a crossroads for traffic bound for Clear Lake and Ukiah in the coast range. About 1,900 people live in this town with its rail sidings, storage tanks and farm supply businesses.

Sacramento Valley Museum, on the west edge of downtown Williams, deals with life at the turn of the century as farms were developed. It includes a general store stocked with authentic merchandise. A picnic area is next to the building. Open Friday through Wednesday, 10:00 a.m. to 5:00 p.m.

In the far western foothills between Lodoga and Stonnyford is **East Park Reservoir,** the first Federal reclamation project in the country. The lake is stocked with warm water fish and is a local recreation area.

West of Maxwell is a remnant of the days when cattle grazed the vast grassland of this county. The **Stone Corral**, six miles west on a county road, was used to gather in the herds at round up time; it dates to 1846 and perhaps before. Nearby are some of the famed Colusa **sandstone quarries** which supplied rock for major buildings in San Francisco.

For more information, contact the **Colusa County Chamber of Commerce,** Box 1027, Colusa, CA 95932. Telephone (916) 458-2541.

Princeton by the Sea

Accommodations

PILLAR POINT INN
380 Capistrano Road
Princeton By The Sea, CA 94018
Tel.   (415) 728-7377
Visa, MasterCard and AMEX are accepted.

Watch the fishing fleet come in at sunset, soak in a steam bath dream away in a thick feather mattress, and wake up hungry for a real treat of a breakfast.

Built in 1985, The Pillar Point Inn stands as the only bed and breakfast Inn on the Bay Area peninsula to take advantage of the spectacular Pacific Ocean views. Set alongside Pillar Point Harbor, home of Northern California's most active fishing fleet, the inn has quickly become one of the area's most popular places to spend a getaway vacation. Each of the Cape Cod style rooms have bay windows overlooking the harbor. Each of the rooms are lavishly decorated with provincial furnishings and colorful tilework, downstairs rooms even have steambaths. Every room has old world comfort such as a fire place to curl up to, as well as the conveniences of today's world, including a videocassette recorder, color television and refrigerator.

Get comfortable, relax, and gaze out over the waters and the boats below. You can be sure it will be more than a fleeting glance.

PRINCETON INN
P. O. Box 429
Princeton By The Sea, CA 94018
Tel. (415) 728-7311
Hrs: Tue. - Sat.   11:00 a.m. - 10:00 p.m.
            Sunday   10:00 a.m. - 9:30 p.m.

Whether it's turn of the century charm in dining and accommodations, or vintage rock and roll, the Princeton Inn belongs on any hit parade.

Originally built just after the 1906 earthquake as a hotel, the inn's main draw is its fine dining with reasonable prices in an uncrowded and unhurried atmosphere in the newly renovated restaurant. Travelers still enjoy a bed and breakfast with cozy rooms, country furniture, fresh flowers and complimentary newspapers. Every Friday and Saturday the Inn offers live music and dancing to hit tunes of the 50's, 60's and 70's in the lounge. If your taste leans more to jazz, drop in on the first Sunday of every month for an afternoon of swing jazz that has fans coming from miles around. From the menu, try the pan fried chicken breast in lemon honey sauce, prime rib served with pastry and cheese stuffed tomato, or the curried seafood clam bake.

From Benny Goodman to Johnny B. Good the Princeton Inn is a "Best Choice" to swing into for a good time.

Restaurant

SHORE BIRD, 390 Capristrano Road, Princeton-By-The-Sea, California. This Cape Cod cottage restaurant overlooks Pillar Point Harbor and features fresh fish, seafood specialties, and homemade desserts.

CONTRA COSTA COUNTY

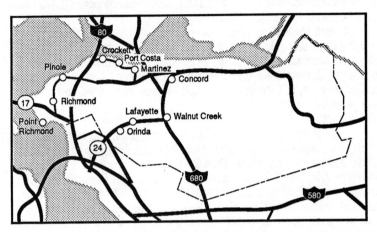

Contra Costa, the "coast opposite" in Spanish, now includes 733 square miles of land bounded on the west by the San Francisco and San Pablo bays, on the north and east by Suisun Bay and the San Joaquin River's old channel. Alameda County lies to the south.

Once the industrial powerhouse for the larger cities, a place to build oil refineries, outfit and service vessels of all sizes on its protected shoreline, Contra Costa has a vitality all its own in the 1980s. Havens of homes for commuters dot the valleys along the freeway leading east from Oakland, while Walnut Creek and Concord attract their own commuters drawn to offices which choose a place away from the fog and convenient to dozens of smaller residential communities. There were 656,000 people living in Contra Costa in 1980. Population estimates show newcomers continue to flock here, perhaps at 2,000 a year since the census was taken.

The industrialization of this arid peninsula between the San Joaquin delta and the bays leading to San Francisco can be traced to railroad promoters, a 283 mile pipeline carrying crude from the Kern County oil fields, and the demands of World War II production. Towns like Nitro, Giant and Hercules hosted the explosive-makers for a war. Point Richmond, still struggling to realize its developers' dreams, played host to four shipyards and a five-fold increase in population in less than one year.

Three distinct zones make up the county. The coast is seventy miles of frontage, bustling with oil refineries, and maritime enterprises from Richmond on San Francisco Bay to Antioch, opposite the confluence of the Sacramento and San Joaquin rivers. The delta has flat, intensely-farmed islands secured behind earthen dikes, and countless waterways prowled by pleasure boaters and teaming with waterfowl. Its flanks are brown with dried grass most of the year, its innards laced with coal and silica, Mount Diablo pokes 3,849 feet above sea level in the middle of the county.

Spanish ranchos with cattle dominated the inland country and the arable delta land until gold miners moved east from San Francisco, bringing the founding of Martinez and Pittsburg. A demand for wheat turned cattlemen into grain producers. The county was named and created, one of California's first twenty-seven, in February 1850. Martinez was designated county seat. Three years later much of the bay shore, south of Albany, and the Livermore Valley was removed from the county to form Alameda County.

Much of the modern history revolves around transportation patterns servicing the urban centers of the bay area. Railroads made the county's ports transcontinental shipping points. On a tonnage basis, about half of the ocean shipping entering San Francisco Bay is worked at Contra Costa docks.   The completion in 1937 of the first of three highway tunnels through the Berkeley Hills made Contra Costa's secluded valleys exclusive commuter communities. Now trains from Bay Area Rapid Transit, BART, run west from Concord on the same route, speeding commuters to and from San Francisco. Agriculture, once the mainstay of the local economy, today uses about one percent of a work force in excess of 210,000 persons.

ATTRACTIONS

Mount Diablo State Park and **Black Diamond Mines Regional Preserve** are good starting places for any Contra Costa tour. When the air is clear you get a panorama of the entire county, the bays and delta. The mining area, once California's largest coal extraction site, has tours offering geologic and archaeological information.

Huckleberry Botanical Regional Preserve is 130 acres near Oakland off Skyline Boulevard with a self-guiding trail leading past several rare plants growing in natural settings.

Broines Regional Park is a major facility above the reservoirs on San Pablo Creek. Its 5,030 acres include a nature area dedicated to John Muir, viewpoints where hikers can see much of the Contra Costa bay shores, trail systems and an archery range. A trail leads from here all the way to **Mount Diablo State Park.**

128

Near El Sobrante on the road to San Pablo Reservoir is **Kennedy Grove Regional Recreation Area,** a 95 acre site developed for family activities and hiking.

Brooks Island, a seventy seven acre mass of land off Richmond's inner harbor, has several Indian shell mounds estimated to be about 2,500 years old. A regional park is under development here.

Point Pinole, one of several regional shorelines on San Pablo Bay, offers a pier which reaches 1,225 feet from shore, giving fishermen special opportunities. There is a fee for shuttle service from the inland parking lot to the pier.

Contra Loma Linda Regional Park on the river, one mile south of Antioch, is a swimming beach with fishing, boat launching and picnic facilities.

South of Brentwood on Marsh Creek is the **"Stone House" of the Rancho Los Medanos,** home of John Marsh. He was the first American settler in the county and California's first licensed medical doctor. Marsh hardly got to live in his three-story house of native stone; he was murdered by four neighbors in 1856. Restoration of the mansion may preclude more than just exterior views.

Concord Pavilion is an indoor-outdoor concert site for big-name entertainers located off Kirker Pass Road. More than 5,000 people can watch from a grassy slope, and over 3,700 reserved seats are available. Ticket information available by calling 676-8742 (67-MUSIC!)

Antioch

Antioch, located on the south shore over looking the islands which mark the meeting of the Sacramento and San Joaquin River, was settled by farmers who arrived by schooner. Its early days as a port revolved around shipping farm products of the area. The town was named in 1851, reportedly after a discussion of Biblical names appropriate to the peaceful countryside.

Benicia

The Contra Costa north shoreline has several small cities boasting a lot of history. From the earliest American days on San Francisco Bay, these sheltered waters attracted a ship-oriented people. Benicia, with its deep water anchorage on the Solano County side of Suisun Bay, is mentioned in an early military report as more favorable than San Francisco and "above the fogs." Interest in Benicia caused the founding of Martinez on the south shore, the Contra Costa county seat. Ignatio Martinez reportedly wanted to steal the march on Benicia, and he did. Shell Oil Company picked the site for its refinery. The Carquinez Straits bridge was opened in 1927, an engineering marvel of the time spanned the straits. It is 314 feet above the water, and the piers holding its span reach 145 feet below the water to rest on a sandstone bed rock.

Concord

Fernando Pacheco and his brother-in-law Francisco Galindo made two tries at laying out the town site for what is now a sprawling community of more than 105,000 people. Their first location on the family's Rancho Monte del Diablo was 25 feet above sea level and flooded out, its wharf stranded by silt from shipping just a decade after platting in 1855. They moved two miles east toward Mount Diablo, gained 40 feet of elevation and called the place Todos Santos. The next year, in 1869, residents renamed the town Concord. It became a center for the nut, fruit and poultry producers of the Ygnacio Valley.

When Concord incorporated in 1905, coal and gypsum mining were well underway on the mountain to the rear. Oil refining, chemical production and steelworks came later. Freeways and BART made this a bedroom community for other bay area employers, a valley of mostly single family homes and shopping centers. The climate is mild, with temperatures in the low nineties during summer and mid-fifties in winter months.

Attractions

Several private and public golf courses are in the valley. **Buchanan Field Golf Course** is next to the municipal airport, **Diablo Creek Municipal Golf Course** is on Port Chicago Highway.

Mount Diablo, a regional attraction, is reached from roads leading out of the city into a combination of state park and regional reserve of the coal and gypsum mine sites.

Concord Pavilion, on Kirker Pass Road at the east city limits, provides a setting for famous entertainers and indoor facilities for many local performing arts groups.

For detailed information, the **Concord Chamber of Commerce** is at 1982 Concord Avenue, Concord CA 94520. Phone 685-1181.

Restaurants

THE GREY FOX INN
1821 Concord Avenue
Concord, CA 94520
Tel. (415) 687-5380

The unassuming Grey Fox Inn sits shaded by a roadside grove of orchards on the outskirts of Concord's active downtown. The decor of the converted hostelry is similar to that found in many bed and breakfast inns of the wine country. Colonial style furniture surrounds the entry area and main dining room. Blush pink tablecloths and subdued track lighting provide a cozy, relaxed ambiance which is enhanced by the cordial, friendly staff who make you feel as if this is your home away from home. As the softly flowing jazz plays in the background and you sit down to dine, you will realize that home could never be like this.

If it's lunch you've come for, try the cold poached salmon, served with a cucumber salad and an herb mayonnaise seasoned with cilantro, dill and garlic. Try the Vol Au Vent, a tasty, tender veal in a mushroom and red wine sauce layered over a flaky pastry shell. The dinner menu emphasizes fresh fish dishes, although there are a number of delicious pasta, veal, pork, lamb, beef and poultry dishes as well. For an appetizer, try the Champignon Farci crab, tender button mushrooms stuffed with sweet crab meat, herbs and spices. A couple of especially recommended entrees are: Paupiettes of sole, consisting of poached fillet of sole wrapped around crab, bay shrimp and bay scallops covered in a creamy fish veloute or seafood Croustade, which is a light, puff pastry shell filled with crab meat, shrimp, scallops, mussels and clams topped with a light, lemony sauce. Wine lovers will be happy to know that the Grey Fox makes a special effort to locate obscure but superior wineries which add a special quality to your meal.

This stellar restaurant, featuring well executed meals at reasonable prices, has a magnetism of warmth and hospitality, making The Grey Fox Inn the "Best Choice" in Concord.

(See special invitation in the Appendix.)

OSAKA JAPANESE CUISINE
2650 Monument Boulevard
Concord, CA 94520
Tel. (415) 676-1017

For over ten years, Osaka Japanese Cuisine has been producing the kind of Japanese cuisine that keeps their loyal leagues of admirers happily returning. The reasons for the success of this popular restaurant range from the warm atmosphere and attentive, courteous service, to the uncompromising attention given to the integrity of the well prepared menu.

The Osaka's decor is an interesting montage of ship-house tables, Kabuki wall art and dolls celebrating the Japanese opera. In you choose to dine in more authentic surroundings, retire to the Tamati room. There, dining atop beautiful handmade vermillion tables and seated shoeless on Tamati floor mats, you can enjoy Japanese fare as it was meant to be enjoyed. The chef, Mitsu Ngimini, does a Sukiyaki which is a wondrous combination of tender aged, slice beef and assorted vegetables in a flavorful sauce. Mitsu also displays a light touch in his Tempura with just the right amount of golden crust surrounding tender, yet crunchy vegetables. The Donburi dishes are other favorites here at Osaka.

Concord is a nice, quaint area with a relaxed ambiance and friendly people. Osaka is a reflection of that community, a friendly comfortable restaurant reproducing the cuisine artistry of Japan. Stop by and join their league of admirers.

(See special invitation in the Appendix)

RED ROBIN, Sun Valley Mall, Concord, California. World famous hamburgers, sandwiches, BBQ, libations.

Crockett

California-Hawaiian Sugar Refining Co. picked Crockett for its West Coast processing plant where ships could easily offload the raw sugar from Hawaii. In 1884, Starr Flour Mill opened what was then the largest mill on the coast, and a sugar beet refinery opened in 1898 was the first unit of the big C and H plant.

132

Attractions

The **John Muir Ranch** is two miles south of Martinez on Franklin Canyon Road. From here the famed naturalist wrote of his travels in the mountains of the west.

Port Costa, located on the shore between Martinez and Crockett, was a port town repeatedly swept by fire. One of five commercial buildings left standing after the last fire is a warehouse filled with craft shops. Other buildings have smaller businesses serving tourists who stray off the main highways to Carquinez Scenic Drive.

Crockett Historical Museum, on Loring Avenue just west of the C and H Sugar Refinery, is in a restored railroad depot. Information on tour times can be obtained from the **Crockett Chamber of Commerce,** 787-1155.

Antiques

THE ANTIQUE FLEA, 1520 Pomona Street, Crockett, California. Furniture from around the world.

MIKE MAGYAR, 1400 Pomona Street, Crockett, California. Open seven days a week. Fireplace mantels, pinball machines and neon!

VICTORIAN ANTIQUES, 1400 Pomona Street, Crockett, California. 7,000 square feet, chuck-full.

Attractions

ALDO RAY FAN CLUB, P. O. Box 427, Crockett, California. Telephone 787-1157. Call for information. Lots of movie star memorabilia.

Delicatessen

VALONA MARKET AND DELI
1323 Pomona Avenue
Crockett, CA 94528
Tel. (415) 787-2022
Hrs: Mon. - Fri.   7:00 a.m. - 7:00 p.m.
       Saturday   10:00 a.m. - 6:00 p.m.
       Sunday   10:00 a.m. - 6:00 p.m.

A real old fashioned deli and market, the Valona takes great pride in the freshness and quality of their homemade salads, sandwiches, and deli items.
Plan your picnic or party with just one stop at the Valona. In addition to an impressive menu selection, you can pick up those little extras you know you'll need. There's also a full range of imported and domestic beers, a large selection of fine wines, and sodas for the kids.
Call ahead to order for your picnic or party and relax assured of the finest, freshest and best of the deli world.

Frames

THE APPLE FRAME SHOP
1319 Pomona Street
Crockett, CA 94525
Tel. (415) 787-1157
Hrs: Wed. - Sun. 12:00 noon - 4:00 p.m.

A picture is worth a thousand words but, the frame is the final statement! At The Apple Frame Shop, owner Don Allen can make that statement better than anyone else around. His special interest and caring attitude are reflected in his expert framing.
Fine art, posters, tapestries, mirrors; if it needs to be framed, Don can do it. At this shop there is a huge variety of frames available, from elegant gold leaf to slick, bright high tech.
Frames and framing are not the only visual delight here, check out the German beer steins and Toby mugs. Serious collectors will find signed, numbered steins and copies of originals. Need advice on your collection--ask Don Allen.
Don's excellent service and attention to detail set him apart from the ordinary. Look for the Apple Frame Shop with the beer-stein mural and prepare to smile.

Restaurants

THE ROSY KITCHEN
1207 Pomona Avenue
Crockett, CA 94528
Tel. (415) 787-1628
Hrs: Mon. - Fri. 7:00 a.m. - 5:00 p.m.
       Saturday   7:00 a.m. - 3:00 p.m.
       Closed Sundays

A favorite memory is of waking up to a house filled with the smell of coffee and the aroma of breakfast being prepared. Rosina Austria and her son Stanley M. Austria, the owners of The Rosy Kitchen, have captured that same wholesomeness in their kitchen--fortunately for us, the kitchen is open to the public. Once inside you know why people have come from miles away to start their day here.

Sit down to a fulsome breakfast and catch up on some of the local news and gossip. The menu shows lots of appetizing omelets, including Rosy's special omelet with diced ham, bell pepper and onions. All breakfasts are served, at reasonable prices, with home-fried potatoes and toast.

At lunchtime, take a seat by the window and watch the townspeople as they go about their daily business, or, enjoy the posters and framed words of wisdom that decorate the walls at Rosy's. You will feel at home here. It's a place for the entire family.

YET WAH MANDARIN CUISINE
20050 Highway 40
Crockett, CA 94525
Tel. (415) 787-3011
Hrs: Sun. - Thu. 11:00 a.m. - 10:00 p.m.
       Fri. - Sat.   11:00 a.m. - 11:00 p.m.

"The Chan Family welcomes you to Yet Wah." For those who love authentic Mandarin Cuisine, that welcome smile is just the beginning of a delectable experience. Yet Wah offers more than three hundred authentic dishes from every part of China.

Award winning dishes, an elegant atmosphere, traditional Chinese spices and old family recipes combine to make Yet Wah deservedly famous. From the "Imperial Dinner", featuring Maine lobster to the "Jade Garden Dinner", vegetarian, you'll find Oriental treats to excite and delight the senses of even the most stoic of diners.

135

Yet Wah also features a panoramic view of the Carquinez Bridge, a large cocktail lounge, and entertainment with dancing on Friday and Saturday nights. Let the Chan Family welcome you to Yet Wah, and you'll be the one with the smile.

Lafayette

Books

THE STORYTELLER
23 Lafayette Circle
Lafayette, CA 94549
Tel. (415) 284-3480
Hrs: Mon. - Sat.   10:00 a.m. - 5:00 p.m.
        Thurday   10:00 a.m. - 7:00 p.m.
Visa and MasterCard accepted.

Reading is an important subject that should be stressed to children. By prompting young ones to read and enjoy reading, we better our contemporary society and definitely increase the potential for our future generations. All of this is the reason that The Storyteller exists, to help children to understand the value of reading.

The Storyteller, for children and parents alike, features children's literature of all types, as well as informative books for adults about the reading material available to the children and even books involving general parenting concerns. It's a true child motivation center, providing activities related to the literature that they have read at home and school, the goal being to excite them to read further. One of their most successful programs is a series of monthly Bedtime Stories, where children dressed for bed with a pillow and blanket curl up on the floor for an evening of stories and a cookie. At the same time parent discussion groups are held in a separate room.

The dedicated owners of the store each hold a specialist credential in reading instruction from the California State Department of Education. They work with local school districts and both have served as consultants in children's literature. Come down to The Storyteller and see how the future of the nation is being molded.

Clocks

CLOCKS, ETC.
3401 Mt. Diablo Boulevard
Lafayette, CA 94549
Tel. (415) 284-4720
Hrs: Mon. - Sat. 10:00 a.m. - 5:00 p.m.
Evenings by appointment.
Mastercard and Visa are accepted.

Hickory dickory dock. The mouse ran up the...lock? No, that's not right. How about sock? Not that one either. Hmmm? There's got to be an answer. Oh, that's it, clock! Well, where can we get one? At Clock's, Etc. you can experience the stunning effect of viewing over 500 clocks in one store.

Clock's, Etc., in business over eleven years, has every kind of clock imaginable, imported from all over the world. Miniatures, desk clocks, wall, mantel, Cuckoo clocks, pocket watches and Grandfather and Grandmother clocks are all displayed in this store. Also, there's a creative gift selection featuring barometers, music boxes, nautical items and quality antique furniture imported from Europe. Some of the special services provided by Clock's, Etc. include a locater service to search for a specific item in clocks or antiques, a complete restoration service for clocks, music boxes and barometers, plus in home service for large clocks.

Clock's, Etc. has a layaway and a ninety day, no interest financing plan available for your convenience. Okay, now we've got the clock. Where can we get the...Gerbil? No, that's not right.

(See special invitation in the Appendix)

Nursery

ORCHARD NURSERY AND FLORIST, INC.
4010 Mt. Diablo Boulevard
Lafayette, CA 94549
Tel. (415) 284-4474
Hrs: Mon. - Fri. 9:00 a.m. - 5:30 p.m.
Saturday 8:30 a.m. - 5:30 p.m.
Sunday 9:00 a.m. - 5:00 p.m.
MasterCard, Visa and Discover cards are accepted.

Plants. People use them to decorate their homes, offices and patios. They're colorful, natural, fragrant and help to create a more interesting

137

environment for all to enjoy. Plants come in all sizes, shapes and varieties, and a wide spectrum of colors. At Orchard Nursery and Florist has the plant you're looking for, as well as a unique and elegant gift shop in The Lazy K House, a complete selection of patio furniture for comfortable outdoor living, and when it comes to the holidays, one of the biggest Christmas displays in Northern California.

In the nursery you will find quality plant material and a complete selection of all the items you need to ensure a healthy and well kept garden. A highly experienced staff will assist and advise you on all your outdoor and indoor selections. At Orchard you will also find a full service florist shop featuring arm-loads of fresh and artificial flowers, houseplants, wire service and an excellent display of flora arts. Then take some time to roam through The Lazy K House, truly a source for the exceptional. There you will find inspiration for decorating your home and a gift for every occasion. You can browse through each of the beautiful rooms while enjoying a cup of freshly brewed coffee.

Come on in and visit Orchard Nursery, Florist & Lazy K House. You're sure to be delighted by all the treasures they have collected just for you.

Restaurants

KAFFEE BARBARA
1005 Brown Avenue
Lafayette, CA 94549
Tel. (415) 284-9390
Hrs: Breakfast and Lunch
          Mon. - Sun.   7:00 a.m - 3:00 p.m.
       Dinner
          Tue. - Sun.   From 5:30 p.m.
Visa and MasterCard are accepted.

What's that building over there, the one that looks like a castle? Are those delicious smells coming from the same place? The answer to the first question is Kaffee Barbara, and the answer to the second is, yes. If just the structure and beautiful aromas of this restaurant attract your attention, wait until you go in!

At Kaffee Barbara, in the style of a German country cottage, freshness, quality and service are stressed. The owner presides over the kitchen with her German background and everything's made from scratch! The luncheon menu features a full selection of salads, combination sandwiches, quiche and a daily special, with tempting desserts. Dinner menus are changed

138

daily, each offering a choice of six to eight entrees and several pasta specials. All the dinners include soup or salad.

The dining area is attractively divided into three cozy rooms and the aroma of their special coffees whets the appetite. On warm days or evenings you may elect to dine on the lovely outdoor patio. Ahhh! Good food in a terrific atmosphere.

LUKES
3474 Mount Diablo Boulevard
Lafayette, CA 94549
Tel. (415) 283-3561
Hrs: Mon. - Sat.   Lunch from   11:00 a.m.
                    Dinner from   5:00 p.m.

If the order of the day is cozy, intimate dining in a quiet atmosphere with congenial hosts, Lukes fits the bill. Amy Franklin and Gary Lucas are the owners; they are also lifelong friends whose longtime desire was to open a restaurant serving deliciously original food in a romantic, rustic dining room. With special touches of etched glass and a wood burning, rock fireplace, the mood is set for a relaxing meal. Lukes menu is every bit as inviting as its atmosphere.

For lunch, shrimp Louie or chicken Piccata with breast of chicken, lightly sauteed in a sauce of butter, white wine, lemon, capers and served with fluffy rice pilaf and a garden fresh vegetable are favorites. If it's dinner you're seeking, come in, kick back by the crackling fire and begin your meal with a mood setting cocktail and a tempting appetizer. Lukes offers three pasta dishes and three chicken dishes, as well as a fresh fish of the day on a daily changing list of blackboard specials. Additionally, New York steak and a scrumptious grilled pork chop with bourbon sauce and raisins are house specialties. To round off your meal try desserts by Mary Ann. She uses old, private family recipes to create specialties such as pecan pie with bourbon sauce, Kahlua cheesecake and Ameretto cheesecake. For dancing after your dinner, stick around for top dance hits from the '40s, '50s and '60s played by a live combo.

Whether you're in the mood for a light lunch, full course dinner, cocktails or good dancing fun, Lukes is the "Best Choice" in Lafayette.

TOURELLE
3565 Mt. Diablo Boulevard
Lafayette, CA 94549
Tel. (415) 284-3565
Hrs: Restaurant
    Lunch   Tue. - Fri.   11:30 a.m. - 2:30 p.m.
    Dinner Tue. - Sat. 5:00 p.m. - 10:00 p.m.
    Brunch Sunday   10:00 a.m. - 2:30 p.m.
    Cafe   Tue. - Sun. 11:00 a.m. - 11:00 p.m.
Visa, MasterCard and AMEX are accepted.

The beautiful French red brick structure of Tourelle clearly bespeaks the ambiance you will find inside this charming setting. Upon entering the brick courtyard with it's lovely fountain, you will find the most amazing working kitchen displayed in full view behind leaded glass windowpanes. A choice of casual or elegant dining awaits you on either side of the courtyard.

For the casual diner, The Cafe is an informal, bright and airy bistro. Here one can dine on marvelous cassoulets, wonderful stews, innovative pastas, glorious seasonal pizzas and delectable desserts. If it's elegant dining you're looking for, The Restaurant is a synthesis between classical and Nouvelle cuisine, called cuisine Moderne. In this section of Tourelle you can dine on truly exquisite and very innovative dishes. The food, flawlessly created, is beautifully presented in good sized portions. Reservations are required for the restaurant.

For wine lovers, there is a selection of forty-two wines by the glass. The wine list has received the prestigious *Wine Spectator Award,* given to only a hand full of restaurants in the world. Whether dining in the cafe or the restaurant, Tourelle is a definite "Best Choice."

The country around Lafayette offers splendid scenery and drives and hikes through public lands. Lafayette is in a natural area certainly worth getting to know better, yet is very close to many of the major bay area population centers.

GETTING TO KNOW LAFAYETTE			
a.m.	Orchards Nursery	Best Plants	Laf/Nurs
a.m.	Clock's, Etc.	Best clocks	Laf/Clock
p.m.	Tourelle	Best bistro lunch	Laf/Rest
Spend your afternoon touring such scenic areas as the Biones Regional Park, or, continue with your shopping.			
p.m.	Storyteller	Best children's	Laf/Book
p.m.	Kaffee Barbara	Best German	Laf/Rest
p.m.	Luke's	Best food&dance	Laf/Rest

Martinez

Antiques

ASILEE TELFER ANTIQUES, 610 Ferry Street, Marinez, California. Estate purchases. Jewelry, furniture, china, linens and oil paintings.

CREEKSIDE
826 Main Street
Martinez, CA 94553
Tel. (415) 228-4773
Hrs: Mon.-Fri. 10:00 a.m. - 5:00 p.m.
Open daily during November and December
Visa, MasterCard are accepted.

Housed in a 1800's vintage building in down town Martinez, Creekside offers fine antiques combined with today's design ideas.
In addition to fine European antique furniture, Creekside offers design services and carries collectibles of all kinds including, teddy bears, glassware, silver and duck decoys. Straw flowers, both dried and silk, are ready to take home for that special touch of color. Pictures are another favorite, as are the homemade candies. The back room is devoted to an interior design studio with wallpaper books lining one wall. Joanne Dunivan's expert staff can help with design ideas and selection of wall paper to make that business or home like no other.

141

As a one-stop antique and design studio, Creekside can help you put a touch of the 1800's with a taste of today.

MARTINEZ ANTIQUE MART
516 Ferry Street
Martinez, CA 94553
Tel. (415) 228-8175
Hrs: Mon.-Sat.   10:00 a.m. - 5:30 p.m.
       Sunday   12:00 noon- 5:00 p.m.
Visa and MasterCard are accepted.

With twenty-five antique dealers offering their wares in a historic 10,000 square foot building, you're sure to find that treasure you've been seeking.

It takes a good hour just to browse through this huge collective. If you are a regular antique shopper, the affordable prices may surprise you. Downstairs you'll find a large selection of American and European collectibles ranging from clocks, silver, lamps, china, dolls, figurines, jewelry and bric-a-brac. There's a good selection of quality furniture. Upstairs is a "Grandma's attic" with all kinds of homey treasures, including old toys and clothing.

It may not be the biggest in the area, but Martinez Antique Mart is your "Best Choice" for collectibles and antiques.

THE VILLAGE GREEN
627 Main Street
Martinez, CA 94553
Tel. (415) 228-5161
Hrs: Mon.-Fri.   9:30 a.m.- 5:00 p.m.
      Saturday   10:00 a.m.- 4:00 p.m.
Open daily during winter holiday season.

The Village Green is definitely not a place time forgot. The assortment of old and new clocks is one of the special features of this shop. You can buy a cuckoo, a wall clock, a table top clock, and even a stately grandfather clock. Owners Marge and Ken Munger have created a fascinating assortment of merchandise which she calls "an eclectic blend--a little of everything." There are even gourmet coffees, teas and spices.

Supporting that theme, at the back of the store is a collection of hand made quilts and quilted bags, including a diaper bag. There's also an assortment of museum quality jewelry and a variety of collectible spoons, thimbles, figurines, English bone china, and coffee mugs. Detailed pen and ink

Contra Costa County

sketches of local scenes grace one of the front walls, as well as an assortment of Martinez souvenirs.

So you find yourself in Martinez, there is no time like the present to stop in and see what makes this place tick.

Collectibles

NYBORG CASTLE GIFTS AND COLLECTIBLES
6662 Alhambra Avenue
Martinez, CA 94553
Tel. (415) 930-0200
Hrs: Mon.-Fri.   9:30 a.m.-6:30 p.m.
       Saturday   10:00 a.m.-6:00 p.m.
November and December
       Sunday   12:00 noon-4:00 p.m.
Visa and MasterCard are accepted.

If a man's home is his castle, then the collectibles at Nyborg Castle will make everyone at home.

Located just five miles from downtown Martinez in the Virginia Hills Shopping Center, this charming gift store specializes in limited edition collector plates, Hummel figurines and Precious Moments figurines. If you're looking for one in particular owner Bea Nyborg can order plates dating back to a 1908 Royal Copenhagen. Other specialities include miniature carousel horses and houses, and a full selection of gifts and greeting cards. Special ordering, shipping, complimentary gift wrap, hospitality and friendly service are the keys to the success of Nyborg Castle.

Expect a royal welcome, the drawbridge is down at this castle, your "Best Choice" for collectibles.

(See special invitation in the Appendix.)

Orinda

Gifts

CABBAGES & KINGS, 1 Camino Sobrante, Orinda, California. Gifts, antiques, estate jewelry; all in a cute shop with friendly service.

143

Restaurant

CASA ORINDA
20 Bryant Way
Orinda, CA 94563
Tel. (415) 254-2981
Hrs: Mon. - Fri. 4:00 p.m. til closing
Visa, MasterCard and AMEX accepted.

The Casa Orinda is a sixty year tradition in the Bay Area. The original owner, Jack Snow, collected an amazing amount of original western art and firearms. These are still in evidence in the informal setting of this restaurant. The western theme has been carried through in the menu. Honest food is what you can expect to find here. Owner John Goyak stated, "none of our customers want changes to the menu. So we go along with it."

That is why you find consistently good tastes, quality-fresh entrees like New York steaks with onion rings, mesquite charcoal grilled fish, home made pasta--cooked to your order, their famous fried chicken, prawns, chicken liver saute, baked lasagna, veal piccata, hickory smoked ham, or the melt-in-your-mouth chicken with gravy, mashed potatoes, vegetables, soup or salad, biscuit and honey...just like it has been on the menu for all these many years.

Their full service bar is a friendly place to adjourn after dinner. If you're looking for a good home cooked meal in a friendly atmosphere, you cannot do better than the Casa Orinda.

LA BEAU'S BAR & GRILL, 436 Ferry Street, Martinez, California. Open Monday thru Sunday from 11:00 a.m. Authentic Creole cuisine. Live entertainment Friday, Saturday and noon on Sundays.

THE ALBATROSS, 15 North Court Street, Martinez, California. Monday thru Sunday, lunch and dinner; specializing in seafood.

Pinole

Delicatessen

THE NEW DELI
624 San Pablo Avenue
Pinole, CA 94564
Tel. (415) 724-5335
Hrs: Mon. - Fri.   6:00 a.m. - 7:00 p.m.
      Saturday   11:00 a.m. - 4:00 p.m.
      Sunday   11:00 a.m. - 3:00 p.m.

After a long climb, the young man finally reached the mountain peak, where upon lived the mystic. Mustering his courage, the young man asked the venerable one the question he had been wanting to ask all of his short life. "Master, what must I do to serve you?" Rapid in his response, the old man stated, "You must go to New Deli, my son." The boy, his head filled with the thoughts of adventure, asked, "When do I begin my journey to the Old Country?" The mystic glanced at the boy and responded. "No, you must go to The New Deli in Pinole, California and get me a roast beef sandwich, for I am hungry."

The New Deli, though not in India, is indeed rare. Not only are all of their foods homemade and fresh, but they also cook their own deli meats. Owners Jennifer and Tom Cote, feature such creative dishes as lasagne, spinach pie and several varieties of hearty soups. Home grown herbs grace their creations and enhance the already delicious flavor. They also feature a full range of vegetarian foods. In fact, you'll find many of The New Deli's sandwiches in natural food stores throughout the Bay Area.

The New Deli also offers catering services for parties or special occasions. You can enjoy your meal in their clean, bright kitchen like atmosphere or take it home with you. This deli has quite a reputation, and even those who live on the highest mountain peaks know about the good food.

(See special invitation in the Appendix.)

Florist

CALVERA FLOWERS
610L San Pablo Avenue
Pinole, CA 94564
Tel. (415) 724-3640
Hrs: Mon. - Sun. 10:00 a.m. - 7:00 p.m.

Should a florist be in business because they love flowers? Many people might have a difficult time answering this question, but for Jamie Oceguera, the answer is an undeniable yes! Jamie first began Calvera Flowers so that he could buy flowers for himself.

Calvera Flowers is an of old fashioned florist shop that generates feelings of good will in all of it's customers. Here, you'll find all of the traditional services including custom floral arrangements, wire services and a plethora of gift items. A large selection of plants, classic dolls, clocks, cards, wrapping paper, music boxes, crystal, vases and many more delightful objects are included in the inventory.

At Calvera Flowers you can always count on quality, selection and service. All of this, at prices reasonable enough for any pocket book, is an unheard of phenomenon in the flower business these days. Stop by Calvera Flowers, pick up a bouquet or gift and share in Jamie's enthusiasm.

Restaurant

ALFONSO'S MEXICAN RESTAURANT, 624 San Pablo Avenue, Pinole, California. Seafood, steak and Mexican food. Full bar service.

Pittsburg

Pittsburg was named after the Pennsylvania city, when, in 1911, Columbia Steel Co. opened here. Other steel makers followed, along with chemical manufacturers and others drawn by the ability to have their own deep-draft pier next to the factory. An ambitious developer, Jonathon D. Stevenson, named the town New York of the Pacific when it was platted in 1849. The next year a wag observed it still "a three-house town."

Coal mined on Mount Diablo was exported through Pittsburg docks for over thirty years, and fishermen made this their port until industry arrived in 1910.

Point Richmond

Jewelry

OSCAR LUGO, FINE JEWELRY, 155 Park Place, Point Richmond, California. A fine manufacturer of jewelry, retail and wholesale, custom design and repairs.

Restaurants

THE BALTIC RESTAURANT
135 Park Place
Point Richmond, CA 94801
Tel. (415) 235-2532
Hrs: lunch: Mon. - Fri.   11:30 a.m. - 2:30 p.m.
     dinner: Mon. - Thur.   5:00 p.m. -10:00 p.m.
     dinner: Fri. - Sat.   5:00 p.m. - 10:30 p.m.
                Sundays   5:00 p.m. - 10:00 p.m.

The San Francisco Bay Area is famous for its' fine foods and restaurants, yet one must experience "The Baltic" to know true inspiration in authentic Tuscany cuisine.

Edward and Ronald De George, the owners, chose an historical landmark building to house this emporium of good food. The atmosphere at The Baltic is old world elegance, fine lace curtains, wood paneling, and plush carpeting create a warm and inviting ambiance. Combine this with the traditional hospitality of Italy, and a choice of indoor or garden deck seating and you have a pleasurable experience in store.

The De George family bring the finest ingredients to their kitchen to create the true taste of Tuscany. Mouth-watering pasta, tender veal, and the freshest of fish and seafood...all dishes are prepared to order.

The wines are specially chosen by Edward De George for use at the restaurant. You will find one of the largest selections (in California) of Italian, Californian, and French wines right here. It's a wine lovers heaven!

The Baltic is a rare treat for romance, business, or just good old-fashioned fine Italian dining. *Buon Appetito!*

HOTEL MAC
50 Washington Avenue
Point Richmond, CA 94801
Tel. (415) 233-0576
Hrs: Lunch: Mon. - Fri.   11:30 a.m. - 2:30 p.m.
     Dinner: Tue. - Sat.   5:30 p.m. - 10:00 p.m.
            Sunday   4:30 p.m. - 9:00 p.m.
     Brunch: Sunday   10:30 a.m. - 2:30 p.m.
Visa, MasterCard, AMEX and Diners Club are accepted.

The Hotel Mac is a 1911 historic landmark. It was originally owned by Kate Riordon, one of California's first woman suffragettes. The "Mac" was nearly destroyed in a 1970 fire, but community interest and effort effected a complete restoration in 1978. Now the stained glass windows sparkle, the hand-polished mahogany and oak gleam, and the custom-built bar seems to stretch into the next county.

Every evening the chefs prepare delectables to tempt your palate. Oysters on the half shell, Pacific red snapper, shrimp teriyaki, or a delightful selection of pasta dishes. Choose your dessert from an assortment of fresh cakes, pastries, pies, and tortes; all prepared by this staff. The wine list, to complement your dinner, is most impressive. There are more than 200 labels to choose from!

When near Point Richmond and you're looking for an enjoyable place to dine, be sure to stop at the Hotel Mac. It's one of the "Best Choices" you can make.

Porta Costa

Antiques

MARTHA'S MADNESS, 17 Canyon Lake Road, Port Costa, California. Fine antiques, art deco and fun gifts.

Restaurant

BULL VALLEY RESTAURANT
14 Canyon Lake Drive
Porta Costa, CA 94569
Tel. (415) 787-2244
Hrs: Wed. - Fri.   5:30 p.m. - 9:00 p.m.
　　　 Sat. - Sun.   5:30 p.m. - 10:30 p.m.
MasterCard and Visa are accepted.

Port Costa may not be on your California map, however it is easy enough to reach by car; just take the Crockett exit off I-80, continue three scenic miles east and you will arrive in the quaint old town of Port Costa. Before you visit the antique shops, start your day at the Bull Valley Restaurant on Canyon Lake Drive for champagne brunch or return later for an intimate candle light dinner.

The varied brunch menu will delight your palate. Eggs Benedict with special house Hollandaise sauce, crepes stuffed with crab meat or shrimp, topped with a light cream sauce, not to mention Huevos a la Valle de Toros - a delicious omelette topped with mild cheddar cheese and Ranchero salsa to name just a few of the exotic choices. The Chateaubriand is a sumptuous dinner feast for two, which includes a choice of filet of beef prepared to your taste and carved at your table with Caesar salad, vegetable du jour, potatoes du jour and Bull Valley Inn's famous home baked bread. The dinner menu includes dishes such as rainbow trout stuffed with bay shrimp, veal Parmigiana served with garlic buttered pasta, crisp roasted ducking Polonaise and the famous New York steak broiled to perfection. Weather permitting have lunch in the charming garden, it's truly beautiful with moss covered bricks and colorful flowers.

If you are a connoisseur of fine dining, it's well worth the drive just to visit the Bull Valley Restaurant.

Richmond

This is a developer's city, with the population now less than 90,000 after some hectic boom years during World War II when barracks and temporary housing took care of at least 110,000 people drawn to work at the four ship yards operated by Kaiser. A total of 1,490 ships slid down the ways here before the construction halted.

Augustin S. Macdonald visualized development here during an 1895 duck hunting trip, looking across at the San Francisco Peninsula. He reasoned a railroad ferry from Point Richmond could save Southern Pacific twelve miles over its proposed ferry route to the city. Eventually the Santa Fe Railroad completed ten miles of fill over tide flats and constructed an 800-foot pier from which to handle rail cars moved by water to San Francisco. By 1902 Standard Oil Co. had masses of oil tanks on the hillside next to its Richmond refinery and Macdonald's town site was a money-maker.

From it's rapid growth, then rapid exodus after the demand for war materials was over, Richmond's municipal government was hard pressed. The rapid recovery earned the community an All American City designation in 1952. Today, as the only city in Contra Costa county with a charter, Richmond also has the distinction of having a full-time mayor as well as a city manger. The economy today reaches beyond the port, including research laboratories, regional postal and Safeway Stores distribution points, and diversification by operators of the oil refineries.

Auto transportation to Marin County uses the Richmond-San Rafael Bridge, completed in 1956. The span is four-and-one-half miles long, and took four years to build. It is operated by the state Toll Bridge Authority.

Attractions

Richmond Museum, 400 Nevin Avenue, is open Fridays and Sundays, 1:00 p.m. - 4:00 p.m. Among the exhibits is the first Ford auto off the company's Richmond assembly line in 1931, and pictures of Ellis Landing, the first wharf in Richmond harbor.

Marina Bay Harbor, 1349 Marina Way South, has public boat launching facilities and information on fishing in San Pablo Bay and the Carquinez Straits.

Lawn bowling and other facilities are at **Nicholl Park,** on Thirty-second Avenue at Macdonald Avenue. Competition Tuesday, Thursday and Saturday starting at 12:30 p.m. Sunday matches at 1:00 p.m. Nicholl is one of twenty seven parks in the city system.

Franklin Canyon Public Golf Course is in Rodeo, on Highway 4. Telephone 799-6191.

One of the largest Indian shell mound burial sites on San Francisco Bay is located on **Harbor Way South.** Archaeologists from the University of California who excavated the site estimate 10,000 bodies could have been in the mound.

Richmond Art Center is located on the Civic Center Plaza. Galleries display local work and a non-profit art school is operated here.

For further information, contact the **Richmond Chamber of Commerce,** 234-3512.

Sport

SHARP BICYLE
2800 Hilltop Mall Road
Richmond, CA 94806
Tel.   (415) 222-8004
Hrs: Mon. - Fri.   10:00 a.m. - 6:00 p.m.
      Thu.   10:00 a.m. - 8:00 p.m.
      Saturday   9:00 a.m. - 5:00 p.m.
      Sunday   2:00 noon - 5:00 p.m.
Visa, MasterCard, AMEX and Discover card are accepted.

The Bay Area is where off road bicycling began, back in days when fat tired machines were still called klunkers. At Sharp Bicycle you will find state of the art equipment with alloy components and eighteen speeds with even entry level models.

You can get everything from tricycles to tandems at this full service shop, including clothing and accessories, but the specialty is mountain biking. With names like Peugeot, Nishiki, Trek, Ritchey, Fisher, Ibis and Ross, you know they talk quality, as well as value. All employees are riders themselves, know where the best rides are, ask about the local guide service.

So if you have visions of getting to the top, gear up at Sharp Bicycle for fun cycling.

(See special invitation in Appendix.)

Walnut Creek

High rise buildings sprout above tree-lined streets in this East Bay city of about 55,000. A crossroads between the routes leading from Oakland to the San Joaquin Valley and those connecting ports on Suisun Bay with San Ramon Valley farming areas, the first house went up here in 1849. For most of its life the community was little more than a shopping center for nearby orchardists. It incorporated as a 500 acre city in 1914, but did not experience rapid growth until the commuter days of the past two decades. City limits now

151

include over 19 square miles. Walnut Creek is home for regional office complexes which draw commuters here instead of sending them west.

Your "Best Choice" for tracing the history of this community is George Emanuels' "Walnut Creek, Arroyo de las Nueces," published locally in 1984.

Attractions

Shadelands Ranch Historical Museum at 2660 Ygnacio Valley road is operated by the city and the **Walnut Creek Historical Society.** Open Wednesdays 11:30 a.m. - 4:00 p.m. and Sundays 1:00 p.m. - 4:00 p.m.

Alexander Lindsay Junior Museum, 1901 First Avenue, has a collection of tame native animals for touching and petting. Call 935-1978 for hours and program information, including outdoor education field trips.

For further information, call the **Walnut Creek Chamber of Commerce,** 934-2007.

Antiques

PARKSIDE ANTIQUES
1299 Parkside Drive
Walnut Creek, CA 94596
Tel. (415) 947-0770
Hrs: Mon. - Sat.   10:00 a.m. - 6:00 p.m.
       Thursday   10:00 a.m. - 8:00 p.m.
       Sunday   12:00 noon - 5:00 p.m.

Folks of the past century never would have dreamed that their furniture, knick-knacks and other everyday items would be so sought after in the future. Well, much to their would be surprise, that's what antique collectives are all about. If you love antiques, you'll be in Seventh Heaven at Parkside Antiques in Walnut Creek.

15,000 square feet are devoted to displaying unique and beautiful antiques from forty-five of the area's top dealers. The showroom features a complete line of fine furniture for your home or office. You'll find items from France, Austria, Belgium, England and the United States. China, clocks, linens, antique lighting and kitchen primitives are but a few of the accessories to view. There's also a wide variety of floral arrangements and decorator items available at Parkside Antiques.

The owners bring over ten years experience in the antique business to make Parkside Antiques a quality collective store. Prices are highly competitive and the selections are staggering. Come and visit Parkside Antiques and share in the lovely surprise this place has to offer.

Apparel

CAROLYN PARKER DESIGN
1218 Boulevard Way
Walnut Creek, CA 94595
Tel. (415) 944-5155
Hrs: Tue. - Fri. 1:30 p.m. - 5:30 p.m.
         Saturday 10:30 a.m. - 4:00 p.m.
Visa and MasterCard accepted.

Carolyn Parker and Robineve Adler, designers, have chosen this medium to display their love of art and the art of dressing. The glamor in movies of the 30s and 40s is very real to them. This is evident as you browse through their design studio to look at the retail attire of soft and easy day wear, elegant evening clothes, and fantasy dance wear. The array is made from the finest of imported fabrics--at close to wholesale prices.

The ambiance of the shop serves as a wonderful background to their clothing. Diaphanous white drapes, silk moire, French chairs, mirrored walls and handmade silk roses spilling out of Art Deco vases. An atmosphere which is appreciated by their sophisticated clientele.

Some of the garments have beautiful appliques of leaves, geometric designs, or flowers. You have seen them on television personalities such as Candice Bergan, Ali McGraw, and on Annie Potts on CBS' show "Designing Women".

If you are looking for a special, dream gown for a wedding, party, or a complete wardrobe, it is available here. You can also find their clothing at Saks Fifth Avenue, I. Magnin, and Nordstrom. But why not shop here? You may just get a chance to talk to these two talented and interesting women in person.

Entertainment

THE PUNCH LINE, 120 Petticoat Lane, Walnut Creek, California. One of the newest and best comedy clubs around. Two drink minimum.

153

Restaurant

MAXIMILLIAN'S
1604 Locust Street
Walnut Creek, CA 94596
Tel. (415) 932-1474
Hrs: Dinner   Mon. - Sun.   6:00 p.m. - 11:00 p.m.
     Lunch   Mon. - Sat.   11:30 a.m - 3:00 p.m.

Ten years ago, Max Wolfe saw that the time was right to bring up-scale dining to the ever growing suburban town of Walnut Creek. After bringing his twenty years of gourmet experience to this great location, Walnut Creek residents and anyone else who happens into Maximillian's couldn't be happier that Max made the move.

Dining here, although decidedly up-scale, is light and informal. The menu features California products and an abundance of fresh fish dishes. The tasty seafoods include such selections as grilled filet of Bodega Bay silver salmon and grilled Alaskan halibut steak. Other favorites include veal Piccata, rack of lamb Gastronome and Tounedos of beef Daniel. Each dish is created with the zeal of a skilled artist and the result is consistently innovative meat and fish entrees. The red carpeting, oak paneling and seasoned brick lend just the right touch of refinement and elegance to your delicious meal.

Overall, Maximillian's is Max Wolfe. That is, the restaurant reflects his dedication to presenting genteel cuisine complemented by caring service and romantic surroundings. A perfect place for a perfect evening.

Wine

PRIMA CAFE AND WINE SHOP
1522 N Main Street
Walnut Creek, CA 94596
Tel. (415) 935-7780
Hrs: Mon. - Fri.   11:30 a.m. - 3:00 p.m.
     Saturday   11:30 a.m. - 8:00 p.m.
The bar remains open until 8:00 p.m.
Visa and MasterCard are accepted.

You may sip before you buy in this combination wine shop and cafe which offers outdoor dining, and knowledgeable comment on the many wines stocked here.

The lunch trade finds a soup and salad menu, with a few other favorites. In the evening the kitchen turns out snacks which can go with a sampling of the vintage, or be turned into a light meal. This is a place to learn about wines without becoming embarrassed. The staff is ready to share information if asked, and to respond to your personal preferences after you try a type of wine.

This is your "Best Choice" in the East Bay for getting the wine to fit your pallet, one of the few places where you can sample and nibble before buying, without going off to the wine country.

While touring this historic area and enjoying the vistas of open ranches and fertile orchards, do take the time to visit with the businesses that provide the bulwark to Walnut Creek's retail trades:

WALNUT CREEK TOUR			
a.m.	Parkside	Best antique	Waln/Ant
a.m.	Carolyn Parker	Best fashion	Waln/App
		sightseeing	
p.m.	Prima Cafe	Best picnic	Waln/Wine
		sightseeing	
p.m.	Maxmillian's	Best supper	Waln/Rest
p.m.	Punch Line	Best laugh	Waln/Ent.

DEL NORTE COUNTY

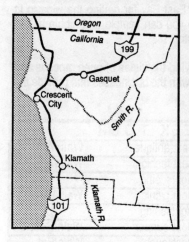

Tucked away on the farthest corner of California's Northcoast, Del Norte is a sparsely populated county of vast redwood forests, two scenic rivers, and a small port city. The coastal plain north of Crescent City supports dairy cattle and growers of Easter lily bulbs. With public ownership tying up most inland timberlands in the rugged Klamath Mountains to the east, lumber and plywood production has declined in recent years. The port, once a major transfer point for petroleum products barged in and lumber barged out, now concentrates on sport and commercial fisheries.

Spanish ships called here regularly in the early 1800s attempting to set up whaling stations. Jedediah Smith, the fur trapper who roamed the west, came through by land in 1828 and now is honored by the Smith River in the northern county and a state redwood park in a scenic bend of that river fifteen miles east of Crescent City. The Smith River trail was a major supply route for the gold mines located in Southern Oregon, and is now the route of U.S. 199, a highway over the Siskiyou and Klamath Mountains. Rainfall averages seventy inches a year at Crescent City, concentrated in the winter months, and twice that on the mountains to the rear, making the Smith and Klamath Rivers flashy streams subject to extreme flooding. The Klamath, which rises in Oregon, remains on its lower reaches a major residential area for small groups of Indian people, and a great source of salmon and steelhead which spend most of their lives in the Pacific Ocean.

The California State Prison System is changing the economy of Del Norte, which now has a population of just over 18,000 people, all but 3,100 of them residents of rural communities and farms. A massive prison that will house 2,200 inmates began construction in 1987 at Malarkey Forest, a redwood grove north of Crescent City on U.S. 101. An estimated 1,570 jobs will result when the facility is fully operational.

Del Norte County

ATTRACTIONS

Harold Del Ponte, a former county supervisor, operates a **drive-through redwood tree** on Highway 169 at the Terwer Valley ramp off U.S. 101. A survivor of logging, the 700-year-old tree is 15 feet in diameter at the base. Open all year, daylight hours only. Telephone (707) 482-5971.

One of those creations of imagination and nature is the **Trees of Mystery** attraction on U.S. 101 north of Klamath. Huge sculptures of Paul Bunyon and Babe the Blue Ox grace the parking lot, while inside the park are several other themes which play upon the giant redwood grove. Open all year. Telephone 482-3503.

At the port, east of Crescent City proper, is **Undersea World,** a commercial aquarium which specializes in fish and mammals of the North Coast. Telephone 464-3544.

The **Del Norte Historical Society** operates a museum in Crescent City on H Street, telephone 464-3922. On the southernmost tip of the peninsula, in Crescent City, is **Battery Point Lighthouse**, another society-sponsored museum. You get there only at low tide, by walking. Open daily. Telephone 464-3089 for hours when the tide will be out.

The **Redwood Parks** are combined in state and federal management. **Redwood National Park Headquarters** has a complete information center at Second and K Streets, Crescent City, for both operations. Attractions include a wild seashore south of town, and the state's traditional campgrounds at **Mill Creek** inland. **Relim Redwood** has a demonstration forest and working lumber mill next to the coastal redwoods. Inland are the **Jedediah Smith Redwoods**, a large holding purchased and given by private timber companies. Howland Hill Road, east from Crescent City, off Humboldt Road, provides an unique drive through this old forest.

Lakes Earl and Talawa, north of Crescent City on county roads, provide miles of beach access, plus fishing and camping around two freshwater lakes just behind the line of dunes. Camping is available on undeveloped sites of this state park. Call 443-4588. From Crescent City, Northcrest Drive to Old Mill Road, then west. From U.S. 101, west on Morehead road, then north on Lower Lake Road, west on Kellogg Road.

For more information, contact the **Del Norte Chamber of Commerce,** 1001 Front Street, Box 246, Crescent City CA 95531. Telephone 464-3174.

Crescent City

Gift Shop

COAST IMPORTS
425 L Street Suite A
Crescent City, CA 95531
Tel.   (707) 464-9294
Hrs: Mon. - Sat.   10:00 a.m. - 6:00 p.m.
         Sunday   1:00 p.m. - 6:00 p.m.
Mastercard and Visa are accepted.

It's time to go gift shopping and you're not sure as to where you want to go. In fact, you aren't really sure what to buy. You want a store that has a wide variety of items both unique and ordinary. This way you can just browse through and are assured of finding something. The name of the gift shop you're looking for is Coast Imports in Crescent City.

At Coast Imports you'll find such things as cards, mugs, potpourri, brass dinner bells, Spiritual Shy incense, sea shell wind chimes, prints, bowls and many brass items. Turn up the next aisle and you'll find even more gifts including jewelry, wicker, clocks, perfume oils, wind socks, lamps, door mats and a fun toy selection with stuffed animals, dolls and much more.

You may surprise yourself when shopping at Coast Imports by being able to complete the entire shopping list. Coast Imports is a unique store that will please both the shopper and the people the who receive the gifts.

Park

UNDERSEA WORLD
Highway 101 South
Crescent City, CA 95531
Tel.   (707) 464-3522
Hrs: Winter   9:00 a.m. - 4:00 p.m.
         Summer   9:00 a.m. - 8:00 p.m.

The deep, mysterious ocean, covering seventy percent of the world's surface, is the wellspring of life. Many of it's fathomless bottoms are unexplored, leaving questions as to what may lurk there. Fascinating! At Undersea World you will be awed by viewing one of the last frontiers in a most comfortable manner.

At Undersea World an experienced guide takes you through a wide pathway, down to the deep viewing tank's sandy bottoms. Everything is explained as you watch sharks glide through the water and observe sea anemones capturing prey. There are perch, flounder, rock fish, sebasty, wolf eel, octopi and many more. Over 5,000 living species in their natural habitats can be studied here. For amusement, feed the *Eumetopias Jubata*, that's sea lions for those not up on their Latin. Watch them dive and play as you toss them their favorite food.

For schools and large groups, there's a special group rate. Also, there's a gift shop and full service restaurant with banquet facilities. Undersea World is an educational experience, one where you can examine some of the mysteries of the Mother Sea.

(See special invitation in the Appendix.)

Restaurant

THE CAPTAIN'S TABLE
170 Marine Way
Crescent City, CA 95531
Tel. (707) 464-9414
Hrs: Mon. - Sun.   4:00 a.m. - 10:00 p.m.

The Captain's Table, appropriately named with its nautical decor, is located on Citizens Dock and features breakfast - all day, lunch, and a varied dinner menu.

The Pancake Breakfast Sandwich is a special feature, and all of the pastries are made from scratch. Dinner comes with soup or salad and potato or rice and entrees include selections such as New York steak, roast beef and veal cutlets, as well as a complete seafood menu. The Captains own Special Newburg is a combination of shrimp, crab and lobster, or one may select stuffed flounder, trout or poached cod.

The Captain's Table features a wine list and carries imported beers. There are accommodations for children under twelve years old, and be sure to inquire about the daily special. Whether it's four bells, eight bells or more bells, there's a hearty breakfast waiting in the galley at The Captain's Table!

(See special invitation in the Appendix).

Klamath

Park

TREES OF MYSTERY
15500 Highway 101 N
Klamath, CA 95548
Tel.   (707)   487-5613
Hrs: Daylight

There's a place in California that the Indians considered taboo. They called it "The place of spirits." Trees grow into strange shapes and the air is filled with an ominous silence. Braves avoided it like the plague. Feel adventurous? Want to go in? It's called the Trees of Mystery and it's only open during daylight hours.

In every forest you will find strange growth, but nowhere are there so many wonders in one location. The trail is approximately one mile and on it you'll see such things as The Family Tree - twelve living trees supported by one trunk, The Elephant Tree - a tree that looks like an elephant in a kneeling position, The Upside Down Tree - two separate trunks, each with it's own root system, one growing through the other. The Lightning Tree - a tree shaped like a lightning bolt, as well as many other bizarre growths.

The Trees of Mystery also has a museum featuring one of the finest and largest private collections of Indian artifacts in the western half of the United States. There's even a gift shop to buy your souvenirs. It's a strange mixture, Indian taboo land and Indian Artifacts - one that has to be seen to be believed. You will leave there with a "Spirit" of wonder.

Restaurant

BABE'S IRON TENDER AND MOTEL TREES
Trees of Mystery
U.S. 101
Klamath, CA 95548
Tel.   (707) 482-3152 Motel
       (707) 482-5585 Restaurant
Hrs: Mon. - Sun.   7:00 a.m. - 9:00 p.m.
       Lounge open to 11:00 p.m. weekends

Babe the Blue Ox, dwarfed by a red-shirted Paul Bunyon, look toward the restaurant and motel from their permanent place at the entrance to Trees of Mystery. The twin statues help set the old-time logging theme of the motel and restaurant operated by Ben Cravey and John Thompson.

There's a new look to Babe's. The restaurant is squeaky clean, the carpet new, and in the kitchen, where beef served up in Paul Bunyon helpings held the sway, Ben has introduced some Cajun cooking to go with the North Coast's own seafoods and some imported items. Now you'll find crawfish pie, along with the sixteen ounce rib eye steak.

The motel provides a handy overnight stopping place for those who want to see more of the redwoods the next day, or enjoy one of Del Norte County's best beaches a couple of miles from the motel. By 1988, the new Babe's will have a 2,000 square foot addition for the expanded lounge, all of it under the eye of the giant statues peering across the road.

GLENN COUNTY

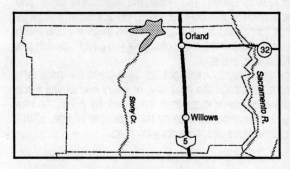

California had its legends in the post gold rush era. Hugh J. Glenn, a physician turned wheat rancher and cattle king, was one of them. This is his county although he did not live to see the designation.

Squeezed between a narrowing Sacramento River Valley's west bank opposite Chico and the first crest of the Coast Range Mountains, Glenn county was carved off from its southern neighbor, Colusa, in 1891. Dr. Glenn had 55,000 acres here under dry-land wheat cultivation. His headquarters, established in 1867, was at Jacinto. It is now little more than a wide spot in the road. The doctor was murdered by an employee in February, 1883.

Elevations are sixty five feet above sea level at the Sacramento, over 7,000 feet on the northern peaks of the Coast Range. Hot summers, and mild, moist winters mark a weather pattern with the growing season at 262 days that suits many crops. Stony Gorge Dam, an early Federal Reclamation Project, and Black Butte Reservoir, a flood control project, provide local waters for irrigation. The Tehama-Colusa Canal brings more water to this northern portion of the California rice bowl. Livestock, and livestock feed crops, are major sources of income. Several thousand acres of almond orchards are in the county.

One of the large natural gas fields discovered in recent decades, Beehive Bend, is located five miles east of Willows. I-5 and the parallel tracks of what is now the Southern Pacific Railroad are on the western side of the cultivated area of the county, with a network of roads from the interstate east to Highway 45, the other north-south route. Orland and Willows, both with populations under 5,000, are the only incorporated cities in this small, 1,319 square mile county of 21,350 people.

ATTRACTIONS

In Willows is the **Mendocino National Forest Headquarters.** Much of the coast range to the west is part of the forest, with dozens of campgrounds and reservoirs in the 867,000 acres of public lands which covers several counties. Contact Supervisor's Office, Mendocino National Forest, 420 East Laurel, Willows CA 95988. Telephone (916) 934-3516.

Willows, an agricultural center whose population remains static at 4,800, is a focal point of the sheep industry in the Sacramento Valley. It was named for a clump of Willows on which travelers guided themselves while crossing the flat lands. The land mark was the only dependable watering place for stock for great distances in the early days. The water hole, about a mile east of town, has long since been filled in.

Two popular fishing areas within the valley are **Black Butte Reservoir** and many locations along the banks of the Sacramento River. The 10,776 acre **Sacramento Wildlife Refuge** is on the southern boundary of the county, one of three major Federal wildlife refuges in the valley. Best viewing of ducks and geese is during the last weeks of November and early December. More than 175 bird species have been identified in the valley and many are in residence in the refuge.

On the south bank of **Hambright Creek,** which is located between Stony Creek and Orland, are the ruins of a **pioneer adobe** which were rooted up by treasure hunters. Granville P. Swift built the home on what became Murdock Ranch. Folklore said he found gold on the Feather River and brought it to the adobe and hid it. The building site, under oak trees 100 yards east of the railroad tracks, now shows nothing but excavations of the later-day gold hunters.

Near Elk Creek, a mountain community which supported logging and lumber mills, is **"Bidwell Hill,"** where John Bidwell camped in 1844 while searching the western valley for ranch lands. A monument made of redwood is atop the little hill, which is about one mile from town, across Stony Creek.

Orland Irrigation District was organized shortly after passage of the 1887 act which created the Federal Reclamation Service. The 20,000 acres served by waters stored in the upper canyon of Stony Creek were the first in the nation to actually get water under the federal act as a demonstration of

163

Glenn County

the program. South of Orland are what were the grain fields of Dr. Glenn's
ranches. Among the new crops coming from the area is clover seed.

For more information, contact the **Glenn County Chamber of Commerce**,
West Wood at Murdock Street, Willows CA 95988. Telephone 934-7994.

HUMBOLDT COUNTY

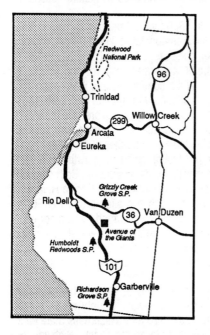

In a state with very small counties, Humboldt is large, rich in history and scenic spots which make it a destination for travelers and a commercial and industrial hub for California's Northcoast. Within its 3,579 square miles are seven incorporated cities, a busy deep-draft port, a national park, a chain of state parks, and one of the most flood-prone river basins in the Western United States which gets rainfall of over 100 inches a year on much of its back country valleys and mountains. Nearly 110,000 people live in the county.

With an eye on the tourist, three cities actively display their heritage of a Victorian era. Eureka, the largest, is a bustling port connected by bridge to a peninsula where pulp mills, plywood and lumber plants create the area's industrial payrolls. Arcata, the college town and first county seat, has a story-book plaza with President William McKinley's outstretched arms in statue form reaching over knots of young people who play beneath. Ferndale, built to serve the dairy farmers of the Eel River bottoms, presents an entire small town of change-of-century buildings.

More than 100 miles from north-to-south, Humboldt has several distinct geographic areas. The entire county jiggles at times from earthquakes, even though it lies north of the extension of the San Andreas fault. Two plates which grind on that fault extend out to sea after reaching Shelter Cove in the south county. Many historic buildings were torn down after damage from an earthquake in the early 1950s.

The county's mountain ranges and river valleys lie in general northwesterly directions, presenting repeated obstacles to winter storms brought in from the Pacific Ocean. Flood plains of the Eel and Mad Rivers and creeks flowing into Humboldt Bay make up pasture for a substantial dairy industry. Patterns of bald hills alternating with forest are made for cattle operations, and the huge quantities of rain prompt phenomenal regrowth of trees when harvested. Rain also triggers landslides which make it expensive to keep open highways and railroads, and have resulted in historic losses of property during flooding.

Humboldt Bay was discovered in 1806 by an American captain sailing for the Russian-American Company. Half a century later, Hans Buhne, captain of a coast-wise trading company vessel, began regular calls in the bay in 1850. He named it for Alexander von Humboldt, a German explorer and scientists then the object of world-wide acclaim. While coastal Indians were peaceful, inland tribes were not and a military presence was maintained from 1854 through 1870. The Hoopa Indian Reservation, a thirty-six square mile mountain preserve on the Trinity River to its confluence with the Klamath, and several rancherias were designated for remaining Indians in treaties of the times.

Lumbermen who could turn the plentiful redwood old growth into a vast assortment of products came next along with the dairy farmers. Both shipped to San Francisco, first by sea and later by the Northwestern Pacific Railroad, a single-track line which winds its way through the slide-prone Eel River Canyon. The redwood groves of the upper Eel River, warmed by summer sun, became popular vacation spots for city residents. Many are now state parks, as venerable in modern times as the redwoods are in historic time. California's prison system maintains a network of work camps from which inmate work crews travel to keep up the parks and fight forest fires.

Highway travel in the county is tied in with U.S. 101 which makes the north-south connection, most of it four-lane freeway. County roads reach remote areas in the south county, including the Sinkyone Wilderness State park and federal public lands in the King Range, both on the coast. Highway 36 provides one route inland from Fortuna to Red Bluff. Highway 299 is the other cross-mountain route, going from Arcata to Redding.

ATTRACTIONS

Prairie Creek Redwoods State Park straddles U.S. 101 at the far northern boundary of the county. By 1989 a freeway will bypass the giant redwood groves and a former orchard that is home base for a large herd of Roosevelt Elk which can be seen from the car. A county road leads to the beach and stops within a short distance of the fabled **Fern Canyon** where towering sandstone walls are covered with several varieties of ferns. Elk are in residence on the beach, too. Two **campgrounds**, **interpretive programs** and a **nature museum** are at park headquarters off U.S. 101. Nearby is a county fish hatchery raising 1.5 million salmon each year. Open all year. Telephone (707) 488-2171. Area park headquarters, with information on the south county and wilderness parks, too, is 443-4588.

The tallest trees in the world are in **Redwood National Park's Redwood Creek** unit. From Orick, take Bald Hills Road east. A trail-head off to the right serves an 8.5 mile hiking trail up to the big grove. From a parking lot on the road, further up the grade, a park service shuttle bus takes people to a **viewpoint** where a short trail drops down to the base of the trees. South of Orick, visible from U.S. 101 at Freshwater Lagoon is the **Redwood Information Center** of the National Park Service, where shuttle bus tickets are sold. Open all year, expect to walk in the rain during winter months. Telephone 488-3461 for information.

Trinidad, an old village west of U.S. 101 is on a plateau above the ocean. The harbor was charted, but not entered in 1595. Heceta and Bodega, two Spanish explorers, sailed into the sheltering head lands for the first time on Trinity Sunday, June 1775 and named the anchorage. The first permanent American residents on the Humboldt coast built here in 1850 and made it the seat of the now abolished Klamath County.

This was a whaling station from 1923 through 1929. A long wharf provides unloading for local fishing boats, which are launched over a beach of cobbles with large wheeled carriers and then tied up at buoys when not working. There is a picturesque light house, a cross marking the historic Spanish discovery monument, a small museum and two state parks to the north which provide access trails down the cliffs to isolated beaches. The **museum**, 5298 Trinity Street, has no established hours, you just call 677-0186 for an appointment. The **Humboldt State University Marine Laboratory** has an aquarium on Edward Street, with public viewing Monday through Friday 8:00 a.m. to 5:00 p.m. during the school year. For other Trinidad information, write the **Trinidad Business Association**, Box 847, Trinidad CA 95570.

Blue Lake, a small town on the Mad River, just off Highway 299, is typical of the communities which grew up supporting large lumber mills as railroad logging boomed in the late 1800s and continued until after World War II. The Arcata and Mad River Railroad, founded in 1854, ran from a wharf in Arcata through Blue Lake to the company mill town at Korbell. The **Blue Lake Depot** is now a local museum, open Tuesday and Wednesdays from 1:00 p.m. to 4:00 p.m. and other hours by contacting the city hall, 668-5655.

The **Hoopa Tribal Museum** is located in the Hoopa Shopping Center, Highway 96, eleven miles north of Willow Creek. Indian art and history are part of the exhibits. Open October through April Monday through Friday and May through September Monday through Saturday, 10:00 a.m. to 4:00 p.m. Telephone (916) 625-4110.

A county road leading south west from Arcata, or the Highway 255 bridge over the bay from Eureka, takes you to **Samoa**, the long peninsula making the north spit of the bay and now home of Simpson and Louisiana Pacific Company paper mills. Developers named Samoa in 1892 when the local news included dispatches about two chiefs fighting for control of the island nation of Samoa.

Lumber mills had the advantage of railroad delivery of logs and deep-draft wharfs on the shore side for exporting the finished products. **Louisiana Pacific** keeps up the tradition of its predecessor the Vance and Hammond Lumber Co. by running a neatly-kept company housing project behind the big mill complex. The L-P Samoa Cookhouse serves three meals a day, family-style, to the public and is a popular tourist stop which includes a museum. Rebuilt several times, the Samoa mills actually use very little of the space in the sprawling buildings seen from the cookhouse. Call 442-1659.

Both the north and south **jetties** at the entrance of the bay can be reached by car over rough roads. North Jetty road from Samoa leads around the U.S. Coast Guard headquarters. South Jetty road is a sandy path from Hookton Road south of Fields Landing and is a popular camping spot for recreation vehicles. Ask before walking the jetties, under some tidal conditions waves roll over the concrete surface and could sweep away the unwary.

Loleta is a tiny and prosperous farm community west of U.S. 101 between Fields Landing and Fortuna. A family-run cheese factory offers tasting and tours. **Loleta Cheese Factory**, open Monday through Friday 9:00 a.m. to 5:00 p.m., Saturday 10:00 a.m. to 4:00 p.m., and Sunday 12:00 noon to 4:00 p.m. Located at 252 Loleta Drive (the main street coming in from the freeway). Telephone 733-5470.

A short drive off U.S. 101, approaching Fortuna is **Fernbridge**, site of a creamery and store, and what was at the time of construction, the largest concrete **bridge** of its kind. Built in 1911, the span carries all traffic over the Eel River to Ferndale and communities on the south coastal sections. It is the object of controversy since a 1985 state engineering report declared "structural members are cracking and failing." Preservationists rushed a protective bill through the legislature. Photos of bridge construction are on display at Ferndale Meat Co., 376 Main Street.

Scotia, just off U.S. 101, is headquarters of the venerable Pacific Lumber Co. which figured in a 1986 hostile takeover that ousted family ownership and shareholders dating back before the turn of the century. This is the **worlds largest redwood mill**, and a self-guiding tour is available at the offices on Main Street, Monday through Friday from 7:30 a.m. to 10:30 a.m. and 12:30 p.m. to 2:30 p.m. During summer months a **company museum** is open, ask for directions to it. Telephone 764-2222, extension 247 for tour and museum information.

Many of the redwood groves in state parks, including the scenic Fern Canyon of Prairie Creek are donations from **Pacific Lumber Co.** holdings. Like many lumber companies, they took 160 acre timber claims from the federal government, then through exchanges with other owners blocked up ownership for economical forest management. Humboldt Redwoods Park to the south took 17,000 acres of Pacific Lumber Co. timber at the time of its formation.

Many of the redwood groves, and most of the small towns and tourist attractions south of Scotia, are on **Avenue of the Giants**, a thirty-three mile portion of highway bypassed when U.S. 101 became a freeway. Swimming, fishing and exploring the waysides are part of the attraction in this big tree country dotted with overnight accommodations. Pacific Lumber Co. has a **demonstration forest** which shows how rapidly redwood grow back after cutting, located at the Jordan Creek interchange five miles south of Scotia. Contact Avenue of the Giants Association, Box 1000, Miranda CA 95553. Telephone 923-2555.

Due west of Humboldt Redwoods Park on Mattole Road is the coastal community of **Petrolia**. The first oil well in California was drilled in 1861, and shipments began on a commercial basis in the summer of 1865. After a brief life the wells dried up and the sleepy community is now part of a vast area where residents are trying to re-establish self-sufficient farms and small woodlots.

Garberville is the informal capital of southern Humboldt's inland area where warm summers and big trees create attractive long-term vacation locations. It is also the center of a nationally-publicized area where illegal marijuana crops are cultivated and police raiders come in each summer to seize plants before they can be sold. Humboldt Redwoods State Park, north of town, has nearly 300 **campsites. Richardson Grove** to the south has 169 sites plus rustic cabins. Several commercial resorts are in the area.

West from here is **Shelter Cove**, a small resort and fishing village at the foot of a steep bluff, and the **King Range Wilderness Areas.** Contact the **Garberville/Redway Chamber of Commerce**, Box 445, Garberville CA 95540. Telephone 923-2613, or the **Eureka/Humboldt County Convention and Visitors Bureau**, 2112 Broadway, Eureka CA 95502-2189. Telephone 442-3738.

Arcata

This city of 12,300 dates back to a time when the Mad River entered Humboldt Bay to the west, making a natural landing which the founders in April 1850 christened Uniontown in a wave of abolitionist sentiment. Pack trains left the docks here for mines located up the Trinity and Klamath rivers. This was the county seat in 1853, and seven years later took the name Arcata, said to mean "landing" in the local Indian tongue. When the lumber mills picked deeper draft sites on Eureka's waterfront, commercial activity shifted there and so did the courthouse, in 1856. The Mad River was later put in a channel straight to the sea, and much of its meandering and sometimes flooded bottom land was reclaimed for choice dairy pastures.

Humboldt State University, which has a campus among redwood trees on the east side of Arcata, started as a teacher's college in 1913. Among its top technical programs are forestry and marine biology specializing in North Coast resources.

Arcata's Plaza is a center of attraction in a town full of Victorian buildings. At Eighth and H is the building pioneer merchant Augustus Jacoby started in 1857 which later became the flagship of the A.Brizard chain of stores in mines and company towns throughout the region. This is now Jacoby's Storehouse, a group of small stores and restaurants with no hint that at one time Arcata's residents holed up here when Indians were on the warpath.

Attractions

The **Arcata Hotel**, on a diagonal walk across the plaza from Jacoby's building, past the bronzed statue of President William McKinley, looks much as it did in its heyday. A ground floor restaurant is set with white table cloths and fresh flowers, the busy barroom buzzes with activity, and a room clerk in the lobby is ready to rent out a refurbished room from his desk surrounded by pictures that testify to things as they were early this century. On the other diagonal of the plaza, giving an eclectic mix are Arcata Muffler and on the far side a very modern Bistrin's clothing store.

Pacific Art Center is in the old creamery at 1251 Ninth street. Plays are performed by a semi-professional company in residence. Call 822-0828 for current programs.

The **Arcata Marsh and Wildlife Sanctuary** is at the edge of town on an old land fill now used to reclaim waste water. **Audubon Society** members conduct tours at 8:30 a.m. each Saturday morning, meeting at the North Coast Environmental Center near the Foot of "I" Street. Call 822-6918.

There's a **self-guiding tour** of Arcata's architecture put into brochure form, available at the Chamber of Commerce offices and several locations on the plaza. One of the restored houses includes a **city museum**, call 822-3619 for museum hours.

Humboldt State University offers campus tours by contacting the admission office, call 826-3011.

For more information, contact the **Arcata Chamber of Commerce**, 1052 G Street, Arcata CA 95521. Telephone 822-3619.

Accommodation

PLOUGH AND THE STARS COUNTRY INN
1800 27th Street
Arcata, CA 95521
Tel. (707) 822-8236

The Plough and the Stars Country Inn is a pastoral retreat where country comfort awaits you. This historic 1860's farmhouse is set on two acres with three common rooms and five guestrooms. There's plenty of room both inside and out. It's a place of casual comfort where a traveler will feel at home.
A true bed and breakfast inn, The Plough and the Stars offers a variety of hospitable and personal services to accommodate your traveling needs, whether they be business or pleasure. Continental breakfast is included with your stay, as well as evening snacks. If there is a big event coming up, no worries, entire Inn booking is available. Also, there are facilities for wheelchair

171

guests. The Pough and the Stars is perfectly located, being close to fishing, beachcombing, Redwood Parks, white water rafting and bicycling.

Have you ever heard of proper Cream Tea? It's wonderful and comes from Devonshire, England. They've got it, you'll love it, everything about The Plough and the Stars Inn is exquisite. It's more than a place to slumber; it's a suitable place for awakening.

RAMADA INN
4975 Valley West Boulevard
Arcata, CA 95521
Tel.   (707)   822-4861 or
        (800) 2RAMADA Toll Free
All major credit cards are accepted.

Located in the heart of Redwood country, The Ramada Inn is in close proximity to National and State Redwood Parks, fishing, beaches and museums.

The inn has a pool and health club, dining facilities, a coffee shop and The Mill Lounge, which features live entertainment on Friday and Saturday evenings from 9:00 p.m. to 2:00 a.m. For special events, banquets and conventions, three meeting rooms can accommodate up to 350 and staff experts can assist in planning and servicing.

Near-by Humboldt Bay boasts generous catches of crab, salmon, shrimp and albacore, and local rivers and streams provide sport for rainbow, steelhead, German brown trout and salmon fishermen. Beachcombers will delight in driftwood, gem stone or giant "Razor" clam finds, or a pleasant day may be spent browsing through the Samoa Cookhouse or Clark Memorial Museum. With a variety of activities and excellent, dependable accommodations, your next trip to Redwood Country should include Arcata Ramada Inn.

Antique

ARCATA EXCHANGE
777 8th Street
Arcata, CA 95521
Tel. (707) 822-0312
Hrs: Mon. - Sat.   10:00 a.m. - 6:00 p.m.
          Sunday   2:00 noon - 4:00 p.m.

As a boy of ten, Keith Newcomer started in the antique and collectible business with a red wagon he pulled from door to door, buying and selling from neighbors. Eventually he retired is wagon in favor of his "Barter's Smarter" van. Today with the help of co-owner Kristine Long and a lifetime of experience, his keen eye for quality and philosophy of keeping prices low has evolved into a wonderful shop - Arcata Exchange.

Some of the fantastic relics you'll find are, lamps, end tables, pianos and other musical instruments, rugs, wicker furniture, willow furniture, solid oak antiques and unfinished hardwood furniture. Precious antique dolls and reproductions, fascinating Greek mythological dolls, figures and mugs, and even old juke boxes are displayed.

One of Keith's interests is surfing. In addition to owning some of the first surfboards (circa 1900), he also stocks new boards, wet suits and wax. Keith is always on the lookout for a reason to go surfing, so he also offers lessons.

When you visit Arcata Exchange, be ready for quality, low, low prices, lots of fun and special attention from Keith and Kristine.

(See special invitation in the Appendix.)

Bed & Breakfast

THE LADY INN
902 14th Street
Arcata, CA 95521
Tel. (707) 822-2797
Hrs: Mon. - Sun. 8:00 a.m. - 8:00 p.m.
After hours please call.
Mastercard and Visa are accepted.

The historical Lady Ann Victorian Mansion, referred to as the Stone House, was built in 1886 by Wesley Stone. This elegant mansion is situated overlooking the town and Humboldt Bay. Stately in appearance, The Lady Ann is decorated throughout with antiques and other charming touches to create the warmth and comfort of the inn.

This bed and breakfast inn features six tastefully decorated guestrooms. Two of the rooms have private baths, while the other four share bathrooms. There's also a parlor with a grand piano, other instruments and parlor games. Breakfast is served in the dining room or kitchen and tea is served in the comfortable sitting room around the fire. The atmosphere is relaxing and invites conversation with new friends. Enjoy daily newspapers, magazines, books, fresh cut flowers, wine and Humboldt cheese. The Lady Ann is within walking distance to restaurants, fine shops, evening entertainment and the Redwood Park.

Bicycles are available as are picnic baskets for outings at the beach or the redwoods. Your hosts will treat you as their friends and answer any questions concerning The Lady Inn or Humboldt County. For a relaxing and comfortable stay, visit The Lady Inn while traveling through Arcata.

Gift

ALLIGATOR BALLOONS
791 8th Street
Arcata, CA 95521
Tel. (707) 822-4141
Hrs: Mon. - Fri.   10:00 a.m. - 6:00 p.m.
          Saturday   10:00 a.m. - 5:30 p.m.
          Sunday   12:00 noon - 4:00 p.m.

What would you think if, when answering the door, you were greeted by an alligator delivering balloons? Well, not a real alligator, but someone dressed as one. An authentic alligator probably couldn't hold balloons anyway. However, they could probably be tied to the teeth. Wait a minute! What is this all about? It's about Alligator Balloons in Arcata.

Truly a unique gift shop, Alligator Balloons specializes in fun. The owner dresses up in alligator, cowboy or cowgirl, Mae West and punk rocker costumes to deliver balloons to anyone you wish. Along with balloons, there are many other items in this shop including cards, mugs, bumper stickers, party goods, metallic puzzles, zany ball point pens, party napkins, plates and little car watches.

For the person with a sense of humor, this store is sure to amuse. Send a friend some appropriate balloons via an alligator courier. Don't think about what you would do if an alligator knocked on your door; but think about how a

174

friend would react to the dilemma. Whatever the occasion, Alligator Balloons will provide the laughs.

FRANKLINS
813 H Street
Arcata, CA 95521
Tel. (707) 822-1444
Hrs: Mon. - Sat. 9:30 a.m. - 5:30 p.m.
MasterCard and Visa are accepted.

In Arabic, the word for gift is *Hadeeya*. In French, it is *Cadeaux*. You will find the word is native in any language throughout the world because gifts and gift giving are a part of every nation, culture and time period. You will also find places to buy gifts almost anywhere on the globe, but none quite like Franklins in Arcata.

The owner of Franklins is constantly changing products to carry whatever it is the patrons are looking for. Mugs, children's clothing, children's books, educational toys, candles, kitchen accessories, office supplies, greeting cards, stationery, as well as dried and silk flowers are but a few of the store's many items. They also have novelty gifts including ceramics, potpourri, imported crystal, jewelry, glassware and handmade wheat boxes from China. There are even people on staff to do floral arrangements.

The owners twenty years of experience show in the product line and great prices you can find at Franklin's. So, even if you can't say gift in ten languages, you know you can visit Franklin's when looking for that special gift. Empty handed is a phrase that doesn't exist at Franklins.

POTPOURRI
1062 G Street
Arcata, CA 95521
Tel. (707) 822-5635
Hrs: Mon. - Sat. 10:00 a.m. - 6:00 p.m.
Bank Americard, Visa and AMEX are accepted.

The knights of King Arthur's roundtable - Percevil, Bors, Gawain and Galahad, all went on a quest for The Holy Grail. For years they traveled the land, encountering harsh climates, starvation and evil adversaries. They never gave up, and the Grail was found. Do you ever feel like your on a quest for a certain article that you just can't seem to find? Well, good news bold people, your quest lies at an end. Potpourri is where your sought after item rests.

Potpourri is a wonderful little shop loaded with country charm, as well as every item imaginable for your or a friend's home. Displayed throughout the store are many handmade articles crafted by local artists. Candle figures, pictures, mugs, unique pottery, jewelry, porcelain figurines, decorative lamps, music tapes and books are only a few of the many items in the shop. Also, there are candle holders, cotton rugs from Georgia, brass items and a huge selection of collectables.

So, you see, there really is an Avalon! Modern times have made quests much easier and had Galahad stumbled into Potpourri, King Arthur's castle would have had a few less empty nooks and turrets.

(See special invitation in the Appendix)

Restaurant

GOLDEN HARVEST CAFE
1062 G Street
Arcata, CA 95521
Tel. (707) 822-8962
Hrs: Mon. - Sat.   6:30 a.m. - 9:00 p.m.
            Sunday   7:30 a.m. - 3:00 p.m.
MasterCard, Visa and AMEX are accepted.

Anytime, any attire, any meal for any reason! That sums up the why's and wherefore's of this delightful cafe! Serving hearty breakfasts, tasty lunch and zesty dinners, the cafe specializes in high quality at reasonable prices, good service and a very relaxing atmosphere.

The Sunday Brunch menu offers some unusual specialties such as the Divers Delight - oyster, scallops, or shrimp sauteed with eggs and spinach, topped with chopped bacon, or tantalizing confections such as the French Almond Kiss or Peach and Cream Cheese Blintzes. The dinner menu is nicely varied beginning with a well priced pasta selection. There are several steak dishes and unusual chicken recipes such as Harvest Country Chicken - broiled breast of chicken with ham and melted jack cheese smothered with brown sauce and mushrooms. The Seafood Lovers Plate serves up deep fried shrimp, scallops and snapper.

So, whether it's to drop in for a frosty beer or to indulge in a complete dinner, try the Golden Harvest Cafe. You'll love it. Ask anyone!

(See special invitation in the Appendix).

Sport

ADVENTURE'S EDGE
650 10th Street
Arcata, CA 95521
Tel. (707) 822-4673
Hrs: Mon. - Sat. 10:00 a.m. - 6:00 p.m.
Visa, MasterCard and AMEX are accepted.

In the beginning, Adventure's Edge was created to provide outdoor enthusiasts with an outlet for sports products. From this humble start has grown not only a retail store stuffed with everything you could need for your adventures, but also a source of information.

Owner Stephen O'Meara and his staff use their knowledge and experience to make this shop a year round resource. Stephen calls Adventure's Edge and "adult toy store," featuring supplies for camping, backpacking, bicycling, cross country/downhill skiing and river touring. Even quality brands such as, North Face, Blue Puma and Moonstone, are tested by the staff to assure that only the best equipment is offered and that it will perform as expected.

Adventure's Edge will furnish information and directions for trails, paths, skiing trails and general suggestions on places to explore in the area. Repair service for any merchandise is also provided to guarantee customer satisfaction. A newsletter is published several times a year to provide you with updates on equipment, techniques and hot spots.

Eureka

This grand city of California's North Coast tells a story in its population, certified at 24,103 in the 1980 census. Twenty years before it was nearing 30,000 people in the post-war boom of the timber industry. Since then, with the slow down in demand for product, the population has declined. The local economy is now emphasizing retailing and increased tourist trade. Giant mills which sent redwood boards clanking out to two years of air-dried curing for top quality lumber are gone. Where the Holmes-Eureka mill was at Bucksport, with its big ocean shipping docks, a modern regional shopping mall sprouted in 1987, the third mall in the crescent-shaped business district hugging the bay.

A concrete bridge, completed in 1971 to cross the bay, has one footing where the Dolbeer Carson mill dried its lumber; a span comes down on the former farmland of Woodley's Island where a new sport-fishing marina berths boats by the dozens. It lifts above another channel of the bay to the newly-christened Indian Island, abolishing the name Gunther which townspeople put on it to forget the February 25, 1860 massacre in which every living remnant of two Indian tribes was killed by self-appointed militiamen. The final span rises above the oyster beds to the Samoa Peninsula where paper mills dwarf the old sawmills.

At the south end of town, Fort Humboldt, headquarters for the regular army which came here to keep the peace between settlers and Indians, looks out from its bluff at the stacks of an oil fired electrical power plant and the third unused stack of a nuclear powered unit. It was shut down amid fears that an earthquake might damage the reactor vessel so carefully installed in 1960, the dawn of a new age in energy. Today, cogeneration plants, turbines spinning with energy from steam made by woodchips ground out of forest wastes pick up the load of the idle nuclear plant. Constant among all of the contrasts are the charming Victorian homes and the sparkling Old Town Eureka which stays the same and keeps attracting more visitors.

Attractions

The old Buhne Hardware and ship chandlery at 422 First Street lives on as **Humboldt Cultural Center**. Rotating art shows are presented here, and performing arts take center stage each Friday evening. Telephone (707) 442-2611.

Other parts of **Old Town**, on first and second streets, reflect the same careful restoration of buildings. At 143 M Street is the penultimate Victorian, the **Carson Mansion** built in 1884-85 to keep skilled workers on the payroll during a slow time in the lumber business. Now a private club, the house is widely known through photographs including national advertisements for the house paint used on its exterior. The **Eureka Chamber of Commerce** has a detailed guide of the old buildings, residential and commercial, at its Old Town visitors Bureau offices, 1034 Second Street.

Woodley Island, the first stop on the Samoa Bridge, has many colorful boats in the new marina along with offices for the Port of Humboldt Harbormaster and the Cafe Marina which features local sea food. From the marina, you can check progress on the celebrated development project which was to create a grand hotel on the old **Dolbeer Carson Mill** site next to the bridge. Steel pilings were sunk before the project ground to a halt leaving a landmark for the curious.

At the Foot of C Street is one of the many commercial fish processing areas along the waterfront. This was the **Tom Lazio Fish Co.** for many years. It featured a restaurant just off the packing line. Now the restaurant remains, and processing is carried out elsewhere.

Once passenger ferries were busy on the bay taking workers back and forth to the mills at Samoa and Fairhaven. Now the **passenger ferry** gives seventy five minute tours from the foot of C Street from mid-June through mid-September at 1:00 p.m., 2:30 p.m., and 4:00 p.m. The ferry Madaket **charters** the rest of the year, and she makes a "cocktail" cruise at 4:00 p.m. during the summer operating hours. Call 444-9440.

Coast Oyster Co., at the Foot of A Street, offers tours of when its plant is operating. The oyster beds were created on tidal flats twenty five years ago by bringing "seed" oysters from Japan. Tour hours are 9:00 a.m. to 2:30 p.m. Telephone 442-2947.

Eureka Inn, at Seventh and F Streets, is a full block of Old English manor-style buildings erected in 1922 and now on the National Register of Historic Places. The Inn, a full service hotel, welcomes visitors to its lobby and public rooms. Telephone 442-6441 for information and reservations.

The **Clarke Museum**, Third and E streets, is in a classic building now stuffed with artifacts of Indian residents and later arrivals on the bay, collected in large part by Cecile Clark who taught history at Eureka High school from 1914 through 1950 and has her work continued by a non-profit corporation. Open Tuesday through Saturday, 10:00 a.m. to 4:00 p.m. Telephone 443-1947.

In Old Town at 1410 Second Street is the **Maritime Museum**, tracing shipping on the bay. The building stands on what was once tide flats until waste material from sawmills created a springy land fill. Open seven days a week, 11:00 a.m. to 4:00 p.m. Telephone 444-9440.

Old time logging equipment is gathered outside, military and Indian history inside the remaining building at **Fort Humboldt State Historic Park**. It's tricky to find this old post on the bluff at the south of Eureka. From U.S. 101, turn east on Highland Avenue then turn left on Fort Avenue, which curves into the park. Open daily during daylight hours, year around. Telephone 443-7952.

Sequoia Park, on W Street south of Harris Street, preserves a redwood grove right in the city. There is a local zoo here, and a **Zoological Society** with regular natural history programs and field trips. For zoo information, call 442-6552. The current Zoological Society offering can be learned by calling the same number.

For additional information, the **Eureka Chamber of Commerce** has a visitors bureau in Old Town, 1034 Second Street. Telephone 443-5097.

Accommodation

THE EUREKA INN
7th and "F" Streets
Eureka, CA 95501
Tel.   (707) 442-6441
AMEX, Visa, MasterCard, Diner's Club, Carte Blanche
and Eureka Inn cards are accepted.

"Romantic" and "elegant" best describe the architecture of The Eureka Inn. This Tudor style building is listed in the National Historical Landmark Register. The staff of this lovely inn is proud of the historical significance of the inn and strives to "Keep A Great Tradition Alive" through constant renovation.

The lobby is graced with beautiful custom made carpeting and a massive fireplace. The first floor boasts a Rib Room Restaurant, the Palm Lounge, Coffee Shop, spa and saunas. The Colonnade and Westchester Rooms provide a charming atmosphere for banquets. Each of the 110 spacious guest rooms is unique with charming features such as, quilts on the beds. Some offer fireplaces and the Honeymoon Suite, its own spa. There are family rooms and fifteen different types of suites. For a relaxing afternoon or evening, enjoy the garden court graced with a heated swimming pool. Limousine and consierge services complete the luxurious feeling of these fine accommodations.

The Coffee Shop restaurant offers scrumptious breakfasts of eggs Benedict or Belgium waffles to start the day. The award winning Rib Room serves lunch and dinner with such popular items as fresh salmon, prime rib, veal picatta, roast duckling Gran Marnier, among other popular beef, poultry and seafood dishes. The wine cellar offers the most extensive selection in Northern California with over 200 varieties from which to choose. Save room for a dessert with tempting creations of cherries Jubilee or banana Foster. The

Rathskeller offers a genuine German Pub atmosphere. A large variety of beers, entertainment and food are available in this theme restaurant.

Since 1922, this "Best Choice" hotel, The Eureka Inn, has been pampering visitors to the area with finely appointed rooms, superb cuisine and meticulous service.

FIRESIDE INN
1716 5th Street
Eureka, CA 95501
Tel. (707) 443-6312
MasterCard, Visa, Discover Card, Diner's Card and
AMEX are accepted.
Children and pets welcome.

The old world atmosphere of the Fireside Inn is comfortable and spacious. The generous use of knotty redwood and the gigantic flagstone fireplace gives a pleasant warmth to the lobby. One of the interesting features of this motel are several huge palm trees gracing the grounds. Travelers are so intrigued by the size of the thriving trees, especially because they are so far north, that they collect the fallen seeds to take home and plant.

Large family units that can accommodate up to six people are available. Kitchens are available in some rooms, providing functional and relaxing accommodations. Coffee is served in the lobby in the mornings.

The Fireside Inn is conveniently located near Eureka's Old Town, fine restaurants and is just a few miles from the beach. This motel is frequently homebase for families ready to hit the beach with the kids and the dog. The beach is popular for clam digging, kite flying, cookouts, long, leisurely walks and, travelers frequently bring their three wheel R.V's.

RED LION MOTOR INN
1929 4th
Eureka, CA 95501
Tel. (800) 547-8010
Visa, MasterCard, AMEX, Diner's Club and Discover
cards are accepted.

During your travels along the Northern California coast, Red Lion Motor Inn will provide comfortable, spacious accommodations. The architecture and Victorian decor was designed to complement the beauty of the area.

Beautifully appointed rooms with oversized beds provide a spacious area to relax after a day on the road. Individually controlled air conditioning, color TV and direct dial phones are standard luxuries.

The elegant dining room serves delicious food for breakfast, lunch and dinner. Dinner offers a fine selection of seafood and gourmet entrees such as steak Diane. After dinner succumb to your desire for a pastry, cherries Jubilee or a scoop of Haagen-Dazs ice cream.

For superior room accommodations, luxurious amenities and professional friendly service your "Best Choice" in Eureka is the Red Lion Motor Inn.

Art

THE ART CENTER
211 "G" Street
Eureka, CA 95501
Tel. (707) 443-7017
Hrs: Mon. - Fri.   9:00 a.m. - 5:30 p.m.
           Saturday   9:30 a.m. - 5:30 p.m.
           Sunday   12:00 noon - 4:00 p.m.
Visa and MasterCard accepted.

The Art Center, established in 1972, is a recent lodger in a building with a diverse history. The Buhne Building, constructed in 1885, was considered to be one of the finest of its time. In the past, various areas of the building served Eureka as a telegraph office, gym facility, water district office and bank. The walls of the building are two-foot-thick brick set on granite slabs, and the mortar for the masonry was strengthened by cement brought around The Horn from Belgium. The columns and pilasters are solid cast iron, as are the decorations on the face of the structure. None of the large earthquakes have weakened or changed its composure.

The owner, Ann Pierson started The Art Center because of the lack of availability of artist's supplies in this area. Their art department now provides a complete selection of materials geared toward the professional artist, graphic artist, student and hobbyist.

Popularity provided for further expansion to encompass gift items like local crafts, pottery, etched glass and photographs. A compliment to the gift section is an array of exciting cards and wrapping papers.

Additional customer request resulted in the formation of the 1200 square foot frame room that offers a large selection of frames and ready-made mats. The services here include mat cutting and decoration, mounting of prints and photographs, glass and board cutting, canvas and needlework stretching, assembly of artwork into frames, calligraphy, conservation work, and specialty services such as the restoration of paintings or frames, preparation of portfolios, and the mounting of exhibits.

The natural evolution in this progression seemed to be a need for a art gallery. Now three small galleries grace The Art Center. The Main Gallery is a permanent, revolving display area which primarily shows the work of local artists, an Annex is used for irregularly scheduled shows and theme presentations and the Center Gallery is reserved for one-person or small group shows which generally change each month.

The Art Center seems to match the Buhne Building in its stability, acclaim and beauty.

EUREKA ART AND FRAME
530 E Street
Eureka, CA 95501
Tel. (707) 444-2888
Hrs.   Mon. - Fri.   10:00 a.m. - 5:00 p.m.
       Saturday   11:00 a.m. - 4:00 p.m.
Visa, MasterCard and American Express are accepted.

Looking for a lasting momento of your journey through Northern California; one that will bring back fond memories and complement the decor of your home? Eureka Art and Frame has a large selection of art in a variety of styles and subject matter.

This cozy gallery is packed with prints, posters and silkscreens by some of the finest, nationally known artists of our time. The owners of the gallery, Paul and Linda Baries, are also the publishers for artists John Wesa and Lyn Walton. Because of this working relationship with the artists, you can gain first hand knowledge of the creativity and effort that went into the art that will grace your home.

Because Paul and Linda love collecting and displaying art, they work with the customers to assure that the best framing and care available goes into each piece. Eureka Art and Frame has over 300 frame styles from which to choose, with same day service, if needed, on framing or, if you prefer, will ship your selection anywhere in the country.

HUMBOLDT'S FINEST
417 2nd Street
Eureka, CA 95501
Tel. (707) 443-1258
Hrs.   Summer   Mon. - Sun.   10:30 a.m. - 5:30 p.m.
          Winter   Mon. - Sat.   10:30 a.m. - 5:30 p.m.
Visa and MasterCard are accepted.

Humboldt's Finest, located in Old Town Eureka, has an elite selection of products handcrafted from natural resources of the area. The spacious, redwood and oak panelled shop has dozens of windows to provide the perfect natural light to set off the works of art on display.

Owners Bruce Braly and Kelan Fawson are proud of the local talent that produces some of the finest art and crafts available. Wood carvings, pottery, beautifully etched glass works, niobium jewelry and a large assortment of earrings are among the treasures of Humboldt's Finest. Fine crafted furniture is used for displaying such treasures as handmade cribbage boards and ceramics. Upstairs is an art gallery where paintings and sculptures are presented.

Bruce and Kelan invite you to the center of the redwood empire in this clean and unspoiled, sea side community to visit this "Best Choice" craft store, Humboldt's Finest.

INDIAN DEVELOPMENT COUNCIL
241 "F" Street
Eureka, CA 95501
Tel. (707) 445-8451
Hrs: Mon. - Sat. 10:00 a.m. - 5:00 p.m.
Visa, MasterCard, AMEX, CitiCorp and Discovery cards

This is a non-profit organization that was established in 1976 to promote the economic well-being of Indian people residing in Humboldt, Del Norte, Siskiyou and Trinity Counties. The Council provides a retail outlet for authentic Indian arts and crafts and thereby supports the continued Indian pride in culture and heritage.

Located in the historic Carson Block Building, which is being restored to its original 1896 condition; including the famous Ingomar Theatre...the Indian Development Council brings current displays of custom-made southwest silver and turquoise jewelry, fine, Northern California Indian basketry, pottery and bead work.

These articles are authentic in their antiquity of design...and imbue us all with pride in our "shared" American heritage. Visit the Indian Development Council and take home a piece of America's past.

With a legacy built upon timber, shipping and fishing, the port of Eureka today is a major center for wares created within Northern California. Its shops and art are sure to satisfy you with regional products, as the following tours will attest.

EUREKA ART TOUR			
a.m.	Red Lion Inn	Best breakfast	Eur/Acc
a.m.	Indian Council	Best Indian craft	Eur/Art
a.m.	Eureka Art & Frame	Best gallery	Eur/Art
p.m.	Luna's	Best Mexican	Eur/Rest
p.m.	Humboldt's Finest	Best furniture	Eur/Art
p.m.	Art Center	Best art	Eur/Art
End your tour at a restaurant having two things for which Eureka is known-- seafood and a sea view.			
p.m.	Waterfront	Best seafood	Eur/Rest

Bank

BANK OF LOLETA
4th and F Streets
Eureka, CA 95501
Tel. (707) 445-3051
Hrs:

Mon. - Thu.	10:00 a.m. - 3:00 p.m.
Friday	10:00 a.m. - 6:00 p.m.
Saturday	10:00 a.m. - 1:00 p.m.

"The Difference in Banking Today!" is at the Bank of Loleta, with personal service and six locations in Northern California to serve you. The bank takes pride in serving the area as the only community bank, but also strives to accommodate the needs of travelers.

When you are far from home and need financial resources, what a relief it is to find friendly people at a bank ready to help. The bank is on line with The Federal Reserve Bank and can receive and dispatch wire money transfers anywhere in the country. Cash advances on Visa, MasterCard and AMEX Gold Card can be made, as well as cashing and selling traveler's checks and foreign exchange for Canadian currency.

In an effort to meet your needs, the bank is open on Saturday. Be sure to take advantage of the friendly, professional services available at Bank of Loleta with branches in Arcata, Eureka, Ferndale, Fortuna, Loleta and Scotia.

Car

AVIS RENT-A-CAR
McKinleyville Arcada/Eureka Airport
McKinleyville, CA 95521
Tel. (707) 839-1576
Hrs: Mon. - Fri.   8:00 a.m. - 9:00 p.m.
          Saturday   9:00 a.m. - 6:00 p.m.
          Sunday   9:00 a.m. - 9:00 p.m.
All major credit cards are accepted.
And,   **JIGGS USED CARS**
4th and "B" Streets   1312 N Crest Drive
Eureka, CA 95521   Crescent City, CA 95531
Tel. (707) 443-1670   Tel. (707) 464-8325
          BEATS WALKIN
4th and B Streets
Eureka, CA 95501
Tel. (707) 443-2070

The well known slogan, "We Try Harder" is honored at all the convenient locations of Avis, even at the "Beats Walkin" location.

You'll find only new Plymouth product cars (nothing over four months old) at the Avis Rent-A-Cars in Eureka and Crescent City from Dodge Colts to stretch limousines. Corporate rates are recognized and there are special weekend rates. At "Beats Walkin" used cars are offered at lower prices.

In addition to trying harder, Avis provides "Service By The Man, Not The Company", which assures that you will be given every consideration by the friendly, professional staff at this "Best Choice" car rental.

(See special invitation in the Appendix.)

Chamber of Commerce

EUREKA CHAMBER OF COMMERCE
240 E Street
Eureka, CA 95501
Tel. (707) 443-1947
Hrs: Tue. - Sat. 12:00 noon - 4:00 p.m.

Clarke Memorial Museum was originated by Cecile Clarke, a history teacher in Eureka from 1915 - 1950. Her passion for the heritage of the area prompted her to collect and display artifacts from the shipping, logging, agriculture and railroad industries, as well Indian collections. The museum is divided into three main galleries each with a theme.

The Main Hall was originally the bank building and is now listed with the National Register of Historical Places. In this building, which has high ceilings and a breathtaking skylight, is an extensive selection of vintage clothing, weapons, furniture and maritime memorabilia.

Nealis Hall, dedicated to the Native American cultures of the area, has the largest display of Hoopa, Karuk and Yurok basketry in the country. By viewing the collection of baskets, you can learn much about the art of weaving. In addition to the baskets, there are displays of regalia including headdresses with accompanying displays of the birds from which the feathers were taken.

Displays can be found in The Emmerson Curly Room. An ongoing program of temporary exhibits is maintained throughout the year. Regional, history, custom and textile, and Victorian decorative arts are among the subjects featured.

Clarke Memorial Museum is a non-profit organization that offers free admission to the public. Donations are gratefully accepted at this fascinating, fun "Best Choice" in Eureka.

Gift

THE INSIDE TRACK
133 Waterfront
Eureka, CA 95501
Tel. (707) 442-7323
Hrs: Summer   Mon. - Sun. 10:00 a.m. - 9:00 p.m.
         Winter   Mon. - Sun. 10:00 a.m. - 4:00 p.m.
Bank Americard and MasterCard are accepted.

A 1910 Pullman sleeping car is the home of a most unconventional shop - The Inside Track. The emphasis of the shop is on small, portable gifts, many of them crafted in the area, for travelers to take or send home.

Among the gifts are redwood bowls, keychains, magnets, signs, bells, boxes and thimbles exhibited on wooden fruit crates, dynamite boxes and Moosehead beer cartons. Charmingly displayed on an old fashioned stove range are a variety of kitchen gadgets. A fine selection of silver and abolone jewelry is also available. The owners of this amazing shop also operate a farm and orchard; summer time offerings include peaches, apples and vegies intermingled with the gifts.

The staff of The Inside Track is friendly and the approach to business is addressed with humor. You really must visit this unusual, "Best Choice" gift shop.

THE IRISH SHOP
334 2nd Street
Eureka, CA 95501
Tel. (707) 443-8343
Hrs: Mon. - Sat.   9:30 a.m - 6:00 p.m.
         Sunday   1:00 a.m - 4:00 p.m.
And,
45050 Main Street
Mendocino, CA 95460
Tel. (707) 937-3133
Hrs: Mon. - Sat.   10:00 a.m. - 6:00 p.m.
         Sunday   10:00 a.m. - 5:00 p.m.
Visa, MasterCard and AMEX are accepted.

With its emerald green carpeting, white walls and wooden fixtures, The Irish Shop has a charming warmth. Owner Connie Young has assembled lovely imports from Ireland, Scotland, Wales, Iceland, Australia and New Zealand.

Gorgeous hand-knit sweaters, scarves and mittens for men, women and children are carried, as well as men's dress hats and caps. Displayed in the shop are a wide variety of blankets from small lap to queen size. Classic women's apparel from Gieger of Austria is featured, as well as creations by Richard Malcolm, Jimmy Hourihan, Henry White and Max Pierre. Accessories such as hats, scarves, belts and jewelry will complement and add to any woman's wardrobe. Waterford, Royal Tara and Belleek china, along with gourmet foods from Ireland, Scotland and Australia round out the unique offerings of Connie's shops.

Connie, who treats customers like guest in her home, will ship your purchases anywhere in the country and offers complimentary gift wrapping.

RAINBOW BALLOONS AND GIFTS
527 4th Street
Eureka, CA 95501
Tel. (707) 445-2156

Hrs:	Summer	Mon. - Thur.	10:00 a.m. - 6:00 p.m.
		Fri. - Sat.	10:00 a.m. - 9:00 p.m.
		Sunday	12:00 noon - 5:00 p.m.
	Winter	Mon. - Sat.	10:00 a.m. - 5:30 p.m.

Visa, MasterCard and Discover Card are accepted.

Located in downtown Eureka, near beautiful Old Town, is a delightful shop called Rainbow Balloons and Gifts. Owner Toni Beccaria started her shop in 1982 by delivering special balloons in costumes such as Miss Piggy and clowns. This endeavor started as a hobbie, but with $300 dollars and scores of ideas she has created an adventure in fun.

"Whimsical, classical and a bit tacky," is how Toni describes Rainbow Balloons and Gifts. The shop boasts the largest balloon inventory in the area, plus you will find a huge section devoted to cards of every imaginable sort including "adults only" varieties, joke and gag gifts, t-shirts for anyone on your list, hats and games galore. Costumes, masks, (including famous personalities), and costume accessories, is yet another section to explore. There is also a full service salon and tanning booth in the back.

Toni invites you to "come on in and have a good time" and munch free popcorn while browsing through her "Best Choice" gift shop.

THE STUMP HOUSE
1108 Broadway
Eureka, CA 95501
Tel.   (707) 445-2471
Hrs: Summer   Mon. - Sun. 8:30 a.m. - 7:00 p.m.
            Winter   Mon. - Sun. 8:30 a.m. - 5:00 p.m.
Visa, MasterCard, American Express and
Discover Cards are accepted.

The Stump House, located in the heart of the Redwoods, is just that, a
building made from stumps of redwood trees. Built in 1902 , the exterior looks
like a big log. Inside, you will be awed by the beauty of the natural wood interior
and the unique, locally made gifts.
     No trip through the Redwood National Forest would be complete
without a souvenir. The natural beauty of redwood shines through in the
handcrafted bowls, salt and pepper shakers and candleholders. Carvings of
figurines and exquisite clocks will add to the decor of your home. Oil lamps for
your table or wall adorn the shop along with chain saw sculptures.
     Owner Harry Freeman invites you to visit and learn more of the history
of The Stump House and the surrounding area. Harry strives to provide the
best possible service by providing the little extras such as free gift wrapping,
shipping and is delighted to accommodate special orders. This attention to
detail and the quality gift items make The Stump House a "Best Choice" in
Northern California.

EUREKA GIFT TOUR			
a.m.	Inside Track	Best variety	Eur/Gift
a.m.	Irish Shop	Best sweaters	Eur/Gift
p.m.	Weatherby's	Best lunch	Eur/Rest
p.m.	Rainbow Balloons	Best jokes	Eur/Gift
p.m.	Stump House	Best in redwood	Eur/Gift
p.m.	Adventure's Edge	Best sport	Eur/Sport

For added variety, mix your shopping with a trip to Arcata, just across the bay from Eureka.

EUREKA / ARCATA PLAY TOUR			
a.m.	Clarke Memorial	Best museum	Eur/Museum
a.m.	Smith Ice Cream	Best lunch	Eur/Ice Cream
p.m.	Alligator Balloons	Best party item	Arc/Gift
p.m.	Franklin's	Best ed. toys	Arc/Gift
p.m.	Potpourri	Best pottery	Arc/Gift
p.m.	Arcata Exchange	Best collect. doll	Arc/Gift

Ice Cream

SMITHS' ICE CREAMERY & EATERY
1338 Myrtle Avenue
Eureka, CA 95501
Tel. (707) 443-0101
Hrs: Mon. - Thur.   11:00 a.m. - 10:00 p.m.
              Fri. - Sat.   11:00 a.m. - 11:00 p.m.
Sum.   Sunday   12:00 noon - 10:00 p.m.
Win.   Sunday   2:00 p.m. - 10:00 p.m.

Leave your diet-mentality at home...you are about to enter the confines of the best manufacturer of homemade ice cream in Humboldt County. Rich (16% butterfat content), smooth, luscious, cold/refreshing, melt-in-your-mouth ice cream; on a homemade waffle cone, in a soda or nestled amidst fruit, flavored syrup, real whipped cream and nuts. Or, try the locals favorite, the Smitty Bar. GO ON...you deserve it! Also, homemade yogurt and non-dairy frozen desserts available.

Larry and Nancy Smith have been the proprietors of this ice creamery for the past three years. They make sure the service is fast and courteous and the surroundings clean and welcoming. Dine outdoors in the warm and colorful patio area.

For your lunch and dinner selection, Smith's provides a daily hot dish along with homemade soups, lightly tossed and full-dinner salads, like fresh crab, cob or taco; charbroiled hamburgers, hot dogs, sizzling hot garlic french fries, deli-style stacked-sandwiches and homemade pies.

191

Humboldt County

The Petal Pusher Flower Shop, offering fresh, live flowers, shares this location. Smiths' Ice Creamery & Eatery...purveyors of fine products for all your senses.

(See special invitation in the Appendix.)

Museum

CLARKE MEMORIAL MUSEUM
240 E Street
Eureka, CA 95501
Tel. (707) 443-1947
Hrs: Tue. - Sat. 12:00 noon - 4:00 p.m.

Clarke Memorial Museum was originated by Cecile Clarke, a history teacher in Eureka from 1915 - 1950. Her passion for the heritage of the area prompted her to collect and display artifacts from the shipping, logging, agriculture and railroad industries, as well Indian collections. The museum is divided into three main galleries each with a theme.

The Main Hall was originally the bank building and is now listed with the National Register of Historical Places. In this building, which has high ceilings and a breathtaking skylight, is an extensive selection of vintage clothing, weapons, furniture and maritime memorabilia.

Nealis Hall, dedicated to the Native American cultures of the area, has the largest display of Hoopa, Karuk and Yurok basketry in the country. By viewing the collection of baskets, you can learn much about the art of weaving. In addition to the baskets, there are displays of regalia including headdresses with accompanying displays of the birds from which the feathers were taken.

Displays can be found in The Emmerson Curly Room. An ongoing program of temporary exhibits is maintained throught the year. Regional, history, custom and textile, and Victorian decorative arts are among the subjects featured.

Clarke Memorial Museum is a non-profit organization that offers free admission to the public. Donations are gratefully accepted at this fascinating, fun "Best Choice" in Eureka.

Restaurant

CAFE WATERFRONT
102 "F" Street
Eureka, CA 95501
Tel. (707) 443-9190
Hrs: Summer   Mon. - Sun. 11:30 a.m. - 10:00 p.m.
           Winter   Mon. - Sun. 11:30 a.m. - 9:00 p.m.
Visa and MasterCard

At First and "F" Street, at the foot of "F" Street and overlooking the bay...the Cafe Waterfront.   Unpretentious, relaxed, lots of windows that overlook the Humboldt Bay and the boats that ply the waters, hardwood floors, lots of antiques and tables covered with lace cloths. A lulling ambiance when you consider that one hundred years ago this was a bustling brothel!

Now, Diane Smith and Barbara Brown are the proprietors of this oyster bar and grill. The cafe has proved so popular that they're adding 1500 square feet on the second floor.

Lunch is served until 5:30 p.m. The daily specials are all made from scratch, appetizingly presented and very reasonable. For the adventurous, the locals choose oyster shooters, as the preface to dinner. The forte here is seafood: oysters, steamer clams and fresh-caught fish, however, they are also reputed to prepare the best N. Y. steak in Humboldt County.

One of the three fun bartenders will serve forth the brew and commentary from the old-fashioned bar.   Mixed drinks and wine are available...just slide onto one of the stools, put your feet up on the brass rail and enjoy.

At the Cafe Waterfront: a view, a great meal, and for the adventurous, oyster shooters!

(See special invitation in the Appendix.)

LUNA'S MEXICAN RESTAURANT
1134 5th Street
Eureka, CA 95501
Tel. (707) 445-9162
Hrs. Mon. - Sat. 11:00 a.m. - 9:00 p.m.
Visa and MasterCard are accepted.

Luis and Ruby Luna have created a Mexican restaurant that offers delicious recipes that can be found only at Luna's. Luis and Ruby opened their cafe style restaurant in 1979, bringing with them ancient recipes from their homeland.

Whether you choose Huevos Rancheros for breakfast, chicken or turkey en mole for lunch or try their special recipes such as enchilada Azteca or tacos and enchiladas made with crab, you can be assured that the freshest ingredients are used. Only vegetable oil is used when frying and the corn and flour tortillas are homemade.

Delicious homemade desserts, friendly service and a very comfortable atmosphere combine to make this a "Best Choice" - Luna's Mexican Restaurant.

WEATHERBY'S
1906 4th Street
Eureka, CA 95501
Tel. (707) 442-0683
Hrs: Mon. - Sat.   11:00 a.m. - 10:00 p.m.
         Sunday   12:00noon - 10:00 p.m.
Visa, MasterCard, Diners cards are accepted.

In 1946 Mrs. Weatherby and her fisherman husband started a fresh fish market. The only food served was her fresh crab sandwich, Mae's homemade chowder and homebaked pies. As their reputation grew the location expanded. Enlarged to a fifty-four seat restaurant, it was purchased in 1975 by Perry and Maureen Clevenger.

Weatherby's has a rustic clapboard exterior, reminiscent of seashore architecture, with a large flashing neon crab sign; the restaurant is still small, but big on freshness, quality and very friendly service. Under Perry and Maureen's guidance the menu selection has expanded to encompass gourmet specialities such as, souffles, clam pot pies, seafood crepes, fresh pasta, Italian dishes, Swedish meatballs with parsley sauce, quiche, seafood, hot roast beef and meatball sandwiches. A luncheon special is the Crepe of the Day and the Quiche of the Day...chef's choice.

For dinner you might start your meal with a dish of the homemade clam chowder or local oysters, poached in a champagne Hollandaise sauce, or lightly-battered, deep-fried fresh vegetables to dunk in a Teriyaki sauce. The entrees of chicken Teriyaki or fresh red snapper, sauteed with herbs, mushrooms, tarragon and parmesan cheese would be nicely complemented by an espresso or cappucinno. Finish your repast with a selection from the deep dish or fresh fruit pies that are made daily. A local favorite is the walnut pie. Simply delicious! Not to be slighted, for your attention, is the Kahlua almond cheesecake, the mousse cake of the day and chocolate or strawberry mousse. Yum.

Much of the local color of Humboldt County, Eureka and the original founders of Weatherby's is depicted by the photographs adorning the walls. The ambiance here is relaxed and unassuming...the seafood is still as fresh as in the days when Mr. Weatherby went fishing.

Sport

ADVENTURE'S EDGE, 408 "F" Street, Eureka, California. An "adult toy store" with all the supplies for camping, backpacking...any outdoor sports. See fuller story under Arcata listing in this book.

Ferndale

Just thirty-five feet above sea level and a short distance from the mouth of the Eel River, this little town of 1,400 people is as conscious of river conditions as of its heritage as a well-preserved Victorian town. Many of the homes have first floors raised several feet above ground level, to avoid flood waters in the living room. At times, the milk from cows in the Eel River bottoms has gone to market by boat or not at all when the wandering secondary channels of the mighty stream fill up around Ferndale.

From a cabin built here in 1852 sprang a home of substance in 1860, a post office the same year, all at the Seth Shaw farm which became the town site. Most of the stores now on Main street date from the 1870s, and all operate today. Two modern additions are several buildings at the county fairgrounds and a housing project for personnel working seven miles west at the U.S. Naval Station at Centerville Beach. The fair started here in 1897, but now sports much newer grandstands and exhibit halls. The navy set up its off-shore listening post in the late 1950s.

Attractions

Ferndale Museum mirrors the life of the people who called this "Cream City," including a reference collection of the local newspaper from 1878 to the present. In the museum is the seismograph station that helps pinpoint frequent earthquakes, most of which are centered off shore as the North American and Pacific Plates grind together in the marine extension of the San Andreas fault. Open February through December on a Wednesday through Saturday schedule, from 11:00 a.m. to 4:00 p.m. Open Sundays from 1:00 p.m. to 4:00 p.m. Telephone 786-4466.

Main Street is a walking and looking tour, with attractions from old-fashioned stores complete with authentic labels, to a working butcher shop that custom cuts for the area farmers. Write the Ferndale Chamber of Commerce for an informational map, or pick one up when you arrive in town.

South from Ferndale, on Mattole Road, is a loop drive which leads to the pioneer oil town of **Petrolia**, then east to U.S. 101 at South Fork in **Humboldt Redwoods State Park**. West, at Ferndale, is a short side trip to **Centerville Beach**, where a memorial cross marks the spot where the steamer Northerner drifted ashore in 1860 after striking a rock the day before near Cape Mendocino. Thirty eight people died in this early tragedy of the Humboldt Coast. The Mattole Road leads south over vast range land kept green by heavy rainfall and frequent fogs. Petrolia's oil, the first pumped in California, was sent to a refinery in San Francisco in 1865. Occasional wildcatters have since returned but the little field three miles east of town has yielded no more commercial wells. **Cape Mendocino**, the most westerly point in the continental United States is on the drive, a land mark for sailor since 1542 as land fall of the trans-Pacific route of Spanish galleons working the Manila trade. A lighthouse, 400 feet above sea level, was built here in the 1860s to aid mariners. It could be seen twenty eight miles to sea.

Local tour maps and detailed information from the **Ferndale Chamber of Commerce**, Box 325, Ferndale CA 95536. Telephone 786-4477.

Trinidad

Accommodation

BISHOP PINE LODGE
1481 Patrick's Point Drive
Trinidad, CA 95570
Tel. (707) 677-3314
MasterCard and Visa are accepted.

Everybody's got to sleep. No matter how long you're able to stave it off, sooner or later the body will shut down and sleep will claim you. It's always like this on the road. Caffeine supplements only work for so long. So, when you feel the inevitable coming on, and are near Trinidad, You're in luck. The Bishop Pine Lodge offers the accommodations so desperately needed.

This Triple A approved establishment features thirteen cottages, some with kitchens, queen size beds and color T.V.'s with HBO. There's also a playground for the kids and a barbeque for preparing your own steaks. When waking up in the morning, get a little exercise by hiking the eight acres of redwood trails. If an inspiring view is what you'd like to see, there's a trail that goes to the cliff overlooking the beach.

Yawn, stretch and come alive. Ahh! that was a good night's sleep. See how much better your feel when rested? That car seat feels entirely different now that you've been separated from it for more than five minutes. The Bishop Pine Lodge is a welcome relief that you will remember for some time.

LIGHTHOUSE MOTEL, 3360 Patrick's Point Drive, Trinidad, California. This charming four-room motel overlooks the ocean, and owners Bill and Lorie Hensen treat you as if you were a guest in their own home. Cable television is in all rooms.

Restaurant

COLONIAL RESTAURANT
1658 Patrick's Point Drive
Trinidad, CA 95570
Tel. (707) 677-3001
Hrs: Restaurant
           Tue. - Sat.   5:00 p.m. - 9:30 p.m.
           Sunday   4:00 p.m. - 9:00 p.m.
          Lounge
           Mon. - Sun.   3:00 p.m. - 12:00 midnight

During the late 1970's Katherine Dilling, while visiting her daughter, went to eat at Colonial Restaurant. She ended up buying everything on the menu. In fact, she liked it so much she purchased the entire retaurant! She now puts her forty years of experience into making it the best eatery in the area.

When dining by candlelight in this homey restaurant, you can choose from a delightful selection of entrees, such as sirloin tip, many kinds of seafood, filet Mignon, prime rib, chicken, vegetarian dishes and many more. All dinners come with homemade bread, soup du jour, green salad and your choice of potato or rice pilaf. Of course, for some, no meal is complete without a good wine. Following that tradition, the wine list is quite extensive.

This restaurant has come a long way since that fated day when Katherine purchased it, a long way in the right direction. Drop by the Colonial Restaurant, dine on delicious food, partake of fine wine and enjoy the casual atmosphere. Be careful though, this is how Katherine got started.

(See special invitation in the Appendix.)

SEASCAPE RESTAURANT
Bay Street (at the pier)
Trinidad, CA 95570
Tel. (707) 677-3762
Hrs: Mon. - Fri.   7:00 a.m. - 9:00 p.m.
           Sat. - Sun.   7:00 a.m. - 10:00 p.m.
           Summer: 6:00 a.m. - 10:00 p.m.

It's hard to get seafood any fresher than at the Seascape Restaurant. The commercial boats unload their catch at the foot of the pier where the restaurant is located.

The restaurant and pier are owned by Joellen Hallmark.

The pier was built in 1944 and is one of the few privately owned piers on the west coast. The restaurant has been a local landmark for over twenty-five years.

Chefs Gene Cave and Joe Christian invite you to try one of the excellent breakfast, lunch or dinner items. The menu is extensive and encompasses seafood (steamed clams, smoked salmon, shrip Louie, broiled lobster, scallops & filet mignon, a bay platter or oyster fry) and landlubber specialties such as Tournedos, a 5 or 8 oz. filet mignon, chicken Stroganoff or a wonderous steak sandwich plate).

Stop by for the full course dinner or just a friendly cup of coffee, the Seascape offers a picturesque spot to study the varied activities of the fishing harbor.

(See special invitation in Appendix.)

LAKE COUNTY

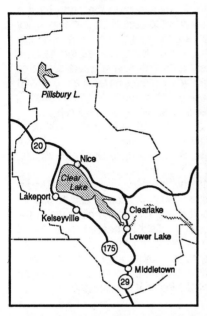

The coast range mountains cradle Lake County, providing the basin for the largest freshwater lake entirely within the state. Waters from the lake, drawn on for orchards and crop land on the rolling hills surrounding it, find their way to the Sacramento River through Cache Creek's outlet near the town of Lower Lake. Within the county over the first crest of hills north of the big lake is the headwaters of the Eel River. It runs from Lake Pills-bury north, entering the Paci-fic Ocean south of Hum-boldtBay.

Lake County's mountainous location keeps it offthe beaten path of modern travelers, but that was not so in days before the Spanish explorers and those who followed.

Indians came here for seasonal camps, digging roots on the lake shore near what is now known as Tule Lake alongside Highway 20 at the western county line. Obsidian tools fashioned from flows crystalized on the south flanks of Mount Konocti and implements made from other stone deposits circulated widely among California's Indian people who traded with residents of the lake. Archeologists date some camps as 10,000 years old.

The first written record of the lake country comes from journals of Ewing Young, a trapper who crossed the coast range in 1832 on his way north. Almost twenty miles long, the lake is dominated by the volcanic Mount Konocti at the southwestern shore. It towers 3,000 feet above water level. Mexican land grants reached into the county, but it was not until 1852, after statehood, that settlers resolved things with the Indian residents. When the state's first counties were formed this was part of Napa as were the three big land grants. An act of the legislature in 1861 split the counties. Lake fell heir to 1,262 square miles, including the agricultural lands around the lake and mountains, some of them 7,000 feet above sea level, in forests reaching many miles to the

199

north. Resorts developed within a few years and there are now an estimated 180 boat rental locations within the county.

The county lies far enough inland to escape heavy rainfall which soaks more westerly sections of the coast range. Upper Lake records about twenty eight inches of rain a year. Many of the mountains to the north have a combination of rain and snow and supply water to several Sacramento Valley stream systems. The elevation at Clear Lake tempers summer heat, with July averages about seventy four and January forty four degrees for the daily high. This has been California's top pear district for several years. Orchards also produce large quantities of walnuts, while some vineyards are over 100 years old.   Dozens of small farms sell direct at roadside stands offering traditional vegetable crops and specialties such as honey and goat milk.

The current county population is about 50,000 with over 15,200 living in the sprawling city of Clearlake voted into existence in the fall of 1980. Lakeport, the county seat, is the only other incorporated city in the county. There are eighteen small communities.

Highway 20, which links U.S. 101 north of Ukiah with I-5 at Williams, provides the primary transportation route through the county and across the coast range. Highway 29, from Lakeport south, follows the old route to the Napa Valley. California's largest geothermal field harnessed for electrical production is at The Geysers, a former resort on the remote southwest boundary of the county which can be reached only by a county road leading west from U.S. 101.   U.S. Forest Service roads provide the primary access to the forest lands north of Clear Lake including the Indian Valley country.

ATTRACTIONS

There were eighteen islands in the lake before massive reclamation efforts of more recent years. One, **Bloody Island** between Upper Lake and Nice on Highway 20, was the scene of an 1850 massacre of more than 100 Indians in retribution for the killing of two whites, the first settlers in the county. Beyond **Buckingham Park** on the south shore is **Anderson Island,** where the remaining Indians fled until a treaty could be worked out. Now privately owned, this was the summer home of Alden Anderson, a former lieutenant governor of the state.

Obsidian deposits sought by Indian tool makers remain. One is on Battle Rock Road a few miles south of Kelseyville. Local rock shops will provide directions to those public sites currently open for rock hounds. Much of the mineralization comes as a result of the ancient volcanic activity which formed Mount Konocti.

200

The **area information station** is located at the Lakeport off ramp from Highway 29, and honors George Hoberg. With his brothers, Hoberg developed the massive Hobergs Resort which serves up to 1,000 convention delegates at a time. Hoberg lobbied for better highways in California. Information services are offered from April through October on a Monday through Friday schedule.

Vineyards were among the first agricultural ventures in the Lower Lake area, and the **Langtry House,** in Guenoc Valley near Middleton, recalls the heritage. A British actress, Lillie Langtry, bought the place in 1888 and imported a wine-maker from the Bordeaux district of France. Call (707) 987-2129 for tour information and directions.

Clear Lake State Park is north of Kelseyville on Soda Bay Road. There are campsites, boat launching and swimming areas on the lake shore and a wildlife refuge on Soda Bay. An Indian nature trail identifies plants used by the original inhabitants. Telephone 279-4293.

Lake County operates seventeen **parks** at communities all around Clear Lake. Facilities range from simple swimming beaches to elaborate recreation complexes. Call 263-2295 for a park directory. For more information contact the **Lake County Chamber of Commerce,** 875 Lakeport Boulevard, Lakeport CA 95453-5498. Telephone 263-6131.

Clearlake

Developers, spurred on by interest in resort-type properties, created the residential communities of Clearlake Highlands and Clearlake Park. When the area incorporated in 1980, the Federal Census listed 4,983 residents of what it called the Clearlake community. After the state completed a more recent counting of noses, the residents within the boundaries of this new city, among the oak trees, totalled 15,200 residents. Several resorts and private recreation areas are inside the new city, along with a hospital, luxury hotel and a business district.

Cache Creek, the outlet for Clear Lake, is just south of the community and one of the oldest settlements, Lower Lake, keeps its identity near by. Geologists say the original Clear Lake drained to the west into the Russian River but a land slide blocked the way. The waters rose and spilled out to form marshes and then make their way into the Cache Creek waterway. A private dam was built here in 1866 to store water for sale to downstream customers but the resulting flood angered farmers. They took the Clear Lake Water Co. to task first with litigation then with a two-day project in 1868 that removed the log dam.

Attractions

Anderson Marsh State Historic Park was established in 1982 on the former cattle ranch and tule marsh at the south end of the lake. Thirty prehistoric archeological sites are documented on the park. The **Cultural Heritage Council**, Box 3217, Clearlake CA 95422, telephone 944-4421, operates a volunteer field program within the new park. Look for the park entrance just south of the Cache Creek bridge on Highway 53.

The new **Cache Creek Dam**, located away from the lake downstream from the community of Lower Lake, can be seen today. It was built in 1914 and regulates outflow to irrigation customers.

Sulphur Bank Mine was on the peninsula near Clearlake Park. This was an important source of mercury for California's gold miners. Nearby, on the point is **Borax Lake**, where the mineral was discovered in 1856 and actively mined for a few years before operations were transferred to **Little Borax Lake** across the water at Buckingham Point.

For more information contact the **Lake County Chamber of Commerce**, 875 Lakeport Boulevard, Lakeport CA 95453-5498, or call the **Clearlake Chamber of Commerce** at 994-3600.

Accommodation

BEST WESTERN EL GRANDE INN
15135 Lakeshore Drive
Clearlake, CA 95422
Tel.   (707)   994-2000
         (800)   528-1234 USA
AMEX, MasterCard, Visa, Diner's Club and Discover cards are accepted.

The El Grande Inn is reminiscent of the famous colonial hotel Francais in Guadalajara, Mexico. With a tiled roof, high atrial courtyard, flower draped interior balconies and handsome open beam construction, it's easily the region's most beautiful hotel. Sounds intriguing doesn't it? Well, read on.

Just over two years old, this inn has sixty-eight spacious and impeccably apointed rooms, some with lake views. Twenty-three of the rooms are suites with wet bars and refrigerators, upholding Best Western's penchant for comfort and quality. You can enjoy El Grande's spa-type indoor pool, relax with a sauna, or perhaps soak in the outdoor jacuzzi. For meals, the inns La Granda Restaurant serves a complete cuisine to satisfy the most discriminating palate. The lounge showcases live entertainment on weekends and dancing in the court yard.

For banquets, the inn is equiped with a downstairs facility capable of accommodating more than 150 people. Upstairs is a forty-person conference room with a tele-conference feature. Nearby you'll find golfing, fishing in Clear Lake, boating, wine tasting and more. Whew! This is some place. For any event, You'll find Best Western El Grande Inn very accomodating.

THE COVE RESORT MOTEL, 2812 Lakeshore Boulevard, Lakeport, California. Clean room, friendly proprietors, television, and a magnificent view of Clear Lake.

Cobb Mountain

Bed & Breakfast

BROOKHILL INN, 17655 Highway 175, Cobb Mountain, California. Tucked away against Cobb Mountain, this four-bedroom hide-away spot not too far from The Napa Valley is surrounded by forest and wildlife; guests may enjoy hiking nearby Boggs Mountain State Forest trails.

Kelseyville

Restaurant

ANNE'S COFFEE SHOP, 3990 Main Street, Kelseyville, California. You might call Anne's Coffee shop a throb in the heartbeat of Kelseyville. Come for news, breakfast, or lunch, and the unforgettable homemade pies.

Wine

KONOCTI WINERY
Highway 29 and Thomas Drive
Kelseyville, CA 95451
Tel. (707) 279-8861
Hrs: Mon. - Sat   10:00 a.m. - 5:00 p.m.
          Sunday   11:00 a.m. - 5:00 p.m.
Mastercard and Visa are accepted.

Benevolent Mount Konocti towers above Clear Lake and the surrounding landscape. Ten thousand years ago, Konocti erupted with fury, sending smoke and ash miles into the air. Now slumbering, it is after this mountain that Konocti Winery is named. Founded in 1974 by a group of small vineyard owners, the winery (pronounced Ka-nock-tie) has been making award winning wines for nearly a decade.

As are all of Lake County's wineries, Konocti Winery is fairly young compared to many of these in the Napa and Sonoma valleys. The reason has to do with the region's past. Recognized more than a century ago as an excellent grape growing area, Lake County saw it's first few vines planted in the 1870's. Thirty years later there were 5,000 acres in production. The wines made from those vineyards consistantly garnered top honors at prestigious international competitions and Lake County eventually became known as one of the finest wine producing regions in the world. Then came Prohibition and the county's thirty-six wineries were abandoned and the vineyards where uprooted. In the 1960's growers began to restore Lake County's prominence by replanting vineyards with premium wine grapes.

The owners of Konocti Winery decided to concentrate on growing grape varieties especially well suited to the unique climate and soils of the area. Sauvignon Blanc, Cabernet Sauvignon, White Riesling, Zinfandel, Cabernet Franc and recently, Chenin Blanc, Merlot and Chardonnay are among the varieties grown. Konocti wines have taken top awards at such national competitions as the Orange County Fair, the Los Angeles County Fair, the San Diego National Wine Competition and the Farmer's Fair of Riverside.

At Konocti Winery you will be able to linger over these fine wines in a beautiful redwood tasting room, which also features a selection of quality wine related gifts and picnic foods. Visitors are invited to sit back and relax in the walnut orchard surrounding the tasting room. A variety of events including live music occasionally during the summer and an annual Harvest Festival the second weekend in October are open to the public free of charge.

Lakeport

The entire lake, and its surrounding mountains, can be seen from this town, started in 1861 when William Forbes donated forty acres of his ranch on which to build a county seat. For a while they called it Forbestown before adopting the name Lakeport. Some 5,200 people live here on tree-lined streets. Originally this community supported the largest Bartlett pear acreage in California and until the 1920s most of the pear crop was picked, sulfur-treated and sun dried. Today, many adults have chosen Lakeport as a retirement home, swelling the population by fifty percent in less than ten years.

Private education had such a strong tradition when the community began that it was not until 1901 that Clear Lake Union High School district formed. It rented the Lakeport Academy buildings on Hartley Street which burned in 1928. The courthouse, completed in 1871, remains in use as the county museum. Packing houses testify to the the continuing importance of the fruit and nut production in the county.

Attractions

Lake County Museum, on Main Street between Second and Third streets, has a reference library used by researchers and exhibit rooms showing several Indian artifacts and information on early farm life in the county. Open Wednesday through Sunday from May through September, and Wednesday through Saturday the rest of the year, from 10:00 a.m. to 4:00 p.m. Telephone 263-4555.

For more information contact the **Lakeport Chamber of Commerce**, 875 Lakeport Boulevard, Lakeport CA 95453-5498. Telephone 263-5092.

Gift

THE GOLDEN ACORN
185 Main Street
Lakeport, CA 95453
Tel.   (707) 263-5454
Hrs: Mon. - Fri.   10:00 a.m. - 5:30 p.m.
       Saturday   10:00 a.m. - 3:00 p.m.
Closed Sundays. Visa and Mastercard are accepted.

Here is a place beautiful enough to produce envy among the vast majority of Northern Califorma gift shop proprietors.   Owned and operated by Barbara Carter, The Golden Acorn has been in business since 1975. Barbara possesses a degree in art and combines this knowledge with good taste and experience to provide an emporium full of fine gifts.

Variety is a key to the popularity of The Golden Acorn.   The shop features a range of items from inexpensive ceramic potpourri warmers to limited edition porcelain collectables by the likes of Royal Irish Dresden and Delft.   Here too, you will find Gorham's famous porcelain dolls and figurines, as well as the porcelain animals of Artesania Rin Conda, a superb studio owned by two Uraguayan brothers.   Not to be passed by are the Marui company's exquisite porcelain birds of prey (available at remarkabley competitive prices.)

The Golden Acorn has clocks by Benchmark and New Haven, goldware by Valerio and crystal by Atlantis.   Other names with which you might be familiar include Hummel, Fenton and Harvey Knox.   Barbara carries a fine selection of gift and greeting cards, art prints, tableware and items for the bath.   There is a gorgeous enclave with many and varied brands of china, silverware, glassware, towels, soaps and even brass bathroom fixtures.

Be sure to take plenty of time to browse through this delightful "Best Choice" of Northern California.

Restaurant

ANTHONY'S
2509 Lakeshore Boulevard
Lakeport, CA 95453
Tel. (707) 263-4905
Hrs: Lunch Thu. - Tue.   11:30 a.m. - 2:30 p.m.
      Dinner Thu. - Tue.   5:00 p.m. - 10:00 p.m.
Closed Wednesdays
All major credit cards accepted.

    Anthony's, an intimate dinner house specializing in Italian cooking and American entrees, is located in a lovely natural setting by Clear Lake. All the foods are created with a distinctive flair in an elegant atmosphere of red carpet, black velvet drapes, white lace tablecloths and hand blown oil lamps.

    The wonderful ambiance is only the tip of the iceberg at Anthony's. The menu features such dishes as veal Scalloppini, a meat ball platter, egg plant Parmigiana, mini Filet Mignon, prime rib every night and lobster, brace of quail and Poor Man Surf and Turf. Anthony's also showcases over seventy-five pasta dinners! The seafood is is truly a rapture of the deep with frog legs included in the listing. To top it all off, the chef has over twelve years of experience and makes everything from scratch, using only the freshest ingredients.

    Anthony's is the type of restaurant that attracts diners from near and far away. Bring yourself or the whole family and enjoy an unforgettable gourmet experience.

Sport

    GUIDED BASS FISHING TRIPS BY RON SNEED, 825 Jerry Drive, Lakeport, California. By appointment all year with successful tournament angler. Clear Lake is one of the best largemouth bass lakes in the nation.

    LEE'S SPORTING GOODS, 380 Lakeport Boulevard, Lakeport, California. Hunting, fishing, camping equipment, sportswear, archery supplies, trophies.

Lower Lake

Wine

STUERMER WINERY/ARCADIA
P. O. Box 950
Highway 29
Lower Lake, CA 95457
Tel. (707) 994-4069
Hrs:　　　Winter　　　Thu. - Sun.　　　10:00 a.m. - 5:00 p.m.
　　　　　　Summer　　　Mon. - Sun.　　　10:00 a.m. - 5:00 p.m.
Visa and MasterCard are accepted.

"You are invited to visit the winery and taste our award-winning wines. Someone is always available to talk with you and show you the facility. We welcome you!" say the family partners of Stuermer Winery.

Located just off Highway 29 in the rolling hills south of historic Lower Lake, tours and tasting are offered at the winery tasting room and a picnic area is available. Stuermer Winery has gained international recognition for its premium Cabernet Sauvignon and Sauvignon Blanc table wines. The finest grapes are selected exclusively from Lake County Vineyards and hand picked to ensure maximum quality.

Clear Lake, the largest natural lake within California and a popular recreational retreat is located just three miles north of the winery. A scenic drive from the Bay Area or Sacramento, Stuermer Winery offers a pleasant diversion from the workaday world. Stop in, tour the winery, and enjoy a leisurely picnic lunch accompanied by a bottle of your wine tasting favorite!

Middletown

Wine

GUENOC WINERY, 21000 Butts Canyon Road, Middletown, California. This winery sits in a valley once owned by famous actress Lillie Langtry amid 270-acre Guenoc Vineyards. Wines include Chenin blanc, Chardonnay and more.

Nice

Game

KABATIN INDIAN BINGO
1545 Highway 20
Nice, CA 95453
Tel. (707) 275-0344

B-Seven..I-Twenty-eight...N-Three...G-Twelve...O-One. As each of the numbers were called your hands were moving deftly across the board placing a marker here and a marker there. Then, with a rush of adrenaline, you notice five squares in a row are marked on your board! You inhale sharply and your hands are shaking slightly as you yell out, "Bingo!"

Scenes like this are typical at Kabatin Indian Bingo, where there's big money to be won. A single game can be worth as much as $25,000. The parlor, if you can call a 28,000 square foot building a parlor, seats 1,300 people. Although quieter, it's like a Las Vegas casino, with the thrill and anticipation hanging thickly in the air. There's no limit on the winnings you can take away. Along with the games, you'll find a wonderful little gift shop and The Bingo Basket snack bar, where there's everything from full dinners to light snacks.

There is always a security staff on duty and the parking lot is both paved and well lighted. The parlor is a project of the Robinson Rancheria Pomo Indian Tribe, who invite one and all to come in and have some fun. Feel lucky? Well, go ahead and make your day.

LASSEN COUNTY

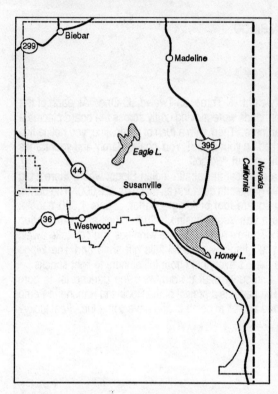

Peter Lassen is an historic figure of some conflicting virtues, but his name rests on a 4,553 square mile county in the northeast portion of the state, and on a major peak and national park which are mostly in neighboring Shasta County. Like the historians' tales of Lassen, the map makers and creators of county boundaries had a hard time getting things together. Lassen, a blacksmith, came to California in 1840 and took up a Spanish grant in what is now Tehama County near Red Bluff. He blazed a northern wagon trail off of the Applegate Trail (see Modoc County) and some reports have him striking off while the wagons fended for themselves among Indians living along the Pit River.

Whatever the facts, Lassen was dominate in history of the lands beyond the upper Sacramento Valley, and his namesake county was organized in 1864 from parts of Plumas and Shasta Counties with Susanville as the county seat. Nevada makes up the eastern border, Modoc County the north, the forty-third meridian the east, and the border of forest rising above Honey Lake on the Nevada side extending westward in a zig-zag fashion the southern boundary. Susanville is the only incorporated community in this county of 21,600 residents.

Issac Roop settled on Honey Lake in 1851, and when Lassen was killed by Indians while at his ranch near Honey Lake in 1859, Roop took up the cause of honoring the Danish pioneer. Roop is remembered for his harsh defiance, first of a California-Nevada border, then of authority from neighboring counties. Winters are harsh here, summers warm. Once out of the basin around Susanville, forest covers the entire county. Cattle dominate the basin agriculture. One major highway, from Mount Shasta on the north, passes through Susanville to reach Reno. U.S. 395 stays east of the mountains as it heads north to Alturas, and south to Reno.

ATTRACTIONS

Nobles Pass, about ten miles northwest of Lassen Peak and now part of the National Park, was an easier route west than the dangerous Lassen Trail down the Pit River. A marker noting the Nobles Pass turn off is on U.S. 395 near Viewland, north of Susanville, and another is in the Susanville Park, Highway 36, west of Susanville, and it follows part of the route, then it jogs north paralleling the alignment of Highway 44.

At the Elysian Valley, six miles south of Susanville on Richmond and Wingfield roads, is the **Lassen Monument** put on Lassens grave in 1862. He built a cabin near here in 1855 which burned in 1896.

Eagle Lake, the second largest natural lake within California, sixteen miles northwest of Susanville on County Road A-1, has several recreation sites for fishing, camping and water sports. Campgrounds are maintained by the U.S. Forest Service and Bureau of Land Management.

About forty recreation sites are exclusively on National Forest Lands in the county. Contact **Lassen National Forest**, 55 South Sacramento Street, Susanville CA 96130 or telephone (916) 257-2151.

Westwood, a small lumber town on Highway 36, was the site of one of California's bitter labor disputes. The Red River Lumber Co. ordered a seventeen and one-half percent wage cut in July, 1938 and the International Woodworkers of America took 600 workers out on strike while another company-backed union wanted to stay on the job. A confrontation with an estimated 2,000 men resulted, the IWA people and their families were driven from town, about half returned a week later. Timber continues to dominate the economy today.

For general information, contact the **Susanville Chamber of Commerce**, 75 North Weatherlow Street, Susanville CA 96130. Telephone (916) 257-4323.

Susanville

Smoke from the lumber and plywood mills greet travelers approaching this town of 6,500 people from the Nevada side. Honey Lake, which rises and falls with the runoff of snow from the mountains, lies in the foreground and several smaller farming communities can be seen in the vast basin to which Isaac Roop came in 1853. He built a store on the Nobles Road, and the town took the name of his only daughter, Susan.

The area was so isolated from the rest of California in the early days that Roop and his neighbors formed their own government by agreement and called it the Territory of Nataqua. When the Plumas County sheriff came up here in 1863 to enforce a boundary he was met by armed settlers who were so insistent that the legislature obliged the next year by creating a county and designating Susanville its county seat.

The town today speaks to its environment. Sierra forests are on the west side of town and mix with the residential district, while the pastures and hay fields are on the other side, all of it connected by a broad main street with busy stores which tell of servicing people who live on ranches a considerable distance from town.

Attractions

Roop's **log cabin** is in the **city park** on Weatherlow Street, where the locals call it "Fort Defiance" in memory of the Sagebrush War which earned them a town and a county. The **William H. Pratt Memorial Museum**, next door, has exhibits tracing those days of defiance. Open daily, 10:00 a.m. to 4:00 p.m. Telephone (916) 257-3850.

For information, contact the **Susanville Chamber of Commerce**, 75 North Weatherlow Street, Susanville CA 96130. Telephone (916) 257-4323.

MARIN COUNTY

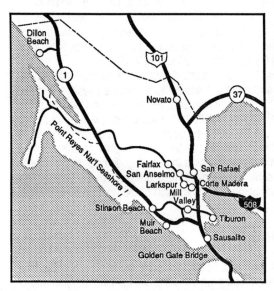

There are two Marins to see in this 523-square mile peninsula which forms the north anchor of the Golden Gate. One is a coast, still primitive in places, peopled by farmers and city folk gone back to the land. The other, on a corridor up U.S. 101 from the bridge, is a series of cities providing services to thousands of residents commuting into San Francisco.

Towering between the two coasts is Mount Tamalpais, whose twin peaks reach 2,600 feet above sea level and create a rain forest on its east slopes, causing redwood forests to march down most canyons on its flanks. Rugged headlands at the Golden Gate are dotted with old coast artillery positions never used, now part of the Golden Gate National Recreation Area. To the north on the coast is Bolinas Bay and its protected lagoon, and the low plateau of Point Reyes which is all a National Seashore.

Drakes Bay and estuary, where some historians say Sir Francis Drake beached his ship for repairs in 1579, provides a study in changing elevations of this coast. It is part of the National Seashore. While historians debate the log book entries on Drake's landing--some say events took place several hundred miles north of here--the Point Reyes area is rich in natural history and National Park Service interpretation points to help understand it.

On the bay side of the county, Angel Island stands guard off Tiburon, its military camps and batteries now a California State Park reachable by ferry boat. The bay and Petaluma River make up the eastern boundary of the county. One of the bay shore features, just south of the Richmond-San Rafael Bridge, is Point San Quentin, location of a state prison of the same name which has drawn national attention. One of its more noteworthy escape cases involved two prisoners who built their own canoe and paddled south into the swift Corte Madera Creek moorages, reportedly waving to a guard tower as they cleared the prison waterfront.

Marin County takes its name from that of a Lacatuit Indian chief. Mission San Rafael Archangel, founded in 1817, began the modern settlement of the county. An 1834 report shows over 1,250 Indians were working at the mission. Buildings on the site today are restorations of the original, located on the campus of Dominican College which was founded in 1890.

The cities are small by urban standards, Novato is the most populous at about 50,00 residents, and most are tucked into sheltered valleys oriented toward the bay or ocean. One community, Sausalito, is curved on the hills under the Golden Gate, a quaint town of 8,500, just a picturesque ferry boat ride away from the city. San Rafael, the county seat since the first state legislature designated Marin and twenty-six other original counties, has a population of about 45,000. Its landmark is the courthouse designed by famed architect Frank Lloyd Wright. Dairying and fishing are about the only original occupations left now, supporting a small fraction of the nearly 230,000 Marin residents.

ATTRACTIONS

Golden Gate Bridge Vista Point, located at the north end of the fifty-year old bridge, provides sweeping views of the orange-painted span and of the former military posts below it.

The **Golden Gate Recreation Area's** headlands offer other views of the rugged entrance to the bay and are open all year. Follow signs to Marin Headlands, Forts Baker, Barry and Cronkite.

Tours of the **Bonita Point Lighthouse** may be taken with reservations. Call 331-1540 for recreation area information.

Mount Tamalpais provides a view of the entire bay area and is accessible by car all the way to its summit. Camping and other facilities are scattered about the state park on the mountain. **Muir Woods National Monument** is on the slopes, best reached by driving less than four miles west from Mill Valley. Hiking trails and a scenic ridge-top road make these places easy to enjoy.

Stinson Beach on the Pacific Ocean just south of Bolinas Bay has over 4,500 feet of sandy beach. It attracts surf fishermen, tide-pool explorers and the curious to the western flank of Mount Tamalpais.

Audubon Canyon Ranch is three miles north of the beach on State Highway One, a preserve for egrets and other birds including Great Blue Herons.

Tomales Bay State Park, four miles north of Inverness, and campsites within **Point Reyes National Seashore** provide bases for exploring a low headland once used for grazing of dairy cattle. The seashore information center and museum is at Point Reyes Station. Call 663-1092 for information.

Marin French Cheese Company is on the coast near the junction of the Novato Road and the Point Reyes-Petaluma Road. Camembert, brie and other cheeses made here. Tours from 10:00 a.m. to 4:00 p.m. For groups over ten, please call 762-6001 for reservations.

San Quentin Prison on Highway 17 at the west approach to the Richmond-San Rafael Bridge, has a shop selling prisoner-made handicraft items. Open 10:00 a.m. to 6:00 p.m. daily.

China Camp is a ramshackle place on the bay, reached off North San Pedro Road from San Rafael. About 10,000 Chinese were said to live here about 100 years ago, and their fishermen netted shrimp from the bay. Fishing regulations tightened in 1910, ending the harvest.

The **Old Dixie School House** at 2255 Las Gallinas Avenue, Marinwood is now a museum. Its career as a school began in 1864. Call 479-8881 to arrange a visit inside the school. An archaeological preserve dedicated to the **Miwok Indians** is adjacent. Artifacts dating back 3,000 years were uncovered in a shell mound. Call 479-5501 to arrange a tour.

Belvedere and Tiburon

Belvedere and its neighbor Tiburon are small towns sharing the point which juts into San Francisco Bay immediately inside the Golden Gate. About 2,300 people live in Belvedere, making it the smallest incorporated municipality in Marin County. It may also be one of the most affluent if a Bank America report is correct in listing the average home value here at $625,000. Tiburon is the ferry landing, and has a population of 7,800.

Both towns occupy the point which makes up the north arm of Richardson Bay, while another exclusive community, Sausalito, is on the south arm. Sausalito began with a sea captain's pilot service to whaling ships entering the bay. Belvedere's history opened with farmer Israel Kashow's wharfs and facilities for sun-drying cod fish brought in from the Bering Sea.

Ownership of the small island, it is now linked to the main peninsula, passed to the Belvedere Land Company in 1890. It developed the lagoon, marketed the exclusive lots, and provided a harbor for yacht clubs, including the San Francisco Yacht Club which stands on the site of the Belvedere Hotel.

Point Tiburon began its career as a ferry terminal in April, 1884. By year's end there was a post office and a saloon. Trains for California's Northcoast came here to a busy rail-yard. Passengers and freight shuttled across the bay on boats and barges. A shipyard specialized in construction of ferry boats operated here before the turn of the century. Residential development swelled the population after World War II, and the town finally incorporated in 1964. The area around the ferry landing is a popular one for tourists.

Attractions

Richardson Bay Audubon Center is located on Greenwood Beach near Tiburon. An eleven acre preserve of ponds and shelter for birds adjoins an 1877 home moved here and restored. Eight hundred acres of bay shore make up a large bird sanctuary open Wednesday through Sunday from 9:00 a.m. to 5:00 p.m.

Old **Saint Hillary's Historic Preserve** is near the center of Tiburon. The Gothic church was consecrated as a Roman Catholic mission in 1888, a **botanical garden** with 210 plant species grows next to it.

On Beach Road in Belvedere is the ship SS China's social saloon, saved for its beauty when the 1886-vintage sidewheeler was scrapped out at a Tiburon yard. Used for a private home until 1978, it is now open to the public, and called the **China Cabin**. Call 435-1853 for information.

Paradise Cove County Park on the north side of Point Tiburon has a public fishing pier, picnic tables and a beach.

Angel Island State Park is a short ferry boat ride away from Tiburon docks. Weekend service year around, daily from May 31 through Labor Day, operating from 10:00 a.m. to 4:00 p.m. Hiking trails crisscross this mountainous island which was a coast artillery strong point with guns trained down the entrance of the Golden Gate.

For additional information, contact the **Tiburon Chamber of Commerce,** Box 463, Tiburon CA 94920. Telephone 435-5633

Corte Madera

Accommodations

CORTE MADERA INN
1815 Redwood Highway
Corte Madera, CA 94925
Tel.   (415) 924-1502
       (800) 622-0797 CA
       (800) 227-4368 USA
AMEX, MasterCard, Visa, Carte Blanche, Diner's Club
and Discover cards are accepted.

The Corte Madera Inn is your "Best Choice" for friendly, comfortable accommodations in Corte Madera. The clerks are out going and very helpful and the decor provides a warm, contemporary ambiance in a spacious lobby and fireplace.
The Inn has 110 guest rooms including two room suites, all beautifully appointed. All rooms have remote control color TV with HBO. There is an Olympic size swimming pool and two spas, as well as an exercise room. Four conference rooms are available with catering provided for up to 200 people. The Peppermill Inn is conveniently located on the grounds for your dining pleasure. There is a small playground for children, in-room babysitting service and children under seventeen stay free. Most rooms face the courtyard and have balconies or porches. There are over a hundred chairs lining the swimming pool area plus a ping-pong table for your enjoyment. Guest laundry facilities are also provided.
The Corte Madera Inn is conveniently located to shops, restaurants and the theater. Be sure to stop and enjoy the luxury and pampering the staff will extend.

217

Restaurant

MARIN JOE'S
1585 Casa Buena Drive
Corte Madera, CA 94925
Tel. (415) 924-1500
Hrs: Mon. - Fri.   11:00 a.m. - 1:00 p.m.
      Saturday   5:00 p.m. - 1:00 a.m.
      Sunday   4:00 p.m. - 12:00 midnight
AMEX is accepted.

The Della Santini family, noted epicureans and acknowledged chefs, have been in association with good foods and fine wines since 1886. They arrived in California at the turn of the century and created Marin Joe's in Marin County in 1954. Marin Joe's, made famous by their outstanding Italian cuisine, currently enjoys a reputation of fine dining in Corte Madera.

Marin Joe's features a menu that is out of this world. Some of the specialities include Spiedini with wild rice, scallops Brochettes, prawn Brochettes, Panzotti, baked lasagne, oysters Doree and many, many more. The Della Santina family knows that good food is inseparable from good wine...one complements the other. With this in mind, they offer over eight types of wine, seventy-seven varieties in all! The ambiance at Marin Joe's is truly delightful, with a piano bar for entertainment.

A restaurant that has been in business for over thirty years is a positive sign of it's continuing excellence; experience molds perfection. Come on in and visit Marin Joe's to enjoy a delicious meal, a quality wine and an unmatched atmosphere. *Buon Appetito!*

SOUTHWEST GRILL, 303 Corte Madera Town Center, Corte Madera, California. Southwest cooking; a blend of Mexican, American, Indian and Spanish cuisine.

STOYANOF'S RESTAURANT
The Village at Corte Madera
1736 Redwood Highway
Corte Madera, CA 94925
Tel.   (415) 924-8981
Hrs: Mon. - Sun. 11:00 a.m. - 10:00 p.m.
AMEX, MasterCard and Visa are accepted.

Greece is a beautiful country with many beaches, outdoor cafes, ancient structures and, of course, fine foods. It is such fun to walk all day, admiring the sites and the beautiful Mediterranean coast. And it's great, after being on the move all day, to settle down and relax while eating a Greek meal in an atmosphere of bliss. This is the kind of enjoyment Stoyanof's Restaurant in Corte Madera offers.

The ambiance of Stoyanof's is extremely inviting with it's lofty ceiling, tall Grecian columns, aqua accents and white walls adorned with vivid color prints of Greece. It really does provide for that bright, airy, Mediterranean mood. There's even an outdoor umbrella patio like so many of the tavernas in Greece. Using only the freshest California ingredients, chefs prepare creative and unusual Greek and California dishes including Mousaka, Calamari, traditional Avgolemono soup and the house speciality, Mesquite-grilled fish.

Greek desserts are not to be forgotten. They have several of the favorites, such as Baklava and fresh fruit tarts. Authentic Greek restaurants are experiences not to be missed. Come to Stoyanof's and let them transport you to Greece, a magical land full of exquisite foods. *Yassu Filos!*

Fairfax

Restaurant

DEER PARK VILLA
367 Bolinas Road
Fairfax, CA 94930
Tel. (415) 456-8084
Hrs: Wed. - Sat. Dinner   5:30 p.m. - 10:00 p.m.
      Sunday   4:00 p.m. - 10:00 p.m.
MasterCard, Visa and AMEX are accepted.

Few places can boast the combination of qualities that make a restaurant incomparable as can Deer Park Villa. Steeped in history, family tradition and surrounded by lush beauty, this "Best Choice" offers genuine hospitality and fabulous fare as well.

The Deer Park Villa was remodeled in 1922 from a hunting lodge and much of the original structure remains, creating a rather unique atmosphere. The menu features a variety of meals including pasta, veal, steak, chicken and prawns. Succulent prime rib and broiled swordfish are two of the evening specials that are sure to please. There are several a la carte items to choose from, all served with an appetizer, vegetable or pasta of the day. The portions are abundant, so bring a hearty appetite. To complement your meal, a fine selection of wines is available.

Besides the exceptional dining, Deer Park Villa has a comfortable cocktail lounge which opens onto a redwood deck, available to private parties and outdoor dining. Catering services are also available. For any occasion, Deer Park Villa remains the foundation for celebration and fine dining.

PUCCI'S RISTORANTE ITALIANO, 35 Broadway, Fairfax, Califronia. Superb Italian cuisine.

Larkspur

Accommodations

LARK CREEK INN
234 Magnolia Avenue
Larkspur, CA 94939
Tel. (415) 924-7766
Hrs: Lunch   Tue. - Sat.   11:30 a.m. - 2:30 p.m.
               Sunday   11:00 a.m. - 2:30 p.m.
      Dinner   Tue. - Thu.   5:30 p.m. - 9:30 p.m.
               Fri. - Sat.   5:30 p.m. -10:30 p.m.
               Sunday   5:30 p.m. - 9:30 p.m.
All major credit cards are accepted.

The Lark Creek Inn, a gracious turn of the century edifice, is a charming reminder of by gone days of elegance and leisure. Originally constructed in 1888 as a family residence, the house was brought to new life and restorated by the Gotti family, owners of San Francisco's famous Earnie's restaurant. Diners quickly found their way to the pleasant yellow and white building, where they could dine under a high glass dome, shaded by towering redwoods by day and lighted by the moon and stars at night. Upstairs, is a small, private banquet room, ideal for wedding rehearsal parties and business meetings. During the warmer months, dining expands to the garden, beside a creek, where umbrellas shade luncheon guests and candles glow at night.
Fresh fish and local produce are featured on the menus, as well as savory house specialities such as roast duckling with strawberry or orange sauce, herbed fettucine with porcini mushrooms, broccoli, smoked chicken, garlic and goat cheese, and Pacific prawns sauteed with Dijon mustard, herbs and mushrooms in cream. The wine list features fine varietals from choice California vineyards. Dining at Lark Creek Inn blends the trend towards fresh, light, regional foods with the tradition of grace and excellence of service.

Restaurant

BLUE ROCK INN
507 Magnolia Avenue
Larkspur, CA 94939
Tel. (415) 924-5707
Hrs: Mon. - Sat.   11:00 a.m. - 11:00 p.m.
       Sunday   4:00 p.m. - 10:00 p.m.

The Blue Rock Inn, now a restaurant serving the finest in Italian cuisine, used to be a two-story Queen Anne style hotel dating back to 1895. It sat on the main route, where stage coaches would roar by with the sound of thundering hooves leaving a trail of dust in their wake. The hotel was quite a looker in those days and remains so today as a restaurant and Historical Landmark.

The manager who is also the chef of Blue Rock Inn, delights his customers with the help of other family members by serving what they feel is the key to superb dining, texture and taste. Offered are over forty delicious entrees, along with three to four daily specials. While the House Speciality is eggplant Parmigiana, you may elect to choose from many traditional favorites, such as veal Scalloppine, chicken Cacciatora, fettucine, tortellini, canneloni or lasagne. All of this, coupled with their delectable wines, desserts, salads and soups, is the reason many walk away unable to finish all of their portions.

Among other delightful features of this majestic landmark are it's Sidewalk Cafe, massive stone fireplace, fresh flowers and linens and the beautiful antique artwork. Overall, from the Old World charm to the food and service that overwhelms, Blue Rock Inn is your stage coach ticket to enjoyment.

Mill Valley

John Reed, holder of the Rancho Corte de Madera del Presidio, built a sawmill here in 1834. It operated for many years, primarily milling the old growth redwood cut from the Widow Creek drainage on the lower slope of Mount Tamalpais. Timbers milled here built the Mexican presidio at Yerba Buena Cove, which later became San Francisco's waterfront. The property went into foreclosure in 1891 after the nearby timbered valley had been logged.

The Tamalpais Land and Water Company bought the town site in 1889, and laid out the town's lots. The company constructed a branch rail line to the North Pacific Coast Railroad's tracks then connecting the Marin towns with the ferry to San Francisco operating from Point Tiburon.

The modern residents of Mill Valley are still tied to the commute. About 12,900 live here, almost all of them in single family homes amongst the second growth redwoods. There is a retail trade district which draws shoppers from a wide area to its interesting specialty stores.

Attractions

In Mill Valley at **Old Mill City Park** are the remains of John Reed's sawmill, the first built in Marin County. Second growth redwood trees now surround the park.

This is the gateway to highway access to Mount Tamalpais with its state parks and **Muir Woods National Monument**. Six point four miles up the **Muir Woods Road** you can see the trestle of the railroad which once took sightseers to the top. Called the crookedest railroad, it had 281 curves between Mill Valley and the 2,608 foot peak.

For more information, contact the **Mill Valley Chamber of Commerce**, 85 Throckmorton Avenue, Mill Valley CA 94941. Telephone 388-9700.

Restaurant

BACI RESTAURANT
247 Shoreline Highway
Mill Valley, CA 94947
Tel. (415) 387-2022
Hrs: Mon. - Fri. 11:30 a.m. - 10:30 p.m.
      Saturday 5:00 p.m. - 11:00 p.m.
      Sunday 5:00 p.m. - 10:00 p.m.
Major credit cards accepted

A restaurant called Baci has people coming back to again and again. One reason is that it's conveniently located on the way to Muir Woods and Stinson Beach, another is the management, which has cultivated a real sensitivity to what people like, and third is the fine Italian food prepared in a wood burning oven.

The high ceilings and spacious dining room, the comfortable chairs and linen covered tables helps create an environment lending itself to a memorable evening. Highlights of the menu are individual sized pizzas with out of the ordinary toppings, home made lasagne and mesquite grilled rabbit. If trying to go light on the calories, you can just forget it when presented with the home made desserts such as white chocolate mousse in berry sauce. Finish off your meal with a a cup of espresso.

Try this Mill Valley restaurant and expect to join the many who go back to Baci time and time again.

THE BUCKEYE
17 Shoreline Highway
Mill Valley, CA 94941
Tel. (415) 332-1292

After four generations in the same family, The Buckeye continues to offer the some of the best in American and German fo o d in the area.

Established in 1937 by the Bush family, today's diners enjoy the same old world comforts and cuisine. Outside the building resembles the high pitch roofed chalets of the Alps. Inside high ceilings, ample windows, candle light and heavy linen on the tables retain that Continental feeling. Featured on the menu are Germanic delicacies such as Wiener Schnitzel, saurbraten, and sometimes duckling and roast goose. Buckeye has a full bar, and serves many imported beers.

For family dining, try the "Best Choice" restaurant run by the same family for more than fifty years.

INDIA PALACE
707 Redwood Hwy.
West side of U. S. 101
Mill Valley, CA 94941
Tel. (415)-388-3350
Hrs: Mon.-Sun.　Lunch　11:00 a.m. - 2:30 p.m.
　　　　　　　　Dinner　5:30 p.m. - 11:00 p.m.

Backed up next to a TraveLodge motel off of U.S. 101, is an unlikely place to find a fine dining establishment of speciality ethnic food. Yet, such is the location of the India Palace where the patron of international tastes will be treated to Indian cuisine prepared by a man whose heritage stems from the land whose meals he serves.

Sarwan Gill, after emigrating to the U.S. at an early age, worked his way towards the dream of owning his restaurant which is realized in the luxuriant decor and exceptional dining of the India Palace. When traveling many people like to seek out the "unknown" spots the locals frequent. This place is a discovery that the local critics found, loved, wrote about, and the Tandoori ovens haven't cooled down since!

If you are cautious about the concept of eating eastern food thinking that plates of curry will burn the roof of your mouth as an uninitiated take the time to stop here and assuage your consternation. If you are familiar with this fare then you know what a treat it can be. Samosas, for instance, are vegetable stuffed pastries which are deep-fired to a light golden brown. They are grease free and come with two sauces, one a blend of mint and the other a combination of tomatoes, tamarind and cayenne; both highlight the spicy pastries nicely. The house specialities are the Tandoori dishes. These meat dishes (lamb and chicken mostly) are marinated a full 24 hours in garlic, yogurt, oil and spices and then slow-cooked in a mesquite-burning oven called a tandoor.

Now that your interest is primed, follow the highway to the friendly community of Mill Valley and find what the locals know about the best Indian dining this side of the Pacific at the Indian Palace.

LE CAMEMBERT, 200 Shoreline Highway, Mill Valley, California. Excellent French-Normandy cuisine.

Muir Beach

Restaurant

THE PELICAN INN
The Pelican Inn
Muir Beach, CA 94965
Tel. (415) 383-6000

Hrs:	Bar		Tue. - Sun.	11:00 a.m. - 11:00 p.m.
	Pub	Lunch	Tue. - Sat.	11:30 a.m. - 3:00 p.m.
		Dinner		6:00 p.m. - 9:00 p.m.
	Pub	Brunch	Sunday	11:30 a.m. - 3:00 p.m.
		Dinner	Sat. - Sun.	5:30 p.m. - 9:30 p.m.

Mastercard and Visa are accepted.

A romantic getaway surrounded by hills and beach, a country inn, reminiscent of sixteenth century England, eagerly awaits your visit. Only twenty minutes from the Golden Gate Bridge, the charming Pelican Inn lies amidst pines and alders between the ocean and the redwoods of Golden Gate National Recreational Area. The Pelican swings it's doors wide for you to come and enjoy it's Tudor bar, country cuisine, peaceful overnight lodging, or for a weekend of elegant feasting and relaxation.

In the tradition of English Country Inns, fulfilling dishes are served for lunch and dinner, as well as afternoon snacks. Enjoy cottage pie, fresh salads, prime rib, rack of lamb and homemade desserts, served before the fireplace or outside on the patio. The sixteenth century panelled bar is well stocked with frothy brews, wines, sherries, ports and is set in the surroundings of brass, low beams, dart boards and pleasant company. This bed and breakfast features snug rooms and private baths accentuated with English antiques, a heavily draped canopy for the bed and a Turkish rug on the floor.

On special occasions, the wenches, minstrels, wine, mead and good food, all come together for a feast that King Henry VIII would have envied. The Pelican Inn provides for a very unique experience, one that will be remembered in the years to come. For fine cuisine, excellent lodging, or a few darts, stop by this inn where English hospitality comes home.

Novato

For most of its history, Novato was the trading center for the fruit and dairy farmers who lived in the uplands of Marin County. In 1857, Joseph Bryant Sweetster and Francis Delong, two founders of the town, claimed they operated the largest apple orchard in the world. There is no record of anyone testing the claim.

Today, swollen with subdivisions for commuters, Novato has over 50,000 residents attracted by its convenient cross-roads location just twenty-eight miles north of San Francisco, and less distance than that to several East Bay locations accessible by the Black Point route around San Pablo Bay. By comparison, the 1940 population was 700.

Portions of five Spanish ranchos are now part of the city. The first developers came in 1888, but the town grew very slowly. Hamilton Air Base, a major field built by the army during World War II, sparked growth. Novato began its expansion after the commuter centers nearer to San Francisco had filled. It wasn't until January, 1960, that Novato actually incorporated as a city.

Attractions

Marin Municipal Water District lakes and lands lie to the west of town, part of 20,000 acres of protected lands with foot, horse and bike paths. For information call 924-4600.

Stafford Lake County Park is three miles from downtown on Novato Boulevard. Fishing, a nature trail and play areas are available

Marin County

Marin Museum of the American Indian, 2200 Novato Boulevard, has outdoor exhibits and a gallery. Open Tuesday through Saturday from 10:00 a.m. to 4:00 p.m., Sundays 12:00 noon to 4:00 p.m. Group tours and special programs available by reservation, call 897-4064.

Novato's local History Museum is at 815 DeLong Avenue in the restored home of the first postmaster, Henry F. Jones. Exhibits include history of Hamilton Field (the former air force base). Open Tuesday and Saturday from 10:00 a.m. to 4:00 p.m. For group appointments at other times call 897-4320.

For more information, contact the Novato Chamber of Commerce, 809 DeLong Avenue, Novato, CA 94948. Telephone 897-1164.

Coffee

BELLA COFFEA
165 San Marin Drive
Novato, CA 94947
Tel. (415) 897-0168
Hrs: Mon. - Fri.   9:00 a.m. - 7:00 p.m.
      Saturday   10:00 a.m. - 6:00 p.m.
      Sunday   12:00 noon - 5:00 p.m.

It is virtually impossible to walk by the Bella Coffea without having the delectable aromas that waft through the air challenge your senses and cause your mouth to water. This delightful shop, owned and managed by Nancy Boccaleoni and Leesa Galassi, had its' origins in their first endeavor of wholesaling coffees to Bay Area restaurants, at trade shows, and through publications such as *Bon Appetite*.
Bella Coffea is stocked with Nancy and Leesa's own coffee extracts that are manufactured for them in Europe.   The coffee beans are roasted, tumbled and air-dried on a screen and then are spilled into the bins while still warm enough to absorb the custom-made extracts. Try the Irish creme liqueur, chocolate mousse, hazelnut or chestnut. Simply divine.
The decaffeinated coffees are made by using the new oil process, as well as the standard method of using water or chemicals to distill the essence of the bean. The oil process results in a coffee that's more flavorful, less expensive and with a lower caffeine level and no chemical content. Currently there are more than forty varieties of coffee sold here.
Coffee is not the only reason so many Bay Area residents flock to the Bella Coffea--the locals will tell you its' because they feel so comfortable in the

226

surroundings--the coffee pot is always on. More in the mood for a cuppa tea???it's here in myriad blends, from chamomile and spiced peach to Earl Grey. Browse the shop and you'll find an interesting array of gift items that are tastefully chosen and displayed. The full line of Krup coffee brewing systems is available.

To go with your cup of coffee or tea try the freshly-baked pastries and confections that are made daily. There is also a full espresso bar with hot or iced coffees. The truffles, turtles, old-fashioned honeycomb and diabetic candy can be purchased by the piece or by the pound.

Do ask, when you stop in, what new, adventurous coffee flavor has been concocted by Nancy and Leesa. You can be sure it will be a "Best Choice."

Gift

BARELEE HARETAGE
1431A Grant Ave.
Novato, CA 94947
Tel. (415) 892-1005
Hrs: Mon.-Sat. 10:30 a.m.-5:00 p.m.

As you enter through the door with the "Welcome Friends" sign on it, you'll feel as if you've stepped into a wondrous treasure chest and became part of the collection. The walls, floors, windows, and ceiling are simply resting places for one-of-a-kind handcrafted items. Amidst the delightful array of unusual gifts is owner Marlee Van Cott, whose effervescent personality seems to animate the entire shop.

For years Marlee dreamed of owning her own store, and worked hard toward that goal. As an excellent seamstress with an eye for design, she always received compliments when she wore her own designs. Eventually, she and her friend Magmar initiated their own small business by having home fashion shows twice a year. Their unique clothing, sewn only with antique fabric, trim, and lace was featured. The wooden items that Marlee's sons (Darren, Keven, and Garret) handcrafted were also shown. After three years, the shows were such a success that Marlee opened a shop. In addition to displaying her own creations, she also displays those of her sons, Magmar, and other artists.

There is a cinnamon scent in the shop that pervades the air. As you enjoy the pleasant aroma, be sure to take your time browsing through the shop and notice the wooden, ceramic,and fabric animals, each with their own distinct personalities. You'll also notice the wall decorations, exquisite old quilts, items made of fine lace, and grand, old furnishings to enhance every room in the house. Explore the shelves and cabinets for intricate ornaments and trinkets. Once

227

you've found that special something, you will delight in the great care Marlee takes to wrap your purchase. She loves to wrap the purchases, and is known for her wonderful bag wraps.

It isn't easy leaving the enchanting world of Barelee Haretage. When you do, however, you will feel richer for having visited Marlee and her shop. The things you buy for yourself and your friends will be treasured possessions that will be appreciated for a long time.

(See special invitation in Appendix.)

Restaurants

THE HILLTOP CAFE, 850 Lamont, Novato, California. Specialize in fresh seafood. Full bar service; happy hour.

THE FILLING STATION
1769 Grant Avenue
Novato, CA 94947
Tel. (415) 897-3800
Hrs: Mon.-Thu.   11:00 a.m.- 9:00 p.m.
       Fri.-Sat.   11:00 a.m.-10:00 p.m.
       Sunday   8:00 a.m.- 9:00 p.m.
Visa, Mastercard, and AMEX are accepted.

The Filling Station, not a place for cars but a restaurant built around the love of cars.

Vintage autos have been a passion for Filling Station owner Steven Keeler since he was given his first car by the sisters at Mercy High School in Burlingame, CA when he was twelve. Steven's wife, Judith, shares his and his son's love for cars and together they have created a fine restaurant around a display of collector parts and cars. Currently a 1912 Model "T" Speedster is in the spotlight.

But, after all, a restaurant is about food, and in this department the Keelers continue their tradition of craftsmanship and attention to detail, which was fostered during the years they owned "Diller's Delicatessens" in Marin and San Francisco. The food is traditional California cuisine, barbecued ribs, chicken, steaks, prime rib, fresh fish, pasta, hamburgers, salads and sandwiches together with a brunch which is served daily until 4:00 p.m., this includes a vast variety of egg dishes. Steven's motto is "You will never leave hungry." All food is made with fresh ingredients and attractively served, but best of all, it tastes great!

At the Filling Station, the decor is for car buffs, but the food is definitely for everyone.

(See special invitation in the Appendix)

SANTE FE MARY'S SOUTHWEST GRILL
1200 Grant Avenue
Novato, CA 94947
Tel. (415) 898-2234
Hrs: Mon.-Fri.   11:00 a.m.- 1:30 p.m.
         Fri.-Sat.   5:00 p.m.-10:30 p.m.
         Sun.-Thu.   5:00 p.m.-10:00 p.m.
Visa, Mastercard, and AMEX are accepted.

Arizona sand paintings, handmade puppets, oil paintings, and ancient artifacts all serve to infuse Sante Fe Mary's Southwest Grill with the flavor and spirit of our Arizona forefathers.

Owners Tim and Sandra Nelson created their establishment as a spiritual bridge with Arizona's past. They feature authentic traditional Southwest creations to please the palate as well as a sense of adventure. Sante Fe chicken, Neuvo Fry bread, Fajitas, and Texas Hash are a small sample of the excellent lunch and dinner specialties. A full bar serves all the favorite libations. All the food is homemade from scratch including some really wicked chocolate desserts - Millionaire Chocolate Almond Cake with both fudge and strawberry toppings.

Sante Fe Mary could be called the patron saint of abundance and good times, and at her namesake restaurant in Novato her sense of fun is fully expressed.

(See special invitation in the Appendix)

T. J. CORCORAN'S
1535 S Novato Blvd.
Novato, CA 94947
Tel. (415) 892-3474

Hrs:	Lunch	Mon.-Fri.	11:00 a.m. - 2:00 p.m.
	Dinner	Mon.-Sat.	5:30 p.m. -10:00 p.m.
	Dinner	Sunday	5:00 p.m. - 9:00 p.m.
	Happy hr	Mon. -Fri.	5:00 p.m. - 7:00 p.m.

Visa, Mastercard, AMEX, Diner's Club and Discover accepted.

Toddy J. Corcoran was a pub owning Irishman from Ennis, County Claire, Ireland. His place was known far and wide as the place to go for fine food, good drink and lively conversation. Toddy so inspired his nephew Mike Nielsen that he and his wife Sandy have modeled their establishment after Uncle Toddy's pub back in the old country.

Once in the door of T. J. Corcoran's, the atmosphere of warmth and comfort quickly encloses and you have entered the special world of uncle Toddy's. Lunch, dinner and the crowd's attire are all distinctly casual. The sandwiches, omelettes, burgers and tostada grandes are good for lunch and prime rib bones smothered in special BBQ sauce or Irish style corned beef and cabbage are sure winners for dinner. However, this place has much more than great food, the lounge-bar at T.J.Corcoran's features live dance music seven nights a week to top tunes of the 50's, 60's, and 70's.

T. J. Corcoran's is definitely more than just another handsome restaurant, it is a fitting memorial to the charm and personality of the Irish spirit and a very special Irishman uncle Toddy J. Corcoran.

This tour offers an ideal mix of hoofing and treading your way around Novato's environs:

WALKING/ DRIVING TOUR OF NOVATO			
am.	Bella Coffee	Best pastries	Nova/Rest
am.	Barelee Heratage	Best gift	Nova/Gift
am.	Am. Indian Museum	Best gallery	Nova/Att
p.m.	Filling Station	Best Am. lunch	Nova/Rest
p.m.	Stafford Lake	Best walk	Nova/Att
While in Novato, try these "Best Choices" for dinner:			
p.m.	Santa Fe Mary's	Best S.W. food	Nova/Rest
p.m.	T. J. Corcoran's	Best meals/casual	Nova/Rest

San Anselmo

Restaurants

BUBBA'S DINER, 566 San Anselmo Avenue, San Anselmo, California. Home cooking at its best.

COMFORTS
337 San Anselmo Avenue
San Anselmo, CA 94960
Tel.   (415) 454-6790
Hrs: Tue. - Sat.   8:00 a.m. - 6:00 p.m.
           Sunday   9:00 a.m. - 3:00 p.m.

Comforts is an appropriate name for this charming restaurant owned by Glenn and Laura Miwa. The Miwa's and their staff provide you with quality gourmet food with emphasis on an ethnic mixture of menu items and a pleasant, relaxing atmosphere.
For breakfast there are coffee cakes, muffins, scones and croissants all freshly baked. For a heartier appetite, French toast made from Brioche, sour cream waffles, eggs with ham or prime rib hash, huevos, omelets or even Portuguese, Polish or Italian sausage to spice up your eggs are available.
Lunch offers a variety of soups, salads, fresh fruit plates, and entrees such as black bean chili, chicken Okasan, eggplant lasagna, Teriyaki prime rib rolls and pasta. Three or four specials for breakfast and lunch that are not on the menu are available daily.
The subtle lighting, fresh daily flowers and the no smoking policy makes Comforts an elegant, relaxing "Best Choice" restaurant.

THE OLD CLAM HOUSE
85 Red Hill Avenue
San Anselmo, CA 94960
Tel. (415) 456-0139 or 456-5816
Hrs: Tue. - Fri.   11:00 a.m. - 3:00 p.m.
                       5:00 p.m. - 10:00 p.m.
       Sat. - Sun.   5:00 p.m. - 10:00 p.m.
       Happy Hour with hors d' ouevres.
       Tue. - Fri.   4:30 p.m. - 7:00 p.m.

    The Old Clam House Restaurant has been a landmark in San Francisco since 1861 and has now opened in San Anselmo with the same great cuisine.
    The Old Clam House features the freshest foods available. Besides having specials which change daily, there are over a dozen seafood entrees to choose from. Some of the specialties of the house include Steamed Cherrystone Clams Bordelaise, Clam House Linguini in either red or white sauce and a variety of veal or beef dishes served with fresh vegetables and pasta of the day. There are omelets, sandwiches and salads for a light meal. Included with your meal is a cup of clam broth and fresh French bread. Meals are delightfully generous and reasonable priced. An extensive wine list has been prepared with considerable thought towards selection, variety and quality to compliment whatever entree you choose. A full service bar is also available.
    The atmosphere of The Old Clam House is relaxed and intimate. Adjacent to the main building is a splendid cocktail lounge with a sliding glass roof to add to the ambience. The pride and care the staff takes with quality, preparation and service will make The Old Clam House a "Best Choice" in your book, too.

RICCARDO'S RISTORANTE
411 San Anselmo Avenue
San Anselmo, CA 94960
Tel. (415) 457-0616
Hrs: Tue. - Thur.   11:30 a.m. - 10:30 p.m.
       Friday   11:30 a.m. - 11:00 p.m.
       Saturday   3:00 p.m. - 11:00 p.m.
       Sunday   3:00 p.m. - 10:30 p.m.

    A slice of old Italy, rattan-wrapped wine bottles hanging from the ceiling, willing smiles on the faces of the people within, and a pervading aroma of fresh-baked Neapolitan style pizza. *Buon appetito!* You're at Riccardo's.
    Pizza's not quite what you had in mind for the evening? How about linguini with clams or mussels and fresh-grated Parmesan, or a plate of

tortellini in a smoothly accented white sauce? Complement your choice with Valley of the Moon wines, by the glass or by the bottle. The wine board does change weekly.

Chef Richard Crispi, and his assistant chef, Carlos Alverado serve only the very best. Enjoy your evening, and if the face across the room seems familiar--look a little closer as it could be Huey Lewis, Joe Montana, Dwight Clark, Richard Udland of Star Wars fame, or Dr. Dean Edell. They know the taste of good Neapolitan cooking when they eat it...and they do...often.

WINKLER'S RESTAURANT, 198 Sir Francis Drake Boulevard, San Anselmo, California. Fine continental cuisine.

San Rafael

In a county full of bedroom communities, San Rafael is an exception--it supplies perhaps two-times as many jobs as any other community in Marin County. With its satellite communities of Fairfax, San Anselmo, Ross, Kentfield, Greenbrae, Santa Venetia and Marinwood, San Rafael occupies scenic hills covered with oaks and redwood trees, and is steeped in history.

Mission-building priests set up shop here in 1817, and their Mission San Rafael Archangel is today part of the campus of Dominican College of San Rafael. Marin County's courthouse was in the downtown until 1969 when the new Marin Civic Center opened over the hill to the north near Santa Venetia. It's hill-hugging design by Frank Lloyd Wright make the new county offices a stopping point for many tourists.

About 45,000 people live within the city limits, and growth is constrained by the smaller communities nearby. Sir Francis Drake Boulevard takes you west to San Anselmo, the first town to incorporate. An electric railroad linking the Ross Valley with San Francisco ferry boats made this one of Marin's first commute towns--in 1902. Further west on the boulevard is Fairfax, named after Lord Charles Snowden Fairfax, who picked the place for his country estate after tiring of adventure in gold rush California's mines.

Ross, another commuter town, took its name from James Ross who came to California for gold, then made more money as a wine merchant and timber man. Redwood trees were clear-cut before the turn of the century, many have grown back.

Attractions

Point Saint Pedro, six miles east of San Rafael, was the scene of a triple killing during the 1846 Bear Flag revolt. While Captain John Fremont held the Mission San Rafael, his chief scout, Kit Carson, shot down three Spaniards who came ashore on the point.

China Camp State Park and **McNears Beach County Park** are just to the north. **Peacock Gap Golf and Country Club** abuts the parks.

Marin Wildlife Center, 76 Albert Park Lane, is a wild animal refuge which cares for injured animals native to Marin County. The center is open to the public Tuesday through Saturday from 10:00 a.m. to 4:00 p.m.

The famed **Guide Dogs for the Blind** have their headquarters at 350 Los Ranchitos. Tours can be arranged, the public is welcome at monthly graduation ceremonies when blind persons and their dogs demonstrate skills. Call 479-4000 for information.

A replica of the **Mission San Rafael Archangel** is at 1104 Fifth Avenue. It is open daily from 11:00 a.m. to 4:00 p.m.

Marin County **Historical Society Museum** is in Boyd Park, 1125 B Street. Lots of pictures of Marin's recent past. Open Wednesday through Sunday, 1:00 p.m. to 4:00 p.m.

John F. McCarthy Bridge, which everyone calls the Richmond-San Rafael Bridge, provides a sweeping view of the north arm of San Francisco Bay and of the famed San Quentin Prison at the west approach to the bridge. This is a toll span, now thirty years old, designed with two decks to hold traffic.

For more information, contact the **San Rafael Chamber of Commerce**, 1030 B Street. Telephone 454-4163

Accommodations

CLARION HOTEL MARIN
1010 Northgate Drive
San Rafael, CA 94903
Tel. (415) 479-8800

"One-of-a-kind" is an appropriate description of the Clarion Hotel Marin, nestled in the oak-studded rolling hills of San Rafael, and conveniently located off Highway 101 between the Golden Gate Bridge and the Napa-Sonoma wine country.

Visitors will experience luxury, hospitality, and impeccable services, which include airporter and limousine service, car rental facilities, same-day valet service, a beauty shop, a gift shop, and bellman service. For the fitness-conscious visitor, there is a multi-purpose work-out room. Just outside is a large, heated swimming pool and jacuzzi set in the serenity of the beautifully-landscaped courtyard.

Directly off the courtyard is Andaron's Cafe, a splendid restaurant featuring California cuisine. the food is sumptuous, the wine is the best from California wine makers, and the emphasis is on unexcelled service. Before or after dinner, unwind and relax in Andaron's Lounge. Along with Happy Hour and complimentary hors d'oeuvres, there is nightly music, dancing, and popular entertainment. Offering flexible conference and banquet facilities, the Clarion is the perfect setting for successful events for groups up to 400.

For the busy traveling executive and vacationer with especially discerning taste, the Clarion Hotel offers Executive Registry, exclusive to the hotel's fourth floor. The accommodations are deluxe, and personal concierge service is available to secure needed items. The Executive Registry includes access to the lounge with complimentary hors d'oeuvres and premium beverages, plus a complimentary continental breakfast and newspaper.For unsurpassed service and hospitality, stay at the Clarion Hotel Marin.

(See special invitation in Appendix.)

PANAMA HOTEL/RESTAURANT AND INN
4 Bayview Street
San Rafael, CA 94901
Tel. (415) 457-3993

This is the third time around for a venerable fixture in San Rafael which now sports an eclectic decor and menu. Opened as a boarding house and restaurant in 1918, the Panama had a life in the mid-1970s as a funky bed and breakfast, and now is run by two men who operated a bistro in England before taking over here.

Daniel Miller and Paul Morrison offer the overnight guest lodgings in rooms which may have old-fashioned claw-foot bathtubs, or private decks with a view. Reasonable rates include maid service and continental breakfast. Some rooms include kitchenettes. For the restaurant guest their is a choice between eating in a pillared dining room with whirling ceiling fans, or --if the weather is balmy--outdoors in a patio surrounded by lush tropical plants.

Some of the entrees on the menu are beyond diversity. Buffalo chicken wings with blue cheese dip is listed. Panama wontons have a place on this menu, sometimes stuffed with Italian or Mexican fillings instead of the traditional

235

Chinese wonton mix. This is your "Best Choice" for a unique dining or overnight experience.

> **VILLA INN**
> 1600 Lincoln Avenue
> San Rafael, CA 94901
> Tel. (415) 456-4975 or 1-800-453-4511
> Major credit cards are accepted.

The Villa Inn has gone through a major renovation program to better accommodate its overnight guests. The Cherbero family, your innkeepers, come from the Basque tradition of taking pride in the services they offer.

The Villa is affiliated with Friendship Inns and carries a AAA listing. Prices range from $50 to $70 a night(at the time of this publication). Rooms have individually-controlled heating and air conditioning, cable television, direct-dial phones, and more. Outside, there is a solar-heated swimming pool, and a spa as well as an adjacent restaurant and lounge open for breakfast lunch and dinner.

You'll find cleanliness and comfort here, plus the personal greeting of Romain and Normal Cherbero and their son Roland, each ready to show they take pleasure in serving you at their newly renovated Villa Inn.

Bakery

IL FORNAIO, 901 A Street, San Rafael, California. The freshest of morning pastries, homemade pasta and soups. A traveler's delight!

Bed and Breakfast

BED AND BREAKFAST EXCHANGE OF MARIN, 38 Harcourt, San Rafael, California. A reservation service, this exchange can find the right accommodations for you throughout Marin County.

Books

THE COTTAGE BOOKSHOP, 1225 Fourth Street, San Rafael, California. Serving their customers for over thirty years. If you can't find it...ask...they'll find it.

MANDRAKE BOOKSHOP, 910 Lincoln Avenue, San Rafael, California. Over 100,000 books in stock; extra emphasis on mystery books.

Costumes

FANTASY CLOTHING, 835 Fourth Street, San Rafael, California. One thousand costumes to choose from...costumes for any occasion...rent for the night or purchase to keep, or have it custom designed!

Entertainment

NEW GEORGE'S, 842 Fourth Street, San Rafael, California. Finest in local and national touring acts. Emphasize rock 'n roll, rhythm and blues and occasional blues and acoustical shows. Comedy night every Tuesday.

Restaurants

CAFE PRANZO, 706 3rd Street, San Rafael, California. Distinctive and varied cuisine from up-scale Italian to California. Casual yet elegant.

CAFE TANGO
1230 4th Street
San Rafael, CA 94901
Tel. (415) 459-2721
Hrs: Mon. - Sun. 11:00 a.m. - 11:00 p.m.
Visa and MasterCard are accepted.

A tradition of Spain, "tapas" cooking, lives on in this North Bay community at the Cafe Tango, along with musicians and dancers performing the tango and flamenco. The wine bar features premium vintage from around the world.

Tapas, explain the cafe's owners, Ann Walker and Christina Franjetic, are small dishes, a sampler. Several different tapas make up the meal. Folklore has it that a piece of bread is atop each tapas to "keep the spirit of the food" from fleeing before the diner tastes it. Menu selection changes here, depending on availability of ingredients. Chef Antonio Buendia, originally from Barcelona, creates the tapas, often listing the day's selections on a blackboard. Desserts are in the Spanish style, too. Larry Walker, wine critic for the San Francisco Chronicle and Ann Walker's husband, selects the wines. Once a month, he also offers classes, helping patrons match particular wines with about eight tapas.

Favorite tapas available daily include tortilla de Española, a potato and onion omelet, and albondigas con salsa de Almendras, which is meatballs in an almond sauce. You'll find delight in sampling the traditional dishes, the fine wines, and in watching the colorful musicians perform.

DANIEL'S
1131 4th Street
San Rafael, CA 94901
Tel. (415) 457-5288
Hrs: Lunch   Mon. - Fri.   11:00 a.m. - 2:30 p.m.
      Dinner   Mon. - Sun.   5:00 p.m. - 10:00 p.m.

Daniels's in San Rafael is your "Best Choice" for excellent French cuisine prepared expertly by owner/chef Claude Collomb. This charming restaurant is handsomely appointed with wainscotting on the walls, marble tables and accented with brass.

Superb food at extremely reasonable price is the forte of Daniel's. Just a sample of the entrees you can choose from: veal medallions Normande with apples and apple brandy sauce, warm calamari and shrimp salad with avocado and heart of palm, baked oysters with lime and beurre blanc, salmon, snapper, sole, rack of lamb with thyme and garlic, the list goes on and on...

Stop by and visit Claude and enjoy the casual, comfortable atmosphere and tremendous food he will personally prepare for you.

DOMINIC'S HARBOR RESTAURANT
507 Francisco Boulevard
San Rafael, CA 94901
Tel. (415) 456-1383
Hrs: Mon. - Fri.   Lunch   11:30 a.m. - 4:30 p.m.
      Sat. - Sun.   Brunch   10:00 a.m. - 3:00 p.m.
      Mon. - Sun.   Dinner   4:30 p.m. - 10:30 p.m.
Holiday Brunch same hours.

Located on the site of an inn started in 1864 by Dominic Murphy, this restaurant overlooking the San Rafael canal is an institution in the Bay Area. It is now presided over by Dominic Pomilia, his wife Gloria and their four children.

Fresh seafood on the menu comes from fishing boats operated by three Pomilia brothers. The menu also includes Italian style chicken, veal and beef dishes, and pasta, of course. There is a large lounge next to the main dining area and both connect to an outdoor terrace used when weather permits. Dominic's is a three time winner of the Gourmet Diner's Club of America silver spoon award, and a place which attracts celebrity guests.

Dominic's can handle banquet groups of up to 600 people, yet offer intimate dining or privacy in its lounge. There's two an a half acres of parking on one side, and the view of the harbor and city lights on the other side of this famous restaurant.

GULF OF SIAM, 1518 Fourth Street, San Rafael, California. Authentic Thai cuisine and ambiance. Order food spicy or mild. Classical Thai dancing Saturday evenings.

E STREET RESTAURANT, 824 E Street, San Rafael, California. A opulently refurbished Victorian, stunning interiors, iconoclastic menu, Tapas bar in the basement. Exciting spot.

LA PETITE AUBERGE
704 Fourth Street
San Rafael, CA 94901
Tel. (415) 456-5808
Hrs: Tue. - Sat.   lunch: 11:30 a.m. - 2:30 p.m.
                       dinner: 5:30 p.m. - 11:00 p.m.
         Sunday & holidays: 4:30 p.m. - 9:30 p.m.
BankAm, MasterCard, AMEX and Diners cards accepted.

La Petite Auberge, a true restaurant *Francais*. Owner/chef Roger Poli, apprenticed at fourteen years of age to learn his craft. The best chefs on the continent undertook his tutelage. The diners at La Petite Auberge are the recipients of this life-long quest.

The ambiance is provincial French, the mood one of relaxed elegance, the service impeccable, the menu offerings superb. For dinner, perhaps breast of chicken, saute sec with artichoke and mushrooms, or, loin of veal Grenadine with wild chanterelles, and the soupe du jour, tossed green salade with French or bleu cheese dressing, or the Pate Maison, or soles quenelle nantua, or tortellini cream sauce will complete the meal. Complement your selection with an appropriate wine and your choice from the pastry tray.

When visiting La Petite Auberge do note the cover to the menu, it was "drawn and presented to my very favorite restaurant," by the famous illustrator Atherton. An indication of the loyalty of the regular *habitues* at La Petite Auberge.

Marin County

LA MEDITERRANEE
857 Fourth Street
San Rafael, CA 94901
Tel. (415) 258-9123
Hrs: Mon. - Thu.   10:00 a.m. - 9:00 p.m.
     Fri. - Sat.   10:00 a.m. - 10:00 p.m.

One good turn deserved another; so three La Mediterranee cafes deserved another. The San Rafael location of these delightful restaurants complements in every respect its three sisters which in no way betray the formula appearance of other larger chain restaurants. Each one is individually overseen by concerned partners in business.

Entering La Mediterranee the guest is transported to the Middle East for a pleasant dining experience where the air is filled with the savory spices and smells of Greek, Lebanese, and Armenian cooking. Ceiling fans and tile tables lend to the atmosphere of casual fine dining. The menu offers a variety of appetizers, soups, salads, combination dinners, desserts and coffees. With the variety of choices it is convenient to visit La Mediterranee for an espresso and a snack, lunch or a complete dinner. Combination dinners are a favorite choice as they provide the widest possible sampling of the tasty treats served here. One rich entree, the Middle East Plate, includes chicken celicia, salad, a sandwich roll filled with cream cheese and tomato, filo wrapped spinach and feta, rice and a lively ground lamb mixture called a Lule Kebab. This one also comes in a vegetarian style. Mediterranean Meza will give two or more people a healthy sampling of just about everything including Lule Kebab, Dolma, Hummos, Baba Ghanoush, Tabuleh, and much more. Other samplings include baked chicken Pomegranate, quiche of the day, and a variety of filo dough specialities.

All of the La Mediterranee restaurants have been reviewed with high praise by area restaurant critics. The restaurant has also received the San Francisco Restauranteur Award from its peers signifying recognition as an outstanding San Francisco restaurant. Be sure to take the time to stop in at this "Best Choice" in dining while in San Rafael.

240

LE CHALET BASQUE
405 N San Pedro Road
San Rafael, CA 94903
Tel. (415) 479-1070

Hrs:	Tues. - Fri.	Lunch	11:30 a.m. - 2:00 p.m.
		Dinner	5:00 p.m. - 11:00 p.m.
	Saturday		5:00 p.m. - 10:00 p.m.
	Sunday	Brunch	10:30 a.m. - 2:00 p.m.
		Dinner	4:00 p.m. - 9:00 p.m.

Visa and MasterCard are accepted.

This restaurant on the outskirts of San Rafael is a popular spot for local business people drawn by the familiar atmosphere and the European cuisine. Owner Francisco Oroz, who began his restaurant career as a busboy, usually greets the guests and helps out at the tables.

Prices are reasonable, drawing many family groups at dinner time for selections such as chicken cordon bleu, beef Stroganoff, escargo, and frog legs. Several children's plates and a variety of soups are part of the menu. The dining area features a simple decor, is described as cozy, and comfortable. There is seating for about 90 people inside, and another 50 on the terrace when weather permits. Chef Pierre Gavina, a veteran of more than three decades of cooking, presides in the kitchen.

Sundays, a festive Basque-style breakfast tops the brunch menu, creating another attraction for this well known eating place. It's a place for a rendezvous or a family outing.

LE CROISSANT
1143 4th Street
San Rafael, CA 94901
Tel. (415) 456-7669

| Hrs: | Mon. - Sat. | 6:30 a.m. - 5:00 p.m. |
| | Sunday | 8:00 a.m. - 5:00 p.m. |

and,
150 Bellam
San Rafael, CA 94901
Tel. (415) 456-0164
Hrs: Mon. - Sun. 6:30 a.m. - 9:00 p.m.

Mornings, the smell of fresh-baked bread is in the air. The people of San Rafael flock here for breakfast and lunch. The crowds are a tribute to the tradition of "fresh-daily" which Daniel and Mitzi Collomb have earned at their two cafes.

241

The salad dressings are made by Daniel, there's a shopping trip for vegetables each day, and the lemonade is fresh-squeezed at Le Croissant. Omelets, over a dozen are on the menu, and the diet plate are among the favorite dishes in these bright cafes with their friendly staff and penchant for quality foods. Breakfast is served all day long, the luncheon menu is added at 11 a.m. each day. By the time you try Le Croissant, the Bellam location may have added its dinner menu.

This is your "Best Choice" for simple food, served in ample portions at moderate prices. Top off your fresh baked croissant with a cup of espresso for the continental breakfast.

THE LIPIZZANER
1240-42 4th Street
San Rafael, CA 94901
Tel. (415) 459-2202
Hrs: Mon. - Fri.   7:30 a.m. - 10:00 p.m.
          Sat. - Sun.   10:00 a.m. - 10:00 p.m.

Two chefs run this newly remodeled restaurant featuring Viennese and French cuisine, and by reservation, you can even have dinner in their kitchen. The chef's table puts four to six diners where they can watch the cooking staff prepare the dozens of popular dishes which are served with elegance.

The co-owners once created their magic in the kitchens of the Fairmont Hotel in San Francisco. Siegfried Pumberger was executive chef and Josef Roettig prepared the dishes from his native Vienna. Their new venture features an elegant dining room and boutique at street level, and a basement with rooms for business luncheons, banquets and private parties. The boutique includes pastries and baked goods prepared in the modern kitchen. Menus are complete, and on weekends a champagne brunch is added.

Most days, you will find Pumberger greeting the guests and Roettig in the kitchen supervising the chefs. They say The Lipizzaner is a place which brings the "front and back together," so you can enjoy fine food.

ROYAL THAI
610 3rd Street
San Rafael, CA 94901
Tel. (415) 485-1074
Hrs: Mon. - Fri.　　Lunch　　11:00 a.m. - 2:30 p.m.
　　　Sun. - Thu.　　Dinner　　5:00 p.m. - 9:30 p.m.
　　　Fri. - Sat.　　Dinner　　5:00 p.m. - 10:00 p.m.
Visa, MasterCard and AMEX are accepted.

The meals are authentic food of Thailand, the restaurant's story is out of Horatio Alger, a rags- to-riches rise in an adopted country. Royal Thai is a favorite of restaurant critics and growing numbers of repeat customers.

Jamie Disyamonthon and her husband Pat provide over sixty Thai selections on their menu, with the waiters happily translating the Thai name into an English description. The couple met in the United States. A banker and a school teacher in their native land, both were working at a Thai restaurant in San Francisco. Many of the dishes are from Jamie's family recipes, prepared with distinctive spices and very little oil or salt. Even the desserts are special bits of the Orient, featuring goodies such as fresh-made coconut ice cream.

You need to visit the Royal Thai for your own review, but we can tell this is a "Best Choice" for real Thai food, and a meal as graceful as a Thai dancer.

SAN RAFAEL JOE'S, 931 Fourth Street, San Rafael, California. Family dining with unpretentious prices.

Stationery

SHANNON'S HALLMARK
915 4th Street
San Rafael, CA 94901
Tel. (415) 454-6820
Hrs: Mon. - Fri.　　9:30 a.m. - 6:00 p.m.
　　　Saturday　　9:30 a.m. - 5:30 p.m.
　　　Sunday　　1:00 p.m. - 5:00 p.m.

This is a stationary and gift store, and much, much more, located in downtown San Rafael. Shannon's has office supplies, computer software and hardware, gifts and Hallmark greeting cards.

David and Margaret Van Staveren and their daughter Jenny and son David operate the family's business with an eye toward varied interests of their customers. Gift selection is handled by Margaret and Jenny, who gather unusual items for special occasions and provide the wrapping paper and cards to make it a simple stop for you. The rear of the store is taken up by the stationary, office and computer departments. They feature the ability to handle telephone and special orders, and stock a van as the mobile office supply center which drives to your door.

At Shannon's Hallmark, the goal is complete service for the customer. You'll see why it is your "Best Choice" for stationary, gifts and more.

California, and San Rafael, noted for its ability to mix cultures, add refinement through intermingling and *voila* you derive the benefits from the culinary efforts produced:

SAN RAFAEL RESTAURANT TOUR			
a.m.	Le Croissant	Best day-long brkfst	SanR/Rest
a.m.	The Lipizzaner	Best Viennese	SanR/Rest
p.m.	Cafe Tango	Best Spanish	SanR/Rest
p.m.	Daniel's	Best French	SanR/Rest
p.m.	Dominic's Harbor	Best Italian seafood	SanR/Rest
p.m.	La Petite Auberge	Best provincial French	SanR/Rest
p.m.	Le Chalet Basque	Best family dinners	SanR/Rest
p.m.	Panama Hotel	Best unique dining	SanR/Rest
p.m.	Royal Thai	Best Thai	SanR/Rest

Sausalito

This small town just a ferry boat ride from San Francisco has a reputation as an artist's colony, and its main business is retail trade, including catering the the tourists who flock here. As the first community up from the Golden Gate, this town of 8,200 had its roots in serving seafarers and has had a busy history.

Captain William Richardson was the first to settle here, using what is now Sausalito as the base for his business of providing pilot service to the whaling and trading ships bound for moorages in the north bay. Whalers anchored here on a regular basis as early as 1800. Richardson, who married the Spanish commandant's daughter in 1825, held a 19,000 acre rancho.

The name is a misspelling of the Spanish word for willow, which grew on the shore. After San Francisco developed merchants used what was then a fishing village as the place to load the rafts which carried barrels of drinking water to the city. Sausalito's waterfront and ferry landing had a reputation for bawdy houses, saloons and gambling. Smugglers, including Baby Face Nelson, staged their liquor imports through the town during prohibition.

During World War II, shipyards operated here and all of the small military posts were manned by coast artillery units. An estimated 20,000 people worked the 24-hour a day, seven-day a week shipyard operation. When they left, the picturesque town returned to a slower time, with few new houses built and vacancy rates very low among the rentals.

Attractions

Heath Ceramics, 400 Gate Road, makes architectural tiles, gift and tableware. Tours for groups of less than twenty if arranged in advance. Call 332-3732.

U.S. Army Engineers have a working model of San Francisco Bay and the Sacramento-San Joaquin delta located in a warehouse on the waterfront, 2100 Bridgeway. Water is moved to replicate the tides and river flow for analyzing problems on a two acre model of the bay. Public viewing Tuesday through Saturday between 9:00 a.m. and 4:00 p.m.

Waldo Point is the moorage for a sometimes controversial houseboat colony, and includes views of some very unique vessels.

On Bridgeway in the center of town, **Plaza Vina del Mar** sports an old world-style fountain. Several craftspersons combine work and retail sales in downtown shops and arcades.

Sausalito Yacht Harbor is the home of some of the most beautiful modern sailing vessels on the bay. Vintage sailing ships can sometimes be seen here, too.

For added information contact the **Sausalito Chamber of Commerce**, 333 Caledonia Street, Sausalitio CA 94965. Telephone 332-0505.

Accommodations

ALTA MIRA HOTEL
125 Bulkley Avenue
Sausalito, CA 94966
Tel. (415) 332-1350
All credit cards are accepted.

This small elegant hotel atop a Sausalito Hill has welcomed guests since 1895. The present building was put up after a 1926 fire destroyed the original. William Wachter, the current owner, has operated the Alta Mira for over three decades.

Thirty-five guest rooms, all recently renovated, are ready for visitors. They overlook an outdoor dining terrace which can handle up to 200 guests and is often reserved for wedding parties. Cuisine in the restaurant has an international flavor. Along with American favorites for breakfast, one can order Scottish kippered herring. Hot and cold luncheons are on the menu. Evenings, executive chef John McDonald takes over, featuring choice meat and seafood. The beef is Angus, prime, of course. The lamb is the best from California growers.

The Alta Mira makes many lists for its small, elegant atmosphere and top service. Whether as an overnight guest, or one looking for superb dining, you'll enjoy stepping into this villa on the hill where the history of hospitality goes back more than ninety years. Heaven on earth!

CASA MADRONA HOTEL AND RESTAURANT
801 Bridgeway
Sausalito, CA 94965
Tel. (415) 332-0502 Hotel
Tel. (415) 331-5888 Restaurant
Hrs: 24 hour service year around
Restaurant

Hrs:			
	Mon. - Fri.	Lunch	11:30 a.m. - 2:30 p.m.
	Mon. - Sat.	Dinner	6:00 p.m. - 11:00 p.m.
	Sunday	Brunch	10:00 a.m. - 3:00 p.m.

Rooms are much sought after in this inn built in the shell of an old mansion, with a reputation for privacy and service. Reservations for weekend stays should be at least four weeks in advance during the winter, and eight weeks ahead during summertime, mid week stays require much less notice. You can sample the atmosphere by stopping for lunch or dinner without the long wait facing overnight guests.

The Casa Madrona prides itself in giving guests a chance to pamper themselves. Owner-manager John Mays offers rooms at prices ranging from $60 to $275 a night (at the time of this publication). His dining room, with spectacular views and an outdoor deck, offers a gourmet menu. Here, too reservations are advised for dinner. Private parties of up to 150 can be handled. Sample entrees such as grilled medallions of salmon, or chicken prepared with special seasoning. Jill Branch, the pastry chef, bakes bread and a variety of deserts each day.

This is an old-fashioned hotel, ready to pamper you for business or romance, amid elegance and privacy.

SAUSALITO HOTEL
16 El Portal
Sausalito, CA 94965
Tel. (415) 332-4155
Hrs: 24 hour service year around
Visa, MasterCard and AMEX are accepted.

Among the small residence hotels of the Bay Area, the Sausalito has a place by itself, the reputation earned by manager Liz MacDonald, who paces the service to fit your idea of hospitality in years gone by.

The fifteen room Sausalito proudly advises that you will find no telephone or television in your room with its antique furniture. But, Liz will send up a black-and-white TV if you insist and there are phones available upon request. That's only proper since many of her guests are celebrities from the TV and entertainment industry. It was here, holed up in the General Grant room (that's room number one), that Sterling Hayden completed writing his novel, "Voyage," during the winter of 1977.

Special names, and appropriate theme decorations go with every room. The Grant is centered around a bed which the president was said to have slept in. Special touches for guests are part of the ambience of this old hotel just a block away from the ferry boat to San Francisco.

Bar

NO NAME BAR
757 Bridgeway
Sausalito, CA 94965
Tel. (415) 332-1392
Hrs: Mon. - Sun. 10:00 a.m. - 2:00 a.m.

Atmosphere is the best way to describe this Sausalito bar, where the absence of a name became the name. The interior is as it was when the place opened in 1958, and as the word spreads, No Name Bar's reputation increases.

There is no cover charge at this institution, but there is entertainment as diverse as the interests of Sausalito's residents. Friday and Saturday, by tradition, are jazz nights from 8:30 p.m. to 12:30 a.m. Every other Tuesday, there is a poetry reading starting about 7:00 p.m. A telephone call will let you know whether a local poet or a celebrity is in town. Sunday afternoons, the entertainment switches to Dixieland Jazz.

This "Best Choice" in bars made the *Esquire* list of the top one hundred bars in the United States list three years in a row, and rates at the top of the list by the *Pacific Sun*, which surveys the Marin County scene.

PATTERSON'S, 739 Bridgeway, Sausalito, California. Specializing in malt whiskeys and imported domestic beers. Has the single largest malt whiskey collection in the U.S.A. Ambiance is British.

Restaurant

CAT N' FIDDLE, 681 Bridgeway, Sausalito, California. Great food, friendly folk, British feel, serving til midnight.

THE CHART HOUSE
201 Bridgeway
Sausalito, CA 94965
Tel. (415) 332-0804
Hrs: Mon. - Fri.   5:30 p.m. - 10:00 p.m.
        Sat. - Sun.   5:00 p.m. - 11:00 p.m.

An adventure in dining can be extremely agreeable. It's high time for a unique adventure in it's most pleasing aspect at The Chart House. The Chart House, managed by Michael Hoffler, is a restaurant that will keep you coming back time and time again.

Once you taste their exquisite offerings you're hooked. The Chart House specializes in fresh fish dishes, so fresh that you can almost smell the briney deep! And what's more, they also feature an oyster feast every night from 5:30 p.m. to 7:00 p.m.

The building that houses The Chart House is an attraction by it's own merit. Being very old, it confers a sense of antiquity on this nautical restaurant, creating a beautiful, relaxing ambiance. After a visit to The Chart House you'll know the true definition of an adventure in dining.

HORIZONS
558 Bridgeway
Sausalito, CA 94965
Tel. (415) 331-3232
Hrs: Mon. - Fri.   11:00 a.m. - 11:00 p.m.
      Sat. - Sun.   10:00 a.m. - 11:00 p.m.

Much of the magic emitting from this classic three story building evolves from its rich history. Starting out in 1898 as the "San Francisco Yacht Club" it became a boat and storage warehouse, then a sport fishing center, then a fish market and later Juanita's first gallery. In 1961 The Kingston Trio bought the lease and a jazz nightclub known as "The Trident" took its place. They remained lessees until 1980, when they sold the lease back to the creators of Horizons, Ron and Carol MacAnnan, who had owned the building since 1959.

In 1981 it became Horizons, a restaurant with a fabulous view, accented with an interior done in hand crafted wood. It boasts a hand painted ceiling, an abundance of plants, and a strikingly clean and colorful decor. Owned, managed and run by family members, Horizons is a delightful place to dine. Prices are moderate, fish is fresh, and there are a variety of gourmet favorites. Brunch is served until 3:00 p.m. and the lunch favorite is eggs Sausalito, much like eggs Benedict, except made with crab.

A full service bar, elegantly prepared food with superb seasonings and sauces, and a dash of fascinating history, make Horizons a "Best Choice" dining experience.

SEVEN SEAS RESTAURANT
682 Bridgeway
Sausalito, CA 94965
Tel. (415) 332-1304
Hrs: Mon. - Sun. 8:00 a.m. - 11:30 p.m.

"Four strong winds that blow slowly, seven seas that run high..."You'll love the Seven Seas Restaurant, offering an immense variety of seafood and moderate prices in a handsome fifty year old Historical Landmark building. The front and back exterior architecture is original, as are the indoor walls panelled with mahogany, exuding a warm and nostalgic atmosphere. Add to this a breath taking feature, a sliding retractable roof that enables you to dine indoors under the stars.

The dinner menu conveniently runs the range from simple meals to elegant gourmet dinners. Paul De Moss, owner for twenty-eight years, insists on quality of food and service. If the seafood you select is not available fresh at the time, they will help you choose a delicious alternative. There are always wonderful daily specials on the menu, and all selections are ample portions served with fresh ingredients and arranged to stir your appetite. A popular favorite here is "Spaghetti Marinara 7 Seas," consisting of shrimp and crab, sauteed in garlic and butter with green onions and mushrooms over a platter of spaghetti. Yummmm....

Seven Seas runs high on our list. Try a meal here and Seven Seas will run high on your list, too.

ZACK'S BY THE BAY
Bridgeway at Turney Street
Sausalito, CA 94965
Tel. (415) 332-9779
Hrs: Mon. - Fri. 11:00 a.m. - 10:00 p.m.
     Sat. - Sun. 10:00 a.m. - 10:00 p.m.
Bar Mon. - Sun. 11:00 a.m. - 2:00 a.m.

The hamburger earned Sam Zakessian a bit of fame when he opened this restaurant and bar by the harbor over thirty years ago. Now, it is enshrined on the menu as the Zack burger, heading a menu known for its reasonable prices.

The seagulls glide beyond the windows and you watch the boats parade by. Zack's interior takes on a nautical look to match its spot overlooking the harbor. In good weather, dining and cocktails are available on an outdoor patio. Breakfast is served from 10:00 a.m. until noon on weekends, the lounge features live entertainment with no cover charge starting at 9:00 p.m. Friday, Saturday and Sunday.

You'll find the casual atmosphere continues in Sam Zakessian's place, even though it is now a tourist attraction as word spreads about this "Best Choice."

Wonderful! I love these tours and the opportunities they present to see, really see, a new part of the country.

TOUR OF THE MARIN PENINSULA			
a.m.	Le Croissant	Best breakfast	SanR/Rest
a.m.	Shannon's Hallmark	Best occasion	SanR/Gift
a.m.	Historical Museum	Best area intro	SanR/Att
p.m.	India Palace	Best lunch	Mill/Rest
p.m.	Muir Woods Nat'l Mon	Best scenic tour	Mill/Att
p.m.	Sausalito Yacht Harbor	Best seascape	Saus/Att
After hours, try one or both of these "Best Choices."			
p.m.	Zack's	Best bay view	Saus/Rest
p.m.	No Name Bar	Best night show	Saus/Bar

Stinson Beach

Book

STINSON BEACH BOOKS
3455 Shoreline Highway
Stinson Beach, CA 94970
Tel. (415) 868-0700
Hrs: Mon. - Sun. 10:30 a.m. - 5:00 p.m.

This is a book store that can offer something earth-shaking because it's the only bookstore on the San Andreas fault, halfway between Jimmy's Gulch and Dogtown.

Aside from that claim to fame, owners Anne Leary and Annie Rand have built a reputation for making customers feel comfortable. Their selection includes a fine nature collection, a children's room, classics, mysteries, non-fiction, as well as current best sellers in both hardcover and paperback. Gifts, games, toys and a wide range of stationery and cards are also available.

Before you step out on the beautiful three mile beach, grab a good book to read. That's an idea no one can fault!

Restaurant

THE SAND DOLLAR RESTAURANT
3458 Shoreline Highway
Stinston Beach, CA 94970
Tel. (415) 868-0434
Hrs: Mon. - Sat.   Lunch   12:00 noon - 2:30 p.m.
                    Dinner   6:00 p.m. - 9:30 p.m.
      Sunday   Brunch   11:00 a.m. - 2:30 p.m.
      Bar Mon. - Sun.   12:00 noon - 2:00 a.m.

Kicking up the sand during a walk in this friendly northern California community you might find a sand dollar. Sand dollars are always considered a treasure by their finders. Dried, they are a pleasure to look upon and if you happen to break it open, you'll find a second treasure inside of little stars or birds. Maybe you weren't fortunate enough to find a sand dollar on your walk, but there is a still a sand dollar in Stinston Beach you can find on Shoreline Highway that is a treasure, The Sand Dollar Restaurant.

Run by Ken Rand, owner for some twenty years, this comfortable beach-side restaurant gives you a second treasure inside of wonderful fresh fish dinners. "Good basic American cooking ," is how Ken describes his meals with daily specials of fresh seafood. Try the steamer clams, mussels or clams. Summertime brings imported New England lobster. If that salt air has worked up an appetite mid day, then stop on in for a lunch of a Dog on a French roll with a side of great homemade fries.

Become a beachcomber and find The Sand Dollar Restaurant in Stinson Beach for a genuine fresh fish meal. And don't forget dessert - fresh strawberries, cheese cake and mud pie.

Tiburon

See the listing, in this chapter, for the town of Belvedere to read about Tiburon and its attractions.

Accommodations

TIBURON LODGE
1651 Tiburon Boulevard
Tiburon, CA 94920
Tel. (415) 435-3133

Imagine yourself soaking in a European spa and sipping a goblet of wine from your own personal bar, all in the comfort of your hotel room. That's Tiburon Lodge.

Sixteen of the rooms come complete with their own whirl jet fresh water spas, and many come with stocked mini bars. Fourteen new rooms have been added, each with its own theme and special decor such as, the English Tudor, Safari and Parisian rooms. Virtually every other imaginable service is available, too, including babysitting, dry cleaning, check cashing, conference rooms, safe deposit boxes, as well as standard hotel customer services. All you have to do is relax, visit the pool or restaurant and take in the gorgeous secluded scenery.

Only a fifteen minute ferry ride from San Francisco, you'll want to come back again to enjoy the food and peaceful surroundings whether your purpose is business or pleasure. The Mainsail Restaurant adjoining the Lodge offers a complimentary full buffet breakfast five days a week. Hotel guests may enjoy the buffet at half price on Saturdays and Sundays. Excellent restaurants are conveniently located within easy walking distance.

(See special invitation in the Appendix.)

Art

L'ARTISTE STUDIO AND GALLERY
104 Main Street, Ark Row
Tiburon, CA 94920
Tel. (415) 435-3482
Hrs: Summer   Tue. - Sun.   11:00 a.m. - 6:00 p.m.
     Winter   Tue. - Sun.   12:00 p.m. - 5:30 p.m.
Visa, MasterCard, AMEX and Discover cards are accepted.

Art is an expressed feeling or emotion that, once displayed, causes a feeling or an emotion to arise in the subject viewing the art. Imagine this, a beautiful sunrise dawning on the horizon, calling to the earth to awaken after a deep, cleansing sleep. The spirit and feeling of dawn is only one of the essences captured at L'Artiste, a working art studio and gallery extraordinaire.

L'Artiste is owned and operated by Georgianna Stout, who began her growth as an artist at the age of three and exhibited in her first one artist show at the age of ten. Georgianna shares her expertise through workshops held in her studio six months of the year. People from all over the world come to enjoy her beautiful art presented at L'Artiste featuring portraits, regional and wildlife scenes. The mediums and techniques vary, with pastels, oils, watercolors and line drawings being popular. The studio-gallery is housed in Tiburon's most famous historic ark (circa 1895), lending a cozy, inviting environment in which to view the displayed art and artist at work.

The artwork showcased at L'Artiste is the type that stirs the deeper emotions of the soul, an art that captures the aliveness of Georgianna's ever expanding world. Visit L'Artiste and enjoy the tranquility these fine works have to offer.

THE WOODEN PELICAN, 7 Main Street, Tiburon, California. Featuring nautical themes in collectibles.

Books

ALBATROSS II BOOK SHOP
100 Main Street
Tiburon, CA 94920
Tel. (415) 435-1506
Hrs: Tue. - Sun.   11:00 a.m. - 6:00 p.m.
         Friday   11:00 a.m. - 9:00 p.m.
AMEX, Visa and MasterCard are accepted.

Oh, the joys of a good bookstore! To be totally absorbed by the many topics presented is true bliss to any book enthusiast. There's a certain kind of feeling that wells up inside you when surrounded by a few thousand books. This feeling of being in a treasure house is sure to be intensified at Albatross II Book Shop.

When entering the bookstore, you'll be warmly greeted by owner Rose Sharp or her able assistant, Betsy Zelinsky. Then, it's off on the treasure hunt. Books of all types and subjects are featured at Albatross II, providing pleasant distraction until finding the genre that you seek. There's a particularly huge selection of books concerning aviation, as well as a large variety related to California and San Francisco.

For special services, the book shop offers a search for out of print or hard to find books at no charge. They also handle consignments, trades and appraisals. As you can see, to call Albatross II a used book store is quite an understatement. Okay, now that you've got your map, go and find the treasure. Albatross II marks the spot.

THE WATERMARK AT TIBURON BOOKS
13 Main Street
Tiburon, CA 94920
Tel. (415)´ 435-4960
Hrs: Summer   Mon. - Sun.   10:00 a.m. - 7:00 p.m.
         Winter   Mon. - Sun.   11:00 a.m. - 6:00 p.m.

Bookstores have always been a place to browse and peruse leisurely. Bookstores are peaceful places that open horizons to the reader. The Watermark at Tiburon Books is a wonderful example of such a place.

Ed and Roberta Lupton are a genuinely friendly couple whose combined life experiences blend to make them well suited for the business in which they are engaged. A conscious effort is put forth by Ed and Roberta to understand their customer's desires and stock the books so suited. Not only will you find a responsive atmosphere, but also, their books are sold at a very good value, all being discounted ten to twenty five percent.

Having been well traveled, Ed takes a special interest in the travel section of the store which is well stocked. Ed has been known to act as a personal travel consultant. Special orders are welcomed. This comfortable shop has a beautiful view with pleasant music. What better way to explore the bookworm in you?

Florist

MAIN STREET FLORAGARDENS, 116 Main Street, Tiburon, California. In the Ark Row; flowers for the table, a major party, or just because.

Restaurant

THE CAPRICE RESTAURANT, 2000 Paradise Drive, Tiburon, California. Continental/California cuisine, breathtaking view, unhurried atmosphere.

CHRISTOPHER'S, 9 Main Street, Tiburon, California. Restaurant housed in a modern reproduction of the first restaurant in Tiburon. Unsurpassed view, full service restaurants and lounge.

255

THE DOCK
25 Main Street
Tiburon, CA 94920
Tel. (415) 435-4550

What better way to enjoy the San Francisco Bay than on the waterfront? At The Dock you can sit at the water's edge, dine in a cozy atmosphere and watch the sun set over the twinkle of the City's lights. The Dock is a family run business that has been delighting its patrons for ten years. Owner James Quinlivan offers catering and reception facilities and often works with tour groups, a French tour group even meets there for lunch every Tuesday.

The Dock offers delicious meals at reasonable prices. Their specialty, of course, is fresh seafood, try their lobster Thermadore or the fresh clam chowder, or any of the great daily fish specials. Steak and veal and eggs Benedict are also on the lunch menu.

After Sunday dinner patrons often sit around the Piano Bar and join in on the sing-a-long of Oldies that starts about 4:30 p.m. and goes until 9:30 p.m. On other nights you may catch a variety of live jazz music. The Dock is easy to find on Main Street in Tiburon, where Bay meets restaurant. Look for the deer wandering about outside, and enjoy the food, the music, and the service inside. It's a perfect place for enjoying the waterfront.

GUAYMAS
5 Main Street
Tiburon, CA 94920
Tel. (415) 435-6300
Hrs: Mon. - Thu.   11:30 a.m. - 10:00 p.m.
      Fri. - Sat.   11:30 a.m. - 11:00 p.m.
      Sunday   10:30 a.m. - 10:00 p.m.
Reservations are recommended.

Looking for truly authentic Mexican food, not the usual fare of burritos and nachos? At Guaymas, diligent care was taken to find and reproduce recipes that are rarely found in this country.

Everything served is exceptional. A sample of savory menu items includes: Vuelve a la Vida - fresh marinated squid, octopus, shrimp, oysters and clams; Camarones Gigantes Marinados - giant shrimp marinated in lime juice and cilantro and rilled over charcoal; Pico de Gallo - jicama, cucumber and fresh fruit with lemon-chili dressing; Chili Poblano Relleno de Pollo con Salsa de Nuez y Granada - large Poblano chiles stuffed with chicken and raisins topped with walnut sauce and pomegranate seeds; or Pechuga Ranchera con Chile - boned chicken breast with red chile guajillo sauce, milk and milk curds. Desserts are as original as the entrees, with puddings, custards and specialties such as Bunuelos con Platanos Borrachos, Spanish for fritters with "drunken" bananas or Pecado de Chocolate con Ceresas - chocolate "sin".

A spectacular view of San Francisco Bay, bright colors and lots of wood produce a simple yet elegant decor. Guaymas reflects the traditional, regional ambiance of the town on Mexico's Sea of Cortez for which it was named.

ROONEY'S GARDEN CAFE
38 Main Street
Tiburon, CA 94920
Tel. (415) 435-1911
Hrs: Mon. - Thu.   11:30 a.m. - 3:30 p.m.
       Sat. - Sun.   9:00 a.m. - 10:00 p.m.

When hungry people, most of them local, frequent a restaurant as often as they do at Rooney's, you know it has to be good. Owners John Rooney and David Hinman specialize in quality food and good service. Their delightful fresh baked breads are made on the premises, the deli style sandwiches on their menu can be prepared with homemade pumpernickel, Russian or Jewish rye.

John and David admit to having no restaurant experience when they opened the cafe in 1970. So it is indicative of their success that The Chronicle recently featured an article on Hot Salads with a picture of Rooney's "hot chicken salad" created by Chef Dave Hinman.

This lovely little cafe also has garden patio complete with awning for fresh air dining. Homemade breads, deli sandwiches, moderate pricing, and the garden patio all add up to an ambiance you won't want to miss, especially if you're hungry!

SCHINO'S, 16 Main Street, Tiburon, California. Quality Italian cuisine with authentic, homemade sauces featured. Specialties are shellfish and veal.

SERVINO'S, 114 Main Street, Tiburon, California. Italian cuisine with a variety of fresh fish specials daily.

SWEDEN HOUSE BAKERY AND CAFE
35 Main Street
Tiburon, CA 94920
Tel. (415) 435-9767
Hrs: Mon. - Sun. 8:00 a.m. - 6:00 p.m.

If you enjoy espresso, European coffees and delightful European pastries, then you're bound to love the Sweden House. The Sweden House is frequented by Europeans, locals, and tourists. The atmosphere is a casual "come as you are," enjoy the classical music and the tempting pastries, and sit quietly and chat over a cup of gourmet coffee or chocolate.

Breakfast is served all day, and lunch is served from 11:30 a.m. - 3:00 p.m. Select an omelet and a croissant for breakfast, or a salad, soup, and sandwich for lunch. The salads are unique and lavish, with names like "Danish Ham with Asparagus Tips," "California Avocado with Shrimp," and "Tuna with Apples and Celery." Various open faced sandwiches are served on your choice of delicious breads.

After eating, pamper yourself with a steaming cup of cappucccino, cafe Borgia, or gourmet hot chocolate. After eating, pamper yourself with a freshly brewed cup of cappuccino or espresso and enjoy the view of the bay and San Francisco from the deck over the water.

Sport

KEN'S BIKE
94 Main Street
Tiburon, CA 94920
Tel. (415) 435-1683
Hrs: Summer   Mon. - Sun.   10:00 a.m. - 6:00 p.m.
       Winter   Wed. - Sun.   10:00 a.m. - 6:00 p.m.

Bike riding is a fun and healthy sport. There's nothing better than getting on a bike and going for a ride on a warm, sunny day. However, when you're traveling, you don't always have a bike with you. But that's no worry in Tiburon, home of Ken's Bike Shop. Here, you can rent a bike and peddle to your heart's content.

Ken's has all kinds of bikes available for rent to all ages. Some of the racing and touring bikes include BMX, Cruiser, Fuji, Red Line, Mongoose and Custom Wheels. Of course, when you rent these bikes, you are free to adventure anywhere you'd like to go. However, if you don't know where to go, Ken can make some great suggestions, such as the ride via Tiburon's bike path to Blackie's Pasture, the Angel Island ride, Quarry Beach, Overnight rides and many others. Ken will also validate your parking and direct you to the ferry which leaves hourly for Angel Island.

Bicycling is a means of maintaining fitness while enjoying a time that is sure to create beautiful memories. The adventure awaits. All you have to do is visit Ken's Bike Shop, rent a bike and peddle away.

Wine

TIBURON VINTNERS
72 Main Street
Tiburon, CA 94920
Tel. (415) 435-3113
Hrs: Sun. - Thu.   10:00 a.m. - 6:00 p.m.
              Fri. - Sat.   10:00 a.m. - 7:00 p.m.
MasterCard, Visa, AMEX, Discover Card and Carte Blanche are accepted.

Like fine wine, Tiburon Vintners has improved with age. There's still the old-fashioned hospitality, easygoing friendly staff and complimentary wine tasting that founder Rodney Strong started over twenty-five years ago. And now the wines are world class, too!

Open for tasting everyday, Tiburon Vintners invites visitors to choose among nearly fifty Windsor Vineyards wines and champagnes, including many award winners. When you duck under the luxuriant grapevine and enter the hundred-year-old tasting room, you step into a gentler time. A host or hostess welcomes you, invites you to relax with a sample of fine wine, and talks to you about the wines, wine and food match-ups and things to see and do in Tiburon. The celebration of life through wine and the arts is Rod's philosophy and the people at Tiburon Vintners share this spirit.

There is free validated parking right next door in the Main Street Lot. Also, the staff will take phone orders to ship personalized wine gifts for you throughout California and New York. Stop by Tiburon Vintners, aged over twenty-five years, and taste some fine wine in an unparalleled ambiance.

MENDOCINO COUNTY

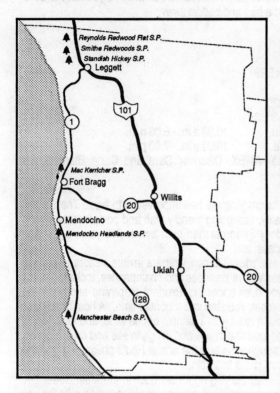

Map labels:
Reynolds Redwood Flat S.P.
Smithe Redwoods S.P.
Standish Hickey S.P.
Leggett
101
1
Mac Kerricher S.P.
Fort Bragg
Willits
20
Mendocino
Mendocino Headlands S.P.
Ukiah
20
128
Manchester Beach S.P.

The name honors Antonio de Mendoza, first viceroy of New Spain. But, like so many of California's twenty-seven original counties, the geographic feature which goes with the name ended up beyond the boundaries described by the legislature of 1850. Cape Mendocino, the farthest west point on the continental United States, is a good thirty five miles north of forty degrees north latitude, the boundary of this giant county. The cape was the first landfall of de Mendoza's Spanish sailors returning from a voyage to the Philippines in 1542.

Mendocino's legal identity crisis did not stop with the legislature of 1850. After creating the county, the state instructed Sonoma County to administer affairs for the vast country to the north. It seemed there were only fifty-five county residents in 1850, and it was not until sawmills began operating on the Big River mouth in 1852 that the population began to climb. In 1859 Ukiah finally got its courts and responsibility for governance of 3,512 square miles of some of the roughest country in the state.

Data for 1872 shows that while the nineteen sawmills of Mendocino County shipped fifty million board feet of lumber, the population was just 8,000 people. The old lumber shipping ports, some of them quite small, and the railroads which brought logs to the mills are part of the charm of the coast which attracts visitors to Highway 1 in increasing numbers. Winding roads now share their asphalt with logging trucks and tourist vehicles.

There is a narrow coastal plain at several locations along the more than 100 miles of ocean frontage of Mendocino County. In some locations vast treeless hills roll up from the small ranches, providing more forage than most commercial livestock operators can use in a season. Sheep and cattle share the grass with deer and elk. Rainfall averages 40 inches a year at the coast, and when summer temperatures turn hot inland, fog is pulled over the grasslands and the pockets of redwood timber, dripping moisture which sustains green growth all year.

The county's population of 66,700 has remained stable for many years. This reflects the transition of lumber, plywood and particle-board plants to more efficient machinery and the reaction to recent down-turns in the demand for forest products. Tree fruit are usually the top value farm crop, followed by cattle, grape sales, and wine production. Coastal villages, hit by several years of poor offshore fishing conditions, bustle with a growing tourist trade. Several recreational homesite subdivisions increase the population on a seasonal basis. Inland, newer reservoir projects, created primarily to control flooding on the Russian River, have increased water-related recreation.

Three distinct ridges of coast range mountains parallel each other, all on a north-south alignment with valleys that gather huge quantities of water, then find a path to the sea. The Russian River drains to the south, creating the largest interior valley. The Eel River drains to the north, marking the next mountain-valley-mountain system east of the Russian. Cutting across the first coastal barrier are the shorter Garcia, Navarro, Albion, Big and Noyo Rivers which provide the passes which connect the inland valleys with the sparsely-populated coast. Redwood and fir forests are on the damper locations, pine and oak the drier sites. Summer temperatures are very hot, the winters mild but very wet. Snow seldom remains for long on the coast range, usually melting into storm runoff with the next surge of rain.

The mountains and their interior valleys are frequently scoured by flood waters. Landslides tied with major storms change the landscape from time to time and dump large silt loads into many streams. Rainfall in the mountains is sixty inches a year or more, while the Russian River Valley at Ukiah averages just under thirty six inches of precipitation. It has a 224-day growing season, well suited to grapes, tree fruit orchards, and hay production.

Cayetano Juarez, a militia leader of the Mexican Alta California government, received a large land grant to what is now Ukiah and the surrounding valley in 1845 but it is not clear that he farmed the Yokaya Rancho. Part of it was a large Indian settlement. The name came from an Indian word, later spelled as "Ukiah." Many Indians of the area were moved to the Round Valley about 1858. Ukiah started just two years before that. A census in the 1930s shows that Indian people from fifteen different tribes were then resident on the Round Valley Reservation, which continues in operation.

ATTRACTIONS

Sinkyone Wilderness State Park, accessible from Usal Road north of Highway 1, is the "lost coast" of Mendocino and Humboldt counties. A 21-mile foot trail links old ranches, provides access to private beaches and waterfalls. Campers must bring their own water purification devices or boil all drinking water. Usal Road, county road 431, continues north where Highway 1 turns east over the mountains to Leggett. Call (707) 247-3318 for information on back country permits.

Rockport and **Westport** are former lumber shipping points. Rockport has a few weathered buildings, but Westport retains some New England-style reminders of its heyday. Settled in 1864, Westport had two big wharves completed in 1878 to take a major role in lumber shipping. North of town is a beach with primitive camping. Call 937-5804 for information.

Geology of the coast comes alive at **Jughandle State Reserve** just north of Caspar on Highway 1, part of a larger Caspar Headlands State Beach. Five separate terraces cut by waves when the Pacific Ocean was at higher levels, can be seen climbing the trail up the Jughandle Creek canyon. At the top is a stunted forest where the shortage of nutrients results in dwarfed trees. Permits are required to enter the headlands. Call 937-5804.

Little River, a quaint community now catering to visitors, is typical of the small ports which developed in the redwood exporting days. Erosion cut through the rock providing a narrow entrance which coastwise schooners, and now commercial fishing vessels, can enter, with care, to reach sheltered moorings.

Van Damme State Park, a favorite for SCUBA divers, is about three miles north. This is a popular spot for rock fishing in the ocean, and trout fishing on the four miles of Little River inside the park boundaries. Hikers can find a canyon lined with ferns, and a forest of mature trees less than shoulder high because of the tough growing conditions. Call 937-0851 for park information.

Albion and **Elk** are little ports similar to that of Little River. Here small coastal steamers could enter to work the lumber waiting on the docks built under the rocky cliffs. Both communities offer popular overnight and eating facilities.

The coastal plain widens at **Manchester** to allow some farm lands. This little community is a center for livestock ranches in the hills.

Manchester State Beach runs form the entrance of the Garcia River north for more than a mile. Diving off shore, ocean fishing and camping draw people.

Just south is **Point Arena,** a major landmark for coastwise vessels. The lighthouse includes a **museum** open to the public. Trails lead down the basalt cliffs to tidepools. Call 937-5804. A store was opened in 1859 in the little village of Point Arena on Highway 1, where cypress trees provide windbreaks for houses. The community incorporated as a city in 1908 and supports dairy farms in the area.

Gualala, a small port town left over from the lumber days, is on Highway 1 at the Sonoma County line. This vacation town developed a reputation as an art colony. It has river beaches for swimming, and a steelhead fishery which attracts sportsmen for the annual migration from the ocean. The sawmill operated here for over 50 years, closing in 1920. A wood-frame hotel built in 1903 became the center of the town's new life as showplace for area artists.

The **Navarro River Valley** provides one of the primary routes from the coast inland, with Highway 128 starting at Highway 1 south of Albion. Highway 128 joins U.S. 101 just north of Cloverdale, passing **Hendy Woods State Park** with its old growth redwoods, **Booneville**, a center for apple growers and several wineries. **Anderson Valley Chamber of Commerce,** Box 275, Booneville CA 95415 has detailed information on attractions.

Hopland, on U.S. 101 in an area of intense farming which gave the town its name, is on the site of an ancient Indian settlement called **Sanel.** Hops were planted here in 1858, and air-dried in barns long before commercial driers were introduced. Stephen W. Knowles, the first hop producer, is said to have received thirty cents a pound. Wine grapes now replace the hops here. Call 744-1015 for area information.

The Geysers, site of the massive geothermal field managed by Unocal, is reached by a county road just north of Cloverdale. A viewpoint, fourteen miles east of U.S. 101, overlooks the steam turbines which are actually located in Lake County. Open all year to the viewpoint. Unocal provides information on the fields through their Communications Department, Box 7600, Los Angeles CA 90051.

For more information, contact the **Mendocino County Chamber of Commerce**, Box 244, Ukiah CA 95482. Telephone 462-3091.

Fort Bragg

On what is a sparsely-populated coast, Fort Bragg is a busy town of over 5,000 residents. The Mendocino Indian Reservation was established here and the military post above the Noyo River designated to supervise the treaty. Soldiers came in 1857, and named their camp for Braxton Bragg a hero of the Mexican War. The historical marker at 321 Main Street locates part of the post and a museum in the only remaining military building that recounts this time in history.

The Indian Reservation was dissolved and the fort declared surplus in 1867. Investors quickly bought the place as a town site. The harbor provided by Noyo River, and the coast range rail connection by the California Western Railroad resulted in a busy community. Union Lumber Co., which later sold to Georgia Pacific Corp., built a huge sawmill. Its reforestation nursery is on Main Street, where seedlings have been grown since 1922 to replant cut-over lands.

The false-front stores, churches in the New England style, and cottages with gables make the town picturesque. Noyo, the town to the south of Fort Bragg, is home to commercial fishermen and charter boat operators. Most lumber shipped by water nowadays goes by barge rather than coastal steamers.

Attractions

Mendocino Coast Botanical Gardens, 18220 North Highway 1, is a formal garden set on seventeen acres. Rhododendrons are among the plantings which make the spot famous. Operated by a non-profit association. Open daily. Summer hours 9:00 a.m. to 5:00 p.m., winter from 10:00 a.m. to 4:00 p.m. Call (707) 964-4352.

The **Stone Painting Museum**, 26800 North Highway 1, features art combining semi-precious stones and paintings. Open Wednesday through Monday, 9:00 a.m. to 4:00 p.m. in the summer. Call 964-9540 for winter hours.

MacKerricher State Park, Highway 1 three miles north of town, has sandy beaches and lots of camping spots.

The **California Western's Skunks** operate from here, reversing their schedules to Willits, and half-day excursions to Northspur. Call (707) 964-6371 (see listing under Willits).

Maps for a **walking tour** of interesting downtown buildings are available at the Chamber of Commerce offices. For more information, contact the **Fort Bragg-Mendocino Coast Chamber of Commerce**, 332 North Main Street, Fort Bragg CA 95437. Telephone 964-3153.

Accommodation

**OLD COAST HOTEL
HOT PEPPER JELLY CO.**
101 N. Franklin Street
Fort Bragg, CA 95437
Tel. (707) 964-6443
Hrs: Restaurant
         Lunch   11:00 a.m. - 2:00 p.m.
         Dinner   5:00 p.m. - 9:00 p.m.
    Shop   9:00 a.m. - 5:00 p.m.

What does hot pepper jelly have to do with a good night's sleep? Only that they're the products to two business that share the same roof that really clicked when they got together.

The result is a good family run hotel, comfortable rooms and good meals, and a specialty food shop featuring some of the best locally produced treats. It all started with Joanna and Bob Santos' idea to return the one hundred year old Coast Hotel to its original purpose as a travelers' accommodation with touches of old world charm, instead of the boarding house it had been for years. Not long afterwards, Carol opened up her shop Hot Pepper Jelly Co. to market her line of Cajun style hot pepper jellies. She ended up also running the cafe and drawing more customers to the restaurant with the aromas of Creole specialties such as jambalaya, gumbo, red beans and rice.

If your hunting for charm, this "Best Choice" offers the best of true European charm (no private baths), and new world Louisiana style cooking.

(See special invitation in Appendix.)

Bed & Breakfast

GREY WHALE INN, 615 North Main Street, Fort Bragg, California. Fort Bragg's first B&B. the inn has large, artfully decorated rooms with lovely views. Breakfast is a delicious full buffet, and the innkeepers offer a wealth of information about the area.

Art

NORTHCOAST ARTISTS, 330 North Franklin Street, Fort Bragg, California. A cooperative of eleven of the north coast's talented artists which features pottery, ceramics, sculpture, prints, batiks, jewelry, painting, and natural fiber art.

Restaurant

EGGHEAD OMELETTES OF OZ, 326 North Main Street, Fort Bragg, California. Over 40 varieties of omelettes, plus pancakes, breakfast plates, and fresh juices. At lunch, enjoy half-pound burgers, unusual sandwiches, and generous portions of homemade potato salad. Open seven days, 7 a.m. - 2 p.m.

THE RESTAURANT
418 Main Street
Fort Bragg, CA 95437
Tel.　(707) 964-9800
Hrs:　Lunch　Thu. - Tue　　　　11:30 a.m. - 2:00 p.m.
　　　　Dinner　　Thu. - Tue.　　5:00 p.m. - 9:00 p.m.
　　　　Brunch　　Sunday　　　　10:00 p.m. - 1:00 p.m.
MasterCard and Visa are accepted.

In the modern world it's easy to forget that there's more to a good restaurant than the facade. Too many times, people work under the assumption that all it takes is a little flash and dash to become an overnight sensation. At The Restaurant, they haven't forgotten that there is a craft to be mastered.

In this dining establishment you won't see any fine china or crystal stemware. In fact, both inside and out, the decorations are simple and eclectic. What you'll find at The Restaurant is great food at surprisingly reasonable prices. The Restaurant's menu is changed regularly, so specific recommendations are difficult to make. But items you'll definitely want to sample when they're available include the Cajun seafood crepes, made with an understanding of what Cajun food is supposed to be and the Creme Brulee, a sweet creamy delight. Offering a wide variety, The Restaurant takes pride in not limiting themselves to one type of cuisine.

The Restaurant, as implied by the name, is a simple establishment serving terrific food. They strive for a comfortable atmosphere so that the patrons can thoroughly enjoy their meals. It is, simply put, a "Best Choice."

Mendocino

The weathered buildings of this unincorporated town of 1,000 residents spread over a knoll on the northern arm of a bay which is the mouth of Big River. Buildings look to be copies of a New England village, which, historians say, they are. Away from the tight little center of town, the lots are large, with vegetable and flower gardens flourishing in the lee of houses and fences.

The coast's redwood industry started here. A crew sent in 1851 to salvage the cargo of a vessel wrecked nearby came back reporting how close the timber was to navigable waters. Harry Meiggs of San Francisco had a chartered vessel return the next year. Aboard, when it anchored in July 1852, was machinery for a sawmill that he had ordered from New England. He bought out the river's only homesteader, making payment with proceeds from his first shipload of lumber. California Lumber Co. which started here later sold out to the Union Lumber Co. and became part of the present Georgia Pacific holdings.

One of the town's landmarks is atop the Masonic Hall, a sculpture from a single block of redwood depicting the symbols of the secret lodge. The Presbyterian Church, looking like a transplant from the east coast, is nearby. Both were built in the 1860s. South of town is the former Silas Coombs house built in 1853, which now charms guests as the Little River Inn.

Attractions

Kelly House Historical Museum, 45007 Albion Street, is housed in a home that was constructed in 1861. There is a small library, histories of many other structures in the area, and a collection of photographs. Open daily 1:00 p.m. to 4:00 p.m. Phone (707) 937-5791.

Ford House Museum, on Main Street, was built in 1854, and provides local information. Nearby is the **Chinese Joss House** constructed in 1855. Several small shops and art galleries greet those who walk the tiny downtown.

For more information, contact the **Fort Bragg-Mendocino Coast Chamber of Commerce**, 332 North Main Street, Fort Bragg CA 95437. Telephone (707) 964-3153.

Ukiah

Pears and grapes do splendidly in this warm valley of the upper Russian River. Surrounding forests produce redwoods in the west, Douglas Fir in the east; sustaining a continuing wood products industry. The primary manufacturing of Masonite, a pioneering pressed-wood board developed in the 1950s, came as added utilization of the Mendocino timber resources.

It was not until 1856, six years after this became a county on paper, that there was even a cabin on the site of Ukiah. Shortly after Samuel Lowery put up his cabin on the old Yokaya Grant, he sold out to A. T. Perkins. There were 100 people living here by 1859 when the county government was relocated from Sonoma County.

There are wineries located in three nearby valleys. The town itself has some very fine Victorian houses. Painter Grace Hudson's home, dubbed the "Sun House," is a local attraction and the historical society operates the Held-Poage Home. Several facilities serve overnight and daytime visitors. The city, largest in the county, has 12,000 permanent residents.

Attractions

The **Ukiah International Latitude Observatory** was established here in 1898 for a scientific study of the stars. Other observatories at Gaithersburg, MD, in Japan, Turkestan and Sardinia are also precisely at thirty nine degrees eight minutes north latitude. That, in Ukiah, is the south end of town on the old highway. Observers for the International Geodetic Association made simultaneous observations of selected stars, establishing the accuracy of the latitudinal grid which map makers and mariners use.

East of Ukiah, on a county road, is what remains of the **Ukiah Vichy Springs**. A report of 1888 said bathing in the waters "renders the skin soft." Fire destroyed the resort buildings which were just three miles from the center of town and took their names from the Vichy district of France.

The Terraces, now in disrepair, were an internationally-famous garden of native plants established by Carl Purdy in 1900. Purdy gathered California wild flowers and propagated them on his parent's farm located eight miles east of Ukiah.

Sun House, South Main Street, was the home of Grace Carpenter Hudson, a famous Pomo Indian painter. A museum shows original paintings, artifacts and basket work. Call 462-3370 for museum hours.

For information, and wine tour maps, contact the **Greater Ukiah Chamber of Commerce**, 495 East Perkins Street, Ukiah CA 95482. Telephone (707) 462-4075.

Willits

This one-time center for area logging operations is 1,360 feet above sea level in a valley which has become the division point for the Northwestern Pacific Railroad. Self-propelled passenger cars, dubbed the "Skunks" by the California Western Railroad's fans, travel the forty miles from here west to Fort Bragg at the coast. A community corporation based in Eureka handles the tracks north of here while the Southern Pacific Railroad operates the branch line to the south as part of its giant system.

The first settlers did not reach here until the 1860s. Kirk Brier of Petaluma built a store in 1865, and sold it to Hiram Willits, an old-timer who arrived in Mendocino County in 1857. His name went on the papers when the town incorporated in 1888. It now has about 4,300 residents and another 6,500 live in recreational subdivisions which are scattered in the Little Lake Valley.

This marks a break in the terrain and climate from the interior valleys to the south. Temperatures are cooler, there is fifty inches of rain a year, and snow whitens the hill and sometimes the valley floor almost every winter. Most of the area drains north to the Eel River's tributaries.

Attractions

Admiral William Standley State Recreation area is fourteen miles west of Laytonville on Branscomb Road which connects to the coast at Westport. This on the headwaters of one fork of the Eel River. Call (707) 247-3318 for park information.

Round Valley Indian Reservation, on Highway 162 east of Laytonville, provides a trip to two other forks of the Eel and a look into the river canyon where Northwestern Pacific Railroad tracks are sometimes carried away by winter landslides. The reservation, a 50,000 acre valley, has a tribal center in **Covelo** with a gift shop. National Forest campgrounds are east of the valley.

269

Mendocino County Museum is in Willits. Exhibits deal with Indian and pioneer logging, and living history players bring the early redwood days to life during summer months.

Black Bart Rock rises above U.S. 101 11.2 miles south of Willits. A mail stage was robbed here, one of twenty-seven coaches victimized by the lone bandit between 1875 and 1883 when a laundry mark identified him as Charles Bolton, a San Francisco man who said he was a mining engineer. Bolton did time in San Quentin, highway makers noted the incident when they routed the Redwood Highway within view of the rock.

The Skunk offers two train rides in the summer, one a half-day affair to Northspur deep in the coast range, the other a trip all the way to Fort Bragg. Summer Saturdays there is a wine and barbecue special. Winters, the diesel car makes daily trips to Fort Bragg. Steam trains run once a month during the summer. Contact California Western, Box 907, Fort Bragg CA 95437. For reservations telephone (707) 964-6371.

For more information, contact the **Willits Chamber of Commerce**, 15 South Main Street, Willits CA 95490. Telephone (707) 459-4113.

MODOC COUNTY

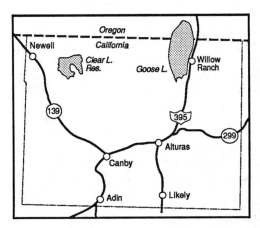

Tucked away in the far northeastern corner of California, Modoc County covers over 4,000 square miles split off from the even larger Siskiyou County located to the west. About 8,600 people live here, most making their homes on ranches or in small rural communities. All of the western portion of the county is in a geologic region called "Modoc Plateau" which takes its name from the many small volcano cones and resulting accumulation of lava and ash creating an undulating landscape rising from 3,000 feet above sea level in the fertile bottoms of the former Tule Lake to 8,000 feet where the Warner Mountains form a sharp wall on the east. The Surprise Valley, site of the first pioneer settlements, lies beyond the Warners on what is an extension of the Great Basin country of Nevada.

Modoc is the name of a proud Indian people who lived south of the Klamath tribes in Oregon. They once roamed the headwaters of the Pit River, a stream with steady water flows in very dry country. The people of Surprise Valley, having problems of their own with the Piute Indians living around Ft. Bidwell, and those living at Dorris Bridge or Dorrisville on the Modoc's side of the mountains, in 1874 successfully petitioned to have the county separated from Siskiyou. The next year, the Modocs, unhappy with their treatment on the Klamath Reservation, came south, touching off the Modoc Indian war with its battlegrounds in Lava Beds National Monument.

Modern Modoc County is a switching point for the Southern Pacific and Burlington Northern railroad routes linking Klamath Falls and Reno. Alturas, the county seat, has a population of 3,025 and serves as a trade center for cattle ranches on the east face of the Warners and in Surprise Valley. Farming is concentrated around Tule Lake near the Oregon border where although the growing season is short--about seventy-five days from last frost to first frost--the rich former lake bottoms yield prize potatoes and premium alfalfa hay.

ATTRACTIONS

Fort Bidwell, on the county road north of Cedarville, was founded in 1866 and is now the tribal headquarters for a large group of Piute Indians living over a considerable area. The general store once supplied the military post here, and hot springs on a nearby ranch were a spa in days gone by. Several old mines, from a brief gold and silver boom just after the turn of the century, may be seen on the pass east from Bidwell Mountain, open only in summer months. For information contact the **Fort Bidwell Store** at (916) 279-6366.

Fandango Pass, on a county road which heads west two miles south of Fort Bidwell, marks one of the toughest grades on the Applegate and Lassen Trails opened in 1846. A stone marker at the summit recites the history. The road winds down on the old wagon track to the west, meeting U.S. 395 on the shore of Goose Lake where the Lassen Trail branched south to California and the Applegate north to Oregon. Pass closed in the winter.

Bloody Point, seven miles east of Tule Lake on the Johnson Ranch, was the scene of repeated Indian attacks on wagon trains. To the west, actually in Siskiyou County except for a small boundary strip, is **Lava Beds National Monument**. On a high bluff of sandstone, projecting out over the old lake bed, on that eastern boundary are the **Tule Lake Petroglyphs**. Painted by prehistoric Indians who predated the Modocs, the petroglyphs are interpreted by naturalists working in the monument area.

In **Cedarville** is the oldest building in Modoc County, the **Cressler and Bonner Trading Post**. Built in 1865 as a store, it is now surrounded by trees in a park located almost in the center of the tiny crossroads town. Bonner, one of the storekeepers, maintained the road from here to Alturas for a decade before the new county took it over in a dispute that led to succession of Modoc from Siskiyou county.

Goose Lake, which straddles the California-Oregon state line, has a joint park on the lakeshore at **New Pine Creek**; a town half in Oregon, half in California. That's because the original surveyor made massive errors which now are monumented into property lines. The entire community is really in California, but neither the residents nor the State of Oregon acknowledge the survey error....which California has tried to resolve for several years.... to no avail.

For information, contact the **Modoc County Chamber of Commerce**, 522 Main Street, Alturas CA 96101. Telephone (916) 233-2819.

Alturas

Until 1874, when Modoc County divided from Siskiyou County, this little rural community was called Dorris Bridge. The legislature, reacting to a petition from residents gave it the name Alturas, Spanish for "heights" in June, 1876. The town is 4,372 feet above sea level. Poplar trees shade the residential streets, and the wide Main Street is laid out where the main road came through town after joining routes to the south and west. There is a colorful hotel, undergoing renovation, and the gray stone office building which was headquarters for the narrow gauge railroad line that served here for years.

The railroads dictated part of Alturas' recent history. It is on the main line of two roads linking Reno and Klamath Falls and is the southern terminus of the spur line now owned by Lake County, Oregon which brings lumber from the Goose Lake country into the system. At one time, much of the tracks were narrow gauge, causing reloading of freight. Lumbering is the major source of income, supplementing the retail trade which support tourist and livestock enterprises.

Attractions

Offices of the **Modoc National Forest** are on Main Street. Detailed information on hunting and fishing opportunities are available, along with maps of campgrounds.

The **Modoc County Museum**, 600 South Main Street, provides displays and a large collection of reference material on the area. Open daily during the summer, other times by appointment. Telephone (916) 233-2944.

For information, contact the **Modoc County Chamber of Commerce**, 522 Main Street, Alturas CA 96101. Telephone (916) 233-2819.

MONTEREY COUNTY

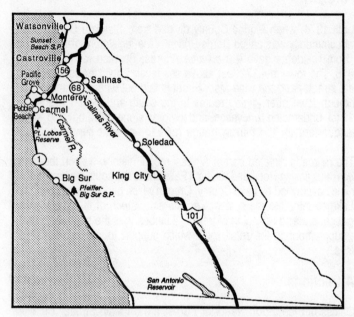

Two major mountain ranges, some of the most fertile agricultural soils, a large bay with a rich fishery, and some of the most scenic coast-line vistas make Monterey special among the California's fifty eight counties. It is also one of the largest in area, with 3,303 square miles, and the most historic in terms of recorded history.

The county is bounded on the north by Santa Cruz and Santa Clara counties and the Pajaro River. On the east, the boundary snakes southward on the first crest of the dry Diablo Range of mountains. A surveyor's offset from the thirty-sixth parallel, used to mark boundaries of many of California's twenty-seven original counties, is the south county line reaching from the mountains west through the Army's Camp Roberts on U.S. 101 over the Santa Lucia Range to a wild coast. That coastline, often punctuated with cliffs rising dramatically from the sea, is the western boundary and the setting for Highway 1, a scenic path sometimes severed by major landslides.

Nearly all of the Santa Lucia Range is in government ownership, either as part of the Los Padres National Forest, or the Hunter Liggett Military

274

reservation used as an inland maneuver area by troops stationed at Fort Ord on Monterey Bay. In the valley between the two ranges, the Salinas River feeds irrigation ditches of countless farmers. Two major reservoirs, Lake San Antonio and Lake Nacimiento, store water near the headwaters of the Salinas to augment its seasonal flow. The farms of the Salinas Valley are famous for their lettuce and other crops, a heritage recorded by novelist John Steinbeck. The port cities still have commercial fishermen and charter boat operators plying a trade which predates most farming.

For all of its size, Monterey county is sparsely settled except in the immediate area of Monterey Peninsula. The county has about 300,000 people. Some 81,000 of them live in Salinas, and 110,000 in the small crescent around Monterey Bay which includes a full Army Division stationed at Fort Ord, and military personnel assigned to several teaching facilities in the city of Monterey. Farming, military and tourist-related activities make up the basic parts of the county economy.

The bay, city and county take their names from Puerto de Monterey. The name honors Conde de Monterey, viceroy of New Spain in 1602 when the explorer Sabastian Vizcaino dropped anchor here. Vizcaino sailed with instructions to find the Bahia de los Pinos discovered in 1542 by Juan Rodriquez Cabrillo. New Spain's first permanent ground party in California came ashore here to stay, October 2, 1769. By the next year, Gaspar de Portola had the presidio open for his soldiers, and Father Junipero Serra opened the Franciscan order's second California mission on the other side of the ridge, overlooking the Carmel River.

Monterey was the Spanish capital of Alta California, a lively town built near the presidio. From here, troops and civilians sponsored by the government went out to build three more presidios. The Franciscans used the Mission San Carlos Borromeo del Rio Carmel as the base for all of their Northern California settlements erected in the next half-century.

Ships in the Pacific trade called at the busy port to resupply, creating a demand for farm products which centered on what is now the Salinas River, but until after statehood was called Rio de Monterey.

The days of Alta California ended in 1846 when U.S. Naval Commodore John Sloat declared Monterey to be a United States possession. But, all of the property rights set up in the Spanish and Mexican times survived to give a foundation to the bay area and its surrounding river valleys.

Sardines gave Monterey a reputation for its canneries along the waterfront. The little fish were shipped to national markets for over 100 years. When the sardines disappeared from the bay's waters in the 1940s, a happening which still confounds biologists, the buildings sat idle for years. Today, shops and the huge Monterey Bay Aquarium occupy much of the space once used for fish processing.

The coast south from Carmel is the Big Sur, a forbidding region during storms, and a place of visual wonderment now accessible by Highway 1. Big Sur itself is a community thirty miles from Carmel, marked by a large grove of redwoods and some small restaurants. Three state parks are along the way, and from Pfeiffer-Big Sur park there is access into the rugged Los Padres National Forest.

ATTRACTION

Soledad, site of a state prison, and a small farming community on U.S. Highway 101, has two points of interest. To the west beyond Los Coches Ranch, are the crumbling walls of the Soledad mission squatting next to a modern chapel.

To the east on Highway 146 is **Pinnacles National Monument,** a collection of volcanic spires bared by erosion. Camping and picnic areas are available. The monument can be very hot during summer months.

Mission San Antonio de Padula, on county road G14 southwest of King City, is fully restored. Founded in 1771, it fell to ruins by this century before careful reconstruction began. At one time the mission claimed 50,000 sheep and 50,000 cattle on its books. A grist mill, wine vat and other reminders of the agricultural work of the friars are on display.

Moss Landing, on Highway 1 north of Monterey, dates to 1853 when barges began working the Salinas River upstream to King City. Small shops, three state beaches and the giant Pacific Gas and Electric generating plant ring the picturesque harbor. For information contact the **Moss Landing Chamber of Commerce**, Box 41, Moss Landing, CA 95039. For moorage information, and charter boat operators, call **Moss Landing Harbor District**, 633-2461.

On Highway 156 at Highway 1 is **Castroville**, a small community set among the deep green fields of artichokes. Southern Pacific created rail yards here for its coastal branch lines. Several roadside vegetable stands and stores in town offer artichokes and other locally grown produce. For information contact the **Artichoke Advisory Board**, 10351 Merritt Street, telephone 633-4411.

Charter boats regularly sail for year around cod fishing, and seasonal whale watching and salmon trips. At Monterey, most operators are based at Fisherman's Wharf. Three operators are Monterey Sport Fishing, 372-2203;

Randy's Fishing, 372-7440; and Sam's Fishing, 372-0577. Other charter boats work from Moss Landing and Capitola.

Several wineries are located in the Salinas Valley, one in the Carmel Valley. Tour information is available by writing the local association; several farms require reservations for vineyard tours. Grape growers and vintners are part of **Monterey Wine Country**, Box 1793, Monterey CA 93942. Telephone 375-9400.

Specialized tours of all Monterey County attractions can be organized through **Steinbeck Country Tours, Limited**. They can be reached by mail at Box 22848, Carmel CA 93922, or by calling 625-5107.

Seven public golf courses are located in the peninsula area, including the famed **Spyglass Hill** and **Pebble Beach** links with their championship eighteen hole layouts. Courses, with club house numbers for tee times and reservations are, **Laguna Seca**, 373-3701; **Pacific Grove Municipal**, 375-3456; **Pebble Beach**, 624-3811, extension 239; **Peter Hay Par Three**, 624-3811 extension 228; **Rancho Canada**, 624-0111; and **Spyglass Hill** 624-3811 extension 239.

The famed **17-Mile Drive** is a toll road circling the forested part of the peninsula, and linking Pacific Grove with Carmel past exclusive residential and recreation areas. The Pebble Beach Company operates this private preserve, and generally allows traffic on the toll road at all times.

Monterey County operates nine parks outside the urbanized areas including **Laguna Seca** off Highway 68, with a world-class road racing course which is home for the Paul Newman and British School of Racing teams, camping available, call 424-1971. **San Lorenzo Regional Park** east of King City interprets farming of the Salinas Valley, campsites are booked through the Leisuretime system, telephone (916) 962-CAMP. **Jacks Peak Regional Park** is a hiking and nature trail area overlooking Monterey Peninsula west of Highway 68. **Toro Regional Park** is six miles from Salinas with views of the valley and several camping spots. Water sports are featured at the reservoir parks of **San Antonio and Nacimiento** in the south county. For information and reservation at all parks except San Lorenzo and Laguna Seca, call (800) 882-CAMP.

For additional information, contact the **Monterey Peninsula Chamber of Commerce**, Box 1770, Monterey, CA 93942.

Big Sur

Accommodations

BIG SUR LODGE, at the Pfeiffer Big Sur State Park. Spacious wooded surroundings, cabins, pool and sauna. No pets.

VENTANA INN, Highway One, Big Sur, California. High on a cliff above the Big Sur coast, the restaurant and all 40 rooms have exquisite views. Private terraces, heated pool, saunas, and lots of privacy lure guests back for repeat visits.

Art

COAST GALLERY
Highway 1
Big Sur, CA 93920
Tel. (408) 667-2301
Hrs: Mon. - Sun. 9:00 a.m. - 5:00 p.m.
Extended summer hours.

Situated on Scenic Route One along the California Pacific Coastline, is the historic showplace for Big Sur artists and craftsmen. The Coast Gallery, standing beneath towering trees and beside the stream of Lafler Canyon, provides the unique environment for Big Sur's artworks of excellence.

The historic showplace for Big Sur artists and coastal craftsmen since 1958, Coast Gallery opened to exhibit such residential notables as Henry Miller, Benny Bufano, Jean Varda, Harry Dick Ross, Bezalel Schatz, Gordon Newell, Louisa Jenkins and Loet Vanderveen. Today, Coast Gallery exhibits carefully selected works of more than 200 artists and craftsmen, including some of the finest marine art available in the country. Included are works by Richard Pettit, George Sumner, Christopher Bell, London and Ballou, and Randy Puckett. Other prominent exhibitors are Carol Setterlund and Wah Chang. Particularly noteworthy is the display of lithographs by Henry Miller, the only ones presently available on the open market. The Coast Gallery's touring shop also carries a wide selection of books by this famous writer/artist.

Whether you view the fine sculpture and paintings or watch the resident candle-maker at work, you're sure to find an oasis of scenic beauty outside and man made beauty within.

Restaurant

NEPENTHE, Coast side of Highway, Big Sur, California. Lunch and dinner served in the beamed dining room overlooking the Pacific. Outside terraces, firepit, live music and dancing.

Carmel

By official count, the population of Carmel-by-the-Sea was 4,707 in the 1980 census. As a practical matter, that many visitors may stroll the sidewalks, patronize the branches of national stores, and frolic on the beach during a typical summer weekend. Tourists invade this place. Carmel residents pride themselves in being a "village," which includes no house numbers, narrow streets among the little cottages built years ago, and political fuss over selling ice cream to go or electing a movie-star mayor.

Clint Eastwood, chosen mayor in a much publicized 1986 election, later endeared himself to residents by purchasing the farm which straddles the Carmel River and is within the county jurisdiction. Some had worried that developers would turn the backyard of the famed Carmel mission into a subdivision. Things stay the same in Carmel, which is much of its charm.

The Carmel Valley is a green spot of pastures and orchards between the steep slopes of the Santa Lucia Mountains. Fifteen miles above the village is San Clemente Dam, built in 1921 to insure a water supply for the farmers and the townspeople. Homes in Carmel Valley Village now mix with the farmland.

Attractions

Basilica Mission San Carlos del Rio Carmelo includes the mission church begun in 1770 by Father Junipero Serra. His remains are there, and the process of designating the famed padre a saint of the Catholic church nears completion. A small museum is inside the enclosed garden. To find the mission when driving south from Monterey on Highway 1, go to the second signal light in Carmel, and turn right on Rio Road. Open Monday through Saturday 9:30 a.m. to 4:30 p.m., Sundays 10:30 a.m. to 4:30 p.m. Masses daily. Call 624-1271.

Point Lobos State Park is on Highway 1 south of town. This rocky promontory is a place in which to get a feel of the Big Sur coastline if you do not have time to travel its length. Climates divide here, making this the southernmost habitat of Monterey cypress, and the northernmost sighting of the brown pelican of Southern California. Open daily.

Two sparkling beaches are a short walk from the village center. **Carmel River State Beach**, south of town is flat and gives a choice of fresh or salt water swimming. At the foot of Ocean Avenue is the **Carmel Bay City Beach**, where short cliffs of rounded boulders delineate a sloping beach of white sands. Both beaches have free access at all times.

For information, contact the **Carmel Business Association**, a Box 4444, Carmel CA 93921. Telephone 624-2522.

Accommodations

THE COBBLESTONE INN, Junipero Street, Carmel, California. A country inn hideaway with twenty-four superior rooms with fireplace, private bath, color T.V. and phone. Delicious breakfast and afternoon hors d'oeuvres included.

HIGHLANDS INN
Just south of Carmel on Highway 1
P.O. Box 1700
Carmel, CA 93921
Tel. (408) 624-3801

Perched on a pine covered hillside overlooking one of the world's most magnificent seaside vistas, Highlands Inn is rich in history and tradition. The inn has been a Carmel landmark since 1916, a gathering place for artists, hideaway for celebrities, a romantic setting for weddings and honeymoons and always a popular destination retreat. The Highlands Inn combines style and sophistication to create an extraordinary ambiance.

General manager, Peter Komposch is proud of the hotel's service, superb accommodations, fine dining and unduplicated amenities and locale. All guest rooms are complete with fully equipped kitchens, wood-burning fireplaces, outdoor decks or balconies. Sumptuous spa suites feature spacious dressing area, hydro massage tubs and plush terry cloth robes.

Spectacular views are accessible from every perspective at Highlands Inn. Whether it's the glass-walled, tree-top Pacific's Edge dining room featuring fresh California cuisine; the executive style meeting facilities with panoramas of the Big Sur Coast, the outdoor hot tubs looking out over an ocean punctuated with brilliant sunsets, or the interesting deli cafe, The California Market, all the views are magnificent!

Stay at the Highlands Inn above the drama of rocks, surf and sand with its sweeping 180 degree panorama of the Pacific Coast. You can enjoy the luxury of a self contained resort hotel or use Highlands Inn as a convenient base to explore the marvelous attractions of neighboring Carmel and the Monterey Peninsula.

INNS BY THE SEA
P.O. Box 101
Carmel, CA 93921
Tel.   (800) 422-4SEA - Inside California
        (800) 433-4SEA - Outside California

Inns by the Sea features five inns in Carmel and two in Monterey with a wide variety of rooms and suites to fit your traveling needs. All seven inns are clean, comfortable, moderately priced, centrally located, very charming and each delivers complimentary continental breakfasts and the newspaper to your door each morning (Carmel only). Please refer to the Monterey section for a description of the Inns in Monterey.

Just a stroll from famous Ocean Avenue, the Wayside Inn is a perfect setting for your stay in Carmel. Close to shops, yet a world apart, this Inn reflects the old world charm still alive in this lovely coastal village. The Inn's spacious rooms and suites are great for the whole family, many have kitchens and fireplaces. The Wayside Inn is located at Mission and Seventh Streets.

Fresh flowers in your room with a garden like setting outside your door, the Candlelight Inn mirrors the charm and serenity of Carmel. With its cozy fireplaces and country inn decor, the Candlelight is a haven away from home. Spacious rooms, some with kitchenettes and suites and connecting rooms are provided. The Candlelight Inn is located on, San Carlos between 4th and 5th Streets.

Carmel is famous for its charm which is reflected by the Carriage House Inn with its country inn feeling, fresh daily flowers, spacious rooms with open-beam ceilings, fireplaces and comforter quilts to keep you cozy and warm. Pamper yourself in the luxurious Japanese style sunken bathtub or relax in the heated pool. The Carriage House is conveniently located on Junipero between Seventh and Eighth Streets.

Nestled among the oaks with a garden highlighted by a large heated pool, Svensdgaard's Inn will set you worlds apart, while being a short walk from shopping and restaurants. Many rooms are spacious with wood burning fireplaces, some offer kitchenettes and adjoining rooms for families. Svensdgaard's Inn is located at San Carlos and Fourth Streets.

Across the street is the Dolphin Inn with its combination of luxury, good taste and traditional atmosphere. The spacious rooms are designed to please with fireplaces, king size beds and in-room movies. After a day of sight seeing, relax in the Dolphin's heated pool. Just a short walk to many shops and restaurants, the Dolphin is also found at the corner of Fourth and San Carlos Streets.

Inns by the Sea is unique in that you can call one toll free number to choose from a variety of Inns offering comfort, beauty, excellent service, moderate prices and convenient locations. Call Inns by the Sea to reserve an unforgettable escape and ask about their special Honeymoon Package.

Antiques

LUCIANO ANTIQUES, San Carlos and Fifth Street, Carmel, California. Enjoy the collections from a worldwide traveler. European, Mid-East and Oriental.

Apparel

R.K. SHUGART
On Dolores between 7th and 8th
Carmel, CA 93921
Tel. (408) 624 -7748
Hrs: Mon. - Sat. 10:00 a.m. - 5:30 p.m.

R.K. Shugart is Carmel's most exclusive and uniquely designed shop specializing in extraordinary women's fashions. Ungaro, Norma Walters, Go Silk, Shamask and Changes by Theodore are among the finest European and American designers featured exclusively by R.K. Shugart. Fashions range from sportswear to evening wear, as well as a complete array of accessories, including jewelry, scarves, belts and handbags.

Housed in the most contemporary, extravagant building in Carmel, R.K. Shugart has established itself as an innovator in the fashion industry. Shop in elegant, luxurious surroundings, where gold-leafed fixtures accentuate the latest fashions and accessories to enhance and complete your wardrobe. Wall to wall mirrors and oversized sofas create plush, comfortable fitting rooms. Indulge in a cup of freshly brewed espresso or sparkling water and sample an assortment of imported chocolates and pastries while browsing.

You'll receive expert advice and fashion consultation from the exceptional and well trained staff at R.K. Shugart. Private showings and consultations are available by appointment. Unequaled excellence and luxury, as well as exquisite clothing and accessories await you at R.K. Shugart.

RITTMASTER
Pine Inn Shop
Ocean Avenue and Monte Verde
Carmel, CA 93921
Tel. (408) 624-1147
Hrs: Mon. - Sat. 10:00 a.m. - 5:30 p.m.
and,
Normandy Inn Shop
Ocean Avenue and Monte Verde
Tel. (408) 625-6611
Library Shop
Ocean Avenue and Lincoln
Tel. (408) 624-4088

Since 1970, Gloria and Richard Rittmaster, along with their son, Greg and daughter, Jennifer have brought a unique selection of the finest designer collections to their shop in Carmel by the Sea.

The scope of their collections run from ladies sportswear, dresses, coats, suits and evening wear through furs, sporty and dressy, on to designer shoes and complete accessory collections including jewelry, hosiery, bags and belts. This well balanced mix is drawn from the best Europe and America have to offer. Featured choices from Germany are Escada, Laurel, Louis Feraud, Breustle and Mondi; from Italy, Hettabretz, Giusi Slaviero and Mimmina. French selections are Yves St. Laurent and Leonard, Paris. American clothes from unique designers Jhane Barnes, Jonathan, Judy Hornby, Nancy Heller, Joan Vass and Donna Parker.

Men's clothing is only found at the Normandy Inn Shop, where the same high standards are maintained. The selection includes designers such as Giorgio Armani, Hugo Boss, Valentino, Lubiam, Breco's and Zanella from Italy just to name a few. You will find sportcoats, suits, dress and sports pants, lots of suede, leather jackets, sweaters and even furs are offered.

Don't miss Rittmaster in Carmel for the best choices in both ladies and mens wear from the best designers around the world.

Art

BENNET STUDIOS, Carmel Plaza Shopping Center, Carmel, California. Large and exclusive gallery featuring bronze sculptures by artists Bob and Tom Bennet. Well known as one of the finest foundries in the nation.

COTTAGE GALLERY
Sixth and Mission
P.O. Box 335
Carmel, CA 93921
Tel. (408) 624-7888
Hrs: Mon. - Sun. 10:00 a.m. - 5:00 p.m.

Nestled in one of Carmel's most attractive courtyard settings is Cottage Gallery. This gallery houses an outstanding collection of original works of art displaying landscapes, figuratives, genre pieces, still lifes, seascape and city street scenes. Styles represented range from detailed realism to impressionism. Traditional American folk art is exhibited as well. In addition to original oils, watercolors and acrylics, the gallery displays unique sculptures in bronze, soapstone, wood and porcelain. The quality of the work exhibited is consistently high. Cottage Gallery is known for its exceptional value in quality art.

The gallery is warm and inviting, with a quiet charm characterizing the general feeling of Carmel itself. The staff is informed and helpful in making browsers feel welcome.

Artists shown at Cottage Gallery represent a wide spectrum of the artistic community in terms of stature and recognition. You will see outstandingly talented younger artist's work displayed alongside that of artists whose works have been accepted into permanent museum collections.

Inquiries may be directed to the owner Mr. George Goff. Be sure to take in this "Best Choice" art gallery at lovely Carmel by the Sea.

GWS GALLERIES
26390 Carmel Rancho Lane
Carmel, CA 93923
Tel. (408) 625-2288
(800) 255-6677 CA
(800) 843-6467 USA
Hrs: Mon. - Sat. 10:00 a.m. - 5:30 p.m.
Sunday 12:00 noon - 5:00 p.m.

What does it take to be a "Best Choice" art gallery? Something like GWS Galleries, one of two in the United States, it is a product of The Greenwich Workshop in Southport, Connecticut. Since 1972 it has become a nationally recognized fine art publisher concentrating on art related to the out of doors. Wildlife, Western, nautical, aviation, landscapes and seascapes are where their artists tend to concentrate.

Most emphasize representational or realistic art. Displayed are a diverse array of media, including oils and watercolors, strikingly set next to bronzes, carvings, ceramics and other forms of sculpture. All the works here are by top nationally recognized artists, most of whom are under exclusive contract. There is a display of William S. Phillips' aviation art which is shown in the Smithsonian Air and Space Museum in Washington, D.C. You will also find paintings by nationally known artists Bev Doolittle, Frank McCarthy, and Howard Terpning, bronzes by Mike Curtis, and wood sculptures by Dave Alexander of Oregon. Also on display are paintings of the Rocky Mountains by Tucker Smith, and prints of impressionist James Verdugo, outdoor artist Peter Parnall and the ever popular Carolyn Blish. Leading landscape artists displayed include Wilson Hurley and Peter Ellenshaw.

The story of talents at GWS Galleries goes on and on, but the point is that you won't find a wider mix of nationally acclaimed representational artists anywhere else on the West Coast. GWS Galleries also offers signed and numbered limited edition prints published by their parent company, The Greenwich Workshop. The gallery also offers framing and related art services. Hard to top... that's a "Best Choice."

LYNN LUPETTI GALLERY
6th Avenue between Dolores and Lincoln
P.O. Box 5776
Carmel, CA 93921
Tel. (408) 624-0622
Hrs: Mon. - Sun. 10:00 a.m. - 5:00 p.m.

Carmel is full of wonderful galleries, but this is one of a kind. No ordinary seascapes there. Lynn Lupetti Gallery is the home of the "Magic People" as artist Lynn Lupetti calls her fantasy characters.

Employing renaissance technique Lupetti combines fantasy with extraordinary realism to express themes of love, magic and nature. Most of her subjects are women and children handled with a special knowing born of intuition. Her art is uplifting. Lynn Lupetti beautifully shares her own memories which enable all people to recapture precious moments of childhood past.

Lynn and her husband, Edward Lohmann, welcome the opportunity to answer questions and show visitors around their intimate and friendly gallery. You'll also enjoy the work of several of their favorite artists who exhibit their work there.

285

Monterey County

SIMIC GALLERIES
Corner of San Carlos and 6th Streets
P.O. Box 5687
Carmel, CA 93921
Tel. (408) 624-7522
Hrs: Mon. - Sun. 9:00 a.m. - 10:00 p.m.

Since 1980, painter/owner/agent Mario B. Simic has been offering a selection of fine art that is exclusive to this gallery. Whether you seek ultra-realism, American-European Impressionism, or traditional classicism, Simic Galleries will meet your artistic tastes.

With over ninety artists now under contract, Simic represents artists listed in world renowned art publications. Works by Eugene Garin, Wendell Brown, Dave Dalton, and James Fetherolf are displayed in this outstanding gallery, as well as works by Antoine Blanchard, Edouard Cortes, Galien Lalove, Dani, Jean-Claude Guidou, Roberto Lupetti and many others.

Mario Simic has devoted his life to the world of fine art. Not only does he offer some of the finest art pieces available, Simic also stands behind the art and supports his customers who come from a broad cross section of society. Every piece is supplemented with a certificate of authenticity, as well as regular valuation appraisals. Simic believes that art not only adds beauty and dimension to the world, but that it is also a sound investment. Simic Galleries is undoubtedly a "Best Choice" gallery.

WALTER/WHITE FINE ARTS
P. O. Box 4834
On 7th between San Carlos and Dolores
Carmel, CA 93921
Tel. (408) 624-4957
Hrs: Mon. - Sun. 10:30 a.m. - 5:30 p.m.
       Summer extended evening hours.
And,
San Carlos at 5th
Carmel, CA 93921
Tel. (408) 624-4390
107 Capitola Avenue
Capitola, CA 95010
Tel. (408) 476-7001

Walter/White Fine Arts is a gallery dedicated to exhibiting the works of the finest contemporary glass artists in the world. The gallery focuses on

286

the new American "Studio Glass-Artists" and the best in contemporary wood and jewelry designers from the United States.

Many of the artists showing at Walter/White are represented in the permanent collections of the finest museums across the country and around the world. This includes the Smithsonian, Metropolitan, Corning, Toledo, Tokyo, Kunsthandverkan, and Museum of Modern Art in New York.

The large audience of collectors, and public support of these artists, has resulted in numerous expositions in Germany, Japan, and traveling tours in other foreign countries. Magazine articles in *Life, Sunset* and *New West* have added to the clamor. You can see examples of these beautiful works of art right here in Carmel.

The hand-blown glass of Walter/White Fine Arts ranges in size from small, elegant perfume bottles and paper weights, to pieces that are quite large and stunning, such as the William Morris, salmon colored "Standing Stone" and several "Sea Forms" from the internationally noted Dale Chihuly. The variety between the shapes and styles to be found here is endless and enjoyable to view.

This studio houses the largest collection of art glass on the west coast. You'll find extraordinary vases, sculpture, and contemporary jewelry. There's hardwood furniture, prints, paintings, and paperworks. View the best, when in Carmel.

Bed and Breakfast

THE COBBLESTONE INN, On Junipero between 7th and 8th, Carmel, California. Country Inn offers twenty-four rooms, romantic and comfortable rooms with fireplace, private bath, color television and telephones.

VAGABOND'S HOUSE
Fourth and Dolores
Carmel, CA 93921
Tel. (408) 624 -7738 (same for all)
and,
SAN ANTONIO HOUSE
San Antonio between Ocean and 7th Street
Carmel, CA
LINCOLN GREEN HOUSE
Carmelo at 15th Street
Carmel, CA

All three of these beautifully unique Bed and Breakfast Inns are owned and operated by the same people, and each offer a unique setting that reflects

287

the beauty and character of the village of Carmel. All provide a complimentary Continental breakfast each morning.

Situated in the heart of Carmel, the Vagabond's House is a charming English tudor country inn surrounding a courtyard dominated by large oaks, lush with camellias, rhododendrons, hanging plants and ferns. Accommodations include eleven unique suites, each with fireplace and private bath.

The Lincoln Green Inn, Elizabethan in style, with its manicured English country garden, offers four English roofed cottages painted white with forest green trim and shutters. The names Robin Hood, Maid Marian, Little John, and Friar Tuck distinguish the separate accommodations. Each has a large living room with cathedral beam ceiling, Carmel stone fireplace, bedroom, kitchen and full bath.

One block from Carmel Beach and conveniently close to the famous Ocean Avenue is gracious San Antonio House. Surrounded by flowering shrubs, tree shaded lawns, flowering walkways and stone patios, this genuine country inn offers the hospitality provided by Jewell Brown, Carmel's Innkeeper of the Year. Two and three room suites are complimented by antiques and private collection artwork, and each has a private entrance, bath, fireplace and stone patio.

Don't miss these wonderful inns if you want to fully enjoy your stay in Carmel. Romance, comfort, beauty, and charm abound for your pleasure!

Art Galleries

ATELIER GALLERY, On Dolores near Sixth, Carmel, California. Exhibiting a wide variety of paintings, etchings and lithographs by world renowned artists.

HANDWORKS, Dolores near Sixth, Carmel, California. A unique collection of home furnishings and small accessories inspired and created in America by artisans.

LOREN SPECK ART GALLERY, on Dolores near Fifth, Carmel, California. Finest in realism, original oil paintings are executed in the technique of the Old Masters.

MINER'S GALLERY AMERICANA, Corner of Lincoln and Sixth, Carmel, California. One of Carmel's largest and finest galleries. Represents over sixty-five of America's best contemporary artists.

THE WESTON GALLERY, Dolores and Lincoln, Carmel, California. Fine 19th and 20th century photographs from the leading gallery of its kind.

Delicatessen

MEDITERRANEAN MARKET
Corner of Ocean and Mission
Carmel, CA 93921
Tel. (408) 624-2022
Hrs: Mon. - Sun. 9:00 a.m. - 6:00 p.m.

To fully enjoy the natural beauty of the Carmel and Monterey areas a picnic outing is a must!! Mediterranean Market, owned by the Coniglio family, is your picnic center for finding a beautiful array of quality goods.

Start off by choosing one of the many handmade picnic baskets, then begin filling it with the tasty delicacies offered. There are many fine imported bottled and canned goods such as olives, pates, mushrooms and caviar. Accompany these snacks with a wide selection of gourmet crackers and freshly baked breads and rolls, meats and cheeses from all over the world offered by the pound or sliced. Make your own sandwiches or ask the Coniglio's for one of their creations. Homemade salads, an assortment of fine chocolates and pastries and an enormous selection of wines from every wine producing country, as well as fine California wines compliment your picnic. There are also gourmet cooking materials such as herbs, supplies and grind your own blend of fresh roasted coffee beans and teas from which to choose.

For friendly, old style service in a market overflowing with goodies, visit the Coniglio's Mediterranean Market.

Jewelry

CONCEPTS
Mission at Sixth
Carmel, CA 93921
Tel. (408) 624-0661
Hrs: Mon. - Sat. 10:00 a.m. - 5:00 p.m.
         Sunday   10:00 a.m. - 4:00 p.m.
and,
600 Stanford Shopping Center
Palo Alto, CA 94304
Tel. (415) 329-8118

Concepts is a gallery of contemporary designer jewelry. Their international reputation for being dedicated to unique designs and the art of jewelry make this "Best Choice" a must in Carmel and Palo Alto. Concepts takes a leading role in the revival of the arts and crafts movement, in the advancement of jewelry as a recognized art form, and in establishing the United States as leader in designer jewelry.

The designs featured at Concepts are unusual, exciting and well made by highly trained professionals with a flair for individuality. Young talent is encouraged and promoted with one person exhibitions featuring artists from across the country and Europe. The work is displayed in an environment that is stylish and pleasingly comfortable. To top it off, the sales staff are well informed, helpful and congenial.

Plan to stop at Concepts to view jewelry art by some of the most exciting designers working today.

Restaurants

ANTON & MICHEL
P.O. Box 1766
On Mission between Ocean and Seventh
Carmel, CA 93921
Tel. (408) 625-6526
Hrs: Lunch   Mon. - Sun.   11:30 a.m. - 3:00 p.m.
      Dinner   Mon. - Sun.   5:30 p.m. - 10:30 p.m.
              Sunday brunch   10:00 a.m. - 2:00 p.m.

Come and find out why Anton & Michel in Carmel has become an institution among Carmel locals for fine dining in an elegant setting. Nestled on Mission Street in downtown Carmel with it's large back window facing the serene Court of the Fountains, Anton and Michel has been serving fine food and spirits for over seven years. You will enjoy the fire burning in the lounge beautiful surrounding decor.

Anton & Michel is known for it's rendition of rack of lamb, but chef Jai Lal also creates delicious dishes from the fresh catches in Monterey Bay such as salmon, scampi Marinara and other seafood specialties. You can choose from wonderfully creative chicken, veal and beef dishes all cooked to perfection. The extensive wine list provides for excellent accompaniments to your meal.

The beautiful lounge offers a place to sit back, relax and enjoy your favorite aperitif or after dinner drink in an unhurried and serene environment.

Anton & Michel is where you will enjoy a multitude of tastes and aromas enhanced by the classic decor and the Court of the Fountains. Don't miss this "Best Choice" to further your pleasure at Carmel by the Sea.

CASANOVA'S, Fifth and San Carlos Streets, Carmel, California. One of the most romantic restaurants in Carmel, featuring fine French and Italian Mediterranean cuisine.

COLLAGE, Sixth Street, Carmel, California. International cuisine with appetizers such as baked Brie in dill sauce, Carpaccio and Escargots and entrees featuring sushi, homemade pasta dishes, fresh seafood, duckling and calzones. Patio dining is available.

**GENERAL STORE
AND FORGE IN THE FOREST**
5th and Junipero
Carmel, CA 93921
Tel. (408) 624-2233
Hrs: Mon. - Fri.   11:30 a.m. - 1:30 a.m.
         Sat. - Sun.   10:30 a.m - 1:30 a.m.

What used to be an old general store back in 1910 is now an excellent restaurant. Also in 1910, there was a forge in the forest that used to serve as a blacksmith's shop where skilled artisans fashioned horseshoes. Now though, these two are combined to make the General Store and Forge in the Forest, one of the most habited night spots in Carmel.

The General Store, furnished with antique marble and hardwood tables, is an intimate restaurant, set under a beautiful molded tin ceiling, serving delicious food. The menu includes a variety of creative appetizers, soups and salads, and entrees including fresh seafood, pasta dishes, chicken and duck dishes, beef, lamb, and veal dishes.

As if The General Store wasn't enough, there's also The Forge in the Forest, one of the most popular drinking establishments in Carmel. Thinking of your dining and drinking pleasure, they have an outdoor patio featuring a large brick fireplace, and an authentic rosewood bar from an old gold rush saloon. From 1910 to now, things sure have changed, but only for the better at General Store and the Forge in the Forest.

IT'S BUDS PUB, Su Vecino Court, Carmel, California. A traditional British style pub serving British, American and Irish favorites. Fresh local seafood, aged beef dishes and other tasty treats.

JIMMY'S AMERICAN PLACE
26344 Carmel Rancho Lane
Carmel, CA 93923
Tel.   (408) 625-6666
Hrs: Mon. - Sat.   Lunch   11:30 a.m. - 3:00 p.m.
                     Dinner 5:00 p.m. - 11:00 p.m.
       Sunday   Brunch 10:30 a.m. - 3:00 p.m.
                     Dinner 4:00 p.m. - 10:00 p.m.

To experience all-American cuisine and atmosphere at its best, try Jimmy's American Place in Carmel.   The decor is stark black and white and gray with big band era sound waves in the background. The clean, crisp decor will impress you with its quality of taste and style as will the cuisine.

The menu boasts beef and seafood dishes, as well as regional entrees with an international accent. The oyster bar, potato sides, salads, soups and desserts are of top quality. Nightly specials are prepared to perfection and old favorites such as lamb chops with potatoes and gravy are so tender you won't need a knife. The fresh green salads are topped with a special sweet-tangy dressing. You can smell the wood burning grill which is used to cook the meat. Finish off your meal with an American dessert - hot apple pie a la mode.

Jimmy's is your "Best Choice" for delicious homemade food in an atmosphere that is delightful.

KATY'S PLACE
P.O. Box 7467
Mission between Fifth and Sixth
Carmel, CA 93921
Tel.   (408) 624-0199
Hrs: Sun. - Thur. 7:00 a.m. - 2:00 p.m.
       Fri. - Sat.   7:00 a.m. - 4:00 p.m.

Katy's Place in Carmel has become a traditional meeting place for local residents. Homestyle cooking, friendly service and old fashioned prices are not a thing of the past at this comfortable breakfast house.

Katy's specialties include homemade blueberry, banana and bran muffins, seven types of eggs Benedict in delicious Hollandaise, fresh raspberry, blueberry or strawberry waffles and pancakes, blintzes with berries, real corned beef hash and an array of delicious omelets.

Known for it's breakfasts, Katy's also serves a great lunch. Choices include burgers, sandwiches and salads, along with daily specials.

While you are in Carmel, be sure to stop by for a terrific breakfast or lunch at Katy's. Delicious hearty breakfasts are served all day.

RIO GRILL, Route One and Rio Road, Carmel, California. Plays to a full house. Mainly contemporary American grill, but with great style and wit.

ROBATA GRILL AND SAKE BAR
3658 The Barnyard below the windmill
Carmel, CA 93923
Tel. (408) 624-2643

Hrs:	Cocktails	Mon. - Sun.	4:00 p.m. - 2:00 a.m.
	Dinners	Mon. - Sat.	5:00 p.m. - 11:00 p.m.
		Sunday	4:00 p.m. - 10:00 p.m.

Reservations for six or more required.

Traditional Japanese cooking emphasizes fresh foods prepared on an open grill before the eyes of hungry diners. Robata follows this tradition with culinary perfection. Besides the unsurpassed cuisine, rustic dark wood walls are accented by Japanese kites and the expert staff are dressed in traditional kimonos and robes.

Diners can sit at the counter to observe the endless activity of artistic Japanese cooks as they prepare meals or choose the privacy of a table. On warm evenings Robata offers outdoor dining. The menu at Robata is a combination of traditional Japanese dishes and regional foods which creates a unique choice. Indulge in the endless list of appetizers from Sashimi to barbecued eggplant or the freshest from the sea at the Sushi Bar. Sip hot sake from the extensive sake list to enhance this memorable evening.

Robata is your "Best Choice" for fine, Japanese dining in the Monterey area.

THE PINE INN, On Ocean Avenue between Lincoln and Monte Verde, Carmel, California. Fine American cuisine.

Carmel, historically noted for its view, architecture and artists presents this tour option to partake of all three:

Culture Tour of Carmel			
a.m.	Point Lobos State Park	Best seaside	Car/Att
a.m.	Katy's Place	Best breakfast	Car/Rest
a.m.	Cottage Gallery	Best original oils	Car/Art
a.m.	Concepts	Best jewel art	Car/Jwly
p.m.	Jimmy's American	Best lunch	Car/Rest
p.m.	Walter White Fine Arts	Best sculpture	Car/Gall
p.m.	Rittmaster	Best fashion	Car/App
p.m.	Carmel River State Beach	Best swim	Car/Att
p.m.	Mediterranean Market	Best beer/wine	Car/Deli
End your tour with a seaside stroll, then enjoy yourself at dinner			
p.m.	Anton & Michel	Best lamb	Car/Rest
p.m.	General Store	Best specials	Car/Rest
p.m.	Robata 's	Best Japanese	Car/Rest

Monterey

This is the oldest community in California that is not named after a patron saint. Nestled against a bay where sea lions and sea otters charm visitors, it is flanked on the flat lands by massive convention centers blending into the old town which began with the Spanish government in 1770. Modest homes of fishermen and others march up the hill toward exclusive housing areas on the ridge which shelters the town from winter's southwesterly storms.

By the thousands, Californians and others pick this small city as a destination, often drawn as much by the writings of Monterey County native John Steinbeck as the span of history reaching back to discovery of the bay in 1542 by a Portuguese navigator under contract to the Spanish, Juan Rodriquez Cabrillo. The Cannery Row made famous by Steinbeck's novel is a favorite tourist destination, competing for attention with the Old Customhouse and first stores of the Spanish pueblo.

The U.S. Army still uses the Presidio of Monterey for a school, the U.S. Navy runs a post-graduate school here, the Defense Language Institute serves all military services, and Monterey Institute of International Relations has a post-graduate civilian program based on language and learning foreign cultures.

Attractions

Downtown Monterey is an urban **State Historic Park,** with headquarters at 210 Olivier Street. Ten buildings, preserved to the years in which they were originally built, are close enough together for two easy walking tours. One group is near Fisherman's Wharf and the Old Customhouse. The other includes homes on Jefferson and Pearl streets. Call 649-2836 for hours.

Fisherman's Wharf offers snacks and fine dining amid fish markets and charter boat offices. There is a resident raft of sea lions and flocks of sea gulls competing for snacks which tourists buy from fish vendors. Open year around. A city parking lot to the right of the wharf next to the small boat basin offers easy access to both facilities.

Allen Knight Maritime Museum, 550 Calle Principal, has displays of Monterey Bay's rich history. Open daily 10:00 a.m. to 4:00 p.m. from June 15 through September 15. Hours the rest of the year are Monday through Friday 1:00 p.m. to 4:00 p.m. and Saturday, Sunday 2:00 p.m. to 4:00 p.m. Call 372-2608 for museum information and other buildings shown by the **Monterey History and Art Association.**

On Presidio of Monterey is a **U.S. Army Museum,** and an old Indian burial grounds. Open Thursday through Monday, 9:00 a.m. to 12:30 p.m. and 1:30 p.m. to 4:00 p.m.

The city operates **Colton Hall,** Pacific Street between Jefferson and Madison Streets, as a museum. It is the site of California's 1849 constitutional convention. Open daily 10:00 a.m. to 5:00 p.m. Telephone 375-9944.

On Cannery Row, the former **Hovden Cannery** was converted to an internationally-recognized aquarium in 1984. Tide pools are recreated complete with waves and shore birds, sea otters swim among the kelp, and a gray whale is in residence. Reservations are recommended during the summer season. Open daily, 10:00 a.m. to 6:00 p.m. Call 375-3333.

For further information, contact the **Monterey Peninsula Chamber of Commerce,** Box 1770, Monterey CA 93940. Telephone (408) 646-8822.

Accommodations

HOTEL PACIFIC
300 Pacific Street
Monterey, CA 93940
Tel. (408) 373-5700
     (800) 554-5542

The Monterey Peninsula's newest and finest luxury hotel, located in the beautiful heart of historic Monterey, awaits your desire for unsurpassed accommodations. The Hotel Pacific, conveniently located a short walk from Fisherman's Wharf and the famed Path of History, is a classic adobe structure boasting 104 rooms and an atmosphere that will bring you back time and again.
The main hall is adorned with original works of art, distinctive artifacts, exquisite antiques, hand tile floors and Indian rugs. Every guest room has its own design following the same South West motif. Each room is an executive suite consisting of a separate sleeping area, with the softest and most comfortable feather bed you will ever experience, a sitting and dining area, a wood-burning fireplace, a wet bar and refrigerator, TV with remote control and telephones. The luxurious bathrooms offer separate shower and bath complemented by fluffy terrycloth robes and towels and the finest in toiletries. You will enjoy the panoramic view of Monterey Bay from your private balcony or patio. Each morning, a complimentary Continental breakfast is served in the guest salon and the morning paper is delivered to your room.
Everything about the Hotel Pacific is the best. For an unforgettable getaway, stay at Hotel Pacific for the ultimate in luxury.

INNS BY THE SEA - MONTEREY
P.O. Box 101
Carmel, CA 93921
Tel. (800) 422-4SEA Inside California
     (800) 433-4SEA Outside California

Inns by the Sea features five inns in Carmel and two in Monterey with a wide variety of rooms and suites to fit your traveling needs. All seven inns are clean, comfortable, moderately priced, centrally located, very charming and each delivers complimentary continental breakfasts and the newspaper to your door every morning (Carmel only). Please refer to the Carmel section for a description of the Inns in Carmel.
At the El Adobe Inn you are moments away from an exciting fun filled vacation. The El Adobe Inn has an open air hot tub and sun deck for your pleasure. All the rooms are beautifully decorated, quiet and offer direct dial

phones and color television with Showtime. The El Adobe Inn is located just off Highway One at 939 Munras Avenue.

The Cypress Gardens Inn in Monterey is also moments away from the many historical and recreational attractions that this area has to offer. Beautifully landscaped, Cypress Gardens boasts the largest swimming pool in the area, as well as a relaxing hot tub. All the rooms are nicely decorated and offer direct dial phones and color television with Showtime. The Inn is conveniently located at 1150 Munras Avenue off Highway One in Monterey.

Inns by the Sea is unique in that you can call one toll free number to choose from a variety of inn offering comfort, beauty, excellent service, moderate prices and convenient locations. Call Inns by the Sea to reserve a very memorable vacation on the beautiful Monterey Peninsula.

SPINDRIFT INN
652 Cannery Row
Monterey, CA 93940
Tel.   (408)   646-8900
        (800) 841-1879

In the midst of Monterey's historic and picturesque Cannery Row, you will find a magical world of elegance and hospitality right on its very own beach. This is the luxurious Spindrift Inn. Come see why it has been named one of the five best hotels in the world for its interior design. You get an idea of what is to come upon entering the lobby which has hand tiled floors, Oriental carpets, distinctive antiques, original art and a charming wood burning fireplace.

Each guest room is different and provides you with a perfect blend of luxury, convenience and comfort. Traditional furnishings, hardwood floors, original art and a marble bath enhance this elegant setting. You'll enjoy the romance of a fireplace and an inviting window seat. The armoire reveals the remote control, color TV, an honor bar and refrigerator. For your ultimate comfort, all rooms feature a goose down feather bed, comforter and pillows. Cotton, plush terrycloth robes, pastel linens, nightly turndown service complete with Swiss chocolates, special toiletries, soaps and even a second telephone are also provided. A fresh, fragrant rose and the daily paper accompany your complimentary Continental breakfast. Indulge yourself in afternoon tea, pastries, wine and cheese all complimentary.

Be sure to take time to enjoy the Spindrift's beach or the view from the private roof top garden. The Spindrift Inn is your "Best Choice" in Monterey for luxury, comfort and service.

VICTORIAN INN
487 Foam Street
Monterey, CA 93940
Tel. (408) 373-8000
       (800) 232-4141

Looking for a unique inn located centrally to all the great attractions of Monterey? Stay at the Victorian Inn where classic luxury and gracious hospitality await you at this "Best Choice" for accommodations.

All guest rooms have fireplaces, remote control TV with HBO and cable. Some have ocean views and all have private patios or balconies. A second phone in the bathroom, separate vanity, shower massage, special toiletries and lush thick towels are additional amenities.   Start your day with a Continental breakfast while you plan your tour of such attractions as Cannery Row, the Monterey Aquarium and famed Fisherman's Wharf. In the afternoon enjoy complimentary wine and cheese in the parlor and a relaxing soak in the garden hot tub.

Pampering luxury and beautifully appointed accommodations await you at Victorian Inn.

Apparel

KOKO COLLECTIONS
415 Alvarado
Monterey, CA 93940
Tel. (408) 649-5656
Hrs: Mon. - Sat. 10:30 a.m. - 5:30 p.m.

For the past three years, Kyung Hi Levin, owner and operator of Koko Collections in Monterey, has been showing the finest in hard to find top women's fashions. Many fashion coordinators display their beautiful one-of-a-kind designs here.

Most of Kyung's customers are from the San Francisco Bay Area, who seek and find places such as Koko Collections that boast unique lines of women's clothing. They come back time and again for the classic lines from the finest in fabrics. You will find originality and quality at a fair price.

Koko's features unique designs from innovative Italian, Japanese and French designers using a variety of natural fabrics. People who know their fashions call this the most exciting boutique in Monterey.

Entertainment

FIRST NATIONAL FOG BANK SALOON, 638 Wave Street, Monterey, California. Step out on the dancefloor, live music in a rustic setting. Rock, blues, jazz and funk. Full bar and appetizers.

Kites

WINDBORNE KITES
585 Cannery Row
Monterey, CA 93940
Tel. (408) 373-7422
Hrs: Sun. - Thu.   10:00 a.m. - 6:00 p.m.
       Fri. - Sat.   10:00 a.m. - 9:00 p.m.
Visa, MasterCard, Discover Card and AMEX are accepted.

Kites provide one of the least expensive, yet most enjoyable hobbies for children from 2-102 years old. Kite flying is quiet, non-polluting, inoffensive fun that ties the enthusiast with the elemental natural forces of wind, weather, and terrain.

Windborne Kites in Monterey boasts the biggest and best selection of kites in the country! They stock kites for the novice through the expert flyer. Aficionados will find a wonderful selection of exclusive artist designs displayed in the store along with an extensive selection of two string stunt kites, as well as traditional American and Oriental styles. The staff, kite flyers all, are always delighted to share their knowledge and enthusiasm for kite flying with anyone who asks. All kites and windsocks are chosen for their quality and flyability and are guaranteed.

Every weekend, Windborne Kites and the California Kite Group sponsors a kite fly on Monterey Beach along Highway 1 at Canyon Del Rey Boulevard. The informal kite fly starts around noon, weather permitting. Bring your kites, the wind is free! Everyone is welcome.

Mall

EDGEWATER PACKING COMPANY
Cannery Row at Prescott
Monterey, CA 93940
Tel. (408) 649-1899

The Edgewater Packing Company houses numerous delights, and you'll want to allow yourself plenty of time to explore the nooks and crannys of this Cannery Row attraction. The brainchild of Dick O'Kane, the Packing Company features food, fantasy, and a flavor of times gone by.

See the west's fastest carousel, with thirty-four horses, two zebras, two chariots - all hand-carved. It delights and entertains kids from one to one hundred. After your carousel ride, taste Oscar Hossenfelder's Fabulous Formula ice cream, hand-made in small quantities on the premises from 1890's recipes. The Warehouse Restaurant is unlike any other, with an antique delivery truck in one corner. Family meals are the speciality, with children's menus, and high quality at reasonable prices. Another restaurant at the Packing Company is Hossenfelder's Fabulous Restaurant, boasting over 4,095 omelette combinations, homemade french fries, and a wide range of meals and snacks. Leave your arcade addict to try the antique games and the latest electronic marvels while others in your group explored the magic shops, novelties shops, candy store and cookie store. Later, you can capture yourself in costume at the photo shop. Don't miss the 1915 Seagrave fire truck, from the San Francisco World's Fair.

Come back again and again to the Edgewater Packing Company, since one visit will only whet your appetite to explore and play in this fantasy land which expands and improves each year.

(See special invitation in the Appendix.)

Restaurant

THE CLOCK GARDEN RESTAURANT
565 Abrego Street
Monterey, CA 93940
Tel. (408) 375-6100
Hrs: Mon. - Sun. 10:00 a.m. - 1:00 a.m.

Take a break from sightseeing in the beautiful Monterey area at the Clock Garden Restaurant in the old part of town. For history buffs, the building's history goes back to the 1800's when it was a stable for the Old Adobe building across the street.

Relax in the beautifully landscaped garden patio, heated on chilly nights, or gather around the garden pond to watch the movement of the fish and water greenery. A collection of antique clocks and glassware is displayed for your pleasure.

The Clock Garden offers tasty meals throughout the day and evening. Breakfasts and lunches start at 10 a.m. are are served until the early bird dinners begin at 4:00 p.m. Choose their famous burger and grilled Reubens, the delicious seafood crepes or imaginative fresh salads. Early bird specials come with soup, salad or artichoke, entrees include tempura-style Calamari, real roast turkey and trimmings, boneless leg of lamb, and fresh seafood dishes. Try the Clock Garden's chicken breasts stuffed with apple and almond dressing, veal piccata, or maybe their famous spareribs. There is also a complete selection of fresh seafood. Top your meal off with a delicious homemade dessert!

Come to the Clock Garden, enjoy the unique setting, delicious food, and the friendly people of Monterey at this "Best Choice" restaurant.

CONSUELO'S MEXICAN RESTAURANT
361 Lighthouse Avenue
Monterey, CA 93940
Tel. (408) 372-8111
Hrs: Mon. - Thu.   11:30 a.m. - 9:30 p.m.
         Fri. - Sat.   11:30 a.m. - 10:00 p.m.
         Sunday   11:00 a.m. - 9:30 p.m.

Consuelo's Mexican Restaurant is located in a Victorian mansion built by Harry Green as a summer residence in 1886. Tucked away from busy Lighthouse Avenue behind trees and flowers, the restaurant is an island of calm. The house was converted into a restaurant with family pictures and period furnishing by owner Ken Bales in 1969. High ceilinged rooms, three on the second floor, are papered in red and white flocked wallpaper. A patio is ready for warm weather luncheons.

Selections at Consuelo's range from fresh seafood prepared Mexican style, to charbroiled specialities such as fajitas, or traditional favorites such as tacos, enchiladas, flautas, and chile rellenos. The house speciality desert is Adobe Pie, a mocha almond ice cream in a chocolate crust, topped with fudge and whipped cream. A children's menu is available.

Consuelo's reputation for food and service keep visitors and locals returning, so be sure to call for reservations on weekends and during summer

301

months. At this "Best Choice," you'll enjoy the finest Mexican cuisine in a historical Monterey setting sure to delight you.

DAVID WALTON'S BEAU THAI
807 Cannery Row
Monterey, CA 93942
Tel. (408) 373-8811
Hrs: Mon. - Sun. 11:00 a.m. - 10:00 p.m.

David Walton's Beau Thai is in an old cannery, but one forgets about the days of old Monterey on entering this little corner of Thailand. David lived in Thailand on and off during the past twenty years, and with his partners Jamlong and Kovit Busadee, co-host and chef, and the rest of the Thai staff, the restaurant provides Thai authenticity and hospitality.

Over forty tasty Thai dishes attract "in the know" locals who come often to enjoy the unique cuisine, as well as pleasing visitors fortunate enough to find Beau Thai. Thai cooking is unlike other Asian styles with its invisible dimension of flavors.

The Bangkok court cuisine does not disrupt the balance of the many delicate tastes and flavors and dishes can be prepared for tastes ranging from mild to Thai hot-hot. Beau Thai is a great place for parties, business meetings, or a quiet rendezvous. Enjoy the selection of imported beers and California wines at prices as reasonable as the rest of the menu.

Make your reservations early to secure your escape to this increasingly popular taste of Asia in Monterey, David Walton's Beau Thai.

DOMENICO'S, 50 Fisherman's Wharf #1, Monterey, California. Overlooking the Yacht Harbor, fresh fish and the finest meats grilled on an open hearth.

JUGEM, 409 Alvarado Street, Monterey, California. Right in the downtown, Japanese cuisine. Sushi, teriyaki, tempura and sukiyaki.

SANDBAR & GRILL
Municipal Wharf #2
Monterey Yacht Center
Monterey, CA 93940
Tel. (408) 373-2818
Hrs: Mon. - Sun.   11:30 a.m. - very late
                         6:30 p.m. - very late piano bar
        Sat. - Sun.   10:30 a.m. - 4:00 p.m. brunch
        Mon. - Fri.   4:00 p.m. - 5:00 p.m. happy hour

For fine food, spirits and fun, get away to the Sandbar & Grill. Strategically tucked below the dock level, you'll find a theatrical hideaway awash with local color and a spectacular view of Monterey Harbor and the local fishing fleet.

The Sandbar's huge, friendly bar always welcomes you. Whether it's lunch, dinner, or just a snack, the Sandbar expertly prepares fresh seasonal seafood dishes and BBQ chicken, ribs, Philadelphia cheese steaks, calamari and other tasty delights to fulfill your culinary desires.

Some of the daily specials might include fettucini and fresh bay scallops in a basil cream sauce, paper-wrapped halibut with lime butter sauce and sauteed mushrooms, or grilled calamari. There's a tasty variety of appetizers: deep fried artichoke hearts, Escargot, or fried mozarella in a marinara sauce. Weekend brunch includes specialties like eggs Monterey with grilled calamari, eggs, English muffins, eggs, crab or salmon Benedict, crab cakes Rio--all this served with cottage fries and fresh fruit! The regular menu can also be ordered from during the brunch.

The prices are reasonable and the dishes are prepared to perfection. Enjoy their nightly piano bar for a sing-a-long or just good listening music. Don't miss this "Best Choice". You'll enjoy culinary delights and good spirits while watching sea lions and otters playing among the fishing boats.

SARDINE FACTORY, 701 Wave Street, Monterey, California. Serves only the finest meat entrees and the freshest Eastern and local seafoods prepared in a Continental style.

SURDI'S RESTAURANT
2030 Fremont Street
At Routes I and 68
Monterey CA 93940
Tel. (408) 646-0100

Hrs:			
Breakfast	Mon. - Sun.	7:00 a.m. - 2:00 p.m.
Lunch	Mon. - Sun.	11:15 a.m. - 2:00 p.m.
Dinner	Mon. - Sun.	4:30 p.m. - Closing
Brunch	Sunday	10:00 a.m. - 2:00 p.m.

When Northern and Southern Italian cuisine is desired, Surdi's is a definite "Best Choice" among Monterey locals and travelers to the area. Bob and Dottie Surdi offer hearty portions of a wide variety of Italian specialities and have earned themselves a respected reputation among those who appreciate Italian food.

A few of the entrees on the Surdi's menu include Cioppini, fettucini Alfredo with prawns, Tortellini Alla Panna, and chicken Monterey - boneless breast of chicken sauteed in browned butter with artichoke hearts, fresh mushrooms, a hint of garlic surrounded with a creamy sauce. All dinners include homemade soup or salad, and freshly baked garlic bread. Italian and Monterey county wines are featured at the dining table, and in the cocktail lounge. There is an award winning salad bar, an antipasto bar and a fresh fruit bar.

Surdi's also offers an American breakfast menu, and an Italian luncheon buffet feast. Sunday brunch is a speciality and offers traditional egg dishes and Italian specialities. Groups, banquets and weddings are welcomed.

In Monterey, Surdi's is your "Best Choice" for authentic Italian cuisine and affordable prices in a great atmosphere.

WHALING STATION INN, 763 Wave Street, Monterey, California. Reservations a must. Bouillabaisse is a gourmet's delight, steaks are reputed the best on the peninsula.

The distinctive California blend of young and old, Spanish and American, seashore and landscape is the enticement of Monterey. Experience its historic and modern charm with this tour.

The Charm of Monterey Tour			
a.m.	Hotel Pacific	Best breakfast	Mon/Acc
a.m.	State Historic Park	Best walking tour	Mon/Att
p.m.	Koko Collections	Best fashions	Mon/App
p.m.	Fisherman's Wharf	Best lunch area	Mon/Att
p.m.	Windborne Kites	Best flying	Mon/Kite
p.m.	Seventeen Mile Drive	Best sunset drive	Mont/Att
p.m.	Sandbar & Grill	Best piano bar	Mon/Rest

Pacific Grove

This is a delightful town, clustered on the north shore of Monterey Bay west of the bustle and commercialism of the Cannery Row District. Pleasant homes, a trail above the low cliff from which sea otters can be seen, and the rare ground-granite pebbles of the beach at Lighthouse Point give the place a special quality. Its downtown business district, astride a broad avenue, speaks to times past when life was not as busy.

Novelist Robert Louis Stevenson, who lived on the peninsula at one time, called Pacific Grove "dreamlike."

Monarch butterflies winter here from November through March, and the return is greeted by citizens with a butterfly festival the second week of October. There is a $500 fine for persons "molesting butterflies."

Attractions

Point Pinos Lighthouse, at the western end of Lighthouse Avenue, was built in 1872. Breakers crash into the rocks here, grinding decomposing granite to brown pebbles instead of sand. A view point and walking area are open at all times. Low tide lets explorers walk among the rocks to a point usually far offshore amid the wonders of tide pools, birds and sea lions.

Asilomar Estate, to the south of the point, is now a state park operated for conventions and retreats. The Young Women's Christian Association developed the site when Pacific Grove pushed religious conferences out of

305

town. Several striking buildings are part of the estate, which can be seen without being a conference participant.

The **Pacific Grove Museum of Natural History**, Forest and Central Avenues, was founded in 1881. Animals of Monterey County are featured in exhibits, the butterfly's life cycle is explained, and the sea otter comeback described. Open Tuesday through Sunday, 10:00 a.m. to 5:00 p.m. Telephone 372-4212.

For details, contact the **Pacific Grove Chamber of Commerce**, Box 167, Pacific Grove CA 93950. Telephone (408) 373-3301.

Accommodations

THE CENTRELLA, 612 Central Avenue, Pacific Grove, California. Experience old-fashioned grace and hospitality. Bed and Breakfast accommodations.

THE GOSBY HOUSE INN
643 Lighthouse Avenue
Pacific Grove, CA 93950
Tel. (408) 375-1287
      (800) 342-4888

Built in 1887 by J.F. Gosby, The Gosby House Inn has made its share of contributions to the history of the Monterey area. When the Del Monte Hotel burned to the ground in 1894, Mr. Gosby opened his home to lodgers, the house has operated as a hotel ever since. This charming house, listed on the National Historic Register, has names with historic significance for each of its twenty-two guest rooms.

Each room is beautifully appointed with an abundance of wood, cozy comforters, dainty wall paper and adorned with fresh flowers and a bowl of fruit. Accommodations range from one to three rooms some with fireplaces and most with private bathrooms. Complimentary breakfast and afternoon tea with hors d' oeuvres and sherry are graciously provided. The staff is on hand to bring you the morning paper, shine your shoes and even select a bottle of wine from the private wine cellar. Additionally, your hosts will make arrangements and reservations at restaurants, one of sixteen area golf courses, tennis courts or the theater.

For a taste of history, romance and ultimate pampering enjoy The Gosby House Inn, your "Best Choice" for accommodations in Monterey.

THE GREEN GABLES INN, 104 Fifth Street, Pacific Grove, California. A romantic Queen Anne style mansion with five upstairs bedrooms, a two room suite and carriage house with private baths and fireplaces. Enjoy morning breakfast with a panoramic view of the bay.

Art

SITE 311 - CONTEMPORARY FINE ARTS, 311 Forest Avenue, Pacific Grove, California. Displays fine contemporary art in a full range of mediums such as paintings, sculpture, fibrework, photography, paper sculpture and more.

Restaurants

LA PROVENCE
105 A Ocean View Boulevard
American Tin Cannery
Pacific Grove, CA 93950
Tel. (408) 649-0707
Hrs:

Lunch	Mon. - Sun.	11:30 a.m. - 2:30 p.m.
Dinner	Mon. - Sun.	6:00 p.m. - 9:30 p.m.
Music	Fri. - Sat.	
Sunday	Brunch	11:00 a.m. - 3:00 p.m.

For traditional cuisine from the south of France in an atmosphere that is reminiscent of the French Riviera, try La Provence in the American Tin Cannery. Owner and chef Pierre E. Coutou, a native of France, has over thirty years of education and experience in the business and has created a special world of dining pleasure in this old factory building overlooking the bay.

There is a panoramic view of Monterey Bay through the large two story factory windows, indoor/outdoor umbrella tables, rattan chairs, picturesque murals and plants that give the atmosphere an informal feeling.

Whether you go for lunch or dinner, there are tasty dishes to tempt your taste buds. Start with a wonderful array of traditional and creative hors d'oeuvres or unusual homemade soups, then enjoy a delicious pate sandwich, a salad nicoise, or entrees like sea scallops and Mahi Mahi baked in a paper bag with dry vermouth, cream julienne of leek and carrot, oyster mushroom fresh pasta or delicious renditions of boneless chicken, breast of duck, rack of lamb, medallions of veal or fine aged Angus beef dishes. All entrees come with salad vinaigrette and special potatoes or pasta. Homemade desserts and a wonderful wine list accompany this heavenly cuisine. Don't miss La Provence for a delicious sunny lunch in a unique setting or a romantic star-light dinner.

On weekends there are the sounds of a guitarist and a vocalist in the background and at Sunday dinner a local dance troupe with a special prix fixe dinner. La Provence will provide for a most enjoyable experience in fine dining.

THE OLD BATH HOUSE, 620 Ocean View Boulevard, Pacific Grove, California. Romantic 1930's style wood and etched glass decor with ocean view dining and full service antique bar. Excellent Italian and French Continental cuisine and extensive European and California wine list.

PEPPERS MEXICALI CAFE, 170 Forest Avenue, Pacific Grove, California. Combined Mexican, Latin American and Californian cuisine featuring fresh seafood, combos and a variety of salsas. Extensive regional wine list and tasty specials.

Pebble Beach

Accommodations

LODGE AT PEBBLE BEACH
17 Mile Drive
Pebble Beach, CA 93953
Tel: (408) 624-3811

A world apart...quiet luxury, casual elegance and unpretentious charm are combined with modern amenities at the 161 room Lodge At Pebble Beach. Outside your window are views of Pebble Beach's eighteen hole golf course and the beautiful Carmel Bay. All the rooms boast up-scale VIP pleasantries and most are accentuated with fireplaces.

Adjacent to The Lodge, the shops at Pebble Beach offer the finest in goods and services including a post office, service station, bank, real estate office, drug store, golf shop and a variety of top quality speciality shops. The Tap Room is down the hallway from the lobby and is patterned after an English Pub. The Gallery restaurant and bar, situated across from The Lodge above the retail shops, serves excellent cuisine and is also available for receptions or conference groups staying at The Lodge. The Cypress Room serves three meals daily and offers beautiful views of the eighteenth green. Club XIX offers French cuisine on the outside terrace for lunch or elegantly presented indoors each evening.

This is a top, world class resort that offers the best of every vacationing desire. Come stay at The Lodge at Pebble Beach and enjoy the great shopping, dining, golfing, tennis and the magnificent beauty that attracts so many visitors to this area of California.

Art

COAST GALLERY, At the Lodge, Pebble Beach, California. Featured are watercolor paintings and marine artists.

Salinas

Tens of thousands of acres around the city produce lettuce and other crops which thrive on the temperate climate and sandy soil of this broad plain of the Salinas River. Many of the farms irrigate by pumping from shallow wells which tap subsurface flows of this meandering stream.

Salinas is a major shipping point for agricultural produce, and is now home for well over 80,000 people. Several industrial and commercial operations also are located in or near the city.

Elias Howe, a sometimes carpenter and church deacon, in 1856 put up the first building in what was to be Salinas. His "Half Way House" was a store and inn. The Salinas post office opened two years before on James B. Hill's Rancho Nacional.

The shift of commerce inland from Monterey brought the county seat here in 1872. A city was incorporated two years later.

Attractions

Boronda Adobe, on Boronda Road at Laurel Avenue, was built in 1848 and is now restored. Open Sundays 1:00 p.m. to 4:00 p.m. Call 757-8085.

A Victorian house which was home of Salinas' first mayor, the Baker House, 238 East Romie Lane, is now restored. Open the first Sunday of each month from 1:00 p.m. to 4:00 p.m., and other times by appointment. Call 757-8085.

The city's library honors author John Steinbeck. Located at 110 West San Luis Street, it contains original manuscripts and other exhibits. Call 758-7311 for hours.

Steinbeck House, 132 Central Avenue, is the author's birthplace. A local charitable guild operates a luncheon-only restaurant here featuring vegetables and other products of the county. Two sittings Monday through

Friday, 11:45 a.m. and at 1:15 p.m. Call 424-2735. A gift shop in the basement is open Monday through Friday from 11:00 a.m. to 3:00 p.m.

Southeast of Salinas is the company town of **Spreckels**, platted in the late nineteenth century around a sugar beet factory operated by the Spreckels family. The factory closed in 1982, people continue to live in this planned community.

For further information, contact the **Salinas Area Chamber of Commerce**, 119 East Alisal Street, Salinas CA 93902. Telephone (408) 424-7611.

Restaurant

STEINBECK HOUSE
132 Central Avenue
Salinas, CA 93901
Tel. (408) 424-2735
Hrs: Lunch.   Mon. - Fri.   11:45 a.m. and 1:15 p.m.
       Gift shop.   Mon. - Fri.   11:00 a.m. - 3:00 p.m.
Visa and MasterCard are accepted.

John Steinbeck, famous for his novels about poor, oppressed California farmers and laborers, never imagined his home being full of people eating foods from the house cookbook. That's what happening right now; his beautiful Victorian residence has been transformed into a restaurant and giftshop, and you're invited.

This unique restaurant offers a chance to experience what it was like back in the days of Steinbeck's childhood, and at the same time, enjoy a delicious meal with a tasty homemade dessert to follow. The Best Cellar Gift Shop affords an opportunity to purchase gifts, antiques and books; it's all owned and operated by volunteers, with proceeds going to local charity groups.

The Steinbeck House is available for private parties, brunches, or receptions. This is one of those rare places that is a definite must on any agenda, and because of this reservations are recommended.

(See special invitation in the Appendix.)

Seaside

Nestled on the south side of Fort Ord, with Highway 1 to its front and a single access to the beach on Canyon Del Rey Road, Seaside is a far different community from that envisioned by its founder. John L. D. Roberts, a physician turned land developer, subdivided his 160 acre ranch with the intention of creating a community to rival the peaceful Pacific Grove.

Roberts was designated Seaside postmaster, and with his wife served 42 years. He also served long terms on the Monterey school board and county board of supervisors. When he died in 1949, Roberts was 88 and his town spread over several times the area of the original ranch. It is the commercial heart of the Monterey peninsula, providing space for businesses that do not fit the other communities.

When the Chamber of Commerce counted in 1986, there were sixteen auto dealerships here, along with over 485 other businesses. Seaside has about 38,000 residents including the 14,000 soldiers and their dependents living on Fort Ord.

Attractions

Fort Ord, on Highway 1, was the site of basic training for soldiers by the tens of thousands, and is now home for an Army Division. Its sand dunes at the ocean's edge provide prime hang glider and kite flying country.

There are 21 parks in Seaside. **Roberts Lake,** located off Canyon Del Rey between the railroad tracks and Highway 1, commemorates the town founder. Beach access is at the foot of Canyon Del Rey

Fremont Boulevard in Seaside has a reputation for the best variety of ethnic restaurants on the peninsula. Vietnamese, soul food, and other specialties are offered on this strip of eateries.

For information, contact the **Seaside-Sand City Chamber of Commerce,** 505 Broadway Avenue, Seaside CA 93955. Telephone 394-6501.

NAPA COUNTY

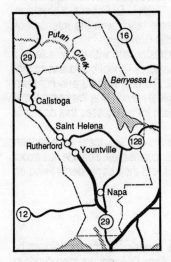

Once much larger with all of Lake County in its bounds, Napa now contains 744 square miles of the Napa River Basin. The commanding height at the valley's upper end is Mount Saint Helena, 4,344 feet above sea level with the summit in neighboring Sonoma County but much of the land mass within Napa. Lake Berryessa, a U.S. Bureau of Reclamation reservoir of giant proportions, lies on the northeast edge of the county. Within a few short miles, the Napa river reaches sea level in a broad, meandering channel that empties into the San Pablo Bay arm of San Francisco Bay.

The Napa Valley is famed for its wine grapes thriving in a climate of hot, dry summers and moist winters. The city of Napa is part of the industrial triangle of Vallejo and Fairfield in Solano County plus Napa.

Scrap iron, salvaged in the bay area, is brought to the Kaiser Steel plant for processing into oil drilling platforms, pipe and other massive items. Napa continues to grow rapidly, offering a short commute to other job centers in the North Bay, and over the hill in Fairfield. There are now more than 100,000 residents in the county, over half of them living within the Napa city limits.

The Napa name came from the Spanish interpretation of an Indian tribal name. Historians are unsure about what the word really means, but they found references as early as 1795 in records of the Mission Dolores at San Francisco. One account says most members of the tribe resident of the Napa Valley died in an 1838 smallpox outbreak and all remaining tribal members were dead by 1870.

Actual exploration of the valley came in 1823 when Francisco Castro and others scouted locations for a new mission. They settled on Sonoma, and designated what is now the site of Napa for the mission cattle operations.

The first resident of the upper valley was George Calvert Yount, a fur trapper from North Carolina who worked at the missions and in 1835 settled among the Indians. Records from the time indicate parts of six tribes had villages in the area. Yount took an 11,814 acre grant to Rancho Caymus in 1836 which included what is now Yountville, named in his honor.

Edward Turner Bale, surgeon aboard an English ship that called in Monterey, took an 1843 grant to Rancho Carne Humana from what was by then the Mexican Alta California government. The communities of St. Helena and Calistoga are within this large grant. For years the mill on the Bale ranch, with a giant water wheel, produced flour from wheat fields that preceded the vineyards of the region.

Napa was one of the twenty-seven original counties created by the legislature of 1850. The county seat has always been Napa. Until the bay area's industrial growth during World War II, the county remained bound to an agricultural economy. Crops emerged as grapes growing in the valleys and a substantial cattle grazing industry based on the hilly foothills and the ability of irrigated lands to produce hay and pasture. Food processing and manufacture of leather goods were among the first commercial ventures. Miners have taken mercury and silver from the older mountains, salt from lagoons in tidewater, and clays for pipe and other products from old river silts. The limestone of the hills forms cavernous storage warehouses for wine, and a source for some diatomatious filter material.

Napa State Hospital, with 2,600 employees, is the largest payroll in the county, followed by Mare Island Naval Shipyard, a commute away in neighboring Solano County. Napa itself has vacant land zoned for industrial development and three industrial parks in the county lie south of the city.

The growing season is 217 days long, measured at St. Helena in the center of the wine country. That means that many grape growers worry about frost protection in the spring, when vines develop early under mild temperatures and the ground is wet by about thirty-three inches of winter rains. January has a mean temperature of forty-six degrees, July of seventy one. Much of the mountain rainfall in the east county is captured by Lake Berryessa and sent out of the basin to Solano County fields along Putah Creek. The newly-developed North Bay Aqueduct, part of the California Water project, augments the flows of the Napa river for farmers in the west county. Rainfall at Napa is about ten inches less a year than at St. Helena, and the summer temperatures average eleven degrees warmer.

Getting around in the Napa Valley is a matter of traveling in the north-south direction of the rivers, or driving over winding mountain roads which connect the main valley and its neighbors. Highway 29 comes north from Vallejo through the valley and on up over the shoulder of Mount Saint Helena above Calistoga. Highway 128 begins at Geyserville on U.S. 101 in Sonoma County and meets 29 at Calistoga. Two east-west routes across the North Bay counties, Highways 37 and 12, cross far below the imposing hills to the north.

The continuing urbanization of Napa County is a factor in local politics. County supervisors, bent on preserving the agricultural land so attractive to vineyards, put a twenty acre minimum lot size on divisions of farm land and a forty acre minimum on hillside partitions. None-the-less, in 1987 county officials predicted that 150,000 people will live in Napa county by 1990.

ATTRACTIONS

The wineries and related attractions draw thousands of visitors to the Napa Valley each year. The Winegrowers of California, through their Wine Institute, 165 Post Street, San Francisco, CA 94108 produce a special **winery travel guide**. Telephone (4l5) 986-0878. About 25,000 acres of grapes are in the Napa region, with Cabernet Sauvingnon the leading vine among seven principal varieties grown. Over 100 wineries open to the public were listed in the most recent directory. Many visitors prowl the roads without a specific destination, driving in to wineries as the fancy catches them.

Mont La Salle, on Mount Veeder Road northwest of Napa, is one winery which has been closed to visitors except by appointment. This is the Novitiate of Christian Brothers. Telephone (707) 963-4480 for current information on tours.

Oakville, a major crossroads on Highway 29 north of Yountville, has fashioned itself into a winery village. From here to the west is one of the famed winding hill roads of the wine country, Oakville Grade Road to Glen Ellen in the Sonoma Valley. It offers views of both valleys and of vineyards clinging to hillsides. The Robert Mondavi Winery in Oakville sponsors a **chamber music festival** each summer and its lunches and dinners in the restaurant are often so crowded that reservations are suggested. Call 963-9611.

Robert Louis Stevenson State Park, on Highway 29 seven miles north of Calistoga, is a day use area which provides views of Mount Saint Helena. Over 3,000 acres is within the park, providing hiking trails into the coast range foothills at about 2,200 feet above sea level. The famed author once lived in the Napa Valley and wrote about the mountain toll house, and remained for a time in a miner's cabin at the old Silverado Mine. A granite marker and spoils from the tunnel mark the site. Telephone 942-4575.

Resorts and campsites line the 168-mile shoreline of **Lake Berryessa**, reached on Highways 121 and 128. The lake is named for Sixto Berryessa, part owner in a 35,000 acre rancho that was not legalized until 1863 and is now flooded by the waters stored behind Monticello Dam. There is a park headquarters on Knoxville Road with information on the area. Telephone 966-2111.

Pope Valley, tucked off in the north county, is a small community which has commercial cattle ranches nearby. The Aetna Springs, one of the areas many old resorts, is on Pope Valley Road as it winds northwesterly to Butts Canyon. Pope Valley Winery, 6613 Pope Valley Road, is open 10:00 a.m. to 5:00 p.m. Saturdays and Sundays only. Rustridge Vineyard and Winery, which is open 8:00 a.m. to 5:00 p.m. daily, is on Lower Chiles Valley Road 3.3 miles south of its junction with Pope Valley Road. Telephone 965-2871.

For additional information, contact the Napa Valley Tourist Information Center, 4076 Byway East, Napa CA 94559. Telephone (707) 257-1112.

Calistoga

The name of this city of 4,000 is better known than its location, on Highway 128 near the northwest boundary of the county. Bottled water from its mineral springs is widely sold, it remains a resort town with bubbly spring water, mud bath treatments, and a nearby geyser which performs on schedule, just like the one in Yellowstone National Park.

"Someday I'll make this place the Saratoga of California," developer Sam Brannan intended to say when he bought the springs in 1859. His tongue slipped, according to a biographer, and the phrase came out "the Calistoga of Sarafornia." The name stuck. Brannan put up twenty-five cottages, a hotel and some palm trees. The venerable palms remain today at what later became Pacheteau's Hot Springs. Indians, it is said, used a word which meant "oven place" to denote the underground energy of Calistoga.

Brannan also operated a store, which did a land-office business, since he came on the heels of the area's brief silver rush. He sponsored a branch railroad to reach his resort, and formally opened the Calistoga Hot Springs in 1868. Brannan is credited with encouraging others to plant the hillsides with cuttings from top wine grape varieties of the time.

Attractions

Napa County Historical Museum, on Washington Street, began in one of Brannan's original resort cottages. The newer Sharpsteen Museum building next door has a scale model showing how the first resort looked, along with other exhibits of the area history. Open daily.

The winding **Petrified Forest Road** west of town leads past a small tourist attraction with a **museum** and **picnic area**. The petrified Forest was created when redwood trees fell, probably as a result of volcanic eruptions, and minerals replaced the wood. Open daily.

California's version of **Old Faithful Geyser** is at 1299 Tubbs Lane. The private park has an admission fee and is the site of weddings and picnics, plus viewing the 350-degree water breaking from the ground every forty minutes. Some eruptions splash bubbles and foam sixty feet above the mouth of the geyser. Telephone 942-6463.

Calistoga's airport is home of a **glider center** which offers rides for twenty minutes or more, and sail plane piloting instructions. Open 9:00 a.m. to 7:00 p.m. in the summer, and 9:00 a.m. to sunset in the winter. Call 942-5592.

The Napa Valley Railroad's old **Calistoga Depot** is a shopping center with fully-restored rolling stock outside. In addition to restaurants and shops, the depot has offices for a **hot air balloon company** providing rides over the valley and the local chamber of commerce which has maps for walking tours of the resort town.

Several wineries are close by Calistoga. There are six spas here including the **Calistoga Spa Hot Springs**, 1006 Washington Street, which was Brannan's second venture for visitors and now has a forty-nine unit motel on the premises.

Calistoga Mineral Water Co., which bottles the widely sold sparkling water, has offices at 1477 Lincoln Avenue. Telephone 942-6295.

For information, contact the **Calistoga Chamber of Commerce** at the Calistoga Depot, 1458 Lincoln Avenue, Calistoga CA 94515.

Accommodation

DR. WILKINSON'S HOT SPRINGS
1507 Lincoln Avenue
Calistoga, CA 94515
Tel. (707) 942-4102
Reservations strongly suggested. Two day cancellation
is required.

Located in Calistoga, is an ultimately pampering, luxurious health spa know as Dr. Wilkinsons Hot Springs. Built in July of 1952 , by Dr. John Wilkinson and his wife, Edy, the natural mud baths and massage facilities have become so well known, they are soon to be featured on a segment of "Lifestyles of the Rich and Famous."

In Calistoga, for over one hundred years, treatments with naturally heated mineral waters and steam combined with volcanic ash have helped sufferers of arthritis and tension. These naturally heated waters and mud are one of the oldest therapies known to man. The Indians of this area were known to congregate to soak in the mud and hot water. Today, people young and old travel to Calistoga to rest, relax and "take the waters." You have your choice of mud baths, mineral whirlpool baths, natural mineral steam rooms, blanket wraps and massage. If you are under doctors care, please check before taking treatments. Dr. Wilkinson employs both male and female California State Certified therapists.

The accommodations at Dr. Wilkinson's Motel range from bungalows with complete kitchens to spacious rooms with twin, queen or king size beds. The rooms with kitchens are fully equipped with stove, oven, refrigerator and utensils. All rooms have individually controlled air conditioning, color TV and telephones. Most of the rooms have mini-refrigerators and all have coffee makers. Complimentary Calistoga Mineral Water is offered upon check in and daily maid service is provided. All the comforts you expect, plus a few more. There are three beautiful pools for the exclusive use of the motel guests, one indoor and two outdoor. Baths are available from 8:30 a.m to 3:30 p.m daily and massage from 9:00 a.m. - 4:00 p.m.

MOUNT VIEW HOTEL
1457 Lincoln Boulevard
Calistoga, CA 94515
Tel. (707) 942-6877

Mount View Hotel has an ageless elegance, with treasures from the Art Deco Period such as, smoked etched and beveled glass, marble statues and attractive antiques.

All rooms have private baths, and private dining rooms or conference facilities are available. "Wine, Dine, Don't Drive" packages are available year round and include accommodations for one night, dinner for two and a bottle of Napa Valley wine delivered to your room. (Prices vary with season.) A pool and cabana area provide a romantic setting; lounge chairs surround the sparkling pool and lush plants provide a cool ambiance.

Be sure to enjoy the luxury of the hotel's dining room, with soft lighting, crisp white tablecloths, ceramic vases and candles adorning the tables. The breakfast menu features homemade waffles, bran muffins, petite filet of beef and a fiesta plate with scrambled eggs and salsa in a flour tortilla and granished with sour cream and black bean sauce. For lunch, try delicacies such as, warm spinach and confit of duck salad with raspberry vinegar dressing, an Andoville sausage sandwich on a French roll, half a roasted chicken with sweet ancho chili sauce or a Mount View salad. Elegant dinner entrees are roast double breast of chicken, sauteed steelhead trout, medallions of veal, Tournedos of beef, scallops, rack of lamb or a fantastic sliced loin of pork with a carmelized onion relish.

Everything you could need is found at Mount View Hotel. For information on local attractions such as, gliding, ballooning, hot springs, mineral baths, geysers, wineries, cycling trails and more, be sure to inquire at the desk. The concierge will be happy to make arrangements for you.

Napa

Fifteen miles up the Napa River from San Pablo Bay, the stream is still navigable. The city built here as an agricultural processing point has sprawled into a life of its own. There are now almost seventeen square miles within city limits, and at last estimate 54,500 people lived here. Don Salvador Vallejo took his Rancho Napa grant in 1838, sold off the back country and retained about 3,000 acres on which a small Mexican community grew.

Settlers were reported here in 1832, before the land grant, and the town site was purchased in 1848 by Nathan Coombs. First this was the water shipping point for timber taken in the valley, then the outfitting center for the brief silver mining boom of 1858. From 1860 on, trade with the large and growing vineyards boosted the town's economy.

Visitors here say that despite the growth of recent decades, the courthouse square remains an "oasis of peace." Large shade trees cover the older residential areas, and many buildings dating back to early days remain, including the courthouse built in 1856.

Attractions

In the spring and summer, **guided walks** of the landmarks in Napa are offered on a regular basis. Call (707) 255-1836 for information.

Grapes are far from the only produce grown in this fertile valley. A **Farmer's Market** on Atlas Road operates from early summer through the fall, giving visitors a chance to sample the produce. Several roadside stands are located in farming areas.

Napa State Hospital, on Magnolia Drive off Highway 221, is on the old Rancho Tulucay grant lands. The 1869 state legislature launched the venerable hospital by sending a commission to view insane asylums in the United States and Europe. In 1872 Napa was chosen site of the hospital designed by the commission after viewing programs for the mentally ill. The first patient was admitted in 1875.

At the junction of Silverado Trail and Soscol Avenue in southeastern Napa, **Adobe Road** marks the site of the headquarters of Rancho Tulucay. It was here that Cayetano Juarez built his adobe in the 1840s. Only three adobes of that vintage have survived in the entire Napa Valley.

For information, contact the **Napa Chamber of Commerce**, 1900 Jefferson Street, Napa CA 94559. Telephone (707) 226-7455.

Accommodation

THE CHATEAU HOTEL
4195 Solano Avenue
Napa, CA 94558
Tel. (707) 253-9300
Reservations suggested. No pets please.
No charge for children under twelve.

In the upper reaches of the town of Napa, just off Highway 29 at West Salvador Avenue, lies The Chateau Hotel. All the charm of a French Provincial inn have been combined with modern conveniences to provide a warm and relaxing stay in this enchanting valley.

The Chateau Hotel is a two story structure with 115 comfortable rooms including six suites and ten non-smoking rooms. There are also ten rooms designed for the handicapped. Beautiful decor graces every room with color coordinated furnishings and sophisticated art adorning the walls. All the rooms have heat, air conditioning, direct dial phones, color TV, in-room movies, full baths, oversized beds and refrigerators in most rooms. Valet laundry, dry cleaning, free parking, Budget-Rent-A-Car and an on call physician are also provided. You are invited to enjoy a complimentary breakfast of coffee, juice, pastries, yogurt and fresh fruit and, an evening wine social.

General manager, Jackie Lawrence welcomes guests and arranges activities such as, rides in a hot air balloon, wine tours, cycling and mud baths or massages. Don't forget your swimsuit, the hotel has a heated pool and spa. The hotel also offers one day film processing.

With all these amenities, The Chateau Hotel is your "Best Choice" in Napa Valley.

EMBASSY SUITES HOTEL
1075 California Boulevard
Napa, CA 94559
Tel. (707) 253-9540

The newest addition to Napa Valley's culinary and lodging options is the Embassy Suites Hotel. The decor of the hotel is light and airy throughout, accomplished by imaginative use of skylights. The balcony is adorned with lush greenery and Spanish tile; the courtyard is inviting with bright, cheerful colors and lovely swans gracing twin ponds. A large fire burns warmly in the lobby and overstuffed sofas beckon with promises of extreme comfort. A well stocked gift shop will provide momentos of your stay.

Every suite offers a bedroom and parlor featuring French country decor, wet bar, micro-kitchen, two color TVs, two telephones and a living room sofa bed. Available to guests are two landscaped atriums, an indoor swimming pool with spa, a steam room and sauna. Complimentary breakfast is served in Swan Court and, in keeping with the generous hospitality of the Embassy Suites Hotel, a complimentary cocktail hour is held from 5:30 p.m - 7:30 p.m in Swan Court.

The Embassy Suites Hotel has a superb luncheon and dinner menu with only hand selected, corn fed beef featured. Daily specials are offered on the diversified menu. Try melt-in-your-mouth ribeye steak or a scrumptious seafood fettucini in a sherry cream sauce. One of the most popular entrees is the Fajitas sizzling skirt steak. Finish your meal with a selection from the Chocoholic Emporium or fabulous cheese cake all made fresh. There is an elegant lounge with piano music featured on weekends and eight spacious meeting rooms in the entry area.

General manager Gary Ettinger and his staff are eager and polite, providing service as refined and elegant as the hotel itself. Be sure to enjoy the pampering charm of this "Best Choice" in Napa Valley, the Embassy Suites Hotel.

Bed & Breakfast

THE WEBBER PLACE
6610 Webber Avenue
Yountville, CA 94599
Tel. (707) 944-8384

A homey Napa Valley farmhouse, circa 1850, is now The Webber Place Bed and Breakfast Inn. Diane Bartholomew is the gracious hostess who will make your stay relaxing and fun. From the foot pedaled organ to the brass beds with Eider Down comforters, The Webber Place is filled with antiques.

Four rooms with old world charm are available, most have big claw foot bathtubs with brass fixtures for relaxing after a long day. The Honeymoon Suite is on the first floor with its own entrance for privacy. A large veranda encircles the house with antique rockers and chairs of solid oak for leisurely reading or watching the world go by. The grounds are surrounded by romantic gardens and lush lawns. At almost any hour of the day, you are greeted by luscious aromas emanating from the kitchen; the home baked rolls and muffins are a special breakfast treat.

The Webber Place is within walking distance of excellent restaurants and shops. Nearby attractions include wine tasting, hot air balloon rides, bicycling and hang gliding. Be sure to visit Diane and take advantage of her elegant and pampering accommodations.

Gift

S. CLAUS
Highway 29
Napa, CA 94558
Tel. (707) 944-9627
MasterCard and Visa are accepted.

At S. Claus the spirit of Christmas lasts all year. Just seconds from the town of Yountville is this charming Christmas store.

Ornaments from all over the world made from porcelain, wood, spun glass, fabric and more can be found. Nutcrackers, pyramids, creches, music boxes, stuffed toys, antique figurines are also displayed. There is always a tree decorated for the season. In February, the lovely tree is covered with red hearts. A Valentine tree? Yes!! You may have a picture of your child with Santa, and a coloring book and candy cane for the kids.

The adjoining Grapevine Room features souvenirs of the wine country and the Nutcracker Sweets Cafe serves hot, homemade soup, quiche and tempting triple chocolate tortes. S. Claus has recently planted a Christmas tree farm, so it will truly be the place for one stop Christmas shopping. Stop in and say hello to the manager Edie Allen and gracious Denise Vinegas, who will be happy to treat you to Christmas year round.

Restaurant

D.D. KAYS RESTAURANT AND LOUNGE
811 Coombs Street
Napa, CA 94559
Visa and MasterCard are accepted.

Located in downtown Napa, opposite the Historic Courthouse is an epicurean dream. D.D. Kays Restaurant and Lounge, the name is a derivation of the owner's names - David Fyfe and David and Ken Cummings. The decor has a 1930s look featuring French art deco bar (circa 1928) and multi-lighted glass bricks.

D.D. Kays features a form of California novelle cuisine that is attractively served, temptingly unusual and satisfyingly filling. Page D'Agostino, the chef extraordinaire, has mastered the fine art of sauce preparation. The roasted garlic served with Sonoma goat cheese, fresh crisp

Bermuda onion slices, tomato wedges and toast pieces is a sumptuous appetizer. His breast of chicken Anastasia served floating on a heavenly lemon sauce and veal and prawns tarragon are spectacular. A special dish you can ask for is Pasta con Lumache made with escargot, mussels and enoki mushrooms with a deliciously flavored pasta.

For friendly, elegant atmosphere and superb food, modestly priced, your "Best Choice" in Napa Valley is D.D. Kays Restaurant and Lounge.

ELMERS
4175 Solano Avenue
Napa, CA 94558
Tel. (707) 255-4447

The familiar long, low rambling building that houses Elmers Colonial Pancake and Steak House is a welcome sight to travelers hungry for a delicious meal. The exterior is beautifully landscaped with colorful flowers; the interior is tastefully decorated, the first sensation you experience upon entering Elmers is the aroma of great food.

A full breakfast menu includes pancakes with luscious variety: buttermilk, potato, corn, wheat, pineapple, banana, dollar, blueberry buttermilk, pigs in a blanket and a huge German specialty. Other options include: blueberry, strawberry cream, pecan, ham, bacon or sausage waffles. Swedish, blueberry, sour cream, Dutch apple or Oregon cheese blintzes are other tempting choices. Luncheon at Elmers features a daily special with sandwiches, salads or "light" fare offered. Dinners of prime rib or pork chops with baked potato and salad are equally scrumptious.

Elmers is your "Best Choice" for a relaxing, filling meal stop in Napa.

JOSEPH MATHEW WINERY
1171 Main Street
Napa, CA 94558
Tel. (707) 226-3777

Today's society has come to hold a high regard for antiquities of the past. At Joseph Mathews Winery, modern day restoration techniques have enhanced the beauty of this over-a-century-old complex in downtown Napa. A restaurant, oyster bar and wine bar are all found in this charming building.

Start your adventure by sampling wines from the Napa, Sonoma and Mendocino wineries or relax in the Sherry Oven Restaurant and Seafood Bar. Downstairs you can enjoy live piano music while you sip your favorite beverage and relish such delicacies as crab nachos. The upstairs area is more formal, only wine and brandy are available. The dinner menu changes nightly and features

323

choices such as, grilled Catalina swordfish, Colombia River sturgeon, salmon, New York Steak with Etoufee sauce, lamb chops, pheasant and even sauteed medallions of antelope.

Greg Carey, the manager, and his staff strive to satisfy your every desire at this "Best Choice" for elegant dining.

THE RED HEN CANTINA
5091 Saint Helena Highway
Napa, CA 94558
Tel. (707) 255-8125
Hrs: Mon. - Sun. 11:00 a.m - 10:00 p.m.

A great place in Napa for super food and to watch hot air balloons is The Red Hen Cantina. On an open deck in front of the restaurant are multi-colored umbrellas and colorful directors chairs. Featuring Mexican cuisine, with willing señoritas to watch over your every need, the enchanting building is filled with pleasant aromas.

Be sure to try the Red Hen Burger, a twelve ounce lean ground beef patty seasoned and wrapped in a warm flour tortilla with Monterey Jack cheese and sauteed mushrooms. Camarones Rancheros made of jumbo shrimp sauted with tomatoes and green peppers, served with rice beans and a salad is a popular dinner entree. The Cantina Lounge is available for your favorite beverage to complement your meal.

The Red Hen Cantina is in a red complex that also houses a dress shop, and antique shop, both worthy of visit before or after you enjoy your meal.

SPEERO'S RESTAURANT AND TAVERN
1775 Clay Street
Napa, CA 94558
Tel. (707) 2155-4744

Located in the Old Carriage House on the Noyes Mansion site is Speero's Restaurant and Tavern. The building has been refurbished and decorated by owner Spiro Drossos, showing off his distinctive good taste. Spiro was weaned in the restaurant business by his parents, owners of the popular Penguins Restaurant in Napa.

Spiro's inventiveness and sparkling personality have made Speero's the most popular watering hole in town. His Poker Limousine Run and Nuts and Bolts Swingles Night are much enjoyed and talked about locally. Occasionally, Spiro plans other activities such as, String Golf tournaments. He sets up a portable bar in a golf cart, for each drink you buy, you get a six foot length of string. Each string enables you to get six feet closer to the hole when putting. The more you drink, the better your handicap??? Well, you get the idea.

Spiro's menu is primarily American with some exotic Greek touches. A scrumptious Sunday brunch is a popular adventure. Be sure to visit Speero's Restaurant and see what fun Spiro has cooked up!

The hills of Napa County hold some of the finest wineries in the world. A trip to the area should include sites within the city of Napa as well as some of the natural attracitons about the countryside. This tour offers some suggestions.

NAPA TOWN & COUNTRY TOUR			
a.m.	Elmer's	Best breakfast	Napa/Rest
a.m.	S. Claus	Best gifts	Napa/Gift
a.m.	Napa Valley Park	Best scenery	Napa/Att
p.m.	Red Hen Cantina	Best Mexican	Napa/Rest
p.m.	Napa Co. Wineries	Best tour	Napa/Att
Make your day better with evening drinks and dinner.			
p.m.	D & D Kays	Best sauces	Napa/Rest
p.m.	Joseph Mathew	Best California	Napa/Rest
p.m.	Speero's	Best tavern	Napa/Rest

Rutherford

Accommodation

AUBERGE DU SOLEIL
180 Rutherford Hill Road
Rutherford, CA 94573
Tel. (707) 963-1211
MasterCard and Visa are accepted.
Dinner reservations are required.

High above the vineyards of Napa Valley in the little town of Rutherford, lies a bit of old Europe known as Auberge Du Soleil. Owners Claude Rouas and the Moana Corporation have outdone themselves. This thirty-three acre site near the famous Rutherford Winery contains the now famous restaurant and thirty-six rooms contained in nine buildings. Warm and welcoming, General Manager, Adair Borba-Thoms runs Auberge Du Soleil like clockwork, her organized touch is evident in the smooth running operation in both the hotel and restaurant.

All of the rooms are designed with fireplaces, television, wet bar and decks that overlook the beautiful Napa Valley. Room rates which range from $180 to $420 per night (at the time of this publication), include Continental breakfast for two, and the use of the swimming and tennis facilities. All the rooms are done in gracious designer colors of yellow, peach and pink.

Chef Michael Cornu, born and raised in Paris, was trained in Cannes, Orleans and Geneva before he came to the United States. Chef Cornu is largely responsible for the introduction of California Eclectic Cuisine, which has become a hallmark of many of the Napa Valley restaurants. (Imitation is the purest form of flattery.) Luncheon prices range from $20 to $25, dinner is a fixed price of $45.00 (at the time of publication) and offers light and creative fare. A full complement of wines, as well as cocktails, is available in the dining room and the lounge. Private parties for up to eighty people are held in the "White Room", paneled with mirrors to reflect the light and views. Adjacent to the restaurant is the intimate "Club Room" which seats up to twenty people for dinner, or serves as a private cocktail lounge.

RANCHO CAYMUS INN
P. O. Box 78
Rutherford, CA 94573
Tel. (707) 963-1777
Visa and MasterCard are accepted.

Beautiful, eighty year old white oak, from a weathered barn in Ohio, has been reborn into the exquisitely unique Rancho Caymus Inn. The fine old barn was painstakingly dismantled and taken to Napa for the construction of the inn by designer and owner Mary Tilden. Mary sent two talented Napa Valley carpenters, Joe Savage and Gray Brandl, to Ohio where they spent thirty-five days tackling the huge task of dismantling the barn without harming the wood. Joe and Gary custom made the inn's doors, stairways, railings, cabinets and hand hewn beams throughout the building. The old wood has its most dramatic effect in the inn's inner courtyard; huge exposed beams support the second floor balcony, while the old mortise and tendon beams have become posts lining the entire second floor.

Rancho Caymus Inn has nine glorious stained glass windows, hand carved black walnut beds and wrought iron lamps designed and crafted especially for the inn by Ecuadorians. Tables and dressers hand carved in Guadalajara and vibrant colored bedspreads, wool rugs, wall hangings and pillow covers dyed and woven by the Salazaca and Otabalon Indians of Ecuador grace the rooms.

The inn has four master suites with Jacuzzi tubs, fireplaces, full kitchens and large balconies which are ideal for longer get away. The Hastings Suite has two bedrooms to accommodate larger parties.

The Caymus kitchen serves breakfast in your room, balcony or in the gardens. Champagne brunch is also available. The menu features omelettes, home baked bread, Mimosas, espresso and daily specials.

Come share the wonder of Rancho Caymus Inn in the beautiful Napa Valley. Two nights minimum stay required for weekends and holidays during the summer.

St. Helena

This small town marks the center of the wine country, and has about 5,000 residents. The Seventh Day Adventists operate Pacific Union College on a 2,800 acre campus that includes farms and businesses operated by the church. Residential areas of town have houses about forty years old, and more than a dozen wineries are within the far-reaching city limits.

The town takes its name from Mount Saint Helena at the head of the valley. No one is sure how the name came to the mountain, but researchers believe it came from a Russian vessel, Saint Helena, which described the peak during a coastwise exploration in the 1840s. Settlers in the valley called it Devil's Mount for some time, a name abandoned by Henry Still who founded the town in 1855. The post office, created in 1858, made the name official.

Attractions

The **Napa Valley Wine Library** is a special collection in the St. Helena city library on Library Lane. Reference work on viticulture, oenology, and historic information on origins of California varieties of grape stock.

Berringer Vineyards just north of town on Highway 29, provides an example of the excavation work used to convert limestone hillsides into constant-temperature cellars for aging of bulk wines after fermentation. Tours from 9:30 a.m to 4:00 p.m., September through May, and from 10:00 a.m. to 5:00 p.m. in June and July. No tours during August, the big harvest month. Call (707) 963-7115.

The **Pacific Union College** campus, seven miles east of town, includes an extinct volcano which retains subterranean heat. A well tapped to 600 feet, some years ago, recorded a uniform 97 degree temperature.

Napa County

One of the most ambitious restoration projects in recent years is underway next to Highway 29, three miles north of St. Helena, at **Bale's Grist Mill State Historic Park.** The thirty-six foot tall overshot water wheel and grist mill erected by Edward Bale in 1846 is being put back into operation. Work should be complete by 1988; with the mill again turning out flour as it did for farmers of the upper valley who sold to the miners. Grist stones were locally mined, timbers for the original three-story structure were milled from trees cut nearby. The Native Sons of the Golden West made the original restoration in 1925. Call 942-4575 for an update on reconstruction work.

Bothe-Napa State Park is one mile north of the grist mill. It includes camping facilities and a swimming pool open in summer months. Call 942-4575 for park information.

For additional information contact the **St. Helena Chamber of Commerce,** Box 124, St. Helena, CA 94574. Telephone (707) 963-4456.

Wine

NAPA CREEK WINERY
1001 Silverado Trail
St. Helena, CA 94574
Tel. (707) 963-9456

For warm, generous hospitality in the Napa Valley, visit owners Jack and Judy Schulze at Napa Creek Winery. Jack has spent his life in the wine industry, first with his father at Gibson Wine Company, then at Beringer Wineries. On a visit to Napa Valley, Jack discovered the Sunshine Meat Packing Company on the Old Silverado Trail. Jack purchased and refurbished the building into a first class operating winery.
In 1980, the winery was born and has won The International Wines and Spirits Tasting Award for their Cabernet Sauvignon. The Napa Creek Cabernet has a royal endorsement for the HMS Yacht Brittania, the ship that brought Queen Elizabeth to the United States in 1984. The winery produces other fine wines including Johannisberg Reisling, Gewurztraminer, Merlot and Chardonnay. The label on Napa Creek Wine is as rich as the wine itself, printed on gold embossed paper, it stands out amongst the rest of Napa's wineries.
Napa Creek Winery gives generous portions for tasting and, Jack has developed a unique gift box for giving wine and shipping. Be sure to enjoy this experience while touring Napa Valley.

328

Yountville

The land mark of this old town is a huge winery building now called Vintage 1870 at 6525 Washington Street. It houses a collection of specialty shops and restaurants. George Yount, the pioneer of Napa County, built a blockhouse for protection from Indians when he settled here on his 1836 land grant. There is no record that the eighteen-foot square building was ever raided. In fact most accounts indicate the local Indians liked Yount and happily worked on his rancho.

Veterans organizations joined in 1881 to build a home for disabled soldiers of the Mexican and Civil Wars. The facility, on the southern side of town on California Drive, was made a state Veterans Home in 1897 and continues to serve veterans today.

The town of 3,000 is eight miles north of Napa, and marks the start of the intense vineyard culture which makes the Napa Valley famous. It is also at the end of the commute to North Bay plants and businesses and has a new luxury home subdivision called Pinewood where prices start at $200,000 and go upward.

Attractions

Domain Chandon, on California Drive near the Veterans Hospital, offers tours of its sparkling vintage operations. Lunch and dinner are served at a restaurant on the premises. Call (707) 944-2892 for reservations.

For information, contact the **Yountville Chamber of Commerce**, Box 2064, Yountville CA 94599. Telephone (707) 224-2937.

Accommodation

VINTAGE INN
6541 Washington Street
Yountville, CA 94599
Tel. (707) 944-1112
Pets allowed with refundable deposit.

In Napa Valley, the age of elegance has returned in the form of the Vintage Inn. The inn was built in 1985 as part of the Vintage Estate. The exterior of the twenty-four, two story buildings is done in wood and kiln brick. The interiors have been gracefully decorated with white pine furniture and hand-painted fabric, creating a feeling of charming warmth. This eighty room inn, located on a three and a half acre parcel of land, has blended a small town village aura with the convenience of a full service hotel.

Included in the eighty rooms are eight mini-suites with alcove area and wet bar, sixteen non-smoking rooms and one room fitted for the handicapped. All rooms have private verandas with handcrafted furniture, a fireplace with Italian marble seat, oversized king and queen size beds, color TV, radio, refrigerator complete with a split of welcome wine, in-room coffee and tea, a whirlpool spa-bath and double sinks with beautiful Italian marble. Other amenities include spacious gardens with waterways, tennis courts and a sixty foot lap pool with spa.

Also located on the estate is the Vintage 1870 complex which houses delightful shops and, restaurants for fine dining. The Vintage Inn Hot Air Balloon, one of the largest hot air balloons in Napa Valley, is available for a one hour flight each morning.

With its graceful elegance, convenient location to shops and restaurants and scores of amenities, the Vintage Inn is a "Best Choice" for accommodations in Napa Valley.

VINTAGE 1870 COMPLEX
6525 Washington Street
Yountville, CA 94559

In 1970, the Old Groezinger Winery and Distillery, in Yountville, were restored with loving care into the Vintage 1870 Complex. This beautiful old brick building houses a variety of shops and restaurants. A listing of some of the shops you'll enjoy browsing and restaurants for fine dining follows:

Gerhard's Sausage Kitchen - specializes in authentic European sausage. Twelve types of fresh, homemade sausage are available, no preservatives or fillers are used. Also carried are over fifty varieties of sausage from around the Bay Area. Sausage will be packed in ice for travelers.

Halliday Bookstore - located upstairs in the complex, has the latest bestsellers in both cloth and paperback. Specialties are books and magazines on wine with publications appealing to the connoisseur, as well as the casual consumer.

The Vintage Cafe - situated in the historic Yountville Railroad Depot. Enjoy a hamburger with an ice cold beer and fresh garden salads. Features a wide variety of grilled and cold sandwiches with a view of the rolling hills and vineyards from the large outdoor deck.

The Barrel Cellar - features the largest selection of wine openers and accessories in Napa Valley. Full lines of the finest crystal from all around the world and an extensive line of Napa Valley t-shirts and sweatshirts are available.

Touch of Gold Bath Shop - gifts for the traveler, wine soap and bubble bath with a large assortment of sunglasses and beach towels also displayed.

Eye of the Needle - carries unique needlework, sewing projects and creative ideas. Specializes in counted cross stitch, needlepoint, quilting, fabric, lace and trim. Full line of embroidery floss and Persian wool.

The Yountville Pastry Shop - located in the courtyard, the bakery offers a wide variety of European style baked goods including: handmade truffles, tortes, fresh fruit tarts and wedding cakes. Enjoy a cup of espresso or cappuccino while you relax on the charming patio.

Depot Gallery - owned and staffed by local artists with paintings, prints and ceramics exhibited.

The Grapes of Brass - distinctive brass gifts and decorative items for the home or office, at competitive prices.

Wee Bit O Wool - Irish and Scottish imports for men and women. Fashions of mohair, lamb's wool and cashmere in coats, capes and handknit sweaters.

The Toy Cellar - an old fashioned toy shop with collectable bears, dolls, educational toys, kites and unusual imported items for kids.

Golden Eagle Bazaar - antiques with emphasis on fine glassware, china, primitives and collector's items. Offers the finest in Scandinavian and European imports and gifts.

The Country Mouse - a charming cottage tucked in a corner on the first floor. It is full of handcrafted country gifts, dried floral wreaths and arrangements. For the "do-it-yourself" person, a large assortment of flowers, supplies and instructions are provided.

The Unicorn - has something for everybody, from the fanciful to the practical. Posters, pictures, sculptures, collectables and gifts. Features Dr. Tom Clark, Beatrix Potter, Artesania Rinconada, Jan Hagara and many local artists. The Napa Valley's original Cairn dealer.

The Blue Canary - specializes in music boxes, carrying over 400 styles, many made on the premises. An unusual find is the large number of replacement musical movements, with over 260 different tunes available.

Hanzel and Gretel - a unique children's clothing store specializing in outstanding clothes for boys and girls size infant through fourteen.

The Cooks Corner - a deli featuring California gourmet food products, fresh roasted coffee beans, meats, cheeses, exotic herbs and spices. The kitchen store carries a full line of bakeware, gadgets, cookware, cutting boards and kitchen gifts and accessories.

Vintage Country Treasures - the shop carries home furnishings with a flair, maided and rag rugs, pottery, clocks, dolls, dicery ducks, lamps and welcome signs.

Napa County

Basket Bazaar - noted for its interesting assortment of basketry culled from the wicker markets of Europe and Asia by the owners, George and Margaret Sterling. Baskets from Africa, the Philippines and South American countries create an ever-changing display of handwoven products. Special items such as, paper maché animals and flowers add more fun to the shop.

Washington Street Restaurant - housed in the old Groezinger family mansion. Chef Joe Mayhew brings a fresh concept to his food. Says Joe, "I consider the visual sense a vital part of the palate, it enhances the whole dining experience." The taste and presentation of the entrees prove that Joe lives up to his philosophy.

Restaurant

THE DINER
6476 Washington Street
Yountville, CA 94559
Tel. (707) 944-2626

Some of the best meals in all of the Napa Valley can be found at The Diner. Bring a hearty appetite, the portions are plentiful. Cassandra Mitchell, the owner, is proud of her menu which features home-grown produce, homemade breads and sausage. The Diner decor reflects the good taste of Cassandra, with white walls and works by local artists adorning the walls. A combination of track lighting and old fashioned globes show off the authentic diner styled counter.

Start off the day with a bowl of hot, old fashioned oatmeal or omelettes of any description. Other popular breakfasts are smoked sausage links, two eggs and special home-fried potatoes or huevos rancheros. Espresso coffee and Mimosa are available to complement breakfast. Lunch features a variety of salads, soups and sandwiches such as, a delicious reuben, a burger on a French roll or perhaps a Paul Bunyon special made of ground chuck on a French roll with fries and a green salad. For dinner, specialties of the house are tostada grande, quesadilla, enchiladas and carne asada which consists of charbroiled strips of steak with avocado salsa and hot corn tortillas. Homemade breads such as, raisin walnut, whole wheat and cottage dill round out any meal. Desserts of chocolate torte, New York cheesecake and ice cream sundaes with homemade sauces will tempt even the most dedicated dieter.

Cassandra and her staff are friendly and professional. The charming atmosphere and the great food make The Diner your "Best Choice" for dining.

332

PLUMAS COUNTY

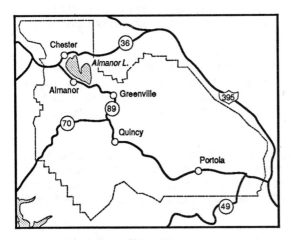

Tucked away at the northern end of the Sierras, where the mountains squat down to a forested plateau intermixed with steep ridges and signs of more recent volcanic activity, this is the headwaters of the Feather River, El Rio del las Plumas in Spanish. Explorer Luis Arguello put the title on the stream because of the water fowl seen in the lower reaches. When Plumas was peeled off of Butte County in 1854 it was the mountains that got the name, not the marshy bird habitat far below. Some canyons in this part of the Feather are 2,000 feet deep. Where Highway 70 crosses the Sierra divide at Beckwourth Pass it is just 5,212 feet above sea level, one of the lowest gaps in the entire range.

Modern Plumas county includes several reservoirs and hydroelectric power plants, including Pacific Gas and Electric Company's scenic Lake Almanor near Chester. Its water is reused by nine turbine stations located down the canyon. Lumber, milled from timber harvested on the Plumas National Forest, is the prime source of income to the area, followed by revenue from livestock grazing on meadows and a few lower elevation ranches. The county has a population of 17,340 people. Many live around Quincy, an unincorporated community of 6,500. Portola, the only city in the county, has about 1,900 people with little change in population in the past thirty years.

ATTRACTIONS

Plumas-Eureka State Park, on a county road five miles west of Blairsden, is an early winter sports area. Hard rock mines once dotted the mountains. Millions of dollars in gold was milled at this site in a structure which is preserved. A museum includes displays of other mining works. Campsites are developed. Telephone (916) 836-2380.

LaPorte, on the county road west of the park, is a ghost town on a ridge, with the Union Hotel and Wells Fargo office said to still be waiting for customers. The town faded quickly when hydraulic mining was outlawed in 1883. A small monument on the west side of the village marks the first gold strike and the emigrant trail south.

Quincy includes some buildings dating to 1855. Like other towns with frame construction, fire destroyed much of the original town created on James H. Bradley's ranch after the county was formed. The first school house, built in 1857, is two miles east of the center of town on the campus of a modern school.

Plumas National Forest operates several campgrounds and recreation sites in the county. Call 836-2575 for information.

For more on the county and its communities, contact the **Plumas County Chamber of Commerce,** Box 1018, Quincy CA 96971. Telephone (916) 283-2045.

SAN FRANCISCO CITY-COUNTY

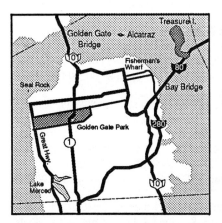

Spread over forty-six square miles of a peninsula which guards one of the world's largest land-locked harbors, San Francisco is a dynamic place, almost all of it urban save for a few coastal points. It welcomes commuters who labor by day in towering office buildings, and a steady stream of business people and tourists drawn to countless attractions and its centers of commercial,financial and political power.

Nurtured in the bustle of the gold rush, San Francisco became California's only city-county in 1856 when most of what is now San Mateo County was a lawless land where the criminals of the city fled, and the sheriff seldom followed. The legislative solution was the creation of a new county to the south, shrinking San Francisco to boundaries of land claims then associated with the city.

It welcomes commuters who labor by day in towering office buildings, and a steady stream of business people and tourists drawn to countless attractions and its centers of commercial, financial and political power.

San Francisco Bay is an ancient stream basin, now submerged beneath sea level, but still the pathway California's two largest rivers--the Sacramento and San Joaquin--follow to the sea through the water-scoured opening in a line of coastal mountains.

The opening, named "Chrysopylae" or Golden Gate by John C. Fremont, is difficult to spot from the sea. Strong tides sweep through it. The water is 357 feet deep under the Golden Gate Bridge, but seventy percent of the bay behind the gate has depths of less than eighteen feet, and much of the bay's area is exposed as muddy flats by the twice daily low tides.

Just south of the city, slicing to the northwest out to sea, is the crack of the San Andreas fault, providing sometimes jolting reminders that this city of 679,000 residents is still under geologic construction. Sand, blowing over the coastal Great Highway provides other reminders of the forces of nature at work.

Temperatures are mild, with sunny skies seen during about sixty-five percent of the daylight hours each year; but fogs and about twenty-inches of rain annually year create another reputation. Tule fogs rise on the bay during winter, and thick walls of white fog come in from the ocean to cool summertime temperatures.

The peninsula on which San Francisco occupies the northern tip is about thirty miles long. Measured across the city, the peninsula is seven miles wide, rising from piers and mud flats on the bay side to imposing hills over 900 feet above sea level, then sloping westward to ocean beaches and surf-pounded cliffs.

A grid of north-south city blocks now covers much of the city, sliced by angled streets and additions creating unique triangular lots and a layout which sometimes confuses visitors. Freeways move autos swiftly around the periphery of the city, while California Highway One on Nineteenth Avenue and U.S. 101 on Van Ness Avenue provide north-south arterial linkage.

History and modern landmarks intermix in the changing city. Indians, who had a culture based in part on mussels harvested from the bay, lived for at least 2,500 years in camps on estuaries and creeks. Explorers, trying to rediscover the Puerto San Francisco described in logs of Spanish Galleons sailing the Pacific in the 1500s, tried for two centuries to find the bay. Part of the overland expedition of Don Gaspard de Portola finally spotted the waters in 1769. Six years later as Franciscan friars established what is now Mission Dolores, the vessel San Carlos entered the Golden Gate to anchor in the lee of the Marin headlands. Construction of the Presidio of San Francisco began in 1775, too.

Whaling ships and those in the China trade soon called at the bay to resupply. In 1835, Yerba Buena Cove, located beneath the land fill of what is now the financial district of the city, became a place for trading with the Spaniards and buying food grown on mission farms. Hudson Bay Company, the northwest fur traders, for a brief time had an agent at Yerba Buena, buying pelts. The Treaty of 1848 gave California to the United States. Discovery of gold in the Sierra foothills the next year launched an historic boom which transformed the little port and the townsite then laid out from the cove west to the Presidio.

Tumultuous times marked the first quarter century after the first legislature named the city and county in 1850. Fires swept the frame buildings periodically, law enforcement at times was in the hands of vigilante committees, and the Tenderloin district bounded by Broadway, Clay and Grant streets to the waterfront earned San Francisco a nickname of the "wickedest city in the world." The Southern Pacific Railroad dominated the next quarter century, a time of commercial expansion, ferry boats and booming connections with world trade.

336

The earthquake of April 18, 1906 halted the city in its tracks. Physical damage from the forty-eight second main shock was limited to buildings in the financial district. When the gas works exploded a short time later, the resulting fire burned out of control for three days, destroying 28,188 buildings. Three-hundred fifty thousand people were homeless, 3l5 known dead, and 352 listed as missing to this day. San Francisco rebuilt, in the form we see it today. The 1915 Panama Pacific International Exposition was the first showcase of the rebirth; some of its Greco-Roman buildings remain and the Marina district's homes, harbors and greens for kite-flyers mark the site.

The tallest tower on the skyline is Transamerica Pyramid, reaching 853 feet above 600 Montgomery Street, one of several steel-frame buildings put up in the building boom after World War II. The city's commanding bridges, over the bay to Oakland, and across the Golden Gate to Marin County, both began construction in 1933. It took four years to complete the Golden Gate, three to route the bay bridge through a rocky tunnel on Yerba Buena Island and over the spans on each side.

San Francisco is a city of neighborhoods, many tied to ethnic populations, others linked with developments. Parks and plazas break up its neighborhoods, and one--Golden Gate Park--is a testimony to slow conversion of sand dunes into a massive regional recreation area. While those who struck it rich in mines, trade or transportation built the striking mansions of Nob Hill, Russian Hill and Pacific Heights, most of the city's residents are working people with a heritage of strong support for organized labor. Their homes, many on lots only twenty-five feet wide, march over the hills and down the slopes.

SAN FRANCISCO/FINANCIAL DISTRICT

Wealth and power are concentrated on Montgomery Street, dubbed the "Wall Street of the West." William A. Richardson, the navigator who left a British whaling ship in 1822 and became harbormaster of Mexican Alta California's Yerba Buena port in 1835, first did business here under a ship's canvas held up by four redwood timbers.

Today that giant of gold rush days, Wells Fargo with its newly merged string of Crocker Banks, contends for clients with the Bank of America, successor to A.P. Giannini's Bank of Italy which was founded to serve emigrant businessmen and workers drawn to the city.

337

ATTRACTIONS

Stagecoach and all, **Wells Fargo** has a museum of its gold-rush history in the bank's headquarters building at 420 Montgomery Street. Open Monday through Friday from 9:00 a.m. to 5:00 p.m.

The **Federal Reserve Bank** at 101 Market Street offers what amounts to a factory tour of their check processing and vaults. Call 974-3252, or write since there is often a waiting list and tours fill weeks in advance. At the lobby level is a huge exhibit of how the U.S. economy works. Open Monday through Friday 9:00 a.m. to 4:30 p.m.

Pacific Heritage Museum is in the Bank of Canton Building at Commercial and Montgomery Streets. Displays change frequently, showing the role of immigrants from the Pacific rim in California's history. Open Monday through Thursday, 1:00 p.m. to 4:00 p.m.

Chevron presents the story of oil processing in a working exhibit at its big headquarters building, 555 Market Street. Open Monday though Friday, 9:00 a.m. to 4:00 p.m. Closed on holidays.

Visitors Information Center is on Market Street at Powell, just a short walk from the Financial District or Union Square. Teleguides, a free service showing attractions in the neighborhood, are at several downtown locations.

BART, Bay Area Rapid Transit, has a station at New Montgomery and Market Streets. The regional train system with express bus extensions in the East Bay, provides quick transportation to several attractions outside of the district.

SAN FRANCISCO/EMBARCADERO

Like a ribbon of concrete which stopped flowing, the Embarcadero Freeway loops north from downtown and spills its cars on Battery Street a few blocks below Telegraph Hill. San Franciscans, in a political storm which recalled their roots of this port city, decided to keep traffic at ground level. These piers, in the days before the 1939 outbreak of war in the Pacific, were the U.S. connection to over 200 steamship companies.

The waterfront's commercial area wraps itself from China Basin and the Army Street Terminal on the south to Fisherman's Wharf and Aquatic Park on the north. Yerba Buena Cove, the first port, became clogged with wooden-hulled ships abandoned in gold rush times, and is now filled out to the present wharf line. Nowhere can the modern-day changes be contemplated more easily than at the foot of Market Street.

The Ferry Building, with a stylish clock on each side of its tower, was built in the 1890s and became the busiest passenger terminal in the nation as commuters and transcontinental rail travelers passed through its halls. By 1958, the Southern Pacific Company suspended passenger ferry service on the bay. The Embarcadero freeway now casts its shadow, literally, on the stately building each morning. Today it is the World Trade Center, bustling with people bent on the economic development of the entire Pacific Rim.

ATTRACTIONS

Colt Tower, atop Telegraph Hill, provides a vantage point for the entire sweep of the waterfront. A semaphore once signaled ship arrival information relayed from Golden Gate to those running the piers below the hill. A memorial to Lillie Coit, the tower was completed in 1933.

Charter boats operate out of Fisherman's Wharf and two other locations on a daily basis. Operators include Captain Ron's 285-2000, Lucky Lady 826-6815, and Wacky Jacky 586-9800.

Bay boat tours are offered from three locations. Blue and Gold sails from Pier 39 at Fisherman's Wharf, 781-7877; Hornblower Yachts docks at Pier 33, 434-0300; and Red and White works out of Pier 41, 546-2810. A **helicopter tour** operates out of Pier 43 at Fisherman's Wharf, 332-4482.

Ferry boats provide crossings to Marin County on a regular basis. The Red and White boats out of Pier 41 call at Sausalito, Tiburon and Angel Island State Park, 778-1880; and Golden Gate Ferries, working from the old Ferry Building at the Foot of Market, makes the Larkspur and Sausalito run, 332-6600.

On Pier 39, a mall extending over the water, is **The San Francisco Experience**, a multi-media show of the city's history which includes jiggles beneath the seats of the theater when the earthquake is reported. Daily shows from 10:00 a.m. to 7:30 p.m. and evenings at 8:15, 8:45, and 9:15 p.m.

The Wax Museum at Fisherman's Wharf, 145 Jefferson Street, has nearly 300 celebrities and scenes depicted in its galleries. Open daily 10:00 a.m. to 10:00 p.m. weekdays and 9:00 a.m. to 11:00 p.m. Friday and Saturdays most of the year, with a 9:00 a.m. daily opening during summer months.

339

Carousel Museum of San Francisco, 633 Beach Street, displays carousels made between 1880 and 1920. Most figures are carved from wood. Open daily 10:00 a.m. to 6:00 p.m.

Levi Strauss has its original factory on the Embarcadero near pier 23. Factory tours are offered by reservation on Wednesdays, call 544-6777.

At **Aquatic Park** is the **National Maritime Museum,** full of ship models and other displays. **Fort Mason Center** includes a research library and more displays. On the **Hyde Street Pier** are a collection of restored vessels. The Museum is open 10:00 a.m. to 6:00 p.m. daily except Christmas. Hyde Street Pier has similar hours. Call 556-2904 for information on activities here.

Moored at Pier 43 is the **USS Pampanito,** a 312-foot submarine commissioned in 1943. It is open daily from 9:00 a.m. to 9:00 p.m.

The **square-rigged S/V Balclutha,** is tied up at Pier 43. This is the surviving vessel of those which regularly made the Cape Horn sail from east to west coasts. Decks are open for walking. A museum below deck should reopen in August, 1987.

Embarcadero Center, on Battery Street at Sacramento, includes over 175 shops and the Hyatt Regency Hotel. On the third level is a Cable Car Museum.

At the north end of Embarcadero is **Ghiaradelli Square,** the old chocolate factory building converted into a retail and restaurant center with outdoor entertainment. It is on Beach street just west of Fisherman's Wharf.

On Beach street at Leavenworth street is another shoppers' paradise, **the Cannery,** remodeled out of the plant Del Monte opened in 1894. Rounding out this trio of massed shops is **The Anchorage,** created on Fisherman's Wharf itself, offering boutiques amongst the fish markets.

SAN FRANCISCO/NORTH BEACH

Columbus Avenue, marching off to the northwest in a diagonal from the financial district, provides the main street of this famous neighborhood. Russian Hill lies to the west, Telegraph Hill to the east. The beach is no where to be found. The name came from a beach at the foot of Powell street which was filled in to the present wharf line in 1881! Some city chronicles also dub North Beach as "Little Italy" or "Latin Quarter."

The road connecting the old Spanish presidio with the village at Yerba Buena Cove once passed this way. When immigrants from France and Italy came ashore at the North Point docks, many settled into this valley which some farmers from Italy had occupied as early as 1830. Here, Columbus Day is an event, and the night clubs on Columbus Avenue have launched many a career in the entertainment world.

Russian Hill has some of the city's most interesting Victorian mansions. It is also traversed by the steep section of Lombard Street which turns up in many television and movie stories shot with San Francisco backgrounds. Ten tight turns take an auto down this picturesque roadway.

ATTRACTIONS

On Green Street at Jones Street is a **block of houses** dating to 1850 which escaped the many fires, including that following the 1906 earthquake.

The Octagon House, 2645 Gough Street, was built in 1861. It is operated as a museum by the National Society of Colonial Dames. Open the second Sunday, and second and fourth Thursdays of each month from 12:00 noon to 3:00 p.m. Call 855-9796 for information, or write for group reservations.

Washington Square, on Columbus Avenue at Union Street, is a place to catch the local scene and select a lunch from a deli fronting the square. The bronze statue of Benjamin Franklin carries some curious inscriptions on the drinking water fountains, placed their by the donor who was a temperance advocate.

Next to the square is the **Church of Saints Peter and Paul,** built in 1922, then finished in 1940 with terra cotta mosaics of Columbus landing in America and the poet Dante at work.

North Beach Museum is on the mezzanine floor of the Eureka Savings building, 1435 Stockton Street. Open during banking hours weekdays.

Club Fugazi, 678 Green Street, presents the ultimate in long running shows called "Beach Blanket Babylon...." These reviews began in 1975 and the show is changed from time to time with topical gag lines and seasonal twists. Shows at 8:00 p.m. Wednesday through Saturday. An extra 10:30 p.m. show Friday and Saturday. Sundays at 3:00 p.m. and 7:30 p.m.

Cable Car Museum, power house and car barn at Washington and Mason streets. The three-level barn is a showplace for the municipal railway, part of a restoration dedicated in 1984. The original cable car is on display and a movie explains how the things work. Open 10:00 a.m to 6:00 p.m. daily.

SAN FRANCISCO/CHINATOWN

Just north of the Financial District is Chinatown, home of perhaps 35,000 of the people of Chinese heritage living in the city, and social and business headquarters for many more of them. Grant Avenue provides the main street, and there is a photogenic gateway to the neighborhood near the intersection of Grant Avenue and Bush street.

The neighborhood stretches north to Columbus Avenue and is about three blocks wide, offering markets trading in oriental foods unknown to many occidentals. Some residents cling to the dress of their homeland, and can be seen walking with dignity on the busy sidewalks. There are Chinese temples, clubs and business offices.

Most buildings date from restoration after the 1906 fire swept through the district. San Francisco's first Chinese immigrants came in 1848, passengers on the brig Eagle. Clipper ships brought an estimated 25,000 residents fleeing from famine and revolt in Kwangtung province who provided the first Chinatown with its residents.

ATTRACTIONS

Saint Mary's Square is a little park on California Street which was, in days before the fire, a house of prostitution that offended the Paulist fathers of the church across the way. A statue of Sun Yat-Sen, father of Chinese independence, is here. The old **Saint Mary's Church** was dedicated in 1854 and survived the fire; the red brick and iron work were shipped in from the east coast.

Kong Chow Temple, 520 Pine Street, is entered through what is called the passageway of peace. Stories of the Six Dynasties are told in wood carvings decorating the third-floor sanctuary. The original temple for people from the Kong Chow district was established in 1857 and dynamited to check the spread of the 1906 fire.

At 720 Washington Street is **Buddha's Universal Church,** a modern structure completed in 1961.

The **Chinese Historical Society**, 17 Adler Place, presents museum exhibits on the Chinese role in the gold rush and western expansion which followed. Open Tuesday through Saturday 1:00 p.m. to 5:00 p.m.

Art of China is displayed at the **Chinese Culture Center**, on the third floor of the Holiday Inn at 750 Kearny Street. Exhibits change regularly, and community activities take place here, too. Open Tuesday through Saturday from 10:00 a.m. to 4:00 p.m.

SAN FRANCISCO/NOB HILL

Nob Hill, which California Street climbs leaving the downtown area, and Pacific Heights, the next hill to the west on California, became places for the homes of the rich. Landmarks abound, and tales of the new rich who kept it are retold in the buildings. The California Street cable car line provides easy access.

Nob Hill, took its name from the "nabobs" who followed the 1856 example of Dr. Arthur Hayne and built their homes on a site with a view. Hayne's home became the site of today's Fairmont Hotel on Nob Hill. Other residents with riches included Leland Stanford, Mark Hopkins and Charles Crocker.

Pacific Heights developed later, and now sports a unique upper class tradition of San Francisco, the guesthouse. Mansions have been turned into resident clubs, with a lifestyle some-what akin to those who first lived in multi-million dollar homes built for folks such as Rudolph Spreckels of sugar fame; his mansion is located at Pacific and Gough streets.

ATTRACTIONS

Whittier Mansion, 2090 Jackson Street, is an 1896 Victorian of red sandstone imported from Arizona. Headquarters of the **California Historical Society**, the mansion is open Wednesday, Saturday and Sunday from 1:00 p.m. to 5:00 p.m. Call 567-1848 for information and group tour reservations.

Haas-Lilienthal House, 2007 Franklin, was occupied by the family of businessman William Haas until 1972; when it was donated to the Foundation for San Francisco Architectural Heritage. An 1886 structure with towers and decorated gables, it is a city landmark. Open Wednesday form 12:00 noon to 4:00 p.m., Sunday from 11:00 a.m. to 4:30 p.m. Call 441-3004.

Pacific Union Club, California at Mason Streets, is in the only residence on the hill to escape fire damage from the 1906 earthquake. James C. Flood built the brownstone with earnings from his stock exchange deals. Two of the city's oldest "gentlemen's clubs" joined and operate the mansion.

At 1051 Taylor Street is **Grace Cathedral**, with an illuminated cross 230-feet above the hilltop. It is the seat of the Episcopal Church in Northern California. Regular choral and organ concerts are presented here, with musicians drawn by excellent acoustics and a famed organ. Call 776-6611 for a schedule.

SAN FRANCISCO/CIVIC CENTER

Civic Center, a group of major buildings constructed after the fire, and downtown, clustered around Union Square seven blocks to the north, are two of the city's most visited areas. Both carry marks of a massive architectural style popular when architect Willis Polk and others designed the city rebuilt after the earthquake and fire.

The City Hall at Polk and Grove streets is testimony to the people who were building massive parks on sand dunes, reaching to the Sierras for their own hydroelectric and water supply, and drilling two-mile tunnels for street cars under the Twin Peaks.

Golden domed, city hall rises sixteen feet, two-and-five-eights inches taller than the U.S. Capital, as every guide book has probably noted since the place was dedicated in December, 1915 with the King and Queen of Belgium in attendance.

Amidst the bustle of shoppers drawn to Geary and Powell streets is the two-point-six acre Union Square with its ninety-seven foot high granite monument to the U.S. Navy's Manila Bay victory in the Spanish American War. Massive hotels and department stores surround the grassy square, interspersed with much smaller shops that have well-known names.

ATTRACTIONS

Eight buildings make up the main attractions of **Civic Center**. The renaissance city hall was, at last count, offices for nearly 1,300 employees from the mayor to the dog license sales clerk. Beneath the plaza is **Brooks Exhibit Hall**, a 90,000 square foot place for trade shows and convention exhibits.

To the west is the new **Louise Davies Symphony Hall**, the grand **War Memorial Opera House**, and a rehearsal hall serves both. Call Ticketron for

344

performance reservations. The opera operates a benefit gift shop at 190 Grove Street. Tours of the entire **Performing Arts Center** are offered on Mondays from 10:00 a.m. to 2:30 p.m.

San Francisco Symphony performs at Davies Hall, Van Ness and Grove, call 431-5400 for program information.

San Francisco Opera performs at the Opera House, Van Ness and Grove, call 864-3300 for program information on one of the world's most talented opera companies.

In the **War Memorial Building** on Van Ness Avenue at McAllister Street in Civic Center is the **San Francisco Museum of Modern Art**. From abstracts to architecture, exhibits change regularly. Open Tuesday through Friday from 10:00 a.m. to 6:00 p.m., with a Thursday evening opening to 10:00 p.m. Saturday and Sunday 10:00 a.m. to 5:00 p.m. Closed holidays.

The **San Francisco Library,** Larkin and McAllister streets, has a massive collection. History buffs and researchers visit the city History Room and Archives on the third floor, where exhibits change frequently. Days and hours vary, call 558-3949.

Music Hall Theater, 931 Larkin Street, presents a long-running lampoon of President Ronald Reagan called "Rap Master Ronnie." The political cabaret act goes on Tuesday through Friday at 8:00 p.m., Saturday at 7:00 p.m. and 10:00 p.m., Sunday at 3:00 p.m. and 7:00 p.m. Call 776-8996.

Lunchtime Theater on Union Square, 430 Mason Street, stages one-act plays Wednesdays and Thursdays at 12:00 noon, offering entertainment for shoppers. Call 421-6162 for current show information.

The **Joseph Dee Museum of Photography,** 47 Kearny Street, presents a collection of photos dating back over a 150 year span of time plus monthly displays. Open Monday through Friday 9:00 a.m. to 5:00 p.m.

Constructed in 1905, the **U.S. Courthouse** and **Post Office** at Seventh and Mission Streets is in the Italian renaissance style. It is the seat of the Ninth United States Circuit Court of Appeals which hears appellate cases for the Western United States.

Old Mint, at Fifth and Mission Streets, is a bit out of the Civic Center. Restored rooms and pioneer coins are on display, along with a stack of gold

San Francisco City/County

bullion worth $4,000,000. Open Monday through Friday, 10:00 a.m. to 4:00 p.m.

Mission Dolores, Sixteenth and Dolores Streets, is southwest of Civic Center, south of Market Street. This is probably the oldest building still standing in San Francisco. Open daily from 9:00 a.m. to 4:00 p.m.

SAN FRANCISCO/WEST

From the Marina District with its yacht harbors on the Golden Gate, around the ocean coast and vast residential areas ventilated by sea breezes to the bay at Hunter's Point, San Francisco has much to offer beyond its often-visited downtown. We'll take a quick tour starting on the Golden Gate, just scratching the surface of these fascinating and historic places.

The Marina includes the site of the Panama-Pacific International Exposition, and part of its buildings are preserved at the foot of Lyon Street, including the stately Palace of Fine Art, standing guard over duck ponds.

To the west is the Presidio of San Francisco which has been fortified in one way or another since 1776 when the Spaniards completed construction of their military headquarters. Venerable buildings and houses tell a story of times long gone by. The military still operates this as its west coast headquarters. The south approach to Golden Gate Bridge is carved off the large presidio holdings of the U.S. Government.

Lincoln Park guards the northwestern tip of the peninsula. The city's largest art museum, California Palace of the Legion of Honor is on a knoll with a view of what San Franciscan's call Lands End, and the ocean beyond. The wreckage of several ships remain beneath the cliffs, and below Point Lobos, the westernmost tip of land, sea lions are usually in residence on the rocks. Also in wreckage are the famed Sutro Baths and Ice Rink built in 1896 by the late Adolph Sutro. Still receiving guests is the Cliff House, one of many to occupy the site since 1863.

Marching inland from the ocean like a green finger of trees and grass in a sea of homes is Golden Gate Park with its world-class zoo on one end and Kezar Stadium, first home of the San Francisco Forty Niner football team at the east limits. The city received title to a vast wasteland of sand dunes in 1868, calling Fredrick Omsted, Sr. to help lay out a regional park. The designer of New York's Central Park settled on 1,000 acres, and it took the next fifty years to complete.

Real estate developers tackled the dunes around the park, stabilizing sand into the Richmond District to the north, and finally in the 1930s the Sunset District to the south. Across the neck of the peninsula toward the bay, smaller neighborhoods seem to tumble on top of each other with the folds of

346

the hills. Candlestick Park, the breezy home of the baseball Giants and football Forty Niners, is a reclaimed land fill. The last big neighborhood of the city is Hunter's Point with a U.S. Naval Yard in mothballs and thousands of residents living in housing which sprang up to support workers at the yard.

ATTRACTIONS

Stern Grove, Nineteenth Avenue and Sloat Boulevard, is a gift to the city in which 25,000 people can gather outdoors for weekend concerts. Most of entertainments' big names have played the picnic-eating crowds at one time or another since 1938. Call 398-6551 for program information of the summer schedules. Eucalyptus and redwood trees make this a pleasant walk in the off season, too.

Giants baseball schedules at **Candlestick Park** can be checked by calling 467-8000. Visitors will probably want to take public transportation to the ball park. For Forty Niner football information, call 468-2249, also at Candlestick.

Marching inland from the ocean like a green finger of trees and grass in a sea of homes is **Golden Gate Park** with its beach and Dutch windmill at one end and Kezar Stadium, first home of the San Francisco Forty Niner football team at the east limits. The city received title to a vast wasteland of sand dunes in 1868, calling Fredrick Olmsted, Sr. to help lay out a regional park. The designer of New York's Central Park settled on 1,000 acres, and it took the next fifty years to complete.

San Francisco Zoo is in Fleishacker Park, Forty Fifth Avenue at Sloat Street. Among the new attractions is a $7 million primate center, added among the landscaping modeled after a famed German zoo. Open 10:00 a.m. to 5:00 p.m.

At Lands End, the **Palace of the Legion of Honor,** contains a unique collection of works by French artists, probably the largest displayed in this country. Open Wednesday through Sunday from 10:00 a.m. to 5:00 p.m. Follow the signs to Lincoln Park from Geary Boulevard.

San Francisco Crafts and Folk Art Museum is in the Richmond District at 626 Balboa Avenue. Commentary on current customs or events may be among the works on exhibit in this small gallery. Open Wednesday through Friday from 12:00 noon to 5:00 p.m. Saturday, Sunday from 1:00 p.m. to 4:00 p.m.

Two art museums are side-by-side in **Golden Gate Park,** enter off of Tenth Street from Fulton Avenue. The **Asian Art Museum** features the Avery Brundage collection and works of artists from mid-east and eastern cultures. Open Tuesday through Sunday, 10:00 a.m. to 5:00 p.m. Call 558-2993. The **M.H. de Young Memorial Museum** features old masters and an expanding American collection. Open Wednesday through Sunday 10:00 a.m. until 5:00 p.m. Call 221-4811.

California Academy of Sciences **Natural History Museum and Aquarium** and **Morrison Planetarium** are in a large building south of the two art museums in Golden Gate Park. Call 221-5100 for information on events. The aquarium has a large, diverse collection of marine life. Models of man in natural situations are part of the natural history display along with a working demonstration of earthquakes. Open 10:00 a.m. to 5:00 p.m. daily. Planetarium sky shows are at 2:00 p.m. on Monday through Friday. Weekends, shows go on hourly from 1:00 p.m. through 4:00 p.m.

Next to the Palace of Fine arts on Lyon Street at Marina Boulevard is **The Exploratorium,** a hands-on museum of science which fills a huge warehouse and lets the curious children and adults spend hours discovering natural phenomena. Open Wednesday through Friday 11:00 a.m. to 5:00 p.m. Saturday and Sunday, 10:00 a.m. to 5:00 p.m. Call 563-7337 for information and reservations for the Tactile Gallery exhibit.

Fort Mason Center, Laguna and Marina Boulevards just east of the Marina, has several collections of special significance to ethnic groups. **Museo Italo Americano,** dedicated to the Italian-American culture, is in Building C, open Wednesday through Sunday from 12:00 noon to 5:00 p.m. Call 673-2200. **African-American Historical and Cultural Society** traces history of blacks in California, also in Building C. Open Tuesday through Saturday, 12:00 noon to 5:00 p.m. In Building D is the **Mexican Museum,** including lots of art work from pre-Hispanic to contemporary Mexican-American artists. Open Wednesday through Sunday from 12:00 noon to 5:00 p.m. Call 441-0404.

San Francisco Fire Department **Pioneer Museum** is at 655 Presidio Avenue. Equipment and memorabilia from the city's first volunteers formed in 1849 to more modern times included. Open Thursday through Sunday from 1:00 p.m. to 4:00 p.m.

Fort Point, built on the site of a Spanish artillery battery guarding the entrance to the bay, is constructed to handle 120 cannon. It is under the approach of Golden Gate Bridge, reached off of Lincoln Boulevard to Long Avenue. Open daily from 10:00 a.m. to 5:00 p.m.

Presidio Army Museum, Lincoln Boulevard at Funston Avenue on the presidio, is in a hospital building erected in 1857. Open Tuesday through Sunday, 10:00 a.m. to 4:00 p.m. Call 561-4115 for information.

Out in the bay, reachable by the Oakland Bay Bridge, is **Treasure Island Museum**. On the site of the Golden Gate Exposition held in 1939 and 1940, the museum records sea and air service in the Pacific. Pan American Airways China Clipper seaplane flights originated from here. Open daily, 10:00 a.m. to 3:30 p.m.

For more information on the city, contact the **San Francisco Visitor Information Center**, 900 Market Street, San Francisco CA 94101. Telephone (415) 391-2001.

Accommodations

AIRPORT EXECUTIVE INN
275 S Airport Boulevard
San Francisco, CA 94080
Tel.   (415) 873-3550
        (800) 482-4174 CA
        (800) 482-6868 USA
All major credit cards are accepted.

The definitive accommodation for busy executives, the Airport Executive Inn offers a wide range of facilities to ease the heavy load of those intent on the pursuit of upward mobility. Only three minutes from the airport, five minutes from Candlestick Park and the Cowpalace, and fifteen minutes from downtown San Francisco, this hotel offers more than the perfect location.
Available with an array of banquet and convention facilities from the fully appointed, 1475 square foot Presidential Room and adjoining Board Room, to spacious executive conference rooms, the Airport Executive Inn also specializes in services to facilitate and ease its guests. These include free airport limousine service, the Exec Health Club with a weight room, sauna and hot tub, room service galore, and modem-operated communication links with your office, just to name a few.

If you are just passing through San Francisco on business, or plan to host a fully catered banquet or conference, the Airport Executive Hotel should be first on your list.

THE FAIRMONT HOTEL
Atop Nob Hill
San Francisco, CA 94106
Tel. (415) 772-5000

The Fairmont Hotel has been home to presidents and kings for decades. It boasts an opulence and stated elegance that rivals the great palaces of European aristocracy. Quiet grandeur is reflected in mahogany, marble, and a red, black and gold motif, underscoring majestic comfort and protected serenity.

The Fairmont contains 700 luxurious guest rooms and suites, six restaurants, six cocktail lounges, a pharmacy, bank, drug store, doctor on call, and an additional range of services rivaling any in the world. Traditionally, the Fairmont has captured almost every award, including the AAA Five Diamond Award, Meetings and Conventions Gold Key Award, and the Travel Holiday Award for its superb Squire Restaurant. The famous Venetian Room Supper Club also presents some of the greatest entertainers in the world.

This hotel has made an immense commitment to excellence in the grandest tradition, and its staff-to-guest ratio approaches one-on-one. Considered a city within a city, one need never leave the Fairmont in pursuit of life's necessities. Or luxuries.

FOUR SEASONS CLIFT HOTEL
495 Geary Street
San Francisco, CA 94102
Tel. (415) 775-4700

Conveniently located two blocks from Union Square in the heart of the city's theatre and shopping district, the Four Seasons Clift Hotel has won both the Mobil Five Star and AAA Five Diamond awards for service and overall excellence. Amenities traditionally offered to guests include full concierge service, soft terrycloth robes, hair dryers, mini bars and complimentary weekday limo service to the financial district.

Among the hotel's array of gathering places are the world renowned Redwood Room bar and French Room restaurant, both famous for their beauty and courtly service. Business guests also enjoy the large variety of meeting and working environments provided especially to meet their needs, including a business center.

The guests list traditionally is filled with today's most famous celebrities and those who appreciate the ultimate in taste and service. For these, the Four Seasons Clift Hotel is famous.

HOTEL MARK TWAIN
345 Taylor Street
San Francisco, CA 94102
Tel.   (415) 673-2332
        (800) 622-0873 CA
        (800) 227-4074 USA

Mark Twain once said, "The coldest winter I ever spent was a summer I spent in San Francisco." However, present day guests can find cozy shelter from the city's chilly wind in the Hotel Mark Twain.

Sporting all the amenities, valet service, coffee makers in every room, direct-dial telephones, a sun deck, conference room, and restaurant, the hotel also offers surprisingly affordable rates. Built in 1928, it has, over the last fifteen years, been completely refurbished with new carpets, drapes, bedspreads and furniture.

Centrally located near San Francisco's famous Union Square shopping and theatre district, the hotel is ideal for the budget minded traveler who is interested in clean, comfortable accommodations at a price which will allow them to enjoy the rest of San Francisco's many attractions.

(See special invitation in the Appendix.)

HYATT REGENCY SAN FRANCISCO
5 Embarcadero Center
San Francisco, CA 94111
Tel.   (415) 788-1234
Telex: 170698
All major credit cards are accepted.

A magic hotel! The Hyatt Regency in San Francisco is bigger, better, and more exciting than life! You are dazzled from the moment you enter the soaring atrium lobby (containing well over 5,000 plants) until you reach the Equinox, the city's only revolving rooftop restaurant and lounge where visitors can take a 360 degree tour of San Francisco without leaving their seats.

The magic extends to its affordable rates and fantastic location in exciting Embarcadero Center. Within minutes of your luxurious room you can

351

visit exotic Chinatown, bustling Pier 39, famous Fisherman's Wharf, or take a ferry boat cruise. And the rest of the city is only a cable car ride away!

Best of all, the magic is the Hyatt Regency itself. You are treated in a Grand Manner that says more than San Francisco. It says"Hyatt." No other makes this fabled city more accommodating!

THE KING GEORGE HOTEL
334 Mason Street
San Francisco, CA 94102-1783
Tel. (415) 781-5050
       (800) 556-4545 CA
       (800) 227-4240 USA
       (800) 345-4240 CANADA

Located in the heart of San Francisco, The King George Hotel features tradition, charm and economy. Charm is well reflected in the Bread & Honey Tea Room located above the lobby, which offers a selection of delightful afternoon teas, including the King George High Tea. You may order a carousel of assorted finger sandwiches accompanied with tea biscuits, toasted crumpets and jam, a tipsy truffle and the King George special blend tea. For international flavor, visit the famous Ichirin Japanese restaurant adjacent to the hotel.

The 143 guest rooms are tasteful, quiet and finely appointed. Even though the rates are reasonable, The King George Hotel does not skimp on what it considers the vital necessities, full valet, porterage and concierge services are readily available.

Inquire about the King George's special vacation packages. The "Union Square Delight" includes deluxe accommodations for two nights, theatre tickets for two, continental breakfast, a discount booklet for nearby Pier 39, and afternoon English High Tea. There are also a "Gourmet Get-Away" and special three-night packages available to help you economize while enjoying the best of San Francisco.

(See special invitation in the Appendix)

MARK HOPKINS INTER-CONTINENTAL HOTEL
Number One Nob Hill
San Francisco, CA 94l08
Tel. (415) 392-3434
All major credit cards are accepted.

The Mark is one of San Francisco's landmarks, with 366 guest rooms and 26 suites appointed in the tradition of fine hotels. Designed to give its guests a view, the central tower and wings spread over the Nob Hill landscape, giving spectacular views of the bay and the city.

Now over sixty years old, the Mark Hopkins has an international reputation. Shops, an art gallery, car rental agency and more are available on the lover levels. The award-winning Nob Hill Restaurant provides breakfast and lunch to the clanging of the California Street cable car, which incidentally is an easy ride to the Financial District and other attractions of the city. Atop the hotel is the world famous Top of the Mark skyroom for cocktails and entertainment and unparalleled view of the area.

Your "Best Choice" for lodging in the Bay Area is among the world's finest hotels, a landmark atop famed Nob Hill.

THE QUEEN ANNE HOTEL
1590 Sutter Street
San Francisco, CA 94109
Tel.   (415) 441-2828
        (800) 262-2663 CA
        (800) 227-3970   USA

The Queen Anne is the mansion built in 1890 by James Fair, one of those who made a fortune in Nevada's Comstock lode. Now it is a famed small luxury hotel, offering just forty-nine rooms and suites with service that matches the Victorian surroundings.

Guests are treated to afternoon tea and continental breakfasts in the morning. Business clients use three rooms for meetings and gatherings. Groups of from ten to eighty persons are treated to meals and events known for fine service with an attention to detail.

This is your "Best Choice" among San Francisco's smaller luxury hotels, a place for relaxation which is a few steps away from many of the city's attractions.

(See special invitation in the Appendix)

RAMADA RENAISSANCE HOTEL
55 Cyril Magnin Street
San Francisco, CA 94102-2865
Tel.   (415)   392-8000
          (800)   228-9898
All major credit cards are accepted.

The spectacular Ramada Renaissance Hotel is located in the heart of downtown San Francisco, just two blocks from Union Square and one block from the cable cars.

This award-winning hotel offers 1,005 luxurious rooms and suites with breathtaking San Francisco views, enhanced by a $1 million art collection, a stunning four story atrium, health club, two restaurants, two lounges, room service, Concierge, and private access accommodations in the Renaissance Club located on the top floors of this thirty-two story hotel.

The Lobby and public areas provide a tasteful and relaxing atmosphere for guests amidst travertine marble, crystal chandeliers, Oriental carpets and the sounds of a classical grand piano drifting upward from the atrium.

The Renaissance offers Standard, Business Class and Renaissance Club guestroom categories. All rooms have bay windows that open to fresh air and all are neatly appointed and above average size. Business Class and Renaissance Club accommodations feature premium rooms, upgraded amenities and added personal services. The hotel also features twenty meeting rooms, including the elegant Renaissance Ballroom for meetings, conventions and banquet functions.

The tasteful ambiance and personal character of this unusual hotel, combined with its convenient downtown location, make the Ramada Renaissance a luxury hotel second to none in San Francisco. Elegance, not extravagance.

THE RAPHAEL HOTEL
386 Geary Street
San Francisco, CA 94102
Tel.   (415)   986-2000
          (800)   821-5343
Visa, MasterCard, AMEX, Diners Club, Carte Blanche cards
are accepted.

Just off Union Square, The Raphael is convenient. Management prides itself in elegance at reasonable rates, with service in the European tradition.

You'll enter a lobby through frosted glass doors etched with the fleur-de-lis of France. There's a crystal chandelier, high backed chairs with velvet cushions, and antique furniture. Rooms are offered in three sizes, all recently

354

renovated. The Raphael's location makes it a splendid headquarters for business or pleasure while in San Francisco, with easy access to public transportation and just a quick walk to the attractions of Union Square.

This smaller hotel on Geary Street is a "find" for travelers who want something a bit more intimate than an establishment with rooms by the hundreds.

TRAVELODGE AT THE WHARF
250 Beach Street
San Francisco, CA 94133
Tel. (415) 392-6700

The Travelodge has a lot to offer. It is the only hotel by the San Francisco Bay, it has congenial, friendly atmosphere and a helpful staff who are eager to demonstrate that the Travelodge has the best service anywhere on the wharf. From the moment you enter the country inn style lobby, you are welcomed and are made to feel at home.

The Travelodge has undergone an extensive renovation and remodeling. Each room was improved and refurbished with the most modern facilities for the greatest comfort and convenience. Many of the 250 deluxe guest rooms have ocean view balconies and suites are available. There are shops, Angellina's Restaurant and Jasper's Lounge available for your enjoyment and many of San Francisco's attractions, including Pier 39, cable cars Fisherman's Wharf, Ghiaradelli Square, and more, are within walking distance.

Many of the people who will serve you at the Travelodge have been with the hotel for many years and are dedicated to providing you with the most comfortable and pleasant stay possible.

THE WESTIN ST. FRANCIS
335 Powell Street
San Francisco, CA 94102
Tel. (415) 397-7000

The Westin St. Francis overlooks historic Union Square and is one of San Francisco's most elegant and highly rated hotels. The hotel is visually beautiful, inside and out. The 6,000 square foot lobby is supremely elegant with huge black marble columns and rosewood. The lobby's great magenta clock was the first master clock introduced to the West and was installed when the hotel reopened following the disastrous 1906 earthquake. There are five outside elevators to move guests who stay in the thirty-two story tower to their rooms at 1,000 feet per minute. They provide spectacular views of downtown San Francisco and at night their lights add a sparkling dimension to the after dark skyline.

The luxury and elegance of the St. Francis extends to every room. Rooms are delightfully furnished, appointed and are spacious and comfortable. The service is impeccable and the happiness and comfort of guests is of primary importance to the efficient staff. The hotel is well located for shopping or business and provides ample parking space for its guests.

The Westin St. Francis has received many awards and has been given the highest ratings possible by AAA, the Mobil Travel Guide and *Meetings and Conventions* magazine's Gold Key Award. The superior comforts and services offered at the St. Francis are traditional San Francisco at its finest. This great monument at Union Square is a reminder of the city's rich history and today offers superb luxury, comfort and every modern amenity.

Antiques

CLAIRE'S ANTIQUE LINENS
3313 Sacramento Street
San Francisco, CA 94118
Tel. (415) 931-3195
Hrs: Mon. - Sat. 10:00 a.m. - 5:30 p.m.
Most major credit cards accepted.

Quality and uniqueness make this store notable. Owner Claire Edelstein's specialties are Edwardian and Victorian linens, which she handpicks during trips throughout Europe. Some pieces are from families of nobility. "The antique linens really are pieces of art that are no longer being created," says Claire. "And they are becoming more difficult to find."

Several contemporary lines of linens, exclusive to Claire's, are available in 100 percent cotton and Egyptian cotton. Claire also offers exquisite china, crystal and silver, displayed on beautifully decorated tables fit for royal entertaining. For that very special gift or wedding present, Claire's is a must.

G. J. MURETA'S ANTIQUES
2418 Filmore Street
San Francisco, CA 94115
Tel. (415) 922-5652
Hrs: Mon. - Sat. 11:00 a.m. - 6:00 p.m.
Sunday 11:00 a.m. - 5:00 p.m.

Although San Francisco hosts many antique stores, few can claim the buzzword "eclectic" as accurately as can G. J. Mureta's Antiques. Beauty and

356

diversity are what owner, Gary J. Mureta, provides abundantly for his customers.

The merchandise changes constantly, providing fresh treasures for dedicated shoppers. You can find fine paintings and prints, lamps, beautiful boxes, rugs, and sometimes elderly clocks of rare vintage. Sterling silver jewelry is a specialty, as are Oriental antiques, both Chinese and Japanese.

Gary often purchases pieces from original owners and is happy to provide their history to interested buyers. He ships anywhere in the world and travellers can expect to find their antiques waiting for them upon their arrival home. A selection from G. J. Mureta's would provide a lovely homecoming!

KEITH'S ANTIQUES
3501 Sacramento Street
San Francisco, CA 94118
Tel. (415) 567-5705
Hrs: Mon. - Fri.   11:00 a.m. - 6:00 p.m.
　　　Saturday   11:00 a.m. - 5:00 p.m.
　　　Sunday   12:00 noon - 5:00 p.m.

At Keith's Antiques, the focus is on small, high quality pieces from perfume bottles to some select items of distinctive furniture. Owner Kathleen Hughes, has a home in Heswall Cheshire which serves as a base for buying antiques for the shop. Manager Alison Fagan specializes in blue and white Staffordshire china.

Kathleen and Alison are both very knowledgeable about antiques and are eager to assist their clients in any way they can. And if you can't find what you want, they will scout for a piece on your behalf to meet your needs. Joan Bridwell shares a small part of the shop and also offers a wonderful selection of crystal, silver and high quality antiques.

The shop is full of treasures, making it perfect for browsing. Casual shoppers seeking gifts and serious collectors looking for especially fine pieces all find what they want at Keith's Antiques.

357

A complete tour, for a rapid day...or a meandering two day excursion, of that which San Francisco is noted for: American/European antiques and ART!

S.F. ANTIQUE & ART TOUR		
a.m. Bechelli's	Best breakfast	SanF/Rest
a.m. Magic If Gallery	Best sculptures	SanF/Art
a.m. Claire's Antiques	Best linens	SanF/Ant
a.m. Artiques	Best lithographs	SanF/Art
p.m. A. Sabella's	Best sea salad	SanF/Rest
p.m. Keith's Antiques	Best English china	SanF/Ant
p.m. G.J. Mureta's	Best silver	SanF/Ant
p.m. Wild Wings	Best nature art	SanF/Ant
Try any of these restaurants for a super supper:		
p.m. California Culinary	Best buffets	SanF/Rest
p.m. Cliff House	Best continental	SanF/Rest
p.m. Dante's	Best chowder	SanF/Rest
p.m. Doros	Best dinner	SanF/Rest

Apparel

ARICIE
Lingerie de Marque
50 Post Street
Crocker Center Galleria
San Francisco, CA 94104
Tel. (415) 989-0261
Hrs: Mon. - Fri.   9:30 a.m. - 6:00 p.m.
      Saturday   10:00 a.m. - 5:00 p.m.

Men sometimes feel awkward in lingerie shops. What to buy? Where to look? What size? Where not to look? However, at Aricie, every effort is made to see that male clients are put at ease by a cheerful staff well trained in the art of fitting a female figure and in assisting with special gift selections.

Aricie has everything a woman could dream of from the sexy to the practical, from silk to cotton. Offering over fifty brand names in panties, bras, nightgowns, cashmere robes and other undergarments, Aricie also stocks specialty, one-of-a-kind articles. Included are hand blown and signed delicate perfume bottles, fine handkerchiefs, jewelry, antique lace, silk stockings, hand-beaded garments, and even pajamas for the "Mr."

If you can't find what you want during the day, Aricie boasts yet another feature: popular special evening showings. Both men and women agree that these events "are the civilized way to shop."

BILLYBLUE, 73 Geary Street, San Francisco, California. Updated, but traditional men's clothes of natural fibers. American and European design.

CARNEVALE
2185 A Union Street
San Francisco, CA 94123
Tel. (415) 931-0669
Hrs: Mon. - Sat.   11:00 a.m. - 7:00 p.m.
           Sunday   12:00 noon - 5:00 p.m.
Visa, MasterCard, AMEX and Discover cards are accepted.

This is a store for those who adore clothes. Carnevale specializes in the unusual, focusing on original works from young and upcoming designers. You'll see Carnevale's fashions worn by the "rich and famous," but because the designers are relatively unknown, prices are still affordable.

Sporting a wide variety of elegant and casual fashions, Carnevale also supports them with plenty of unique accessories.

Seasonal fashion shows also provide tantalizing glimpses of today's glittering new trends. If you're looking for the new, exciting, and sometimes outrageous--dance to Carnevale!

CASHMERE'S OF SCOTLAND, Crocker Galleria, San Fanrcisco, California. Mens and womens classic cashmere clothing.

CLOTHES CONTACT - VINTAGE CLOTHING
473 Valencia at 16th
San Francisco, CA 94103
Tel. (415) 621-3212
Hrs: Mon. - Sat.   11:00 a.m. - 7:00 p.m.
           Sunday   12:00 noon - 6:00 p.m.

If you can purchase potatoes by the pound, why not clothes? This innovative idea is exactly what German-born Werner Werwie brought back from Europe and introduced to San Francisco.

Vintage clothing ranging from leathers to silks are displayed attractively on sized racks.   Dressing rooms are provided   for your convenience. The Clothes Contact is just like a department store but for one creative and economical difference: you pay for your wardrobe by the pound! Suits, skirts, hats, sportswear, military wear, dresses--you name it--are available at one low rate per pound. Heavier items such as coats and furs come at a low fixed price.

But remember: allow plenty of time for fun and browsing!

(See special invitation in the Appendix.)

COMME DES GARCONS, 70 Geary Street, San Francisco, California. Trendy Japanese fashion from a great designer.

THE COMPANY STORE
1913 Fillmore Street
San Francisco, CA 94115
Tel: (415) 921-0365
Hrs: Mon. - Fri. 11:00 a.m. - 7:00 p.m.
      Saturday   10:00 a.m. - 6:00 p.m.
      Sunday   12:00 noon - 5:00 p.m.

In this day and age, clothing means much more than it did one hundred years ago. Today, there's sort of a psychology to dressing. People that feel good about themselves usually express it in their apparel. It's a fact that tasteful apparel fits the personalities of those who wish to display self confidence and enthusiasm. This is why so many women with these traits shop for their clothing at The Company Store.

This apparel shop features just about anything the serious minded shopper could want. For example, designs by "Lady-Like," created in their own workshop, present one piece cotton knit dresses for spring. The design comes in raspberry, sand and sky blue. However, spring is only one season. They also carry fashions for summer, fall and winter. The size range is also unusual--8 thru 24. Natural fibers are predominately used in the soft and comfortable fashions.

Along with the terrific selection of delightful clothing, The Company Store is also well stocked with accessories. Hats, belts, stockings, jewelry and much more can all be found here. Due to the simplicity of the styles, accessories are emphasized and the selection is outstanding. It includes designer pieces from all over the world--special emphasis is place on San Francisco designers.

Another plus about this apparel store is the service. The owner and staff are all very courteous and helpful, making it a pleasure to shop here. If you're a woman who feels good about yourself, The Company Store is the establishment to visit for all your wardrobe needs.

COTTON & COMPANY, 3961 24th Street, San Francisco, California. Cotton t-shirts, sweats and clothing in original designs.

COTTONTAIL AND ME
1820 Fillmore Street
San Francisco, CA 94115
Tel. (415) 563-8262
Hrs: Tue. - Fri.   11:00 a.m. - 6:00 p.m.
       Saturday   11:00 a.m. - 5:00 p.m.
Visa, MasterCard and AMEX are accepted.

A Fairy tale come true! Cottontail and Me overflows with adorable clothes and toys for children between the ages of "brand new" and six years. The clothes range from designer wear to play clothes, with many selections available in comfortable 100 percent cotton.
When buying for the shop, owner Elizabeth Tana says, "I put myself in the customer's place." A mother herself, Elizabeth knows what is important when choosing clothes, gifts and toys for little ones.
Gift selections are vast, including cuddly teddy bears, quilts, bibs, jewelry, wall hangings, chairs and hobby horses. Everything you could possible imagine for the nursery is available, and if you have a special request, Elizabeth will be happy to order it especially for you.

GLAD RAGS, 3985 24th Street, San Francisco, California. Natural fiber clothing, 100% cotton, silk and wool.

JAY BRIGGS, 61 Post Street, San Francisco, California. Updated traditional men's clothing store.

JOSEF ROBE
Pier 39
San Francisco, CA 94133
Tel. (415) 781-4767
Hrs: Mon. - Sun. 10:30 a.m. - 8:30 p.m.

It all began when actor Michael Ferral was recuperating from surgery and wanted a special sort of robe. His wife, actress Marrian Walters, put her knowledge of theatrical costume designing to work and created the original Josef Robe, one that opens on the side. Soon they were in full production and sales zoomed after being featured in Playboy magazine. Customers come from as far away as Europe and Australia.

What is so special about these robes? Excellent craftsmanship and unique design! The robes are ankle-length and each one is sized. There is no "one size fits all" at Josef's. The weight and construction are serious matters, and they have their own method of sewing and binding these long-wearing items.

New designs are being added to the roster and soon Michael and Marrian plan to offer robes made of a 1903 terrycloth from Turkey. Prices vary according to style and color combinations.

LE BEAU MONDE, Embarcadero 3 on Cannery Row, San Francisco, California. Contemporary women's clothing; primarily sportswear.

MARIMEKKO
50 Post Street
San Francisco, CA 94104
Tel. (415) 392-1742
Hrs: Mon. - Sat. 10:00 a.m. - 6:00 p.m.
Visa and MasterCard are accepted.
and,
Stanford Shopping Center
Palo Alto, CA 94304
Tel. (415) 327-6111

Timeless clothing designs, cut from fabric which has been called works of art, set apart this unique apparel store. The clothing is complemented by tasteful fashion accessories for the exclusive clothing designs in wood and sterling silver.

Finnish artists, who staged a renaissance in 1950s, created the first fabrics for Marimekko. Clothing patterns came out of the same simple school of design, with an emphasis on comfort. The clothing is fashioned from knits, silk-screened cottons, and woven patterns. Items for the home include silkscreened cotton fabric by the yard, classic furniture by Alvar Aalto, and museum quality glassware featuring free form vases.

Some say a trip to Marimekko is as pleasing as a visit to a museum of modern art. We can say this is your "Best Choice" for fine apparel and accessories, and makes a visit to the Crocker Galleria on Post Street worthwhile.

M. J. MILLER, 4 Embarcadero Center, Podium level, San Francisco, California. Active sportswear for tennis, golf, swimming, running and more.

MUDPIE, 1699 Union Street, San Francisco, California. Unique items, mostly European, mostly fun sports clothes.

MY FAVORITE CLOTHING & SHOE STORE, 37 Drumm Street, San Francisco, California. Bargain clothes, four floors of them.

OBIKO
794 Sutter Street
San Francisco, CA 94109
Tel. (415) 775-2882
Hrs: Mon. - Fri.   10:00 a.m. - 6:00 p.m.
         Saturday   10:00 a.m. - 5:00 p.m.

Handmade apparel and accessories, most of it created by California custom designers, are featured at this small shop. Jewelry on display is described as "breathtaking."
Owner Sandra Sakata draws on fabric artists, weavers and jewelry designers for her luxurious selection of wares. To be part of Obiko's suppliers, she says, the artists must create in a unique and highly individual manner. Many of the designs are one of a kind, fashioned by artists who also display in art galleries and international museum shows.
Women looking for clothes that are for celebration will find this small Sutter Street shop their "Best Choice" in a city known for its fine apparel stores.

RABAT, 4001 24th Street, San Francisco, California. Women's clothing, accessories and shoes.

SAYS WHO?, 1626A Union Street, San Francisco, California. Clothing for the generous woman. In natural fabrics and great colors.

363

THE TAILORED MAN
324 Stockton Street
San Francisco, CA 94108
Tel. (415) 397-6906
Hrs: Mon. - Fri.   9:30 a.m. - 6:00 p.m.
     Saturday   9:00 a.m. - 5:30 p.m.
     Sunday   12:00 noon - 5:00 p.m.
All major credit cards accepted.

The Tailored Man, conveniently located on Union Square, offers knowledgeable service and quality clothing of exceptional fit. This elegant store, furnished with comfortable leather couches and oriental carpets, has three floors of exceptional apparel. President Peter Domenici is committed to bringing the finest in quality and service to his customers and The Tailored Man has built a solid reputation for made-to-measure clothing over the past two decades.

The courteous and professional staff (fluent in five languages) will help you select from a vast assortment of European and American designer lines in every size. Each suit is marked by a master tailor, who will supervise the alterations and be on hand for your second fitting. There is a fine ready to wear department in addition to custom tailoring and shirt making.

From neckwear to formal wear, from handmade Italian suits to designer socks, you will find the best in men's apparel at The Tailored Man.

WILKES RASIFORD, 375 Sutter Street, San Francisco, California. Men and womens clothing, imports and some American designerwear.

ZOE
2400 Filmore Street
San Francisco, CA 94115
Tel. (415) 929-0441
Hrs: Mon. - Sat.   11:00 a.m. - 7:00 p.m.
     Sunday   12:00 noon - 5:00 p.m.

How many items of clothing have you bought one year only to discover the next year, because of fads in colors, that you can't find anything new to match? Tired of shops that carry trendy clothing in which you wouldn't be caught dead? You'll find the solution to these problems at Zoe.

Classic, simple lines in basic colors have been assembled by owner Trish Pillsbury with the goal of providing her customers with clothing that easily coordinates. The timeless elegance of her sweaters, skirts, slacks and dresses will add to your wardrobe and provide a foundation on which to build for years to come. Versatile is a key word at Zoe and extends to the prices which range from inexpensive to sophisticated.

This beautifully designed shop has plenty of windows that provide natural light allowing you to see the true color of the clothing. The airy feeling is further enhanced by bright, white walls and sharp, clean architecture. The combination of classic clothing and the personal attention Trish gives makes Zoe your "Best Choice" for investment shopping in San Francisco.

This tour provides for all the special people in your life--including yourself.

THE CLOTHES OF 'FRISCO			
a.m.	New Joe's	Best breakfast	SanF/Rest
a.m.	Aricie	Best lingerie	SanF/App
a.m.	Marimenko	Best cotton knit	SanF/App
a.m.	Obiko	Best clothes art	SanF/App
p.m.	Old Swiss House	Best Swiss lunch	SanF/Rest
p.m.	Josef Robe	Best robes	SanF/App
p.m.	Clothes Contact	Best prices	SanF/App
p.m.	Cottontail and Me	Best children's	SanF/App
p.m.	Carnevale	Best selection	SanF/App
p.m.	Zoe	Best classics	SanF/App
	After your spree, choose from three very different restaurants to celebrate your style!		
p.m.	Yamato Restaurant	Best Japanese	SanF/Rest
p.m.	Umberto Ristorante	Best Italian	SanF/Rest
p.m.	Neptune's Palace	Best sea & cheese	SanF/Rest

Many of the world's finest clothing designs can be found only in San Francisco. This tour highlights some of the shops where you can expect to discover that one-of-a-kind find.

Art Galleries

ARTIQUES
2167 Union Street
San Francisco, CA 94123
Tel.   (415) 929-6969
Hrs: Mon. - Sun. 10:30 a.m. - 6:30 p.m.

Although a visit to Union Street requires no special purpose, art collectors will want to come to peruse the fine works available at Artiques. Their motto, "Quality art at affordable prices" is diligently upheld, which is evident in the displays of the gallery.

The enormous popularity of Maxfield Parrish is supported by Artiques, as an entire corner of the gallery is devoted to original lithographs in original frames by this artist.   You don't have to be an Art Deco collector to appreciate Louis Icart, his works transcend any classification. Icart paintings and signed etchings are always displayed, such subjects as "Paris Flowers" and "Madame Butterfly" in all their splendor. At Artiques, there is always some of the finest examples of the exacting detail inherent in the process of stone lithography, something that many collectors revere.   There are wonderful works by Toulouse-Lautrec, circa 1927 and several by Alphonse Mucha, circa 1905.

A wide concentration of original oils is headed by Grant Wood, as well as members of the Barbizon school.   California artists from the 1880's to the 1940's are also featured, such as noted masters Cooper, Hosmer, Dawes, Valencia and Welch. Also, you will discover superb oils by European artists such as Carl Jonnevold, whose "A Fjord" is greatly admired.

Professional restoration and exquisite framing is available at Artiques. Their six month lay away allows you to plan ahead for giving art or adding to your own collection. Artiques is a "Best Choice" journey into the world of pleasure of fine art.

BIORDI ART IMPORTS
412 Columbus Avenue
San Francisco, CA 94133
Tel. (415) 392-8096
Hrs: Mon. - Sat. 9:30 a.m. - 6:00 p.m.
Visa, MasterCard and AMEX are accepted.

You'll find Biordi's exclusive shop in the heart of San Francisco's Italian district.   What better location for fine, hand-painted Majolica pottery and cookware imported directly from Italy? A bridal registry is provided for the exclusive and fashionable hand-painted dinnerware. Besides the elegant dinnerware, you'll also find a rich selection of treasures from candlestick holders to chandeliers. Fabulous gifts available include pieces from De Simone, the artist from Palermo, and platters by Deruta.

Everything is personally selected by the owner, Gianfranco Savio, and displayed to perfection in a shop designed by Marquis Associates, reflecting its own artwork and simple, classical style.

There is no other shop quite like Biordi, many discriminating shoppers come from out of state. For your convenience, Biordi will ship anywhere in the world. Dare to visit Biordi Art Imports. You'll be sure to fall in love!

THE MAGIC IF GALLERY
4 Embarcadero Center
San Francisco, CA 94111
Tel.   (415) 362-4500
Hrs: Mon. - Fri.   9:30 a.m. - 9:30 p.m.
          Saturday   10:00 a.m. - 9:00 p.m.
          Sunday   10:00 a.m. - 5:00 p.m.
Visa, MasterCard and AMEX are accepted.

If your life is getting too serious, and you just want to have some fun, The Magic If Gallery is the place to visit.

Twenty-five artists from different parts of the country work daily to produce fantastic soft sculptures that come from the whimsical imagination of fantasy land. Whether its a six foot Do-do bird, a sea dragon, parrots, palm trees, hand puppets, hot air balloons, fish, fairy tale posters, pillow cases, greeting cards or a five foot butter sculpture - nothing in the gallery is ordinary.

Your "Best Choice" for fun and fanciful art is The Magic If Gallery.

SCRIMSHAW GALLERY, LTD.
Pier 39, K-12
San Francisco, CA 94133
Tel.   (415) 986-2309
Hrs: Mon. - Sun. 10:30 a.m. - 8:30 p.m.

You might meet Paul Harvey or John Denver adding a piece to their collections if you stop by Scrimshaw Gallery on Pier 39, where owner Mike Attaway offers California's largest collection of original and limited edition pieces of this American folk art.

Twenty Scrimshanders, etching each piece by hand on fossilized ivory from Alaska, are represented in this gallery. Every collector's taste and budget can be met, with pieces ranging from $10 to $8000 in an assortment of jewelry, knives, money clips, spoons or special orders.

Scrimshaw Gallery, Ltd. also features other art of a maritime theme, bronze whale sculptures by Randy Puckett, original paintings and water colors by Larry Foster, the best known U. S. cetacean artist who illustrates for National Geographic, Encyclopedia Americana and The Smithsonian, and nautical lithographs in limited editions by Wells, Hoyne and Stobart.

THE VICTORIAN SHOPPE
Pier 39, P-2
San Francisco, CA 94133
Tel. (415) 781-4470
Hrs: Mon. - Sun. 9:30 a.m. - 9:30 p.m.
Visa, MasterCard, AMEX, JCB, and personal checks accepted.

The Victorian Shoppe is one of the most unique specialty shops to be found anywhere. It is filled with Victorian houses done in more than a dozen media, including watercolored lithographs, ceramics, needlepoint, cross-stitch, wood art, cantaglios, fabric art, and more. Artist Debbie Patrick produces seventy-five percent of the merchandise in the shop which she and her husband, Jim who renovates real Victorian homes, opened in 1978.

The watercolored lithographs are one of Debbie's most popular creations. Each lithograph is printed on a specially treated paper, hand watercolored and then signed and dated on the day it is painted. There are many different style houses available, in many different colors. After you have made your choice, the lithograph is matted in whichever of fifteen different complementary colors you choose and, if you wish, framed while you wait. A history of each house is included, describing style characteristics and items of unique historical significance.

The prices on the artwork at The Victorian Shoppe are very reasonable and the helpful staff will ship your purchase anywhere in the world, or securely package it in a sturdy cardboard portfolio complete with handle so you can take it with you, if you wish. This is a delightful place to browse and find a wonderful remembrance of your trip to San Francisco.

VORPAL GALLERIES, 393 Grove Street, San Francisco, California. Paintings, drawings, prints, sculpture, photography, ethnic jewelry, weavings and tapestries representing over fifty artists including Picasso.

WEST OF THE MOON
3464 Sacramento Street
San Francisco, CA 94118
Tel.   (415) 922-4650 American Indian
        (415) 346-4141 African, Oceanic
        (415) 346-4111 Pre-Columbian
Hrs: Wed. - Sat. 12:00 noon - 6:00 p.m.
And by appointment

West of the Moon, Lost Art Gallery and New World Antiquities offer a unique combination of primitive art under one roof. Three remarkable men, each an expert in his own field, have combined their talents and expertise to present authentic ethnic art from Africa, the Americas and Oceania. The works found here were produced by people to show their devotion to their gods, they are one of a kind masterpieces.

Mark Wm. Clark is a specialist in Pre-Columbian art, featuring the Maya. He will know the history of any piece that interests you and gladly share his expertise. Dave DeRoche specializes in traditional artifacts of Africa, the Americas and Oceania. American Indian art, including a large variety of Navajo weaving, is presented by Fred King. If you are a collector, it will be difficult to make a decision, everything is priceless, unusual and desirable. The collection changes constantly and if they don't have what you are looking for, they will direct you to someone who does, or find it for you.

You will always find one of the proprietors available for consultation and whether you are a beginning collector or a lifetime connoisseur, you will appreciate the knowledge and quality at West of the Moon.

Attractions

NEIMAN-MARCUS DOME, 150 Stockton Street, San Francisco, California. *The Glass Ship*, erected in 1901, stained glass dome is focal point of Rotunda.

RED AND WHITE FLEET
Pier 41 Fisherman's Wharf
San Francisco, CA 94133
Tel. (800) 445-8880
Hrs: Call for departure times

Red and White Fleet offers you the seven best cruises on the San Francisco Bay. Since each cruise is a different, memorable adventure, plan to take more than one!

369

Golden Gate Bay Cruise - a wonderful way to take in views of the skyline, hills and historic monuments of The City. Highlights are sailing under the Golden Gate Bridge, past Alcatraz and Angel Island and along the waterfront.

Sausalito/Fisherman's Wharf Ferry - cruise from Fisherman's Wharf, the lovely National Historic Landmark full of shops and art displays to Sausalito, the "Riviera" of America.

Walking Tour of Alcatraz - only with Red and White Fleets can you stroll around "The Rock" and visit the cell blocks of the twelve acre prison and grounds.

'Round The Rock Cruise - listen to the fascinating stories of Frank Heaney, the former prison guard, who hosts this adventurous cruise.

Angel Island Ferry - pack a picnic and spend the day viewing the former U. S. Army cannon emplacement of the Civil War and one time major U.S. Immigration Center.

Marine World Africa USA Cruise - take the high speed catamaran and experience thrilling encounters with killer whales, dolphins, sea lions and non-stop shows and exhibits.

Tiburon Ferry - at the tip of a peninsula, spend an afternoon shopping in this sparkling seaside village that commands a beautiful view of San Francisco.

Automotive Services

COASTSIDE TIRES
1639 Taraval
San Francisco, CA 94116
Tel.   (415) 566-6960
Hrs: Tues. - Fri.   9:00 a.m. - 5:30 p.m.
          Saturday   9:00 a.m. - 1:00 p.m.
Closed Sunday and Monday.

Coastside Tires owner, David Sharp, knows everything there is to know about tires. "In today's self-service world of gas stations," he says, "people don't take the time to check their tires like they should." That's why Coastside Tires welcomes you to bring in your car for free air, free inspection, and free rotation.

Specializing in Remington and Sumitomo brands, David also can obtain any special brand or size you need to keep your vehicle running safe and sure.

David's world is tires: repair, sales and service. He's eager to share it with you and offers fair prices and conscientious service. In this world where we depend upon our automobiles so much, a motorist couldn't ask for more.

Bed and Breakfast

BED and BREAKFAST INN, 4 Charlton Court, San Francisco, California. An English inn, elegant and unique.

EDWARD II INN AND CARRIAGE HOUSE
3155 Scott Street
San Francisco, CA 94123
Tel. (415) 922-3000
Hrs: Office Mon. - Sun. 8:00 a.m. - 11:00 p.m.
Visa, MasterCard, AMEX

ROMANCE! Imagine a traditional English country architecture complete with window shutters, flower boxes, and traditional banners. Imagine mauve and white wicker, floral prints, and antique wood tables graced with charming dried floral arrangements. Imagine low cost Pensione rooms, or lavish Carriage House suites complete with whirlpool baths, canopied beds, and wet bars. Sheer romance!

Located in the fashionable Marina District, the hotel was built to host guests attending the Panama-Pacific International Exposition of 1915. The three story European-style Inn was in the forefront of the bed & breakfast phenomena on the West Coast and remains today as a citadel to gracious living.

Continental breakfasts are offered by the in-house Italian- French bakery, located in the lobby. Sumptuous European dining is available in the Marina Cafe. Taste the romance and charm of the past in this charming environment.

(See special invitation in Appendix)

JACKSON COURT
2198 Jackson Street
San Francisco, CA 94115
Tel. (415) 929-7670

Graciousness, elegance and luxuriousness are keywords when describing this beautiful Bed and Breakfast. It's old San Francisco charm at its highest. Each guest is impressed by the soothing and serene elegance when they enter the courtyard and proceed to the library parlor. The library, a sanctuary in tones of forest greens, welcomes you with a large fireplace. Ten guest rooms and suites are decorated with attention to old world luxury. The Garden Court boasts a fireplace and handcrafted wood panelling. The Blue Room, cool and

371

serene, lures you with its 17th Century Renaissance sofa and brass porcelain bed. Every room is equally unique and compelling.

A lovely complimentary breakfast is served every morning and full concierge services are rendered faithfully with the intent to make you feel at home in romantic San Francisco. Once home to Luciano Pavarotti and Mikhail Baryshnikov, the converted brownstone mansion in the scenic Pacific Heights district awaits your pleasure.

THE MONTE CRISTO BED AND BREAKFAST
600 Presidio and Pine
San Francisco, CA 94115
Tel. (415) 931-1875
Open all year. Major credit cards are accepted.

The elegantly restored Monte Cristo was originally built in 1875 as a saloon and hotel. It's colorful history includes serving as a bordello, a refuge after the 1906 earthquake and as a speakeasy during Prohibition. Located two blocks from Victorian shops, restaurants and antique stores on Sacramento Street, the Monte Cristo is only about ten minutes to any other point in the city. The proprietor, Frances Allan has the ability to make you feel welcome and right at home.

Each room is individually decorated, the wallpaper, pillows, bedspreads and linens have been selected to blend and create a stunning impression. Every room has it's own unique features such as a 250 year old wedding bed or a sunken, tiled tub. There are also handsome antiques and oriental carpets throughout the house. You will enjoy your stay at this "Best Choice" of San Francisco.

PETITE AUBERGE, 863 Bush Street, San Francisco, California. The romantic ambience of a French country inn snuggled in the downtown area. Fireplaces in every room and gracious service. Breakfast features homemade breads, pastries, freshly squeezed juices, and wine or tea is served in the afternoon.

THE WHITE SWAN INN, 845 Bush Street, San Francisco, California. Combines the charming serenity of an English garden inn and graceful sophistication. Tasteful rooms feature curved bay windows, antiques, fireplace and private baths. Delicious full breakfast and afternoon tea with hors d'oeuvres.

Bath Accessories

BUBBLES
3391 Sacramento Street
San Francisco, CA 94118
Tel. (415) 923-0512
Hrs: Mon. - Sat. 11:00 a.m. - 6:00 p.m.

At Bubbles, owner Laura Ng has created a pretty shop that has bath accessories from the dramatic to casual, high tech to ultra feminine, traditional to contemporary.

Laura is more than happy to assist those looking for ideas when redecorating or needing advice choosing a certain type of soap or gift. She carries top of the line towels and bath carpets from large sizes to small rugs. Shower curtains of every design are beautifully displayed, as well as pedicure sets, personal bath items, brass towel racks, mirrors, bath taps, shelving, bath salts and potpourri galore. Laura will also design gift baskets for you and ship them anywhere in the country.

No matter what type of accessory you seek, Bubbles is a "Best Choice," fun place to browse.

Candy

CONFETTI LE CHOCOLATIER
Embarcadero Center #4
San Francisco, CA 94111
Tel. (415) 362-1706
Hrs: Mon. - Sat 10:00 a.m. - 6:00 p.m.

Ah! Chocolate! The sheer, luxurious debauchery of chocolate as it melts slowly and drowns your taste buds in dulcet sensations of pleasure. Have I gotten your attention? Confetti le Chocolatier deserves full attention. A grand and beautiful shop located in the posh Embarcadero Center, Confetti offers one of the largest selections of European chocolates in the world!

From intense and heavy French chocolate to light, creamy Swiss, their principal selection features Moreau, Pierre Koenig and Joseph Schmidt, among many other hand-selected chocolates from some of the world's most renowned chocolatiers. Presentational gift boxes are also unique and sophisticated. An example, "Boite a la Rose" (Rose box) contains handmolded chocolates filled with lush rum truffles and hazelnut pralines, complemented with foilwrapped raspberry and cream de casis pieces, all embossed with a rose motif and

373

wrapped in a white, enameled box tied with a silk ribbon and adorned with a silk rose.

If you are one of America's chocolate gourmets, or looking for the definitive gift, or just searching for intense excitement of the palate, a visit to Confetti is a must.

(See special invitation in the Appendix.)

China and Crystal

WATERFORD - WEDGWOOD SAN FRANCISCO
304 Stockton Street
San Francisco, CA 94108
Tel. (415) 391-5610
Hrs: Mon. - Sat. 9:30 - 5:30
Visa, MasterCard, AMEX, Diner's Club and Carte Blanche.

As the name implies, this store specializes in Wedgwood China and Waterford Crystal. San Francisco had the first Wedgwood store in the United States and this store carries a complete line of Wedgwood chine and crystal. Manager Karin Wolff is committed to serving her customers and stands behind every product they sell.

Wedgwood carries every pattern exported to the USA and will help you locate anything you want that is not in stock. Occasionally a potter from the factory visits the store, which allows the customer to have a selection autographed. Although the specialty here is china with the Wedgwood name, they also carry Midwinter, Adams and Coalsport, which are divisions of Wedgwood, Waterford crystal and a selection of interesting oven cookware.

No matter what your fine china needs, Wedgwood is the place to shop. The extensive selection and the quality caring service will delight you.

Coffee House

THE BLUE DANUBE COFFEE HOUSE
306 Clement Street
San Francisco, CA 94118
Tel. (415) 221-9041
Hrs: Mon. - Sun. 9:00 a.m. - 12:00 midnight

Remember the Left Bank? Remember Greenwich Village? Remember the artists and writers locked into intense conversations over an endless succession of steaming cups of espresso? Remember the laughter, the easy friendships, the regulars, and the exquisite opportunities for people watching? Remember the classical music and jazz? And the paintings by local artists that decorated the walls?

You can experience all that and more at the Blue Danube Coffee House. The mood is European: a small sidewalk cafe with seating available inside. Fine coffee, including espresso, cappuccino, and freshly ground house blends complete the mood. Also available are selections of wine, beer, and freshly squeezed juices which complement your choice of hot soup de jour, excellent Brie, fruit and cheese boards, sandwiches, pastries and good company.

Spend a lazy afternoon or evening at the Blue Danube Coffee House. It's a splendid blend of past and present with a European flavor.

Entertainment, Live Music

CLUB FUGAZI, 678 Green Street, San Francisco, California. Versions of the funny musical revue *Beach Blanket Babylon* has been playing at the club and delighting fans for over thirteen years.

THE GREAT AMERICAN MUSIC HALL, 859 O'Farrell Street, San Francisco, California. Top names and local talent. Comedy, jazz, country, rock music.

THE PUNCH LINE, 444 Battery Street, San Francisco, California. The best and latest in comedy. Two drink minimum. Deli food.

ROCKIN' ROBIN, 1840 Haight Street, San Francisco, California. Dance to fifties rock and roll with a DJ. Filled with 1950's memorabilia. Weekend cover charge.

WOLFGANG'S, 901 Columbus Avenue, San Francisco, California. Traditional San Francisco nightclub, bar, restaurant with changing entertainment.

Florist

ACRES OF ORCHIDS
Rod McLellan Co.
1450 El Camino Real
South San Francisco, CA 94080
Tel. (415) 871-5655
Hrs: Mon. - Sun.   8:00 a.m. - 5:00 p.m.
       Tours   10:30 a.m. & 1:30 p.m.
Tours take approximately one hour.

Orchids by the thousands are grown each year in the vast greenhouses of this South San Francisco company, which offers tours and a retail sales shop for the curious. The first family greenhouse went into operation in 1888 as a hobby. Now it is a show place drawing visitors by the thousands and shipping cut flowers and orchid plants by the millions each year.

Today, you can learn how orchids are bred scientifically, by cloning tiny cuttings from parent orchids. It's far different from flower production when the McLellan family went from dairy farming to commercial flower growing in 1895. The third generation's Rod McLellan took the business to its specialty of raising blooming orchid plants for sale to the public. The showplace greenhouses here are backed up by another facility at Watsonville which produces, among other plants, eucalyptus and roses on a wholesale basis.

With about sixty greenhouses, in South San Francisco, in various stages of production, the tour attractions will vary by year or season. Reservations are requested for groups of four or more people. Special tour times can be arranged for conventions, clubs, etc. To find the Acres of Orchids greenhouses, located south of I-280, take the Hickey Boulevard exit to El Camino Real. Off the Bayshore Freeway (U.S. 101) exit on I-380 to I-280, then take Hickey Boulevard exit.

Food

EICHELBAUM & COMPANY
2417 California Street
San Francisco, CA 94115
Tel. (415) 929-9030
Hrs: Tue. - Fri. 8:00 a.m. - 9:00 p.m.
Visa and MasterCard are accepted.

The definitive in gourmet "take out" food, this cozy neighborhood store draws satisfied customers from far and wide. For those who do not feel like cooking, Chef Eichelbaum offers a rich selection of French, California, Asian and Italian cuisine to take home, or sample at the few tables available for those who can't wait till they get home.

If you are planning a picnic, just a couple hours notice will result in an attractive and tasty box lunch consisting of a wide choice of specialties, including Oriental chicken salad, stuffed grape leaves, brie cheese, fresh fruit, chocolate brownies and a french loaf with butter.

Chef Eichelbaum's menus change frequently. You may find roast loin of pork with blueberry sauce or baked chicken stuffed with wild rice and hazelnuts. The desserts are wonderful, as are the quiches, and every entree is packed in aluminum foil for easy reheating. Eichelbaum & Company is the answer for gourmets on the run.

Furniture

CONCEPTS
398 Kansas Street
San Francisco, CA 94103
Tel. (415) 864-7776
Hrs: Mon. - Sat.   10:00 a.m. - 6:00 p.m.
        Sunday   12:00 noon - 5:00 p.m.

Concepts is well named, offering exciting, new design "concepts" for your home furnishing plans. If you're furnishing a new home, or refurnishing an old one, you'll want to visit Concepts' showroom at Showplace Square and talk with their creative and knowledgeable staff.

Today's contemporary furnishings offer a plethora of shapes, colors and textures to delight the senses. Choosing from fine Italian leathers, plush upholstery fabrics, and the sheer, clean lines of glass, at Concepts you can create a living environment that will delight you for years to come.

New ideas handled with flair are a specialty at Concepts. For those who might need a little extra assistance, a design service and in-home consultations are available. If you've never before considered contemporary design, a trip to Concepts is recommended. It may change your whole lifestyle.

FILLAMENTO
2185 Fillmore Street
San Francisco, CA 94115
Tel. (415) 931-2224
Tel. (415) 931-2224
Hrs: Mon. - Sat.   10:00 a.m. - 6:00 p.m.
      Thursday   10:00 a.m. - 8:00 p.m.
      Sunday   12:00 p.m.- 5:00 p.m.
Visa, MasterCard and AMEX are accepted.

This is a store which deals in fashion, primarily for the home, but also for yourself. The furnishings and accessories are contemporary and offer the most creative choices for your home.

The departments of the store have a home-like look to them, including fresh flowers to set off the furnishings grouped in departments. You can visualize things for a kitchen, or as they might look on your table set for a festive dinner. Seasonal gifts are functional, the look stylish. Owner Iris Fuller and her staff members are extremely creative, well informed and eager to help.

Lifestyle may be the best way to summarize Fillamento's offerings. With the help of the staff you will find the correct furnishings and accessories to fit your lifestyle.

LIMN COMPANY
457 Pacific Avenue
San Francisco, CA 94133
Tel. (415) 397-7474
Hrs: Mon. - Fri.   9:30 a.m. - 5:30 p.m.
      Saturday   11:00 a.m. - 5:30 p.m.
and,
Ligne Roset By Limn   Limn Extra
821 Sansome Street   44 Berry Street
San Francisco, CA 94111   San Francisco, CA 94107
Tel. (415) 397-7471

If you are looking for exciting furniture and other exotic items, Limn Company is the place to go. With an illustrious reputation in design, this store offers contemporary furnishings that will stand the test of time to become classics.

The goal of this store is to bring the design trade to the general public, with availability for all price ranges. There is furniture from Herman Miller, Knoll and other American classics, as well as the finest furniture from this century. You will find unusual furnishings, from wall hangings to tables, desks, sofas, beds, art, out-of-the-ordinary jewelry, fabulous lighting systems, neckties and even magnets. Limn Company offers design and space planning, installation and delivery. The staff is image oriented and conscientious, seeking to craft long term solutions for spaces and the people who live and work in them.

Limn's is a showroom with a blend of modern art and functional furniture solutions. You will want to visit more than once, since the displays and inventory are constantly changing. Also visit Ligne Roset By Limn where you will find the finest in contemporary French storage and upholstery. For bargain shopping visit Limn Extra, Saturday only, where many, many people find great design at reduced pricing.

MICHAEL ANTHONY
1549 California Street
San Francisco, CA 94109
Tel. (415) 776-0340
Hrs: Mon. - Fri.   10:00 a.m. - 6:00 p.m.
          Saturday   11:00 a.m. - 5:00 p.m.
Visa, MasterCard, and AMEX cards accepted.

When you step through the French doors into the world of Michael Anthony you are going to want to take one of everything with you to complement your home. The exquisite taste exhibited in the selection on display explains why his interior designs grace the pages of so many well-known magazines.

From custom-made furniture to aromatic potpourri, you will find irresistible items that need to be a part of your home and lifestyle. Lamps that are one-of-a-kind, handmade lampshades, fabulous fabric pillows to go, baskets of every shape and size, imported pottery, candle holders,Spanish battle glass, and a unique selection of porcelain

You will find endless decorating ideas, that unique gift you've been hunting for, fun accessories and peerless quality. The shop is strategically located near the end of the California Street cable car run; so you could combine two of San Francisco's "Best Choices".a cable car ride and Michael Anthony.

379

Dorothy said it best, "There's no place like home." So remember where your heart is while you are in San Francisco and take the time to look for that "something special" to make your house more of a home.

SAN FRANCISCO'S HOME DECOR TOUR			
a.m.	Bubbles	Best bath	SanF/Bath
a.m.	Incredible Xmas Store	Best Xmas items	SanF/Gift
a.m.	Concepts	Best design	SanF/Furn
a.m.	Oasis Energy Systems	Best purifier	SanF/Water
p.m.	Eichelbaum & Co	Best grmet picnic	SanF/Food
p.m.	Limn Co	Best fixtures	SanF/Furn
p.m.	Michael Anthony	Best accessory	SanF/Fur
p.m.	Biordi Art	Best kitchen appl	SanF/Kit
p.m.	Judith's	Best nutrition	SanF/Kit

Gift Shops

THE BAY COMPANY
211 Jefferson
San Francisco, CA 94133
Tel. (415) 775-2146
Hrs: Mon. - Sun. 9:00 a.m. - 11:30 p.m.
Visa, MasterCard and AMEX are accepted.

The Bay Company, located on the main corner (Jefferson and Taylor) of Fisherman's Wharf, is San Francisco's largest and most fascinating souvenir store.

Wonderful gifts to amuse and titillate friends back home can be found in every section of this colorful shopping oasis. Sportswear, chocolates, posters, postcards, stuffed animals, children's clothing and much more.

CIRCLE OF FRIENDS
1604 Haight Street
San Francisco, CA 94117
Tel. (415) 626-9733
Hrs: Mon. - Sat.   10:00 a.m. - 6:30 p.m.
        Sunday   11:00 a.m. - 6:00 p.m.

Welcome to a true find! Like grandmother's attic, Circle of Friends creates the magic of discovery from gifts and jewelry, to over 1000 different greeting cards. Owners Cheryl and Joseph Wagner buy most of their treasures directly from artists, thus assuring quality and originality.

Most of their gift items are handmade and include Indian artifacts, unique jewelry, mugs, posters, candles and masks. Then, if you think you've seen it all, go upstairs. There you'll find silkscreened T-shirts, notions and soaps, kites and flowers. There's something for everyone.

Visit Circle of Friends for the unusual in gifts and the extraordinary in service.

(See special invitation in the Appendix.)

EGGCENTRICITY
1848 Fillmore Street
San Francisco, CA 94115
Tel. (415) 931-1848
Hrs: Mon. - Sat.   11:00 p.m. - 6:00 p.m.
        Sunday   12:00 noon - 4:00 p.m.

Eggcentricity specializes in magnificent and unusual gift items. Owner Barbara Johnson possesses the taste and eye of a true artist, passing on the benefits of her creative selectivity to discriminating shoppers.

Although it is obvious that you will find a lavish selection of decorative eggs: scrimshaw, mouth-blown glass, and eggs of every description, the exciting selections just begin there. Along with lotions, soaps, massage oils, and a full spectrum of specialty items for the bath, you'll find a wide display of fine hand-crafted ceramics, Russian lacquer boxes, baskets, crystal, candles, and much more.

Eggcentricity provides a potpourri of the unusual in a shopping environment that will make you want to return again and again.

San Francisco City/County

THE INCREDIBLE CHRISTMAS STORE
2800 Leavenworth Street
Across from the Cannery at Fisherman's Wharf
San Francisco, CA 94133
Tel. (415) 928-5700
Hrs: New Year's to Easter
      Mon. - Sun.   10:00 a.m. - 6:00 p.m.
     Easter to New Year's
      Mon. - Sun.   9:30 a.m. - 9:30 a.m.

Ever wonder where your true love found partridges in a pear tree and milk maids a'milking? Chances are they visited the Incredible Christmas Store at Fisherman's Wharf!

Owner Aan Silverstone has accumulated Christmas related gifts and decorations from over twenty countries. Included are nativity scenes from Italy, porcelain cherubs from France, and brightly colored wheat straw birds, pandas and tropical fish ornaments from China. Scattered throughout the store are amazing Christmas trees wearing remote controlled high-tech lights that can be programmed to flash in any creative manner. Wide selections of Christmas music (including reggae) are available on tape, compact disc, and record.

But Christmas doesn't end after December! Twenty-five flavors of fresh fudge (a specialty being fudge dipped in Oreos) are available daily, ready for shipping throughout the United States. There are also several thematic gift sections, the Dog, Cat & Mouse Corner especially for pet gift selections, and the Teddy Bear Den, with loveable bears available in every conceivable shape and size. Its Christmas all year round at The Incredible Christmas Store!

ONLY IN SAN FRANCISCO
Pier 39
P.O. Box A01
San Francisco, CA 94133
Tel. (415) 397-0122
Hrs: Mon. - Sun. 8:30 a.m. - 11:30 p.m.
Visa and AMEX are accepted.

There are souvenir shops by this hundreds in this city. Out on Pier 39 at Only in San Francisco, you'll find just about every popular souvenir plus a wide selection of gifts for the folks back home.

The way to find your gift can be as simple as telling a staff member what sights you liked in the city, or the tastes and interests of the person for whom the gift is intended. You can also do as many customers do, browsing through this unique store moving from post cards to tee shirts, coffee mugs to shopping bags. There are ten cent items here, and a few that top $60.

This is your "Best Choice" for a memento of San Francisco for the folks back home, and if you live here, it is the place to find the full selection Giants' and Forty-Niner memorabilia.

STAR MAGIC - SPACE AGE GIFTS
4026A 24th Street
San Francisco, CA 94114
Tel. (415) 641-8626
Hrs: Mon. - Thu.   11:00 a.m. - 7:00 p.m.
        Fri. - Sat.   11:00 a.m. - 9:00 p.m.
        Sunday   12:00 noon - 6:00 p.m.
Extended hours during summer and holiday season.

Star Magic is a futuristic gift shop offering space age gifts that are both scientific and spiritual. The shop is uniquely painted to resemble the solar system, with unusual lighting to heighten the effect. Soft celestial music plays as you wander from section to section browsing among the ample and unusual selection of gifts offered here.

Star Magic is divided into sections and labeled to help the shopper easily understand what is available. The astrophysics section has telescopes, binoculars, moon globes, stars for the ceiling and more. In the geophysics section you will find relief maps, crystal growing kits, books on the earth and other unique items. The pre-historic section is a favorite of the youngsters who visit the shop, with its selection of dinosaur models and related products. There is a metaphysical section with lots of books and videotapes. A section full of new age albums, tapes and CD's. Additionally, there are gemstones and crystal jewelry, plus an assortment of holograms, prismatics, kaleidoscopes and a high tech exec section with futuristic clocks, lamps and desk top accessories.

The Star Magic staff is courteous, knowledgeable and anxious to help you and answer all your questions, but you never feel pressured and are encouraged to browse and absorb the ambiance of this unusual gift shop.

As with clothes, so it is with small, personal gifts, San Francisco has many things found nowhere else. These novelties are a tribute to this city and to the people who create them. Many of the gifts found at the following businesses are distinctively Californian, created by the cultural, climatic and historical diversity alive and well in San Francisco.

	SAN FRANCISCO GIFT TOUR		
a.m.	Oggetti	Best desk item	SanF/Stat
a.m.	Only in San Francisco	Best S.F. item	SanF/Gift
a.m.	Eggcentricity	Best potpourri	SanF/Gift
a.m.	Bay Company	Best import	SanF/Gift
p.m.	Hamburger Mary's	Best S.F. lunch	SanF/Rest
p.m.	S.F. Opera	Best fine art gift	SanF/Music
p.m.	Orvis-San Francisco	Best sport equip	SanF/Sport
p.m.	Shades	Best sunglasses	SanF/Glass

You really cannot expect to get all your gift shopping done in one day in San Francisco. These "Best Choices" for gifts will give you added variety.

	SAN FRANCISCO GIFT TOUR TOO		
a.m.	Acres of Orchids	Best live plant	SanF/Park
a.m.	Glenda Queen	Best gold jewelry	SanF/Jwry
a.m.	Confetti le Chocolatier	Best chocolate	SanF/Candy
a.m.	Blue Danube	Best coffee	SanF/Coff
p.m.	Neiman-Marcus Rotunda	Best lobster san.	SanF/Rest
p.m.	Woods	Best stuffed toys	SanF/Toy
p.m.	Wines of California	Best accessory	SanF/Wine
p.m.	Puppets on the Pier	Best puppets	SanF/Toy
p.m.	Maxwell's Plum	Best elegance	SanF/Rest

Jewelry

THE ENCHANTED CRYSTAL
1771 Union Street
San Francisco, CA 94123
Tel. (415) 885-1335
Hrs: Mon. - Sat.   10:00 a.m. - 6:00 p.m.
       Sunday   12:00 noon - 5:00 p.m.

The Enchanted Crystal has the most dazzling array of natural quartz, leaded crystal and art glass that you are likely to find anywhere in the world.

Highly prized in many cultures for its esthetic, metaphysical and scientific qualities, the emergence of interest in natural rock crystal in and around the Bay Area has made The Enchanted Crystal a virtual haven for crystal lovers. The display theme within the store is constantly changing, and the window displays are planned months in advance, however you'll always find a large selection of fantastic and one of a kind items like carved dragons, fairies, unicorns, sea goddesses or carousels displayed in pyramid show cases. In addition to the natural crystal balls on incredible hand crafted stands, The Enchanted Crystal has one of the largest crystal balls in the world!

The Enchanted Crystal also has an extensive collection of carved decorative figures, stained glass windows, crystal pyramids, carved jewelry, and a great assortment of antique and contemporary pieces, as well as many crystal geodes in their natural state. Each piece is individually selected and many are created exclusively for The Enchanted Crystal by artisans in Europe, Central and Latin America, the U.S., and the Orient. Whether left in its natural crystalline state or faceted into brilliant jeweled gems, the beauty of natural rock quartz is unmistakable. You have to see The Enchanted Crystal to believe the selection.

(See special invitation in the Appendix.)

GLENDA QUEEN-UNION STREET GOLDSMITH
1763 Union Street
San Francisco, CA 94123
Tel. (415) 776-8048
Hrs: Mon. - Sat.   11:00 a.m. - 5:45 p.m.
       Sunday   12:00 noon - 4:45 p.m.
Most major credit cards are accepted.

Historically, mankind has always loved and prized gold. At Glenda Queen-Union Street Goldsmith, you'll be able to indulge yourself with a dazzling visual feast of sparkling, shimmering creations that represent the original creativity of over forty Bay Area artists!

Most of the selection displayed is one-of-a-kind. You'll see engagement and wedding rings, earrings, necklaces, bracelets, and other adornments. Precious and exotic, non-precious gems are used to advantage. Specialness abounds and you can be assured that your selection is unique, just as you are unique.

If you love the unusual, in tastefully created fine jewelry, that you can treasure for a lifetime, treat yourself to a visit to Glenda Queen-Union Street Goldsmith.

Kitchen Equipment

JUDITH ETS-HOKIN CULINARY CO.
3525 California Street
San Francisco, CA 94118
Tel. (415) 668-3191

Judith Ets-Hokin offers one of the most comprehensive and multi-faceted solutions to any kitchen dilemma. If your cooking skills are dubious, attend the Judith Ets-Hokin Cooking School - one of the best in the area for learning culinary basics. Here nutrition principles, spice application, and the basic understanding of recipes are taught through a series of lecture demonstrations and practical assignments.

Having a party? Judith Ets-Hokin's catering department, The Party Solution, is standing by to assist you from soup to nuts, as well as offering a fully equipped party facility complete with a dance floor.

For picnic or cocktail party needs, the Judith Ets-Hokin Deli is prepared with a wide variety of ready-to-go delectables. The retail kitchen shop also stands ready with a bridal registry for unique cooking equipment, as well as as a large selection of perfect gifts for the bride-to-be. Explore all the options at Judith Ets-Hokin's. You won't be disappointed!

Linens

SCANDIA DOWN SHOP
1546 California Street
San Francisco, CA 94109
Tel. (415) 928-5111
Hrs: Mon. -Fri.   10:00 a.m. - 6:00 p.m.
      Saturday   10:00 a.m. - 5:00 p.m.
MasterCard, Visa, AMEX and Discover cards are accepted.

The staff of Scandia Down Shop, believes "the bedroom should be your retreat to comfort and lived-in luxury." They do their best to provide her customers with every need to meet that vision.

Picture being enveloped in the soft warmth of down comforters and pillows on your own feather bed covered with a wool sleeper pad, designer sheets, wool throws and pillow shams. Anything you can dream of for your sleeping pleasure Scandia Down likely has it in a wide selection of the highest quality available. If not, the custom workroom can create it! And it's cleaning and restoration service guarantees you years of continuous usage. Rest assured, Scandia Down can supply years of comfort and repose.

Recordings, Classic

SAN FRANCISCO OPERA SHOP
199 Grove Street
San Francisco, CA 94102
Tel. (415) 565-6414
Hrs: Mon. - Fri.   11:00 a.m. - curtain time
      Saturday   12:00 p.m. - curtain time
      Sunday   12:00 p.m. - 6:00 p.m. (in season)
Visa, MasterCard and AMEX cards accepted.

The Opera Shop has established a worldwide reputation as the place to find the new, the rare and the unusual, as well as all the familiar things relating to the performing arts.

The huge selection of opera, classical and ballet videos is astounding. The royal Opera performs *La Boheme*, *Spartacus* by the Bolshoi Ballet, music from the Royal Opera, the Metropolitan, A.B.T. and hard to find Russian operas are among the titles listed. Records and tapes your passion? From Verdi's immortal *Rigoletto* with Alfredo Kraus, Sherrill Milnes and Beverly Sills to the newest *Don Carlos* with Placido Domingo and Katia Ricciarelli--it's here.

387

The gift selection is endless. Silk scarves, opera glasses, volumes of color plates, books of all varieties, t-shirts, tote bags, sweatshirts, coffee mugs, towels, diaries, or an address book with notes playing across its cover--it's here.

Once here--you'll spend hours musing amongst the greats, take the time to enjoy a cup of cappuccino at the Espresso Bar, and remember the Opera House slogan, you'll "take home more than memories from the San Francisco Opera Shop."

Restaurants

A. SABELLA'S
2766 Taylor Street
San Francisco, CA 94133
Tel. (415) 771-6775
Hrs: Mon. - Sun. 10:30 a.m. - 10:30 p.m.

Fisherman's Wharf and A. Sabella's restaurant are inseparable traditions: both romantic and both famous. The Sabella family has operated its excellent restaurant on the Wharf since 1887, and for the past 100 years treasured family recipes and culinary traditions have been handed down to each succeeding generation. Today it is host Antone Sabella and his brother, Michael, a trained chef, who maintain these high expectations. Present day diners are not disappointed!

Famous Sabella specialty is, of course, seafood--fresh and zesty. Favorites include the Sabella Special Pirate Salad, loaded with fresh crabs and shrimp, as well as garnished with jumbo shrimp and lobster. Another is sand dabs Meuniere. Or how about the Antone: thinly sliced swordfish, stuffed with shrimp, baked in butter wine sauce, and capped with a taste tantalizing white sauce and Parmesan cheese. For those who are seafood surfeited, A. Sabella's also feature steak, veal, and exceptional preparations of pasta.

What better way to spend an evening than to luxuriate in A. Sabella's burgundy-toned, two-tiered dining room overlooking romantic Fisherman's Wharf, while enjoying a truly sumptuous dinner?

BANK EXCHANGE & PARK EXCHANGE
600 Montgomery Street
San Francisco, CA 94111
Tel. (415) 885-4605
Hrs: 8:00 a.m. - 4:00 a.m.

Where to go for one of the hottest disco scenes in the city and a popular lunch spot? The Bank Exchange and Park Exchange, located at the foot of the Transamerica building!

A gracious choice of salads, light food, reasonable prices and quick service attracts business people and tourists alike. Completely surrounded by glass walls and glass ceilings, you can see the moon at night. Very European in style, 10,000 square feet of space has sound computerized light tracking and not-to-be-believed stereo sound.

At night the Bank Exchange magically transforms to the Park Exchange, a gorgeous Greek gazebo where one can dance, drink, enjoy appetizers such as oysters, pate and cheese, or simply relax in a beautiful park setting. D.J.'s choreograph the latest in pop music to keep you moving under the moon. The Bank Exchange and Park Exchange..it's HOT!

BECHELLI'S COFFEE SHOP
2346 Chestnut Street
San Francisco, CA 94123
Tel. (415) 346-1801
Hrs: Mon. - Sat.   7:00 a.m. - 4:00 p.m.
            Breakfast and lunch
        Sunday   8:00 a.m. - 3:00 p.m.
            Breakfast only

Bechelli's has grown by leaps and bounds since its opening in 1977, but it retains what has made it such a favorite among the people on the Marina - a homey atmosphere, good food and pleasant people. When you walk through the door of this cafe, the first thing you notice is the look of an old style diner with booths. The quality of the delicious food and comfortable atmosphere is matched only by the owners, Mark, Jan and Patrick Bechelli, who attribute their success to listening to and implementing suggestions by customers.

Breakfast is served all day, which gives you plenty of opportunities to sample the thirty different kinds of omelets. There are also great homefries, other egg dishes and buttermilk pancakes. Lunch starts at 11:00 and Bechelli's is well known for their superb sandwiches and hamburgers. The hamburgers are a special treat, because the meat is ground fresh by the meat market across the street. Topping your meal are wonderful desserts homemade by Jan.

With all this going for it, it's no surprise that they had to enlarge the restaurant to accommodate the crowds. You might be tempted to get your food to go, which you can, but you'll find the atmosphere so pleasant you'll want to sit down and stay awhile!

BERTOLUCCI'S, 421 Cypress Avenue, South San Francisco. A family-run restaurant for over fifty years. Cuisine is traditional Toscara.

CALIFORNIA CULINARY ACADEMY
625 Polk Street
San Francisco, CA 94102
Tel. (415) 771-3500
Reservations are a must.

Here is a new experience in culinary exploration! Enjoy the expertise of tomorrow's master chefs as they perfect their skills in this European-modeled culinary academy.

Gourmet delights are created for the public in a charming, turn-of-the-century reconverted theatre. From the large skylight above, light dapples along the upper balcony seating area down to the lower level where diners can watch the student chefs at work through the glass walls of the kitchen.

The meal and buffet menus are dazzling. Appetizers include Galantine of squab in aspic. Entrees might be saute d' Agneau Chasseur--sauteed lamb hunter style; an excellent Escalope de Veau Normandie--sauteed veal cutlet with apple in calvados sauce; or quail with morels. Buffet tables groan under elaborate gelatins, roasts, pates, terrines, to name but a few gastronomic titillations. This is not to be missed.

CHA CHA CHA TAPAS BAR AND CAFE
1805 Haight Street
San Fransico, CA 94117
Tel. (415) 386-5758
Hrs: Mon. - Sun. 11:00 a.m. - 11:30 p.m.

San Francisco, well known as a cultural gathering center, is home to a most charming restaurant, a restaurant which in and of itself is a cultural extravanganza. Interested yet? Well, to ease the suspension, the name is Cha Cha Cha Tapas Bar and Cafe. But before you rush down, read on and learn more about this fabulous restaurant.

Cha Cha Cha offers a varied menu with an international flair. Choose from many delicious Tapas, such as shrimp in a spicy clam sauce; New Zealand mussels with marinara sauce; chicken tenderloins grilled and served in a mustard sauce; and sauteed mushrooms with fresh herbs, garlic and butter. But that's not all, they also have delicious hamburgers with plenty of cheese and toppings. Some of the main courses include roasted Cuban pork with Arroz con Grie and black bean sauce; pan fried trout with Cajun spices and jalapeno butter; and a steak sandwich with grilled onions, to mention a few.

For libations, they've got wines, beers and the all-time favorite, Sangria. Then, to top it all off, partake of a truly delicious dessert in Cha Cha Cha fashion. This restaurant is a "Best Choice" in San Francisco.

THE CLIFF HOUSE
1090 Point Lobos
San Francisco, CA 94121
Tel. (415) 386-3330
Hrs: Mon. - Sun.   9:00 a.m. - 10:30 p.m.
     Fri. - Sat.   9:00 a.m. - 11:00 p.m.
     Bar open until   1:30 a.m.
Visa, MasterCard and AMEX are accepted.

Steeped in history, the Cliff House has been serving hungry and thirsty San Franciscans and visitors since 1850. Destroyed initially by an explosion after a dynamite-laden ship crashed into the cliffs below, the restaurant has been rebuilt and renovated many times over the years. What hasn't changed is the lively atmosphere, caring service and the great view of the ocean and Seal Rocks.

The Cliff House consists of two restaurants, a deli, a bar, a lounge and a gift shop. The main floor restaurant is the Seafood and Beverage Co. For starters, you might try the prawns sauteed with feta cheese or Fried Calamari. For a light meal, try the Sutro Crab Louis or the Ben Butler, crab meat crowned with cheddar cheese and broiled to perfection on dark rye. Continental dishes such as, Chicken Jerusalem, Breast of Chicken Marsala, Stuffed Filet of Sole with crab and shrimp, Curried Shellfish, Scallops Saute or Deep Fried Oysters are further tempters.

The Upstairs restaurant features forty-five omelettes served with Potatoes Lyonnaise, fruit garnish and an English muffin, and other lighter fare during daytime hours. Dinner items include a wide variety of pasta and seafood dishes such as, Fettucine al Pesto Siciliana and Scallops Saute.

Not dynamite, earthquake or fire can destroy this historic "Best Choice" restaurant in San Francisco - the Cliff House.

DANTE'S SEA CATCH
Pier 39
San Francisco, CA 94133
Tel. (415) 421-5778
Hrs: Mon. - Fri.   11:30 a.m. - 10:00 p.m.
     Sat. - Sun.   11:00 a.m. - 11:00 p.m.

Floor to ceiling bay windows allow you to enjoy the panorama of the Pier 39 Yacht Harbor and San Francisco's Bay Bridge, while dining on a wide array of skillfully prepared fresh seafood. If you wish a more cozy atmosphere, you are invited upstairs to Vito's Bar to experiment in front of the fireplace with specialty drinks and delicious appetizers.

Chef Danny Comforte, a graduate from the New Jersey Culinary Institute of America in Hyde Park, has been creating gastronomic masterpieces ever since Dante's Sea Catch opened eight years ago. His crab Cioppino and clam chowders are award winners!

For fresh seafood, fine Italian cuisine, friendly service, reasonable prices, and one of the best views in San Francisco, Dante's Sea Catch at Pier 39 is the place to go.

DOROS
714 Montgomery Street
San Francisco, CA 94111
Tel. (415) 397-6822
Hrs: Mon. - Fri.   Lunch 11:30 a.m. - 2:30 p.m.
    Mon. - Sat.   Dinner   6:00 p.m. - 10:30 p.m.
All major credit cards are accepted.

Doros offers the epitome of fine dining. Owner and stellar host, Don Dianda, works closely with award-winning, executive chef, Paul Bermani, to assure the quality of the kitchen. They have combined their talents so well, in fact, that Doros has been chosen as one of limited number of restaurants in the entire country to be included in the Dining Hall of Fame by *Nation's Restaurant News*.

The cuisine is inspired, spanning fettuccine al Alfredo, Roman style, to planked Chateaubriand, sauce Bernaise, and including spectacular desserts flambé.

Opulence and luxury begin at the door with valet parking. The cardinal-carpeted dining room is rich with crimson leather booths and black leather chairs, walls of dark panelled woods, and delicate lace over linen tableclothes. Original 18th Century oil paintings grace the walls in both the dining room and spacious lounge.

392

Don is proud of his wine cellar. One of California's largest, containing over 2,000 cases, it boasts treasured vintages from California and France, with Italian and German choices as well. Doros is a dining experience not to be missed.

EMPRESS OF CHINA
838 Grant Avenue
San Francisco, CA 94108
Tel. (415) 434-1345
Hrs: Mon. - Sat.   Lunch   11:30 a.m. - 3:00 p.m.
                         Dinner   5:00 p.m. - 11:00 p.m.
          Sunday   12:00 noon - 11:00 p.m.

Experience an explosion of senses in the Empress of China. Stroll through the Empress Garden Court, San Francisco's only high rise Chinese roof garden restaurant, and bask in the reflection of the Dowager's own garden with its banks of seasonal blossoms surrounding a marble fountain. Or dine in the Golden Court Room, featuring Chinese shadow boxes and ornate peacock feathered chandeliers from past dynasties. Visit the Emperor's Chamber, an elegant V.I.P. room with red silk walls, marble topped teak tables and historic temple arch. The main dining room offers dignity and serenity in a lavishly gilt atmosphere enhanced by impressive carvings depicting the four seasons. Each dining area gives you a kaleidoscope view of the city from Nob Hill to the Bay.

This High Mass for the senses is further titillated by an opulent menu which has been the winner of Holiday Awards for many years. Superb regional dishes from Szechuan, Manchuria, Shanghai, Mongolia, and Peking provide taste sensations that rival the exciting decor.

When in Chinatown, make Empress of China your choice for splendorous dining in unforgettable surroundings. It's another world you won't want to miss.

FIVE HAPPINESS, 4142 Gary Boulevard, San Francisco, California. Mandarin and Schezwan cuisine.

FRENCH ROOM
at the Four Seasons Clift Hotel
495 Geary Street
San Francisco, CA 94102
Tel. (415) 775-4700

Hrs:	breakfast	Mon. - Sun.	7:00 a.m. - 10:00 a.m.
	lunch	Mon. - Sat.	12:00 p.m. - 2:00 p.m.
	dinner	Mon. - Sun.	6:00 p.m.- 10:30 p.m.
	brunch	Sunday	11:00 a.m. - 2:30 p.m.

A palatial setting, where the centuries seem to roll-back and you feel yourself carried to a world of elegance. A classic, romantic luster suggest 18th century Louis XIV. Gaze upon panels painted in the style of Fragonard and Boucher whilst seated upon embroidered chairs.

Luxury and Continental cuisine combined. Crisp Belgian waffles for breakfast, lovely omelets, pancakes with macadamia nut, banana, pecan toppings. Or, for the daring, smoked salmon on toasted bagels.

Lunchtime experience California and Nouvelle cuisine. Pan-fried Dungeness crabcakes with garlic Aioli, California seafood Bouillabaisse, or a smoked salmon omelete with Alfredo sauce and chives. Dinners are traditionally superb. A light Duckling consomme with fresh vegetables Quenelles or perhaps fricassee of sweetbreads and black chanterelles. Alternative cuisine is routinely offered for people who are counting calories and watching their cholesterol and sodium.

The primary entree at The French Room has long been the roasted rack of lamb with thyme, rosemary and roasted garlic. The French Room, among an elite corp of restaurants which blend architectural glamor and culinary marvels which define the art of fine dining.

HAMBURGER MARY'S
1582 Folsom at 12th Street
San Francisco, CA 94103
Tel. (415) 626-5767
Hrs: Mon. - Sun. 10:00 a.m. - 2:00 a.m.
Visa, MasterCard and AMEX are accepted.

The "South of Market" area is a melting pot for all of San Francisco's cultures. Its reasonably priced housing was what originally attracted the eclectic mixture of life styles, from artists to punk rockers, gays and apparel designers to the yuppie set. If you are a "people person" and want to be part of the "scene," Hamburger Mary's is your "Best Choice."

The full-service bar is always lively and crowded, the music rocks out, the hamburgers are great, a Super Salad would feed an army, all desserts are homebaked, breakfast is served anytime, the kitchen is open till 1:15 a.m., and as co-owner, Rose Christensen stated, "the food is good and the prices are cheap."

What more could you want? San Francisco flavors in a funky and fun decor, people, food and drink...what a life...Hamburger Mary's.

HARRIS'
2100 Van Ness
San Francisco, CA 94109
Tel. (415) 673-1888

Hrs:	Mon. - Fri.	Lunch	11:30 a.m. - 2:00 p.m.
		Dinner	5:00 p.m. - 11:00 p.m.
	Saturday		5:00 p.m. - 11:00 p.m.
	Sunday		4:00 p.m. - 10:00 p.m.

Epitomizing the popular slogan, "Beef: real food for real people," Harris' provides Iowa and Nebraska's corn fed, dry aged, top choice beef in an orgy of various cuts and popular preparations. Forget nouveau, California, or any other fad cuisines! Owner Ann Harris believes beef reigns supreme. Judging by the popularity of Harris', so do a vast number of others.

Although the restaurant is spacious and elegant, it is also unusual. A display case that looks over the avenue actually is a working meat case filled with selections of the highest quality of well marbled beef ready to be prepared for the customer, or sold separately at retail prices.

The main dining room, a top-of-the-art testament to the 1950s, contains a massive mural by Barnaby Conrad. A majestic mahogany bar to the right of the dining room also has a mural depicting highlights of San Francisco. To the right of that is a skylit garden room for parties up to 100. To the rear of the restaurant are several private rooms ready to accommodate anywhere from a dozen to several dozen private party-goers. Harris' popularity is a reality and reservations are recommended.

HOUSE OF PRIME RIB
1906 Van Ness Avenue
San Francisco, CA 94109
Tel. (415) 885-4605
All major credit cards accepted

An American extravaganza of the beef persuasion! Each year, ninety tons of eastern corn-fed beef are cured with a secret herb blend from

England, packed in rock salt, and roasted in seasoned ovens at the House of Prime Rib. Thick slices of juicy prime rib then are carved to order from shiny service carts at tableside and served to enthusiastic devotees of beef-at-its-best.

Americana prevails with a carefully selected wine list, featuring California's great red wines, and the paramount choice suggested to accompany exquisite American beef being the Spring Napa Valley Cabernet Sauvignon. All dinners are served with salad, mashed potatoes, dreamy Yorkshire pudding, creamed spinach, and fresh horseradish sauce.

Enjoy this culinary feast in the casually elegant atmosphere of brass-etched glass, pastel shades, and glossy-rich woodwork. The House of Prime Rib is an institution as American as apple pie, even though their specialty pecan pie is well worth the extra calories!

INDIA HOUSE
350 Jackson Street
San Francisco, CA 94111
Tel. (415) 392-0744
Hrs: Mon. - Fri.   Lunch   1:30 a.m. - 2:00 p.m.
                    Dinner   5:30 p.m. - 10:30 p.m.
      Saturday   5:30 p.m. - 10:30 p.m.

The mystery of India comes alive in the elegantly appointed main dining room of India House. Indian throw rugs beckon you to your private table. Ornate wall hangings, the pervasive perfume of exotic spices, and the subtle light from flickering flames seduce and reinforce an ancient magic. India House is renowned for its "tandoori" dishes (cooked in fired clay tandoor ovens), as well as tangy creations in curry. A house curry specialty is the lamb Khorma. A highly recommended tandoori is the chicken Tikka, succulent and boneless chicken served on a sizzling platter. Specially prepared vegetarian dishes are also featured, including Samosas: vegetable-filled pastries served with a tempting variety of sauces for dipping.

A *Holiday Magazine* award-winning restaurant, India House offers not only romantic alternatives to the noise and quick gratification of today's chrome and plastic world of dining, but offers it with cultural and culinary panache.

(See special invitation in the Appendix)

THE IRON HORSE
19 Maiden Lane
San Francisco, CA 94108-5490
Tel. (415) 362-8133
Hrs: Lunch Mon. - Sat. 11:30 a.m - 4:00 p.m.
Dinner Mon. - Sun. 5:30 p.m. - 10:30 p.m.

What do Frank Sinatra, Tony Bennett, Rod Stewart, Gene Hackman, Robert Young, Loretta Switt, Clint Eastwood, Pat Paulsen, Mayors Alioto and Christopher, Governors Brown and Duekmaijin, Los Angeles' Raiders owner Al Davis, and several Spanish Consulates have in common? Answer: The Iron Horse restaurant with its excellent contemporary Northern Italian cuisine, old world warmth, and "New York Club" decor.

Join this litany of famous people and enjoy the results of chef Thomas Walsh's culinary expertise, as well as owner John Kukulica's disarming charm. Revel in fresh fish, veal, large seafood salads, boneless quail, traditionally created pasta dishes, and taste-tempting sauces. A favorite "drop in and dine" for dignitaries, visitors, and stars alike!

JULIUS CASTLE
1541 Montgomery Street
San Francisco, CA 94133
Tel. (415) 362-3042
Hrs: Mon. - Fri. 11:30 a.m. - 10:00 p.m.
Sat. - Sun. 5:00 p.m. - 10:00 p.m.
All major credit cards are accepted.

High atop scenic Telegraph Hill, famous Julius Castle was built in 1921. As the pages of the city's history slowly turned over the years, the castle remained obdurate, mellowing, aging and silvering with time. Diners can enjoy its opulent heritage while seated in Queen Ann chairs at gothic tables in the Victorian wood paneled main dining room. A panoramic view unfolds below.

Restauranteur Jeffrey Pollack and chef Daniel Lewark offer a classical continental menu, supported with a wide selection of international cuisine. A vintage wine list is augmented by the availability of rare scotches and cognacs. A third floor dining room, complete with fireplace and outdoor deck, is available for private parties.

By day or night, Julius Castle weaves a luxurious tapestry of magic, mood and service in this splendid castle.

L'ENTRECOTE DE PARIS
2032 Union Street
San Francisco, CA 94123
Tel. (415) 931-5006
Hrs: Mon.-Sat.   11:30 a.m. - 12:00 midnight
       Sunday   11:30 a.m.- 10:00 p.m.
Visa, MasterCard, AMEX and Diner's Club are accepted.

Parisian perfection here in the good old U.S. of A.? You'll swear you are in the legendary Cafe de Paris in Geneva or L'Entrecote de Paris in Paris as you tantalize your taste buds on the world renown L'Entrecote sauce. The creation of the late Monsieur Freedy Dumont, this sauce features a magnificent blend of twelve mysterious ingredients kept secret through the years. Today the sole possessor of this enchanting sauce's legacy in the United States is San Francisco's L'Entrecote de Paris.

The completely Parisian character of the restaurant is evident with the pink tablecloths accenting the main interior dining area. A romantic glassed-in terrace borders the sidewalk and sports frosted lampshades, lovely white chairs and a towering palm tree - a favorite place for lovers to gain a glimpse of French ambiance while enjoying the fine cuisine. The preferred meal is the inimitable Entrecote-tender New York strip served sizzling in its tray of lovely sauce, warmed by candles from beneath and accented with authentic, thin french fries, or pommes frites as they are called. Beyond the intrigues of the Entrecote, a full menu beckons your selection. Caesar, Nicoise, Maison, Tomates et Thon and other salads are all implicitly fresh and tastefully presented. Light specialties include L'Escargot du Cafe de Paris, Saumon Fume, Oyster Brian, Steak Tartare, and several succulent Canard aux Framboises, tender duck smothered in a wonderfully sweet red raspberry sauce. Another popular entree is the La Brochette de Coquilles St. Jacques - plump sea scallops wrapped in bacon on a skewer with fresh mushrooms. Renown desserts such as La Poire Belle Helen which features a pear poached in syrup, served with ice cream and topped with chocolate sauce, or any of the other French dessert sensations are a must to complete your meal.

While the sauce is a secret at L'Entrecote de Paris, not so the charm and the exacting French cooking. Treat yourself to the "Best Choice" in Parisian dining - without going to Paris.

L'ETOILE, 1075 California Street, San Francisco, California. Stylish dining featuring nouvelle cuisine prepared by Chef Bougard. French African style lounge with Peter Mintun at the piano. Excellent California wine list and an extraordinary French cellar.

LA MEDITERRANEE
2210 Fillmore St.
San Francisco, CA 94115
Tel. (415) 921-2956
Hrs: Mon. - Thu.   11:00 a.m. - 10:00 p.m.
           Fri. - Sat.   11:00 a.m. - 11:00 p.m.

    In a city of many ethnic restaurants, La Mediterranee stands apart from the crowd in both quality and value. The management's motto is, "The smallest things make the biggest difference." Not only does this mean an attention to detail, but one of the smallest things is the price.
    This original location of four area restaurants by the same name, La Mediterranee on Fillmore street is wedged unobtrusively between other storefronts and the authentic Middle East atmosphere is as pleasant as the food is exceptional. Ceiling fans hum lazily over bright tile tables and the air is rich with the pungent smell of cooking spices as espresso machines hiss occasionally in the background. At first look at the menu, the uninitiated may a bit overwhelmed by the many fine choices. A good recommendation would be to opt for the Mediterranean Meza which will give two or more people a healthy sampling of just about everything including Lule Kebab, Dolma, Hummos, Baba Ghanoush, Tabuleh, and much, much more. A sure winner for dessert is a heavenly treat called Datil Amandra,which is a date stuffed filo pastry served with hot whipped cream and shaved almonds.
    La Mediterranee has been reviewed with high praise from many Bay area restaurant critics. In 1983 it received the San Francisco Restauranteur Award from its peers signifying recognition as an outstanding San Francisco restaurant. Be sure to take the time to dine at this delightful cafe with locations also in Berkeley, San Rafael and on Noe Street.

LA MEDITERRANEE
288 Noe Street
San Francisco, CA 94114
Tel. (415) 431-7210
Hrs: Tue. - Thu.   11:00 a.m. - 10:00 p.m.
           Fri. - Sat.   11:00 a.m. - 11:00 p.m.
           Sunday   Brunch Only

    When traveling in an international city it is appropriate to eat internationally. For fine casual dining, La Mediterranee on Noe Street, will transport the diner overseas to the Middle East with Greek, Lebanese and Armenian cooking.

Simply but effectively decorated, one senses an authentic Mediterranean flavor to the surroundings in the plain tile tables, ceiling fans, hanging lanterns and Mosque-shaped cutouts in the wall. Upon perusal of the menu, you will find many ethnic dishes that are as authentic as the surroundings. A good recommendation would be to opt for the Mediterranean Meza which will give two or more people a healthy sampling of just about everything including Lule Kebab, Dolma, Hummos, Baba Ghanoush, Tabuleh, and much, much more. A sure winner for dessert is a heavenly treat called Datil Amandra, which is a date stuffed filo pastry served with hot whipped cream and shaved almonds. If that sounds like a bit much for you, there is a smaller combination called the Middle Eastern Plate, which comes in a vegetarian style as well. Don't forget to complement your meal with a fine wine from their modestly priced wine list.

A sister to La Mediterranee on Fillmore Street, the Noe Street location, along with Berkeley and San Rafael locations, has been reviewed with high praise from many Bay area restaurant critics. The restaurant has also received the San Francisco Restauranteur Award from its peers signifying recognition as an outstanding San Francisco restaurant. Be sure to take the time to dine at this delightful cafe when in San Francisco.

LE ST. TROPEZ
126 Clement Street
San Francisco, CA 94118
Tel. (415) 3870408
Hrs: Mon. - Sat. 5:30 p.m. - 10:00 a.m.

France's loss is San Francisco's gain. Fabulous restauranteur, Jean Baptiste, has created one of the most intimate and authentic French chateau atmospheres, outside France, at the elegant Le St. Tropez. Romance abounds, enhanced by a warm fireplace, volumes of Balzac stacked over archways, wood beam candelabra, antique copper pots on the walls that catch the light from flickering oil lamps on the tables, and the muted sound of a popping cork.

The menu rivals the lush decor. The menu changes seasonally and specials are offered daily. You may want to begin your meal with raviolis de Crabe au Basilic: delicious homemade raviolis stuffed with tender shredded crab and draped with a light butter and wine sauce. You may choose the salade de Canard Landaise from the litany of creative salads. This features duck from southwest France mixed with dainty potatoes and delicate walnut oil.

Superb entree selections draw accolades from the cognoscenti of French food. For example, experience the excellent Saumon Saute a Minutefresh filet of salmon sauteed with fresh garlic, ginger and black pepper. Or try the Longe de Veau Grille, a melting tender grilled veal loin that is enriched with a zesty pine nut sauce. The list goes on, topped only by luscious, homemade desserts. Le St. Tropez is recommended for being out of the mainstream and offering exceptional cuisine in a luxurious atmosphere.

LICK'S LTD, 3600 16th Street, #2, San Francisco, California. Espresso bar, fresh soups, salads and quiche. Outstanding desserts.

THE MAGIC FLUTE
3673 Sacramento Street
San Francisco, CA 94118
Tel. (415) 922-1225
Hrs: Mon. - Fri.   Lunch 11:00 a.m. - 2:00 p.m.
      Mon. - Sun   Dinner   5:30 p.m. - 10:00 p.m.

There's an elegance to this famed San Francisco restaurant where the furniture and interior are in the European style, the background music is from the classics, and the owner himself seats most of the guests who come in from stylish Sacramento Street.

Philip LaCavera says fine cuisine is a family tradition, while the diners who come here may comment as much on their host's friendliness and the grace of his tuxedo clad waiters. A luncheon favorite is chicken cacciatore, a boneless breast of chicken sauteed with fresh vegetables topped with a sauce created with Parmesan cheese. Dinner entrees expand to seafood and veal dishes. Pastas are on both menus, along with desserts made in the Magic Flute kitchens.

This is the place for relaxing and enjoying the LaCavera family's recipes amid surroundings as classical as the cooking and the service.

MARGARITAVILLE
1787 Union Street
San Francisco, CA 94123
Tel. (415) 441-1183
Hrs: Mon. - Sun. 11:00 a.m. - 2:00 a.m.
Visa, MasterCard, AMEX accepted

Looking for an elusive "piece of the sun" while in San Francisco? Look no farther than Margaritaville, where the festive atmosphere of vibrant colors, potted plants, murals and a tropical fish aquarium will brighten your day.

Margaritas are the most popular drink, especially during happy hour, made from what the menu calls, "just the right amounts of tequila, Triple Sec and sweet and sour" blended with your choice of flavors such as banana, strawberry, melon, peach, pineapple and traditional lime.

The menu offers the traditional fare of tacos, enchiladas, tostadas, nachos and an appetizer of chalupas. Special entrees like carne asada made from sirloin steak marinated and served with grilled onion, guacamole and sour cream; or chicken mole - a breast of chicken smothered in a sauce of peanuts, chocolate, chilis, herbs and spices will tempt your taste buds. Or, savor the most popular item on their menu, sizzling Fajitas, prepared for you at any time of the day or evening.

Besides offering a paradise-like atmosphere and wonderful food, Margaritaville is a community oriented establishment that has a designated driver program, whereby the person elected to drive, and not drink, is given their meal and soft drinks at no charge (only for a party of four or more). Margaritaville participates in Courtesy Cab programs during the holidays and continuously partakes in promotional programs and events in the city.

MAXWELL'S PLUM
Ghirardelli Square
San Francisco, CA 94109
Tel. (415) 441-4140
Hrs: Mon. - Sun.   11:30 a.m. - 11:00 p.m.
      Sun. Brunch   11:30 a.m. - 4:00 p.m.

Everything about the award-winning Maxwell's Plum is spectacular. Huge windows overlook the San Francisco Bay. The opulence of the magnificient crystal chandeliers, the breathtaking Tiffany glass ceiling in the main dining room, the handcrafted wood carvings, etched panels of glass, over 100 brass gaslights, and an endless display of art works; decoratively, this is one of the most elaborate restaurants ever created in San Francisco.

There's a Cafe within which serves lighter meals, no dress code, the service is incredible, a full-service bar, three sumptuous banquet rooms for those special occasions, and a lavish Sunday Brunch.

The General Manager, Carlo Galazzo, is justifiably proud of the setting that surrounds the heart of Maxwell's Plum...the kitchens and professional chefs that prepare the fabulous foods for which this establishment is noted. Remember the best meal of your life...that's the daily fare at Maxwell's Plum.

MAYE'S OYSTER HOUSE
1233 Polk Street
San Francisco, CA 94l09
Tel. (415) 474-7674
Hrs: Mon. - Sat.   11:30 a.m. - 10:00 p.m.
          Sunday   2:00 p.m. - 10:00 p.m.
MasterCard, Visa and AMEX are accepted.
Free parking across the street.

Oysters come French fried, broiled, and in stews. There are oysters ala Bordeaux, too, but what started as an oyster house in the market at California and Market Streets in 1867 is as well known by local residents for its steaks, chops and seafood.

This is the second oldest restaurant still in continuous operation in the city. George Maye, who opened the saloon and chop house in the market, gave his name to the enterprise. It relocated to Polk street after the 1906 earthquake, and to its present quarters in 1930. You'll be greeted by Gigi Fiorucci, one of the present owners, and be seated in a room with paneled walls decked with photos, paintings and prints. Service is prompt, the menu expanded to include pastas, chicken and veal in the Italian tradition.

San Franciscans flock here for lunch and dinner, drawn by good food, the decor which has the mark of a friendly club, and the delightful service of Gigi and Phyllis Fiorucci.

(See special invitation in the Appendix.)

NEIMAN MARCUS ROTUNDA RESTAURANT
150 Stockton Street - Fourth Floor
San Francisco, CA 94108
Tel. (415) 362-4777
Hrs: Mon. - Sat. 11:00 a.m. - 5:00 p.m.

The domed Rotunda of this department store is the landmark of Union Square. The Rotunda Restaurant and Cafe offers two unique menus for their two seating areas.

Since the store opened in 1982, eating here may have become more popular than shopping. Both offer a touch all their own. In the Rotunda, appetizing specials are prepared daily, the most popular items include a Lobster Sandwich with shallot dressing, and Duck Confit - served with polenta and shitaki mushrooms. Breads and popovers are baked fresh daily. The waiters clad in tuxedos match the elegance of the Rotunda dome with its gold leaf over plaster detail work. The restaurant features a spectacular view of

403

Union Square. If you choose the cafe, the menu tends toward sandwiches and salads, service is quick. Full bar service is available throughout.

The afternoon menu is served from 3:00 p.m. - 5:00 p.m. with delicious desserts and sandwiches available. Be sure to make reservations. Lunch or afternoon, Neiman-Marcus offers one of our "Best Choices" for the San Francisco experience.

NEPTUNE'S PALACE
Pier 39
San Francisco, CA 94111
Tel. (415) 434-2260
Hrs: Mon. - Fri.   Lunch   11:00 a.m. - 4:00 p.m.
                    Dinner   4:00 p.m. - 11:00 p.m.
     Sat. - Sun.   Brunch   11:00 a.m. - 3:00 p.m.
                    Dinner   3:00 p.m. - 11:00 p.m.

A stay in San Francisco should always be accompanied by a meal at a fine seafood restaurant. No better place to enjoy a fine meal of fresh seafood than Neptune's Palace perched on the end of picturesque Pier 39 over looking the whole of San Francisco bay. Lunch or dinner affords a lovely view of the Golden Gate Bridge and surrounding water front.

Luncheon menu selections include specialities such as shark Scallopine, lightly grilled and served over fresh vegetables. Or fresh fillet of stuffed salmon filled with Neptune's special cheeses. On the lighter side there is seafood quiche and, for the traditionalist Neptune, serves the Palace burger. Fine dining at night fall offers a change of menu with steamed clams, oysters Rockefeller and a supreme prawn cocktail for openers. Guests have a wide choice of fresh seafood entrees some samplings of which are salmon sesame, Petrale sole Chardonnay, Fisherman's Cioppino, and a juicy selection of steaks all prepared to perfection and served in style to match the refined atmosphere.

Seafood and San Francisco, they go together. Don't miss this outstanding dining establishment on your stay at the Bay.

404

NEW JOE'S
347 Geary Street at Union Square
San Francisco, CA 94102
Tel. (415) 989-6733
Hrs: Mon. - Sun. 7:00 a.m. - 1:00 a.m.
Visa, MasterCard, AMEX, Carte Blanche and Diners cards.

Generous portions at moderate prices all day long are the hallmark of this comfortable Geary Street restaurant and lounge which caters to the shoppers and theater goers. New Joe's is operated by Jeffrey Pollack, well known in San Francisco's entertainment world.

Pollack operated San Francisco's largest nightclub, the Old Waldorf. He now operates four restaurants in the city, and has as partners in the New Joe's venture rock promoter Bill Graham and Bill Thompson of Starship. There are booths here and a counter with stools, overlooking the open kitchen. Tables are set on starched linen cloths, the room decor is accented with burgundy hues. Salads are famous here, as is the traditional Italian cuisine, the grilled meats have the flavor of mesquite charcoal, and the desserts run from fruit tarts to chocolate tortes.

New Joe's is the kind of place San Franciscans come back to over and over again, drawn by the good food and the friendly atmosphere.

NOB HILL RESTAURANT
Mark Hopkins Inter-Continental Hotel
Number One Nob Hill
San Francisco, CA 94108
Tel. (415) 392-3434
Hrs: Mon. - Sun. Dinner 6:00 p.m. - 10:00 p.m.
All major credit cards are accepted.

The view of San Francisco's skyline and lights of the bay can be breathtaking as you dine in the stately Nob Hill Restaurant. The food offered there is such a unique combination that it has a name all its own, fitting of the setting--new American.

Bits of what are known in gourmet circles as California, French and oriental cuisines are woven into the Nob Hill Restaurant's recipes which use the season's finest offers, seasoned by fresh herbs grown on the protected grounds of the hotel and inspected daily by Chef Peter Morency. In addition to the regular wine list, there is an American wine list to complement the cuisine, drawn from top vintages of the country's thirty-four wine producing states.

The consistent excellence of the food combined with the ambiance created by piano entertainment, expert waiters in black tie, Wedgwood china

405

and perfect roses on every candlelit table, has distinguished the Nob Hill Restaurant as one of San Francisco's very finest.

THE OLD SWISS HOUSE
Pier 39 203 "C"
San Francisco, CA 94l33
Tel. (415) 434-0432
Hrs: Mon. - Sun.   Lunch 11:30 a.m. - 4:00 p.m.
          Mon. - Sun.   Dinner   5:00 p.m. - 10:00 p.m.
Visa, MasterCard, AMEX and Diners are accepted.

Pier 39, reaching out into the bay with its collection of tourist attractions, may seem like an odd place for a European restaurant. The Old Swiss House is a replica of a Swiss chalet, where owners Roger and Marianne Braun grew up in their native Switzerland.

You'll find wienerschnitzel with dumplings, traditional lamb, fowl and fish dishes here. Full luncheons are complemented by soup and salad, offerings for light eaters, with lighter prices. At the top of the dinner menu is a rack of lamb for two. The dining rooms, and cocktail lounge complete with fireplace, are Swiss; the view of the bay and bridge are San Francisco.

The Brauns are both graduates of Swiss restaurant management schools with a decade of experience there before coming to San Francisco. Their Old Swiss House is as new as the Pier 39 development, but the tradition and decor in this charming chalet brings the flavor of the old country to the bay.

RESTAURANT 101
101 California Street
San Francisco, CA 94111
Tel. (415) 788-4101
Hrs: Lunch Mon. - Fri.   11:30 a.m. - 2:30 p.m.
          Dinner   Mon. - Sat.   6:15 p.m. - 10:00 p.m.
AMEX, Carte Blanche, MasterCard and Visa are accepted.

If you are travelling with the family, you'll want to arrange babysitting for an elegant outing to the Financial District at Restaurant 101. Celebrate San Francisco in this discriminating dining establishment where the extensively French trained chefs seduce your tastebuds and your eye.

Expect the unexpected on the daily original menus for lunch and dinner. The unique cuisine is a combination of traditional meats, such as duck, veal, lamb, calve's liver or quail, presented in very untraditional combinations of new light sauces and lavish vegetable medleys. Savor, for instance, the veal chop infused with roasted garlic or the noisettes of tender lamb filled with mushrooms and basil on a bed of red and green peppers, rings of onion, and tomatoes. The kitchen's own angels' hair pasta, a regularly featured selection, bears witness to Italian refinements as well. Desserts receive very special attention from Austrian pastry chef, Gerhard Michler, who continues the theme of unique combinations with such graceful endings as a raspberry soup of fresh fruit puree and champagne, or the chocolate and mango mousses served with fresh mangoes marinated in gingered orange sauce.

The tasteful table settings, the airy ambiance, the imaginatively chosen wine list, and the first rate service all add to the popularity of this sophisticated but unintimidating French restaurant, making reservations essential.

THE SAILING SHIP RESTAURANT
Pier 42 Embarcadero at Berry
San Francisco, CA 94107
Tel. (415) 777-5771
Hrs: Tue. - Sun. Cocktails   5:00 p.m.
                    Dinner   8:00 p.m.

This glamorous vessel began its colorful career in 1908, trading in the North Atlantic. During World Wars I and II, she carried munitions and food supplies to the Allies. In between those conflicts, she was acquired by rum-runners to bootleg liquor during Prohibition! She was discovered by Hollywood and featured in over twenty-five films including, "Mutiny on the Bounty," "Hawaii," "High Wind in Jamaica," "Stowaway" and "Barbarassa." In 1968, Dolph Rempp bought The Sailing Ship from Columbia Pictures and landbounded it in an earthquake proof cradle alongside the San Francisco Bay, one half mile south of the Oakland Bay Bridge.

This famous craft, now named The Sailing Ship Dolph Rempp, has been converted into an elegant dining establishment, specializing in fresh seafoods such as, The Grand Array of Local Selections, Dungeness crab, Santa Barbara mussels, Louisiana crab cakes, whole live Maine lobster, Catalina swordfish, Washington Silver salmon, as well as Iowa milk fed veal, Nevada tenderloin medallions of beef, Idaho lamb rack, Black Angus filet mignon with Sour Mash Whiskey sauce and daily specials. The menu also includes a variety of hot and cold first courses and salads, a soup de jour and delectable desserts headed by the famous chocolate and fresh fruit souffles. The marvelous American Regional menu conceptualized by the owner and created by Executive Chef Patrick Giddings, is presented beautifully by his staff in the galley.

Internationally renowned for its excellent cuisine, it also offers a cozy cocktail lounge, nightly jazz pianist and plenty of parking. This San Francisco landmark restaurant combines all the elements one could desire in memorable dining, incredible surroundings, candlelight, excellent service by courteous tuxedoed staff, ambiance, entertainment, plus exceptional cuisine and wine. It can boast of having one of the largest champagne cellars in the country and is considered Northern California's most romantic restaurant. The Sailing Ship Dolph Rempp is also fantastic for large and small parties, weddings, receptions, luncheons, banquets, luaus, picnics and other gatherings!

THE SHADOWS
1349 Montgomery Street
(Telegraph Hill)
San Francisco, CA 94133
Tel. (415) 982-5536
Hrs: Mon. - Sun. 5:00 pm. - 10:00 p.m.
Visa, MasterCard, AMEX, and Carte Blanche are accepted.

The Shadows Restaurant perches on the side of Telegraph Hill, one of the most picturesque and intriguing spots in the city. It commands a sweeping view of San Francisco Bay, especially the cozy loft dining room on the second level. The restaurant is in a house that is more than 100 years old and has recently undergone a renovation that turned it into a romantic French hideaway. Nicely spaced tables are set with pink linen, candles and red roses in pretty crystal vases.

The delightful atmosphere and lovely decor of The Shadows is more than matched by the cuisine offered by owner Jeff Pollack, manager Jean Dupret and chef Dan Lewark. Contemporary French cuisine is the house specialty. Begin your meal with one of the unusual hors d'oeuvres, such as Asiette de Poissons Fumes a La Tomate - various smoked fish served with tomato sherbet, then perhaps Soupe de Brie Gratinee - Brie cheese soup, followed by Salade d'Endive et Artichaut - Belgian endive with artichokes. The choice of entrees is varied, with seafood, veal, duck and lamb available. There is something for every taste and the desserts are the perfect end to your memorable meal.

This delightful restaurant with it's spectacular views, charming and romantic decor, and wonderfully prepared and served French cuisine will delight you, just as it has been delighting diners for over a hundred years.

SUTTER 500 RESTAURANT AND CAFE
500 Sutter Street
San Francisco, CA 94102
Tel. (415) 362-3346

Hrs:	Lunch	Mon. - Sat.	11:30 a.m. - 2:00 p.m.
	Dinner	Mon. - Sat.	6:00 p.m. - 10:00 p.m.
		Sunday	5:30 p.m. - 9:00 p.m.

The Sutter 500 Restaurant offers more than just a restaurant, it also has a cafe, a bar and the "International Corner" bookstore. The restaurant is discreetly tucked away behind the bar for private, intimate dining. The emphasis is on modern French cuisine with a California accent. Meat, fish and seafood are offered, all prepared with the freshest ingredients, and an innovative use of the fresh produce available in California. Chef Hubert Keller is classically trained and brings his special touch to such choices such as roasted salmon and medallions of lobster wrapped in spinach leaves with a red wine sauce.

For those who prefer a more casual approach to dining, there is the cafe. Located on the corner of Sutter and Powell, it has sliding bay windows which are open wide on warm days and offer diners uninterrupted "people-watching" while enjoying the excellent cuisine in the cafe. For those in a hurry, the bar offers a quick lunch, the Sutter Express. Proprietor Jean Gabriel has created three different dining experiences under one roof and each is distinctive and enjoyable.

The International Corner Bookstore has been on this corner since 1974 and offers the best source of international publications in San Francisco, according to Herb Caen. They also offer travel books, including books in foreign languages. There are lots of fashion magazines, both domestic and foreign. Sutter 500 offers unique browsing and dining and shouldn't be missed by those seeking a distinctively San Francisco experience.

SWISS LOUIS
Pier 39 Building E #204
San Francisco, CA 94133
Tel. (415) 421-2913
Hrs: Mon. - Sun. 7:30 a.m. - 10:30 p.m.
All major credit cards accepted

Swiss Louis has been a San Francisco tradition for years. It was originally located on Broadway, but moved to its present location on Pier 39 in 1978. It has a panoramic view featuring Alcatraz, the Golden Gate and Bay Bridges, the Yacht Harbor, Coit Tower and the city. Sal Chiavino, Swiss

Louis's owner, joined the restaurant in 1966, bringing with him a wealth of training and knowledge gained in Italy where he was born and apprenticed as a chef. He and the present chef, Aldo, are committed to serving their customers the best food possible.

Swiss Louis' emphasis is on Northern Italian cuisine and many of the selections are originals developed by Sal when he was the chef. They offer wonderful seafood, as well as veal, rack of lamp, pork chops, delicious pasta and more. The menu is extensive, with fifteen fish and fifteen pasta entrees alone. Chef Aldo is continually creating new and exciting dishes. He's happy to personally suggest one of his "special" entrees and welcomes your comments.

For an enriching dining experience, whether you want a leisurely meal while enjoying the unexcelled view, or a quick snack so you can get back to your sightseeing, be sure to try Swiss Louis. You won't be disappointed.

TOKYO SUKIYAKI
225 Jefferson Street
San Francisco, CA 94133
Tel. (415) 775-9030
Hrs: Lunch Sat. - Sun.   11:30 a.m. - 4:00 p.m.
         Dinner   Mon. - Sun.   4:00 p.m. - 11:00 p.m.

This truly authentic Japanese restaurant was established in its present location at Fisherman's Wharf in 1954 by owners Noboru and Yoshiye Nojima. Not only the food at Tokyo Sukiyaki is authentic, the interior of the restaurant was all built in Japan. The private Japanese style dining rooms, tatami rooms, behind sliding doors are especially pleasant. Seating is provided on woven reed floor mats surrounding low tables, all from Japan. Western style seating is available for those who prefer it. The Japanese experience is continued by the kimono-clad waitresses, all of whom speak Japanese. This is a very popular place with people visiting from Japan.

The main chefs at Tokyo Sukiyaki were all trained in Japan and offer only the most authentic Japanese cuisine. The menu is beautifully printed in Japanese on rice paper, but fortunately for western diners is also translated into English. There is a very long list of appetizers. In Japan it is common for people to sample many appetizers when dining in a fine restaurant. There are many entrees to choose from, featuring chicken, beef and seafood, and several appetizers and an entree make a delicious meal.

The restaurant's location on Fisherman's Wharf offers a truly spectacular view. Soft, soothing Japanese music plays as you enjoy your wonderfully delicious, authentic Japanese cuisine. Tokyo Sukiyaki offers you a truly Japanese experience in dining.

San Francisco City/County

TUBA GARDEN
3634 Sacramento Street
San Francisco, CA 94118
Tel. (415) 921-TUBA
Hrs: Mon. - Fri.   11:00 a.m. - 2:30 p.m.
     Sat. - Sun.   10:30 a.m. - 2:30 p.m.
Private parties available evenings

When Anthony La Cavera and Ben Wenske opened Tuba Garden in Presidio Heights, they were one of the first to think of converting the city's Victorian Homes into splendid dining establishments. Lunch and brunch are served in the main dining area, the courtyard patio and a quaint carriage house built in the 1800's is used for banquets and receptions. The restaurant features marble topped tables, oak floors, baskets, flowers and each month a different artist's works are displayed and offered for sale. A fountain adorns the patio where the tuba, after which the restaurant was named, is displayed.

Thanks to Ben's expertise, he was once chef for the Prince of Liechtenstein, the food offered is excellent. A specialty is onion soup, served in a crock and topped with a rich layer of imported cheese. The chicken salad Hawaiian is a favorite and there are platters of cheese and fruit and distinctive sandwiches available. Brunches offer eggs Benedict, cheese blintzes, quiche Lorraine, Belgian waffles, omelettes and much more. Desserts are all homemade and are scrumptious, particularly the Chocolate Mousse Cake.

The food is original and delicious, the ambiance is charming and relaxing, the service couldn't be better, and all in all Tuba Garden is a "Best Choice" for lunch or brunch in San Francisco.

UMBERTO RISTORANTE ITALIANO
141 Stewart Street
San Francisco, CA 94105
Tel. (415) 543-8021
Hrs: Lunch   Mon.-Fri.   11:30 a.m.- 2:30 p.m.
     Dinner   Mon.-Sat.   5:30 p.m.-11:00 p.m.
     Bar   Mon.-Sat.   11:30 a.m.-12:00 midnight
MasterCard, Visa, AMEX, Carte Blanche Diner's Club cards.

Experience San Francisco lore in the making. Umberto Menghi, called the James Bond of cooking by many of the avid followers of his television program The Elegant Appetite, confesses his Toscana regional recipes reflect the newest of the traditions because they set new trends all the time. When you step down into the cellar level on Stewart Street, one block from the Ferry

411

Building, into an old world atmosphere of cool Mediterranean pillars and arches, you begin an unforgettable experience.

The soft lighting, the Italian terra cotta tiles, pink linens and elegant silk flower arrangements create an intimacy enhanced by a pianist who performs nightly. The simplicity of the decor is reflected in Umberto's recipes which are prepared with his traditionally light sauces consisting of vegetable, fruit and meat juices blended with wine and lemon. Under the attentive direction of budding restauranteur Giovanni Cesaratto, special care is taken to obtain only the freshest ingredients daily to add the greatest authenticity to the Menghi recipes. Giovanni personally recommends the Tagliatelle Di Mare, tossed with fresh seafood and fish veloute or the delectable lasagna Di Mare-black lasagna pasta filled with assorted seafood and baked in a scrumptious lobster and cream sauce. An excellent appetizer is the calamari Fritti consisting of pan-fried squid ringlets served with tasty diced onions, parsley and their original dill dip. Patrons continually rave about the fish preparations Gamberoni Umberto and scampi al Chardonnay. The latter presents plump prawns sauteed and served with a spectacular chardonnay wine sauce. Particularly pleasing are Umberto's veal recipes, such as the Bistecchina Di Vitello Nocciata - a delicious veal steak in a delicate walnut sauce. Or try the Medaglioni Di Vitello Alle Mele, featuring medallions of veal loin sauteed with sliced apple and grappa brandy. Utmost consideration is given to the selection of fine wines, both domestic and Italian, to complement any selection, while homemade desserts, espresso and cappuccino are excellent ways to complete your meal at Umberto.

This restaurant was once one of San Francisco's best kept secrets. But no more! It is indeed fast becoming a subject of lore. "Best Choice" for truly unique dining.

VICTOR'S
St. Francis Hotel
35 Powell Street
San Francisco, CA 94102
Tel. (415) 397-7000
Hrs: Mon. - Sun. 6:00 p.m. - 11:00 p.m.

Located on the thirty second floor of the Westin St. Francis Hotel, Victor's restaurant is a tribute to the master chef, Victor Hirtzler, who served at the hotel from 1906 to 1926 and introduced haute cuisine to the West Coast. The view is breathtaking, diners enjoy a glittering, romantic panorama of the city. The lighting is subdued and each table elegantly set with pink linen, stemware, and candles in silver and glass holders.

The menu features superlative American and California nouvelle cuisine with an emphasis on fresh local produce, poultry, fish and beef prepared with a light, natural hand. The entrees change daily in accordance with the fresh ingredients available. There are numerous choices of appetizers, soups and salads. You might begin your dinner with poached filet of baby salmon, followed by an unforgettable soup, such as lobster bisque and then a salad of endive with delta crayfish and wild rice and continue with an entree of Bodega Bay sturgeon with saffron broth and fresh fennel. Of course there is a superb wine cellar from which to pick the best wine to complement your dinner.

Everything at Victor's is perfect, from the view, to the service, to the delightful cuisine. Victor's is justly proud of the over eighty years of culinary excellence which make it one of the best and most memorable restaurants in San Francisco.

YAMATO RESTAURANT AND SUSHI BAR

717 California and Grant Avenue
San Francisco, CA 94108
Tel. (415) 397-3456
Hrs: Tue. - Fri.   Lunch   11:45 a.m - 2:00 p.m.
       Tue. - Sun.   Dinner   5:00 p.m. - 10:00 p.m.
Major credit cards are accepted.

Yamato Restaurant and Sushi Bar has maintained the vanguard of innovative Japanese dining for the last forty years. Yamato is located on the California Street Cable Car line just above Grant Avenue on the edge of Chinatown. Japanese travelers from all over the country and even visitors from Japan come to Yamato. Owner Ryozo Ishizaki has established an atmosphere favorable for guests to experience Japanese cuisine. Ryozo commissioned Walter Harada to design such a restaurant, one of charm and artistic intensity. The sushi bar is done in pine and ever changing exhibits of Ikebana flower sculptures are an authentic Japanese work of art.

The menu includes a special five course gourmet dinner designed with the Emperor in mind. An Imperial dinner includes soup, salad, tender chicken marinated in Yamato's special sauce, cooked on bamboo skewers with green pepper and onion, shrimp tempura, and beef Sukiyaki consisting of thin sliced beef, fresh mushroom, bean cake, yam noodles and fresh vegetable all cooked at your table.

Attention to detail marks Yamato Restaurant as a superior dining experience. Be sure to visit Yamato's Restaurant and Sushi Bar in Century Plaza Hotel, Century City when visiting Los Angeles. As further proof of Yamato's excellence, a kitchen is maintained at the San Francisco International

Airport that prepares inflight meals for Japan Airlines and caters for other airlines.

Fine dining is a San Francisco tradition and certainly worthy of its own 'tour.' So, what follows is not a tour as such, but a listing of some of the choicest restaurants in San Francisco along with a house specialty. Wherever you go you are sure to enjoy the atmosphere, service and food of your best choice.

SAN FRANCISCO RESTAURANT TOUR		
Any of these meals will taste twice as good after you return from any of the Red & White Fleet's seven tours of the bay area. For details, see the Red & White's SanF/Att entry.		
Harris'	Best beef	SanF/Rest
Maye's Oyster House	Best oysters	SanF/Rest
Margaritaville	Best Mexican	SanF/Rest
The Magic Flute	Best chicken cacc	SanF/Rest
Le St. Tropez	Best French	SanF/Rest
L'entrecote de Paris	Best Entrecote	SanF/Rest
Julius Castle	Best Continental	SanF/Rest
The Iron Horse	Best pasta	SanF/Rest
India House	Best "tandoori"	SanF/Rest
House of Prime Rib	Best prime rib	SanF/Rest
Nob Hill Restaurant	Best "new American"	SanF/Rest
Empress of China	Best roof garden	SanF/Rest

Shopping Mall

NEIMAN-MARCUS, 150 Stockton Street, San Francisco, California. Land mark dome, dining in the Rotunda Restaurant, shopping on several floors.

Sporting Goods

ORVIS-SAN FRANCISCO
166 Maiden Lane
San Francisco, CA 94l08
Tel. (415) 392-1600
Hrs: Mon. - Sat. 9:30 a.m. - 6:00 p.m.
MasterCard, Visa and AMEX are accepted.

Orvis is an outfitter who does business through attractive mail order catalogs from a headquarters next to a trout pond in Vermont. Here on Union Square in San Francisco you can step into the magic of those catalogs, and while there is no pond handy for testing the action of a new fly rod, there is a waterfall, cascading by as you walk down the stairs to the lower level of this fine sporting goods store.

Classic equipment--guns, rods, reels, and flies--and classic sports clothing make up much of the inventory. There are items for a home, yours or as a gift, or the summer cabin. There are gift items for any outdoors person, including observers of wildlife as well as hunters. Friendly sales people are ready to explain how things work, swap stories of the "one that got away," and guide you to the books, videotapes and references for more about your sport.

If you are an Orvis catalog reader, a stop at the store is a must. This is also a place for browsing for any visitor to Union Square, a place where the sound of a real waterfall takes you away from the city and into the outdoors, if only while you experience the Orvis magic.

Stationery and Wrapping Paper

OGGETTI
1846 Union Street
San Francisco, CA 94123
Tel. (415) 346-0631
Hrs: Mon. - Thu.   10:00 a.m. - 6:00 p.m.
       Friday   10:00 a.m. - 8:00 p.m.
       Saturday   10:00 a.m. - 6:00 p.m.
       Sunday   11:00 a.m. - 6:00 p.m.
Visa, MasterCard, AMEX, and Discover cards are accepted.

Oggetti, a one-of-a-kind specialty store, offering an extensive selection, exclusively, of the highly popular Florentine paper products. This award winning shop proves the notion that the best comes in small packages, since there is less than 550 square feet of space.

415

Packed with literally hundreds of paper "upholstered" items, boxes of every size, shape, color and pattern, or picture frames, notebooks, photo albums, and a variety of other home and desk accessories.

The common denominator of Oggetti's merchandise is that it is all covered, in whole or in part, with Florentine paper--which is a decoration process invented by the royal bookmaker to Louis XIII in the 17th century is called "papier a cuve" as each sheet of paper is dipped in a special basin which contains a solution of water and herbs to which color has been added. The blending of the liquids, using a variety of tools, results in a one-of-a-kind design on each sheet.

Whatever you single out, your gift will be tasteful and unique. One-of-a-kind, just like Oggetti.

Sunglasses

SHADES
1645 Market Street
San Francisco, CA 94103
Tel. (415) 863-5454
Hrs: Mon. - Sat. 10:30 a.m. - 6:00 p.m.
All major credit cards are accepted.

Here is a specialty shop to cool your eyes. Shades in San Francisco is a store that is devoted exclusively to the needs of sunglass wearers. Whatever it is in sunshades for your eyes, they have it.

With over a thousand pairs on display, Shades has the most complete selection around. Starting with prices as low as two dollars on up to exotic designs, you can select from a vast variety of glasses that include ski, motorcycle, fashion, jockey, designer, hard to find styles, woodies and a large selection of original 1950 and 60 glasses. As a special note of interest Shades maintains a museum of bizarre and amazing glasses. If for some unknown reason they don't have what you're looking for in stock they will order it for you. Also phone orders are gladly accepted.

Shades definitely has what you need in sunglasses. You can choose from brand names like RayBan, Vuarnet, Revo, L.A. Eyeworks, Parche-Carrera and American Optical. So, give the friendly folks at Shades a call or better yet stop in and tell them you read about them in "Best Choices".

(See special invitation in the Appendix.)

416

Toys

PUPPETS ON THE PIER
Pier 39
San Francisco, CA 94l33
Tel. (415) 781-4435
Hrs: March - December
         Mon. - Sun   10:00 a.m. - 9:30 p.m.
       January -February
         Mon. - Fri.   11:00 a.m. - 7:30 p.m.
         Sat. -Sun.   10:00 a.m. - 9:30 p.m.
Visa, MasterCard and AMEX are accepted

This is a puppet store. An exclusive puppet store, the likes of which you probably can not find anywhere on the West Coast.

Hand puppets and marionettes of all sizes and shapes are on the shelves, with proprietors Jim and Debbie Patrick inviting visitors to touch and try. These cute little fellows are, for the most part, inexpensive. Whether it is a gift for a child back home, or getting a story ready for production in a puppet theater, you'll find this a fun place to shop, one of the many attractions on Pier 39.

Smiles abound as the puppets are demonstrated, and visitors shown the skills of managing a puppet. Telephone and mail orders of specialty puppets are welcomed.

WOODS AND WOODS BASIC BROWN BEARS
444 De Haro Street
San Francisco, CA 94107
Tel. (415) 626-0781
Hrs: Mon. - Sat. 10:00 a.m. - 5:00 p.m.

Eric and Merrilee Woods both agreed that there were no stuffed toys for boys. Merrilee started making stuffed corduroy and denim airplanes for her son. The idea caught on and soon Merrilee was making stuffed toys for neighborhood stores.

Today, Woods and Woods Basic Brown Bear Factory is located in the Showplace Square in San Francisco. They are now producing all kinds of stuffed toys in addition to the Fluffyfliers; Colonel Teddy, Beary Godmother, Grandma and Grandpa Bears, Chocolate Moose, "Mom", the Mother Goose, and the most popular of all the - Basic Brown Bear.

This is a unique opportunity to watch the toys come alive as they are cut, sewn, and stuffed at the factory workshop. On quiet days, they might even let you stuff a bear or two yourself! School groups or large parties interested in a "formal" tour are encouraged to call for an appointment.

Water Purity System

OASIS ENERGY SYSTEMS
445 Kirkham Street
San Francisco, CA 94122
Tel. (415) 731-7009
Hrs: Mon. - Fri. 10:00 a.m. - 6:00 p.m.
Weekends by appointment
Credit or time payment plan.

Jim Walters runs Oasis Energy Systems from his home. Don't look for a high gloss, flashy storefront. That wouldn't be Jim's style. As an avid traveler of this world, an explorer of not-oft traveled footpaths, Jim has evolved a deep respect for our world and its endangered ecology. His philosophy is, "to provide a clean, healthy, economical environment for the home and the people that inhabit that home."

As William Ruckelshaus, the U.S. EPA Director, stated, "The number one environmental problem--is chemical pollution" of our country's waters. The World Health Organization estimates that "60% to 90% of human tumors are environmentally induced and that a pure water source would eliminate 80% of all world illnesses." And lest you think this is a global and not American problem, you should read some of the pertinent literature that Jim has available regarding water pollution-related deaths and illnesses caused in California and the rest of the country.

Jim has sought to address this problem. He is a distributor for Multi-Pure, the most effective drinking water system in the world. It's compact, fits underneath your sink or on the countertop, effective--removes toxic metals, minerals, asbestos, e. coli bacteria, and chlorine, as shown by laboratory tests. The final product? Well people who use the system say "it tastes like spring water."

Used, now, in hospitals, major universities, laboratories, by the U. S. military, foreign embassies, major airlines, and in recreation vehicles, apartments and homes worldwide. Take an active role in protecting your environment...call or write Jim for a free, no obligation information packet today.

Winery

WINES OF CALIFORNIA
Pier 39 Space B1
San Francisco, CA 94133
Tel. (415) 989-1357
Hrs: Mon. - Sun. 10:30 a.m. - 8:30 p.m.

Sal Chiavino, owner of Wines of California, carries no less than 600 different types of wines exquisitely displayed. Sal travels California searching for new varieties from smaller vineyards to add to his collection.

Ninety-nine percent of the wines are from California. Sal feels that California wines are superior to those from Germany and France. He explains that dedication and hard work by the vintners of the area have produced wines that rival even the masters of Europe. At Wines of California, your taste buds can delight in anything from a dry Chardonnay to Cabernet. Accessories from racks to bottle stoppers are handsomely displayed with even hard to find items such as an old fashioned picnic basket complete with table cloth, napkins, wine glasses, opener, cheese board, knife and storage container available. Gourmet condiments are also displayed.

Sal's gracious hospitality include complimentary cheese and wine tasting. A free catalogue will provide you with resources for purchasing wine from Sal long after you have headed home.

SAN MATEO COUNTY

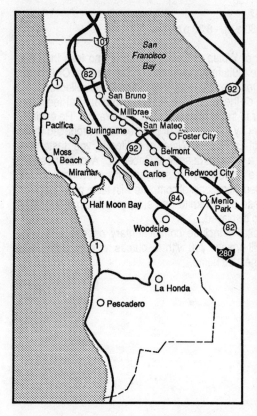

The mid-section of the San Francisco Peninsula takes its name from the Spanish designation of Saint Matthew, and for the early years of mission life and even into California's early statehood, this 447 square mile jurisdiction was part of other domains. Mission Dolores, the first agricultural enterprise in what is now the city of San Francisco, had its rural sheep ranch called San Mateo. Politically, the state legislature trimmed the county from San Francisco in 1856, six years after statehood.

It was a touchy time, since the wild peninsula was a haven for criminals. Records of the first county election show the bad guys of the times wanted their town, Belmont, designated county seat. Redwood City won out after the state supreme court invalidated the vote and ballots were cast again in 1857. The coast from Pescadero south was part of Santa Cruz county until 1868. Residents convinced the legislature it was easier to ride twenty miles over a mountain to the county seat in Redwood City than take the Gazos Creek trail and thirty more miles on the coast to reach Santa Cruz and the courthouse.

San Mateo, the city, was platted in 1863 when the San Francisco-San Jose Railroad was under construction. That rail line, and the historic El Camino Real of earlier times set the development pattern for the county.

People are concentrated in the area from the bay west to the first ridge line. Then after the rift valley which is the earthquake-prone San Andreas fault, redwood forest covers the Santa Cruz mountains as they dip toward a sparsely-settled coast. On the bay side, the common county boundary with Santa Clara splits Palo Alto and Stanford University, then takes to the ridge and township lines, doglegging westward to the beach just north of Big Basin Redwood State Park.

About 590,000 people now live in the county, most of them on its west slopes in cities which seem to run into each other. Daly City, south terminus of the Bay Area Rapid Transit (BART) trains which link the peninsula with the East Bay, is the most populous city, with 79,000 residents. San Mateo has almost as many citizens, and the communities of South San Francisco and Redwood City count over 50,000 persons each.

Coastal fogs dominate the summer weather of Half Moon Bay and other towns along Highway One. On the west slope, summer is mild with temperatures warmer than San Francisco and fog far less frequent. During winter months, the mountains help create ample rainfall to green up the pastures of the country manor horse ranches and the lawns of the smaller residential developments. Many homes, designed to hug the hills, are shaded by native trees and landscaped with native plants, forsaking traditional lawns altogether for what could be described as modern comforts in a subdivided forest.

The log of the British vessel Blossom, reporting an 1827 overland trip from Yerba Buena to Monterey, described the area around San Mateo Creek as like "a nobleman's park." Today many families of the moneyed equivalent to nobility make their estates in San Mateo. Among the first was William Ralston of Bank of California fame. He transformed a hillside ranch at Belmont into a country home which by 1868 could handle 120 guests down for the weekend.

Much of the industrial engine of the peninsula is in the Daly City and South San Francisco area. The county's top employer is United Airlines which runs regional shops at San Francisco International Airport, and generates about 8,500 jobs. Ampex Corporation, in the advance on magnetic tape technology, is the largest employer in Redwood City.

ATTRACTIONS

Virgin redwoods are preserved in **Memorial Park,** oldest in the county park system. Located on Pescadero Road a few miles east of the coast, it can be reached by Highway 84 from Redwood City or Alpine Road off of Skyline Drive. Camping, picnic and swimming facilities in this forest. Call 879-0212 for campsite reservations.

421

On the south boundary of San Francisco is the 2,064-acre **San Bruno Mountain county park.** This rugged area has many plants and animals which have lost their homes to the urbanization of the peninsula. Park entrance is off Guadalupe Canyon Parkway.

Fitzgerald Marine Reserve is a collection of tidal rocks with an interpretive center. From Moss Beach, go west to the foot of California Street.

Skyline Boulevard has historic and scenic interests. It represents the first regional transportation planning venture by local government; starting in San Francisco on the coast at Lake Merced, then skirting the city's reservoirs in the San Andreas rift, and finally mounting the ridgetop of the Santa Cruz mountains which make a boundary between Santa Clara and Santa Cruz counties.

Sweeny Skyline Preserve, east of Pacifica next to Skyline College, provides a viewpoint of ridge, bay and ocean. Follow signs to the college, park in student lot three and follow the signs.

In Belmont, which began life as a camp for outcasts from San Francisco, is the palatial **Ralston Hall** on the campus of the College of Notre Dame. Financier William (Billy) Ralston completed his country house in 1868. It is fully restored, open for tours by appointment. Call 593-1601, extension 6.

Half Moon Bay on the coast offers a glimpse of farmland developed by Portuguese settlers, and a town with a Spanish flavor. **Spanishtown Historical Society** offers tours by writing them at Box 62, Half Moon Bay, CA 94019. More informal tours can start at Cunha's Grocery with purchase of the local guidebook.

The editorial offices and gardens of **Sunset Magazine** are in Menlo Park, 80 Willow Road. Call 321-3600 Nearby are the gardens of the Allied Arts Guild, which includes a tea room, at 75 Arbor Road. Call 325-3259.

Colma is the cemetery city, famed for its subdivisions of cemeteries for many San Francisco residents. Take Hillside Boulevard south in Daly City to reach Colma, or from the Bayshore go west on Randolph Boulevard to Hillside. San Francisco's Board of Supervisors forced the out-of-county burials with an 1897 ordinance halting interment in the city. Colma, already site of one cemetery, now has thirteen plus one for pets. The town, with about 500 living residents, and 1,000,000 graves, was incorporated in 1924. Florist shops and monument works do a brisk business here.

The famed **Tanforan Race Track** opened in San Bruno in 1899. When aviators wanted to test the concept of aircraft carrier flights in 1910 they came to Tanforan with a Curtis biplane which then flew to the bay, landing on a platform erected on the battleship Pennsylvania. The buildings, alongside El Camino Real, burned in 1964 and the land went to developers. Tanforan Park is now a regional shopping center.

Hillsborough, the millionaire's community, is southwest of Burlingame. **Woodland Theater** gained fame for its summer Sunday symphony concerts. The town's founders said there would be no sidewalks, stores, saloons or hotels, a drive through today will show you the legacy.

For additional information, contact the **San Mateo County Convention and Visitors Bureau**, 888 Airport Boulevard, Burlingame, CA 94010. Telephone (415) 347-7004.

Belmont

Antiques

BELMONT COUNTRY STORE
700 Ralston Avenue
Belmont, CA 94002
Tel. (415) 593-8267
Hrs: Mon. - Sat.   10:00 a.m. - 5:30 p.m.
        Sunday   12:00 noon - 5:00 p.m.

Without a doubt, the most recognizable building in Belmont is the large pink store next to the railroad tracks that parallel El Camino Real. Originally built in 1870 as a general store, and employed as a retail business for more years than any other building on the peninsula, this landmark has been the home of Belmont Country Store Antiques Collective since 1982.

With approximately sixty dealers spread out over more than 20,000 square feet, Belmont Country Store is one of the largest antique collectives in Northern California. Within the confines of Belmont Country Store are antiques of every type and period, including American Country, English, French, European, rustic, formal and Art Deco. There are dealers for furniture for every room of the house, clocks, jewelry, quilts, rugs, vintage clothing, old bubble top gasoline pumps, phonographs, vintage Coca-Cola dispensers and just about every collectable imaginable.

A full time and highly trained staff separate from the dealers is always standing by to assist you with any questions you may have. So, the next time you're searching for the perfect accent piece, save yourself some time and go to Belmont Country Store.

Restaurant

THE VAN'S
815 Belmont Avenue
Belmont, CA 94002
Tel. (415) 591-6525
Hrs. Mon. - Sat.   11:30 a.m. - 11:00 p.m.
        Sunday Brunch   10:00 a.m. - 3:00 p.m.
Visa, MasterCard and AMEX.

The Van's restaurant has a very interesting history. In 1915, the Pan American Exposition was held in San Francisco to commemorate the opening of the Panama Canal. It was a gala event with many nations building exhibits, peoples from around the world came to the city to celebrate. After the exposition, all of the buildings were dismantled..except two. The Palace of Fine Arts and the Japanese Tea House. The latter was barged down the river to its new location and is now known as The Van's.

Over the years the building continued its tradition for the unique. During Prohibition it served as an illegal saloon...later a reputed gambling house, and later still it was questionable as to the use of the upstairs bedrooms.

Continuing with tradition, The Van's creates the unique with food, like the barbecued pork back ribs, tender and juicy, and prime USDA steaks cooked to order on an authentic Mexican oak charcoal broiler. Other specialties include Australian lobster tails, T-Bone or Porterhouse steaks plus many other delicious seafood and barbeque dishes.

Just returned from the theater and want something light? The Van's has a special mini-menu, served from 11:00 p.m. to 1:00 a.m., just finger foods and light snacks.

The Sunday Champagne Brunch is an elegant and pampered experience. Assorted baked goods, fresh fruit and complimentary champagne await you, as you begin your dining experience and ponder the colorful beginnings of this fine, unique dining establishment -- The Van's.

Burlingame

The streets are wide, the avenues long, stretching from the bay to the hills in what was probably the first town in the west to gain a reputation for its "country club life." Anson Burlingame, late the minister to China when he spent a weekend at Billy Ralston's Belmont estate, liked the area so well he bought an 1,100 acre place for a villa. Ralston subdivided part of his own estate into five acre lots for what he envisioned as a summer colony for San Francisco's elite. The country club came in 1893 for entertainment of the rich land owners. Some say it was the first country club in California. In 1908 there was enough of a business district to bring about incorporation of a city.

Today about 26,000 live in the city, many employed by the businesses which serve San Francisco International Airport, a scant three miles away. Three industrial and business parks add to the local job base. But, its tree-lined streets and old mansions still provide an attraction to visitors. The exclusive Hillsborough is next door, an incorporated community which has allowed only five schools in town in addition to its residences which have an average value of $600,000 per house and half-acre minimum lot sizes.

To the north of Burlingame lies Millbrae, a city of 20,000. This newer community is still growing in size. Its merchants provide support to enterprises at San Francisco Airport, and its homes house people working in many peninsula communities.

Attractions

Kohl Mansion, 2750 Adeline Drive, is an English Tudor-style residence completed in 1914 on a forty acre site. It is typical of many country estates of the period. Now used for a girl's school, it is open for tours by appointment. Call 591-7422. If you wish, the tour will include light refreshments fitting to the baronial English theme of the place.

Coyote Point Regional Park is on the bay at Peninsular Avenue. The complex includes a local museum, a large yacht harbor and the **San Mateo Municipal Golf Course**. Call 573-2593 for park information, 347-1461 to reach the golf club house.

For more information, contact the **Burlingame Chamber of Commerce**, 306 Lorton Avenue. Telephone 344-1735.

San Mateo County

Accommodations

SAN FRANCISCO AIRPORT MARRIOTT
1800 Old Bayshore Highway
Burlingame, CA 94010
Tel.   (415) 692-9100
          (800) 228-9290 USA/CANADA

A world class hotel, the magnificent San Francisco Airport Marriott offers at once the convenience of being located at the San Francisco International Airport, while only minutes away from the excitement of San Francisco, as well as all Bay area business and industry.

Graciousness and luxury are the key words here. Full concierge services, a fully equipped health club with saunas, an indoor pool, rooms and suites lavishly equipped with special features and extra VIP services are but a few of Marriott's attributes. Business and entertainment needs are met with a selection from twenty-eight meeting rooms, five conference rooms and five meeting suites. Marriott also offers the largest Grand Ballroom between San Francisco and Los Angeles. Best of all, in-room video checkout allows for a hassle free departure in only minutes!

There is no need to go further for fine dining and entertainment. Gourmets will favor Veronique's, where fresh seafood, veal and lamb specialties are enhanced by over 100 wine selections. Orchids offers abundant Sunday brunch and luncheon buffets, and those wishing more excitement should visit either the View Lounge or the Bay Watch Lounge. This truly is a hotel to meet your every need.

HOLIDAY INN/CROWN PLAZA, Burlingame, California. Fine quality accommodations, restaurant and gift shop.

Art

POTCARRIER AMERICAN INDIAN ARTS
347 Primrose Road
Burlingame, CA 94010
Tel. (415) 348-0178
Hrs: Tue. - Sat. 10:00 a.m. - 5:00 p.m.
Also by appointment.

When it comes to American Indian Art, one name stands out among the rest. It's the name of one of the country's finest galleries specializing in American Indian artwork. Here you won't find imported copy pieces because only authentic, hand-made native American arts and crafts are on display at Potcarrier American Indian Arts in Burlingame.

At Potcarrier American Indian Arts there is a wide selection of Southwest Indian pottery, Navajo rugs, baskets, sand paintings, and Kachina dolls. Also, there are many fine examples of traditional and contemporary jewelry, primarily from the Navajo, Hopi, Zuni, and Santa Domingo Reservations. If you're looking for information, there is a large selection of books concerning Indian Art, or you can just ask the owners; they know the lore and can answer any question you might have.

If you are a collector, gift seeker, or just enjoy viewing beautiful artworks, then Potcarrier American Indian Art is sure to please. Being "Best Choice" is certainly a feather in their cap.

Bakery

COPENHAGEN BAKERY AND CAFE
1216 Burlingame Avenue
Burlingame, CA 94000
Tel. (415) 344-4937
Hrs: Mon. - Sat. 6:00 a.m. - 6:00 p.m.

What did Greek slaves teach to the Romans, and what did the Roman emperor Trajan do with this knowledge? Don't know? Well, the answers are baking and a school of baking, respectively. There's probably many other things you didn't know about baking, but that's not important. The important thing to know is where to go for baked goods, and that's Copenhagen Bakery.

At Copenhagen Bakery, whether it's bakery goods, sandwiches, soups or salads, everything is made with the freshest ingredients and the greatest care. That's right, it's more than just a bakery, Copenhagen's also has a cafe. A few of the sandwiches from the cafe are breast of turkey, Black Forest ham, smoked salmon, pastrami and many more. Some of the baked items include many types of bread, such as white, whole wheat, Squaw, French, light rye, pumpernickel and Dutch Crunch. As if that's not enough, they've also got cookies, cakes, homemade Danish and many other sweet treats.

Is it any wonder that Copenhagen Bakery has become the hub of activity in Burlingame? The Romans learned quite a bit from the Greeks, but had they taken lessons from Copenhagen's they wouldn't have slammed the oven door and fallen.

Candy

AIDA OPERA CANDIES
1375 Burlingame Avenue
Burlingame, CA 94010
Tel. (415) 344-3333
Hrs: Mon. - Sat. 10:00 a.m. - 6:00 p.m.
Visa, MasterCard and AMEX are accepted.
Mail orders are accepted.

Watch candy being made the "way Grandpa did" at this gourmet candy shop located in Burlingame's fashionable Crosby Commons shopping arcade. Aida Opera Candies has recently celebrated its fortieth anniversary of serving quality candies. Using old world techniques, the grandson of Anthony Perry Basques, who operated a little shop on Mission Street in San Francisco years ago, hand dips chocolates, making small batches and working in public view whenever possible.

Using the highest quality ingredients available, such as fresh butter and cream, natural flavorings, fine liqueurs and rich domestic and imported varieties of chocolate, the Basques family carries on the traditions of making exquisite candies. Among their specialties are raspberry rocky road, made with homemade marshmallow, dark chocolate, walnuts and raspberry flavoring. Aida Opera Candies is also famous for chocolate and divinity fudge, almond bark, fresh peanut brittle and a wide variety of truffles. Available also are unique seasonal gift items.

Named for a candy that was popular in the thirties, Aida Opera Candies creates a divine treat that springs forth fond memories of old fashioned delights.... just like grandpa used to make!

PRESTON'S CANDIES AND ICE CREAM
1170 Broadway
Burlingame, CA 94010
Tel. (415) 344-3254
Hrs: Mon. - Sat. 10:00 a.m. - 9:00 p.m.
Sunday 12:00 noon - 6:00 p.m.

Since 1946 Preston's has reigned as one of the supreme candy makers in the Bay Area. In fact, when you consider the numerous awards extended to Preston's it is impossible to deny their status as one of the select candy makers in the West. The small, handmade batches they produce ensure that personal attention is paid to each and every bite. Recent awards include the 1983, 1984, and 1985 Grand Champion Medallion of the International Truffle

Competition. The Best New Piece of Candy award was also won by Preston's in 1984 and 1985.

Truffle lovers simply must make Preston's their primary choice. Each of the eight selections features the unmistakable smoothness and melting quality for which Preston's is famous. The luscious Amaretto, chocolate chocolate, mocha, rum, Grand Marnier,cognac and raspberry varieties are gourmet candy delights that bring great satisfaction every time you try them. Tours of the production area are available by appointment. It is fascinating to watch them as they create, from scratch, their wonderful nuts and chews, haystacks, all milk and dark chocolates, coffee caramel, orange creams, non-pareils and other yummy confections.

Molded chocolate comes in the shape of an airplane, cable car, a horse, or... how about a Rolls Royce? There are chocolate greeting cards for thank yous, or anniversary, birthday or holiday. For the sports-minded, a catcher's mitt, baseball, football, bowling ball and pin, skis, and more... at Christmas time you can buy a 2-1/2 foot Santa, at Easter the 3 foot bunny. The list of choco-possibilities is endless.

There are cute novelty gift items for kids, like boats and trucks filled with candy. Adults enjoy the elegant crystal candy dishes, excellent receptacles for Preston's confections.

Preston's commitment to quality carries through to their high grade, homemade ice creams. Thirty flavors. By the cone, dish, or handpacked. In a sundae, milkshake, split or float. Ice cream elitists savor Preston's ice creams.

Coffee

COFFEE BISTRO
1170 Burlingame Avenue
Burlingame, CA 95125
Tel. (415) 347-1208
Hrs: Mon. - Thu. 7:00 a.m. - 9:00 p.m.
     Friday   7:00 a.m. - 11:00 p.m.
     Saturday   8:00 a.m. - 10:00 p.m.
     Sunday   10:00 a.m. - 8:00 p.m.

Almost everyone knows a good place to go to relax, study, meet friends, read or just sit quietly and think. However, when on the road, places like these are hard to find. So, when you're traveling in or around Burlingame, looking for an establishment like this, go to Coffee Bistro.

At Coffee Bistro, in an atmosphere of cozy white rooms laced with gray piping, you'll find a delightful menu full of homemade entrees. Their real stars are the delectable meatloaf and their scrumptious tuna salad. Also, there's

429

homemade coffee cake and delicious banana nut bread. Naturally, everything is made with the freshest ingredients and the greatest care is taken in the preparation of all. Of course, one can't forget the coffees, that rich brew that always seems to hit the right spot.

Places like Coffee Bistro are nice to find when in need of a good cup of coffee, a delicious meal and a relaxed, comfortable atmosphere. It's a "Best Choice" where you're always welcome.

Collectibles

THE DOLL PLACE
1202 Broadway
Burlingame, CA 94010
Tel. (415) 579-3939
Hrs: Tue. - Sat. 11:00 a.m. - 5:00 p.m.
All major credit cards accepted.

The Aztec emperor Montezuma, the Spanish conqueror Cortes and Queen Victoria, besides being prominent rulers, all had something in common. They all collected dolls. It is a very old hobby that not only exists today, but has recently surpassed stamps and coins to become the most popular collectible hobby in the United States.

At THE DOLL PLACE the wonderful world of modern doll-collecting awaits. Avid collectors and beginners, and even those looking for a toy, can choose from a wide selection in this interesting showroom.

The staff, each of whom brings with her the expertise gained from years of building personal collections, assist the visitor in choosing from a variety extending from a thirteen dollar Ginny doll to a wax-over-porcelain German doll valued at $2,900.

Ann Parsons, owner of The Doll Place, considers her shop an art gallery and delights in showing visitors the state-of-the-art contemporary doll collection that is housed there. There are also many cards and doll-related gifts including miniatures available to the shopper.

(See special invitation in the Appendix)

Delicatessen

BROTHERS DELICATESSEN AND RESTAURANT
1351 Howard Avenue
Burlingame, CA 94010
Tel. (415) 343-2311
Hrs: Sun. - Tue.   8:00 a.m. - 7:45 p.m.
     Wed. - Sat.   8:00 a.m. - 9:00 p.m.

At long last there is a real New York delicatessen on the West Coast, the likes of which will send your tastebuds into a frenzy. Here's a restaurant in the tradition of the finest delis in The Big Apple, with that ambiance native New Yorkers have come to take for granted.

The sandwiches are large and packed full of corn beef, lean and juicy pastrami and just the right amount of spice. And, would you believe, a half-doner Kosher pickle. What a rarity. Also featured are tasty Reuben sandwiches on toasted pumpernickel with melted Swiss cheese, sauerkraut and fantastic corn beef. The tongue sandwich is another treasure in these parts and featured at Brothers. Hungry yet? How about chicken in a pot or Matzo Brie cooked to perfection. And for dessert, there's the wonderful cheesecake, strudel and many other fine pastries.

Owners Sam and Kathy Hou, when asked how they do it, respond with, "We listen to what our customers have to say. We ask them what they like and how they like it prepared. The rest is easy. Great service and a big smile." Brothers Delicatessen and Restaurant, for that New York meal in more than a New York Minute.

Gift

BARE NECESSITIES
291 Primrose Road
Burlingame, CA 94010
Tel. (415) 344-3700
Hrs: Mon. - Sat. 10:15 a.m. - 5:30 p.m.

Did you know that the word perfume comes from the Latin roots "Per," meaning through, and "Fumus," meaning smoke? Perfumes have been found in the tombs of Egyptian pharaohs. They soaked fragrant woods and resins in water and oil, then rubbed the liquids on their bodies. However, since then, perfumes have become much more sophisticated and at Bare Necessities you can see why.

Bare Necessities is a charming shop with a wonderful selection of more than fifty essential perfume scents. And what's even better, after a few simple questions from Christine, the shop's owner, these scents can be custom blended into lotion to suit your skin type. Other items featured include bath salts, bath and shower gel, men's and women's soaps, men's shaving products, herbal skin care, gift baskets, home fragrances, hand painted clothing and much more.

Throughout the store are many antiques intermingled with the gift items, creating a charming atmosphere. Christine is a delightful lady who has a way of making you feel very welcome. Stop in for a visit and enjoy the heavenly scents of Bare Necessities.

ELECTRIC AVENUE
1350 Burlingame Avenue
Burlingame, CA 94010
Tel. (415) 343-2219
Hrs: Mon. - Fri.   10:00 a.m. - 8:00 p.m.
       Saturday   10:00 a.m. - 6:00 p.m.
       Sunday   12:00 noon - 5:00 p.m.
MasterCard, Visa and AMEX are accepted.

Gift shopping can be fun or it can be tedious. It really all depends on the shop that you're browsing through. If you happen to find a shop that has a little of everything, then it's great. Not only can you find that special gift, but you can have fun. Electric Avenue in Burlingame is one such shop where you're sure to enjoy yourself.

Here is the store of the eighties, retail entertainment, leading the way for others to follow. Electric Avenue with it's blue and gray decor is an ever changing gift shop. From the room in the rear featuring unusual and colorful wall hangings, to high quality gift items in the front, you're sure to find an item to please anyone. There are a wide selection of T-shirts, a neon gallery, Art Deco, gag gifts, tricks, fine paintings, nostalgic gifts, trend setting items and even inflatable air guitars which are only a few of the unique wares this gift shop has to offer.

To tell you more would ruin the surprises that are in store for you. Come and experience them soon at Electric Avenue. A place to shop for yourself or someone else while having fun.

(See special invitation in the Appendix.)

FOUR GREEN FIELDS, 1107 Burlingame Avenue, Burlingame, California. High quality Irish imports. A very good selection.

KING CHARLES WORLDLY GOODS, 1217 Burlingame Avenue, Burlingame, California. An excellent gift shop with an unusual selection of items.

SERPIL'S
1429 Burlingame Avenue
Burlingame, CA 94010
Tel. (415) 342-1114
Hrs: Mon. - Sat.   10:00 a.m. - 5:30 p.m.
     Sunday   12:00 noon - 5:30 p.m.

Everyone knows of the country of Spain, but do they know that Spain is famous for Llardro´®? Llardro´® is a beautiful, skillfully-crafted ceramic, displaying various scenes of life. Often humorous, and always eye-catching, Llardro´® is definitely treasured in a collection or individually. Where can you find one? At Serpil's Distinctive Gift Shop. Serpil's carries the largest selection of Llardro´® on the West Coast - approximately 400 pieces at any one time.

The gift shop also features other high quality gifts, such as French Crystal by Lalique, American Porcelain by Boehm, David Winter Cottage Collections, Andrea Birds and Swarovskii pieces (made with 32% lead crystal.)

Now that you know where to get a Llardro´®, (especially Limited Editions) come in and browse. At Serpil's you can surround yourself with a beautiful part of Spain that would have made Don Quixote envious. The service at Serpil's is friendly, and they aim to please everyone.

(See special invitation in the Appendix.)

Jewelry

WHITE DOVE JEWELRY EXCHANGE
270 Lorton Avenue
Burlingame, CA 94010
Tel. (415) 347-3540
Hrs: Tue. - Sat. 10:00 a.m. - 6:00 p.m.

Jewelry has been a means of displaying wealth and status since time began. Fascination with rare minerals and gemstones has, at oft times,

433

amplified the quality of mankind's greed, as well as, generosity. However, leave these lofty thoughts to the philosopher and king. Because jewelry doesn't require abstract thoughts; it just requires an eye for beauty, and you're sure to get an eye-full at White Dove Jewelry Exchange.

This store has a tremendous variety of diamonds, gemstones, pearls, gold, silver, and many other pieces of jewelry. Several items on display are hand-made by the owner including antique reproductions. Some of the services offered by White Dove Jewelry Exchange are: custom mounting, jewelry repair, and video appraisals. All merchandise and repair are 100% satisfaction guaranteed.

At white Dove Jewelry Exchange there is an atmosphere of soft lights, plants, and large sofas. Customer comfort is important to them, and they are considered more valuable than any stone in the store. So you see, the king and philosopher are thinking along the wrong avenue, they should be on the one where White Dove Jewelry Exchange is located.

(See special invitation in the appendix)

Kitchen Articles

THE OCCASION PLACE
275-277 Primrose Road
Burlingame, CA, 94010
Tel. (415) 342-8396
Hrs: Mon. - Sat.   10:00 a.m. - 6:00 p.m.
    Sunday and evenings by appointment.

The first thing a chef will tell you about a kitchen is that it has to be well stocked; you can't open a can without an opener, nor can you boil water without a pot. The second necessity for a kitchen is a person who knows how to cook. Without these prerequisites a kitchen is just another room. The Occasion Place, seeing a need for this, provides the equipment and training needed for a first-class kitchen.

When you enter The Occasion Place, you will be amazed at the tremendous selection of cooking utensils and other accessories they carry. It is stocked, wall to wall, with every cooking convenience imagined. You name it, The Occasion Place has it. To the rear of the store is the kitchen, completely outfitted and ready to cook. In this kitchen, students are taught by the area's finest professional cooks, who take their jobs seriously.

Schedules and reservations for classes can be obtained by phone or picked up at the front desk. If you want to improve your cooking skills in a grand fashion, or need anything for the kitchen, stop by The Occasion Place. They're sure to whip something up for you.

(See special invitation in the Appendix.)

Restaurants

CAFE RICO, 1219 Burlingame Avenue, Burlingame, California. A charming place offering good food, espresso and delectible desserts.

ENTRE, 525 California Drive, Burlingame, California. Full range menu. Eat here, or take-out.

MARIA'S PASTA, 1464 Fox Plaza Lane, Burlingame, California. Best pasta take-out in the Bay area

PAYTAYA PRINCESS, 430 Airport Boulevard, Burlingame, California. Features Thai cuisine. Superb.

Wine

PRESTIGE FINE WINE & LIQUORS
1300 Burlingame Avenue
Burlingame, CA, 94040
Tel. (415) 342-0570
Hrs: Mon. - Wed.   9:00 a.m. - 9:00 p.m.
       Thu.- Sat.   9:00 a.m. -10:00 p.m.
       Sunday   10:00 a.m. - 6:00 p.m.

Wine generally is divided into six classes: appetizer, red, pink, white, dessert, and sparkling. It's value can range from almost nothing, to extremely high. Over one billion gallons were produced in France last year. Wine is an important subject in Europe, as well as, Northern California, and Prestige Fine Wines & Liquors in Burlingame, is one of the centers of attraction for this interesting topic.

Prestige Fine Wine & Liquors boasts of having the largest selection of California wines in the Bay Area, as well as an extensive shelving of quality champagnes. For the connoisseur, they also deal in vintage ports, some dating back to 1943. If you are an imported beer drinker, this store can satisfy any discriminating taste, having beers from Germany, Belgium, France, Finland, England, Australia, and many other countries. In all, over 200 varieties from around the world. Even bar supplies and party accompaniments are available to equip the home bar.

Prestige Fine Wines & Liquors is a varied store, in as much as they carry over 2,500 video tapes for rental. Whether it's sitting at home with that special person, or for a momentous occasion, this wine store can supply for that delightful touch at which the Europeans are adept.

(See special invitation in the Appendix.)

Daly City

San Francisco borders Daly City to the north, and the Pacific Ocean makes its west boundary. For many years farms dominated this area with lettuce, artichokes and plants grown for the floral trade. Rapid growth has propelled population over the 80,000 mark as it becomes a suburban residence for people working in the city or in the plants of neighboring South San Francisco.

The 1906 fire brought exciting times to this farming community named after John D. Daly, a dairy farmer. Hundreds fled to the hills here to watch the city burn. There was a more desperate gathering in 1859 when holders of original land grants attempted to remove squatters from the land. They built a fort, located a cannon, and chased off the owners. It wasn't until 1866 and a California supreme court ruling that title to Daly City became clear.

South San Francisco is an industrial giant with about 50,000 residents located east of Daly City. G.F. Swift, the meat king, started the town with a packing company. When the Fuller Paint Company opened a factory in the 1890s the industrialization was set, and by the turn of the century steel mills were fabricating beams and plates for the area's growing ship-building industry.

Attractions

Serramonte Shopping Center is one of the Bay Area's most popular. Located on Serramonte Boulevard off I-280, it features suburban branches of many San Francisco stores.

Thornton State Beach is shared with San Francisco. **Fort Funston** , established during the Spanish American War, was part of this former military reservation. Skyline Boulevard starts its southward journey here. A famous duel between U.S. Senator David Broderick and Judge David Terry was fought on the county line in 1859. There are markers and a plate telling the story of the senator's death.

Oyster Point Marina, on the bay side of Forbes Industrial Park in South San Francisco, includes a large park behind the wharfs which attract people with picnic lunches from the nearby office buildings.

San Francisco's **Cow Palace** is actually in San Mateo county, located on Geneva Avenue off the Bayshore Freeway. Sporting events and livestock shows which go back to the roots of South San Francisco's stockyard days are scheduled at the Cow Palace.

For more information, contact the **Daly City Chamber of Commerce**, 244 Ninety Second Avenue, telephone 755-8526

Foster City

This small community which hangs on the tide flats at the west approach of the San Mateo Bridge, is a tribute to the land use planners and developers of the 1960s. They conceived of a planned community, and made it work. Incorporated in 1971, it now has about 24,000 residents scattered among its water-oriented housing, connected by bike paths and neatly laid out streets.

Over 500 businesses are located on the commercial and industrial land laid out by the developers of Metro Center, Vintage Park and Bridge Landing. At last count, Foster City had nine churches, 9,448 residential housing units including rentals and plush waterfront condominiums.

Attractions

Bridge Landing is being developed as a restaurant and office site with views of the metropolitan skyline. It is at the foot of the San Mateo Bridge, with the master plan calling for three restaurants and a seven-story hotel at the intersection of Third Avenue and the state highway which leads across the bridge.

For information, contact the **Foster City Chamber of Commerce**, 1124 East Hillsdale Boulevard, suite 116. Telephone 573-7600.

Restaurants

THE CUSTOM HOUSE, 979 Edgewater Drive, Foster City, California. Decor suggests a customs post in India, superb views, mesquite-broiled steak and seafood are house specialties.

BEETHOVEN'S PIZZA
1080 D Shell Boulevard
Foster City, CA 94404
Tel. (415) 570-2253
Hrs: Mon. - Thu.   11:30 a.m. - 9:00 p.m.
       Fri. - Sat.   11:30 a.m. - 11:00 p.m.
       Sunday   4:00 p.m. - 9:00 p.m.

If Beethoven walked the Earth today, his Teutonic tastebuds would light up at their first test of this pizza generated in his name. Beethoven's Pizza has one of the finest pizzas on the peninsula. You can order it by phone and have it delivered free to your door within thirty minutes, or you can visit the restaurant to enjoy your meal.

When first entering Beethoven's Pizza, you will be greeted by very serene Italian decor with soft classical music playing in the background. One of the best pizzas served at Beethoven's Pizza is the classic combo, an eight topping delight. You can create your own from the extensive list of fresh toppings, including pepperoni, pineapple, olives, onions, salami, sausage, ground beef and so many others that you may find it necessary to choose. There's an abundant salad bar plus an extended menu, along with beer and wine or mineral water to go with the meal.

Beethoven may have been deaf, but there are no indications that his taste buds were diminished. It's too bad he's not here to partake of this superb pizza. Who knows what new symphonies might be inspired.

(See special invitation in the Appendix.)

SENOR PEPE'S
1288 E Hillsdale Boulevard
Foster City, CA 94404
Tel. (415) 349-7373
Hrs: Sun. - Thu.   11:30 a.m. - 10:00 p.m.
       Fri. - Sat.   11:30 a.m. - 11:00 p.m.
All major credit cards are accepted.

Friars and caballeros once trod the El Camino Real (King's Highway) along the California coastal valleys. In a land rich with Mexican lore it is only fitting to tether your burro outside the welcome walls of Señor Pepe's in Foster City. Enter into a land south of the border where no expense has been spared in recreating the feel of Old Mexico. Out on the veranda, stroll in the evening air while enjoying the breathtaking view overlooking a lovely lagoon.

The dinners are in harmony with the decor, prepared from age old recipes imported from Mexico's señoras. Each dish is individually prepared using only the finest and freshest of ingredients. All of your traditional favorites are on the menu and so are many other *comidas muy buena* like Carne Asada and Camarones a la Mazatlan.

Senor Pepe's in Foster City only the first in three locations in the Bay Area; so *amigo* be sure to spur your burro to any or all of the locations including San Mateo and Cupertino.

Half Moon Bay

Accommodations

HALF MOON BAY LODGE
2400 S Cabrillo Highway
Half Moon Bay, CA 94019
Tel.   (415) 726-9000
        (800) 528-1234
        (800) 368-2468
Visa, Mastercard , Diner's Club, Carte Blanche, Discover
and AMEX are accepted.

Major hotel luxury and small town coastal ambiance create a unique vacation opportunity only thirty-five miles south of San Francisco. Half Moon Bay Lodge is a member of Best Western and has received the AAA Four Diamond Award, making it your "Best Choice" for accommodations. Snuggled comfortably on coast Highway 1, the Half Moon Bay Lodge offers its guests large rooms, king and queen size beds, direct dial phones, color cable TV, in-room refrigerator, private balconies, heated pool, indoor whirlpool spa, and (in one-third of all the rooms) romantic fireplaces. The hotel is close to private beaches, beautiful meadows, and horseback riding facilities.

Located on the fourth fairway of the Half Moon Bay golf course designed by Arnold Palmer himself, the Half Moon Bay Lodge is an excellent base from which to explore the rugged California coastline and then relax and unwind in the luxury of this fine hotel.

(See special invitation in the Appendix.)

Bed and Breakfast

MILL ROSE INN
615 Mill Street
Half Moon Bay, CA 94019
Tel. (415) 726-9794
Visa, Mastercard and American Express are accepted.

There are a number of lodging establishments along the peninsula coastal region, with bed and breakfast inns being the newest additions. In Half Moon Bay, the first bed and breakfast and without a doubt, still the finest is the Mill Rose Inn.

Outdoors there is a beautiful English style garden that fills the air with the scent of over 200 varieties of roses, as well as other flowers. In the sitting room inside the main entrance you will find luxury highlighted by the large, comforting fireplace, elaborate furniture and singing canaries.

The true luxury and charm of Mill Rose Inn can't be fully appreciated until you are introduced to your room. Every room is personally decorated by the owners and hosts Eve and Terry Baldwin to be like a scene out of a romantic fantasy. All of the rooms are named after varieties of roses and have private entrances, beautifully appointed private baths, king or queen sized brass or canopy beds, fireplaces, complimentary brandy and sherry, antique furnishings, telephones, color cable television, plush robes and a refrigerator with complimentary beverages. In addition, each room has it's own features such as handpainted tiling, oversize tubs for two and a broad scattering of live plants, flowers and decorative watercolors.

In the morning, you can enjoy a delicious champagne breakfast with fresh fruits and juices, freshly baked French pastries, coffee, plus quiche, omelets or crepes. Breakfast can be brought to your room or you can enjoy the lovely breakfast room overlooking the garden. In the afternoons, Eve and Terry serve complimentary wine and cheese. Also included in your stay is the use of the enclosed garden, gazebo whirlpool spa. The Baldwin's suggest you reserve a time for the use of the spa because to assure privacy only one party is allowed in at a time.

For a romantic, luxurious getaway, be sure to call the Baldwins and enjoy this heavenly bed and breakfast.

OLD THYME INN, 779 Main Street, Half Moon Bay, California. A historic Victorian home, beautifully restored. Complimentary wine in the evenings, full breakfast in the morning.

Book

BAY BOOK AND TOBACCO COMPANY
Strawflower Village Shopping Center
80 N Cabrillo Highway
Half Moon Bay, CA 94019
Tel. (415) 726-3488
Hrs: Mon. - Thur., Sat.   10:00 a.m. - 7:00 p.m.
         Friday   10:00 a.m. - 9:00 p.m.
         Sunday   11:00 a.m. - 6:00 p.m.
Visa and MasterCard are accepted.

When Kevin Magee was growing up near Half Moon Bay, there weren't any bookstores in town or even a decent library. Of course there have been a lot of changes made in the area in past years, not the least of which is that Half Moon Bay now has one of the best bookstores in the entire Bay Area, owned and operated by Kevin Magee.

When opening his store in 1979, Kevin wanted to combine his love of reading with his love of fine tobacco, but knew it was unusual to put the two together. Kevin knew that the only way it could work was to maintain high standards in all sections of Bay Book and Tobacco Company. This unique combination has received praise not only from pipe smokers, lovers of fine cigars and bibliophiles, but also from the wholly independent magazine *Consumer Checklist,* which rate Bay Book and Tobacco Co. as one of the ten best bookstores in the Bay Area.

For the discriminating fan of fine tobacco, Bay Book and Tobacco Company has a selection of the world's best cigars stored in a walk-in humidor. All of the cigars are the finest, hand rolled varieties imported from around the globe. Kevin has created eight of his own blends of top grade pipe tobaccos, naming them for local parks and towns. All the necessary accessories are available including a choice collection of briar pipes.

The selection of books is even more complete and impressive. Bay Book's carries over 30,000 titles without making customers feel cramped. As a result of careful, direct from the publisher ordering (a rarity for bookstores) the staff has learned to fill each section with a wide enough variety that even some specialty stores can't compete. Every staff member goes through an extensive training program so that they can help you find any book in the store and recommend related or alternative titles.

Kevin and his staff strive to provide the best service possible, so if there is something you are having difficulty locating, they will special order any book in print and assure you of its prompt delivery.

Luggage

BUFFALO SHIRT CO.
315 Main Street
Half Moon Bay, CA 94019
Tel.   (415) 726-3194
Hrs: Mon.-Sat.   10:00 a.m.-6:00 p.m.
          Sunday   10:00 a.m.-5:00 p.m.
Visa, Mastercard, and AMEX are accepted.

An unswerving dedication to quality and versatile, useful products have made the Buffalo Shirt Company a national success story.

Owner, entrepreneur, Bob Mascall opened the Buffalo Shirt Company retail store in 1978 when the demand for his handmade, sturdy canvas bags outgrew his home workshop. By adding several lines of top quality, natural fiber clothing (Pendleton, Woolrich, Timberline), enlarging his canvas bag variety, and mail order mass marketing, Bob rapidly built his successful enterprise. Today those same canvas bags are individually made by caring craftspeople on the premises along with luggage, "carpenter's bags", back packs, shave kits, log carriers, and briefcases all made of 100% cotton fabric in a wide variety of colors and with a lifetime money back guarantee (for the original purchaser). Buffalo Shirt Company also produces its own line of canvas clothing made of a light weight yet extremely durable cotton fabric. The store features a section devoted to locally grown and produced products and foods.

While strolling through Half Moon Bay, stop at Buffalo Shirt Company where quality, durability, and value made this store a business success.

Park

RANCHO CANADA VERDE
2700 Purissima Creek Road
Half Moon Bay, CA 94019
Tel. (415) 726-6011
Visa and Mastercard are accepted.

The world takes on new meaning when viewed from the back of a horse. Time seems to slow down and much more of the unnoticed beauty of Nature becomes visible as horse and rider make their way through forest and meadow. Rancho Canada Verde offers trail riding through some of the most beautiful country in California. Trails meander through the 650 acre Rancho Canada Verde ranch and through much of the adjacent 1,800 acre Purissima Creek Open Space District. Manager Bruce Hamilton and his staff work with the horses and riders to guarantee that before they hit the trail, they work smoothly together as a team. The horses are gentle, healthy, responsive, and well trained to insure an exciting and safe journey. Choose from hourly trail rides to overnight camp outs at an authentic former cowboy bunkhouse. Western and English riding instruction is also available from the competent staff.

Whatever your riding ability, from tenderfoot to experienced rider, horseback riding at Rancho Canada Verde is just what the doctor ordered to recapture the tranquility of the natural, unhurried rhythm of life on the trail.

Restaurants

McCOFFEE
522 Main Street
Half Moon Bay, CA 94019
Tel. (415) 726-6241
Hrs: Mon. - Sun. 9:00 a.m. - 6:00 p.m.
Visa and MasterCard are accepted.

Every small town has its special place or "hangout" where the locals comfortably congregate and Half Moon Bay is no exception. In Half Moon Bay the hangout is McCoffee, owned and operated by Elizabeth McCaughey.

As in the name McCoffee is a gourmet coffee store but it is also much more. Since 1976, it has been one of the main social centers of the community. Every morning dozens of local people drop in for an espresso, coffee and freshly baked croissants. In the afternoon, many of them return for great sandwiches made with quality meats and a choice selection of cheeses. And

443

throughout the day a steady stream of patrons pick up fresh-roasted coffee beans, imported chocolates, imported cheeses, teas, pates, and wines or come by just to sit at a table and soak up the heady community atmosphere. A fully operational old fashioned soda fountain has been added to further enhance the friendly environment.

For the traveller with a hunger for the true taste of coastal life, McCoffee presents a tasty slice of the authentic Half Moon Bay living.

THE SWEDISH PLACE
2320 South Cabrillo Highway
Half Moon Bay, CA 94019
Tel. (415) 726-7322
Hrs: Mon. - Fri.   11:00 a.m. - 10:00 p.m.
       Saturday   8:00 a.m. - 10:00 p.m.
       Sunday   10:00 a.m. - 10:00 p.m.
Visa, Mastercard, AMEX, and other major credit cards
 are accepted.

In 1981, Mr. Magnus Helberg looked at a quaint gift shop in Half Moon Bay and envisioned creating a restaurant which would capture the flavor and spirit of his native Gotenberg, Sweden. After some negotiations, Magnus prevailed upon the gift shop owners to transform their store into a classic model of a country Swedish restaurant complete with manicured grounds, antique light fixtures, Swedish flags, and a large stone fireplace.

Having been a chef in Sweden, Magnus prepares traditional Swedish favorites such as Swedish meatballs, Gravlax, cabbage rolls, and many dishes he has created such as filet of beef stuffed with Gorgonzola cheese. Seafood, however, is what makes the Swedish Place such a standout with the locals. Your waiter will not only recite for you the catch of the day but will ask you how you would like it prepared (poached, fried, served with caviar, garnished with crayfish sauce are only some of the options). Before leaving be sure and visit the gift shop on the patio and view the beautiful painting of a street scene from Magnus' home town.

In Half Moon Bay, visit with Magnus at the Swedish Place and let him delight you with the culinary creations from his native land and from his own imagination.

Wine

OBESTER WINERY
12341 Highway 92
Half Moon Bay, CA 94019
Tel. (415) 726-9463
Hrs: Mon. - Thu.   12:00 noon - 5:00 p.m
          Fri. - Sun.   10:00 a.m. - 5:00 p.m.
Visa, MasterCard and AMEX are accepted.

Situated just half an hour from San Francisco Airport on the scenic drive to Half Moon Bay is Obester Winery. Half the fun is the beautiful drive and the rest awaits you upon arrival. Paul and Sandra Obester will be your hosts and delight in showing you around their lovely winery.

The rural setting invites you to relax and enjoy a picnic on the tables that are available while you sample the award winning wines that the Obesters produce. Every wine from 1977 to 1985 has been awarded a gold medal for excellence. The varieties of wine are Chardonnay, Johannisberg Reisling, Gewurtztraminer, white Zinfandel and Cabernet Sauvignon.

Be sure to visit the Obesters and sample the wines in the warm and friendly tasting room and discovery for yourself the simple truth about fine wines; that is, a good wine is a good wine because it tastes good from first sip to the last drop.

La Honda

Sport

TROUTMERE, Highway 84, La Honda, California. Perfect introduction to fishing for all ages. Poles, gear, bait provided. Catch is cleaned and packaged for you.

Menlo Park

Accommodations

STANFORD PARK HOTEL
100 El Camino Real
Menlo Park, CA 94025
Tel.   (800)   368-2468
       (415)   322-1234
All major credit cards are accepted.

Step into a lavish world that will put you at your best for business or pleasure. On the Bay Area peninsula, first class accommodations are few, but the Stanford Park Hotel is among them.

This Four-Diamond hotel combines personalized service with lavish decor and architecture. Outside the building shines elegance with its fountain, and its strong architectural style using cedar shingles, dormer windows and copper covered gables. The hotel is built around a series of courtyards and most of the rooms overlook at least one of them, providing a peaceful, calming view. Inside the rooms, many with vaulted ceilings and fireplaces, you find amenities such as, a dry bar, two telephones, and even a computer hookup. You have access to the pool, whirlpool spa, sauna and an indoor exercise room. If you need to go out for the day, the staff will arrange a free shuttle service to many of the area's business centers, shopping areas, restaurants and attractions in Palo Alto, Menlo Park and Stanford University. Although room service is available, you are invited to come down and dine in the hotel's excellent restaurant, The Palm Cafe, which serves Continental and California cuisine.

Thanks to Stanford Park, you can step up to first class accommodations on the Peninsula.

Antiques

KAREN'S ANTIQUES
712 Santa Cruz Avenue
Menlo Park, CA 94025
Tel. (415) 326-9404
Hrs: Mon. - Sat. 10:00 a.m. - 5:00 p.m.
Visa and MasterCard are accepted.

When Karen Wiebel decided to sell some of her family's antique glass, something became very clear to her. Few dealers knew much about this speciality.

With a commitment to knowing her merchandise Karen started her own shop in 1975. Today it is one of the largest independently owned antique shops on the Peninsula. There are 4,000 square feet of show space. The store has gone well beyond glass ware and is separated into a series of rooms, each furnished with antiques from a different style, era or setting. Browse through bedrooms, dining rooms, and sitting rooms and select from pieces of American Country to French or English formal.

To insure having something for everyone and every budget, Karen makes two buying trips to England every year. That means the level of quality remains consistently high. Whether its fine furniture or glassware, porcelains or collectibles, the quality is what shines through at Karen's Antiques.

(See special invitation in the Appendix.)

Book

KEPLER'S BOOKS AND MAGAZINES
821 El Camino Real
Menlo Park, CA 94025
Tel. (415) 324-4321
Hrs: Mon. - Thu.   10:00 a.m. - 11:00 p.m.
     Fri. - Sat.   10:00 a.m. - 12:00 midnight
     Sunday   9:00 a.m. - 10:00 p.m.
Visa and MasterCard are accepted.

In 1955, pacifist Roy Kepler opened the first paperback bookstore on the San Francisco peninsula. Kepler's belief in freedom of speech and thought ran directly contrary to the popularized paranoia of the mid 1950s. A time when certain ideas were considered "dangerous."

Kepler's philosophy was reflected in his bookstore. Kepler's Books, in the 1960s, offered alternatives to the youth of the day, both in substance of the books stocked and in the style of its operation. It was a happening place. Kepler's was one of the few places where you could walk out with a London Times in one hand and Chairman Mao's "little red book" in the other.

Today, Kepler's continues to stock books of every category of human thought and for every stretch of the imagination. In all, some 50,000 titles in 140 categories fill the shelves. Kepler's also offers a large selection of foreign and domestic magazines and newspapers.

As part of Kepler's ongoing events, quality authors of national and regional renown, regularly go to the store to read from and discuss their books. Several local literary and poetry groups, including Stanford University's Stegner Fellows attend meetings at Kepler's.

Furnishings

LA BELLE FRANCE
705 Santa Cruz Avenue
Menlo Park, CA 94025
Tel. (415) 323-6766
Hrs: Mon. - Sat. 10:00 a.m. - 5:30 p.m.
All major credit cards are accepted.

Ever dream of filling your home with 18th and 19th Century French style furniture? And then dream you could do so for about the same cost as ordinary furniture? Well pinch your self, it's all possible at La Bell France.

Dominique Sanchot had that same dream. After working for several years as an interior designer, she learned that a small number of craftsmen and artisans working in France were specially licensed to create fine reproductions of period furniture from the Louvre. She located these furniture makers and brought some of their work back to California where she opened La Belle France. Because the pieces are not actual antiques, the prices are affordable. They also have amenities King Louie could never dream of, like the 18th century armoire that opens into a a fully equipped entertainment center and wet bar.

Visit La Belle France and find fine French furniture of your favorite era, and have it in a pinch.

(See special invitation in the Appendix.)

Pizza

APPLEWOOD INN
1001 El Camino Real
Menlo, Park, CA 94025
Tel. (415) 324-3486
Hrs: Tue.-Sat.   5:00 p.m. - 11:00 p.m.
      Monday   5:00 p.m. - 10:00 p.m.
      Sunday   5:00 p.m. - 9:00 p.m.

If your style is gourmet, but your taste buds say "pizza," Applewood Inn has the solution for you, caviar pizza and champagne.

Of course if your style is more like traditional pizza, there's that too, but with some of the best crust you've tasted. Complement it with one of eighteen imported beers. For something different, but still very American try the Dallas pizza, featuring BBQ beef, chili, mushrooms, onion and green pepper. Also on the menu is a wide array of fresh pastas, delicious sandwiches, hamburgers, polish sausage and hamburgers. A "must-try" is the Apple Inn's Hungarian goulash with langos, a lightly salted traditional Hungarian fried bread.

Be a little cavalier, have caviar on your pizza at this unusual, "Best Choice" restaurant.

Records

CLASSICAL WAX, 827 El Camino Real, Menlo Park, California. The Bay Area's most complete collection of classical and classical jazz recordings available. Albums, cassettes and compact discs. Special orders for hard to locate recordings.

Restaurants

BRITISH BANKERS CLUB, 1090 El Camino Real, Menlo Park, California. Continental cuisine and a popular lounge.

DAL BAFFO
878 Santa Cruz Avenue
Menlo Park, CA 94025
Tel. (415) 325-1588
Hrs: Lunch   Tue. - Fri.   11:30 a.m. - 2:30 p.m.
      Dinner   Tue. - Thu.   6:00 p.m. - 10:00 p.m.
                Fri. - Sat.   6:00 p.m. - 10:30 p.m.

If a restaurant's wine list is an indication of overall quality, Dal Baffo ranks among the finest. Winner of the 1985 and 1986 Grand Award from The Wine Spectator for having one of the outstanding restaurant wine lists in America. These are not the only honors.

Chef Vincenzo LoGrasso came directly from New York's Waldorf Astoria to open the Dal Baffo with his wife Catherine. The elegant decor features Laura Ashley wall covering and fine furniture. Diners enjoy the ambiance of cozy arched alcoves. The menu is very European with a superb selection of seafood, veal, pasta, beef, lamb and chicken dishes. Some of the intriguing options are frog legs sauteed provencale, swordfish livornesse and breast of pheasant.

With 600 wines to choose from, ranging in price from about $10 to $1,000, you know why Dal Baffo is a winner.

LE POT-AU-FEU, 1149 El Camino Real, Menlo Park, California 94025. Fine French country cuisine, featuring a new menu every day with the freshest California ingredients available.

THE ACORN, 1120 Crane Avenue, Menlo Park, California. Mediterranean cuisine featuring gourmet specialties from France, Italy and Greece.

YUEN YUNG, 639 Santa Cruz Avenue, Menlo Park, California. You'll find Szechuan-style specialities and a daily dim-sum lunch at this popular peninsula restaurant.

Milbrae

CLARION HOTEL. SAN FRANCISCO AIRPORT
401 E Millbrae Avenue
Milbrae, CA 94030
Tel.   (415) 692-6363
        (800) CLARION

The Clarion really is an island a world apart! Eight acres of lavishly landscaped gardens, tree-shaded walks, and heated swimming pool provide an island atmosphere to the surrounding 228 spacious guest rooms and suites. The outdoors follows you inside to the lobby where floor-to-ceiling windows, redwood paneling and rich earth tones complement the hotel's gracious and friendly service.

Enjoy the end of a busy day with cocktails and hors d'oeuvres overlooking the garden in the Rendezvous. Follow with an intimate dinner in the Heathstone, specializing in fine food. Later, in the Lounge, enjoy cocktails and dancing. Try the Nob Hill Court for a knockout Sunday Brunch. Snackers will be accommodated in the off-hours Le Cafe. Or, if you crave the goodies offered by an authentic San Francisco Deli, visit Sac's Third Avenue.

Central to the race track, Marine World, as well as Candlestick Park, the Cowpalace, and downtown San Francisco, the Clarion Hotel is a peninsular island paradise: the airport hotel with "that certain savoir-FLAIR." It's California at its best.

Restaurant

MI TEQUILA, 1595 El Camino Real, Milbrae, California. Mexican food served in a warm, friendly atmosphere that fairly jumps.

Miramar

Restaurant

MIRAMAR BEACH INN, Highway 1, Miramar, California. Coastside night-life center of the Bay Area, featuring an ocean view, fresh seafood and a calendar of live entertainment from dancing to comedy.

Moss Beach

Restaurant

MOSS BEACH DISTILLERY
Beach Way and Ocean Boulevard
Moss Beach, CA 94038
Tel. (415) 728-5595
Hrs: Mon. - Thu.   4:00 p.m. - 10:00 p.m.
         Fri. - Sat.   4:00 p.m. - 11:00 p.m.
         Sunday   10:30 a.m. - 2:00 p.m.
                           4:30 p.m. - 10:00 p.m.
All major credit cards are accepted.

There are several theories as to why Moss Beach Distillery has remained popular for almost six decades. Some feel it is the colorful history dating back to the prohibition days when the restaurant was a retreat for silent movie stars, politicians and notorious rumrunners. Although all of the activities in and around Moss Beach Distillery are now legal, much of the flavor and bustling atmosphere of the olden days still survives.

At Moss Beach Distillery, set atop a cliff high above Seal Cove, every table in the dining room offers wonderful opportunities to watch colorful sunsets on the Pacific, the steady pounding of the surf and an occasional passing whale. Of course, no restaurant could continue to enjoy such sustained popularity without serving exceptional food, and this unique restaurant has some of the best on the West Coast. Owners David and Patricia Andrews insist on only the freshest seafood and meats for their restaurant, and go out of their way to obtain a variety of seafood selections from around the globe, including Australia, New Zealand, Alaska, Hawaii and New England. Chef Mullins then performs his wizardry, creating special sauces and cooking each entree to perfection.

Whatever your reason for visiting Moss Beach Distillery, it will only take one visit for you to decide to come back again. Whether you prefer the history, the view, the ambiance, or the dining, the important thing is that they are all here for you to enjoy.

Pacifica

Gift

COMING ATTRACTIONS BOUTIQUE
1345 Linda Mar Center
Pacifica, CA 94044
Tel. (415) 355-1346
Hrs: Tue. - Fri.   10:00 a.m. - 6:00 p.m.
Saturday   10:00 a.m. - 5:00 p.m.
Sunday   12:00 noon - 4:00 p.m. (Seasonal)

Have you ever heard of a store being opened by popular demand? Well, that's exactly what happened with Coming Attractions Boutique in Pacifica. After six years of Christmas boutiques and having gift parties at the homes of their friends, Ginny Johnson and Carol Salinas finally decided that their selection was getting too large to cart around in their cars anymore, and so were forced to either open a store or cut back the options they could offer their customers.

Deciding to maintain their services, they found an available space in a small shopping center and let their many friends know they were ready for business. The result is a quality gift shop mainly featuring Californian arts and crafts with a selection for every taste and budget. Some of the items you can expect to find in Coming Attractions include homemade candies, beautiful ceramics, porcelains, Fenton glass, stained glass, scented soaps, quilts, lace decorations, potpourri, coffee mugs, a wide variety of country items and much, much more.

If you can't find something you're looking for, simply ask Carol or Ginny. They will be more than happy to put out feelers and do a little searching to keep their customers satisfied. From gift parties to a quality shop, success has always had a way of showing itself in a grand fashion. Stop by Coming Attractions Boutique and see what the coming attractions are for you.

Pescadero

Restaurant

DINELLI'S, 1956 Pescadero Road, Pescadero, California. Greek and American home cooking for breakfast, lunch and dinner. Souvlakis, gyros, soups and fruit turnovers are specialties.

453

Portola Valley

Candy

KONDITOREI
284 Ladera Country Shopper on Alpine Road
Portola Valley, CA 94025
Tel. (415) 854-8616
Hrs: Mon. - Sat.   8:00 a.m. - 6:30 p.m.
       Sundays   10:00 a.m. - 5:00 p.m.

In German, konditorei means confectionery shop. In Portola Valley, Konditorei is a shop that manages to be many things to many people, especially a place to be with friends in a calm atmosphere while enjoying a favorite treat.

Owned and operated by Nick and Patty Badiee, Konditorei is many shops in one. Within their doors, you can choose between ice cream, frozen yogurt, gelato, pastries, imported chocolate truffles, or cake to snack on. You can relax with a hot cup of espresso, cappuccino, tea, or fresh ground coffee, or buy a pound of one of the fifteen varieties of roasted coffee beans to take with you. You can shop to fill a gift basket with a selection of imported foods and chocolates, novelty candies, stuffed animals, coffee and tea accessories, local books, gift certificates, and more. You can even come in and just have a friendly chat with one of the many regular local patrons.

More than anything else, Konditorei is an elegant version of a friendly country store. Only five minutes from Highway 280, Konditorei offers a relaxed atmosphere that has many of the area residents using the shop as a central meeting place. The walls are often decorated with works of local artists, and although most people are happy with the comfortable cane and oak chairs around the glass-top tables, some of the customers prefer sitting in the store's big rocking chair.

Konditorei is the center of many of the area's social events, especially those for the local children. Every holiday, from Valentines Day to Christmas, the Badiee's participate in special festivities, one of the favorites being every Halloween when a local storyteller is brought in to entertain all the children between ages 5 to 105.

Redwood City

Among the residential communities of the peninsula, Redwood City stands out for its longevity, and its industrial capacity. About 350 manufacturing plants are located in the city. It has the only deep water port on the entire southern reach of San Francisco Bay.

It was that water access, which used to extend far inland up Redwood Slough, which gave the city its name and its first business even before the gold rush put the local economy in high gear. Timber, milled on the Mexican ranchos in the foothills, was put aboard ships here. By 1850 when the boom was on in San Francisco, water shipment of lumber became big business. Shipbuilders, wagon makers and blacksmiths also set up shop on Redwood City's own embarcadero.

Since 1857, when court-ordered voting on location of a San Mateo county seat was conducted for a second time, the courthouse has been here. Until that time, local residents had simply called the place "embarcadero." They formally acted to name the city in 1858 after the courthouse squabble became history.

Attractions

Lathrop House, 627 Hamilton Street, was built in 1863 on lots in the original townsite. The Gothic revival home has twice been relocated to save it, and is now operated by Redwood City Heritage Association. Open Tuesday through Friday from 11:00 a.m. to 3:00 p.m. Telephone 365-5564.

Flood Park, located on Bay Road off of Marsh Road south of the city limits, is on an old estate with large oak and bay trees. A picnic grounds and family recreation area are operated by the county park department. Call 363-4021.

For further information, contact **Redwood City Chamber of Commerce**, 1006 Middlefield Road. Telephone 364-1722.

Entertainment

MALIBU FUN CENTER, Blomquist and Harbor Boulevard, Redwood City, California. Test your skills with miniature race cars and golf course, enormous video arcade, and three batting cages!

Gift

A BIT COUNTRY
847 Middlefield Road
Redwood City, CA 94063
Tel. (415) 369-2968
Hrs: Mon. - Sat. 9:30 a.m. - 5:30 p.m.
Visa, MasterCard and Discover cards are accepted.

When Loretta Thomas was a young girl, she tried to talk her mother into opening a specialty gift store so that she could work. Unfortunately, her mother declined, but now you can enjoy the quality of store that Loretta has created in A Bit Country.

As the name suggests, A Bit Country is a shop specializing in country gifts and home accessories. Loretta goes out of her way to find high quality items by small manufacturers and craftspeople. As a result, A Bit Country actually has more variety and better selection than most country stores with twice the space. Just about anything you may desire in country-style gifts are available, including homemade caramels and sasparilla. There are cards, furniture, home decorations such as, punched-tin pictures and handpainted, carved figurines. You'll find toys for the young at heart, tableware, baskets, ribbons galore and much more.

Loretta invites you to stop in, browse and enjoy "Best Choice" shopping at A Bit Country.

Restaurant

BARBAROSSA
3003 El Camino Real
Redwood City, CA 94061
Tel. (415) 369-2626
Hrs: Mon. - Sat 6:00 p.m. - 10:30 p.m.
Reservations are recommended.
All major credit cards are accepted.

Looking for the best restaurant on the Peninsula? It's elegant, formal and delicious. That's what many say about Barbarossa.

For more than a decade host Karl Handwerk and chef Gary Maffia have been setting the standard against which newer restaurants are measured. To make your dining experience memorable, you are surrounded in the rustic charm of natural redwood and the elegance of fine paintings, wrought iron chandeliers. The menu is both enticing and diverse, as indicated by the presence of entrees like veal sauted with morels, or breast of duck served with pear souffle and black currant sauce. Don't pass up a chance to sample one of Chef Maffia's desserts, such as the hazelnut creme in warm chocolate sauce. Barbarossa's wine list includes more than 100 California and French wines. A pre- selected four to five course prix-fixe meal at $27.50 (at the time of this publication) is available each night.

For the best that Peninsula has to offer, look into the Barbarossa for fine dining.

GYPSY CELLER
932 Middlefield Road
Redwood City, CA 94063
Tel. (415) 367-1166
Hrs: Tue.-Sat.   6:00 p.m. - 10:00 p.m.
         Sunday   5:00 p.m. - 9:00 p.m.
All major credit cards are accepted.

If you're not in love already, watch out! Cupid's arrows may be sharp, but a strolling violinist almost never misses.

Gyspy Cellar was opened by concert violinist Jan Novak and his wife Toni in 1976 to give patrons an atmosphere for romance in which to enjoy fine eastern European cuisine. Well traveled diners have commented that the Slovakian entrees are true to their counterparts in the finest of European restaurants. Try the grape leaves stuffed with seasoned beef and rice topped with sour cream. A favorite is the Saslik Enesco, a kabob of tender sirloin marinated for three days in a special preparation of onions, green pepper, bacon and mushrooms served on a bed of rice pilaf.

As you dine Jan will play his violin, accompanied by pianist Ivo Kucera to perform a non stop selection of joyous and romantic tunes. So if there's romance in your fortune, the Gypsy Cellar is the place for you.

REDWOOD CAFE & SPICE COMPANY
1020 Main Street (in the Victorian Gardens)
Redwood City, CA 94063
Tel. (415) 366-1498
Hrs: Breakfast: Mon. - Fri.   7:00 a.m. - 11:00 a.m.
　　　 Lunch: Mon. - Fri.   11:00 a.m. - 3:00 p.m.
　　　 Brunch: Sat. - Sun.   8:00 a.m. - 12:00 noon
and,
OLD GABLES ANTIQUES
1018 Main Street
Redwood City, CA 94063
Tel. (415) 364-1288

Just outside of downtown Redwood City are two beautifully restored antique Victorian homes that make up Victorian Gardens. The Redwood Cafe & Spice Company occupies the 1874 John Diehlman House. Old Gables Antiques is harbored in the 1857 Offerman House. For information on the history of the peninsula area and possible historic home tours...ask Gladys at the Old Gables Antique Shop.

At the Redwood Cafe & Spice Company you can enjoy breakfast and lunch, prepared to provide for your maximum dining pleasure. The three, fully restored to the era, dining rooms and the outside bricked patio, with its striped umbrellas sheltering the Bistro chairs amidst all the lush flowers and the plashing of a fountain, provide the backdrop for your selection from their imaginative menu.

For breakfast choose from many variations of "scrambles," the house favorite is the garden scramble with ham, cheese, tomatoes, and finely minced scallions. It's served with a home-baked bran or blueberry muffin. Or want a delectable? Choose the Swedish oatmeal pancakes with Ligonberries. Select from fresh-ground coffee, regular or decaf, or one of the forty-four varieties of loose tea, regular or decaf too!

Lunch is innovative sandwiches and salads. The house specialty here is the seafood salad with poached red snapper, bay shrimps, hard-cooked egg, and tossed with a creamy dill dressing. Or, try the Southwestern Quiche. *Magnifique!*

The Cafe also houses a country store with a wide variety of coffee beans and bulk teas. There is also a selection of over fifty types of fresh, dried, and prepared spices, plus jams, honeys, and a country sampling of gift items to choose from. All tastefully displayed on antique furnishings like a hutch and doughboy, buffet tables, cupboards, and lighted with glass-shaded lamps.

At the Old Gables Antiques enjoy perusing Gladys' collection of fine American and European antiques; all available at reasonable prices.

San Bruno

Art

DECK THE WALLS
230 Tanforan Park
San Bruno, CA 94066
Tel. (415) 583-8846
Hrs: Mon. - Sat.   10:00 a.m. - 9:00 p.m.
      Sunday   12:00 noon - 6:00 p.m.

Picture this: A shop with a wide selection of fine art prints from the worlds best artists and an equally diverse choice of frames.

Dina and Norman Steinberg operate their business with the idea that service is the single most important element and that their customers are the world's most important people. That is why you can expect to get just exactly you're looking for whether you pick something off the shelf, or need something custom framed.

For that bare spot in your home or office, make it bearable with a poster or print from Deck the Walls.

(See special invitation in Appendix.)

Gifts

DESIGNERS BRASS, 280 El Camino Real, San Bruno, California. Fine quality, classic brass items for the home. Specializing in bath fixtures.

HOTAI, 227 Tanforan Park Center, San Bruno, California. Unusual imports. Products from around the world.

Textiles

YARN CRAFTERS
113 Tanforan Park Shopping Center
San Bruno, CA 94066
Tel.   (415) 871-6540
Hrs: Mon. - Fri   10:00 a.m. - 9:00 p.m.
          Saturday   10:00 a.m. - 6:00 p.m.
          Sunday   11:30 a.m. - 5:30 p.m.

Are you frustrated because you can't find, or match, the color for your next knitting project? Well, don't do anything rash, check Yarn Crafters, where you'll find the largest selection of yarn goods available.

There, is of course, every color of the rain bow in stock, and then a lot of others too in this incredible inventory. The primary yarn manufacturer is Bernet, which assures you of consistent quality. Yarn Crafters also features a full array of accessory items for crochet, knitting, embroidery, needlepoint and hook rugs. You'll find hoops, stretchers, finishing supplies and wall hanging kits. If you are new to these crafts, there are books to help you out, or you can consult with a knowledgeable and friendly staff. One of the best selections of counted cross stitch in the Bay Area.

(See special invitation in the Appendix.)

San Carlos

Antiques

THE COCKNEY CONNECTION, 750 El Camino Real, San Carlos, California. Direct importers of quality English antiques from all eras.

460

Restaurant

SALVATORE'S
1000 El Camino Real
San Carlos, CA 94070
Tel: (415) 593-1000
Hrs: Lunch   Mon. - Fri.   11:30 a.m. - 3:00 p.m.
      Dinner   Tue. - Sat.   5:00 p.m. - 11:00 p.m.
                   Sun. - Mon.   5:00 p.m. - 10:00 p.m.
AMEX, MasterCard and Visa are accepted.

Usually, when you think about fine Continental restaurants with a renowned chef and all the popular touches of elegance, you also start thinking about your pocketbook. But at Salvatore's, the idea is to enjoy good food, a friendly atmosphere and professional service, without worrying.

Salvatore's, in business since 1977, is owned and operated by the Campagna brothers, Duke and Sal, two of the most popular men in this small peninsula community. The menu at their restaurant reflects the Campagna's way of doing business, offering a wonderful selection of taste tempting delights for every palate and every budget. Choose from a variety of dishes including pasta, fresh seafood, chicken, choice beef or milk-fed Provimi veal. Other favorites include Manicotti a la Campagna, veal Stecchine and veal Antonio.

Along with your meal, be sure to select one of the approximately 300 wines from the cellar, including Northern California's largest selection of Schramsberg vintage sparkling wines. At Salvatore's, your pocketbook need not be large, however, your appetite's another story.

San Mateo

This peninsula city is hemmed in by its neighbors, and no longer subject to the rapid growth rate of earlier years. About 80,000 people live here in a combination of older homes and new high-rise buildings.

John B. Cooper, a deserter from the British Navy, gets credit for being the first settler inside what is now city limits. His adobe home was finished in 1851. The town was platted in 1863 to include Cooper's holdings and the estates of four San Franciscans then alternating between city and country living.

Modern San Mateo is connected to Hayward on the East Bay by one of the longest highway bridges in the nation.

461

Attractions

San Mateo County Historical Museum, 1700 West Hillsdale Boulevard, has over 200,000 artifacts in its collections. Open Monday through Thursday 9:30 a.m. to 4:30 p.m., Sundays 12:30 p.m. to 4:30 p.m. Call 574-6641.

Coyote Point Recreation Area is on the bay, and includes a museum for environmental education with a group of live animals on exhibit. Open Wednesday through Friday 10:00 a.m. to 5:00 p.m. Saturday, Sunday 1:00 p.m. to 5:00 p.m.

The first **San Mateo Bridge,** a toll span built by private investors, is maintained, in part, as a fishing pier. It is located off Beach Park Boulevard in Foster City.

Sawyer Camp Trail is a park laid out into the hills where logging once took place. The combination foot, bike and horse trail systems actually link Crystal Springs Road in San Mateo with Hillcrest Boulevard in Millbrae.

Bay Meadows Race Track, on Hillsdale Boulevard off U.S. 101, can handle about 25,000 spectators and continues the peninsula tradition of extended racing seasons which began with the Tanforan track. Call 574-7223.

Bank of America made its branch at Third Avenue and El Camino Real a memorial to the founder, A.P. Giannini. The famed banker's career is shown in artwork at the entrance.

For information, contact the **San Mateo Chamber of Commerce,** 106 South Boulevard. Telephone 341-5679.

Accommodation

DUNFEY SAN MATEO
1770 S Amphlett Boulevard
San Mateo, CA 94402
Tel.   (415) 573-7661
        (800) 228-2121

Dunfey's will enchant you with its old Tudor charm and soft, pastel colors. Casual elegance is noted instantly in any of the 300 guest rooms or 36 suites available for you. Dunfey San Mateo believes that service is important and a friendly Guest Service Manager will be happy to assist you in any way possible with such things as reservations, car rentals, typing services, babysitting arrangements, tours or even helping with the best jogging routes.

Your stay at Dunfey's can be anything you make it: sun drenched by the outdoor pool, relaxed by the cozy fireplace in the Lobby Bar or livened up in the sensational nightclub, Tingles, featuring contemporary dance music.

Dine in Poppies, specializing in cuisine that ranges from fresh seasonal fruits and vegetables to lamb, game and beef, plus the freshest in seafood. Buffet breakfasts are available each morning, champagne brunch on Sunday and "all you can eat" theme dinner buffets including, seafood, Italian, prime rib or lobster are available in Poppies cafe. The Dunfey San Mateo is "the most complete hotel on the San Francisco Peninsula."

LOS PADROS INN, 2940 S. Norfolk Street, San Mateo, California. 113 units, steam room, Jacuzzi, rental cars, shuttle service, free coffee and donuts every morning.

VILLA HOTEL, 4000 South El Camino Real, San Mateo, California. More than just a hotel...a way of life. First class operation.

Antiques

THE COLLECTIVE ANTIQUES, 55 East 3rd Avenue, San Mateo, California. A large antique store that features several sellers--all under one roof.

THE PEDESTAL SHOPPE
201 S B Street
San Mateo, CA 94401
Tel.   (415) 342-5070
         (415) 349-7508 - Repair shop
Hrs: Tue.- Sat. 12:00 noon - 5:00 p.m.
Special appointment.

Once it was a drug store. Now, the entire building is an antique store, with a basement and two floors giving over 9,000 square feet of display space. The repair shop area where restorations are carried out is at a separate location.

Furniture is the stock-in-trade for much of this big store. Oak and walnut pieces for the home and office are on display after careful restoration work in the shop. Besides working over the items headed for the sales floor, Pedestal Shoppe craftsmen offer their services to the general public. Work

463

can be as extensive as complete restoration or as limited as removing a scratch on the finish. Estimates are free.

Jim and Mildred McCarty preside over a slice of Americana in their old building, selecting pieces with care, and filling special orders when you want to match what you already own. You step into the past when you enter The Pedestal Shoppe in downtown San Mateo selling only Americana Antiques.

SQUIRES AND CORRIE
ANTIQUE SLOT MACHINES
373 S. Claremont Street
San Mateo, CA 94401
Tel. (415) 342-6737
Hrs: Mon. - Sat. 8:00 a.m. - 5:00 p.m.
And by appointment.
All major credit cards are accepted.
World wide shipping.

Today's wise investor would do well to visit Steve   Squires' and Glenn Corrie's fascinating shop for the newest in investment collectibles: antique slot machines. Stepping across the threshold is almost like walking into a Nevada casino--except there are no glazed-eyed folk pulling at the one-armed bandits that line the walls.

Specializing in the buying, selling, repair and restoration of old slot machines, Squires & Corrie provide a one-of-a-kind service in the U.S.A. "We're the only ones who do complete factory restoration," says Steve Squires. "We do everything possible to make it as good, if not better, than new, even to manufacturing parts we can't find in our inventory of thousands of antique parts."

The price tag for restoring an antique slot machine can range from $600 to $2,850, depending upon what you wish to have done. And if you wish to have it gold-plated with twenty-four karat gold, it will cost more. However, Steve says that top slot machines can bring $50,000 or more in today's market. This is an investor alert!

Art

LYNWOOD GALLERIES
360 S Railroad Avenue
San Mateo, CA 94401
Tel. (415) 342-3639
Hrs: Tue.- Sat. 9:30 a.m. - 5:30 p.m.

Fine art and fine framing earned Lynwood Galleries their reputation in a few short years. Old masters and contemporary artists' works are sought out by the gallery buyers.

You may find a Rembrandt or Picasso on display here, along with works of dozens of other well known artists. There is also a promise that the staff can research and locate for you works of any specific artist to assist in your selection of just the right piece. The framing shop is a custom operation, doing work for museums, archives and private collectors. A display of frame samples makes it easy to visualize how the work will appear when completed, whether you are mounting a traditional oil or a poster.

Young in its business life, which began in 1985, Lynwood Galleries offers a wealth of experience in fine art through its staff, dedicated to obtaining the best at the best prices.

(See special invitation in the Appendix.)

PENINSULA ART EXCHANGE
2057 San Mateo Fashion Island
San Mateo, CA 94404
Tel. (415) 349-1940
Hrs: Mon. - Fri.   10:00 a.m. - 9:00 p.m.
      Saturday   10:00 a.m. - 6:00 p.m.
      Sunday   12:00 noon - 5:30 p.m.
Visa and MasterCard are accepted.

There's a local connection in this fine art gallery. Owner Luz Maria Hartley is an artist herself, known for realistic and impressionist oils. They share the walls with some of the best known artists in the world.

In this gallery, you'll see many of the famous Vargas girls, the distinctive work of the late Patrick Nagel, as well as mainstream artists Nieman, Erte, Heide, Otsuka, Becker and many others with international reputations. The Peninsula Art Exchange is affiliated with the San Francisco Art Exchange, giving local buyers quick access to works of world famous artists. Prices range from two hundred to two million dollars for the prints and paintings in the inventory of this exchange.

Added services of the Peninsula Art Exchange, are as a brokerage source nationally and internationally to locate and bring art work to the door steps of your home, and custom framing is available, giving you the chance to choose the setting for your painting whether it is a mainstream print artist or an old master.

(See special invitation in the Appendix.)

Books

BETWEEN THE BOOKENDS, 177 West 25th Avenue, San Mateo, California. Bookstore and coffee house.

THE BOOK STORE
132 3rd Avenue
San Mateo, CA 94401
Tel. (415) 343-2751
Hrs: Mon. - Sat. 9:00 a.m. - 6:00 p.m.

Since 1958, Fred Krupp has been tailoring his book store to fit the wide interests of his customers, expanding space and adding books until The Book Store now stocks over 40,000 volumes. Special collections feature local authors, war and history, cookbooks, and publications for children.

Changing with the times, the store now includes audio-recordings of popular books, and a collection of learning tapes. Personalized service here includes special orders on books not in the inventory, even those which are reported out of print, plus mailing of purchases to anywhere in the United States or Europe. There is even a standing offer to exchange books if a customer wishes.

This is a place for best sellers, and just about everything else you may want to read, from reference books to a good novel. And, for those who make The Book Store their "Best Choice," you will enjoy the personal old fashion care the staff will provide. This is not just a store that carries books, but a REAL BOOK STORE!

(See special invitation in the Appendix.)

Collectibles

THE COLLECTOR
140 Hillsdale Mall
San Mateo, CA 94403
Tel. (415) 570-5599
Hrs: Mon. - Fri.   10:00 a.m. - 9:00 p.m.
       Saturday   10:00 a.m. - 6:00 p.m.
       Sunday   12:00 noon - 5:00 p.m.

Some folks collect the porcelain figurines of European children and adults made by Hummel, others are into collecting memorabilia of "The King," Elvis Presley. Helen Liu is into collecting what the collectors want, and making it available to them.

From neat showcases in her Hillsdale Mall store, one can see a huge collection of what collectors want. Helen Liu has been at it for fifteen years, gathering in plates, statues, figurines, music boxes, and even model ships built in bottles. You'll find stone-craft rabbits, cats in a variety of media, pewter ware, and hard to find Jim Beam bottles. In addition to the nostalgic items, The Collectors stocks a wide selection of gift items, priced from two dollars to several hundred dollars.

This is a place for the looker, and the giver of gifts, as well as the collector seeking that one special item to fill out a home display. It is a place to learn what strange things some of us collect.

(See special invitation in the Appendix.)

SHELLEY'S HOUSE OF MINIATURES, 178 West 25th Avenue, San Mateo, California. A great selection of dollhouses, miniatures and supplies.

467

San Mateo County

Games

GAMES & THINGS
2165 San Mateo Fashion Island
San Mateo, CA 94404
Tel. (415) 341-3830
Hrs: Mon. - Fri.   10:00 a.m. - 9:00 p.m.
     Saturday   10:00 a.m. - 6:00 p.m.
     Sunday   12:00 noon - 5:30 p.m.

Walking into Games & Things is like a trip to another world in which fun and competition are the things that count. It's their business, and it shows, making this much more than a toy store.

Here you'll find an extensive collection of backgammon sets. Little ones ready for play on a camping trip or in a car, luxurious ones for an elegant recreation room. Puzzles and solitaire, games old and new have a place on the shelves. The modern electronic tag games are here, along with those military games, mysteries and other challenges for the teenagers and adults. In the book section are volumes on Dungeons and Dragons, and at the counter you can use the store's finder service to locate a specialty item even if it is not in stock.

Part of the magic in browsing through Games & Things comes from discovery of games and toys out of your own past, things you had forgotten were such fun. The place has a magic, too, as you discover how well versed the clerks are in describing the games, letting you measure the challenge and the skill level required as you pick something as a gift or for you own entertainment.

Gift

CHAR CREWS COMPANY
1212 Hillsdale Avenue
San Mateo, CA 94403
Tel. (415) 573-0345
Hrs: Mon. - Wed.   10:00 a.m. - 5:00 p.m.
     Thu. - Sat.   10:00 a.m. - 6:00 p.m.

The brand names are nationally-known, but the prices at Char Crews Co. are often twenty to thirty-five percent off the manufacturer's suggested retail prices. Char Crews offers quality dinerware and gift items.

In the show room are fine china, crystal, and flat ware from Anysley, Coapport, Dansk, Denby, Franciscan, Oneida, Lenox, Haviland, Sasaki, and Wedgwood. Utensils are carried in sterling, silver plate and stainless styles. If you are unable to find the item in stock, Char Crews will special order for you. Their staff is trained to consult with on your gift needs, drawing on years of experience in this specialized field of quality merchandise.

For shoppers who know the merchandise, Char Crews maintains a mailing list to send out information on its sales when their quality items are offered at even more affordable prices.

THE ORIENTAL ELEGANCE
2065 San Mateo Fashion Island
San Mateo, CA 94404
Tel. (415) 571-8989
Hrs: Mon. - Fri.   10:00 a.m. - 9:00 p.m.
       Saturday   10:00 a.m. - 6:00 p.m.
       Sunday   12:00 noon - 5:30 p.m.

The beauty of the Pacific Rim's artists comes alive in this gift shop presided over by Victoria Hrabe, a woman of taste who does her own buying and bargaining.

Fluent in four languages, Victoria sometimes finds herself talking with a shopper who recognizes the art of his native country. The selection is varied. Samurai swords share space with jewelry fashioned from native materials such as horn, seeds or bone. Dresses and kimonos are on the racks, hand embroidered tablecloths on the shelves. And, because you are dealing with the buyer, Oriental Elegance provides a unique opportunity to custom order just about any gift which catches your fancy.

Antique and modern, from Japan to Malaysia and more, this is a gift shop worth visiting, an elegant place that gives you a touch of the Orient.

(See special invitation in the Appendix.)

REFLECTIONS
2234-B San Mateo Fashion Island
San Mateo, CA 94404
Tel. (415) 341-0951
Hrs: Mon. - Fri.   10:00 a.m. - 9:00 p.m.
       Saturday   10:00 a.m. - 6:00 p.m.
       Sunday   12:00 noon - 5:30 p.m.

The glitter in this gift store comes from the glassware and other bright items on the shelves, and the personality of its owner and artist in residence, Moriah Sinclaire.

Moriah is a glassblower and a skilled engraver. When you select a set of glasses, a vase or a plaque, she will finish it off for you with the touch of a craftsperson, not the repetitive form of an engraving machine. Reflections features custom glassware, created by Moriah after consultation with the customer, along with many other gift items sparkling with beauty.

You'll see many samples of Moriah Sinclaire's glass blowing artistry on display here. If one of the pieces creates an idea for something else, she is on hand ready to transform the idea into a very special gift.

(See special invitation in the Appendix.)

Kitchen Articles

COOKS HEADQUARTERS
151 W 25th
San Mateo, CA 94403
Tel. (415) 341-7668
Hrs: Mon. - Fri.   9:30 a.m. - 5:30 p.m.
        Saturday   9:30 a.m. - 4:00 p.m.

This is not your typical kitchen utensil store. Cooks Headquarters has gathered under one roof equipment for the casual cook and the professional chef. You can even buy commercial ranges and institutional-sized pots and pans.

The store features its own line of cutlery and a broad selection of the other tools and gadgets used by experts. There are shelves and shelves of implements, gathered after learning what cooks use and recommend for those special tasks. One of the Bay Area's largest collection of cookbooks is in another part of the store, waiting for you to browse through. And, Cooks Headquarters hosts classes for the curious who want to learn new skills in food preparation, or concentrate on dishes featured in a particular style of cooking.

From casual to gourmet cook, even the person who concentrates on the backyard barbecue, this is your "Best Choice" for ideas, utensils, specialty items, and a look at what the professionals use when they enter a big kitchen.

Nursery

FANCY PLANTS
2234 A Fashion Island
San Mateo, CA 94404
Tel. (415) 572-1860
Hrs: Mon. - Fri.   10:00 a.m. - 9:00 p.m.
       Saturday   12:00 noon - 6:00 p.m.
       Sunday   12:00 noon - 5:30 p.m.

    The lush greenery of the plants and the captivating beauty of the many varieties of orchids adorning the windows of Fancy Plants is but a preview of what awaits you inside. There are plants of every size, shape and color.
    It all started in 1982 when the shop opened as a plant store featuring orchids. Customers were quick to recognize that Fancy Plants was no ordinary plant shop. You will find cattelaya, cymbidiumi and phalanonsis orchids, hanging plants, cacti, silk flower arrangements, potted plants, brick-a-brack, stuffed animals, hand painted birds, mobiles, vases and the largest selection of baskets you have ever seen. There are also supplies, fertilizers and "how to" books galore.
    Fancy Plants believes that everyone's live can be enriched by owning plants, so they strive to provide the very best to help get started exploring the plant world. The staff is very knowledgeable and friendly so you can ask advice when you purchase a new species.

Restaurants

NICK'S ON 25TH
109 W 25th Avenue
San Mateo, CA 94403
Tel. (415) 574-1256
Hrs: lunch: Mon. - Fri.   11:30 a.m. - 2:30 p.m.
      dinner: Mon. - Sat. from 5:00 p.m. on
      brunch: Sunday   10:00 a.m. - 2:30 p.m.
Visa, MasterCard, AMEX and Diner's accepted.
Reservations are recommended.

    Nick's on 25th is a traditional San Francisco-style bar and grill that is highly recommended, by its patrons, for a delicious lunch, dinner, or for cocktails with friends. The trendy black and white motif is complemented by lush greenery and the many framed prints of notables; enjoy your meal under the gaze of Marilyn Monroe, James Dean, Robert Frost, James Stewart, Clark

471

Gable, Albert Einstein, and John Lennon...they would have felt right at home here.

The restaurant features a complete cocktail lounge. Premium wine by the glass is offered. The walls, in the lounge, are lined with signed photographs of famous personages in football, baseball, Hollywood actors and actresses, singers, and celebrities.

Lunch has such taste tempting items as fresh fish, salads, and pasta specialties. Dinner entrees include rack of lamb, blackened rib steak, veal, chicken, and every day a new evening special is presented for your consideration. Nick's pastry chef concocts such delectables as cheesecake, cream pies, fruit tarts and chocolate desserts. Banquet facilities to seat up to forty are available by reservation for your private party or wedding reception.

A "Best Choice" for great, San Francisco-style dining...you're in good company at Nick's on 25th.

THE OLD CLAMHOUSE
33 W 25th Avenue
San Mateo, CA 94403
Tel. (415) 571-1846
Hrs: Mon. - Fri.   11:00 a.m. - 11:00 p.m.
     Saturday   4:00 p.m. - 11:00 p.m.
     Sunday   4:00 p.m. - 10:00 p.m.
Visa and MasterCard are accepted.

It's not fancy. But for a meal at less than ten dollars, this is your "Best Choice" in San Mateo. And for clam chowder, there is no question. It's the best for miles around.

Seafood is the specialty of the house, drawing on a tradition which reaches back to the original clamhouse established in San Francisco in 1861. Meals at the San Mateo branch are like those on the wharf in the city, except that the prices are moderate. Grilled salmon topped with crab meat and Hollandaise sauce is among the favorites on the menu, which also includes a selection of veal and beef entrees for luncheon or dinner.

As you would suspect, shellfish have a big place on the menu. Dishes range from the traditional clam recipes to some featuring mussels. And, in the heritage of the wharf, pasta and sauces add zip to many at this neighborhood gathering spot with a reputation for good food, and good service.

ORCHID GARDEN RESTAURANT, 2318-2322 El Camino Real, San Mateo, California. Excellent Chinese restaurant.

472

POPIES, 1770 South Amphlett Boulevard, San Mateo, California. Located in the landmark Dumfey Hotel, this fine restaurant is a favorite among locals and visitors.

PRINCE OF WALES PUB
106 E 25th Avenue
San Mateo, CA 94403
Tel. (415) 574-9723
Hrs: Mon. - Fri.   11:00 a.m. - 12:00 midnight
      Saturday   12:00 noon - 12:00 midnight
Extended hours on Fridays.

Awarded "the best darts pub in the Bay area," the Prince of Wales Pub has been the center for darts on the Peninsula since 1964 and offers organized play on Monday and Wednesday nights. Owner, Jack Curry, is the 1976 U.S. Champion.

Customers and friends of the Prince are an active lot. This is the only pub that publishes a monthly newsletter, organizes regular speedwalks, sponsors an award winning chili cookoff team and orchestrates well publicized Bay area "pub crawls" in which they visit an astonishing number of pubs via chauffeur driven van.

One especially fun feature is the "Beers of World Club" whereby you ask for a club card and start sampling the variety of imported beers and ales the pub is proud to offer. To complement the selection of beers are fish and chips and banger, as well as an equally well known menu, featuring the famous "Windsor Burger" in its original recipe as it was specially prepared for Edward, the young Prince of Wales, when he visited Del Monico's in New York during 1920. High spirits flourish in this fun loving pub.

(See special invitation in the Appendix.)

RED ROBIN, Fashion Island Mall, San Mateo, California. World famous hamburgers, sandwiches, BBQ and libations.

Shoe Repair

IN & OUT SHOE REPAIR
49 West 42nd Avenue
San Mateo, CA 94403
Tel. (415) 349-6844
Hrs: Mon. - Thur. 9:00 a.m. - 8:00 p.m.
      Friday   9:00 a.m. - 9:00 p.m.
      Saturday   9:00 a.m. - 8:00 p.m.

Honesty, integrity, pride, quality workmanship--these are the words American craftsmen once lived by. It seems nowadays these values are all but forgotten...not true at the In and Out Shoe Repair shop in San Mateo.

Paul and Susan Krause and their children, Amity and Nathan are keeping these values alive today. Paul's beginning in the shoe repair business dates back to 1971. Since that time he's worked for many different companies, always striving for the very best quality possible. In 1984, Paul was recognized for his abilities by winning the coveted National Silver Cup for shoe repair. He was also featured on the cover of *Shoe Service,* a nationally published trade magazine, and with an article about his services.

He now owns his own shop and its set up so that the customer can watch him work; cutting, nailing, polishing and everything in between. Paul uses the most sophisticated and advanced machinery available to assist his skilled hands in making and completing the repairs. The machinery is so advanced that Paul journeyed to Holland for hands-on-training.

No job is too large or too small. Customers can have their shoes repaired while they go shopping or can wait, if they prefer. Custom sandals are made on the premises and as with repairs, same day service is available. 100% satisfaction is guaranteed. Soles and heels can be replaced in as little as fifteen minutes. Drop by with your favorite old pair of shoes and when you leave, they'll be just like new--only better, cause they're already broken in!

The In and Out Shoe Repair carries a full line of accessory items for your leathers and you can have keys made while you wait. Stop by Petrinis Market on 42nd Avenue in San Mateo and say hello to Paul, Susan and the kids.

Tobacco

K. P.'s PLACE, 36 Eat 3rd Avenue, San Mateo, California. Tobacco shop with a good selection of tobacco, accessories and magazines.

Toys

TALBOTS TOYLAND
445 South B Street
San Mateo, CA 94401
Tel. (415) 342-0126
Hrs: Mon. - Sat.   9:30 a.m. - 6:00 p.m.
        Sunday   11:00 a.m. - 5:00 p.m.

Supermarket of toys is one way to describe this downtown store. There is a complete bicycle department, another just as well stocked for hobbies, and others for toys and baby furniture.

There are racing bikes for the professional competitor, training bikes for the beginner, and rack after rack of bicycles for everyone in between. Plus accessories. The shelves of the hobby department offer miniatures and craft sets, electric trains and radio-controlled cars. In the toy department, choices start with coloring books and end with kites, almost like checking over the inventory of Santa's workshop. The newest department stocks furniture for the baby's room; rocking horses to cribs.

This is a place for the young, and the young at heart. Here you'll find a bicycle for the elderly and a pull-toy for the toddler, a supermarket that is your "Best Choice" when looking for a toy store.

Woodside

This is one of those communities which decided to incorporate when the pressures of growth developed. Like Portola Valley to the south, Woodside is a collection of homes on large lots scattered beneath the live oaks and other native trees. It takes its name from the Woodside Store, built in 1854 by Dr. R. O. Tripp, a dentist who came to the woods to recuperate from an illness. The store still has the pigeonhole mail sorting system for the hundreds of loggers who called here for letters while working in the redwood forests.

Up to fifteen sawmills processed the timber taken from here. Woodside residents claim the first English-speaking settlers on the peninsula in the form of John Coppinger, a one-time officer in the Royal Navy who by 1841 had a house of some stature beside Kings Mountain and Woodside Roads.

Today Woodside includes fourteen square miles of rural lands, most of it in lots of from one to three acres with single family homes. The community center is along Woodside Road where three other roads come together.

475

Attractions

Woodside Store still exists at the intersection of Tripp and Kings Mountain Roads, operated by the San Mateo County Park Department. Dr. Tripp's dental offices are restored and the logging days described. For information call the park department, 363-4020.

Filoli House and Gardens, Canada Road, is one of several formal garden showplaces in San Mateo County. Call 364-8300 for current information on visiting hours.

For further information, call the **Woodside Police Department** at 364-1811

Museum

WOODSIDE STORE, Tripp Road at Kings Mountain Road, Woodside, California. Relics of early logging, lumbering and gold-rush days whisk you back to the past.... authentic redwood horse troughs and nineteenth century merchandise are also displayed.

Restaurant

BELLA VISTA
13451 Skyline Boulevard
Woodside, CA 94062
Tel. (415) 851-1229
Hrs: Tue. - Thu.   5:30 p.m. - 10:30 p.m.
       Fri. - Sat.   5:30 p.m. - 11:00 p.m.
       Sunday   4:30 p.m. - 10:00 p.m.
All major credit cards are accepted.

Imagine a romantic restaurant, serving Continental cuisine, set back in the redwoods of Santa Cruz Mountains, which features a panoramic view of the San Fransisco Bay. If such a place existed, it would be a natural choice for anyone seeking a way to celebrate a special event or a special person. Well, it does exist, and Bella Vista is without a doubt the restaurant to go to for those occasions.

From the moment when you are greeted with a sincere smile in the large redwood lined entry lounge where a warming blaze bathes you in dancing light, your unforgettable evening begins. The menu at Bella Vista is a series of delicious entrees beginning with a superb variety of hot and cold appetizers including Oysters Rockefeller, Saumon Fume and Escargot aux Champignons. Some of the most popular entree choices include Filet of Sole Veronique, Veal Jerusalem and Tournedos of Beef a la Rossini. In addition, each night the chef selects and prepares a selection of dishes that can only tempt you further.

To top it off, even diners who protest fullness from their dinner will reassess their appetites when presented with a perfectly baked Souffle filled with chocolate, raspberry or Gran Marnier. For that especially memorable evening, visit Bella Vista. A "Best Choice" in anyone's book.

SANTA CLARA COUNTY

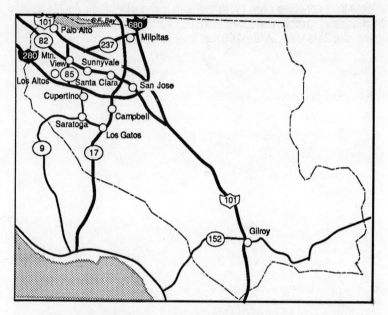

A booming metropolis and a sophisticated farming community share the south bay's most populous county. About 1.4 million people live on the 1,293 square miles of Santa Clara County, nearly one half of them residents of San Jose which grew like a weed in the past three decades and shows signs of continuing its growth.

On the west, the county boundary shares the ridge of the Santa Cruz mountains, reaching south almost to Watsonville where it turns east, first in a river channel and then by precise survey lines drawn to the summit of the Diablo Range of mountains. The mountain crest boundary works its way north, then takes a surveyor's azimuth west to San Francisco Bay's very south tip, following the Coyote River into the bay.

Two formidable mountain ranges, the Santa Cruz and Diablo, create an arid valley which is free of the fogs that bother other communities on San Francisco Bay. Brown foot hills, which receive no rain at all in summer months, march up to the mountains, crested with observatories and experimental radio and radar transmission sites of the scientists who live below. Major freeways

478

come down both sides of the bay to San Jose, and U.S. 101 carries travelers south through the farming area of the Coyote River valley.

Until thirty years ago, Santa Clara County valleys were filled with farms and orchards producing a variety of food. Its hills, basking in the Mediterranean climate, turned out famous wine grapes and seasonal forage for a livestock industry. In 1960, Santa Clara County had 70,000 acres of prunes and 20,000 acres of apricots. Its processing plants turned out the largest dried fruit and canning yield of any area in the state, about seventy-two million quart cans worth. While industrial development began here with the demands for World War II war material, the real expansion is fueled by electronics, giving the name "Silicon Valley" to the country from San Jose to Palo Alto. The boom began with the silicon chip which stores and processes electronic information.

Inventiveness is not new to people of this valley. The first commercial radio station in the country, KQW, was issued its license in 1912. But Herrold Wireless Laboratories actually began experiments in San Jose in 1909, broadcasting with 11,000 feet of wire strung seven-stories up between two office buildings.

Lockheed is the county's largest employer with over 23,000 working its missile and space craft contracts. Right behind is Hewlett-Packard Corp. which had its birth in the genius of Stanford University graduates at Palo Alto. International Business Machines Corporation, IBM, makes its headquarters in a former prune orchard south of San Jose and employs about 13,500 persons.

The history of Santa Clara has its roots in the Spanish soldiers and Franciscan friars who established their missions and forts in the early 1800s. But there is a difference, because San Jose was California's first "civilian" town, a trade center apart from the missions and forts. The Pueblo de San Jose de Guadalupe began in November 1777 when the viceroy sent five families, guarded by nine soldiers, to start a town. Each family received the equivalent of ten dollars a month for the first year while they established their crops. An 1831 report shows 524 residents, little farming, and a lot of cattle running on the marshlands of the south bay.

After the 1846 revolt and American occupation of Mexican California, San Jose was the state's first capital. It is said that legislators complained of poor accommodations during that 1849 session, and by a vote moved the capital and the legislature north to Benicia for the 1851 meeting. Meanwhile, experiments in apricot and prune culture were underway. The trees matured in the 1860s and the orchard economy was born, pushing aside the livestock to ranges in the hills.

The industrial growth after World War II brought more than factories and research laboratories. Subdivisions shoulder-to-shoulder fill much of the valley from San Jose toward San Francisco. Except for a small gap at the county line and Coyote River on the east shore of the bay, more subdivisions march northward toward Oakland. This is the metropolis of Northern California.

ATTRACTIONS

Lick Observatory of the University of California is on the 4,029 foot west peak of Mount Hamilton. You can get a view of the entire county from here. A gift of real estate speculator James Lick, the observatory was completed in 1888, and is reached by a twenty-mile long road from the valley below. Open daily, 1:00 p.m. to 5:00 p.m.; special summer programs each Friday night at 10:00 p.m. Write the observatory at Box 84, Mount Hamilton CA 95140 for summer program reservations. Telephone (408) 274-5062. Mount Hamilton Road branches off Alum Rock Avenue.

Alum Rock Park is on the way to the observatory. This was a famed mineral spa started in 1872. Current recreation opportunities include hiking and horseback riding. Open daily 8:00 a.m. to sunset.

Located in Alum Rock Park is the **Youth Science Institute**, a small natural history museum which sponsors hikes and nature trips in the park. Open Tuesday through Friday 9:00 a.m. to 4:30 p.m. and Saturday 12:00 noon to 4:30 p.m.

Foothills College Electronic Museum, 1235 South El Monte Road, Los Altos Hills, traces the history of vacuum tubes and their solid state successors--transistors and silicon chips. Located just of I-280. Call (415) 948-8590 for current hours.

NASA Research Center, Moffett Field, provides tours by reservations only, two weeks in advance. The world's largest wind tunnel is among attractions along with several current space experiments. Write TA-12/Ames Research Center, Moffett Field, Mountain View CA 94035. Telephone (415) 965-6497. Located off U.S. 101 at Mountain View.

Santa Clara Valley Wine Growers Association, Box 1192, Morgan Hill, CA 95037, provides written information on its nineteen wineries if you send a stamped, self-addressed envelope. The association also welcomes the curious to its monthly dinner meetings where technical information is shared. Call (408) 778-1555 for information.

Splashdown Waterslide, 1200 South Dempsey Road, Milpitas, actually has four waterslides plus several picnic areas. Open daily June through August, weekends in April, May and September. Call (408) 943-9252 for hours.

McClellan Ranch Park, an eighteen acre reserve in Cupertino, preserves some of the old farmland in an area which urbanized from a crossroads farming community. The Baer blacksmith shed and other turn-of-the century ranch buildings are restored. Call (408) 253-2060 for hours.

For additional information, contact the **Chamber of Commerce**, 1 Paseo de San Antonio, San Jose 95113. Telephone (408) 295-9600.

Alviso

Restaurant

MARINA SEAFOOD GROTTO
995 Elizabeth Street
Alviso, CA 95002
Tel. (408) 262-2563
Hrs: Lunch Tue. - Fri.   11:30 a.m. - 2:00 p.m.
      Dinner Tue. - Fri.   5:00 p.m. - 10:00 p.m.
             Saturday   5:00 p.m. - 10:00 p.m.
             Sunday   4:00 p.m. - 9:30 p.m.

A short distance off highway 237 between Interstates 101 and 880 is one of those long recognized establishments that local residents insist upon and visitors are happy to discover. Marina Seafood Grotto, located along the historical waterfront village of Alviso, is amid the old magic from the days when large canvas warehouses, canneries, oyster beds, and poultry shell plants made this the bustling shipping point for San Jose.

The entire restaurant has a pleasing atmosphere. At the entrance is a beautiful aquarium filled with colorful koi and goldfish. The dining room is delightful with subdued lighting during lunch and dinner hours. The crowning feature of the restaurant is a magnificent marlin mounted on the main wall above a scarlet lit fountain.

If you enjoy steak and lobster, this is the place. Try chef Phil Lam's personal choice, the huge and sumptuous calamari steak. The poached sea bass is always in great demand and features mushrooms, chopped green onions, and shrimp capped with a yummy, rich cream sauce. The broiled lobster tail is worth trying also, it's sweet and succulent. Open the menu and you'll find a passbook to an honored tradition of zesty service, great atmosphere, and tantalizing seafood delights.

(See special invitation in the Appendix.)

Campbell

For information and a list of attractions on Campbell please look under the Los Gatos heading.

Accommodations

CAMPBELL INN
675 East Campbell Avenue
Campbell, CA 95008
Tel. (408) 374-4300
Hrs: 24 hour service year around
All major credit cards accepted.

Tucked away, just off busy High 17, at the Hamilton Avenue exit is one of the San Jose area's finest hotels. The Campbell Inn, built in the Spanish Mission style, boasts of its exclusive and private accommodations.

There are one hundred rooms here, including some executive suites with steam rooms connecting to fireplace-equipped living rooms. Weekday rates, set for business travelers are in the medium range, but the Campbell Inn offers three packages to share its luxurious facilities with pleasure seekers. Special rates apply on weekends, for honeymoons and anniversaries; during the winter a two-day, two-night deal even offers some of the deluxe rooms at special prices. Features include a breakfast buffet with dozens of food choices, and VCRs in each room with a 300 tape library from which to choose.

To find this "Best Choice" ask your travel agent for a booking which will include chauffeured transportation from the San Jose Airport which is only minutes away.

Apparel

TRUDY'S
124 The Pruneyard
Campbell, CA 95008
Tel. (408) 377-1986
Hrs: Mon. - Fri.   10:00 a.m. - 9:00 p.m.
     Saturday   10:00 a.m. - 6:00 p.m.
     Sunday   12:00 noon - 5:00 p.m.

Are you getting a little tired of opening the closet only to be faced with the same clothing you've worn for the past few months? Maybe there's a little space in there for something new and exciting? Well, if this is the case, there's no better place to go than Trudy's, the premier women's fashion store in the Bay Area.

From their beginning in 1974, Trudy's has been a major contributor to the ever-changing women's fashions in the Bay Area. Their unending dedication to fine quality at reasonable prices has established them as an eminent factor in the retail clothing industry. You can be assured that if Trudy's introduces a new line, that it will be the very best merchandise selection available. Following in this tradition, Trudy's has recently expanded into bridal and men's formal wear, also in The Pruneyard. They currently carry casual wear, career dress, party dresses, sportswear, wedding attire, clothing accessories and jewelry.

When it comes to fashion and knowledge thereof, Trudy's has it all. After a visit to Trudy's, opening your closet will become a fitting experience.

Art

THE ART EMPORIUM
305 E Campbell Avenue
Campbell, CA 95008
Tel. (408) 374-5082
Hrs: Mon. - Sat. 10:00 a.m. - 4:30 p.m.

A cooperative is a group of people working or acting together for a common purpose. It's a sound principal to combine many abilities in order to achieve a goal that couldn't be reached otherwise. This is exactly what happened at The Art Emporium. A group of artists has banded together to present some of the best art in the area.

The Art Emporium is a most unusual and refreshing art gallery. First formed in 1984, this cooperative is comprised of sixteen artists who enjoy working together, exchanging ideas and growing in their art forms. Works featured throughout the year include realistic and full-range paintings in various media, rustic scenes on saw blades, custom Indian beaded jewelry, portraits, sewn crafts, machine and hand knitting and much, much more. Also featured, is a special showing of a particular artist each month, wherein a whole wall is devoted to their works.

Each artist has a speciality in which he of she excels, and when you combine all sixteen of these specialities into one, it becomes The Art Emporium. Stop by, visit this gallery and see the wonders cooperation can yield.

(See special invitation in the Appendix.)

CHABOT GALLERIES
132 The Pruneyard
Campbell, CA 95008
Tel. (408) 371-6393

For over fourteen years, Chabot Galleries has provided the Bay Area with the most diversified selection of fine quality art available. In order to maintain this outstanding selection, the owners Vaughan and Susan Bigalow travel extensively throughout the world, choosing pieces appealing to the connoisseur or the most discriminating novice.

Your first visit to Chabot Galleries will tell you that this is no ordinary gallery. High ceilings, spacious walls and the perfect combination of lighting, all serve to enhance the many fine works of art that await your approval. Some of the featured artists shown include Leroy Neiman, Eyvind Earle, Albar, Marc Changall, Salvador Dali and R. C. Gorman. Chabot Galleries are noted not only for their expansive selection of fine paintings, but for their innovation as well. They have recently instituted a revolving charge plan so that you may now purchase on credit, making fine art available to everyone.

At Chabot Galleries, the quality fine art, exemplary customer service and affordable financing, makes them truly unique in the world of art galleries. Aesthetically speaking, Chabot Galleries is unequivocally a "Best Choice."

(See special invitation in the Appendix)

Catering

REMINGTON'S, 1730 West Campbell Avenue, Campbell, California. The finest in banquet facilities in the area. Features a full bar, spacious lounge, three dance floors, live music with disc jockeys.

Delicatessen

A & J POLISH DELICATESSEN
1783 South Winchester Boulevard
Campbell, CA 95008
Tel. (408) 379-6167

A menu of Polish recipes passed down for over 400 years, homemade Polish sausage, a wonderful deli and gift section makes A&J Polish Delicatessen a must for the lover of ethic foods and gifts.

In the deli, you'll find canned food from Poland, cookies, jams, candies, pickles and relishes. Polish art, including handmade dolls, hand-carved wooden statues and plates, and oil paintings are available. Greeting cards, records and tapes are offered as well. There is a large selection of Polish books, magazines, and newspapers, and there's also a videotape rental section of the shop.

Try the Pierogi, the Bigos, or Golombki---you'll think you've died and gone to heaven; one visit to A & J Polish Deli and your tastebuds will love you forever. The deli's famous homemade sausage can also be shipped anywhere you'd like.

(See special invitation in the Appendix)

BRITISH FOOD CENTRE
1800 W Campbell Avenue
Campbell, CA 95008
Tel. (408) 374-7770
Hrs: Mon. - Sat. 10:00 a.m. - 6:00 p.m.
     Sunday 12:00 noon - 6:00 p.m.
Visa and MasterCard are accepted.
and,
505 E 4th Avenue
San Mateo, CA 94402
Tel. (415) 347-7498

The British have landed! That is the British Food Centres. A real English market with a selection of food, cooking utensils, books, gifts and novelty items that would make any British merchant proud. And it's right here in America, right in Campbell and San Mateo.

When Billy and Betty Fredlund started the business of selling British antiques in 1976, little did they know they would soon be providing for the local British people a fine variety of products from their homeland. They stock over

2,000 items such as soft drinks, sauces, spices, Indian and Chinese food, jams and marmalades, jellies, pie fillings, cake mixes, cereals and puddings, teas and coffee, chemist supplies, books and atlases, frozen foods and fine quality gifts. These items are also available from the British Food Centre's mail order catalog which can be mailed to you upon request.

Everything in The British Food Centre's stock is from the United Kingdom. They offer food from Scotland, Wales, Ireland and England. The entire staff of the British Food Centre is British and they are ready to extend to you the hospitality they're famous for. So, put on your trainers (tennis shoes) and run down this very minute. Hurry, before a queue (line) develops!

Flowers

SUNSHINE FLOWERS, 2371 South Winchester Boulevard, Campbell, California. Unusual flower shop that is located in the middle of a shopping center! Potted, hanging and fresh flowers.

Gift

JARDIN DE PARFUM
470 The Pruneyard
Campbell, CA 95008
Tel. (408) 371-7644
Hrs: Mon., Thur., Fri.   10:00 a.m. - 9:00 p.m.
      Tues., Wed., Sat.   10:00 a.m. - 6:00 p.m.
      Sunday   2:00 noon - 5:00 p.m.
Major credit cards are accepted.

Delightful fragrances from around the world will delight your senses at Jardin De Parfum. For those with discriminating taste and a flair for the unique, this boutique offers it all.

More than 100 fine fragrances for women and over 50 for men including Arpels, Van Cleef, Pheromone and Caryen are just a few of the many quality perfumes to choose from.

Jardin De Parfum offers full nail and color consultations and a complete line of cosmetics. They also carry a wide array of gift items and are always delighted to assist you in selecting that perfect gift.

When it comes to imported and domestic fragrances, cosmetics, gifts, personalized service and careful attention to providing complete customer satisfaction, Jardin De Parfum is your one stop shop.

KIRKWOOD HARDWARE AND GIFT SHOP
1400 West Campbell Avenue
Campbell, CA 95008
Tel. (408) 379 -7800
Hrs: Mon. - Fri.   8:00 a.m. - 9:00 p.m.
         Sat. - Sun.   9:00 a.m. - 5:30 p.m.
Visa, Mastercard, AMEX are accepted.

The largest independent hardware store in California is not in L.A., San Francisco, or San Diego, but in the pleasant community of Campbell.
Founded in 1965 by the Rampy family, Kirkwood Hardware Store has just about everything the home owner or building trades professional needs for both large and small projects. Troy Rampy manages the store and maintains a large inventory of products and tools easily located in the well stocked, paint, plumbing, electrical, tool, and general hardware sections. His staff is knowledgeable and friendly and will take the time to help solve those little problems that crop up on any job. Literally thousands upon thousands of nuts, bolts, tools, parts, and accessories are at your disposal and available immediately for efficient use. Honesty, integrity, and service are keys to the success of the Kirkwood Hardware Store and are a tradition with the Rampys.
Nowhere are those qualities more evident than in the Kirkwood Hardware Store's gift section. This section operated by Fran Ramby, Troy's wife, features many gifts not normally found in gift shops. She stocks items such as Llardro-Spanish porcelain, Hummel-German figurines, Waterford crystal, Italian furniture, and fine crystal from Germany. These treasures are displayed along with large selections of high quality, well made gifts in all price ranges.
In Campbell when in the market for hardware or gifts, remember the motto on the business cards of the Kirkwood Hardware Store and Gift Shop, "Yes, we have it". The statement is true and your search is over.

(See special invitation in the Appendix.)

Jeweler

FINE DESIGN JEWELERS
880 E Campbell Avenue
Campbell, CA 95008
Tel. (408) 559-7700
Hrs: Tue. - Sat. 10:00 a.m. - 5:30 p.m.

At Fine Design Jewelers, there is an air of excitement, a feeling of elegance and a realization that you have just entered a very special place. Sherry and Donna, the owners, welcome you to their world of fine jewelry, where amidst their world of pink and grey glass showcases, you'll find exactly what you're seeking.

This delightful shop features crystal by KMM Mostny, jewelry by such makers as Goldman and Krementz and special designer items by Alan Revere, Carrie Adell and many others. Of course, you'll also find sparkling diamonds, gemstones, silver, gold, quality watches and several other fine gifts. They also offer a complete repair department, wherein skilled hands breathe life back into your favorite heirloom. For custom design jewelry, the facilities at Fine Design Jewelers know no limit.

Sherry and Donna invite you to come and shop in comfort at their shop where everyone is treated like someone very special. Exquisite selection, charming atmosphere and modest prices aptly describe Fine Design Jewelers. The next time you start to feel a little excited and you don't know why, look up and you'll probably see their sign.

(See special invitation in the Appendix.)

Nautical

THE SHIP'S CHANDLERY
1640 W Campbell Avenue
Campbell, CA 95008
Tel. (408) 866-0170
Hrs: Mon. - Sat. 10:00 a.m. - 6:00 p.m.
Thursday until 8:00 p.m.
Visa, MasterCard, AMEX, Diner's Club and Discover cards.

A gale is blowing up, and the seas begin to churn, white caps curl over to mix with the gray of the angry sea. Ah, but there is refuge ahead. As the cold north wind blows at your backs, the anchor is dropped into the briny waters off The Ship's Chandlery.

At last inside, you are welcomed aboard by Captain Frederick Hall. Fred has decorated the inside of The Chandlery like a ship, complete with deck and wheel. As you listen to the sounds of nautical music, browse through the thousands of items all relating to the sea. There are compasses, barometers, ship's clocks, boatswain's whistles, bells, seaworthy clothing and all varieties of headgear, deck shoes, maps, charts and books. Captain Fred makes custom rigging and performs nautical repairs as well. His gear is so much in demand that he ships it all over the world.

The Ship's Chandlery also has a fine selection of nautical gifts. Gifts, to please everyone, from the most salty sea- goer, to the armchair pollywog. So, the next time you're in need of nautical gear, anchor at The Ship's Chandlery. It's not just any port in the storm, it's the port in any storm.

(See special invitation in the Appendix.)

Restaurants

ANDY'S BARBEQUE
700 E Campbell Avenue
Campbell, CA 95008
Tel. (408) 378-2838

Hrs:	Mon.-Sat.	5:00 p.m.- 10:00 p.m.
	Sunday	4:30 p.m.- 9:00 p.m.
Bar	Mon.-Thu.	3:00 p.m. - 12:00 midnight
	Fri.-Sat.	3:00 p.m.- 1:00 a.m.

Visa and Mastercard are accepted.

Barbequed ribs, chicken, sausage and steaks are the reasons for visiting Andy's Barbeque in Campbell, after tasting these delights, their memory will bring you back again.

Owner Andy Unzen and his family have dedicated themselves to making the best barbequed food anywhere which they have been doing since they opened in 1965. The food is what counts at Andy's Barbeque, in fact Andy challenges his customers to find better barbeque sauce anywhere and so far his challenge has gone unanswered. The atmosphere is comfortable, unpretentious and genuine friendly service is always available.

Be sure and remember to stop at Andy's Barbeque next time you're in Campbell and taste barbequed food at its best.

COOK BOOK, 180 The Pruneyard, Campbell, California. The largest selection of omelets in the Bay Area. Great for breakfast.

EL LUCERO
1875 S Basocom Avenue #730
Campbell, CA 95008
Tel. (408) 559-3680
Hrs: Mon. - Sun. 11:00 a.m. - 9:00 p.m.
All major credit cards are accepted.

Tucked away in the corner of The Pruneyard Shopping Center in Campbell is one of the finest Mexican restaurants you'll find anywhere. The El Lucero generates a very warm and cozy feeling with it's high beamed ceiling, guitars on the wall, soft lighting and well spaced tables that further the intimacy and excellent service.

The menu at El Lucero features a wide variety of Mexican entrees. Everything is made from scratch, using only the freshest possible ingredients. Louise, the owner, states, "My day starts at seven in the morning, buying the freshest produce that we will be using that day. We take extra special care in the preparation of all of our foods because I cook for my customers just as I would for my own family." You can choose to dine in or out of doors at this restaurant that's always looking for new ways to please it's customers.

El Lucero also features a wine list and excellent margaritas. For parties, with a little advanced notice they can provide space enough to accommodate 150 people in warm weather with the patio open. Finding this restaurant tucked away in a corner is like finding your pocketbook behind the couch. El Lucero is always a pleasant discovery for anyone who enjoys delicious Mexican food in an unmatched ambiance.

(See special invitation in the Appendix.)

FIRENZIA, 331 Hacienda, Campbell, California. Excellent Northern Italian food. Decor is elegant.

FUNG LUM RESTAURANT, 1815 South Bascom Avenue, Campbell, California. Fine quality Cantonese cuisine.

490

MARTHA'S VINEYARD
1875 S Bascom Avenue
Campbell, CA 95008
Tel. (408) 371-5060
Hrs: Mon. - Fri.   11:00 a.m. - 3:00 p.m.
      Fri. - Sat.   5:30 p.m. - 10:30 p.m.

Martha's Vineyard, well known for their authentic East Coast seafood and tempting pasta dishes, has become a regular bill of fare for those of discriminating taste.

The cuisine is elegant and yet ambience is casual. Enjoy the relaxing intimacy of the cozy bar complete with fireplace. There is a library room complete with wine racks filled to the brim with fine selections of California wines and beautiful skylights throughout the restaurant which completes the warm atmosphere.

For dinner there are specialties such as blackened Louisiana Redfish with fresh salsa or an Iceland lobster with mint and lime, or a chicken breast, wrapped in pastry with goat cheese, thyme, basil and beurre blanc, or seafood lasagna with crab, shrimp, prawns and smoked salmon, or even baked halibut in filo with fresh asparagus, crab and bernaise sauce and on, and on...

Martha's Vineyard in Campbell awaits you with exquisitely prepared seafood and pasta dishes, uncompromising service and an elegant atmosphere.

Salon

DESIGNERS LIMITED
2523 Winchester Boulevard
Campbell, CA 95008
Tel. (408) 378-7300
Hrs: Tue. - Sat. 8:00 a.m. - 8:00 p.m.

You'll find Designers Limited modestly listed in the local telephone directory, under Beauty, which does them a tremendous injustice. This is certainly not your run-of-the-mill beauty shop, as you'll discover when you make your visit.

The number one goal at Designers Limited is complete customer satisfaction. Customers are dealt with on a one to one basis with each being treated as if they were the most important patron to ever come into the shop. There are over thirty employees to serve you, each a specialist in his or her field. Some of the services are coloring, color analysis, ear piercing, electrolysis, facials, hair design, make-up, manicures, massages, pedicures, perming, sculptured nails, tanning and waxing.

For a special treat, you can try The Great Escape, seven hours of ultimate service in their beautiful salon. Visualize your greatest fantasy and let them help you escape. The Escape consists of a soothing massage, a facial, a manicure and pedicure, hair shampoo and styling and finally, a make-up masterpiece to add the finishing touches to the new you. Designers Limited is not just a salon, it's an experience that must be lived to be appreciated. Stop in today and let them pamper you.

Sport

WHEEL AWAY CYCLE CENTER
402 E Hamilton Avenue
Campbell, CA 95008
Tel. (408) 378-4636
Hrs: Mon. - Thu.   9:00 a.m. - 6:00 p.m.
      Friday   9:00 a.m. - 9:00 p.m.
      Saturday   9:00 a.m. - 6:00 p.m.

Many countries in Europe and Asia don't make everyday use of automobiles. To that, one might say, "That's ridiculous, how do they travel to and from their destinations?" They ride bicycles, that's how. It's much healthier, less expensive and creates no pollution. Many Americans are starting to take up this practice, and they go to Wheel Away Cycle Center to obtain their biking supplies.

At Wheel Away Cycle Center they carry a fine selection of Schwinn, Raleigh, Miatre and Centurion bikes. They have over 1,000 bicycles in stock at all times! For accessories, they have the most extensive inventory in the entire area. Safety equipment, seats, racks and tires are only a few of the items in this store. They've also got the best repair shop in the Bay Area, with full time service men and women on duty every day. The people at Wheel Away Cycle Center are constantly keeping abreast of all the new items coming on the market in order to keep up with the cyclist's needs.

Wheel Away carries bicycles for everyone in the family. From the most advanced cyclist, riding in marathon races, to a young child just beginning to ride for the first time. Bicycles are a great way to get in shape, save money and help the environment. Stop by for a visit and see what you can Wheel Away.

(See special invitation in the Appendix)

Theater

GASLIGHTER THEATER AND SALOON
400 E Campbell Avenue
Campbell, CA 95008
Tel. (408) 866-1408
Hrs: Box Office   Mon. - Sat.   10:00 a.m. - 7:00 p.m.
        Performances   Friday   8:30 p.m.
                              Saturday   6:30 p.m. & 9:30 p.m.
Visa and MasterCard are accepted.

There he is! Look, what's he doing? Oh no, that ugly man in the black cape is tying that poor, innocent girl to the railroad tracks! Horror of horrors, can anyone stop him? Yes, he can, the man wearing the big white hat with that indomitable smile on his face. The villain is foiled, and good prevails once again. This is the type of hilarious entertainment that awaits you at The Gaslighter Theater and Saloon.

You can boo, hiss, throw popcorn at the villains and much more in this Barbary Coast style theater. For starters, make your way to the bar which features domestic and imported beers, wine, soft drinks, candies, hot dogs and many other taste pleasing snacks. Then, when ushered into the theater by one of the local dance hall girls, be seated and prepare yourself for some of the best family entertainment you've ever seen. You'll notice two large baskets of popcorn situated next to your seat that you can use as you see fit, that villain is an awfully nasty critter.

In addition to the regular shows, The Gaslighter Theater offers special packages for groups of thirty people or more. Some packages feature pizza and beer served in the saloon, others feature complete dinners. Come on down to The Gaslighter and lend your support to the protagonist, not to mention the innocent lass.

Toys

D & J HOBBY AND CRAFTS
96 San Thomas Aquino Road
Campbell, CA 95008
Tel. (408) 379-1696
Hrs: Mon., Thur., Fri.   10:30 a.m. - 9:00 p.m.
      Tue., Wed.   10:30 a.m. - 6:00 p.m.
      Saturday   10:00 a.m. - 5:30 p.m.
      Sunday   12:00 noon - 5:30 p.m.

How would you like to control your own submarine; to be able to cruise the depths in complete silence? Or perhaps, you'd rather engineer a train down a difficult section of tracks? If you like these scenarios, then you're sure to be pleased with a visit to D & J Hobby and Crafts.

Darrel and Janet Pozzi own and operate the hobby store that enables you to make a fantasy into reality. Items like radio controlled helicopters, submarines, cars, boats and airplanes are only a few of the interesting items carried in this unique shop. The 20,000 square foot emporium also features over 1,000 model trains, cars and engines, as well as miniature dragons, telescopes, porcelain dolls, doll-house furniture and much more. Each department is staffed by knowledgeable hobby professionals who love what their work.

D & J Hobbies and Crafts is the largest store of their kind in the Western United States. Now we know what the technical geniuses that built Silicon Valley do for fun. Why not, it's terrific. Stop by, board your submarine, sound the diving alarm and take 'er deep.

(See special invitation in the Appendix.)

Cupertino

Coffee Shop

L'EPICURE, 19720 Steven's Creek Boulevard, Cupertino, California. A gourmet food shop that features fine coffees, teas, wines, imported cheese, pate and pastas.

THE ROASTED COFFEE BEAN, 10917 North Wolfe Road, Cupertino, California. Coffee roasted on the premises. Coffee accessories retailed.

Furnishings

**HABERSHAM PLANTATION
COUNTRY STORE**
Vallco Fashion Park
10123 N Wolfe Road
Cupertino, CA 95014
Tel. (408) 255-2275
Hrs: Mon. - Fri.   10:00 a.m. - 9:00 p.m.
      Saturday   10:00 a.m. - 6:00 p.m.
      Sunday   11:00 a.m. - 6:00 p.m.
Visa, MasterCard and AMEX accepted.
As of Sept. 1, 1987 the address will be:
1175 Homestead
Sunnyvale, CA 94087
Tel. (408) 255-2275

The misconception of Silicon Valley is that just because the area is on the leading edge of modern technology, there is no one that appreciates the simpler things that a country lifestyle has to offer. Don't be fooled. One of the most popular stores in Cupertino, for both browsing and shopping, Habersham Plantation Country Store is dedicated to the best of American country.

With over 3000 square feet of space, Habersham's is the largest country store in the Bay Area; it is separated into a series of rooms so that the feeling is one of having been invited into someone's home. The wide, wood-plank floors, abundance of authentic country furniture from New England craftsman, and the decorator accessories provide the setting for a fulfilling shopping experience.

The two couples that own and run the store, Billie and Kell Schmidt and Chris and Betty Van den Heuvel, search out a wide selection of country ware: rag rugs, pewter, hand-dipped candles, cookware, confections, scented items, wooden ornaments, wrought iron tools and copper utensils.

Habersham Plantation Store offers its' customers an array of services. For home decorating you can order a beautiful silk or dried flower arrangement by Kerilyn, or, take advantage of the services of Patricia Rocha, the in-store interior designer who specializes in American County decor. For those couples just starting out, Habersham Plantation Country Store has a bridal registry and a selection of lace bridal accessories.

LORE´ CLASSIC DESIGN
10871 N Wolfe Road
Vallco Village
Cupertino, CA 95014
Tel. (408) 257-2840
Hrs: Mon. - Sat.   10:00 a.m. - 5:30 p.m.
     Thu.   10:00 a.m. - 8:00 p.m.
Sunday by appointment.

Lore´ dispels the myth that custom furniture designed specifically with your needs in mind is exorbitantly expensive. The truth is that at Lore´ Classic Designs you can get exactly what you want for less than you would pay most retailers for a factory produced piece.

At Lore´ you have a choice. You can come into the showroom with an idea in mind or you can call and ask a designer to come to your home to work with you. At the showroom you can select between pre-designed frames or custom design a frame and choose from over 200 upholstery fabrics or leathers.

Along with furniture, Lore´ also carries a variety of other home decorations including lamps, mirrors, accent rugs, objects d'art, and beautiful watercolors by several artists and most prominent, award winning artists. Lore´ Classic Design is definitely a "Best Choice" for shopping and browsing.

Gift

GIFTS UNIQUE, 21269 Stevens Creek Boulevard, Cupertino, California. Decorative and collectible gifts from around the world.

HERITAGE PEWTER, 21269 Valencia, Cupertino, California. Limited edition sculptures by artist Michael Anthony Ricker.

VALENCIA
VALENCIA
10123 North Wolfe Road
at Vallco Fashion Park
Cupertino, CA 95014
Tel. (408) 253-4110
Hrs: Mon. - Fri.   10:00 a.m. - 9:00 p.m.
     Saturday   10:00 a.m. - 6:00 p.m.
     Sunday   11:00 a.m. - 6:00 p.m.

The choices available at Valencia are varied enough that almost everyone will be able to find the perfect item, whether for that special occasion or for day-to-day usage. Owned and operated by Donald and Leah Valencia, the store exemplifies their excellent taste and management style in its' organization of displayed items.

Select from figurines and sculptures in bronze, carved wood, soapstone, and ceramic. It boasts the area's largest selection of sterling silver and amber jewelry. There's glass art in many forms: etched, sculpted, layered, hand-painted, colored, blown, lead crystal, satin, and glazed. Valencia carries an array of special decorations for the home, such as: mobiles, tapestries, wooden boxes, distinctive oil lamps and windchimes.

Beyond the beauty of the works presented, two virtues of the merchandise at Valencia add special value: all items are beautifully hand-crafted by artisans who take the time to care about quality and aesthetics... and as Donald Valencia stated, "If more than one artist if doing the same kind of work, with equal quality, I'll carry the one from California." So, pride of craft and pride of state.

Restaurants

BAXTER'S, 19624 Stevens Creek Boulevard, Cupertino, California. Burgers, chicken and more. Disco dancing seven nights a week.

DEL MONACO, 107 North De Anza Boulevard, Cupertino, California. Mesquite broiled steaks, prime rib, seafood and fresh pasta.

RUSTY PELICAN, 10741 North Wolfe Road, Cupertino, California. Seafood specialties in a South Pacific atmosphere.

Sport

THE MILLPOND FOR SPORTSMEN
10893 N Wolfe Road
Vallco Village
Cupertino, CA 95014
Tel. (408) 996-8916
Hrs: Mon.- Sat.   10:00 a.m. - 5:30 p.m.
      Thu.   10:00 a.m. - 8:00 p.m.
      Sunday   12:00 noon - 5:00 p.m.

If "avid" is a word you use to describe your fishing interest; if the word your wife uses is a lot less polite than "avid"; if you believe that fishing is more than merely weekend recreation but a great metaphor for what is truly no less

497

than a way of life; then pull over in Cupertino. This store is for you. Just look in the window and you'll be lured in to the store.

From beginner's classes in fly-casting to intermediate fly-tying up to advanced rod building, it's all here. All of it! There are even special services available for your age and skill level, from guided tours of top fishing lodges around the world to a call in service to find out who's catching what biting what where. What? No, where!

Cast your line toward The Millpond - you're bound to catch a big one!

(See special invitation in the Appendix.)

Gilroy

Slowly climbing up the Coyote Creek drainage from San Francisco Bay, U.S. 101 reaches an elevation of 190 feet above sea level at Gilroy. This is the heart of the lower Santa Clara Valley's rich farms and truck gardens. The town is named after a ship jumper, John Cameron, who left a vessel at Monterey in 1814, taking the name Gilroy for his California life. Gilroy did well for himself, marrying the daughter of Ygnacio Ortega and inheriting Ortega's Rancho San Ysidro. The city was incorporated in 1870.

This is a major crossroads for east-west and north-south travel, dating back to the Monterey settlement. Pacheco Pass road winds east of Gilroy through the mountains to the San Luis Dam and reservoir which is a key part of the multi-million dollar California Water Project. Hecker Pass road goes west over a scenic mountain route to Watsonville on the Pajaro River. Travelers in a hurry should avoid the twisting Hecker Pass, and go south to where U.S. 101 crosses the Pajaro, then take State 129 west following the Pajaro canyon.

About 27,000 people live in the city, several thousand more on nearby farms. The climate is mild, suited for growing garlic for seed, a product which gives the town a reputation celebrated each July with a Garlic Festival. Garlic production moved beyond seed in 1927 when the C.B. Gentry Chili Powder Company launched dehydration of garlic and onion for concentrates used in food preparation. Other crops of note here include wine grapes, many fermented to premium vintage in local wineries.

Attractions

The **Gilroy Historical Museum**, 195 Fifth Street, is located in the **Carnegie Library** build in 1910. There is a 2,000 volume reference library, and collections showing history of the South Santa Clara County area. Open

Monday through Friday, 9:00 a.m. to 12:00 noon and 1:00 p.m. to 5:00 p.m. Saturday, 1:00 p.m to 5:00 p.m. Telephone (408) 847-2685.

Twelve miles northeast of town is **Gilroy Hot Springs**, once a spa with shuttle stage coach service from the Gilroy train depot. **Coe State Park** is nearby the ruins of the vandalized spa and wells.

Downtown Gilroy has several examples of turn of the century architecture, including its old city hall and Masonic Temple and Strand Theater building. Monterey Street is the starting point for walking tours. Brochures with detailed information can be obtained at the museum or Chamber of Commerce.

Seventeen **wineries** are in the area, most offering tasting rooms and tours. The **Gilroy Visitors and Convention Bureau** will mail a brochure for a self-guiding tour.

Garlic World, 4860 Monterey Highway, is a store specializing in Gilroy's "Garlic Capital of the World" reputation. Garlic in just about every imaginable form is for sale here. Open daily. Telephone (408) 247-2251.

For more information, contact the **Gilroy Visitors and Convention Bureau**, 780 Monterey Street, Gilroy CA 95020. Telephone (408) 842-6437.

Los Altos

Antiques

ANTIQUARIAN SHOP, 220 State Street, Los Altos, California. Fine 18th and early 19th century porcelain and pottery. Paintings, early glass and silver, and fine antique music boxes.

BOOK NEST, 366 Second Street, Los Altos, California. Antiquarian books, leather-bound and used books in all subjects.

MAIN STREET ANTIQUES
351 Main Street
Los Altos, CA 94022
Tel. (415) 941-2967
(415) 948-5147

For many years antiques have been a central part of the shopping in Los Altos. By demanding authenticity and prices that make collecting something affordable, Main Street Antiques has created and maintained standards that attract people from miles around.

This is a wonderful, warm country shop which specializes in quilts and Americana. Some of the antiques generally in stock are 19th and early 20th century hand-pieced quilts from New England and the Midwest, country furniture, early baskets and folk art. Owner Bea Teer goes shopping several times a year to keep her shop well stocked.

Main Street Antiques, located on the second floor at 341 Main Street, is your "Best Choice" for country antiques, quilts and folk art.

MARIA'S, 393 Main Street, Los Altos, California. Country French furniture, fine European pine and English antiques. Quimper, china, sterling, jewelry and other accessories.

ORIENTAL CORNER, 280 Main Street, Los Altos, California. Fine Oriental antiquest including porcelains, furniture, paintings and jewelry.

Apparel

CHLOE
316 State Street
Los Altos, CA 94022
Tel. (415) 949-5558
Hrs: Mon. - Sat. 10:00 a.m. - 5:30 p.m.
All major credit cards are accepted.

At Chloe its what you don't see that counts! Nothing in the world makes a woman feel more feminine and luxurious than fine lingerie...a personal elegance that gives a lady an aura of grace and confidence.

Decorated in peach and lace, the shop specializes in fine lingerie and sleepwear in natural fibers such as silk and cotton and provides a choice selection of domestic and imported undergarments. They have one of the Bay Area's largest selections of Lejoby, the most renowned bra makers in France, as well as selections from Lily of France, Christian Dior, Robes of California,

500

Blanche, Christine Prsenza and Iris. Chloe also carries a nice selection of easy-to-wear and care for styles for casual apparel, turtlenecks and cowls, camisoles and lace collars. There's a cache of accessories, including jewelry, hosiery, garter belts, bridal accessories and robes from terry to silk.

Custom ordering is done gladly as is shipping anywhere in the United States. Once you've found your favorite styles and designer line, owner Marie Stevens will put an information card together for the gentleman in your life. After all...when you ask for "silkies", he should know where to get it for you...right?

Art

SUNBIRD GALLERY
243 Main Street
Los Altos, CA 94922
Tel. (415) 941-1561
Hrs: Mon. - Sat. 10:00 a.m. - 5:30 p.m.
All major credit cards are accepted.

There are still some art dealers with the courage to carry almost exclusively original works, allowing artists to show the full effects of their talents. One of the best outlets for original paintings and sculpture on the peninsula is Sunbird Gallery. It is the largest independent fine art gallery between San Francisco and Carmel and is separated into three sections.

The front gallery features art and artists of the southwest, with a mixture of works depicting western life, wildlife, Indian culture and featured artists are changed regularly. The two smaller galleries house a wider variety of paintings, although there are still many pieces in the western and wildlife themes. In addition, you can browse through marine paintings by Nelson, Pettit or Sumner, and there's an entire section of modern pieces by artists such as W.H. Dietrich, Tim Holmes and others.

In addition to the art, Sunbird Gallery presents occasional lectures about various artists and art forms. Whenever possible, they bring in an artist whose works are currently being featured to meet the public. Every September, Sunbird Gallery hosts a special all western art show especially for lovers of western art. Seeking the original? Go to Sunbird Gallery in Los Altos.

ZYT GALLERIE AND YOUR FRAMING CENTER
ZYT GALLERIE AND YOUR FRAMING CENTER
923 North San Antonio Road
Los Altos, CA 94022
Tel. (415) 948-6770
Hrs: Tue. & Thu.   10:00 a.m. - 9:00 p.m.
Wed., Fri. & Sat.   10:00 a.m. - 6:00 p.m.
All major credit cards are accepted.

Fine artwork enhances a room and reflects the occupants taste and style. Your Framing Center and the Zyt Gallerie provide the fullest opportunity for you to make the most of home or office. The store was originally a custom frame shop, doing high quality work at reasonable prices, but the owners wanted to offer more to their customers. So, they turned a portion of their shop into a do-it-yourself framing center, in which they cut all the materials, from moldings to glass and then gave instruction to people who were willing to put it together themselves.

The newest addition to the shop is Zyt Gallerie, which features top quality artwork such as hand colored etchings, limited edition prints, graphics and prints by such greats as Erte and Ansel Adams and Zyt Gallerie's own artist, Francesca Benevento.

The gallery is run by art director Alicia Searle who also serves as a trained design consultant, working with customers both in the gallery and in their homes and offices to help select the perfect artwork and frames to enhance a room. Reflect the real you....with a fine quality print and frame from Zyt Gallerie and Your Framing Center.

Attraction

HISTORY HOUSE MUSEUM, 51 South San Antonio Road, Los Altos, California. One of the original Los Altos homes restored to its early 20th century refinement. Home of the Los Altos Historical Society and keeper of the local archives.

Books

LINDEN TREE CHILDREN'S RECORDS AND BOOKS
365 1st Street
Los Altos, CA 94022
Tel. (415) 949-3390
Hrs: Mon. - Sat. 9:30 a.m. - 5:30 p.m.
Visa and MasterCard are accepted.

Parents know that the best types of entertainment for children are also educational. Parents and others who care for children will travel from around the Bay Area to Linden Tree, Northern California's most complete store for children's books and recordings.

With thousands of books, records and tapes, including many hard to find 'copies in stock, Linden Tree also carries a large selection of books just for parents, with subjects ranging from nutrition during pregnancy to adolescence. In addition to the books and recordings, Linden Tree also carries a smaller selection of simple rhythm musical instruments so that the children can play along with their favorite records. There is a nice selection of small games and toys to keep youngsters entertained when traveling.

It's the little touches that really make Linden Tree special. A play table in the store keeps small ones occupied while parents shop, and when you come into the store, the staff of Linden Tree will gladly play a record or tape of any artists. Linden Tree = keeping active young minds entertained.

(See special invitation in the Appendix)

LOS ALTOS BOOKSTORE
205 State Street
Los Altos, CA 94022
Tel. (415) 941-0550
Hrs: Mon. - Sat. 10:00 a.m. - 5:30 p.m.
All major credit cards are accepted.

The most pleasing aspect of Los Altos Bookstore, and the one that sets it apart from almost every other bookstore, is the warm and unhurried ambiance. Hardwood floors and a large skylight give the store a homey, inviting feel, and the presence of a small table for children and comfortable sofa for adults lets you know you're welcome. For years Los Altos Bookstore has been one of a handful of bookstores that area people travel to when looking for special titles. The largest section of the store is set aside for children, ranging from cloth books for infants through traditional favorites and many hard to find titles in hardback as well as paperback. The rest of the store is dedicated to non fiction titles including well stocked biographical sections, philosophy, how-to, self help, and a special section for books about California, the west, and more.

In addition to selection and atmosphere there are a variety of services available. If you have difficulty finding a particular title, Los Altos Bookstore will be happy to special order it, and once you have made your selections they will gift wrap at no extra cost. For customers who enjoy reading fictional bestsellers, there is a lending library of current choices. Be sure to look for the bulletin board outside the store headed by "the quote of the week", with lots of space set aside for passerby's intelligent responses to opinions from past literary leaders. Stop in, find a "good read", and on the way out jot a few of your own "words of wisdom" for the world to see!

(See special invitation in the Appendix.)

Clocks

TIME PERIOD
357 Main Street
Los Altos, CA 94022
Tel. (415) 949-1649
Hrs: Tue. - Sat. 10:30 a.m. - 5:30 p.m.
Visa, MasterCard and Discovery cards are accepted.

People are always trying to save it, manage it, invest it, make it, and everyone wishes they had more of it, no, not money! Time! So it only makes sense that the clocks used to keep track of time be the most distinctive you can find.

Time Period has nearly one thousand new clocks, but their specialty is the complete restoration of fine antique timepieces. Because of the high quality of his work, owner Dick Osgood is becoming one of the more respected names among collectors, and is a lecturer who has made three videos for the National Association of Watch and Clock Collectors.

Whether you prefer antiques, reproductions or modern works, Time Period has timepieces for any room in the house, from grandfather and grandmother clocks, hall and wall clocks to alarm and travel clocks. Every piece on display is from makers who care about quality, design and function. Time Period has a clock that will please you...time after time after time!

504

Gifts

B. K. COLLECTIONS, 342 State Street, Los Altos, California. Antique Oriental furnishings, silk flower arrangements, jewelry, brass, frames, photo albums and home accessories.

THE WORKS, 240 Main Street, Los Altos, California. Build your own gift basket with fresh, hand-dipped chocolates, over 100 cheeses, fudge, wine, coffee, tea, mulling spices, meats and more!

T.N. SPICE
4546 El Camino Real
Los Altos, CA 94022
Tel. (415) 941-7363
Hrs: Mon. - Sat.   8:30 a.m. - 9:00 p.m.
      Sunday   11:00 a.m. - 8:00 p.m.
Visa and AMEX are accepted.

T.N. Spice 'n everything....you guessed it! The main focus of this very nice store is, as the name suggests, specialty teas and coffees with over forty types of coffee beans from award winning roasters, a selection of over three dozen bulk teas and almost as many available in tea bags from around the globe. There is also a complete array of accessories for tea or coffee drinking needs.

Locals come in daily for the pleasant atmosphere surrounding the cafe like espresso bar. Current and back issues of popular magazines are available to read and many people use T.N. Spice as a meeting place. They enjoy the hot espresso, cappuccino or ninotchka, a combination of espresso and steamed milk topped with hand whipped cream, dutch chocolate, toasted almonds and grated orange peel, or they may come to savor the best hot chocolate around.

Whatever your reason for coming, don't pass up the fresh pastries and tempting desserts. T.N. Spice is everything nice...and getting better all the time!

(See special invitation in the Appendix).

Jewelry

GLEIM JEWELERS, 350 Main Street, Los Altos, California. Traditional and custom jewelry designs.

LESCAUT, INC.
220 State Street
Los Altos, CA 94022
Tel. (415) 948-9229
Hrs: Mon. - Sat. 10:00 a.m. - 5:00 p.m.
All major credit cards are accepted.

Nothing is more personal or revealing than jewelry. The type, style and amount worn by an individual tells so much about a person's taste and personality. Therefore, great care should be taken in selecting perfect accessories and no one goes to greater lengths than the proprietor of Lescaut, Inc.

At Lescaut the atmosphere is very open and personal. The display of jewelry is presented in several renditions of Thos. Jefferson's desk from Monticello...but with beveled glass tops that allow for looking at the "gems." Wanda Martin, the owner will work with you to find the perfect accents for your personality and lifestyle. There are American and European-crafted works, estate jewelry and one-of-a-kind pieces available through the design creations of her goldsmiths.

The custom jewelry is presented in drawings, hours are spent carefully carving the wax replica (which can be tried on for approval before the final casting is made) and, when the result is presented, you know that the piece is entirely yours.

The offerings in this shop are comparable to Tiffany's of New York. Featured, in the finest quality available, are classic pearls, jade and colored gemstones. Wanda says, "I like to consider the jewelry I sell to be the heirlooms of tomorrow--at today's competitive pricing."

(See special invitation in the Appendix.)

Linens

LINENS OF LOS ALTOS
Table Top, Bedding & Gifts
271 Main Street
Los Altos, CA 94022
Tel. (415) 948-4395
Hrs: Mon. - Fri.   10:00 a.m. - 5:30 p.m.
          Saturday   10:00 a.m. - 5:00 p.m.
Visa and MasterCard are accepted.
Special services: bridal registry, custom table pads, bedding, tablecloths.

A steady stream of customers have been delighting in Linens of Los Altos' extensive selection of table top and bed linens for more than four years now. This fine shop specializes in tablecloths for tables of all sizes and in a choice of easy-care fabrics, 100% linen and cotton, cutwork, damasks, crochets, vinyls and much more. Placemats, napkins, runners and doilies--all conveniently displayed. The range of bed linens includes blanket covers, duvet covers, dust ruffles, hand-woven throws and a constantly-changing selection of accent pillows. In addition, you can find handkerchiefs, gifts and tabletop accessories including crystal and silver. A courteous staff will gift wrap and ship via UPS for the customers' convenience.

Restaurant

ARNO'S, 397 Main Street, Los Altos, California. Continental cuisine in a newly remodeled restaurant.

BEAU SEJOUR
BEAU SEJOUR
170 State Street
Los Altos, CA 94022
Tel.   (415) 948-1382
         (415) 948-1388
Hrs: Lunch   Mon. - Fri.   11:30 a.m. - 2:00 p.m.
          Dinner Mon. - Sat.   5:30 p.m. - 10:00 p.m.
All major credit cards are accepted.

It's difficult to say which is more interesting, the story of Beau Sejour restaurant, or the story of Beau Sejour's owner and chef, Lap Huynh, or whether it is even possible to separate the two. Either way, both are deserving of praise, and that praise has not been lacking, coming from sources such as *Gourmet* magazine, *New West* magazine, and the top newspapers throughout California. The Huynh family's reputation for fine restaurants stretches back over two decades when Lap was owner of the well known Olympia restaurant, serving haute French cuisine to diplomats and officials visiting Saigon. Once in this country, Chef Lap took the opportunity to improve his own cooking skills, studying under famed French chefs Michel Guerard and Patissier Gaston Lenotre.

Beau Sejour's decor is designed to give the feel of dining in a French country home. The menu is full of delicious and distinctive dishes, including three and four course Prix-fixe menus for under fifteen and twenty dollars respectively. The a la carte menu includes such specialties as Saint Jaques au Shitake, Soja et Cylantro - scallops and mushrooms in cilantro sauce, and Veau en Croute - thinly sliced veal, pate de foie gras and mushrooms wrapped in a tender pastry.

The newest addition to Beau Sejour is the cafe and bar on the lower level, serving a creative weekly menu of fresh pastas, sandwiches, seafood, salads and more, direct from Chef Lap's kitchen for under ten dollars. Beau Sejour translates to "good visit", which is precisely what you will have when you dine at this "Best Choice" restaurant.

CAPRICCIO, 4546 El Camino Real, Los Altos, California. Very modern...very Italian...very good.

CHEF CHU'S, 1067 North San Antonio Road, Los Altos, California. Original interpretations of Szechwan.

COLUMBUS STREET RESTAURANT & BAR, 4898 El Camino Real, Los Altos, California. Italian cuisine featuring seafood, milk-fed veal, and fresh pasta.

PENG'S, 4320 El Camino Real, Los Altos, California. Chinese cuisine featuring Hunan specialties.

508

Sport

THE MIDGE
271 State Street
Los Altos, CA 94022
Tel.   (415)   941-8871
       (415)   948-0105
Hrs: Mon. - Wed.   10:00 a.m. - 6:00 p.m.
      Thursday   10:00 a.m. - 9:00 p.m.
      Friday   10:00 a.m. - 6:00 p.m.
      Saturday   10:00 a.m. - 5:00 p.m.
      Sunday   12:00 noon - 4:00 p.m.
Visa and MasterCard are accepted.

There's an old saying amongst fishermen, "To be lucky once is easy, to be lucky all the time you need the right equipment!" For fly fishing, one of the best sources of that consistent kind of luck is The Midge, Northern California's fastest growing independent dealer in fly fishing equipment.

Don't let the size of the store fool you. Although it may appear small, it's packed with enough gear to supply both the weekend sportsman trying to land a few steelhead to the commercial fishermen who rely on quality equipment to make their living.

The Midge is the area's exclusive dealer for many of the lines they carry, including Orvis, Alpine, Steffen, Scott Powr-Ply and Teton. They have an exceptional array of pre-tied flies, rods, reels, fishing apparel and all the equipment needed for the dedicated fly-tier. They offer an excellent selection of services ranging from classes in fly tying and casting to instructional books and tapes, special ordering for any type of fishing, and a complete travel service, including guides for wherever you may want to fish around California or around the country. There is even a phone-in mail order service for any fishing need. So don't be lucky just once...get the right stuff!

(See special invitation in the Appendix).

Toys

LIN'S TOY CUPBOARD
237 A Street
Los Altos, CA 94022
Tel. (415) 948-4511
Hrs: Mon. - Sat. 10:00 a.m. - 5:30 p.m.
Visa and MasterCard are accepted.

There's more to finding good toys for your children than watching the Saturday morning cartoon shows, so turn off the set and head for Lin's Toy Cupboard, a place where there is a wide selection of toys for children of all ages.

At Lin's Toy Cupboard you'll find many toys that aren't in the bigger chain stores. Not only will you see big names like Legge but also lesser-knowns such as Ambi, Battat and Playmobil. Childrens' furniture pieces in Lin's are hand-crafted by people who care about sturdy, lasting furniture.

Although the stock is widely varied, with toys and games for children from newborn through adolescence, there are a few areas where Lin's Toy Cupboard specializes. Creativity is a child's best asset, and Lin's Toy Cupboard carries large amounts of art and craft materials from finger crayons for toddlers to paint sets and model building sets for older children. They also have dozens of windsocks and kites year round, so that you and your children can take advantage of a pleasant day whether it's in June or January. And now...back to *Monsters* of the *Universe*...!!!!

(See special invitation in the Appendix.)

Los Gatos

On the foothills, above the Santa Clara Valley, are several small communities which keep their identities despite the growth going on below them. Los Gatos, incorporated in 1877, has 27,500 residents and a downtown of great charm. The name of the place comes from the Spanish rancho known for the wildcats of the Santa Cruz mountains. Saratoga, Monte Sereno and Campbell are clustered near by.

Saratoga was laid out at the foot of the toll road, now Highway 9, which leads over the mountains to the redwoods. Six miles up the grade is Congress Springs where in 1866 a spa was opened. The town took its name from the famed Saratoga, New York spa.

Monte Sereno is a residential town of 3,500 incorporated in 1957 to preserve the large-lot homesites from further encroachment. Campbell is another modern creation, incorporated in 1952. Over 33,000 people are concentrated on about five and one half square miles along with the offices of Quadrex, a firm which consults on energy consumption.

Attractions

Los Altos History House Museum, 51 South San Antonio Road, Los Altos, is located in an old apricot orchard which covered much of the little civic center of town. Pictures and artifacts from the community's past are on display. Open Wednesday 1:00 p.m. to 5:00 p.m., Saturday 12:00 noon to 4:00 p.m. Call (415) 948-9427.

Villa Montalvo is a gleaming white showplace home and gardens, located at 15400 Montalvo Road, Saratoga. San Francisco mayor James Phelan built the place for weekend entertaining, then left it to the city's art foundation when he died in 1930. A gallery is open Thursday and Friday from 1:00 p.m. to 4:00 p.m., and on Saturday and Sunday from 11:00 a.m. to 4:00 p.m. The gardens are open Monday through Friday from 8:00 a.m. to 5:00 p.m., and Saturday and Sunday from 9:00 a.m. to 5:00 p.m. Call (408) 741-3421.

Hakone Japanese Gardens, 2100 Big Basin Way, Saratoga, are part of another estate. A city park since 1966, the gardens were started in 1917 to complement the home of the Oliver Charles Stines of San Francisco. Restoration work was completed in 1981. Open Monday through Friday 10:00 a.m. to 5:00 p.m., Saturday and Sunday from 11:00 a.m. to 5:00 p.m. Call (408) 867-3438 for information.

Saratoga's downtown caters to visitors with small shops and restaurants, and is listed in California's Historic Landmarks simply as **"Saratoga Village."** Highway 85 will take you to this creekside business district.

Vasona Lake Park, on Blossom Hill Road East of Los Gatos, is a shady recreation spot. There is sailboating on the lake, one of many reservoirs serving the Santa Clara Valley, and a miniature railroad ride for children. Open daily.

Several wineries are in the foothills, from the well-known **Paul Masson** holdings near Congress Springs to several small family operations. Los Gatos Chamber of Commerce will mail winery information.

511

Forbes Mill Museum, 75 Church Street, is located in what is probably the oldest standing building in Los Gatos. Open Wednesday through Sunday from 12:00 noon to 5:00 p.m. Call 395-7375.

The **Campbell Historical Museum**, Civic Center Drive at First Street, Los Gatos, is open Tuesday through Saturday from 1:00 p.m. to 4:00 p.m. Call 379-3060.

For information, **Saratoga Chamber of Commerce**, 20460 Saratoga-Los Gatos Road, Saratoga, CA 95070, telephone 867-0753; **Los Gatos Chamber of Commerce**, 5 Montebella Way, Los Gatos, CA 95030, telephone 354-9300; **Campbell Chamber of Commerce**, 328 East Campbell Avenue, Campbell, CA 95008, telephone 278-6252.

Accommodations

LA HACIENDA INN
18840 Los Gatos-Saratoga Road
Los Gatos, CA 95030
Tel. (408) 354-9230

When choosing accommodations in Los Gatos, La Hacienda Inn is unmatched in atmosphere, comfort and features. This "Best Choice" is reminiscent of the early 1900's when stagecoach travelers stopped in the vicinity to spend the night before completing the long trek over the coastal hills to Monterey Bay.

La Hacienda's unique residential setting provides the traveler with a quiet country atmosphere located midway between Saratoga and Los Gatos. Yet it is close to San Jose International Airport and Highways 17, 280, and 101. The Inn has been owned and operated by the Morosin family for more than twenty-five years. The care and hard work invested in your pleasure and comfort as a guest is apparent.

All the rooms have been beautifully renovated in a Southwestern motif with custom pine furniture. Each room includes a private patio, in-room refrigerators, color televisions, and AM-FM clock radio. Deluxe rooms with stone fireplaces and suites with complete kitchens are available. Guests are invited to enjoy the pool, relax in the spa and stroll in the handsomely-landscaped garden. A Continental breakfast is available daily to all guests.

The famed La Hacienda Restaurant, adjacent to the Inn, serves wonderful Continental dishes superbly tended by their international chefs. Banquet and wedding facilities are available and the piano bar is open every night until 2:00 a.m.

La Hacienda Inn is ideal for travelers who enjoy gracious comfort in an informal atmosphere. The Inn meets the demands of both the corporate and leisure traveler and provides facilities for small seminars. Rates range from $61.00 for a single to $111.00 for a deluxe suite. When you're in the Los Gatos area, try La Hacienda Inn for a wonderful experience.

Antiques

ANTIQUES COLONY
140 West Main Street
Los Gatos, CA 95030
Tel. (408) 354-3484
Hrs: Mon. - Sat.   10:00 a.m. - 5:00 p.m.
     Sunday   11:00 a.m. - 5:00 p.m.

Since 1904 the Opera House has stood on West Main Street. Built and originally operated by Southern Pacific stationmaster, Eugene Ford, it has served as home for numerous groups and businesses. In the early years, until 1916, it was a socially active gathering place, hosting school plays, graduations, political meetings and a theater circuit. In recent years it has been known by antique collectors from all over Northern California as the Opera House Antiques.

Current operators Paul and Linda Dorsa have named it the Antiques Colony, counterpart to their Antiques Colony on San Carlos Street in San Jose. Both are excellent collectives. The Opera House, with its historical location and 35 exhibitors is a favorite in Los Gatos among antiquers. Its personality is formed by the collective character of the exhibitors, with quality evident throughout. Vendors displaying near the front of the shop concentrate on antique furniture--armoires, desks, buffets, many ornately hand-carved with roses, crests and scrolls.

Additionally, you'll select from some exceptional pieces such as I saw on my last visit. Like, Currier & Ives lithographs, scenes of Washington crossing the Delaware, and the signing of the Declaration of Independence. One vendor features artifacts of Northwest Indians, turquoise jewelry and beautiful collector dolls. Another vendor offers oriental items, exquisite cloisonne ring boxes and snuff bottles. There is lovely satin glass, splendid cut crystal, Heisey, depression glass and Tiffany.

Ladies who seek a quality selection of vintage clothing will find 30's through 50's skirts, ruffled dresses, plush velvet suits, hats, coats, scarves and shoes. Primitives abound. Items like teapots, beaters, grinders and muffin pans. There's beautiful jewelry--brooches, rings, bracelets. This is only some highlights of the thousands of excellent collectables available on the bottom floor.

A trip to the loft at the Antiques Colony is always a treat. Art Deco lovers will find wonders galore. Nostalgia. Magnificent oak armoires, brass floor lamps with elegant silk shades...one can almost hear the thrilling arias of singers from yesteryear so rich is the feeling of history and aesthetic pleasure.

The Antiques Colony at the Opera House is one of those wonderful places where posterity is preserved by means of thoughtful handling of an historical structure, and, it's a real favorite of the antique treasure hunters.

DeVILLAR GALLERY, 18400 Overlook Road, Los Gatos, California. Fine antique oil paintings, sculpture and furniture.

PATTERSON'S ANTIQUES
PATTERSON'S ANTIQUES
88 West Main Street
Los Gatos, CA 95031
Tel. (408) 354-1718
Hrs: 11:00 am-5:00 pm 7 days a week

Patterson's Antiques is an old-timer among the raft of antique dealers here in Los Gatos. The Seelering nickelodeon which has been the waypost at Patterson's for the last 15 years delightfully suggests the mood and specialty that have made the shop a unique and popular antique store through the years. Patterson's carries a full line of antiques including furniture, oil paintings, glass ware, dishes and jewelry, but the real attraction is the incredible collection of toys, books, assorted documents and sundry railroad items. The Fetwell Building that houses the shop is itself an antique, as well as a town landmark, dating back to 1908. Once you're inside Patterson's be sure to look up 14' to the beautiful patterned tin work ceiling that is original to this building. Mrs. Patterson and her right-hand, Chuch Bergtold offer warm greetings to shop visitors. With a little prodding, you can enjoy their stories about individual pieces and the antique knowledge they have spent years accumulating. Be sure to ask about the collection of lead soldiers near the rear of the shop. This impressive collection of more than 500 figurines from the 1930s makes up a legion of infantry men and gunners; all are decked in World War I style gear. Close by historic navel recognition models stand in tribute to their days as the playing pieces for World War II planning sessions and Pacific sea battle simulations. Other war memorabilia can be uncovered in the far reaches of Patterson's where train timetables, photographs, menus and reports are stored. War medals of all kinds are much easier to find; they are displayed in a couple of places among the jewelry, collectables and silver spoons displayed in glass cases. Firemans' badges and hats, firehose nozzles along with train conductors' lamps are among the unique collectables available here. If war toys and memorabilia don't interest you, ask about the Bohemian etched glass dinner service from the Leland Stanford estate. This gem sits inconspicuously against the left wall. A closer look reveals a sparkling amber and clear pastoral pattern, delicately and artfully etched around each of the 75 pieces in the collection. The wealth of antique pieces here make Patterson's an adventure to visit.

Apparel

J. ALEXANDER, Old Town, 50 University Avenue, Los Gatos, California. A fine woman's boutique with unique selections of "studded" dresses, jumpsuits and pants created by local artisans.

Art Gallery

EL GATITO GALLERY, 123 West Main Street, Los Gatos, California. Oldest gallery in Los Gatos. Thirty local artists contribute to the gallery. Display of paintings: pastels, oils, watercolors, photographs and jewelry. New show every month.

Bar

CARRY NATIONS, 8 North Santa Cruz Avenue, Los Gatos, California. Seeing is believing. A fun spot!

Body Oil/Scents

BARE ESCENTIALS
54 North Santa Cruz Avenue
Los Gatos, CA 95030
Tel. (408) 354-8853
Hrs: Mon. - Sun.   10:00 a.m. - 6:00 p.m.
      Friday   10:00 a.m. - 9:00 p.m.

At Bare Escentials you can indulge your body with fragrant lotions and rich, soothing oils that make you feel absolutely luxurious. The shop's pure jojoba oil, rich avocado oil and healing aloe and comfrey lotions will leave your skin feeling clean, natural, and refreshed. Like the bright, colorful lupines that grow wild in the neighboring Santa Cruz Mountains, products manufactured and sold at Bare Escentials are nature's own. Pure ingredients--aloe, rosewater, honey and chamomile--produce soaps, lotions, oils and cosmetics that work with your body, beautifying, soothing and healing. A myriad of fragrances and cosmetics can be matched to your own skin type and coloring by salespeople who know and use the products they suggest for you. Custom blended colors and fragrances help to achieve that special look or scent you want. A complete line of pure, packaged Bare Escentials make-up shades and perfume scents are also available.

Top quality and satisfaction are always guaranteed since every product is subject to rigorous testing before it hits the shelves. Diane Richardson created the Bare Escentials product line after searching for a natural make-up that looked and felt good on her own sensitive skin. She tests each new product to her own stringent standards, and only when those needs are met, does it receive the Bare Escentials label.

Diane praises customers for their innovative ideas and curiosity. Many of the shop's best powder shades and fragrance blends started as customer suggestions. Feel free to ask questions and try the "gourmet" products -- "leisure products" such as bubble baths that are scented or, naughty/nice love oils for a delicious body massage.

While you're there, don't miss French Doors, the clothing annex at the back of the store. You'll find one-of-a-kind watersilk jumpsuits and beaded dresses imported from around the world. Pamper yourself--at the Bare Escentials. Beautiful, natural make-up and a chic new outfit. You're worth it!

Coffee Shop

LOS GATOS ROASTING COMPANY, 101 West Main Street, Los Gatos, California. Everything for the avid coffee-drinker.

Linens

THE MAID'S QUARTERS
5 North Santa Cruz Avenue
Los Gatos, CA 95030
Tel. (408) 395-1980
Hrs: Tues. - Sat.   10:00 a.m. - 5:00 p.m.
          Sun. - Mon.   Closed
Call for special hours in December

While strolling through picturesque Los Gatos, a stop at the Maid's Quarters is a must. Claudia Mann, Judy Burgard and Lyn Collishaw opened this beautiful shop seven years ago, and their expertise in bedroom, table top and bathroom design shows throughout the store.

They specialize in domestic and imported bedding, and they regularly work with designers to custom-design bedding and accessories to fit your decor. Such famous lines as Palais Royal, Le Jacquard Francais, Paper White, Brinkhaus and many others fill their store with sheets, comforters, duvet cases, pillows, towels and selected table linens. Displays include beautiful cherrywood beds and other furnishings from the Harden Company.

Although bedding is their specialty, the Maid's Quarters also has unique gift items such as silver and pewter picture frames, handkerchiefs for men and women, fine porcelain, silver and stainless steel serving pieces and flatware, casual and formal dinnerware, imported soaps, lotions and bath accessories, elegant lounging robes and selected baby items.

The friendly staff at the Maid's Quarters are happy to consult with you when putting together your dream bedroom or bathroom. One warning though! a bedroom decorated with items from the Maid's Quarters might make it even harder to get out of bed in the morning.

Pottery

MUD IN YOUR EYE
50 University Avenue
Los Gatos, CA 95030
Tel. (408) 354-8104
Hrs: Mon.-Wed.   10:00 a.m. - 6:00 p.m.
      Thu.-Fri.   10:00 a.m. - 9:00 p.m.
      Saturday   10:00 a.m. - 6:00 p.m.
      Sunday   11:00 a.m. - 5:00 p.m.

If pottery is your passion, then Mud in Your Eye is close to heaven. This shop is loaded with every kind of pottery imaginable, from friendly character mugs and adorable pot critters to gallery quality vases and works of art.

More than sixty artists contribute their works to the large, varied inventory of the store. Owner Kyong Clark and his knowledgeable staff can help you find just what you're looking for. Every piece in the shop is unique since every piece is individually handmade. Browsing is an art in itself at Mud in Your Eye since every nook and cranny is filled with exceptional quality bowls, vases and lamps. Artists such as Marsha Ton have their work featured throughout the store so leave yourself plenty of time to look for hidden treasures.

Items that are both beautiful art and functional houseware are the trademark of Mud in Your Eye, both a household supply establishment and an art gallery

(See special invitation in the Appendix.)

Restaurants

C. B. HANNEGAN'S
208 Bachman Avenue
Los Gatos, CA 95030
Tel. (408) 395-1233
Hrs: Rest: Mon. - Sun.   11:30 a.m. - 12:00 midnight
      Pub: Mon. - Sun.   11:30 a.m. - 2:00 a.m.

This Irish-style pub provides lunch, dinner and cocktails for a large cross-section of the community and has become a popular spot for locals and travelers over the past seven years it has been in business. Johnny Hannegan and Chris Benson own and operate this favorite establishment in the town they were born and raised in.

Chris runs the restaurant section, which boasts a brick barbeque pit with its all-oakwood fire. He serves the tastiest burgers, ribs, and homemade sausage in town. Also served are delicious barbequed chickens, hearty pastrami sandwiches, spicy pizza, fresh green salads and homemade soups. The same menu is served all day long with daily specials like roast turkey, roast sirloin, corned beef and cabbage, and roast leg of lamb, each served with all the trimmings. Lunch and dinner are served on large wooden tables, at the counter facing the barbeque pit or upstairs in the bar overlooking the restaurant. Prices range from $3.00 to $8.00.

Larry runs the Irish Pub upstairs and proudly features more than seventy single malt Scotches from the old country. Besides the full bar and specialty cocktails, the taps are always flowing with Harp Lager, Watney's Guiness Stout and Anchor Steam. The colorful bartenders entertain the customers with their unique backgrounds and knowledge. There's a different crowd at Hannegan's each night, which goes to show that this place welcomes all walks of life.

Hungry and thirsty travelers needing some good company or a late night snack will find great food, drink and fun at C. B. Hannegan's.

ELEGANT BUNS RESTAURANT
15 1/2 North Santa Cruz Avenue
Los Gatos, CA 95030
Tel. (408) 395-0414
Hrs: Mon. - Sun. 11:00 a.m. - 12:00 midnight

You can call it popular demand. The success of the Elegant Buns Restaurant in San Jose led to the opening of this new location. Although the reputation of Elegant Buns rests largely on the tremendous selection of quality burgers, it is well to note that the menu is very distinguished in its variety.

Appetizers such as breaded mushrooms, nacho melt supreme and crispy chicken strips will start out your meal. The salads are prepared with only fresh ingredients. Especially pleasing is the Chinese chicken salad with shredded lettuce topped with delicious marinated chicken, Mandarin oranges, cashews, rice noodles, sesame seeds and a superb dressing. A large variety of sandwiches ranging from barbequed beef to cheese steak will tempt you.

Entrees of deep fried calamari, rib eye steak or mixed vegetable platter and even selections from "south of the border" round out your choices. With all these choices, don't forget the burgers! The half pound burgers have been acclaimed "the valley's best," and they are available on sesame, onion, sour dough, poppy seed, whole wheat and croissant buns. In addition, burgers can be order with lean, ground white meat of turkey rather than ground beef. The elegance of the burgers comes with such items as the caviar burger, makin' bacon burger with cheese or the burger Bernaise.

Such undisguised uniqueness is certainly a prime measure of elegance as are quality, atmosphere and service. If you value these, your "Best Choice" is Elegant Buns for a fine meal and a good time.

IL PASTAIO, 15466 Los Gatos Boulevard, Los Gatos, California. A contemporary Italian cafe that serves some of the best and most creative pasta dishes encountered.

MIMI'S ROOFTOP CAFE
Old Town
50 University Ave.
Los Gatos, CA 95030
Tel. (408) 354-5511

Hrs:	Lunch	Mon. - Fri.	11:30 a.m. - 3:00 p.m.
	Brunch	Sat. - Sun.	9:00 a.m. - 5:00 p.m.
	Dinner	Tue. - Thu.	6:00 p.m. - 10:00 p.m.
		Fri. - Sat.	6:00 p.m. - 10:30 p.m.
		Sunday	6:00 p.m. - 9:00 p.m.

Imported from Old World Switzerland, come the secret delectable culinary delights of Mimi's Rooftop Cafe. The recipes that make up the menu at Mimi's are served in the surroundings and charm of an open air European cafe.

Cozy tables are placed among flowered trusses that cover balcony windows, making this a comfortable stop to enjoy the famed cheese blintzes that are one of Mimi's specialities. Cheese and custard filled, smothered with strawberries and sour cream, these blintzes leave a lasting impression on your tastebuds. They are unique enough to warrant a write up in *Gourmet* magazine. Here also you can enjoy a selection of delicious dinners that are a combination of the best French cooking tempered by California influence of the light fare. Entrees such as sole Bonne Femme are preceded by homemade soup and a fresh antipasto salad with cheese, salami, artichoke hearts and vegetables topped with homemade vinegarette. For lunch, generous sandwiches are featured along with a variety of tasty salads. Saturday and Sunday champagne brunch includes special egg dishes enhanced by freshly made sauces and toppings. Complement your meal with a fine California wine from Mimi's well stocked cellar.

Certainly a stop at Mimi's will leave you with pleasant remembrances of a refreshing atmosphere, casual Continental dining and a desire for more of those delectable cheese blintzs.

(See special invitation in the Appendix)

SOUTHERN KITCHEN
35 East Main Street
Los Gatos, CA 95030
Tel. (408) 354-7515

For the best breakfast in town, try the Southern Kitchen, owned and operated by Dino and Mary Masouris. Dino, a native of Corinth, Greece, has been in the restaurant business in this country for the past twenty years. His Los Gatos breakfast spot has been a favorite eating place for many years.

The Southern Kitchen serves hearty helpings made only from the freshest top-quality ingredients. You will notice that this place is frequented by athletes training for competition. Herb Caen even labeled the Southern Kitchen in Los Gatos the "breakfast of champions" in his column in the *San Francisco Chronicle*. The writer referred specifically to Olympic Gold Medalist, Claudia Losch, who ate here while training for the Los Angeles games.

The popular breakfast menu features a variety of delicious omelets and other egg dishes, along with pancakes and waffles, all served with hash brown, toast or fresh homemade muffins, fresh fruit, grits, and biscuits and gravy. The Southern Kitchen also specializes in banana or strawberry pancakes and waffles. Breakfast and lunch are served all day and include daily specials, such as, BBQ ribs and leg of lamb. Dino's homemade soups make a wonderful accompaniment to a hearty meal.

The staff at the Southern Kitchen is friendly and efficient, and you can't beat the prices. If there is a short wait, customers are served free fresh coffee on the wooden benches outside in picturesque downtown Los Gatos. So whether you are an athlete or just a hungry breakfast lover, the Southern Kitchen is the place for your champion breakfast.

STEAMER'S, FISH AGAIN AND PASTA TOO!

50 University Avenue (Old Town)
Los Gatos, CA 95030
Tel. (408) 395-2722
Hrs: Sun.-Thur. 11:30 a.m.-10:00 p.m.
      Fri.-Sat. 11:30 a.m.-11:00 p.m

For fresh seafood and pasta, no other place comes close to Steamer's, Fish Again and Pasta Too! Locals and travelers favor this "Best Choice" for its daily fresh catches prepared in a variety of innovative and classical styles, and for its fresh, homemade pasta dishes. Pasta selections range from the spicy Biscayan with calamari to the more sublime Carbonara in a delicate creamy sauce.

In addition to serving the best seafood and pasta, Steamer's has an atmosphere that will bring you back again and again. Seafood lovers can watch the chefs and shuckers in action while sitting at the oyster bar, dine in the intriguing Art Deco maritime decor, or sit in the outdoor patio shaded by giant live oak trees, and view historic Old Town and the Santa Cruz mountains.

Try the house favorite, Steamer's Linguine, which combines pasta with bay shrimp, mushrooms, crab, and Parmigiano Reggiano. This dish is so delicious that you'll want to order it each time you visit. But you'll have to give the other pasta dishes a try, as well as the wide variety of fresh seafood catches grilled to perfection. The appetizers are a meal in themselves. You can have raw oysters, clams, fresh jumbo prawns, deep-fried mozzarella cheese in marinara sauce, or the fresh lightly-breaded calamari.

Come to Steamer's, Fish Again and Pasta Too! for a relaxing lunch or dinner. The service is friendly, efficient, and informative. The dazzling desserts, full bar, and extensive wine list all add to a unique dining experience.

T-BIRDS PIZZA
444 North Santa Cruz
Los Gatos, CA 95030
Tel. (408) 395-2525

For classic California pizza that tops all others in the area, come into T-Birds Pizza and watch the undisputed world champion pizza spinner cook up some classic and innovative dishes. Owner Barry O'Halloran has been seen on the Tonight Show with Johnny Carson and other shows demonstrating his championship pizza dough spinning. He has won competitions in San Francisco, Las Vegas and London.

T'Birds not only claims to have the world's best pizza spinner, but owners Barry O'Halloran and Dana Smith claim the best pizza. According to Barry, "We try harder and care more about our pizzas." Only the freshest, top-quality ingredients are used on their pizzas and in unique and classic combinations. Choose among T-Birds' white or wheat and San Francisco sourdough crusts, all topped with their robust and zesty sauce. Try the Real Italian Pizza, which comes from a recipe Barry obtained from an Italian spinning competitor he met in London. It's a thin-crust pizza with olive oil, lightly sauced with extra mozzarella, sprinkled with fresh garlic and topped with fresh sliced tomatoes and grated Romano and Parmesan cheese. Or, try the Mexican-style La Bomba, with refried beans, cheddar cheese, chorizo, red onions and ground beef, topped with lettuce, black olives, fresh tomato, sour cream, salsa and Jalapeño peppers.

T-Birds also serves delicious calzone, handmade dough rolls filled with deli meats, fresh vegetables, T-Birds sauce, and a blend of domestic and imported cheeses. The hot turnover sandwiches contain a blend of cheeses and meats, garnished with tomato, red onion, lettuce, mayonnaise and mustard. To compliment these wonderful dishes, choose from twenty-four ingredients at T-Birds salad bar--topped off with their homemade dressings.

The name T-Birds fits the decor of this "Best Choice" with a fifties mood, featuring booths and background music of your favorite oldies. If you're hungry for pizza, come down to T-Birds to watch the world champion pizza spinner in action. He'll conjure up some of the best pizzas you'll ever taste.

The attractive downtown of Los Gatos, known as "Saratoga Village," and its surrounding area lend themselves admirably to sightseeing and shopping. Combining side trips with shopping and dining, such as those suggested with these two tours, will surely enhance your stay here.

TOUR OF LOS GATOS			
a.m.	Southern Kitchen	Best "all day" breakfast	Los/Res
a.m.	Villa Montalvo	Best garden walk	Los/Att
a.m.	Patterson's	Best documents	Los/Ant
a.m.	Antiques Colony	Best ambiance	Los/Ant
p.m.	Steamer's	Best seafood lunch	Los/Res
p.m.	Bare Escentials	Best cosmetics	Los/Cos
p.m.	Mud in Your Eye	Best pottery	Los/Pot
p.m.	Vasona Lake Park	Best afternoon stroll	Los/Att
p.m.	Hannegan's	Best dinner crowd	Los/Res

Toys

BEARS IN THE WOOD
59 North Santa Cruz
Los Gatos, CA 95030
Tel. (408) 354-6974
Hrs: Tue. - Fri.   10:00 a.m. - 5:30 p.m.
        Saturday   10:00 a.m. - 5:00 p.m.
        Sunday   12:00 noon- 4:00 p.m.

Bears in the Wood is one of the friendliest shops in Los Gatos, where lots of furry little creatures offer warm, fuzzy bear hugs and happy faces to every visitor. Reputed to be the world's first teddy bear store, Bears in the Wood upholds a "strictly bearish" code which specifies bears and bear items as the exclusive concern of the shop. This philosophy brings a wide and imaginative "bear-iety" to the shelves: teddy bear jewelry, books for collectors, teddy ice cube trays and muffin tins, washable bears for babies, A. G. Classic bears that respond when you talk to them, adorable bear cards and bear clothes (for people and bears alike).

There are also roller skating teddies; fuzzy, cuddly bears; itty-bitty bears; great big bears and handmade, signed, numbered bears for serious bear collectors. Before your purchase take the bear test: a big squeeze, hug or cuddle.

In 1976, when Janee McKinney opened her shop, many merchants along the bustling North Santa Cruz Avenue thought she was just kidding when she devoted her shop exclusively to teddy bears. More than a decade later, Janee says that many of the once-skeptical merchants have become her best customers. Howard McKinney, who used to work at a fishing and sporting goods store down the block, chuckled with the other merchants at the idea of a bear store. He thought (unlike fishing poles) bears were not serious business. Today, the married couple work together in the busy shop. According to the McKinneys, bears are like good friends. They always like you and they're always there, no matter what. You can never have enough of them.

On the last Saturday in October, Bears in the Wood celebrates Teddy Roosevelt's October 27 birthday with a super bear bash. Teddy's birthday and the Easter bear-ny coloring contest are two of the biggest events here at Bears in the Wood. But then every day's a bear-abration at this store.

Travel

THE TRAVEL STORE, 56 1/2 North Santa Cruz Avenue, Los Gatos, California. One of the very best travel stores in America. Specializes in gifts, books, necessities and other unique travel-minded articles. Everything you could think of, or, have forgotten at home.

Wine

DOMAINE M. MARION WINERY
300 College Avenue (P.O. Box 2389)
Los Gatos, CA 95030
Tel. (408) 395-7914
Hrs: Mon. - Sun   1:00 a.m. - 4:30 p.m.
     Tour daily at: 1:00 p.m.
Visa and MasterCard are accepted.

History buffs, wine connoisseurs and scenic lovers will all enjoy a visit to this traditional winery, tucked into the side of a terraced hilltop and overlooking quaint downtown Los Gatos. Experience a taste of Northern California's striking beauty and colorful history as well as excellent, reasonably-priced wines.

Domaine Marion Winery, operating at the site of the former Novitiate Winery, meshes the old and new, with its beginnings in the pursuits of the first

524

explorers and modern adventurers. The cavernous, stone winery was constructed in 1888 by a group of willful Jesuits, including a wine maker from Italy, who originally produced altar wines for many of the state's parishes until 1950 when they expanded the winery to include commercial retail wines. In January 1986 the Jesuits retired from the wine industry, leasing the facility to the Domaine M. Marion Winery owned by Dennis Marion whose first experience in the wine business involved selling the best champagne, Dom Perignon, to rock stars like the Grateful Dead and Jefferson Airplane. After years of swirling, sniffing and tasting wines from around the world as a wine retailer and importer, Dennis Marion is now a recognized authority on German Rieslings and French Burgandies. As a wine maker his mission has been to produce excellent wines at affordable prices, which he has been doing since 1978. His success was confirmed in 1984 at the American Wine Competition, where his 1982 Cabernet Sauviqnon earned "best buy" status by outscoring 336 wines according to the taste score-to-price ratio.

The original stone winery proves to be a "Best Choice" for interesting history and truly outstanding wines. Ask about the fire of 1934 - it's a great story! And be sure to take the trek to the hilltop where the Jesuit mission stands. The view from there is fantastic!

(See special invitation in the Appendix)

Los Gatos is certainly well worth spending more than one day in, so prowl awhile longer and enjoy yourself even more in this, city of the 'Cats.

PROWLING ABOUT LOS GATOS			
a.m.	Hakone Japanese Gardens	Best flowers	Los/Att
a.m.	The Maid's Quarters	Best bedding	Los/Tex
p.m.	Mimi's Rooftop Cafe	Best lunch specials	Los/Res
p.m.	Bears in the Wood	Best stuffed bears	Los/Toy
p.m.	Campbell Museum	Best history	Los/Att
p.m.	Domaine Marion Winery	Best champagne	Los/Win
p.m.	T-Birds	Best California pizza	Los/Res

Milpitas

Accommodations

THE BEVERLY HERITAGE HOTEL
1820 Barber lane
Milpitas, CA 95035
Tel. (408)   943-9080
       800-443-4455 (reservations)

The Beverly Heritage Hotel combines the stateliness,comfort, and amenities of a large convention hotel with efficiency rivaled only by the best smaller hotels. Just off Interstate 880, the hotel is easy to find. Relax amidst whirling fans, verdant plams, a lively player piano in the high-ceiling atrium lobby. You can unwind in the wicker chairs, enjoy buckets of complimentary fruit, and read on comfortable sofas in front of the fireplace.

All 201 rooms--from the standard guest room to the studio suite offer value and excellence. Most rooms have king-sized beds, and living room areas. Two meeting rooms seat 205 and 154 persons respectively; three conference rooms hold up to twenty persons.   There is 24-hour beverage service, a weekday newspaper delivered to your door, and free local phone calls. The hotel's Cadillac limo service delivers you to and from the airport.

Brandon's Restaurant and Nightclub in the hotel is so popular, reservations are suggested in the evening. Elegant breakfasts, lunches and dinners plus a show-stopping Sunday brunch make the dining at the hotel unforgettable. In the evening dance to the tunes of disk jockey music playing popular tunes as you glide across the large parquet floor. Two big video screens, comfortable oak booths with cozy padding, brass fixtures, and framed posters set the mood. Let the Beverly Heritage and Brandon's make your stay in Milpitas a getaway you'll long remember.

Bakery

THE HOME COOKERY, 119 North Milpitas Boulevard, Milpitas, California. A bakery, deli, cookware classes and catering.

Florist

MARLOWE'S FLOWERS AND GIFTS
200 Serra Way #50
Milpitas, CA 95035
Tel. (408) 943-1557
Hrs: Mon. - Fri. 7:30 a.m. - 6:00 p.m.

Milpitas claims one of the premiere florists in the entire country, Marlowes Flowers and Gifts. Adelaide Kleier has been in the florist business since 1947 turning out superb arrangements for individuals and custom work for weddings, funerals and parties.

One visit and you'll understand why many Bay area corporations deal only with Marlowes when preparing for banquets or special events. You'll delight in their whimsical balloon bouquets with teddy bears attached for parties. Gourmet baskets include champagne and wine, cheese, sausage, pate, and other wonderful treats. A back room is full of ceramic vases, and a large assortment of wicker baskets assures you the perfect finishing touch for your silk flower arrangement. In the front cooler, spectacular arrangements of ginger, orchids, irises, alstromeria, and many colored mums dazzle your eye. A patio area contains flowing fountains, trellises, and lush hanging vines. You can purchase potted flowers, terrariums, and cactus. You'll be charmed by the elegant porcelain dolls wearing intricate lace dresses and the Avanti line of plush pets. Also featured are Francesca dolls from the Americana collection, adorned in period dress. Bisque carousel figures are elaborate pieces, horses, clowns, bears, tigers. You'll also find porcelain clown dolls, etched glass wine goblets, and music boxes. The shop subscribes to three wire services.

One stop at Marlowes and you'll see why the shop's ranking in the top 200 out of 45,000 FTD florists is a standing well deserved.

(See special invitation in the Appendix.)

Golf

TULARCITOS GOLF COURSE AND RESTAURANT
1200 Country Club Drive
Milpitas, CA 95035
Tel. Golf Course: (408) 262-8813
Restaurant: (408) 262-8870
Hrs: Golf Course: Dawn to Dusk Every Day
                           Except Christmas
        Restaurant: Mon. - Thu.   7:00 a.m. - 9:30 p.m.
                           Fri.   7:00 a.m. - 1:00 a.m.
                           Sat. and Sun.   6:00 a.m. to Dusk

Resident Pro Kim Sandmann calls the Tularcitos Golf Course the best-kept secret in the Santa Clara Valley. Located in the scenic Milpitas foothills, the course offers a panoramic view of the Bay. Gentle rolling hills offer interesting challenges which let the golfer use every club in the bag.

At the course, you'll find a full pro shop, and putting greens and sand traps for practice, and lesson by Kim. Any level golfer will enjoy the full 18-hole championship course challenges here.

Nan's restaurant takes advantage of the exciting view, and Nancy Engstrom's culinary skills entice diners from all over the Valley. The decor at Nan's is romantic, with a wrought-iron Castilian archway, a fireplace, high wood-beam ceiling, and fresh-cut flowers on each table. Lunch with Nancy and enjoy a Monte Cristo sandwich, or an open-face crab sandwich, guaranteed delicious. Dinners are lavish: Choose from scallops Provencal, scampi or prime rib. The Sunday Brunch will bring you back for its array of salads, cracked crab, steamed mussels, clams, prawns, seafood curry and seafood crepes. Anyone for frog legs? Try them at the Sunday brunch, or stick with more traditional fare of omelets, eggs Benedict, beef Burgundy, or the elegant pastries.

Nancy invites wedding receptions, banquets and special theme parties such as luaus. She is an accomplished decorator and will add her special touches to your gathering. Whether you prefer the golfing or the exceptional dining and atmosphere, come and enjoy the Tularcitos Golf Course and Nan's Restaurant.

(See special invitation in Appendix)

Kitchen Articles

HOME COOKERY
119 N Milpitas Boulevard
Milpitas, CA 95035
Tel. (408) 945-8581
Hrs: Mon. - Fri.   7:00 a.m. - 7:00 p.m.
      Saturday   8:00 a.m. - 6:00 p.m.
      Sunday   9:30 a.m. - 5:00 p.m.

Enter a world of just out of the oven croissants, gourmet sandwiches, shiny cookware and useful gadgets, aromatic gourmet coffees and teas, cookbooks, bulk foods and every cooking implement imaginable, you have entered the world of Home Cookery.

Cozy eating areas invite you to breakfast on blueberry muffins, a cinnamon roll, macadamia or fudge-melt cookies. At lunch, enjoy great deli sandwiches, satisfy your sweet tooth on tasty chocolates, and finish off with freshly ground coffee. Cooks are sure to find what they need among the knives, coffee grinders, waffle makers, portable stoves, beaters, sifters, and teapots. A bulk food section features chocolates, whole wheat, yeast, semolina flour, almonds, pistachios, cinnamon, dates, raisins, and sacks of flour for big baking needs.

While you are there, pick up a newsletter and learn what cooking classes are planned for the month. If you are planning a company party, the staff of The Home Cookery will cater it for you. Culinary masterpieces start with a visit to Home Cookery!

Restaurant

LA MILPA
107 N Milpitas Boulevard
Milpitas, CA 95035
Tel. (408) 945-6540
Hrs: Mon.-Thu.   11:00 a.m. - 9:00 p.m.
      Friday   11:00 a.m. - 10:00 p.m.
      Saturday   8:00 a.m. - 10:00 p.m.
      Sunday   8:00 a.m. - 9:00 p.m.

Milpitas is a rapidly-growing community. In recent years, Calaveras Boulevard has adopted a new face as many businesses have opened to serve the expanding population.

La Milpa, located just off this throughway, was opened to provide a warm family restaurant where members of the community could come and enjoy camaraderie as well as home-cooked Mexican meals. Word spread, and today La Milpa boasts patrons far and wide.

Robert Cisneros and Martha Cisneros Perez, brother and sister, grew up with Mexican cooking. Their parents owned two highly-successful Mexican restaurants. When Martha and Robert opened La Milpa, Martha's husband, Ramon, decided to make it a family team and joined them. You can feel the family's warmth in every aspect of the restaurant: the excellent home recipes, the friendly waiters and waitresses, and the kitchen staff; who speak largely in their native tongue, which adds to the harmony and efficiency in their workplace.

The two dining areas are comfortable and subdued with rich maple booths, chairs with cushy burnt orange seats, earth-tone carpets, lots of plants, and amber lamp shades mounted on elegant Castilian iron chandeliers. These generous appointments are an entree to the authentic menu.

All of the food is made fresh from the salsas and sauces to the guacamole. For breakfast, we suggest the Huevos a la Mexicana: a delightful mixture of scrambled eggs, fresh tomato, diced onions and tangy green chile served with beans. The Huevos Con Papas y Chorizo is also delicious, as is the Machaca with its tasty blend of shredded beef, fresh tomato, onion and green chili. The nachos before lunch or dinner are extremely popular, filled high with guacamole and sour cream. A special plate Robert told us about is the Mole´ Enchiladas: two enchiladas loaded with chicken and topped with a delicious mole´ sauce of special spices, chiles and--amazingly--chocolate. Another popular dish is the Gorditas: two fat corn tortillas made from masa dough formed into pockets, filled with beans and beef or chicken, and garnished with lettuce and tomatoes. The whole is then topped with rich sour cream and guacamole. A mexican extravaganza! The fajitas here are supreme. La Milpa pioneered this dish and still maintains its excellence. Nearly 30 combination plates are available for lunch or dinner, as well as a number of a la carte items. You'll love their super-rich creamy flan for dessert, and great wine Margaritas and daiquiris complement your meal.

When La Milpa first opened in Milpitas, it was with a philosophy of gracious home cooking and authentic family atmosphere. Ramon, Robert, Martha, and their crew maintain the same standards today.

If you're visiting...make the visit worthwhile...learn a bit about the county, the town of Milpitas, and the people. That's what a vacation is for, to relax and enjoy new experience.

EXPLORING MILPITAS			
a.m.	Home Cookery	Best pastries	Mil/Deli
a.m.	Tularcitos	Best golfing	Mil/Golf
p.m.	La Milpa	Best lunch	Mil/Rest
p.m.	Marlowe's	Best florist	Mil/Flor
p.m.	Ed Levin Park	Best walk	Mil/Park
p.m.	Beverly Heritage	Best lounge	Mil/Acc

Morgan Hill

About eleven and one-half square miles are inside the limits of this city which takes its name from the owner of a ranch. The current population is nearly 19,000. There are small houses here dating back to the late 1800s, and modern townhouses. City ordinances limit growth, favoring homes with less impact on public services or facilities.

Morgan Hill was the fellow who married the rancher's daughter. Daniel Murphy was a well-to-do man who raised cattle on the rolling hillsides. His daughter Diana married Hill. They later called the place Morgan Hill Ranch, and the name went with the small collection of houses begun here in 1892. Murphy, at the time of his death, owned three million acres of ranch land in three states.

The modern residents of Morgan Hill are putting their future with light industry, seeking firms for its business parks as a supplement to the traditional trade in support of area farms. Orchards around here are famous for the French prune, which was developed in Morgan Hill, then became standard for the Santa Clara Valley prune industry.

Attractions

Henry W. Coe Park is in the mountains directly east of the city. Dunne Avenue leads to the park, taking you past **Anderson Reservoir**, a large lake with several recreation sites.

To the west, off Watsonville Road, are a chain of **reservoirs and parks** along county road G8, which follows Uvas Creek northward, eventually reaching San Jose. Picnicking, swimming and other recreational opportunities.

In the Santa Cruz Mountains northwest of Morgan Hill, and worth the side trip, off Almaden Avenue from San Jose or Uvas and McKean Roads from Morgan Hill, is **Almaden Quicksilver Park**. It its time, this place with its reddish hillsides produced more mercury than any other site in North America. Production began in 1845, and took off with the gold rush--mercury is a traditional method of recovering fine gold--and continued until the turn of the century.

For further details, contact the **Morgan Hill Chamber of Commerce**, 17320 Monterey Road, Morgan Hill CA 95037. Telephone (408) 799-9444.

Mountain View

Antiques

SHIRLEE'S VICTORIAN HOUSE, 100 West El Camino Real, Mountain View, California. Specialists in antique jewelry.

Books

PRINTERS, INC., 301 Castro Street, Mountain View, California. Combination espresso bar/cafe and full-service bookstore that has quickly become the meeting place for area artists and professionals.

Gifts

T. N. SPICE, 331 Castro Street, Mountain View, California. Teas, coffees, spices and lotsa gift items.

Restaurant

COUNTRY GOURMET & COMPANY, 2098 West El Camino Real, Mountain View, California. Wholesome meals, espresso, fine wines and choice desserts.

IMPERIAL GARDENS, 2116 West El Camino Real, Mountain View, California. Cinese cuisine in a garden setting.

LOUISIANA TERRITORY
LOUISIANA TERRITORY
2290 West El Camino Real
Mountain View, CA 94040
Tel. (415) 964-8900
Hrs: Lunch   Mon. - Fri.   11:30 a.m. - 2:30 p.m.
      Dinner   Mon. - Sun.   5:00 a.m. - 10:00 p.m.

At one time or another, most everyone has dreamed of traveling to New Orleans for Mardi Gras. The lively colors, the festive music, down home aroma and spicy flavor of the local cuisine are just the thoughts to lift your spirits on a stormy day! Well, dream no more, Mardi Gras has come to California in the form of a unique restaurant called Louisiana Territory.

The best way to describe the Louisiana Territory is to say it is a celebration of the New Orleans lifestyle. Some of the walls have been painted with street scenes from the famous French Quarter, while others have posters regaling some of the many events that happen throughout New Orleans. The tables are decorated with bright colors, confetti and loads of costume jewelry just begging to be worn by people wanting to join the celebration. A variety of specialty drinks, California wines and Dixie beer are all available at the bar. To complete the scene, a live Dixieland band performs tunes that are conducive to a party mood.

A superb menu of authentic Cajun, Creole and southern style dishes are the primary attraction. The owner, Vince Guasch, has mastered the fine art of spices. So, put on your party hats and come visit Louisiana Territory, where Mardi Gras is not limited to a mere season.

MONTERY WHALING COMPANY, 190 East El Camino Real, Mountain View, California. Fresh seafood and steaks in a spacious, comfortable atmosphere. A live jazz band plays nightly in the lounge.

Palo Alto

A distinguished community, Palo Alto grew up with Stanford University. Now about 94,000 people live inside city limits, and about 12,000 of them work at the university which is one of the county's ten largest employers. The San Mateo and Santa Clara county lines split the area politically.

Much of the city's growth comes from the electronics firms which set up shop in the industrial park on the edge of the Stanford campus. There are nearly three times the jobs here as there are houses in which to live, making Palo Alto a commuter destination of some magnitude.

Stanford also boasts a large football stadium which has been host to one of professional football's Superbowls, and draws 90,000 fans for Saturday afternoon games each fall. People come from many parts of the country for medical treatment at the Stanford Hospital, a research and teaching institution with a wide reputation.

Attractions

Stanford University is an 8,000 acre campus on what was the livestock farm of railroad tycoon Leland Stanford; a memorial to his son Leland Jr. who died at the age of sixteen while overseas. With a thirty million dollar endowment for starters, and an idyllic setting amid huge trees, the resulting memorial is worth visiting.

Hoover Tower is the campus landmark, and provides a panoramic view; open Monday through Saturday 10:00-11:45 a.m. and l:00-3:45 p.m.

The **Museum of Art** has the golden spike which marked Leland Stanford's cross country railroad completion, but more important is the largest U.S. exhibit of Rodin sculptures; open Tuesday through Friday 10:00 a.m. to 5:00 p.m., Saturday and Sunday 1:00 p.m. to 5:00 p.m.

The **Linear Accelerator**, on Sand Hill Road in Menlo Park, gives tours of its atom-smasher, call (415) 854-3300, extension 2204, for reservations. For general campus information and tours, call (415) 723-2560.

Allied Arts Guild, Arbor Road at the end of Cambridge Avenue in Menlo Park, operate a group of shops and tea room as a benefit for the Children's Hospital at Stanford. Open Monday through Saturday, 9:30 a.m. to 5:00 p.m. Call (415)324-2588 for lunch reservations.

Baylands Interpretive Center is at the water's edge east of Palo Alto. Catwalks go out over the tide flats and marshes which are a haven for birds and water-loving animals. Open Wednesday through Friday 2:00 p.m. to 5:00 p.m., Saturday and Sunday from 10:00 a.m. to 12:00 noon. Use Embarcadero Road east from U.S. 101 to reach the parking lot. Call (415) 329-2506.

For community information, contact the **Palo Alto Chamber of Commerce**, 2450 El Camino Real, Suite 100, Palo Alto CA 94306. Telephone (415) 494-2150.

Accommodations

DINAH'S MOTOR HOTEL
4261 El Camino Real
Palo Alto, CA 94306
Tel.   (415)   493-2844
       (800) 982-5852 CA
       (800) 227-8220 USA
Hrs: Dinah's Poolside Coffee Shop
       Mon. - Sun.   6:30 a.m. - 2:30 p.m.
All major credit cards are accepted.

For over thirty years people have been staying at this city hotel with country charm. They know that at Dinah's they will be treated to personal service, a garden setting, and meticulous attention to detail. From the towering redwoods overhead to the flowers around the goldfish-filled lagoon, Dinah's is a place to relax and forget your worries for awhile.

You can choose between the original cabana style poolside or lagoon side rooms, the newer rooms and suites in the three-story tower, or studio or one-bedroom apartments complete with refrigerators, stoves, and a separate laundry room. Each room has its own individual furnishings, artwork, floor plan and flavor.

Although room service is available, its fun to join the other guests, as well as some of the local regulars, for breakfast and lunch at Dinah's Poolside Coffee Shop. Weather permitting, you can even enjoy your meal outdoors on the pool decks.

The key words at Dinah's are service and affordability.   Services include same day valet service, mini refrigerators in all the rooms full of fresh fruit, juices, and sodas, plus free toothpaste, mouthwash, and shampoo for all guests.

Santa Clara County

GARDEN COURT HOTEL
520 Cowper Street
Palo Alto, CA 94301
Tel.   (800)   556-9595 CA
       (800)   824-9028 USA
AMEX, MasterCard and Visa are accepted.

When you're visiting an area and are looking for a nice place to stay, there are usually only two choices: hotels or bed and breakfast inns. The choice can sometimes be difficult because they both have their advantages, but now, in Palo Alto, there's no longer any reason to make that decision because The Garden Court Hotel combines the best features of a major hotel with the charming quality of a bed and breakfast.

The Garden Court Hotel offers an elegance which is sure to make any visit thoroughly enjoyable. Among the array of services unique to the hotel are cozy fireplace lounges where complementary wine and hors d'oeuvres are served every evening, a morning choice of five newspapers from around the nation, overnight shoe polishing and an atmosphere that is pure comfort.

For meals you can eat at Lelands, the hotel's appointed restaurant, serving contemporary American cuisine. This hotel certainly has it all. So, the next time you're in Palo Alto you know you won't have to make the choice of a place to stay; it's already been made for you. The Garden Court Hotel combines the style and comfort necessary to make it the "Best Choice."

HYATT RICKEYS, 4219 El Camino Real, Palo Alto, California. Featuring cottage style suites and marble decorations, a putting green, croquet lawn and parcourse.

Antiques

THE ANTIQUE EMPORIUM, 4219 El Camino Real, Palo Alto, California. A collective featuring quality furniture and collectibles from all eras and all areas of the globe.

Apparel

LAUREN HILL, 603 Stanford Shopping Center, Palo Alto, California. Apparel designed especially for the professional woman.

PRESTIGE, INC.
50 Town and Country Village
Palo Alto, CA 94301
Tel. (415) 324-3559
Hrs: Mon. - Sat. 9:30 a.m. - 5:30 p.m.
AMEX, MasterCard and Visa are accepted.

It's difficult to shop for women's apparel these days due to society's ever changing fashion likes and dislikes. This is in, and that is out; this store carries this, but doesn't have that. Enough! Prestige, Inc. meets the fashion needs of women, from homemaker to top executive, without giving into trendy fads.

Prestige, Inc. has a wide selection of clothing lines to please the businesswomen, casual dresser, or the lady searching for a formal outfit for a night on the town. If you're looking for accessories, this store has the largest selection of hats, belts, and handbags in the Bay Area. The service is keyed to personal attention, and you can expect to be offered a cup of coffee, a glass of wine, or a serving of fresh fruit.

The mother and daughter team at Prestige, Inc. know their profession well, and if you're not exactly sure of what you're looking for, they will help you find the proper fashion accent. Now, there's no more need for running to and fro around town trying to mix and match everything, because it's already done for you at Prestige, Inc.

THE SHORT SHOP, 103 Town and County Village, Palo Alto, California. A complete line of casual and professional clothing expressly designed for men 5'6" and under.

Books

FUTURE FANTASY
2033 El Camino Real
Palo Alto, CA 94306
Tel. (415) 327-9242
Hrs: Mon. - Fri.   10:00 a.m. - 7:00 p.m.
       Saturday   11:00 a.m. - 5:00 p.m.
Visa, MasterCard accepted.

There is another dimension...it is...as vast as the Cosmos and as timeless as eternity. It is the middle ground between night and day...it is a place we call Future Fantasy.

Future Fantasy is a unique bookstore specializing in mysteries, science fiction, and fantasy. In stock are more titles from Asimov to Zelazny than any other bookstore in the Bay Area; many are signed, special, or limited editions. Among special services offered are ordering hard-to-find books at no charge, personalized notification of new title arrivals, and membership in the Insatiable Readers Club which includes a monthly newsletter and earned store credit.

For the dedicated collector or the person who just enjoys reading a good book, Future Fantasy can amply satisfy either. Just remember, when on your way to the bookstore, if you hear a voice that sounds like Rod Serling's, you've gone too far!

PHILEAS FOGG'S
87 Stanford Shopping Center
Palo Alto, CA 94304
Tel.   (415)   327-1754
         (800)   233-FOGG CA
Hrs: Mon. - Fri.   10:00 a.m. - 9:00 p.m.
         Saturday   10:00 a.m. - 5:30 p.m.
         Sunday   12:00 noon - 5:00 p.m.
MasterCard, Visa and AMEX are accepted.

It's a fairly safe bet that you obtained this book because you love to travel. If so, no store could be more appropriate for you than Phileas Fogg's, the most comprehensive bookstore in the United States dedicated to travel and travelers.

Phileas Fogg's, named after Jules Vernes' most famous around the world traveler, has a vast selection of country and city guides, international food and wine books, country road maps and city street plans, atlases and globes, language books and tapes, children's travel books, travel videos and some travel accessories. They even have computer software for travel. Besides such items to help you on your journeys, Phileas Fogg's has large format photo essay books that are great for gift giving and receiving.

Phileas Fogg's can ship anything you select to any city in the world. If you love to travel, or know those who do, start your trip, or their's, with Phileas Fogg's, the store exclusively for the travel minded.

538

PRINTERS INC.
Bookstore and Coffeehouse
310 California Avenue
Palo Alto, CA 94306
Tel. (415) 327-6500
Hrs: Mon. - Sun. 10:00 a.m.- 11:00 p.m.
MasterCard and Visa are accepted.
And,
301 Castro
Mountain View, CA 94041
Tel. (415) 961-8500

There is little doubt that Palo Alto is the cultural center of the peninsula. Equally there are few who will argue with the statement that Printers, Inc. Bookstore and Coffeehouse is the cultural center of Palo Alto.

Printers, Inc., a legend from the day it opened, is the place where Stanford students, professors, poets, artists, and others with active minds meet to participate in lively conversation over a cup of espresso or capuccino. Also on the premises is a well stocked bookstore that features international magazines, and a weekly authors evening where well known, as well as, "up and coming" writers discuss their works.

Printers, Inc. is a place that definitely broadens the horizons of it's patrons. There you can meet some very interesting people, enjoy a fine cup of Italian coffee, or get a good book. Watch out though, capuccino has a tendency to promote waxing eloquent, philosophical discussion, especially at Printers, Inc.

Collectibles

MOVIE MEMORIES
165 University Avenue
Palo Alto, CA 94301
Tel. (415) 328-6265
Hrs: Mon. - Thu. 11:00 a.m. - 7:30 p.m.
Fri. - Sat. 11:00 a.m. - 9:00 p.m.
Sunday 11:00 a.m. - 5:00 p.m.
AMEX, MasterCard and Visa are accepted.

Imagine throwing a party with names on the guest list like Clark Gable, Humphrey Bogart, John Wayne, Marylin Monroe, and several other big name stars! At Movie Memories all of these famous persons are available for invitation.

539

Movie Memories is a memorabilia store of wide variety, carrying everything from reproduced souvenir pin-ups of James Dean, Clint Eastwood, and Mae West, to theater posters of all the modern releases, and even the hard-to-find early releases. Also included are movie stills, promotional photos, press kits, pins, postcards, and a special Disney section.

Movie Memories is happy to work with you on mail orders, and if you send a self-addressed, stamped, legal-sized envelope, they'll send you a free catalog. It's one of those places to find exactly what you've been looking for all this time. You don't have to be a big movie buff to have important people hanging around your house, you just have to know where to go.

(See special invitation in the Appendix.)

TREASURE ISLAND STAMPS
91 Town and Country Village
Palo Alto, CA 94301
Tel. (415) 326-7678
Hrs: Mon. - Sat.   9:00 a.m. - 5:30 p.m.
         Thursday   7:00 p.m. - 9:00 p.m.
All major credit cards accepted.

Do you know what the most popular hobby in the world is today? What hobby has been enjoyed by more people throughout history than any other? If you answered stamp and coin collecting (philately and numismatics, for those in the know) then you're absolutely correct!

At The Coin Broker/Treasure Island Stamps you can begin a new collection, or add a piece of value to your extant congeries. Display cabinets are filled with shelves of currency, coinage, and stamps of every time period, country of origin, design and color imaginable. If you have a question concerning the wares, the owners, knowing their philately and numismatics, are quite capable of answering to your satisfaction.

So, if you're looking for that cherry on top of the cream for your collection, or just want a collectable for investment purposes, The Coin Broker/Treasure Island Stamps, to coin a phrase, is sure to fill the bill.

Delicatessen

SUZANNE'S MUFFINS, 376 University Avenue, Palo Alto, California. Choose from a daily selection of a dozen varieties of muffins. Round out your meal with fresh green salad, fruit salad, homemade soup or Santa Fe chili.

VILLAGE CHEESE HOUSE
157 Town and Country Village
Palo Alto, CA 94301
Tel. (415) 326-9251
Hrs: Mon. - Sat. 9:00 a.m. - 5:30 p.m.

Do you love to cook? Are you frustrated by the difficulty you have in finding key ingredients for recipes you would like to prepare? Village Cheese House in Palo Alto is your "Best Choice", not only for finding those rare ingredients, but also for variety. Owner Richard Staehnke is proud to offer hard to find gourmet items.

One of the widest selection of gourmet items in the United States can be found when you visit Village Cheese House. Cavier, pate, spices, tea and coffee from around the world are featured. Additionally, goodies such as windmill cookies, several different varieties, and chocolates imported from Switzerland and France will satisfy even the most sophisticated sweet tooth. Cheese and meats of only the highest quality are available. <u>Sandwiches!</u> Sandwiches, locally famous and the most popular in the area for the last twenty-seven years will be prepared for you to go, your taste buds will thank you! The walls are lined with more jams, jellies, marmalades, chutneys, honey, flavorings, mustards, vinegars, oils and sauces than you have ever seen. The list goes on with soups, salads, pastas and desserts available to satisfy your cravings. There is a large selection of kitchen accessories and they even carry baskets which will come in handy for picnics on your travels or for gift giving.

Village Cheese House is the place to find the supplies you need to explore exciting new recipes. Stop in and stock up on goodies and then ask the friendly, courteous staff to ship your selections home.

Florist

BLOSSOMS
199 Stanford Shopping Center
Palo Alto, CA 94304
Tel. (415)323-7040
Hrs: Mon. - Fri.   10:00 a.m. - 9:00 p.m.
        Saturday   10:00 a.m. - 6:00 p.m.
        Sunday   12:00 noon - 5:00 p.m.
All major credit cards are accepted.
Phone orders are welcomed.

When you're strolling through the Stanford Shopping Center, take the time to pass along the small section between Macy's and Emporium. There you'll

541

see a deceptively small European-style outdoor flower shop with dozens of fragrant bouquets in front. It's really cute, but that's not why it's one of the best.

Four things keep people coming back to Blossoms time and time again -- value, quality, service, and personality. Owners Jill Slater and Jan Jungnick work hard to maintain the standards that have kept Blossoms so popular for nearly a decade. The plants and flowers they present are the freshest and most decorative available, and they are modestly priced.

Blossoms has a complete floral arranging department with the resources to cater an event of any size. In fact, some of their best customers are the shopping center's major stores, which use arrangements from Blossoms to highlight their own selections.

The staff of Blossoms enjoy their work and will put their talents at your disposal. Every bouquet is decoratively wrapped and each customer given the full attention they deserve. Blossoms is equipped to deliver throughout the mid-peninsula area and is also able to use any of three wire services to have your arrangement delivered anywhere across the nation or to many countries around the world.

(See special invitation in the Appendix.)

Gift

INDIAN VILLAGE
43 Town and Country Village
Palo Alto, CA 94301
Tel. (415) 328-7090
Hrs: Mon. - Sat.   10:00 a.m. - 5:30 p.m.
      Thursday   10:00 a.m. - 7:00 p.m.
All major credit cards are accepted.

American Indian art is more than just jewelry and crafts. It is history wrapped in an intricate display of beauty. Indian art is steeped in symbolism and meaning, each piece representing the expressions of the artisan. Where can you find these works?

At Indian Village, where for the past twenty-four years, the owners have succeeded in providing quality American Indian art and crafts for long time collectors, as well as for first time gift seekers. The owner makes several trips a year to southwest reservations to obtain new items for the store. These include kachina dolls and Navajo weavings. There is also an excellent selection of artwork including, original paintings, limited edition prints, bronze and pewter sculptures, books and artifacts.

The staff at Indian Village is congenial and conversant in providing advice and background for the items. Whether an avid collector or casual shopper, you will be fascinated by Indian Village.

Ice Cream

**BLATZ FOLDED ICE CREAM
AND FROZEN YOGURT**
101 California Avenue
Palo Alto, CA 94306
Tel.   (415)327-4469
Hrs: Sun. - Thu.   11:30 a.m. - 10:00 p.m.
         Fri. - Sat.   11:30 a.m. - 11:00 p.m.

When Rob Blatman opened Blatz Folded Ice Cream and Frozen Yogurt he challenged one of the tenets of America. Ice cream is as American as . . . well, ice cream. Anyone claiming to improve ice cream better be able to prove it, and the proof, in this case, is in the ice cream.

What makes Blatz's ice cream so special? Well, it's true that the ice cream is extra rich. That's not the answer though. The special part comes after you choose your favorite of eighteen flavors, when you get to mix in your choice of freshly chopped walnuts, Snickers bars, Reese's Peanut Butter Cups, M&M's, trail mix, Gumi bears, bubble gum, or a host of other options. As if that isn't enough, the entire concoction is then placed into a freshly homemade sugar cone that is itself almost as delicious as the ice cream.

If, for some reason, ice cream isn't your thing, you're probably not a real American. No matter -- there are plenty of alternatives at Blatz. For the health-conscious there's 100% natural frozen yogurt and high-protein tofutti. You'll find espresso, cappuccino, and natural sodas for your drinking pleasure. You can also get your ice cream served more traditionally, in an old-fashioned milk shake, a New York malted, or a Blatz Bonanza Split with three scoops of ice cream, a banana, and your choice of hot fudge, marshmallow, chocolate, and butterscotch sauces.

Have a real American experience -- come to Blatz with Mom and a flag and have some . . . ice cream!

(See special invitation in the Appendix.)

Jewelry

GLEIM THE JEWELER
322 University Avenue
Palo Alto, CA 94306
Tel. (415) 323-1331
Hrs: Mon.. - Sat. 9:30 a.m. - 5:00 p.m.
MasterCard, AMEX and Visa are accepted.
And,

119 Standord Shopping Center	350 Main Street
Palo Alto, CA	Los Altos, CA
Tel. (415) 325-3533	Tel. (415) 949-1122

Respect is a difficult commodity to acquire; it can't be borrowed, stolen, or purchased. So, when you learn that the Gleim family are among the most respected names in both the jewelry business and the local community, you should understand it is the culmination of years of effort.

Gleim The Jeweler, founded in 1931 and a member of the American Gem Society, has worked diligently to bring high standards to the profession. The store has an excellent selection of traditional jewelry to choose from such as diamonds, colored gemstones, distinctive gold chains, and accessories. There's a full range of services offered to the customer including jewelry repair, custom jewelry design, diamond repair and recutting, appraisals, and a complete estate jewelry service with consultation and purchasing.

When making an investment, one has to be sure of the person they are dealing with, jewelry notwithstanding. With that statement in mind, remember the well respected name of Gleim The Jeweler when in need of jewelry service.

TIMOTHY FIDGE AND COMPANY,
CUSTOM JEWELERS
27 Town and Country Village
Embarcadero Road at El Camino Real
Palo Alto, CA 94301
Tel. (415) 323-4653
Hrs: Mon. - Sat.   10:00 a.m. - 6:00 p.m.
          Sunday   11:00 a.m. - 5:00 p.m.
All major credit cards are accepted.

Timothy Fidge and Company features original designed jewelry made with fine natural gems and precious metals. The designs are unique, the gems are magnificent and the prices are very reasonable.

544

At Timothy Fidge and Company virtually every piece of jewelry on display is designed and created at the store. Owner, Timothy Fidge does most of the designing himself and proclaims his style as "conservatively contemporary." His pieces have won the prestigious "Diamonds Today" national design competition on three separate occasions.

Timothy Fidge and Company has an extensive inventory of loose and mounted gems. They specialize in ideal cut diamonds (diamonds cut for maximum fire and brilliance) and fine quality colored gems. From the rare and exotic gems like Tanzanite and Benitoite to the more easily recognized Emeralds and Sapphires, just about every gem is available.

Timothy Fidge and Company is a member in good standing of the American Gem Society, which promotes education and ethics among jewelers.

This will make a most pleasant gift shopping tour and a chance to find local handcrafted items.

THE PALO ALTO BUY IT YOU LIKE IT TOUR		
a.m. Indian Village	Best Indian Art	Palo/Gift
a.m. Gliem Jewelers	Best jewelry	Palo/Jwly
a.m. Blossoms	Best bouquets	Palo/Flor
p.m. Village Cheese House	Best lunch	Palo/Deli
p.m. D.B. Gaskill	Best leathergoods	Palo/Lea
p.m. Blatz Folded Ice Cream	Best ice cream	Palo/Ice
p.m. Timothy Fidge & Co	Best cust. jewelry	Palo/Jwly
Then, when you are ready for dinner, savor the time you spend and meal you have at either of these two fine restaurants.		
p.m. London House	Best pub	Palo/Rest
p.m. Ming's Villa	Best Chinese	Palo/Rest

Santa Clara County

Restaurants

DINAH'S SHACK
4269 El Camino Real
Palo Alto, CA 94306
Tel. (415)493-9510
Hrs:

Mon. - Fri.	Lunch	11:30 a.m. -	2:30 p.m.
Mon. - Sat.	Dinner	5:00 p.m. -	11:00 p.m.
Sunday	Lunch	11:00 a.m. -	2:00 p.m.
	Dinner	4:00 p.m. -	9:00 p.m.

All major credit cards are accepted.

What does it take to keep a restaurant popular for over sixty years? On the peninsula only one restaurant can provide the answer. Established in 1926 as a take-out chicken outlet, Dinah's Shack has with stood the challenges of time, changing tastes, a growing metropolis, and fad cuisines to remain the number one independent family restaurant in the area.

The secret to Dinah's success is simple: serve consistently good food in large portions at a fair price. Tradition is important, too. Generations of Stanford students and loyal patrons have carved their initials into the wood paneling for more years than anyone can remember.

As it was in the beginning, the specialty of the house is still the Southern-fried chicken, but you'll also find delicious dishes such as veal Oscar, grilled red snapper, and tender steaks from which to choose. If you're hungry, really, really hungry, Dinah's smorgasbord, loaded with over forty carefully prepared dishes, is one of the best in the Bay Area.

Dinah's also offers entertainment Thursday through Sunday evenings, when a concert harpist fills the air with gentle tones and turns your dinner into a romantic rendezvous. Or you can enjoy a pianist and singer in the lounge. Hmmm... maybe that explains who was in the kitchen with Dinah!

(See special invitation in the Appendix.)

FUKI SUSHI, 4119 El Camino Real, Palo Alto, California. Sushi, sashimi and tempura.

GATE HOUSE, 265 Lytton Avenue, Palo Alto, California. Fine Continental cuisine served in a relaxed elegance.

GAYLORD
317 Stanford Shopping Center
Palo Alto, CA 94304
Tel. (415) 326-8761
Hrs: Mon. - Sun.   11:30 a.m. - 10:00 p.m.
          Sunday   12:00 noon - 3:00 p.m.
All major credit cards are accepted.

"India's cuisine is a combination of subtle tastes...fragrant, pungent, and warm spices from all over India are delicately blended to create dishes...each dish has it's own distinctive flavor and aroma. The blending of spices is an age-old, exacting craft indispensable to Indian cuisine." This is an excerpt from the first page of the menu in Gaylord restaurants, and it speaks for itself as introduction.

Gaylord's, conveniently located in the Stanford Shopping Center, and famous around the globe, is the place to go for North India specialties. Their chefs, trained for more than twenty years, create several delicious dishes to choose from including Rogan Josh, Tandoori chicken, lamb, seafood, meatless entrees, and nine varieties of Tandoori-baked breads. Also, included with every meal is a choice of Chutneys.

The atmosphere at Gaylord's is straight out of India; the walls are adorned with authentic artwork, and Sitar music fills the air. So, if you are up for something exotic, don't hop a plane to India, just go to Gaylord's. Passport not required.

LE MEURSAULT, 651 Emerson Street, Palo Alto, California. Crepes and traditional French cuisine. Selection of over 200 wines!

THE LONDON HOUSE
630 Ramona Street
Palo Alto, CA 94301
Tel. (415) 321-0778
Hrs: Tue. - Sat. 11:00 a.m. - 11:00 p.m.
Visa and MasterCard are accepted.

The English are a very reserved people, and are famous for that indomitable "British, stiff upper lip." The harsh demands of life don't seem to bother them very much. A reason for this is one of their daily stress relieving habits...Tea time. It's a break from a busy day to relax in an open and comfortable atmosphere with friends while enjoying a light meal and a cup of tea.

547

The London House, a combination tea room and English shopping center, is a wonderful place to relax. The Tea Room, accented with a warming fireplace, serves several English-style dishes featuring: crumpets, Welsh Rarebit, Cornish pasties, and a daily selection of sandwiches. After 5:00 p.m., the dinner menu offers such things as poached salmon, Irish Guiness stew, and baked ham with pineapple, as well as the day time light fare. For shoppers, The Celtic Shop features antiques and woolens from all over the United Kingdom including kilts, scarves, and tams.

Of course, one can't forget the pub with the traditional dart board, and over fifteen imported lagers, ales, and bitters. The London House is a good explanation as to why the Brits enjoy their tea so much. It's a cultural experience that is a must.

MADDALENA'S, 544 Emerson Avenue, Palo Alto, California. A most elegant restaurant which featues Italian and French cuisine.

MAMA'S RESTAURANT, 379 Stanford Shopping Center, Palo Alto, California. Here, when you take a shopping break, you'll find inexpensive quality dining in an elegant setting.

MING'S VILLA
1700 Embarcadero Road
Palo Alto, CA 94303
Tel. (415) 856-7700
Hrs: Dim Sum Lunch
                    Mon. - Sun.   11:00 a.m. - 3:00 p.m.
         Dinner   Mon. - Sun.   5:00 p.m. - 10:00 p.m.
All major credit cards are accepted.

When someone says, "Ming" a lot of minds automatically associate with the evil villain always being thwarted by Flash Gordon, however, all of that is changing rather abruptly. Now, the name Ming is becoming ingrained upon people's memories in association with Ming's Villa, a Chinese restaurant of such excellence and quality that had the villain eaten there, he surely would have been caught because he would have, from that day, developed a predictable habit...eating at Ming's Villa.

This Chinese restaurant is set apart from all the others in the nation because it is, simply put, the "Best Choice." Everything about this restaurant is elegant, from the imported, custom-made glass panels, to the living mural of aquariums that house the seafood later to be incorporated into the fresh entrees. Teams of world famous chefs create such dishes as Hunan Szechuan,

Beijing, Canton, and more than 100 types of Dim Sum, originally created for the Chinese Imperial Family centuries ago.

The suckling pigs are prepared over a specially built spit in the kitchen, but most of the barbeque preparation takes place in the main dining room so that the patrons can appreciate the art involved. For an incredible evening out, or a famous Dim Sum lunch, Ming's Villa is the spot. You won't see the villain here, but you may develop his potential habit.

THEO'S, 546 University Avenue, Palo Alto, California. Theo's features lots of fresh fish daily, as well as charbroiled steak, lamb and chicken. The full bar serves premium California wines.

Fantasies can become part of your reality with this tour, which features memorabilia, books and other collectables which are just as much of an inspiration as they are a delightful escape.

THE PALO ALTO EXPAND YOUR HORIZONS TOUR			
a.m.	Future Fantasies	Best sci-fi	Palo/Book
a.m.	Phileas Fogg's	Best almanacs	Palo/Book
p.m.	Movie Memories	Best memorabilia	Palo/Coll
p.m.	Dinah's Shack	Best smorgasbord	Pal/Rest
p.m.	Treasure Island Stamps	Best stamps	Palo/Coll
p.m.	Printer's	Best book & coffee	Palo/Book
p.m.	Gaylord	Best India dinner	Palo/Rest

San Jose

This was a small pueblo going on seventy years old when Captain Thomas Fallon rode in July 14, 1846 and hoisted the U.S. flag above town hall. Just four years later, there was hustle in the town; San Jose was an outfitting center for miners traveling to the gold fields in the Sierra Nevada mountains.

The city had boat and stage connections with San Francisco and the East Bay in 1850, using much of the same land routes travelers choose today. Modern San Jose has a busy airport, vast rail yards and freeways atop freeways. Only the water-borne transportation has gone by the wayside in the post-gold rush days.

Annexation pushed city limits outward repeatedly in the most recent decades as residents tried to solve their urbanization problems. Now 160 square miles are inside the city including some sections stretching up canyons chosen by housing developers. There are almost 2,400 acres of parks in the city, where outdoor recreation is a way of life.

Attractions

Happy Hollow Park and Zoo, Kelly Park at Keyes and Senter Roads, has baby animals for petting. Open daily, 10:00 a.m. to 5:00 p.m. Call (408) 292-8188.

San Jose at the end of the nineteenth century is on display in a model at the **San Jose Historical Museum**, 635 Phelan Avenue in Kelly Park. Open Monday through Friday 10:00 a.m. to 4:30 p.m., Saturday, Sunday 12:00 noon to 4:30 p.m.

Native arts of Mexico are displayed at **Hispanic Development Council Cultural Center**, 325 South First Street. Some Central and South American artists also show here. Open Monday through Saturday from 10:00 a.m. to 6:00 p.m.

The **Indian Center of San Jose**, 3485 East Hills Drive has artifacts and displays from many tribes of North America. Open Monday through Friday, 8:30 a.m. to 5:30 p.m. Off White Road, between Alum Rock and Story Roads.

San Jose State University, 125 South Seventh Street, has an enrollment of 25,000, and many exhibits and activities on its campus a short distance from downtown. Call 227-2207 for information. The Student Union, a major attraction for its architectural design, houses an art gallery.

San Jose Center for the Performing Arts, Almaden Boulevard at West San Carlos Street, was designed by the Frank Lloyd Wright Foundation and features a collection of moveable stages to handle several acts in quick fashion. Call 288-7469 for program and ticket information.

Winchester Mystery House, 525 South Winchester Boulevard, is a 160 room Victorian mansion which is a top tourist attraction. Call 247-2101 for tour information.

Raging Waters, 2333 South White Road, is one of the new water theme parks with activities for everyone from toddlers on up. Next to **Lake**

Cunningham Regional Park. Open daily 10:00 a.m. to 7:00 p.m. Telephone 238-9900.

Rosacrucian Egyptian Museum and Planetarium, 1342 Naglee Avenue, contains mummies, other artifacts from Egypt and other mid-east countries, collected by the Rosacrucian Order, a worldwide organization. Planetarium shows are daily at 2:00 p.m. Museum hours Tuesday through Friday 9:00 to 9:40 a.m.; Saturday through Monday, 12:00 noon to 4:40 p.m. Telephone 287-2807.

The **World of Miniature,** 1373 South Bascom Avenue, is a collection of models from home interiors to the waterfront of a Maine seacoast town. Open Tuesday through Saturday 10:30 a.m. to 5:30 p.m. Call 294-4256.

San Jose Institute of Contemporary Art, 377 South First Street, provides a gallery for viewing emerging artists and those with national reputations. Open Tuesday through Saturday from 12:00 noon to 5:00 p.m., open until 8:00 p.m. Thursdays. Call 998-4310.

The **Japanese Friendship Garden,** 1300 Senter Road, offers a teahouse for meetings, and a landscaped garden complete with Koi fish in the ponds. Open daily, 10:00 a.m. to sunset. Telephone 287-2290 for teahouse reservations or a tour guide.

For information, contact the **Chamber of Commerce,** 1 Paseo de San Antonio, San Jose CA 95113. Telephone 295-2265.

Accommodations

HOLIDAY INN PARK CENTER PLAZA
282 Almaden Boulevard
San Jose, CA 95113
Tel. (408) 998-0400

There is nothing better than a central location when you're on a vacation, business trip or attending a convention. And when you get a beautifully appointed interior, luxurious setting and superb dining, you are indeed fortunate. All of this, in combination with it's ideal location, is what attracts so many guests to Holiday Inn Park Center Plaza.
Each of the rooms and suites offers a motif that is fresh and clean, entreating your luxurious rest. The Holidex II computer streamlines your swift and efficient check-in, and free van transportation to and from Amtrack,

Greyhound and San Jose International makes commuting easy. You'll appreciate state-of-the-art telephones, spaciousness of the king suite, and remote control color TV's with H.B.O. Some of the nearby sights include the Monterey Coast, Great America theme park, the Winchester Mystery House and the Santa Clara Valley Winery.

Complete convention accommodations are available, with banquet and conference rooms that seat up to 1000. There are also eight executive rooms for small meetings and seminars. For meals, the elegant Parrot Restaurant serves outstanding cuisine in a terrific ambiance. Well, now that you know about the Holiday Inn Park Center Plaza, you are indeed fortunate. Check-in and check it out and you'll see why.

LE BARON HOTEL
1350 N First Street
San Jose, CA 95112
Tel. (408) 288-9200

Le Baron Hotel offers a wide variety of distinctive rooms and suites. Its sparkling green motif is cool and inviting, and its commitment to making your stay a pleasure always primary.

For moderately priced luxury, there are one and two bedrooms with king, queen or two double beds. Executive junior suites afford 700 square feet of room, wet bar, full sitting room and a separate work area. The Presidential suite provides a whirlpool and sauna, two TVs, three telephones, dining area, sound system and a full wet bar. Le Baron's gracious hospitality extends to special suites, such as honeymoon, men's executive and women's executive. The choice of restaurants and entertainment is as impressive as the variety of rooms and suites available at Le Baron.

The lobby level restaurant, Ivory's, serves exceptional traditional fare for breakfast, lunch or dinner. Its split bamboo panelling, carved animals and cane furniture, provide a relaxing environment. Beamer's, the lobby level cocktail lounge, is the place to go if you feel like dancing. Nine stories above the lobby, is Belvedere Gardens, where you can dine and take in the panoramic view of the valley below. The elegant white gazebo in the center of the room serves as the hub for their famous buffets. Sensational flower arrangements and shimmering mirrors make for a soothing atmosphere. There are always fabulous foods such as leg of lamb, baked honey glazed ham, roast beef au jus, whole salmon or halibut. Entrees are epicurean dreams of chicken Wellington, seafood Newberg, Hungarian goulash, oriental ginger beef and a host of others. The salad bar offers chicken, tuna, huge shrimp, mushrooms, crisp vegetables, cheeses, cut meats and delicious dressings.

Elegant suites, two restaurants, a lounge and spacious meeting rooms with all audio and computer needs furnished, make Le Baron Hotel your "Best Choice" for business or leisure travel in San Jose.

RADISSON HOTEL
1471 North Fourth Street
San Jose, CA 95112
Tel. (408) 298-0100
Visa, MasterCard, Diner's Club, AMEX and Discover cards are accepted.
Reservations requested.

Experience a sophisticated elegance that Louis IV never knew at the Radisson Hotel, where an old world charm that harkens Europe's finest combined with ultra-modern accommodations. The 19th century French theme is seen at every turn with supple golden oak wainscot trim, textured wallpaper, custom designed carpeting and fabulous beveled glass panels. The lobby's two extremely fine French Victorian hutches, a splendid crystal chandelier, palms and beautiful silk flower arrangements set the tempo for the antique appointments throughout the hotel.

Be pampered in one of Radisson's premiere king suites with its marble entry way, solid oak wet bar, recessed ceilings with delicate indirect lighting, custom wood molding, refrigerator, two remote control color television, overstuffed chair with footrest and an ornate armoir. The Radisson tradition continues with such surprising niceties as a jacuzzi, full length Victorian mirror, plush terry bathrobe and a bath equipped with eighteen karat gold plated fixtures and telephone. The Plaza Club level fills even your slightest whim, cookies and milk are served from 9:00 p.m. until 11:00 p.m., the maids turn down the beds, and a little bottle of cognac or brandy is served as a nightcap. The Galle dining room, with its exquisite Victorian beveled glass windows, extends an intimacy sustained by the most pristine French paintings and chantilly lace curtains. Here the highback chairs and scintillating, floral patterned, padded booths reflect a menu that is readily served and proudly presented. It is Regional cuisine at its finest.

A stone's throw from the San Jose airport, downtown, and freeways 880, 101 and 680, there awaits an extraordinary sophisticated French Victorian world. The Radisson Hotel, "Best Choice" for French elegance in accommodations and fit for royalty. Louis IV never had it so good!

(See special invitation in the Appendix)

RED LION INN, 2050 Gateway Place, San Jose, California. Luxurious rooms, excellent restaurants and live entertainment in the lounge.

Antiques

THE ANTIQUARY
1310 Lincoln Avenue
San Jose, CA 95125
Tel. (408) 286-6739
Hrs:　Mon. - Sat.　11:00 a.m. - 6:00 p.m.
　　　　Sunday　　　12:00 noon - 5:00 p.m.

Antiquers will tell you that their favorite shops have certain things in common. Primary is the quality of items. Secondly, they like reasonable prices, always with an eye peeled for a "sleeper." Foremost in their thoughts are those shops which exhibit the first two attributes and also offer a wide selection. The Antiquary owners, Lyndy and S.K. Lim, accede to these desires of collectors. The shop is a collective with numerous dealer exhibits, making this a must on any antiquer's itinerary.

Several dealers feature jewelry, which you will see beautifully displayed in a row of showcases. Ninety percent of it is antique - wonderful cameos, lapis necklaces, sterling silver rings, ivory and diamonds. You'll also find some fine old radios, such as 1933 Sears Silvertone and a 1932 Philco Jr., both in excellent condition. There is a showcase filled with impressive silver, including Victorian cigarette and calling card cases. One prime item is a beautiful and rare sterling filigree thimble holder, dated 1916. A large section in The Antiquary is devoted to high quality vintage clothing. A number of shops carry some rather nice "old clothe," but not true period vintage clothing, in good repair such as silk, velvet and lace dresses, mink stoles, hats of all varieties and more.

A room at the rear of the shop contains some terrific Art Deco cocktail and curio cabinets, as well as oak and pine tables and chests of drawers. Elsewhere there is Depression glass, watch fobs, carved ivory, Oriental collectables, military badges and pins, ruby glass, extremely fine museum quality bronzes and thousands of other collectables.

At The Antiquary, all of you browsers are perpetually welcome to visit this progressive collective.

(See special invitation in the Appendix.)

THE ANTIQUES COLONY
1915 W. San Carlos St.
San Jose, CA 95128
Tel. (408) 293-9844
Hrs: Daily 10:00 am - 5:00 pm

With more than 70 dealers under one roof, the Antiques Colony is an ideal place to browse. The three large showrooms allow room to roam freely and at leisure, and there is something for every collector. Quality antiques and collectibles is their trademark, and they offer extremely accommodating credit terms. In any collective such as the Antiques Colony, the merchandise is bound to change somewhat from day to day, so you are well advised to make your purchases on sight, for the item may not be available upon your return.

When we visited we spoke with a vendor showing marvelous refinished furniture. His pieces were genuine antiques showing rare craftsmanship, many with elegant carvings. There were hutches, pedestals, tables and chairs from early American to French and British makers. The vendor explained that he had studied the refinishing techniques of the European masters and applied them to his work. The results are stunning.

The dealers reflect their personalities in their merchandise, so there's plenty of variety. One dealer, for example, offered perfectly-restored clocks. Several primitives dealers showed such items as church pew, axes, saws, dozens of irons, a cast iron stove, an old sled, washboards, lanterns, two huge wagon wheels, a horse harness and hundreds of kitchen utensils. A cabinet contained brilliant Venetian glass goblets, purple cut leaded crystal, a Mary Gregory decanter and vases, several hobnail pieces, a French opaline capinet had a different orentation, with several old toy trains, carved Chinese wood statues and German porcelain steins. Vintage furniture included Victorian and turn-of-the-century- armoires, bed sets, sofas of various eras, dressers, well-kept and restored utilitarian pieces to some with excellent marquetry.

Other items caught our eye. We were taken by a tall grandfather clock, circa 1840, with eight-day movement, calendar and hand-painted moon phase in a beautiful mahogany cabinet. One splendid rococo mirror with kidney-shaped dresser and matching stool was as unique as it was attractive, and perfectly conditioned. There was a fabulous engraved tilt water pitcher with quadruple silver plate, dated 1883. These were our favorites, but yours could be a piece of jewelry, brass chandelabra, wicker furniture, a rare oil painting or antique doll. As Howard Carter exclaimed when he first peeked inside King Tut's tomb, the first to gaze upon the treasures in centuries: "Wonderful things!"

Santa Clara County

TAPESTRY IN TALENT, 66 North Market Street, San Jose, California. Individually hand-crafted object of art. Ceramics and photography available in this cozy gallery.

THE WILLOW GLEN COLLECTIVE
1349 Lincoln Avenue
San Jose, CA 95125
Tel. (408) 947-7222
Hrs: Mon.-Sat. 10:30 a.m.- 5:00 p.m.

The Willow Glen Collective is one of those shops that instantly catches one's attention with beautiful window displays which offer a hint of the treasures inside. For years, the collective has been known by antique collectors as a storehouse of charming and valuable surprises. Chris Constantino manages the shop. She and eight other women each have their own area and specialty, assuring customers of special find on every visit. The shop is geared for convenience, with wide aisles for good accessibility.

A few examples of the many fine prints and lithographs here are Fox and Fisher, some rare Maxfield Parrish prints, Turner flamingo scenes, and Bessie Pease prints. There are several boxes filled with highly collectible prints, magazine covers, trading cards, etchings, and well-conditioned frames. There are also Irish porcelain tea cups and saucers, a rare old stuffed Mickey Mouse doll, and Hobnail and End-of-the-Day vases displayed in one of the cabinets. You will also find gorgeous Fenton pink and ruby optic baskets and excellent pressed glass pieces. Among the many other entrancing items are collector's spoons, adorable dolls, sparkling jewelry, beaded evening purses, hand-embroidered linen tablecloths and napkins, and vintage clothing.

A favorite display contains cuddly old Steiff plush animals, a Red Riding Hood cookie jar, Disney memorabilia, crystal perfume bottles, Venetian blown glass dancers, Lenox plates, Hummels and Roseville items. Take your time when visiting The Willow Glen Collective, because you'll discover new treasures at every turn.

(Invitation in the Appendix.)

Apparel

THE CRYSTAL IRIS BOUTIQUE
227 N 1st Street, Suite 104
San Jose, CA 95113
Tel. (408) 947-1222
Hrs: Mon. - Fri.   11:00 a.m. - 6:00 p.m.
         Saturday   12:00 noon - 5:00 p.m.
Also by special appointment.

Fine clothing for women, tasteful accessories, fragrances and skin care products, all are displayed here amid antique furniture and beautiful decorative items. Crystal Iris is elegance.

The stylish evening gowns and other apparel stocked here are seen frequently in San Jose restaurant fashion shows, but it is an experience apart to come to the store. Fancy lingerie, high fashion gowns and furs are available, selected by proprietors Doris and Clifford Carter with a particular taste which is reflected throughout the boutique. This is a place for pampering yourself, or choosing a gift for someone very special.

Whether it is a whiff of the cologne Marie Antoinette is said to have used, or a limited edition gown, you can find it at Crystal Iris Boutique. You will find this lovely boutique above the Metro Cafe on San Carlos between 3rd and 4th Streets.

(See special invitation in the Appendix.)

DIVA, 1337 Lincoln Avenue, San Jose, California. Contemporary clothing, shoes and accessories for men and women.

MARJORIE'S INTIMATE APPAREL, 311 Town and Country Village, San Jose, California. Specialty apparel for intimate wear, including support undergarments.

SILK-N-SEQUIN
112 Town & Country Village
San Jose, CA 95128
Tel. (408) 985-7096
Visa and MasterCard are accepted.

All that glitters is not gold, is an old adage that is true to form at Silk-N-Sequin, for this is a shimmering wonderland of some of the most gorgeous sequined tops and dresses you will ever behold. The Silk-N-Sequin line is entirely hand selected and manufactured in India to exacting standards. The two piece sets and tops have a very sophisticated appeal. Many of the gowns feature pearls and beads or beaded fringe sleeves.

At Silk-N-Sequin, custom designing with raw silk is a specialty. Expert sizing and consultation guarantees a look and fit that is perfectly suited to your taste. Much of the fabric is one of a kind and the construction of the outfit is done right in the shop. The elegant silk is of the highest quality...slip into your new outfit and feel like a million dollars! Expert alterations are available and the knowledgeable staff is happy to help with any assistance you may need. Accessories include dressy belts, intricate beaded jewelry, purses, silk scarves and a good deal more.

At your "Best Choice" for clothing, Silk-N-Sequin, layaway and very reasonable prices allow you to have apparel fit for a queen without spending a king's ransom!

SOMETHING TO CROW ABOUT, 107 Oakridge Mall, San Jose, California. Stocked to service the needs of children...fashions and gifts galore.

Art

GALLERY SARATOGA
408 El Paseo Shopping Center
San Jose, CA 95130
Tel. (408) 866-0884
Hrs: Mon. - Wed.   10:00 a.m. - 6:00 p.m.
        Thur. - Fri.   10:00 a.m. - 9:00 p.m.
        Saturday   10:00 a.m. - 5:30 p.m.
        Sunday   12:00 noon - 5:00 p.m.

A unique idea in organization is the co-op arrangement of Gallery Saratoga. Forty local artists work as a unit, holding regular meetings and rotating floor duty in the showroom that displays each of their works. This provides the customers with first hand knowledge of each piece of art.

The themes include endearing still lifes, beautiful, haunting desert scenes, wind swept seascapes and charming views of the country. The primary mediums are oil, acrylic and watercolor with some batiks, soft sculpture, photography, hand painted ceramics and elegant pierced porcelain pieces shown. The front of the gallery is the featured artist section, which changes monthly.

The talent and creative virtues of the artists are evident in the quality and integrity of their work at prices that allow you to embellish your entire home. So come all ye art enthusiasts to Gallery Saratoga and gaze at these works, take them home and place them in their proper places.

J.J. BROOKINGS
330 Commercial Street
San Jose, CA 95112
Tel. (408) 287-3311
Hrs: Mon. - Tue.   By appointment
      Wed. - Fri.   9:30 a.m. - 5:00 p.m.
      Saturday   11:00 a.m. - 5:00 p.m.

There was a time when serious art collectors from the South Bay had to travel to San Fransisco to enjoy a selection equal to their expectations. That changed when J.J. Brookings opened it's doors. Owner Tim Duran, an avid art collector, saw a need for a first-class gallery in San Jose, and J.J. Brookings is his answer.

Tim deals in both the primary and secondary markets, meaning that some of the works have been sold before, while others are new works shown on consignment by the gallery. Post 1960 and contemporary paintings are featured. The impressive list of painters shown includes Andy Warhol, Ed Ruscha, Sam Francis, Ben Schonzeit, Charles Bell and Elena Borstein. The tremendous breadth at J.J. Brookings is evident in the diversity of medias offered. There are paintings, vintage and contemporary photographs, works on paper, sculpture and tapestries by major artists of national and international acclaim.

Most of the works at J.J. Brookings are priced within reach of the individual of average means who wishes to invest in a valued work of art. A variety of consulting services are provided free to individuals and corporations. If you are one who realizes the importance art provides in adding spark to your life, then J.J. Brookings is a guiding light for you.

Attraction

THE MYSTERY HOUSE
525 S Winchester Boulevard
San Jose, CA 95052
Tel. (408) 247-2101

Do you believe in ghosts? Even if you don't now, you will after just one appearance at the Winchester Mystery House. Find out for yourself whether or not spooks walk the beautiful parquet floors, mischievously creak some of the 2,000 doors and rattle a few of the 10,000 windows in this 160-room Victorian mansion.

What possessed the creator of this five-million dollar architectural fantasy? Why did Sarah Winchester, heiress to the Winchester fortune, keep carpenters building twenty-four hours a day for thirty-eight years? It's creepy...the stairs that lead to nowhere and the walls and rooms that are connected to secret passages. It's something that everyone should see for themselves. Guided tours, carried out everyday, lead you into spine chilling mystery as you view this old mansion and two museums featuring Winchester firearms and products.

You'll also enjoy their speciality shop and quaint cafe. Visit The Winchester Mystery House, that is if you've got the heart. But above all, just be sure to take the right stairway...

Books

PHOENIX BOOKS AND ESPRESSO CAFE
17 N San Pedro Street
San Jose, CA 95113
Tel. (408) 292-9277
Hrs: Mon. - Fri.   7:00 a.m. - 12:00 midnight
Saturday   11:00 a.m. - 12:00 midnight
Sunday   11:00 a.m. - 7:00 p.m.

The coffeehouse as a community gathering place had it's origins in seventeenth century England. In London, the early coffee houses were built primarily near universities, and professors and students opted for the popular coffee and open atmosphere as an alternative to stuffy classrooms. It's reasons like these that make Phoenix Books and Espresso Cafe so well frequented.

Extended hours, an enticing menu of exciting pastries, cakes and fresh entrees makes it a perfect place for gatherings. The two level arrangement and extremely well thought out floor plan offers separate environments for a most diverse variety of groups. Downstairs is an espresso bar with ample seating for groups to exchange ideas freely. There is also a separate dining area where you can enjoy entrees like pasta, Greek salads and exotic gourmet juices. Upstairs is the Children's Cultural and Entertainment Center.

Phoenix Books and Espresso Cafe has become an important hub of intellectual, business and artistic life in San Jose. It hosts many special gatherings such as receptions for the San Jose Symphony and the Civic Light Opera. A well stocked general bookstore focusing strongly on philosophical, theological and holistic subjects. The books, cuisine, relaxed environs, vibrant

560

ideas and the superior coffees are Phoenix's way of assisting the community in uplifting it's pleasure, knowledge and awareness.

(See special invitation in the Appendix)

YESTERDAY'S PAPERBACKS
2636 Union Avenue
San Jose, CA 95124
Tel. (408) 559-6006
Hrs: Mon. - Fri.   9:00 a.m. - 7:30 p.m.
      Saturday   9:00 a.m. - 5:00 p.m.
      Sunday   12:00 noon - 5:00 p.m.

Meine dammen und herren, mesdames et messeurs, ladies and gentlemen! The newspapers at Yesterdays Paperbacks speak your language! Offering over one hundred newspapers from around the world and across the country, you may keep up with what's happening in your neck of the woods wherever that may happen to be!

Not only does the shop carry over 12,000 paperbacks in excellent condition, but they are organized in such a way that it is very easy to find the subject you are looking for as well as the title. There is an excellent selection of books at very reasonable prices and if you seek a title they do not have, owners Bill and Kathy Eshnaur will be happy to search out and try to locate the book for you.

Whether you're looking for a book, have books to trade, or just picking out a hometown or country newspaper, stop in at Yesterday's Paperbacks. Wilkommen, bien venu....welcome!

Candy

SCHURRA' S CHOCOLATES
848 The Alameda
San Jose, CA 95126
Tel. (408) 289-1562
Hrs: Mon. - Fri.   9:00 a.m. - 5:30 p.m.
      Saturday   9:00 a.m. - 4:30 p.m

Founded in the same location it now occupies, Schurra's opened in 1912 and goes about the business of creating Santa Clara County's premiere handmade chocolates with pride. Applying the old art of candy making, it has thrived by bringing creative new recipes to the fore mentioned. Current owner Bill Mundy grew up in the area around The Alameda and used to come

561

into Schurra's frequently as a boy to purchase the dainty treats. He remembers his enjoyment well and now relishes the idea of offering the likes of his scintillating long stemmed brandy cordials.

At Christmas time there are wonderful eggnog truffles. Webster may have defined the word delicious after tasting the incredible chocolate dipped strawberries! Generations of customers have loved Schurra's famous old fashioned fudge, Australian glazed fruits, peppermint chews, truffles, fancy creams, nuts and dried fruit. It's difficult to believe what differences exist between machine and handmade candy until you watch a batch of divinity, caramel or chocolate being made and see the addition of every ingredient.

Schurra's Candy Factory is equipped to accommodate large corporate orders for any occasion. They are experts at molding logos and do so for major corporations and hotels. Bill uses some molds that are over a hundred years old and has over sixty for Easter alone. People from all over the world stop in when visiting San Jose; they love to come in and purchase the delicious candies like Bill did as a boy. There's a lot of nostalgia involved. You see, Schurra's has been producing the best candies for as long as anyone can remember!

(See special invitation in the Appendix.)

Clocks

ALMADEN CLOCKS
5371 Camden Avenue
San Jose, CA 95124
Tel. (408) 265-2133
Hrs: Mon. - Sat.   10:00 a.m. - 6:00 p.m.
          Wednesday   10:00 a.m. - 9:00 p.m.
          Sunday   12:00 noon - 4:00 p.m.(Dec. only)
Visa and MasterCard accepted.

Wayne Schaich grew up in a house with 120 clocks--his dad Carl, owned and operated the Clock Haven in San Jose for over twenty years; so it was natural to grow up amidst the sight and sounds of so many clocks. Now, Wayne fixes and sells clocks at his own shop, Almaden Clocks in the Avanti Shopping Center.

This shop contains probably the largest collection of grandfather clocks in Northern California, about one hundred are on the floor at any one time. Three hundred grandfather clocks are in inventory. Why so many? Because their reputation is for reasonable, moderate pricing on these future family heirlooms.

In partnership with Chris Savery, there are now three other clock shops, all located in the Bay area. You'll find new and antique timepieces here in varied styles. Little clocks, big clocks, quiet clocks, and clocks with booming chimes, or travel timepieces, clocks of simple design or those that need a whole mantle for display and admiration.

When you need a clock repaired or adjusted, you can depend on an experienced repair person at Almaden Clocks. Wayne started fixing the clocks in his home long before his father would let him begin the apprenticeship that led to today's reputation as the "Best Choice" for clock repair and clock sales.

Collectibles

COLLECTIBLES OUTLET
1899 W San Carlos Street
San Jose, CA 95128
Tel. (408) 288-6027
Hrs: Mon., Tue., Wed., Fri.   10:00 a.m. - 5:00 p.m.
        Thursday   10:00 a.m. - 9:00 p.m.
        Saturday   10:00 a.m. - 5:00 p.m.
        Sunday   12:00 noon - 5:00 p.m.
Credit cards are accepted.

This is a massive display of collectors items, about 5,000 square feet of shelves and cabinets filled with porcelain figures, music boxes, crystal, dolls, bears and stuffed animals from the world's finest manufacturers, all at discounts of 15% - 60% off manufacturers suggested retail prices.

They can special order almost any pieces not in stock and go to great lengths to find what their customer's want. Showcases often have 200 or more pieces from one manufacturer such as Hummel and LLadro. They will allow you to carefully examine each piece guaranteeing complete customer satisfaction or your money back on all purchases. We really can't list everything available here, or even come close to it. There is even an real antique car on the floor of the Collector's Outlet.

Whatever you are collecting, Bill Lee will probably have it at the Collector's Outlet. It's a browser's paradise!

SU-ELEN'S LIMITED
14 Almaden Plaza
San Jose, CA 95118
Tel. (408) 266-4317
Hrs: Mon. - Fri.   10:00 a.m. - 9:00 p.m.
        Saturday   10:00 a.m. - 6:00 p.m.
        Sunday   12:00 noon - 5:00 p.m.
Thanksgiving through Christmas
        Saturday   10:00 a.m. - 9:00 p.m.

What really distinguishes a shop that features fine collectibles is the proprietor's taste in selections. At Su-Elen's Limited the merchandise is all hand picked and the interior design has rendered the shop beautiful with mauve carpeting and elegant lace curtains. Owner Helen Keenan's selection of collector plates is displayed along the walls on colonial style racks and the thematic focus is country romance, brides and children. Among the porcelain dolls are limited edition Madame Shioa-Yen creations with very smooth faces, Lennox dolls, music box dolls by Julia Rueger, Bradley dolls and many others of very high caliber.

Most impressive are the hand made clay sculptures by Emilio Tezza, whose works have been shown in Milan and Rome and have been described as "great art with a comical approach." Some of his subjects, such as the Rabbi, Don Quioxote and the busy pharmacist will undoubtedly capture your fancy. Another highly unusual line is the hydrostone sculpture with bronze finish. Western artists Remington and Russell are represented in as much detail as the originals. Helen is an authorized dealer for the Emmett Kelly collection of clown figurines and Ceoci porcelain clowns.

The bear collection at Su-Elen's is highlighted by a fantastic full size hand made specimen which fits over a vacuum cleaner and is intricately adorned in a lace dress. It seems to orchestrate the other character bears by North American and the marvelous Raikes bears. A precision mantle clock may be purchased that will be prized for generations. Hundred of items priced from very moderate to expensive have one thing in common, they're all special treasures that will give you considerable pleasure.

(See special invitation in the Appendix).

Delicatessen

LAVILLA GOURMET AND DELICATESSEN
1319 Lincoln Avenue
San Jose, CA 95125
Tel. (408) 295-7851
Hrs: Tue. - Sat. 9:30 a.m. - 6:30 p.m.

Owning Lavilla was once a dream for Ed Palestro. He used to make deliveries there as a sausage maker and salesman, and became fast friends with the owner, who promised to sell the business to Ed upon retirement. When the time came, Ed knew it was a large responsibility to carry on the traditions of the finest delicatessen in the entire area; the clientele wouldn't tolerate the slightest decline. No Problem. The Palestro family continues it's forty year legacy of sheer excellence.

Ed comes in early every morning to prepare fresh fillings and meats for the day. The delicious quarter-pound meatballs are one of his specialities, and he creates their great Ravioli and Lasagne. The macaroni salad, potato salad and a number of gourmet varieties are made fresh every morning from scratch. Garlic olives, cole slaw, tomato salad, marinated mushrooms and specialities like olive loaf, roast beef, ham and gelatina can all be purchased fresh at the counter.

A lovely gazebo-style patio is provided for luncheoners to take their repast on a sunny day. Others can shop among the many well-stocked shelves of imported cookies, fresh sourdough bread, teas, countless pastas, California wines and so much more. People come from all over to shop at Lavilla. They can't obtain these products anywhere else, and they're simply the very best. Stop in and see what forty years can do to produce excellence.

MEYBERG'S DELI AND RESTAURANT
1002 Town and Country Village
San Jose, CA 95128
Tel. (408) 241-2753
Hrs: Mon. - Wed. 7:00 a.m - 9:00 p.m.
Thur.- Sat. 7:00 a.m. - 10:00 p.m.
Sunday 8:00 a.m. - 8:00 p.m.

Owner Harold Meyberg is pleased to converse in English, Dutch, Arabic, Italian, Hebrew, French and Russian and offers foods with as much variety.

Open for breakfast, lunch and dinner, such delicacies as lox omelets, veal bratwurst and eggs, lox and eggs, brisket of beef, short ribs, veal Scallopini, lamb shanks, beef stroganoff, chicken Cordon Bleu, fresh salads, bagels and strudels are some of the meals that customers rave about. In addition to these prepared entrees, you will find a bevy of gourmet foodstuffs including cheeses, meats, coffees, teas, imported chocolates, crackers and herbs. An adventure in imported beers numbering over 220 await you in the coolers, along with sodas, fresh juices and seltzers.

Steeped in the tradition of the best international deli's, Meyberg's is at your service as a "Best Choice" in San Jose.

Entertainment

THE LAST LAUGH, 29 North San Pedro Street, San Jose, California. Live comedy presented by professional comedians. Nightly.

Farm

MISSION ORCHARDS
2296 Senter Road
San Jose, CA 95112
Tel. (408) 297-5056
Hrs: Mon. - Fri. 8:00 a.m. - 4:30 p.m.
November and December, seven days a week.

Since the days of Adam and Eve, fruit orchards have played an important role in the lives of men and women. Grown in the sun's golden rays and nurtured by rich soil, fruit tastes good and provides the body with much needed vitamins. All of this is just as true today as it was in the days of old, and nowhere will you find more healthy, good tasting fruit than at Mission Orchards.

The elegantly packed fruits, candies, cakes, special gift baskets and gourmet treats are ready to be eaten or shipped anywhere you choose. Crown Comis pears, Mission Red apples, Navel oranges, Ruby Red grapefruit and Holiday grapes bursting with flavor are the finest gifts nature can offer. These fruits can be arranged in numerous combinations including the Happy Holiday Assortment and the Dried Fruit Assortment. You can join the Fruit For All Seasons Club and receive sweet oranges, giant nectarines, exotic kiwi fruit, Bing cherries and many more. There is one for every month, shipped by air to ensure perfect arrival.

The dried fruits available at Mission Orchards are unparalleled for natural flavor and beauty of arrangement. Presented in their box or basket configurations, they are as pleasing to the eye as to the palate. This is some orchard! At Mission Orchards you can partake of the fruit without having to worry about any consequences.

Florist

ANNE'S FLOWERS
955 Lincoln Avenue
San Jose, CA 95126
Tel. (408) 287-1133
Hrs: Mon. - Fri.   8:00 a.m. - 7:00 p.m.
      Saturday   9:00 a.m. - 6:00 p.m.
      Sunday   10:00 a.m. - 3:00 p.m.
Visa, MasterCard and AMEX are accepted.

Custom arrangements are the specialty of Sherry White, the skilled florist who operates Anne's Flowers in the Willow Glen neighborhood. You find Sherry listening as the customer describes the decor and the occasion, then creating arrangements which have subtle beauty just right for the place and time.

This shop has a tradition dating back five decades to a roadside flower sales business which grew into the Lincoln Avenue building over thirty years ago. A large display window features some of the skilled arrangements created by the staff, always a new idea as the seasons change. Football mums, fresh bouquets, or funeral and wedding decorations are ready quickly. Orders received by 1:00 p.m. get same day delivery. Gift items, including gourmet fruit baskets, round out the shop's offering.

A friendly florist shop where they listen, then fit the flowers to the occasion, Anne's Flowers make the customer's wishes come alive.

(See special invitation in the Appendix.)

SAN JOSE TOUR			
a.m.	Bear and Doll Garden	Best Bear & Doll	SanJ/Toy
a.m.	Rystad's Ltd. Editions	Best plates	SanJ/Gift
a.m.	Mackey Picture Frame	Best art	SanJ/Frame
p.m.	La Villa Deli	Best lunch	SanJ/Deli
p.m.	Willow Glen Collective	Best browsing	SanJ/Ant
p.m.	Glass with Class	Best art glass	SanJ/Glass
p.m.	The Antiquary	Best collectables	SanJ/Ant
p.m.	Anne's Flowers	Best Florist	SanJ/Flor

SAN JOSE FLORIST
1559 Meridian Avenue
San Jose, CA 95125
Tel. (408) 269-9171
Hrs: Mon. - Tue.   8:00 a.m. - 6:00 p.m.
      Wed. - Fri.   8:00 a.m. - 7:00 p.m.
      Saturday   8:00 a.m. - 6:00 p.m.
      Sunday   11:00 a.m. - 5:00 p.m.
And,
1375 Blossom Hill Road
San Jose, CA 95118
Tel. (408) 265-5960

Flowers are mediums of spiritual enhancement to be purchased where the attitude of the shop reflects the joy you feel when you give flowers. At San Jose Florist there is a sense of peace and a captivating beauty in the shop...the interior sparkles with striking silk flower arrangements, exquisite art glass and is highlighted by intricate lighting.

San Jose Florist is consistently called upon to furnish weddings, banquets and funerals and receives many commendations for their fine work. A family operation with two locations, the shop employs a highly skilled, creative and experienced staff. The refrigerated case, as well as the large number of silk arrangements provide a diverse selection and unusual, exciting artistic designs in a wide variety of styles. An elegant gift store, San Jose Florist features very fine Fenton, Imperial and Bohemia glass. There are decanters and vases, bowls and baskets, and other blown glass pieces. Also, find excellent collectors pieces, impressive in shades of amber, cranberry, purple, blue and green. The Christopher Collection of porcelain ballet figures and angels will delight you. You'll also find some heartwarming glazed porcelain clowns that make splendid gifts.

A full service FTD establishment, San Jose Florist will provide delivery throughout the country. There is every reason to believe in their dedication, professionalism and ability to please.

(See special invitation in the Appendix).

Frames

MACKEY PICTURE FRAME
1396 Lincoln Avenue
San Jose, CA 95125
Tel. (408) 293-3733
Hrs: Mon. - Fri. 9:00 a.m. - 5:30 p.m.
Sat. 10:00 a.m. - 5:00 p.m.

Since 1958 Mackey Picture Frame in Willow Glen, has been the single choice of artists and framing buffs both near and far. The Mackey family has specialized in the framing business through three generations. Bill Mackey learned the trade from his father, and at one time the family ran nine framing studios. Though most of the locations have been sold, three are still operated by Mackey family members. Bill, his wife, Peggy, and son, Sean run the Willow Glen shop, and a daughter and son-in-law operate Mackey Santa Rosa. The Oregon location is the home of the Mackey molding mill which supplies forty percent of the material sold in their own studios as well as numerous framers throughout the state.

Antique dealers, photo studios, needlework shop owners and others have referred their customers to Mackey for years. Their motto is, "You name it, we frame it." Frames range in size from 5 x 7 to 24 x 48 in a variety of woods and finishes, including oak, raminwood, maple, fruitwood, walnut and rosewood. A wide selection of metal frames is also available in a variety of colors and styles.

Mackey Picture Frame includes a gallery with a tasteful selection of beautifully-framed lithos and oil paintings. The gallery includes something for all ages and tastes. Erté and Icart lithographs, signed limited-edition Dali, LeRoy Nieman, Bessie Pease, posters and an assortment of other strikingly framed and matted works of lasting beauty and value. Mackey carries a great selection of unusual lithographs. Or you can order from the various catalogs which contain beautiful reproductions of the old masters and contemporary works.

Give your photo, litho or print a spirited lift. Visit friendly Willow Glen with your favorite framing subject and let the Mackeys add that finishing touch.

Gift

AVERY'S
3666 Stevens Creek Blvd.
San Jose, CA 95117
Tel. (408) 984-1111
Hrs: Mon.-Tue.-Wed.-Sat.   10:00 a.m. - 6:00 p.m.
        Thurs. - Fri.   10:00 a.m. - 9:00 p.m.
        Sunday   12:00 p.m. - 5:00 p.m.

After discovering Avery's, many have asked themselves, "where have you been all my life?" Well, Avery's has been, for quite some time, conveniently located right behind Kiddie World on Stevens Creek Boulevard. Nancy Trainor is the dynamic force behind Avery's, the 16,500 square foot gift specialty store. Her friendly, knowledgeable staff enjoys showing you all of the beautiful items and answering your questions.

If you share a passion for elegance, you'll appreciate the lavish in-stock selection of fine china such as Bing & Grondahl, Royal Doulton, Wedgwood, Noritake, Minton, Lenox, Bernardaud, and more.

There are literally more than 500 different patterns on display at all times, including exceptional stoneware by Heath, Denby of England, Dansk International, and others. The Orrefors from Sweden is remarkable in its sparkling clarity, but you'll find equally brilliant Atlantis bowls and decanters from Portugal, and Waterford from Ireland is featured lavishly in Avery's crystal gallery. Not to be missed is the collections of Lalique, Gorham, Saint-Louis, and Baccarat crystal. Be sure, also, to see the showcase of fine Irish Belleek, Mt. St. Helens blown art glass, and the majestic Lladro porcelain sculptures from Spain.

The phenomenal list of distinguished gift items at Avery's includes elaborate serving trays, creamers and teapots, silverware, ice buckets and fancy flasks, bowls, vanity sets, and candelabras--the selection is amazing! Again, you can depend on the markings: Oneida, Reed & Barton, Wallace International, and Supreme Cutlery. You can also find a complete selection of formal and casual table linens, gourmet cookware, cookbooks, butcher blocks and kitchen gadgets.

Avery's has a silk flower department and the staff will assure you of lasting beauty and uniqueness in the custom arrangements made for you. For overall gift shopping, Avery's is the place. All purchases are gladly giftwrapped upon request. Insured UPS shipping, crystal engraving, and special ordering are available too.

BALLOONS INSTEAD, 228 El Paseo de Saratoga, San Jose, California. Balloon bouquets arranged for any occasion. Delivery available.

THE BUNNY HUTCH
14926 Camden Avenue at Union
San Jose, CA 95124
Tel. (408) 371-1555
Hrs: Mon.-Wed.,
       Fri. & Sat.   10:00 a.m.-6:00 p.m.
       Thursday   10:00 a.m.-8:30 p.m.
Thanksgiving thru Christmas:
       Wed. - Thur.   10:00 a.m.-8:30 p.m.

The Bunny Hutch is nestled in inviting Cambrian Plaza awaiting your discovery. It isn't only what you see when you're at The Bunny Hutch that uplifts your spirits, it is also what you smell--an all-pervasive aroma of fragrant scented spices, colognes, and English soaps. The spacious 3,000 square feet displays American country gifts and oak antique furniture infinitely well. Changing weekly, the displays present new and unique creations of master country crafters from around the country.

A hop down to The Bunny Hutch will net you new surprises every time. Stop by and admire the corner where cuddly stuffed bears and bunnies are perched on the shelves of a beautiful old oak hutch. There's a nice selection of cute cards and coffee mugs. In another section are stained glass lamps, handsewn quilted bunnies, silk flowers, and assorted tins of talc powder. Next, encounter some elegant picture frames with figures of cats, bunnies, and flowers along the perimeter, ring boxes, handpainted plaques, and handsewn pillows. Enjoy the large display of wicker baskets, porcelain hen cookie jars and cups, and Raggedy Anns and Andys.

An upper shelf around the store displays professionally matted and framed scenes of English Country, early American, and Victorian life. The shop also carries a complete supply of wrapping paper and elegant lace ribbon. There are presentations by guest speakers on such topics as "Decorating Your Mantle, Country Style," and "Country Holiday Decorating Ideas." Summer, winter, spring, and fall, The Bunny Hutch brings country into your heart and home.

CANDELA DE ALMADEN
5353 Almaden Expressway Unit 53
San Jose, CA 95118
Tel. (408) 269-6323
Hrs: Mon. - Fri.   10:00 a.m. - 9:00 p.m.
      Saturday   10:00 a.m. - 6:00 p.m.
      Sunday   12:00 noon - 5:00 p.m.
Thanksgiving - Christmas
      Saturday   10:00 a.m. 9:00 p.m.

Candles of just about every size, color and scent attract shoppers to this gift store on Alamedan Expressway. Massive candles cast from original European molds share the display with modern floating candles.

Scents of the candles fill the air as you enter Candela de Almaden. The beauty of tapers, votive candles, and colors from all shades of the rainbow unfold. Denise and David Raumaker offer custom candle making for weddings or similar occasions when you already have a decorating theme which will be complimented by the elegance of candle light. Gift items range from Russian stone carvings to East European porcelains, gold-plate items to crystal, plus stoneware and an army of nutcracker figures ready to march into your home.

Candela de Almaden is a "Best Choice" for exploring as well as buying, a collection of beautiful things waiting to greet you.

(See special invitation in the Appendix.)

DAISY PATCH, 1115 Minnesota Avenue, San Jose, California. Uncommonly fine silk plants, flowers, trees and decorative accessories.

K's, 410 El Paseo Shopping Center, San Jose, California. Extremely fine china, crystal and other precious gift items.

RATTAN N' TEAK, 319 Town and Country Village, San Jose, California. Specializing in Oriental gifts and art objects. Wicker repair, restoration and supplies.

RYSTAD'S LIMITED EDITIONS
1013 Lincoln Ave.
San Jose, CA 95125
Tel. (408) 279-1960
Hrs: Tues.-Sat. 10:00 a.m.-5:00 p.m.
       Open Mon. from Thanksgiving to Christmas

For more than 20 years, Dean Rystad has offered the best selection of collector plates in the Bay Area. Serious plate collectors are attracted to his selection of more than 1,200 limited edition plates. The plates are perfectly arranged by theme and manufacturer. Most Bing & Grondahl, and Royal Copenhagen Christmas plate collectors will find nearly every issue available here. Dean is an official authorized dealer for such lines as Rockwell, the Bradford Exchange, Lenox, Belleek, Hummel, David Winter cottages and others. Through his search service, Dean can locate back issues with a 99 percent success rate. He will order any plate you like, and call you promptly upon delivery.

Gift shoppers will enjoy the variety of interesting dolls, lithographs, bells, Christmas ornaments, collector eggs, Lladro porcelains, and other beautiful items. Time after time you'll want to return to Rystad's for the highest quality collector limited editions and most cordial service imaginable.

TEDDY BEAR EXPRESS
1337 S Winchester Boulevard
San Jose, CA 95128
Tel. (408) 379-2203
Hrs: Mon. - Fri.   8:00 a.m. - 7:00 p.m.
      Saturday   11:00 a.m. - 4:00 p.m.
MasterCard, Visa and AMEX are accepted.

"Paging Doctor Teddy Bear... Paging Doctor Teddy Bear ... to Tommy's Birthday party STAT!" Teddy Bear Express delivers all types and sizes of teddy bears with a free bouquet of balloons and a card expressing your sentiment to anyone for any conceivable occasion.

Teddy bears, of course, are perfectly suitable gifts for people of all ages and occupations. Teddy Bear Express features a doctor, nurse, dentist, executive, aerobic bears, birthday bears and even specialty bears made to order. All you need to make someone's day is a little imagination and Teddy Bear Express!

Teddy bears can be delivered to homes, businesses, hospitals, schools...and Teddy Bear Express will package and ship your selection anywhere nationwide. Teddy Bear Express can also fix up your bears to-go, complete with balloon bouquet to make it beary special. So, visit the bears or just pick up the phone and dial (408) 379-2203 and let the smiles begin!

(See special invitation in the Appendix.)

While shopping for friends back home, don't forget to splurge on yourself. This tour will help you enjoy yourself and San Jose.

SAN JOSE'S PICK & CHOOSE TOUR			
a.m.	Original Joe's	Best steak & eggs	SanJ/Rest
a.m.	Yesterday's	Best paperbacks	SanJ/Book
a.m.	Crystal Iris	Best accessories	SanJ/App
a.m.	Silk-N-Sequin	Best silk fashion	SanJ/App
p.m.	Meyberg's Deli	Best lunch	SanJ/Deli
p.m.	Mackey Picture Frame	Best framing	SanJ/Frame
p.m.	T.J.'s Ice Cream	Best ice cream	SanJ/Ice
p.m.	Schurra's Chocolates	Best candy	SanJ/Candy

Glass

ALMADEN STAINED GLASS
4666 Meridian Avenue at Branham Lane
San Jose, CA 95118
Tel. (408) 978-8300
Hrs: Mon. - Fri.   10:30 a.m. - 7:00 p.m.
     Saturday   10:00 a.m. - 5:00 p.m.
     Sunday   12:00 noon - 5:00 p.m.

This shop has much to offer to anyone interested in beautiful things. Your first impression upon entering is of an art gallery. The place is filled with gorgeous stained glass windows and lamps of every size and shape, as well as numerous smaller items such as, stained glass boxes, suncatchers and terrariums. These items are not only for sales, but also serve as an inspiration to the many hobbyists and professionals who shop for supplies. People looking for a way to dress up their homes or businesses also get ideas from the displays for custom work they may want to have the shop perform. The shop also does expert repair work.

Almaden Stained Glass has helped many people get started in working with stained glass through its Beginner's Class. This course is for people who want to beautify their homes and/or make stained glass projects for their friends or to sell. The folks at Almaden claim they can teach anyone and that no artistic skills are required. Many of their graduates go on to take the more advanced classes offered for the serious student.

The stained glass craftsperson will be especially delighted with this place because of the enormous selection of glass, tools and other supplies. Almaden offers over 600 different colors of glass and thousands of other items used in the craft. The staff is also very helpful and supportive with their extensive knowledge of techniques and materials. They offer wholesale prices to businesses, schools and government agencies. Discounts are available to stained glass students and senior citizens.

This is a special place for the shopper seeking the finest in decorative pieces of stained glass, and for the artisan or the beginner who wonders if the beauty of stained glass is a hobby worth pursuing.

(See special invitation in the Appendix.)

GLASS WITH CLASS
1336 Lincoln Avenue
San Jose, CA 95125
Tel. (408) 286-8098
Hrs: Mon. - Sat. 10:00 a.m. - 5:00 p.m.

Glass, made mostly of sand, soda and lime, is one of man's most useful materials. It can be made into thousands of different objects of various shapes and sizes. As a collectors item, glassware is a highly prized and much sought after commodity. It's easy to find ordinary glass, but to find "Glass With Class" you have to go to San Jose.

Few dealers can create a truly charming atmosphere by blending old and new. Lenore Shelly has achieved this at Glass With Class by extending her expertise and aesthetic sensibilities to create a showroom arrangement that is perfectly integrated. She specializes in American glass and is an expert on Fenton, Cambridge, Fostoria, Duncan and Miller and many others. The back showcase features her extensive Heisey selection with fine etched goblets and an elegant punch bowl among them. Another favorite piece is a beautiful yellow and peach Burmese vase, hand painted with conch shells, seahorses and other marine creatures, signed by the artist.

Lenore began offering primarily glass items, but has expanded her vistas into other areas including handcrafted gifts and beautiful antiques, rare collector dolls and an unsurpassed consortium of miniatures that are absolutely fabulous. This glass shop is a classic where class is literally mirrored off every shelf.

(See special invitation in the Appendix.)

Ice Cream

TJ'S ICE CREAM, FROZEN YOGURT AND GELATO
1375 Blossom Hill Road
San Jose, CA 95118
Tel. (408) 265-7163
Hrs: Sun. - Thu.   11:00 a.m. - 10:00 p.m.
      Fri. - Sat.   11:00 a.m. - 11:00 p.m.

Ice cream, Gelato, yogurt and shakes. Super sundaes, floats, freezes and decorated cakes. For goodness sake, TJ's has them all! Kicking off the cavalcade of delicious sweets is the ice cream. Over fifty flavors, yummy gourmet delights like Oreo Cookie, Nutty Banana, Irish Coffee and Fudge Brownie. Some of the most irresistible of them are made right at TJ's. You'll want to taste their Snickerlicious, M&M Candy Crunch, Butterfinger Bonanza and Rainbow Sherbert. Yes, the bountiful Banana Royale, Fudge Brownie Delight or Cookie Delight come with any topping, whipped cream and of course, a cherry!

Seldom will you find yogurt and ice cream side by side, but at TJ's the best of both worlds is yours. Cone or cup with excellent fresh toppings are available for your yogurt enjoyment. The Walking Waffle cone is huge and holds a five ounce serving of your favorite yogurt or ice cream. Add to that almonds, walnuts, whipped cream.....you've got one good reason why people say TJ's is the greatest!

And what sensational cakes! Wow! Ice Cream, Fresh Baked, Frozen Yogurt and Gelato cakes. There are albums filled with pictures of cakes sporting corporate logos, party invitations, comic book characters, record covers and others. Bring a copy of whatever you've like to have duplicated on a cake top and they'll do it up, or choose from over five hundred ideas from the album samples. Make TJ's your place for satisfying those cravings for the rich and delicious and you'll be in for a reward that will make your taste buds very grateful!

(See special invitation in the Appendix).

Jewelry

JOHN SUMIDA, 416 El Paseo de Saratoga, San Jose, California. Elegant custom jewelry and precious gemstones from one of San Jose's foremost goldsmiths.

LO MONACO'S
2904 Alum Rock Avenue
San Jose, CA 95127
Tel. (408) 251-4100
Hrs: Tue. - Fri   10:00 a.m. - 6:00 p.m.
       Saturday   10:00 a.m. - 5:00 p.m.
and,
3139 Stevens Creek Boulevard
San Jose, CA 95117
Tel. (408) 985-1222

The Lo Monaco generations have long been institutions in San Jose. Virtually no one can remember a San Jose without a Lo Monaco's Jewelers. This is because they have continued to thrive since the time when the native Sicilian, Santo Lo Monaco made his way to San Jose via New York and San Francisco, setting up shop in 1923.

In their sixth generation, this dynamic clan claims utmost integrity and lasting value in merchandise as it's prime measure of prosperity throughout the years. Their customers come back knowing they can count on expert watch and jewelry repairs, remounting, appraising, cleaning and exceptional custom design capabilities. Le Monaco's is an optimum supplier of wedding rings, diamonds, rubies, emeralds, sapphires and other precious stones. You will also find a fine selection of Black Hills gold, Swiss pocket watches and eighteen karat gold tie clasps.

The Lo Monaco's Galleria has become a favorite place for shoppers of high quality gifts, meticulously selected and favorably displayed. Sasaki crystal, decanters, intricate blown glass items and Lladros are only a few of pieces available. The quality merchandise, in combination with service that's beyond reproach,inscribe Lo Monaco's with a sterling reputation that you can bank on.

577

COLLECTIBLE TOUR			
a.m.	Antiques Colony	Best collection	SanJ/Ant
a.m.	Antiquary	Best clothing	SanJ/Ant
p.m.	San Jose Cafe	Best lunch	SanJ/Rest
p.m.	Willow Glen	Best lithographs	SanJ/Ant
p.m.	Collectibles Outlet	Best crystal	SanJ/Coll
p.m.	Weibel Winery	Best winery	SanJ/Wine
p.m.	Victorian House	Best dinner	SanJ/Rest

Records

FLASHBACK RECORDS, 2090 Lincoln Avenue, San Jose, California. Vintage records. A great selection for all musical tastes.

Restaurants

BRENNAN'S TERRACE
95 South Market Street
San Jose, CA 95113
Tel. (408) 288-5015

Beaming with good taste and casual elegance, Brennan's Terrace provides a skyward outlook of the historical downtown center. It's second floor perch is superbly relaxing, offering a tapestry of views that include monuments such as the San Jose Museum of Art, Saint Joseph's Cathedral and the spectacular Fairmont Hotel.

With it's checkered floor, brass and oak full length bar and supremely fresh cuisine, Brennan's Terrace exhorts a special purpose. A commitment to excellence is reflected in the high quality and discernibly fresh ingredients that go into each dish. Some of the entrees include Fettucine Alfredo, veal Scallopine, chicken Molokai and fresh Pasta Primavera. For seafood, try the pepper snapper, Australian lobster tail, scampi-style sauteed prawns or the thick Calamari steak. There's also great soups, salads and side dishes to choose.

Brennan's special blend coffee, espresso, cappuccino and freshly squeezed juices amplify your dining experience. The impeccable wine list features Rieslings, Chenin Blanc, Chardonnay, Cabernet, Zinfandel and many more from premiere California and French cellars. Brennan's Terrace spares nothing in presenting serenity and dreamy relaxation, great libations, and cuisine that speaks passionately to you palate.

CHEZ CROISSANT
51 E San Carlos Street
San Jose, CA 95113
Tel. (408) 297-1233
Hrs: Mon. - Thu.　7:00 a.m. - 6:30 p.m.
　　　Fri. - Sat.　　　7:00 a.m. - 9:30 p.m.
Major credit cards are accepted.
and,
1092 N 1st Street
San Jose, CA 95112
Tel. (408) 297-1102

Tender and fluffy, French pastries come from the ovens of Chez Croissant daily. They are delivered to other restaurants, and here they are fashioned into special luncheon or dinner sandwiches.

Decorated with a Parisian theme, the pleasant Chez Croissant locations downtown and at the San Jose Airport attract folks from afar, drawn by word of the delightful food. Besides the unique croissant sandwiches stuffed with cheeses, sprouts and other fillings, you will find soups, salads, and desserts which do honor to having a French bakery from which to draw. Eclairs, delicately constructed treats with whipped cream, fresh fruit and tender crusts; each dessert becomes reason enough for finding the Chez Croissant.

This is a "Best Choice" for a meal, but we must add a recommendation for the desserts and aromatic coffees, the fruit milk shakes and other bits of flavor that attract people for a snack or a break. A pastry or a meal, this is the place!

(See special invitation in the Appendix.)

D.B. COOPER'S
163 W Santa Clara Street
San Jose, CA 95113
Tel. (408) 279-JUMP

Hrs:	Lunch	Mon. - Fri.	11:00 a.m. - 3:00 p.m.
	Dinner	Mon. - Thu.	5:00 p.m. - 10:00 p.m.
		Friday	5:00 p.m. - 12:00 midnight
		Sat. - Sun.	6:00 p.m. - 12:00 midnight
	Hungry Hour	Mon. - Fri.	4:30 p.m. - 6:30 p.m.

Dining, dancing, and weekday lunches are offered at this spot which honors the missing D.B. Cooper, an airline highjacker who disappeared with his parachute and $200,000 in cash in November, 1971. They say the infamous bandit lives on in San Jose, at least in spirit.

You'll find a modern place done in pinks, blacks and grays with potted palms that are a far cry from the Douglas Fir trees and cold Columbia River which marked where part of the real highjacker's cash was found. The owners, Charles Oliver and Greg Gray, say this is how Cooper would be spending the rest of the loot, if we only knew. The menu is full of memorabilia from the Thanksgiving Eve exit out the rear ramp of a southbound jetliner. The food is a mix of modern and traditional. Hamburgers, hotdogs, Tex-Mex and ribs. Tropical drinks. Rock and roll and top forty music greet dancers swirling under a parachute. Hungry Hour, as D.B. Cooper terms its weekday afternoons, offers light snacks to go with drinks.

This is your "Best Choice" for entertainment, eating, and remembering. In an era where airline highjacking is less-than-pleasant, it lets you recall the decade when America gave the missing D.B. Cooper a legendary status which most of us have forgotten.

(See special invitation in the Appendix.)

EMILE'S
545 S 2nd Street
San Jose, CA 95112
Tel. (408) 289-1960

Hrs:	Tue. - Fri	11:30 a.m. - 2:00 p.m. lunch.
	Tue. - Sat.	5:30 p.m. - 10:00 p.m. dinner.

The term "Superstar" is generally affixed to athletes and well-know movie personalities. But no hall of famer or actor whose Oscars run knee-deep is more deserving of the word than San Jose's own Emile Mooser. It's more than towering talent that elevates Emile above aspiring echelons of great chefs. It's also the powerful charisma and magnanimous hospitality that he exhibits.

Getting his start in Switzerland, Emile's dream came true when he opened this beautiful restaurant in 1972. The stately dining room features tasteful art prints, etched glass dividers and burgundy carpeting. The seasonally changing menu takes into account the availability of the freshest ingredients worldwide. Enjoy such dishes as, Supreme de Poulet aux Crevettes, Coquilles St. Jacques et Crevettes Oriental, Escalope de Veau a la Creme et aux Champignons, Les Ris de Veau au Cabernet Sauvignon and Le Pigeameau au Vinougre de Framboise.

No one should bid adieu to Emile's without sampling one of his famous desserts, such as Le Souffle Au Grand Marnier and La Creation Aux Chocolat Maison. There is also an excellent wine list from Emile's private and most prized wine cellar. Make reservations at Emile's, and enjoy the products of this great man's works.

EULIPIA RESTAURANT AND BAR

374 S First Street
San Jose, CA 95113
Tel. (408) 280-6161

Hrs:	Lunch	Mon. - Fri.	11:30 a.m. - 2:00 p.m.
	Dinner	Mon. - Thur.	5:30 p.m. - 9:30 p.m.
		Fri. - Sat.	5:30 p.m. - 10:00 p.m.
		Sunday	4:30 p.m. - 9:00 p.m.

At Eulipia Restaurant, a California epicurean sublimity is evident in the menu, the mild classical and jazz background music, and the atmosphere that is enticingly lighted, with tasteful art prints along the red brick wall; adding warmth to a dining room appointed with fresh flowers.

A luncheoner will be delighted by a selection of satisfying appetizers like quesadilla with goat cheese and aioli, spinach salad and fried mozzarella with red pepper sauce. The wonderful freshness of the likes of chicken pasta salad with spicy garlic dressing and oriental chicken salad reign supreme. Further favorites such as blackened red snapper and a brimming shrimp tostada entreat every time, and then there are the entrees, pasta shells with sun dried tomatoes and goat cheese are quite popular as is the sensational linguine with lamb sauteed with garlic in olive oil.

Dinners at Eulipia feature a fashionable and refined levity and sophistication. A most appreciated place for theater goers, the menu retains many of the specialties served at lunch with some exciting entrees such as chicken breast with Brie and a roasted garlic sauce, fresh pasta with gorgonzola, vegetables and basil. Satisfy your curiosity with the sumptuous

New York steak. The spinach fettuccine with salmon and dill or the prawns with apples and snow peas also come highly recommended. Led by the splendid chocolate truffle cake, there are also some erstwhile unheard of wonderful, sweet fantasies including, caramel custard and mocha mousse. Employing an epicurean simplicity and grace, great culinary surprises and spritely service, Eulipia Restaurant is a little utopia where dining is an entirely inspiring enterprise.

THE FAMOUS PACIFIC FISH COMPANY
177 West Santa Clara Street
San Jose, CA 95113
Tel. (408) 298-7222
Hrs: Mon. - Fri.   11:00 a.m. - 10:00 p.m.
      Sat. - Sun.   5:00 a.m. - 10:00 p.m.

This building is certainly famous, in fact, a historical landmark.Built in 1887, it once housed the San Jose Mercury News, a ballroom, and several other businesses. But none of the occupants were better suited to it than The Famous Pacific Fish Company. The beautiful brick building houses thick wood beams, painted a cool marine gray, with genuine nautical artifacts. You feel as if you are wrapped in the serenity of a Claude Monet seascape.

The lounge is a lively spot for Happy Hour in downtown San Jose. The Oyster Bar is most convenient, offering delicious delicacies while you sip. Old life preservers, a carved life-sized statue of a sea captain at the stairway, and a brilliant blue marlin mounted on the wall inside a cozy side room are just some of the fine appointments you'll enjoy.

Lunch or dinner is served in the upstairs loft. The cooking area is centrally located, where you can view the chefs as they prepare their famous mesquite dishes. They use the same proven art of mesquite broiling which was perfected in the coastal cities of Mexico, whereby the skewered fish are cooked slowly over mesquite charcoal. The freshness of the fish is legend. They say, "If the fish weren't biting yesterday, they're not on our menu today." Be sure to check the fresh fish board, where you'll know the daily specials are listed: mussels Mariana, Cajun blackened catfish, smoked salmon fettucini--at least three specials every day.

The famous lunch menu includes shrimp and scallop skewers, luscious seafood Louies, grilled Teriyaki chicken, and delicious seafood melts. Try the jumbo Mexican shrimp, trout Piccatta, chicken Dijon, or Procoli Calamari. If it's pasta you want, indulge in one of the superb treats like salmon Alfredo or the Fish Company's linguini.

A favorite among the appetizers is the excellent Ceviche, a mouth-watering white fish marinated in lemon, tomato, onion, cilantro, and spices--a recipe straight from the coast of Mexico. You will enjoy such specialties as chicken Teriyaki, filet mignon, New York steak, Alaskan crab legs, and especially the gigantic twenty to twenty-four ounce lobster tail. The wine list is exceptional. There are eight Chardonnays to choose from, Chenin Blancs, Sauvignons, reds, Zinfandels and more.

You needn't be famous to come here, but when you do, you'll understand why The Famous Pacific Fish Company is the rage in San Jose.

GERVAIS RESTAURANT FRANCAIS
1798 Park Avenue at Naglee
San Jose, CA 95126
Tel. (408) 275-8631
Hrs: Tue. - Fri.   11:30 a.m. - 2:00 p.m. lunch.
      Tue. - Sat.   5:30 p.m. - 10:00 p.m. dinner.

Twinkle twinkle little star...I wish I may, I wish I might, have a gourmet dinner this very night. Poof! Your Fairy Godmother appears and with a wave of her wand you find yourself seated in Gervais Restaurant Francais.

Chef Gervais Henric and his wife Mary Lou, have developed in this restaurant a place where the best French cooking and elegant appointments embellish the palate as well as the aesthetic senses. The entrees enter the annals of great French creations, each showing the magical Gervais hand. Choose from dishes such as Coquilles St. Jacques, rich and sweet scallops sauteed in white wine sauce; the Poulet Financiere, chicken with wine sauce; Escallope De Veau Forestiere, scallops of veal in wine sauce; or the Filet De Porc Charcutiere, a filet of pork with caper sauce. Another delicate favorite is the Caille Grille Vigneronne which is a sensational quail grilled in Cognac.

Desserts include truffles, pastries and a widely prized Moscovit Gervais. The wines, refined and diverse, embrace your meal in grand fashion. In every way, Gervais presents you with the trappings of French gourmet in a sublime dining environment. Ahhh! This is exactly the type of place you were wishing for...*Bon appétit!*

GUNTHER'S RESTAURANT AND CATERING
1601 Meridian Avenue
San Jose, CA 95125
Tel. (408) 266-9030
Hrs: Mon. - Sat. 7:30 a.m. - 8:00 p.m.

New Yorkers have every reason to be proud of their great reputation for delicatessens. Yet, when they come to California they have a hard time finding one that compares to their favorite deli back home. Californians, on the other hand, are happy to have discovered Gunther's, a genuine New York style deli that can also fit their catering needs.

As Gunther's is a family business, headed by Gunther himself, with the help of his wife and four children, all areas of the restaurant's service come under their direction. Gunther supervises all the daily cooking and serving at the restaurant, while daughter Debbie takes care of the catering.

Early risers can enjoy a favorite breakfast such as the lox and onion, cheese or salami omelettes, served with fresh cut home fried potatoes and choice of roll, toast or bagel. For lunch Gunther's always features a prized daily special like chicken Almondine, Salisbury steak or beef Stroganoff. Daily entrees include a terrific knockwurst and sauerkraut, as well as, bratwurst and hot potato salad. Order baked lasagna ala carte, delicious barbecued chicken, or their exceptional brisket of beef. These are served throughout the day along with many sandwiches.

In addition, Gunther's features a special soup each day such as minestrone, cream of spinach, or the incomparable chicken matzo ball. Desserts include an excellent apple strudel, bakalava, German chocolate cake, or macaroons.

Gunther's special catering offers complete consultation resulting in made-to-order buffets or sit down dinners--all according to the customer's budget. A dinner hall that seats 450 is at your service for Gunther's expert catering of weddings, banquets, buffets, receptions, industrial promos, etcetera.

With Gunther's in San Jose, it's a wonder that anyone in these parts would yearn for New York.

HOCHBURG VON GERMANIA, 261 North 2nd Street, San Jose, California. Fine German cuisine and ballroom dancing.

LE PAPILLON
410 Saratoga Avenue
San Jose, CA 95129
Tel. (408) 296-3730
Hrs: Mon. - Fri.   11:30 a.m. - 2:00 p.m. lunch.
      Mon. - Sat.   5:00 p.m. - 10:00 p.m. dinner.

Rising like a fiery comet over the select constellation of fine restaurants, Le Papillon has never looked back to witness its shadow. They realize that the challenge of refining classic French cooking and their own California Nouvelle knows no compromise. Only the freshest and most unique ingredients are used to create such impeccably fine dishes as to resist definition.

The sense of pervading quality and grace begins with a refined dining environment. Utmost propriety is exercised by the maitre d', as well as the service personnel, in a friendly, human manner that is a Le Papillon trademark. The endless entree specialities are legendary, including Linguini Fue de Mer, veal and crab Chiron and the chicken Chasseur. Another classic in demand at Le Papillon is the loin of venison, roasted to a blush and resting on a bed of hunter sauce with a hint of thyme and graced with fresh sauteed Chantrelles mushrooms.

For the exotic, they've got reindeer, bear, rattlesnake, alligator and a miraculous tenderloin, all supremely prepared and served. When your entree has been savored, the desserts are equally tantalizing. At Le Papillon, your happiness and satisfaction are sure to prevail with dishes that exhort a special orbit of inimitable quality.

THE OLD SPAGHETTI FACTORY
51 N San Pedro
San Jose, CA 95110
Tel. (408) 288-7488
Hrs: Lunch   Mon. - Fri.   11:30 a.m - 2:00 p.m.
      Dinner   Mon. - Thur.   5:00 p.m. - 10:00 p.m.
                 Fri. - Sat.   5:00 p.m. - 11:00 p.m.
                 Sunday   4:00 p.m. - 10:00 p.m.

The Old Spaghetti Factory has a unique charm stemming from the vintage brick building in which it is located. During times gone by it served as a warehouse and originally as the San Jose Ravenna Pasta company, a real spaghetti factory. The decor is fascinating with an abundance of wrought iron, a twenty-four foot bar, a 1921 St. Louis street car in one of the dining areas, Tiffany lamps, an old piano/organ, stained glass windows, antique prints and booths constructed from old wood and iron bedposts. The monumental popularity of this restaurant is due to the modestly priced, generous portions of delicious foods it offers.

Choices begin with traditional spaghetti with tomato sauce and continue with secret homemade recipes such as clam sauce, Mizithra cheese and butter, meat sauce and mushroom sauce. There are combinations that allow samplings of two or more sauces; as with all meals these include salad, sour dough bread and garlic butter. Dinners also come complete with coffee, tea or milk and Spumoni ice cream. Zesty sausage, slices of tenderloin, fettuccine Alfredo or spinach tortellini are other premium choices. At lunch time, besides spaghetti and pasta, they serve excellent sausage, meatball and tenderloin steak sandwiches.

For an adventure in classic food, in an atmosphere filled with charming artifacts and relics, The Old Spaghetti Factory is waiting for you in beautiful San Jose.

ORIGINAL JOE'S
301 South First Street
San Jose, CA 95113
Tel. (408)292-7030
Hrs: Mon. - Sun. 11:00 a.m. - 1:30 a.m.

The legacy of Original Joe's is perpetrated by the string of imitators who emulate not only the name but many of the restaurant's famous dishes. Owner Babe Rocca began his career at Original Joe's (founded by his father Louis Rocca in 1937) on Taylor Street in San Francisco. Although Louis Rocca is no longer with us and Babe has divested himself from the San Francisco restaurant since 1956, he and his sons, Matt and Brad, have continued the tradition in downtown San Jose.

There seems to be no limit to the varied menu at Original Joe's. Breakfast specials include Italian sausage and eggs, top sirloin and eggs, and a variety of creative omelets. Try lasagna, barbecued lamb, sirloin tips with risotto, or a crisp salad for lunch. Choose from a selection of twenty-two sandwiches or internationally-known Joe's Special, made with fresh spinach, eggs and ground chuck with mushrooms.

At dinner time, a mood of reserved elegance pervades the dining room of Original Joe's. Savory entrees include veal scaloppini, roast beef, calf's liver with onions and bacon, and pot roast, each served with a choice of french fries, vegetables, spaghetti or ravioli. Other excellent entrees include the 18 ounce New York steak, brochette with mushrooms, pork chops, chicken and seafood. Spaghetti, ravioli and mostaccioli are among the excellent pasta selections at Original Joe's.

Nothing short of moving First Street to some other city could possibly dislodge Original Joe's from its pre-eminence in downtown San Jose.

The original is here to stay.

PAOLO'S
520 E Santa Clara Street
San Jose, CA 95112
Tel. (408) 294-2558
Hrs: Lunch   Mon. - Fri.   11:00 a.m. - 3:00 p.m.
     Dinner   Mon. - Sat.   4:30 p.m. - 10:00 p.m.

It's true that the world is touched by imperfections. But it is nevertheless filled with some perfectly good creations, and Paolo's has claimed some of the best of them. A new concept of perfection is the goal in every dish served, matched by an unfettered commitment to excellence which was begun by founder Jack Allen more than forty years ago.

There are two main dining rooms, both simple, yet elegantly appointed. The front room with it's colored glass windows is especially enjoyed by luncheoners who come to dine on a sunny day. The food is equally enlightening. For appetizers, treat yourself to smoked Oregon trout, Icelandic scampi Livornese or choose from many others. Entrees begin with lobster, scallops and a fine fish of the day. You'll also behold such favorites as chicken Jerusalem, veal Shitake and bouillabaisse Marseillaise. The filet mignon is perfectly broiled and served with an embracing Porcini mushroom sauce.

When it comes time for dessert, they've got what it takes to bring the evening to a pitch. At Paolo's, the service, ambiance and unmatched cuisine make for a perfect dining experience.

RUE DE PARIS
19 N Market Street
San Jose, CA 95113
Tel. (408) 298-0704
Hrs: Lunch   Mon. - Fri.   11:00 a.m. - 2:00 p.m.
     Dinner   Mon. - Thu.   5:30 p.m. - 10:00 p.m.
               Fri. - Sat.   5:30 p.m. - 11:00 p.m.
All major credit cards are accepted.

It is amazing how worlds can be reversed in an instant. One second you're dreaming and suddenly you're awake! This sort of transformation takes place when you enter Rue de Paris. Every detail, from the impeccably prepared cuisine to the the dainty and charming French decor is as if lifted from the core of Paris. The two principal dining areas are blithely lit yet serene, divided as they are by curtains of elaborate chantilly lace.

Luncheon may begin with a selection of elite hors d'oeuvres, soups and salads. The Pate de Canard au Cognac, Soupe a l'Oignon Gratinee and Tomate et d'Avocad are tantalizing preliminaries to the entree. An exceptional seafood

587

choice is the Filet de Sole Veronique. Unyieldingly delicious, it is brimming in a rich saute of butter, lemon and fresh grapes. For a splendid veal preparation, try Escalope de Veau Orloff, tender veal sauteed in sparkling champagne, cream sauce and fresh mushrooms.

The dinner entrees provide exquisite excursions into culinary delights that the critics have continually applauded. Your palate will embrace every morsel! Experience sumptuous Demi Caneton a l'Orange, tender half duck capped with a luscious orange Grand Marnier sauce or Carre d'Agneau Provencale, thick rack of lamb swaddled in a fine garlic crust. The desserts at Rue de Paris are impossible to pass by. Souffle aux Framboises, a fresh raspberry souffle, is bursting with flavor as are the sinfully delicious Patisserie Maison and Fraise Grand Passion. Relax and enjoy a rich espresso with your dessert and cherish your unique Parisian rendezvous!

(See special invitation in the Appendix.)

SAN JOSE CAFE
777 North First Street
San Jose, CA 95112
Tel. (408) 297-7775
Hrs: Mon. - Thur.   11:30 a.m. - 10:00 p.m.
     Fri. - Sat.   11:30 a.m. - 11:00 p.m.
Bar Hrs:
     Mon. - Tues.   11:30 a.m. - midnight
     Wed. - Sat.   11:30 a.m. - 2:00 a.m.
     Wed. - Sat.   (Live entertainment)

Strictly Californian and distinctly San Jose, this renown pavillion is a most enchanting, casual spot for marvelously mixed drinks, nighttime danceable jazz and eminently satisfying cuisine. A rise of seven stories up in the glass elevator heightens your anticipation of the wide skyscape view of the East Hills. There is a sustained grace and roominess, as well as, outstanding views from every vantage of the restaurant and bar. Owner Joe Antuzzi, Jr. shows his deep affinity for the city by displaying enlarged photos of pioneers, street scenes; a gallery of San Jose's past history. The atmosphere is refined by the cool modesty and richness of black painted wood beams, glowing red lamps, and gold trim all around. One dining room features cozy, padded booths, the other features spaced tables set with fresh flowers, wine glasses and perfectly arranged napkins. Elegant rosewood wine cabinets along the walls add a perfect touch of sophistication.

The menu at the San Jose Cafe offers excellent diversity and has so many exciting features that draw regular clientele from business banqueters and legislators to late night couples after the theater. Any of the several great appetizers may be meals in themselves. Try the grilled spiced prawns-- marinated in a fresh lemon and garlic sauce with a tinge of crushed red pepper and a light olive oil, then grilled to perfection. You'll love the traditional Caesar salad. You may, however, immediately gravitate toward the Cafe duck salad, consisting of grilled duck, seasonal greens and fresh fruit, and finished with a terrific sweet and sour dressing. The daily soups are tantalizing surprises. Sandwiches are satisfying portions you'll truly enjoy. A breakthrough in burger greatness has been achieved with the half-pound San Jose Cafe burger.

San Jose Cafe offers two to six daily specials of only the freshest fish. The zesty pastas, fresh linguini and smoked petit poulet and Cajun spiced fettucini come highly recommended. Entrees include splendid beef, poultry, veal and lamp preparations. There are dry-aged prime rib, grilled American lamp chops, and grilled boneless quail to entrance your palate. No menu item is enjoyed by more of the people of San Jose Cafe's patrons than the incredible build-your-own pizza. Choose from anchovies, artichoke hearts, Roma or sun-dried tomatoes, roasted peppers, Pancetta, braised duck or other fantastic toppings.

The San Jose Cafe bar setting is airy and romantic. The bar looks out over a starlit city. The dance floor is always full as the music is lively. You'll swing, swerve and sing when you stop in at the San Jose Cafe bar for the great cuisine, drinks, jazz, and view. It's acclaim is legend.

TASSO'S GARDEN RESTAURANT, 1111 Meridian Avenue, San Jose, California. Cocktails with Continental lunch and dinner. Elegant garden surroundings.

TESKE'S GERMANIA RESTAURANT
255 North 1st Street
San Jose, CA 95113
Tel. (408) 292-0291
Hrs: Lunch   Mon. - Fri.   11:00 a.m. - 2:00 p.m.
         Dinner   Tue.-Sat.   5:00 p.m. - 9:30 p.m.

Seekers of truly authentic German food at its best need look no farther than Teske's Germania Restaurant. Chef Ernst Teske and his wife Marianne came to this country after many years of experience in the restaurant business in their native land.

There are three principal dining areas in addition to a patio, each with its own individual charm. The first features a rustic bar and rich wood panelling, it is very intimate and reminiscent of an old Bavarian inn. The traditional dining room is complete with pictures of wildlife, scenes from Bavaria, a quaint chalet style ceiling and a large cow bell transported by Ernst from Germany. On the walls are mounted buffalo and boar, elk and deer heads, reminders that Ernst is a master hunter as well as chef. The third dining area is strictly elegant. Oil paintings adorn the walls and the fancy green wallpaper and antique cabinets are rich touches. The patio is enhanced by a marble and brick floor, a fountain, sculptured pillars, vines and begonias all in a secluded setting.

Lunches entice you with German dishes that demonstrate Ernst's tremendous talent and versatility. A favorite is the Rouladen, juicy stuffed beef with luscious red cabbage served with fresh homemade noodles. For dinner, sample tantalizing Geschnetzeltes Mit Spaetzle, Sauerbraten or Wiener Schnitzel. The selection of German beers and wines is extensive and discriminating, each offered as a fit complement to your meal. These magnificent German dishes coincide with a hearty hospitality that presides over every bite. With an intimacy and old world charm, this "Best Choice" comes highly recommended.

(See special invitation in the Appendix.)

VICTORIAN HOUSE RESTAURANT
476 S 1st Street
San Jose, CA 95113
Tel. (408) 286-1770

Hrs:	Lunch	Mon. - Fri.	11:30 a.m. - 3:00 p.m.
	Dinner	Mon. - Thu.	5:00 p.m. - 10:00 p.m.
		Fri. - Sat.	5:00 p.m. - 11:00 p.m.
	Brunch	Sunday	10:30 a.m. - 2:30 p.m.
	Dinner	Sunday	4:00 p.m. - 10:00 p.m.

All major credit cards are accepted.

The Victorian House Restaurant is located in a turn of the century brick building that retains a traditional quaint candor. Inside are antiques, all for sale, and genuine Tiffany lamps above the tables. There are exquisite nineteenth century oil paintings on the walls, bountiful hanging greenery, elegant tables with sophisticated settings and beautiful cabinets filled with art glass. The outdoor patio is available for dining on sunny days, a veritable paradise with lavish green plants, dazzling fountains and oak trees that gently canopy the tables.

The menu is as superb as the setting suggests. Lunch begins with fresh stuffed croissants and delectable salads. There is an array of palate pleasing luncheon entrees from which to choose, such as spaghetti with whole clams and sausage or linguini pesto a la Pasquale which boasts owner Patrick Mormon's marvelous pesto with fresh basil and pine nut sauce. Entrees are remarkably diverse and introduce seafood, chicken and veals creations. For dinner, try the Angelo, chicken sauteed in sweet butter and wine with fresh artichoke hearts, mushrooms, garlic and secret Italian herbs, or perhaps the Scalone, a perfect synthesis of scallops and abalone blended into a seafood medallion, dipped in delicate egg batter and sauteed with lemon juice and butter.

A la Carte pastas such as homemade ricotta ravioli, mostaccioli and sausage and cannellone are all uniquely prepared and brimming with flavor. With service that propels such valiant creations, Victorian House claims its rightful high station.

Sport

GO SKATE SURF AND SPORT
2306 L Almaden Road
San Jose, CA 95125
Tel. (408) 978-6479
Hrs: Mon. - Fri.   10:00 a.m. - 7:00 p.m.
          Sat. - Sun.   10:00 a.m. - 6:00 p.m.

Throughout the years the skateboard has changed tremendously. The challenges encountered and the skills necessary to take part in major competitions now equal those of other sports. Daredevil stunts, flyaway antics, judo kicks, 360 degree spins and rocket air variations are all maneuvers that require equipment far beyond the early skateboard's capabilities. But whether beginner or professional, Go Skate answers every call for skateboarding equipment and accessories.

At Go Skate some 150 different models of skateboard decks are available at all times. Choose the wheels, rails, bearing and any other features you like from the widest selection imaginable. Helmets, knee pads, riot gloves and wrist guards are only a few of the accessories this skating shop has to offer. Repair services of all types are also available. But skateboards aren't all they have...Go Skate also caters to surfers and skiers and snow boarders by offering surfboards, skies, snow boards and many types of accessories.

And not to limit the old pastime of roller-skating, you can purchase those skates here too. For clothing, they've got hundreds of shirts and shorts, sandals and beach apparel with designs reflecting the sports represented in the store. In addition to San Jose, stores are located in Santa Cruz, Milpitas, San Mateo, Sacramento and Stockton. So, before going surfing, skiing or snow boarding, be sure to go to Go Skate Surf and Sport first.

MEL COTTON'S
1266 W San Carlos
San Jose, CA 95126
Tel. (408) 287-5994
Hrs: Mon. - Fri.   9:30 a.m. - 9:00 p.m.
        Saturday   9:30 a.m. - 6:00 p.m.
        Sunday   11:00 a.m. - 5:00 p.m.
Visa and MasterCard are accepted.

There are many thousands of South Bay men who remember, when in their childhood, that it was always Mel Cotton's for sporting goods. Whenever they needed a new baseball mitt, sweats for gym class or a new fishing pole, their fathers would take them to Mel Cotton's.

Mel Cotton's, in business since 1946, is a large emporium that serves every facet of the sporting world. The various rooms are all sensibly divided into complete sections. Backpacks, hiking gear, camping equipment, ski accessories, athletic attire of all sorts, baseball, football, soccer, raquetball, tennis and body building equipment are some of the items carried by this store. For the hunter or gun collector, they've got racks of rifles and a window case filled with handguns. Fishing equipment is also featured at Mel Cotton's.

As a rental service, it's possible that Mel Cotton's has never been surpassed. Their winter ski rentals are terrific! You can also rent a canoe, camping equipment and other items. If Mel Cotton's doesn't have it for sale or rent, then you're in for quite a search. Join the crowd and visit Mel Cotton's where, as always, your sporting goods needs will be met.

Textiles

THE BLACK SHEEP
45 Almaden Plaza
San Jose, CA 95118
Tel. (408) 978-2044
Hrs: Mon. - Fri.   10:00 a.m. - 9:00 p.m.
        Saturday   10:00 a.m. - 6:00 p.m.
        Sunday   12:00 noon - 5:00 p.m.

Tapestries, wallpieces and all sorts of yarn creations are gathered here in a massive selection of needlework supplies. Connie Conant works her own magic with needle, thread and yarn in between consulting with her customers who come here for cloth, yarn and craft supplies.

592

The yarn collection takes up an entire room, with skeins and hanks in just about every color and gauge an artist might want. The DMC line of tapestry wool is stocked in all of its colors. There are over 2,000 cross-stitching patterns, another 1,000 or more for knitting and crochet projects. Special holiday theme patterns and finished works are on display so you can think ahead. Fabrics for pillows, clothing and draperies are available, along with just about every size and style of needle one can imagine, and a collection of books.

You'll find the Black Sheep a fun place for classes, for custom framing of your finished work, and for one of the area's largest selections of needlework supplies assembled under one roof.

(See special invitation in the Appendix.)

OAK TREE STITCHERY SHOP, 227 El Paseo de Saratoga, San Jose, California. Needlework and stitching supplies.

Be it food and drink or gifts and toys, San Jose has a plethora of necessary luxuries. The businesses listed in the following tour have among the best of them.

SAN JOSE'S NECESSARY LUXURIES TOUR			
a.m.	Chez Croissant	Best croissants	SanJ/Rest
a.m.	San Jose Florist	Best blown glass	SanJ/Flor
a.m.	Anne's Flowers	Best fruit basket	SanJ/Flor
a.m.	Su-Elen's Ltd	Best porcelain doll	San/Coll
a.m.	The Bunny Hutch	Best gift displays	SanJ/Gift
p.m.	Eulipia	Best Calif. lunch	SanJ/Rest
p.m.	Gallery Saratoga	Best art	SanJ/Gallery
p.m.	Almaden Clocks	Best timepieces	SanJ/Clock
p.m.	Alamaden Stained Glass	Best stained glass	SanJ/Glass
The following stores are open late for your convenience:			
p.m.	The Black Sheep	Best tapestries	SanJ/Tex
p.m.	Avery's	Best selection	SanJ/Gifts
Then, take the necessary steps to a cocktail before dinner.			
p.m.	Famous Pacific Fish Co.	Best seafood pasta	SanJ/Rest
p.m.	Victorian House	Best elegance	SanJ/Rest

Theater

OPRY HOUSE/CLUB ALMADEN
21350 Almaden Road
San Jose, CA 95120
Tel. (408) 268-2492
Hrs: Wed. - Sat.   5:00 p.m. - 1:00 a.m.
            Sunday   10:00 a.m. - 12:00 midnight
Shows   Thu. - Sat.
Visa, MasterCard and AMEX are accepted.
Reservations are required.

One could not imagine a more congenial setting for The Opry House theater. Built by James Randall in 1854, the hacienda style mansion was once the hub of the mercury mining region around which Almaden was born. Now, the old wine cellar and assay office beneath the building serve as a restaurant and saloon, and on the main level The Opry House, theater entertains sellout crowds night after night.

The theater provides raucous, bawdy, baggy pants Vaudeville comedy in a contemporary vein. The crowd loves it, they hiss, boo and toss popcorn at each other, all of which furthers the evening's hilarity. There are also performances by The Barbary Coast Players, featuring Broadway cabaret and melodramas. The Club Almaden restaurant offers five different menus. These are pizza, banquet, dinner show, after show and regular dinner. There is a full bar and lounge where you can raise a few and order a pizza before the show.

Six acres of lovely open grounds along Los Alamitos Creek constitute the idea setting for weddings and company picnics. The children's theater along the creek has facilities for horseshoes, volleyball, ping-pong and barbequeing. Actors dressed up as miners, clowns, pirates, cowboys, sea captains or whatever suits the occasion, entertain for the duration. Since when was so much history, setting and fun wrapped into one? Come and see The Opry House for a time that won't be easily forgotten.

Toys

HEIDI'S TOYLAND AND PERUVIAN GIFTS
224 El Paseo De Saratoga
San Jose, CA 95130
Tel. (408) 374-4592
Hrs: Mon. - Fri.   10:00 a.m. - 9:00 p.m.
      Saturday   10:00 a.m. - 6:00 p.m.
      Sunday   12:00 noon - 5:00 p.m.

Since the beginning of time, toys have played an important part in the life of a child. Toys help them prepare for adulthood and often display the child's special abilities. For these reasons, toy stores abound everywhere. But no toy store is quite as unique as Heidi's Toyland and Peruvian Gifts.

The combined ingenuity of Peruvian born Heidi and her husband Reinhold Hess comes alive through the marvelous surprises at Heidi's Toyland. The inimitable selection of toys focuses on educational varieties from around the world. Snap-lock animals, learning cubes, picture puzzles, letter word blocks and Fisher Price brand toys and games are only a few of the items this shop carries. In addition to the toys, you'll find handcrafted gifts from Peru, Bolivia and Guatemala. Hand woven tapestries, jackets, rugs, hand tooled saddles and hand painted clay pottery are all in the inventory.

Aside from the South American crafts, Heidi's has other treasures from around the globe. Such items as Russian jewelry boxes, Hawaiian soaps and necklaces from Spain. Heidi also provides free gift wrapping. Beauty, fun, education, exotic gift items and delicate crafts are all at Heidi's Toyland and Peruvian Gifts. An altogether exciting variety.

(See special invitation in the Appendix)

BEAR AND DOLL GARDEN
1167 Lincoln Avenue
San Jose, CA 95125
Tel. (408) 292-8422
Hrs: Tues. - Sat. II:00 a.m. - 5:00 p.m.

The Bear and Doll Garden is a little Eden of a place filled with loving and cuddly bears and dolls, all highly collectible. Owners Faith Lowman and Georgia Carlson, are bear and doll experts, and Georgia is a master bear designer and crafter. Most of Faith's North American selection is behind the counter, with plenty of Raikes and Steiffs. Among these a Liberace in his pretty ruffled shirt and rings, Queen Elizabeth, glowing in her fancy gown, or

Cub Canabearal, the astronaut, ready to take off in a gleaming silver space suit. One thing that separates Bear and Doll Garden from other shops carrying stuffed bears is their highly select and unusual lines, such as a Merry Thought bear from England, and a Beefeater in his spiffy red coat and hat. Have Georgia show you the Softy Bears that have zippers in the back of their heads and convert into purses. The Huggable Honey Bears by Caress are supple and soft little fellows with sailor hats who will instantly capture your heart.

Faith and Georgia, members of the Teddy Bear Artists Guild, come in contact with hundreds of other dealers. Faith's son is the originator and director of the guild, so you could say that a love of bears runs in the family. Nobody outdoes Georgia for quality and originality in hand-made bears. Hand-stitched Andrew, a "prince of a bear", is detailed to the fullest degree in a cashmere coat with leather trim and glass eyes. Georgia's Willy Winter bear, most charming in his hand-knitted gray sweater, is a heart warmer.

Special dolls here include such charmers as Dynasty and Bradley, terrific starter collector dolls with sweet porcelain faces. The limited edition Victoria Impex dolls, designed by Cindy McClure, are porcelain and feature marvelous diaphanous wings and silk flowers, like fairies from a childhood fantasy. The most highly-prized hand-sculpted Cabbage Patch dolls by Xavier Roberts can be purchased here under the adopt-a-doll program. Each baby comes with official adoption papers. Delight in the rare Carrole and Zapf dolls from Germany, and the lovely Ginny dolls. Each line has it s own timeless character and delicate wardrobe.

"Bearaphernalia" abounds at Bear and Doll Garden, with swings and highchairs, baby baskets, handmade clothing, and more. Bear collectors will note items like bear earrings, Fimo charms, bear pins, and scrimshaw featuring finely engraved bears. Nowhere will you feel more like you've entered bear and doll heaven than at the Bear and Doll Garden.

With the bear being California's state animal, it only stands to reason bears should be featured in a tour. So, here's one to make your travels and shopping more bearable.

The San Jose "Real Bear" Tour			
a.m.	Le Baron Hotel	Best breakfast	SanJ/Rest
a.m.	Graffiti	Best Crayola Bear	SanJ/Gift
a.m.	Teddy Bear Express	Best teddys	SanJ/Teddy
a.m.	Rystad's	Best ltd editions	SanJ/Gift
a.m.	Bear & Doll Garden	Best selection	SanJ/Toys
p.m.	Teske's	Best German lunch	SanJ/Rest
p.m.	Candela De Almaden	Best European	SanJ/Gifts
p.m.	Happy Hollow Park	Best petting zoo	SanJ/Att
After your tour, bear down on one of these fine restaurants.			
p.m.	D.B. Cooper's	Best dining/dancing	SanJ/Rest
p.m.	Old Spaghetti Factory	Best portions	SanJ/Rest
p.m.	Gunther's	Best N.Y. deli	SanJ/Rest
p.m.	Rue du Paris	Best French	SanJ/Rest

Wine

MIRASSOU
3000 Aborn Road
San Jose, CA 95135
Tel. (408) 274-4000
Hrs: Mon. - Sat. 10:00 a.m. - 5:00 p.m.
  Sunday 12:00 noon - 4:00 p.m.
MasterCard, Visa and AMEX are accepted.

America's oldest wine-making family has it's tasting room nestled comfortably in the east hills of San Jose. Nowhere in the United States do wine-making roots go back as far as they do at Mirassou. Daniel Mirassou and his two brothers Peter and Jim, represent the fifth generation of vinegrowing and wine-making excellence, a tradition that dates back to the 1850's when their ancestors first planted vines in the San Jose region.

Visitors are warmly received in the tasting room, and tours of the winery are encouraged. Guides are well versed in every aspect of the grape crushing, fermenting and aging process and will explain the fascinating history of the Mirassou family. Some notable breakthroughs in wine-making have been

597

developed over the years at this winery which currently produces more than 300,000 cases per year. Distribution is throughout all fifty states and around the world. As one might anticipate from such a rich tradition, the awards won by Mirassou are very impressive.

This winery also hosts special food and wine events including cooking classes, elegant brunches and dinners, an Annual Vintage Winetasting Festival, and an Independence Day Concert and Winetasting Celebration held in July. Their friendly staff is always more than ready to let you know of other exciting, upcoming events. Come visit America's oldest wine-making family and see the pride they take in their wine-making tradition.

WEIBEL WINERY
1250 Stanford Avenue
Mission San Jose, CA 94534
Tel. (415) 490-9914
Hrs: Daily from 10:00 a.m. to 5:00 p.m.

For more than forty years, the Weibel family has made its home at this historic winery, founded by Leland Stanford in 1869. The acquisition of the Mission San Jose Winery in 1945, and later expansion into Mendocino County, has enabled Weibel to maximize its quality and selection. Advanced wine-making techniques and quality control at Weibel continue to represent the best modern technology combined with the time-honored traditions of the wine-maker's art. The Mission San Jose Winery, located just south of the old Spanish Mission, is a registered historic landmark. Visitors are invited to sample their wines in the rustic, large-beamed Spanish-style hacienda where the friendly staff is happy to answer questions about any of the fine wines. Tours are offered on an informal basis during weekdays between 10:00 a.m. and 5:00 p.m. Picnicking on the patio under lush arbored trellises with a glass of excellent wine is encouraged. The isolated vineyards provide a sweeping view of the Mission Range and the Bay below.

In addition to sharing wine tasting with visitors, the Weibel Winery sponsors splendid special events. The popular morning Brunches-In-The-Vineyards begin mid-morning with wine tasting in the winery's private park. The magnificently prepared dinners held on the trellised patio are occasions to join Fred Weibel, Sr. and his master winemaker for discussions on the winery and the fine Weibel wines. Weibel's elegant Starlight Dinners begin in early evening with a sparkling wine reception and hors d'oeuvres in the historic Hacienda Tasting Room. And there are vineyard concerts and other special events throughout the year. Contact the winery and they will send you a schedule of events and reservation forms.

Not surprisingly, Weibel Winery has won a number of awards for its wines, including four gold medals in 1986 at the prestigious Orange County Fair for its 1982 Mendocino Brut Sparkling Wine, 1985 Mendocino County Chenin Blanc, Solera Flor Dry Bin Sherry and Solera Flor Amber Cream Sherry. The Weibel recognition extends to international events as well. In 1986 Weibel was selected as the official winery for the Transamerica Open Tennis Championships, and official producer of champagne for the 1987 America's Cup Challenge.

Stop by and sample the fine products of the Weibel Winery, and when your sipping is through, it's a short distance to the mission, where more great history entreats you.

Santa Clara

In a county of new cities, Santa Clara's history goes back almost as far as that of San Jose. When the town incorporated as Santa Clara in 1852, it contained a few blocks and 1,500 or so residents. Today the city limits enclose 20 square miles, the homes of nearly 93,000 people, and there is nowhere left to expand. San Jose circles the city, except on the west where Sunnyvale shares city limits.

Food processing and electronics are the basic industries here. The fruit industry began with a mission orchard planted about 1780 on a site irrigated by water diverted from the Rio Guadalupe. Earthquakes, by the way, were hard on the mission churches. Three buildings tumbled down in 120 years. The University of Santa Clara, chartered in 1855, took over the mission site and became California's first college.

Several historic homes exist in the city, including one, at 1159 Main Street, which could have been the first factory-built home on the west coast. It was made in New England, sent by ship and erected here in 1851. Modern hotels and the attraction of the Great America amusement park make this a popular city for conventions.

Attractions

University of Santa Clara, with a campus astride The Alameda, a tree-lined street branching off El Camino Real, is full of history and Spanish-style buildings.

DeSaisset Museum has rotating exhibits of fine art, and artifacts from the original mission; call (408) 554-4528.

599

Mission Santa Clara de Asis is on the campus, a 1928 replica of the first mission here; open daily with a self-guiding tour.

The **International Swim Center** where world class athletes work out is at 2625 Patricia Drive. Call 243-7727 for open swimming hours and information on various workouts including synchronized swim teams.

Across from City Hall, at 1505 Warburton Avenue, is the **Triton Museum**. Traveling art exhibits are shown here, from folk to fine art. Call 247-3754 for hours.

One of the oldest adobe houses in California is **The Alameda**. Built in 1790 and once the home of a teacher at the mission Indian school, it is now used by the Santa Clara Women's Club. Open Wednesday, 10:00 a.m. to 3:00 p.m.

A historic Santa Clara **tour book** is available by writing the Chamber of Commerce. The city's historical and landmark commission researched information and sells the book by mail at two dollars a copy.

For more information, contact the **Santa Clara Chamber of Commerce**, 1515 El Camino Real, Santa Clara, CA 95052. Telephone 296-6863.

Accommodations

EMBASSY SUITES, 2885 Lakeside Drive, Santa Clara, California. Limousine service, luxury appointments and an in-hotel restaurant.

SANTA CLARA MARRIOTT HOTEL
2700 Mission College Boulevard
Santa Clara, CA 95054
Tel. (408) 988-1500
       (800) 228-9290
All major credit cards accepted

The Marriott is a landmark of the Santa Clara Valley, towering above the Great America Amusement Park next door. Families on vacation and people here on business make the hotel their homebase while in the San Jose and Santa Clara area.
Located just a few minutes from the San Jose Airport, the Santa Clara Marriott has facilities to please every traveler. For the children, there is a video arcade. An indoor-outdoor swimming pool can be used in any weather. Those interested in fitness can work out on weight machines and other exercise

equipment. Two restaurants and lounges serve guests and visitors here. Lush green plants under arched skylights make Alexander's a special place to dine. Continental cuisine, or extensive wine list, and modern beauty make it one of the most special places in this big hotel.

You can see the landmark building, but until you walk the restaurant row, enjoy the guest rooms and other facilities, you'll have to take our word that this is the "Best Choice" for a headquarters when you come to San Jose or Santa Clara.

(See special invitation in the Appendix.)

THE WOODMARK HOTEL
5415 Stevens Creek Boulevard
Santa Clara, CA 95051
Tel. (408) 446-3030

A most uncommon hotel has come to Silicon Valley. The Woodmark. While it resembles a lovely French country estate, it is, in fact, your opportunity to experience an entirely new class of executive accommodation. There are sixty luxurious rooms and suites, many of them featuring wet bars, fireplaces, bay windows and courtyard views. Tastefully-appointed furnishings and thoughtful touches are to be found here at the Woodmark. Enjoy bedside remote control for 24-channel cable television, a VCR with access to the hotel's library of current and classic films, desk and bedside telephone options and personal computer modem capabilities. In the bath, you'll find a second TV, additional telephone, hair dryer, terry robes, plump towels and elaborate personal care items.

Your stay at The Woodmark includes a full, complimentary buffet breakfast served in a private salon. Guests are free to "raid the pantry" for a complimentary dinner. From late afternoon until midnight, a cozy bar waits ready to serve your favorite cocktails at moderate prices. The hotel services are equally personalized, and include valet services, prompt laundry and dry cleaning, a hotel lending library (which features the top 10 bestsellers, current magazines and new journals), secretarial services and a concierge for personal assistance. The Woodmark also has three conference rooms for business functions.

From its regally-walled perimeter to the landscaped atrium, The Woodmark is truly devoted to the comfort, convenience and privacy of the individual traveler or family. You will receive all this in grand style at The Woodmark Hotel of Santa Clara.

601

Apparel

VICTORIA'S SECRET, 285 Steven's Creek Boulevard, Santa Clara, California. A shop dedicated to providing the finest in lingerie.

Chocolates

GODIVA CHOCOLATIER, 2855 Stevens Creek Boulevard, Santa Clara, California. World renowned chocolates...one's you'd be tempted, if the car wasn't running, to ride a horse to pick them up!

Entertainment

GREAT AMERICA
1 Great America Parkway
Santa Clara, CA 95054
Tel. (408) 988-1776 or (408) 988-1800

With new attractions added almost every season, Great America continues its reputation as Northern California's largest and best known amusement park. The single admission ticket lets you sample the rides and attractions all day long, with entertainment for everyone from toddlers to senior citizens.

A ride of the Sky Tower, near the park entrance, gives you a view of the place plus the Santa Clara Valley, and a brief history. On the plaza you'll find the Pictorium Theater with a screen seven stories high, ninety-six feet wide; the largest in the United States. Especially for the children are the Smurf Woods and Fort Fun theme areas. There's a roller-coaster in the old fashioned style as part of the County Fair theme group, while for the modern youth the Demon takes its passengers through a double corkscrew. Other modern rides which attract lines are the Tidal Wave which does full circle, then reverse loops; the Revolution, which swings out as a pendulum, finally going full circle; and the Edge, where you drop from a 131-foot tower, accelerating to fifty-five miles an hour in the fall.

In between all of the excitement, are several shows at the Grand Music Hall, and several restaurants, shops and arcades. If you haven't been to Great America recently, make it part of an outing soon, and plan to make a day of it.

Games

GAME GALLERY, 2855 Stevens Creek Boulevard, Santa Clara, California. A vast array of games for people of all ages.

Gift

GRAFFITI #2207
Valley Fair Shopping Center
2855 Stevens Creek Boulevard
Santa Clara, CA 95050
Tel. (408) 244-7971
Hrs: Mon. - Fri.   10:00 a.m. - 9:30 p.m.
      Saturday   10:00 a.m. - 6:30 p.m.
      Sunday   11:00 a.m. - 6:00 p.m.

There is always a party atmosphere at Graffiti, with unbridled fun, design and color everywhere. This greeting card and gift shop has gifts that range from outrageous to elegant with an emphasis on contemporary design and off the wall humor.

What lures people into Graffiti is the glow inside. Neon table lamps are displayed along the walls in the shapes of music notes, parrots, Art Deco designs, palm trees and brilliant flamingoes. There's a lot of "touchable" merchandise, which includes inflatables, ceramics, jewelry, masks, clocks, action products and stuffed toys. Graffiti boasts one of the largest mask collections in the bay area with ceramic, feather and hand painted lines. They also have over sixty varieties of candy for you sweet tooths. Anything from a cuddly dog to a vibrant beach bum bear, complete with sunglasses, can be found in the stuffed toy section.

The tremendously upbeat art themes expressed in the gift items are reflected in the thousands of contemporary greeting cards that line the walls. Card lines range from traditional to risque with more concentration placed on adult humor and themes.

This store is guaranteed to coax a laugh out of the most serious shopper and with the wide selection of gifts and cards on the cutting edge of contemporary, Graffiti is a "Best Choice" for fun.

(See special invitation in the Appendix.)

Music Boxes

RICHTER'S, 2855 Stevens Creek Boulevard, Santa Clara, California. Beautiful music boxes from all over the world.

Restaurant

ARTHUR'S, 2875 Lakeside Drive, Santa Clara, California. Serving continental cuisine, with seafood specialties and live entertainment in the lounge.

FISH MARKET, 3775 El Camino Real, Santa Clara, California. Fresh fish daily. Sushi bar.

HEAVEN POP CUISINE
Valley Fair Mall
2855 Stevens Creek Boulevard #2179
Santa Clara, CA 95050
Tel. (408) 241-4150
Hrs: Mon. - Fri.   10:00 a.m. - 9:30 p.m.
Saturday   10:00 a.m. - 6:30 p.m.
Sunday   11:00 a.m. - 6:00 p.m.

The days of rock and roll in the 1950s and 1960s come to mind at this combination soda fountain, restaurant and gift shop in the Valley Fair Mall. Pop art is king, Andy Warhol has his name on the soup of the day, and other artists and singers grace food and drink items.

For the hamburger connoisseur, there were, at last count, seventeen different burgers with flavors from teriyaki to chili. At the door is a blown-up gorilla wearing the official Heaven Pop apron, and inside there's a juke box to play the songs of the decade. Gift items and memorabilia fill the shop, along with gags and toys.

Pop art lives on at Heaven Pop, a place for fun and memories, mixed with good food.

J. R. CHOPS, 2106 El Camino Real, Santa Clara, California. Continental cuisine, elegant settings, private booths available.

LA PALOMA
2280 El Camino Real
Santa Clara, CA 95050
Tel. (408) 247-0990
Hrs: Mon.-Thurs. 11:00 a.m.-10:00 p.m.
       Fri.-Sat.   11:00 a.m.-10:30 p.m.
       Sun.   4:00 p.m.- 9:00 p.m.

There is an art to Mexican cuisine that is usually lost in the "international foods" aisle at the local supermarket. The art is not lost , however, among the chefs at La Paloma.

Rudy and Cindy Parker, owners and third-generation restauranteurs since 1977, have been selecting and blending the freshest ingredients into spicy and delicious traditional Mexican dishes. The menu has such favorites as tacos, enchiladas, tamales, burritos, tostadas and chilis. There are several specialty items that should be sampled also. For a memorable appetizer try the Super Nachos--fresh tortilla chips covered with beans, cheese, jalapeño peppers, black olives, sour cream, and your choice of seasoned ground beef or chicken. Try the very popular Sizzling Fajitas entree--marinated chicken or beef grilled with onions, green peppers and tomatoes. This is served on a hot skillet with cheese, guacamole, pico de gallo, frijoles charro and tortillas. Or indulge yourself with a Fisherman's burrito, a soft flour tortilla filled with crab meat and shrimp and covered with suiza sauce and jack cheese. If you don't have a palate for Mexican food, you can choose a hamburger, cheeseburger or New York steak from the menu. Be sure to save room for dessert--especially the home-made Kahlua pie.

There is more to La Paloma's than just an excellent menu. The heavy-beamed ceilings, rough walls, native arts and crafts, and distinctively arched doorways create the atmosphere of a Mexican villa. At each table you will find a basket of fresh tortilla chips and a bowl of salsa. (The salsa is so good that the recipe was requested for publication in Bon Appetit magazine.) On Friday and Saturday nights a strolling guitarist entertains with a selection of fine Latino music. So, come and enjoy a pleasant atmosphere, exceptional food, prompt service and a reasonably-priced menu.

LONNIE'S BAR-B-QUE
1595 Franklin Street
Santa Clara, CA 95050
Tel. (408) 243-7752
Hrs: Tues.-Fri.   11:00 a.m.-9:00 p.m.
        Sat.   12:00 p.m.-9:00 p.m.

Hidden away in a nondescript cinderblock building on a quiet side street in Santa Clara is a restaurant where you will find some of the best barbequed ribs, chicken, and Louisiana hot links you have ever eaten. Owned and operated by a husband and wife team, Lonnie's Bar-B-Que has, until recently, been a secret hideaway for connoisseurs of great-tasting barbeque.

When talking about Lonnie's Bar-B-Que, the number one thing to know is "the sauce is boss." Using a closely-guarded family recipe, Lonnie makes his own sauce from scratch with more than 40 different ingredients. The result of his efforts is a perfect barbeque sauce, which has a full-bodied flavor that still lets the taste of the meat come through. All the meat is hand-trimmed so that every bite is extra-lean and tasty. The meat is slowly barbequed over charcoal and hickory and carefully basted with the special sauce for a taste that can't be beat. The meat seems to melt in your mouth. Your taste buds and stomach will thank you for treating yourself to this restaurant. It's an experience that just can't be missed.

Directions to help you find Lonnie's Bar-B-Que: from El Camino Real, turn south at Lincoln Ave. or from Highway 280 or Stevens Creek Blvd., head north on Winchester Ave. until it becomes Lincoln Ave. Lonnie's Bar-B-Que is right on the corner of Franklin and Lincoln Avenues.

PEDRO'S, 3935 Freedom Circle, Santa Clara, California. Authentic Mexican restaurant and cantina.

OUT AND ABOUT SANTA CLARA

a.m.	Mariott Hotel	Best breakfast	Sant/Acc
a.m.	Graffiti #2207	Best masks	Sant/Gift
a.m.	NASA Center	Best space show	Sant/Att
p.m.	La Paloma	Best lunch	Sant/Rest
p.m.	Great America	Best park	Sant/Amusement
After your stomach returns from Great America, settle back for food and drink from either of these restaurants or try a telescopic tour of the cosmos.			
p.m.	Lonnie's	Best barbeque	Sant/Rest
p.m.	Heaven Pop Cuisine	Best dinner	Sant/Rest
p.m.	Lick Observatory	Best stargazing	Sant/Att

Saratoga

Antiques

CORINTHIAN STUDIOS
Antiques * Objects d' Art
20506 Saratoga-Los Gatos Road
P.O. Box 385
Saratoga, CA 95070
Tel. (408) 867-4630
Hrs: Mon. - Fri. 10:00 a.m. - 5:30 p.m.
Saturday 10:00 a.m. - 5:00 p.m.
Sunday 12:00 noon - 5:00 p.m.

One of the Bay Area's oldest and most respected names in antiques and fine period furnishings, this twenty-eight year old establishment features an impeccable collection of French, English and American pieces. Plus, impressive displays of beautiful objects d'art, including clocks, silver, china, crystal and a large estate jewelry collection.

Antique collector's of the highest order will find a match-less selection of extraordinary antiques at Corinthian Studios. The owners have the benefit of over thirty years of contacts, throughout Europe, Asia and North America, seeking out the very finest. Corinthian Studio's staff is highly qualified to take you on a trip through the great craftsmanship of the past.

Estates bought and sold. Consignments considered.

Art

GREENLEAF GALLERY
14414 Oak Street
Saratoga, CA 95070
Tel. (408) 867-3277
Hrs: Tues. - Sat. 10:00 a.m. - 5:00 p.m.
      Also by appointment

Janet Greenleaf is a remarkable woman. You'll see why when you stop in and visit her gallery. Janet is a working artist, gallery owner and consultant for corporate and private art enthusiasts. Reflecting Janet's lifelong passion for collectable art, the gallery exhibits the work of more than thirty-five professional artists working in various media. There are gorgeous wildlife etchings and bronzes by Sandy Scott of Texas, brilliant contemporary abstracts by Gregory Deane, Gregory Hawthorne and Andrea Eagleston, and large florals by Janet Greenleaf. Tomi Kobara's rich impressionistic oils and Yuriko Takata's large archaeologically inspired watercolors keep company with unusual handmade paper pieces by Leslie Hoffmeyer and John Greenleaf.

Janet keeps nationwide connections with artists and educates others in art selections with her keen knowledge and art background. Prices suit every budget; Janet's main concern is that each customer, "enjoy the purchase that you make."

Greenleaf Gallery offers complete museum-treatment framing and restoration services, crating, delivery and professional consulting. Art shows, receptions and rotating exhibits take place regularly. If the gallery does not have just what you're looking for, Janet will find it, or commission an artist to execute a piece.

Attraction

VILLA MONTALVO, 15400 Montalvo Road, Saratoga, California. An historical landmark, this 175 acre estate combines art with nature. Gallery features works by well-known and local artists. Peaceful nature trails and vistas.

Delicatessen

ARGONAUT DELI
12866 Saratoga-Sunnyvale Road
Saratoga, CA 95070
Tel. (408) 867-5888
Hrs: Mon. - Sat.   7:00 a.m. - 7:00 p.m.
Sunday   9:00 a.m. - 5:00 p.m.
Closed holidays.

Home-style cooking and a wide variety of meats and cheeses stocked for retail sales set this delicatessen apart.

The meats and cheeses are domestic and imported, purchased by Mike Overhulse. His wife Diane and Jean Carter combine to create the recipes which win notice for their kitchen. There are fresh salads, mustards concocted with a flair, coffee beans and pastas in the well-stocked deli section. Argonaut is an outlet for a local toymaker in a small gift section of the place. There's also a catering service.

This "Best Choice" for homestyle cooking serves you family style at dining tables inside, or at one of two tables outside from spring through fall.

Gift

FANCY FOLK
12241 Saratoga - Sunnyvale Road
Saratoga, CA 95070-3023
Tel. (408) 446-1942
Hrs: Tue. - Sat. 10:00 a.m. - 6:00 p.m.

Fancy Folk is a showcase for over sixty artists and craftsmen; since 1979 featuring truly unique and one of kind treasures. Opened by owner Phyllis Stiles to an be outlet for skilled craftspeople, this shop is filled with originally crafted art from portraits to pottery.

All of the items for sale are made by hand thus ensuring quality and care in each piece. Phyllis takes special pride and interest in her artists and their work. Her enthusiasm spills over into her friendly dealings with her customers, making a visit to this delightful shop a pleasurable past time. The artists featured work in clay, wood, cloth, oil paints, pen and ink, watercolors, precious metals and glass. There are adorable soft sculptures, French country ceramics and dishwasher proof pottery, raku, custom gold jewelry, floral designs... to name just a few articles on display.

609

Stop in to this purely delightful spot on the "Best Choices" list of shops and walk away with a treasure that is truly your own. Just look for the orange canopy, one block south of Prospect on the Saratoga-Sunnyvale Road.

(See special invitation in the Appendix.)

Kitchen Articles

THE BUTTER PADDLE
14510 Big Basin Way
Saratoga, CA 95070
Tel. (408) 867-1678
Hrs: Mon. - Sat.   10:00 a.m. - 5:00 p.m.
          Sunday   12:00 noon - 4:00 p.m.

In 1967, The Butter Paddle opened and the shop stocked just enough copper pots, cookie cutters, molds and aprons to open the doors. Twenty years and a bigger store later, this gourmet kitchen shop is bursting with tools and toys to equip a chef, the kitchen and dining room plus keep the bookshelf full of great recipe books.

One of the special reasons to visit The Butter Paddle is that all the staff are volunteers who donate their time to the store so that the proceeds can go to the Eastfield Children's Center. The center is a home for emotionally disturbed children. In the past few years profits generated have been used to redecorate the children's rooms, refurbish the kitchen and purchase numerous supplies for the center. The staff gives parties monthly for the children at Eastfield. Because they are dedicated to their cause, both the merchandise and the service are excellent.

The following is a brief listing of the inventory at The Butter Paddle: All Clad and Calphalon cookware, decorative and functional copper, BIA Cordon Bleu porcelain, a complete line of tinware, a full selection of Portmeirion, furniture by "From the Mill", Rogar wine vintners, Chicago Cutlery, Oriental and Mexican cookware, Chantal teapots and warmers, oven to tableware that looks like pewter by Wilton Armetale, glassware, specialty food items, water processed coffee beans, gadgets galore, a wonderful selection of cookbooks, free gift wrap and much, much more.

For an amazing display of kitchenware and china, food stuffs and to support a good cause, be sure to go to The Butter Paddle, a "Best Choice" in Northern California.

Nursery

SASO HERB GARDENS
14625 Fruitvale Avenue
Saratoga, CA 95070
Tel. (408) 867-0307
Hrs: Mon. - Sat. 9:00 a.m. - 2:30 p.m.
Call for class and tour information.

Just off the beaten path of downtown Saratoga on a well cultivated homestead acre there exists a garden that grows the largest variety of herbs in the United States

Over a thousand medicinal, culinary and decorative herbs are nurtured by Virginia and Louis Saso in this garden that bears their name. Once in the produce business, Louis discovered the healing quality of herbs thirty years ago and this couple made a commitment to devote their horticultural talents to the benefit of herbs. Both husband and wife are eager to share their knowledge with others. To that end there is an area of the garden that is set aside for classroom instruction.

Louis teaches the practical approach to the culture and use of culinary, medicinal and ornamental herbs, while Virginia shares her knowledge of the culinary aspect of herbs, as well as herb crafts. Her special craft is making everlasting wreaths from flowers and herbs. She also teaches classes in wreath making in the summer and fall. Plants and wreaths are available for sale at the gardens. A yearly "schedule of garden events" will be mailed upon request.

Certainly the classes and formal tours are worth calling ahead to plan, yet, if an impromptu visit is all you have time for you are welcome to stop in and survey the grounds. There are several theme areas in the gardens at the center of which stands a five hundred year old oak that is a testimony to vitality of nature.

Santa Clara County

Restaurant

BELLA MIA
14503 Big Basin Way
Saratoga, CA 95070
Tel. (408) 741-5115
Hrs: Tuesday-Saturday

Lunch	11:30 a.m. -4:00 p.m.
Dinner	5:00 p.m.-10:00 p.m.
Mondays	5:00 p.m.-10:00 p.m.
Sundays	10:30 a.m.- 3:30 p.m.

Closed holidays, except Easter Brunch

What do bread sticks, Seafood Conchiglie, truffles, and croissant pudding have in common? They all have the distinct culinary mark of owner Bill Carlson. His imagination is at play producing delicious "California Italian" cuisine. Bill creates specialties that combine fresh, local ingredients with rich tomato sauces and traditional Italian seasonings. The bread sticks here smell great and taste even better--bars of bread fresh from the oven, topped with butter, garlic, dill weed, and other spices. Cheese and sour cream sauces are served with each bread basket. And that's just for openers.

The Seafood Conchiglie, lasagna, and Bella Mia Scallopini are among the restaurant's best entrées. Fresh herbs from local gardens and clams, fish, and crabs from the neighboring Pacific, plus a touch of Carlson originality, produce semi-traditional Italian dishes with a unique, savory twist. Truffles are Bill Carlson's latest culinary adventure. He dips "liquor balls" and soft mousse centers in rich, dark chocolate the old-fashioned way and gets delicious results. Other desserts, like the croissant pudding merit saving some room.

The ambience of this charmingly restored late 19th-Century Victorian house is just one of Bella Mia's attributes. Inside, tables provide an intimate, yet uncramped feeling. Outside, lovely weather and gorgeous mountain scenery supply two essential makings for enjoyable outdoor dining. Brilliant pink fuchsias, abundant greenery, a small fountain, and space heaters for chillier evenings are part of the lovely outdoor setting. A different jazz band plays in the garden each Sunday during late spring and throughout the summer. The brunch is a favorite weekly event for many locals. People stand in line for pleasant garden tables and inside seats, so be sure to make reservations. Bella Mia--"My Love"--is aptly named.

(See special invitation in Appendix.)

PLUMED HORSE, 14555 Big Basin Way, Saratoga, California. One of the South Bay's oldest and finest restaurants, serving quality cuisine and featuring live entertainment five nights a week. Extensive wine list.

Wine

CONGRESS SPRINGS WINERY, 23600 Congress Springs Road, Saratoga, California. Award winner using grapes grown in Santa Cruz Mountains only. Tours provided to allow visitors to understand fine winemaking.

THE CHOICEST OF SARATOGA

a.m.	Butter Paddle	Best utensils	Sar/Kit
a.m.	Fancy Folk	Best crafts	Sar/Gift
p.m.	Argonaut Deli	Best lunch	Sar/Deli
p.m.	Greenleaf Gallery	Best fine art	Sar/Art
p.m.	Corinthian	Best collectibles	Sar/Ant
p.m.	Saso Herb Garden	Best herbs	Sar/Nurs
p.m.	Bella Mia	Best Cal/Italian	Sar/Rest

Sunnyvale

An estimated 112,000 people now live in the twenty-three square mile city of Sunnyvale in the middle of the Santa Clara Valley. This is the home address for some of the most-familiar names in the electronics and computer world. It houses the only branch of the United States Patent Office, a place for scientists and engineers to cross reference the projects on which they are working.

Rancho Pastoria de las Borregas, or "shepherds of the lambs," once covered much of the present city. Martin Murphy Jr. bought much of the tract and in 1849 put up the first house in Sunnyvale, built from lumber which was sawn on the east coast and brought to the bay by ship. Fig trees cut from those at Mission Santa Clara sheltered the house.

When the railroad was laid up the peninsula, the flag stop was called Murphy's Station, and later Encinal for the oak trees which grow in much of the city. Developer W. E. Crossman, who subdivided 200 acres of the Murphy ranch in 1898, is credited with coining the name Sunnyvale. Food processors

613

and the Joshua Hendy Iron Works gave employment to the people before the high tech invasion of post war years.

Attractions

The **U.S. Air Force Satellite Control Facility**, on Lockheed Way, does control and evaluation of military space vehicles, working with a network of ground stations around the world.

The old is remembered in an **historical district** which is part of the first downtown, at 100 South Murphy Avenue. Restaurants, shops and service businesses occupy what was the center of the farm community early in this century.

Martin Murphy Jr. Park, 230 East California Avenue, has the original homestead, fig trees and all. The house was demolished in 1961, and the ranch lands now play host to lawn bowlers, a community amphitheater for performing arts, and picnic sites. Call 738-5515 for information.

Sunnyvale Historical Museum is in Martin Murphy Jr. Park. Open Tuesdays and Thursdays from 12:00 noon to 3:30 p.m., Sunday from 1:00 p.m. to 4:00 p.m. Call 749-0220.

For information contact the **Sunnyvale Chamber of Commerce**, Murphy and Olive Streets, Sunnyvale CA 94086. Telephone 736-4971.

Accommodations

MAPLE TREE INN
711 East El Camino Real
Sunnyvale, CA 94087
Tel.   (408)   720-9700
         (800)   262-2624   CA
         (800)   423-0243   USA

The Maple Tree Inn has something for everyone. Located close to shopping, restaurants, and family entertainment centers, the Maple Tree Inn offers an attractive, quiet atmosphere with gracious hospitality.
Following a relaxing dip in the lap-sized pool, enjoy your favorite newspaper and a generous "California style" breakfast in the pool-side lounge. Nearly half the Inn has been set aside for non-smokers, and many rooms are designed to accommodate guests with wheelchairs.

One of the best moderately priced hotels in the Bay area, the Maple Tree Inn is your "Best Choice" for accommodations.

(See special invitation in the Appendix.)

RADISSON HAUS INN
1085 E. El Camino Real
Sunnyvale, CA 94087
Tel. (408) 247-0800
Hrs: Mon. - Fri. Breakfast 6:30 a.m. - 11:00 a.m.
                  Lunch   11:30 a.m. - 2:00 p.m.
                  Dinner   5:30 p.m. - 10:00 p.m.
        Sat. - Sun. Breakfast 8:00 a.m. - 10:00 a.m.
All major credit cards accepted

A world of luxury and elegance unfolds when you enter through the doors of the Radisson Haus Inn, past a marble and brass fountain and into the sweeping, three story atrium lobby.

Most of the rooms have views of either the spectacular atrium, or the luxuriously appointed mezzanine lounge atop a slow curving stairway. Every room from the cozy atrium-view rooms to the spacious executive suites personally have been decorated by the owner with only your comfort, luxury and convenience in mind.

A complimentary breakfast buffet is prepared daily, and diverse lunch and dinner menus featuring traditional American and authentic oriental dishes are offered in Radisson Haus Inn's comfortable restaurant.

If you've treated yourself to the special Dynasty Suite with its opulent oriental furnishings, extra-plush carpet and Italian marble vanity and bath, you may not wish to leave your room. The Radisson Haus Inn also has a room service menu available for just such contingencies.

Apparel

KIRKISH'S
198 S. Murphy Ave.
Sunnyvale, CA 94086
Tel. (408) 736-6243

When is a store more than a store? When it's a part of history. And no store is more a part of history in Sunnyvale than Kirkish's. Founded in 1924 by Freda and Michael Kirkish, and run since 1945 by their sons Henry and Robert, Kirkish's is Sunnyvale's oldest retail business. It's also an excellent place to find Western-style clothing for boys and men. The selection includes everything from bolo ties, bandanas, and Stetsons to the peninsula's largest assortment of Western shirts. Square dancers and Round dancers, male or female, can pick up complete outfits plus information on where to find local classes, clubs, and hoe-downs. Kirkish's also carries a wide variety of boots by makers such as Acme, Dan Post, and Tony Lama.

Started as a general clothing store, Kirkish's has a long tradition that few stores anywhere could equal. By staying more in touch with the needs of their customers, Kirkish's survived the threats of shopping malls, trends, and chain stores. Even now, after more than forty years of running the business, Robert and Henry will often greet and wait on their customers personally.

As dedicated as the Kirkish brothers are to their customers, they are just as dedicated to the local community. Improvements to the downtown area are supported whether it means a disruption of normal business because of construction or potential competition. For more than 40 years, Kirkish's has been the area's major outlet for supplying the Cub Scouts and Boy Scouts with a complete line of uniforms and accessories.

Somehow it's comforting to know that in an age of mass marketing and glitzy displays a store can survive simply by being friendly, personable, and selfless. It's good to know that Kirkish's has.

(See special invitation in appendix.)

Art

NORTHERN LIGHTS, ETC
106 Town and Country Village
Sunnyvale, CA 94086
Tel. (408) 737-0487
Hrs: Mon. - Fri. 10:00 a.m. - 5:30 p.m.
Saturday 10:00 a.m. - 5:00 p.m.
Closed Sunday.

Scandinavia comes to America! Half gift shop and half art gallery, Northern Lights, Etc features specialty items from Sweden, Finland, Norway, and Denmark. Owners Kajsa Bergman and Eva Lessem import delicate ceramics and handcrafted glasswork, as well as a wide variety of hand dipped candles, decorative linens, unique Scandinavian jewelry, and many other unusual gift ideas.

The gallery is festooned with prints, painting, lithographs, and glass art by contemporary Scandinavian artists. With rare exceptions, all the art is available for sale to the public.

616

For an exciting opportunity to choose gifts for every home, taste, and budget, visit Northern Lights, Etc and enjoy the very best from Scandinavia.

Books

ANTIQUARIAN ARCHIVE, 160 South Murphy Avenue, Sunnyvale, California. Twice-loved books. Specialists in military history and memoirs, nautical and maritime, Aeronautica, railroadiana and Roycroft books.

NOVA BOOKSTORE, 209 Town and Country Village, Sunnyvale, California. Specialists in future studies, new technologies, science, philosophy and finance.

Entertainment

ROOSTER T. FEATHERS, 157 W. El Camino Real, Sunnyvale, California. Comedy club with shows seven nights a week.

Gift

J.R. MUGGS
1111 West El Camino, #121
Sunnyvale, CA 94087
Tel. (408) 730-4443
Hrs: Mon. - Fri.   9:00 a.m. - 8:00 p.m.
        Saturday   9:00 a.m. - 6:00 p.m.
        Sunday   12:00 noon - 5:00 p.m.

Do you know someone who has an ugly mug? Ever wonder how you, as a friend, could help out? Oh, no, not plastic surgery, that's not what's being discussed; coffee and tea mugs are the issue here, and J.R. Muggs is the place.

This gift shop has a selection of over 10,000 mugs in ceramic, glass, hand-crafted clay, plastic, pewter or porcelain! But wait, not only can you choose from all these mugs, but you also have a choice of over two dozen types of whole bean coffees, including decaffeinated and flavored ones. Any accessories needed? J.R. Muggs has all the best air tight containers, espresso and capuccino makers, brewers, coffee bean grinders, teakettles, ceramic teapots and even English biscuits.

617

After all the decisions have been made, sit down with a fresh-ground, freshly brewed cup of coffee and savor the atmosphere of J.R. Muggs. So you see, in this gift shop you can help yourself out, as well as your friend.

(See special invitation in the Appendix.)

Golf

GOLF COUNTRY
1036 East El Camino Real
Sunnyvale, CA 94087
Tel. (408) 738-GOLF
Hrs: Tue. - Fri.   10:00 a.m. - 8:00 p.m.
      Sat. - Mon.   10:00 a.m. - 5:00 p.m.
Visa and MasterCard are accepted.
and,
1325 Blossom Hill Road
San Jose, CA 95118
Tel. (408) 264-GOLF

Did you know that many golfers in the Bay Area don't shop for their sports equipment in the same place where they golf? Why? It's because they know that quality and the lowest pricing isn't always just around the sand trap. Golf Country might be a little bit off the green, but that's where they go for the name brand equipment at the lowest prices.

Everything the golfer could dream of is at Golf Country including shoes in all styles and sizes, racks of the latest in golf fashion, hundreds of sets of irons and woods, books, instructional tapes, plus gifts and accessory items. There is an indoor putting green to try out the clubs before buying them, and if you do make a purchase, free computerized club fitting. If your clubs need repairing, Golf Country can do it right.

Every employee in the store knows the profession to a tee, so there won't be any unanswered questions to ponder. Golf Country may not be located right off the course, but they can provide the equipment for your ace in the hole.

Restaurants

GALANO'S
1635 Hollenbeck Avenue
Sunnyvale, CA 94087
Tel. (408) 738-1120
Hrs: Lunch   Friday   11:00 a.m - 2:00 p.m.
       Dinner   Tue. - Thu.   5:00 p.m. - 10:00 p.m.
                  Fri. - Sat.   4:00 p.m. - 10:00 p.m.
                  Sunday   4:00 p.m. - 9:00 p.m.
       Closed Monday
Visa, MasterCard, AMEX and Diner's Club are accepted.

Many restaurants boast of long traditions, but to our knowledge there is only one restaurant with heritage stretching back to the days of Columbus, and that's Galano's. The owner of Galano's, himself an award-winning ancestor to a line of master chefs dating back over 500 years.

An unspoken philosophy at Galano's is a simple one, eat well and return often. The menu consists of a combination of traditional favorites and closely guarded family recipes all created in diverse styles. Only the freshest ingredients are used in the following entrees pasta, seafood, chicken, veal, beef dishes and a special childrens' selection.

For relaxing before or after dinner, Galano's has a comfortable, quiet lounge. With restaurants like Galano's close at hand, it's exceedingly difficult to understand why Columbus would want to sail away to a new world.

HUNAN, 793 East El Camino Real, Sunnyvale, California. Featuring Szechuan and Mandarin cuisine in a quiet yet colorful atmosphere.

619

LION AND COMPASS
1023 N.Fair Oaks Avenue
Sunnyvale, CA 94089
Tel. (408) 745-1260
Hrs: Mon. - Fri.   Lunch   11:00 a.m. - 3:00 p.m.
      Mon. - Thu.   Dinner   5:00 p.m. - 9:30 p.m.
      Fri. - Sat.   5:00 p.m. - 10:00 p.m.
All major credit cards accepted

Turn back the clock and step into the luxurious world of the British West Indies during its heyday in the 1920s. A veritable oasis in a high-tech desert, the Lion and Compass offers four distinct dining areas, as well as a long, hand-carved, full service bar which was transported from the famed Lion and Compass pub in Halifax, England.

"The Patio" offers all the tropical wicker and flavor of old Barbados. "The Rose Room" is a fantasy of art deco in shades of robust grays and rose. It's an excellent environment in which to raise hearts and glasses. "The Grill" delights with its modernized version of the classic diner look. Finally, "The Library" suggests F. Scott Fitzgerald might appear at any moment to dine before the large, mirrored fireplace and antique bookcases, enjoying the deep, rich aroma of aged oak and mahogany panelling.

The menu at the Lion and Compass is every bit as complex and stunning as the decor. Classically trained chefs vary the menu daily, specializing in ocean fresh seafood. Even the wine list changes daily as the owners seek the best wines, primarily California, to complement the menu selections. Not to be missed.

RUSTY SCUPPER
1235 Oakmead Parkway
Sunnyvale, CA 94086
Tel. (408) 245-2911
Hrs: Mon. - Fri.   11:00 a.m. - 1:30 p.m.
      Saturday   5:00 p.m. - 1:30 a.m.
      Sunday   5:00 p.m. - 12:00 midnight
Visa, MasterCard, Diner's Club and AMEX are accepted.

It's all at the Rusty Scupper from the excitement of a live DJ and dance music in the lounge, to the enjoyment of fine dining on the patio overlooking a peaceful lake.

The Rusty Scupper's national reputation for freshly cut choice steaks and superb prime rib is further enhanced by their chef's capacity for variety.

The excellent menu also features seafood specialties and a long list of fresh fish flown in daily.

The "happy hour" between 5:00 p.m. and 8:00 p.m. features a complimentary twenty-four foot buffet with salads, hot entrees and a variety of "munchies."

(See special invitation in the Appendix.)

SUNNYVALE CATTLEMAN'S RESTAURANT
502 Ross Dr.
Sunnyvale, CA, 94086
Tel. (408) 734-5566
Hrs: Dining Room:

	Mon. - Fri.	6:00 a.m. - 10:45 p.m.
	Saturday	9:00 a.m. - 10:45 p.m.
	Sunday	9:00 a.m. - 9:45 p.m.
Lounge:		
	Tue. - Sat.	11:00 a.m. - 2:00 a.m.
	Sunday	2:00 p.m. - 12:00 midnight
	Monday	11:00 a.m. - 12:00 midnight

AMEX, Visa MasterCard are accepted.

Well it 's just a little bit of country in the city for you folks out there that want good American cooking for every kind of appetite. Sunnyvale Cattleman's Restaurant has preserved the friendly downhome west. They serve up good food and good times in a relaxed first class western atmosphere.

Come on in; they have something for everybody at breakfast, lunch and dinner. A menu with sixty-five to seventy regular selections and up to thirty daily specials, to boot, has got to have a meal just right for you. Steak lovers can get a cut three inches thick - fourteen ounce sirloins. If red meat does not appeal to you they also have plenty of fresh fish and chicken dishes. Stop on in for breakfast and saddle up the counter for a great meal with friendly cooks and waitresses who <u>will</u> stop to give you the time of day. All around there is a feeling of the old west and comfort. In the lounge a person can join in sing-alongs and dancing while relaxing around the cozy hearth.

Yes sir, for a good honest American value and a pleasant atmosphere Sunnyvale Cattleman's Restaurant is the place you want to go.

Toys

MICKEY'S HOUSE OF SOLDIERS, 601 Capella Street, Sunnyvale, California. The world's largest collection of miniature soldiers on display.

TOUR OF SUNNYVALE			
a.m.	Gold Country	Best golf shop	Sun/Golf
a.m.	Kirkish's	Best western	Sun/App
a.m.	J.R. Muggs	Best coffee mug	Sun/Gift
p.m.	Northern Lights	Best Scandanavian	Sun/Gift
p.m.	Historical Museum	Best history	Sun/Att
End your day or begin your night with dinner at one of Sunnyvale's finest restaurants.			
p.m.	Lion and Compass	Best daily menu	Sun/Rest
p.m.	Galano's	Best tradition	Sun/Rest
p.m.	Rusty Scupper	Best buffet	Sun/Rest
p.m.	Sunnyvale Catleman's	Best western meals	Sun/Rest

SANTA CRUZ COUNTY

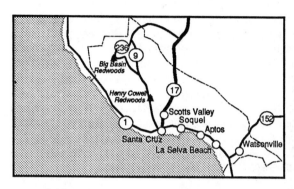

This coastal county is about seventy miles south of San Francisco, and thirty five miles west of San Jose. It attracts visitors from both metropolitan areas, drawn by scenic beaches, ocean fishing, and majestic redwood forests in the rain-drenched Santa Cruz mountains.

The county line, which was adjusted about a century ago, now begins on the north at Big Basin Redwoods Park and heads inland to the crest of the Santa Cruz Mountains, then south to the Pajaro River which flows to the Pacific Ocean. About 446 square miles are inside county boundaries. It is the home of 209,000 people.

Agriculture dominates the economy in the Watsonville area, where the soil and mild temperatures combine with moisture from the ocean to produce truck gardens and orchards with a wide reputation. From the town of Santa Cruz north, tourism is the economic life blood, although a few farms specializing in brussels sprouts and artichokes dot the timbered valleys reaching to the coast.

Don Gaspar de Portola, leader of the Spanish overland expedition which located San Francisco Bay, planted a cross by the banks of the San Lorenzo River in 1769. That Holy Cross gave the city and county its name. A mission Exaltacion de la Santa Cruz was consecrated twenty-two years later.

Civilian settlers were brought ashore in 1797 in a Spanish experiment at pueblo, or community, founding. The model village was less than a success, but the land around it yielded crops which could be sold to the crews of whaling ships which called in Monterey Bay.

Under the California Republic, the town became a busy port. Cattle were shipped from its docks, lumber milled in the forests was exported, and a foundry which actually began operation in 1848 was one of the first to cash in

623

on the gold rush. Elihu Anthony's blacksmiths quickly turned to production of iron picks for the mining trade.

The city of Santa Cruz received its charter in 1866. The Spanish influence remained, and one historian reports the Santa Cruz bull ring was still drawing crowds in 1867. The ring was in the "suburb" of Banciforte, which was annexed into Santa Cruz in 1907.

Tourist attractions had already come to the city by then, and they were enhanced in 1931 when a replica of the Mission Santa Cruz was completed on the plaza--about half the size of the original mission.

Whalers made their mark on the county in other ways besides fostering the first farming ventures. Captain John Davenport, who noted the annual whale migration which brings the seagoing mammals close to shore each year, gathered a crew ashore in the 1850s at Davenport Landing. When the lookout called, they left their cabins and manned the boats, then rendered their catch on the beach. A large cement plant came later, creating the company town of Davenport in 1906. The resurgent community calls itself "New Davenport" these days and like others on Highway One, welcomes visitors.

ATTRACTIONS

Roaring Camp and Big Trees Narrow Gauge Railroad, on Graham Hill Road at Felton, provides train rides on steep grades among the redwoods. Other attractions at the camp, including a vintage steam sawmill, located off the San Lorenzo Canyon Highway, state route 9, east of Santa Cruz. Open daily. Call 335-4484 to check hours.

On Graham Hill Road, you will cross the **Felton covered bridge,** one of only three remaining in Santa Cruz county. It was erected in 1892.

West Cliff Drive north of Santa Cruz takes visitors to **Light House Point,** where a sea lion herd is usually in residence on the rocks below. A museum and gift shop are open Saturday and Sunday from 1:00 p.m. to 5:00 p.m. Displays include story of the butterfly migration to the bay.

Further north on the drive is **Long Marine Laboratory** and **Natural Bridge State Park.** Tide pool aquariums, and the 85-foot long skeleton of a whale, are at the University of California laboratory. Call 429-4087.

At Aptos, a small community south of Santa Cruz, are four miles of beaches and the entrance to **Forest Nisene Marks State Park.** Sugar Baron Claus Spreckels built his Deer Park here in the 1870s, importing deer, elk and other big game animals. Call 335-4598 for information on the state park. A community park is at the turn off for the state park, located in the foothills to the east.

Big Basin Redwoods State Park provides camping and hiking trails among giant trees. A coastal neck is accessible off Highway One, but the park headquarters are far inland, reached by taking Highway 236 northwest from the small community of Boulder Creek. Telephone for campground reservations, 338-6132.

Santa Cruz County has about twenty **wineries,** with seven of them offering tasting rooms. For wine tour information, write to the Santa Cruz Convention/Visitors Bureau , Box 1476, Santa Cruz, CA 95061. Telephone 423-6927, or write for information on tours from the Santa Cruz Mountain Vintners Association, Box 2856, Saratoga, CA 95707.

Aptos

Accommodations

SEACLIFF INN
SEVERINO'S RESTAURANT
7500 Old Dominion Court
Highway 1 and Seacliff Beach Exit
Aptos, CA 95003
Tel. (408) 688-7300

Centrally located in Santa Cruz County and situated just a few blocks from historic Seacliff State Park and Beach, is the Seacliff Inn. The inn was designed and built by local owners who carefully oversee all services provided.
Included in the one hundred and forty tastefully decorated rooms are twelve individually appointed suites; perfect for a personal retreat or a great place to bring the entire family. For your enjoyment, there is a pool, spa and a putting green. There are spacious gardens where you can walk and a Koi fish pond which has a spectacular waterfall.
Severino's restaurant at the inn is a delicious, convenient place for breakfast, lunch and dinner. The Italian decor and warm peach tones of the interior make this a relaxing place to enjoy the view of Monterey Bay. A complete menu offers fresh seafood, chicken, beef, veal, lamb and pasta dishes. Dine outside and enjoy the beautiful weather of the area.
Be sure to visit Seacliff Inn and Severino's for a restful hideaway near the beach at this "Best Choice" in Norther California.

Santa Cruz County

Restaurant

CHEZ RENEE
9051 Soquel Avenue
Aptos, CA 95003
Tel: (408) 688-5566
Hrs: Tue. - Fri.   Lunch   11:30 a.m. - 2:00 p.m.
        Tue. - Sat.   Dinner   6:00 p.m. - 10:00 p.m.

There is a very special dinner house located among the redwoods off Highway One in Aptos, that seems to be a secret known only to restauranteurs and vintners of the Monterey bay area. However, due to the expertise and knowledge of the owners and their dedication to the unsurpassed presentation of fine cuisine, Chez Renee is headed for fame and recognition far beyond the Monterey Bay.

The owners artistic talents are shown off by the beautifully appointed decor of this country house. The main dining room, with it's high arched ceiling, along with the intimate side rooms, creates a warm romantic atmosphere that is complemented by their extensive personal art collection.

At your fireside table you can enjoy such appetizers as duck Ballotine, the restaurant's own smoked salmon, or possibly a pasta such as, Tortellini Renee or fresh fettuccini with Chanterelle mushrooms. Your entree could include one of several Provimi Veal presentations, a Filet Mignon, sweetbreads, or a delicious rack of lamb. Among the daily specials could be that day's preparation of fresh Duckling or the freshest of the local Monterey Bay fish that are available. To complement your dinner, there is a comprehensive and well balanced wine list featuring both the best of California and French vintages. The finishing touch would be a sampling of the house pastries or a warm souffle and an espresso.

So, when you have a choice of restaurants, choose the "Best Choice" and visit Chez Renee for good food, beautiful decor and a friendly atmosphere.

Capitola

This little harbor south of Santa Cruz has a long pier, and is one of the charter boat home ports on Monterey Bay. A resort community of long-standing, Capitola retains its charm.

Soquel Point, with its county beach access, juts out into the bay. The rest of the town curves inland, providing protection from the prevailing winds during summer months. Beaches and cliffs alternate along the shore line. New

Santa Cruz County

Brighton Beach State Park with its campground is at the far south end of the community.

The tradition of a summer home at the beach began in 1869 with the opening of Camp Capitola. By 1885 there was a three story hotel, a dance hall and other facilities built by F. A. Hihn, who sold off residential lots to finance his improvements. About 10,000 people live here year around.

Attractions

New Brighton Beach State Park is open all year. Swimming and surf fishing, several camping spots. The main beach is known as a popular diver's spot, with rock fish, kelp bass and ling cod among the species taken regularly. For information, ask at O'Neill's Surf Shop, 1149 Forty-First Street, 475-4151.

Wharf Charters at the pier offers both sight seeing and deep sea fishing charters. Whale watching is a specialty in season. Call 462-3553 for information.

Fairwinds Charters, 541 Capitola Avenue, provides sailing instruction, chartered sailing trips and cruises. Call 462-2006.

Two of the more than twenty wineries in Santa Cruz County are located close by. **Bargetto Winery**, 3535 A Main Street, Soquel, was established in 1933 and has a creek-side tasting room and gardens. Open daily, 9:00 a.m. to 5:30 p.m. Call 475-2258. On Porter Street in Soquel is **Devlin Wine Cellars**. A tasting room is open daily from 12:00 noon to 5:00 p.m.

For information contact the **Capitola Chamber of Commerce**, 410 Capitola Avenue, Capitola CA 95010. Telephone 475-6522.

Accommodations

THE VENETIANS, 1500 Wharf Road, Capitola, California. Hotel cottages on the beachfront, inexpensive, but clean.

Bed and Breakfast

SUMMER HOUSE, 216 Monterey Avenue, Capitola, California. On Depot Hill, overlooking Capitola Village. Walking distance to beach, shopping and restaurants.

Art

WALTER/WHITE FINE ARTS, 107 Capitola Avenue, Capitola, California. The nation's top glassblowing artists' work is on display here.

Bakery

GAYLE'S BAKERY AND ROSTICCERIA, 504 Bay Avenue, Capitola, California. Best bakery in the area. Famous for baguettes, homemade breads and the deli.

Gift

THE ENCHANTOR
417 Capitola Avenue
Capitola, CA 95010
Tel. (408) 476-4854
Hrs: Wed. - Mon. 10:30 a.m. - 5:30 p.m.

The Enchantor is a magical place filled with fine gifts, toys and dolls, located in a light, warm building with a fireplace and hidden rooms. Owner Marilyn McCurry believes that part of the charm of their shop is the retention of the original beauty of the building.

On display you will find beautiful handmade wooden nutcrackers by Steinbach and Christian Ulbrict. Charleen Kinser's stuffed animals look up at you with their wanting eyes and there is a unique display of Pye In The Skye handthrown pottery by James and Mary Shorba. The Victorian porcelain dolls by Lynda and Alan Marx are sure to catch your eye. There are also handmade wooden firewagons, soft sculptures and music boxes. You won't find a better collection of fine limited editions and one of a kind gifts anywhere else.

The mystical, wonderland of The Enchantor, with its Merlins and wizards, dragons and fairies, will touch your heart.

Restaurant

ANTOINES INN NEW ORLEANS, 200 Monterey Avenue, Capitola, California. New Orleans atmosphere, Cajun, Creole and Italian specialties.

SEA BONNE, 231 Esplanade, Capitola, California. Fresh seafood entrees, tasty chowder and crisp salads. Fine selection of California wines.

Rio Del Mar

Restaurant

CAFE RIO, 131 Esplanade, Rio Del Mar, California. Recently expanded, this secluded beach restaurant is worth the drive! Enjoy fresh seafood and cocktails in a beautiful atmosphere.

Santa Cruz

Marquez de Branciforte, the viceroy of early California, directed a civilian community, or pueblo, be established near the Mission Santa Cruz in 1797. The settlers actually came ashore here in July of that year, and for over 100 years the community of Branciforte existed on the banks of the San Lorenzo River right along with the mission property on the north side.

The name Santa Cruz, however, apparently was what most outsiders applied to the small harbor and surrounding farm land. When California's first twenty-seven counties were created in 1850, the legislature officially called the county and the county seat Santa Cruz. The valley above was the center of a brisk logging and sawmill business.

When the Southern Pacific Railroad reached here early in this century, Santa Cruz businessmen rapidly turned their attention to tourists. Wealthy San Franciscans found sunny weather and a mild climate quite different from their foggy summers. That attraction continues to this day, aided by developments such as a long commercial pier which mixes fishermen with tourists.

Attractions

The **Octagon Museum** at Front and Cooper Streets contains historical displays related to county history. The former Hall of Records building was restored in 1982. Call (408) 425-2540 for current operating hours. A walking tour guide of four historic areas of town is available at the museum, and at Santa Cruz City Hall.

Santa Cruz City Museum, 1305 East Cliff Drive, concentrates on natural history and prehistory of the area. Call 429-3773 for current operating hours.

629

There is still a seaside amusement park here, **The Beach Boardwalk**, located at 400 Beach street. Rides and shops are combined. Open daily from Memorial Day through Labor Day, weekends the balance of the year. Call 423-5590.

On Washington Street, you can visit the **Union Depot** where the excursion trains used to arrive. Now refurbished in a Victorian manner, it has food concessions and other items for shoppers. Open daily. Telephone 425-1910.

An internationally famous garden specializing in begonias is open to the public from June through October. **Antonelli Gardens**, 2545 Capitola Road, reaches the peak of its beauty in August and September. Open Monday through Friday from 8:00 a.m. to 6:00 p.m. Saturday, Sunday from 9:00 a.m. to 6:00 p.m.

The **Art Museum of Santa Cruz County**, upstairs at 224 Church Street, features displays of fine art. Open Tuesday through Sunday 12:00 noon to 5:00 p.m. Thursday evenings open until 9:00 p.m. Telephone 429-3420.

The half-scale replica of **Mission Santa Cruz** is at 126 High street, open daily. Includes a gift shop. Call 426-5686 for hours.

University of Santa Cruz, on the hill above the bay, has an avant garde reputation in higher education circles. Several programs are offered which may fit with visitor's schedules. Call 429-2495. The 2,000 acre campus is off High Street on Glenn Coolidge Road.

For additional information, contact the Santa Cruz County Convention and Visitors Bureau, Box 1476, Santa Cruz CA 95061. Telephone 423-6927.

Accommodations

THE DARLING HOUSE
314 West Cliff Drive
Santa Cruz, CA 95060
Tel. (408) 458-1958
Open all year.

The Darling House is a 1910 ocean-side architectural masterpiece designed by William Weeks. Lit by Tiffany lamps, open hearths, and sun shining through beveled glass, this bed and breakfast is a definite "Best Choice" for those seeking peaceful elegance. The spacious lawn, citrus orchard, towering palms, and blossoms for every season create a colorful display of California splendor.

The Darling House, with its superb location and its authenticity in antiques, is a uniquely enjoyable place to stay. Enjoy all the original fireplaces and fixtures. You'll find an 1899 Tiffany lamp, beautiful Chippendale wood furniture, and other rare antiques.

Owners Darrell and Karen invite you to relax in the evening beside your own hearth, sip a vintage sherry or hot cider, and watch the moonbeams dance on the rolling sea. You will sleep securely to the sounds of the surf. In the morning, sit on the ocean-side veranda or by the fireside in the tiger oak dining room, and sip espresso or cappuccino and feast on nut breads, croissants, and fresh fruits. During the day sail on Monterey Bay, stroll down West Cliff Drive to the lighthouse, or run on a secluded beach. Then feast on fresh cracked crab and dance at the Coconut Grove Ballroom. All these enjoyable attractions of Santa Cruz are within a five-minute walk from the Darling House. Also providing facilities for weddings and group events, the Darling House will give you a timeless escape with unmatched beauty for any occasion.

DREAM INN, 175 West Cliff Drive, Santa Cruz, California. This full-service hotel is adjacent to the wharf, and has a bay view, pool, and restaurant.

Antiques

MODERN LIFE
1531 Pacific Avenue
Santa Cruz, CA 95060
Tel. (408) 429-9011
Hrs. Mon. - Sat. 10:30 a.m. - 6:00 p.m.
        Sunday   12:00 noon - 6:00 p.m.

Department store atmosphere of antiques and collectibles specializing in Art Deco through mid century jewelry, artifacts, clothing and costumes and designer furniture.

Located in the heart of Santa Cruz on the Pacific Garden Mall...Modern Life is a decorating paradise...the collector's dream...the ultimate in shopping for the unique gift. Modern Life was recently voted the Best Antique Store in the "Best of Santa Cruz" contest.

POSSIBILITIES UNLIMITED
1043 Water Street
Santa Cruz, CA
Tel. (408) 427-1131
Hrs: Daily   10:00 a.m. - 5:30 p.m.
         Sun.   11:00 a.m. - 5:30 p.m.

While you're in the Santa Cruz area make sure you stop at Possibilities Unlimited. Well known among antique experts as the top antique store in the area, this Best Choice is a must whether you're in the market for fine antiques and rare collectibles, or just want to browse through the past in this beautifully layed out shop.

Owners Henry and Gini Lu Robinson proudly display their fine collection of oak and walnut antique furniture from the turn of the century along with many other fine pieces from over 20 antique dealers who share in this outstanding collective.

Stepping through the greenhouse entrance gives you a view of the 8,000 square foot showroom and assures you hours of pleasure browsing through the past. As you walk from one room into another, you find yourself transformed into a turn-of the-century living room, an office, or even a kitchen with its rare refrigeration unit, stove, and sinks. On some beautiful old dining tables antique glassware and china are displayed in table settings as if dinner were being served. Next to the kitchen you'll find antique bath tubs, sinks, and bathroom accessories. In a section displaying antique office furniture are many beautiful oak desks and chairs. Henry and Gini Lu have done a wonderful job in reconstructing the past in their shop.

In addition to all the beautiful furniture, you will also find a wide variety of toys and dolls, vintage clothing, costume and antique jewelry, rugs, and other fine collectibles. Possibilities Unlimited also has the facilities to restore your unfinished and broken-down antiques into their original condition.

When you come into Possibilities Unlimited, your eyes will light up at the wide-open showrooms and all the rare and beautiful pieces on display. Come in to browse, or search for that special piece that will give your future a little taste of the past. All the people here are happy to share their wealth of knowledge and answer any questions you might have.

Attractions

SANTA CRUZ BEACH BOARDWALK
400 Beach Street
Santa Cruz, CA 95060
Tel. (408) 423-5590
Call for hours.

The Santa Cruz Beach Boardwalk is the West Coast's only beachside amusement park. Located on Santa Cruz's white, mile long beach, the Boardwalk features a mixture of thrill rides, children's rides, arcades, costume characters, restaurants and an indoor miniature golf course, providing entertainment for the entire family.

Just a brief listing of some of the attractions - the Giant Dipper Roller Coaster built in 1924 with graceful arches, sweeping curves and a seventy foot drop at fifty-five mile an hour speeds; the Classic Carousel merry-go-round built in 1911 now completely restored with hand carved horses characterized by long flowing manes, jewel studded bridles, muscular legs and spirited expressions. Music for the carousel is provided by a 1894 band organ with 342 pipes. During the spring and fall a dance series is presented with big name bands.

Whether it's the thrill of the Giant Dipper, the excitement of the arcade or the beauty and elegance of the Coconut Grove Ballroom, visit the beautiful California coast at Santa Cruz.

B & B

CHATEAU VICTORIAN, 118 First Street, Santa Cruz, California. Open all year, Chateau Victorian features rooms with private bathrooms and fireplaces. Enjoy the hot tub while you're there.

VALLEY VIEW INN
P.O. Box 66593
Santa Cruz, CA 95066
Tel. (415) 321-5195
Call for directions and reservations.
AMEX accepted with prior arrangement
Smoking is discouraged.
No children under twelve.

The coastal mountains of Scotts Valley, ten minutes from Santa Cruz beach, provide a tranquil setting for this get-away retreat which is only two

633

minutes from Highway 17. Valley View occupies a striking house built by a protege of Frank Lloyd Wright, and updated by owner and architectural designer Scott Young and his wife Tricia. The inn reflects the beauty of its surroundings with walls of glass, a full wall of solid mirror in the living room, a kitchen in-the-round and a large redwood deck with a hot tub. All this overlooks thousands of acres of redwood forest.

There are two lovely bedrooms, each with glass doors overlooking the forest, but the Youngs never have them occupied with guests that are unacquainted, so you may be assured of complete privacy. A piano, telescope for star gazing, color cable TV, stereo, lots of extra pillows and cushions for snuggling in front of the massive stone fireplace, plush towels, a full breakfast and much more are provided.

The minimum stay is two nights, the extras include a well stocked kitchen for those private tete-a-tetes, complimentary sherry and white wine, and this "Best Choice" for your vacation won't put a strain on your budget.

(See special invitation in the Appendix.)

Delicatessen

HARBOR DELI AND BAKERY
Corner of 7th and Eaton
Santa Cruz, CA
Tel. (408)-479-1366
Hrs: Mon.-Sun. 7:00 a.m.- 8:00 p.m.

For those of you who have a taste for gourmet delights, Harbor Deli and Bakery in the Santa Cruz harbor area provides a selection of fine European foods. Their vast array of menu choices are complemented by catering service and a unique front door delivery known as "Room Service".

Prepared daily in their own kitchens comes such goodies as soup of the day, natural gourmet sausage, pates of duck, chicken or pork, roasted ribs chicken or cornish game hens and a salad bar of delectable choices where servings are bought by the ounce. Also from their own pasta factory Harbor Deli And Bakery manufactures the makings for such Italian favorites as lasagna, manicotti, pasta con pesto, and canneloni. No deli is complete with out sandwiches and Harbor Deli is no exception offering many truly exceptional sandwiches. Rounding out the meal are a wide selection of domestic and imported wines, champagnes, and beers along with imported cheeses and fresh fruit. Now that your mouth is watering, why not stop in or better yet call for "Room Service" and have your delicious meal delivered to your hotel room, home or boat right there where you're relaxing. If you happen to be having a few hundred friends over for lunch, Harbor Deli can handle that too with their capable catering crew.

So if you're planning a day at the beach, an afternoon of sailing, or are just passing through and savor a meal of distinction, stop in at Harbor Deli And Bakery for this "Best Choice" in dining.

Restaurants

CASABLANCA RESTAURANT AND INN
101 Main Street
Santa Cruz, CA 95060
Tel. (408) 426-4063
Hrs: Mon. - Sun. Dinner   5:00 p.m. - Closing
      Sunday   Brunch   9:30 a.m. - 2:00 p.m.
Visa, MasterCard and AMEX are accepted.

Located on the beach between Santa Cruz Municipal Pier and Coconut Grove, the Casablanca offers twenty-seven guest rooms with private balconies and panoramic views of Monterey Bay. The restaurant features fine dining in a rooms fitted to match the North African theme, complete with potted palms and slow-turning fans high above the tables.

Casablanca is a short walk from the Santa Cruz Municipal Pier and its picturesque shops. Many of its guest rooms have wood burning fireplaces and kitchens. But, with gourmet chefs at work below, you'll probably want to sample some of the seafood entrees for a romantic touch to a weekend or vacation stay here. The extensive menu prepared by executive chef Billy Grippo also features beef, lamb and chicken dishes. Specialties include snapper roasted in a red bell pepper puree, spinach fettucine with scallops and Eastern blue crab, and fresh prawns with mushrooms in a sesame and ginger broth. There is an extensive wine list to complement the menu.

The villa where Main street meets the beach is your "Best Choice" in Santa Cruz for gourmet dining and excellent overnight accommodations. Casablanca is a special place.

CROW'S NEST
2218 East Cliff Drive/Yacht Harbor
Santa Cruz, CA 95060
Tel: (408) 476-4560
Hrs: Mon. - Fri.   11:30 a.m. - 2:30 a.m.
     Saturday   11:30 a.m. - 3:00 a.m.
     Sunday   10:00 a.m. - 3:00 p.m.
AMEX, MasterCard and Visa are accepted.

High above the Santa Cruz Yacht Harbor is a lookout, or "Crow's Nest," maintained by the Coast Guard Auxiliary. It serves as a weather station, observation tower and base for marine rescue operations. Directly beneath this much needed lookout is a restaurant of the same name, but filling a different need.

Sweeping views, a friendly atmosphere and exceptional food have made the Crow's Nest one of the most popular spots on the Monterey Bay. Outdoor decks on both levels provide an excellent vantage point for the parade of boats in and out of the harbor and a ringside seat for the colorful Wednesday evening sailboat races. For lunch and dinner the Crow's Nest offers the freshest local catch, direct from the fishing fleet that berths beside the restaurant each morning, as well as the choicest, specially aged, Midwestern, corn feed beef, lamb and shellfish. Complimentary wine is served with lunch and brunch.

On the second level, the lounge with two outdoor decks offers nightly entertainment in a variety of music. There is also an Oyster Bar, serving diverse appetizers all evening long. Although not needed at the Oyster Bar, reservations are recommended for the dining room. Come down to the Crow's Nest to eat, drink, dance and check out one of the best views on the bay.

INDIA JOZE
Restaurant, Bakery and Catering
1001 Center Street
Santa Cruz, CA 95060
Tel. (408) 427-3554
Hrs: Mon. - Thu.   11:30 a.m. - 10:00 p.m.
     Fri. - Sat.   11:30 a.m. - 12:00 midnight
     Sunday   10:00 a.m. - 10:00 p.m.
Visa and MasterCard are accepted.

Fresh chilies, mint, ginger, garlic and a host of exotic spices gives India Joze food the reputation for flavor which attracts repeat customers by the table full. Founder Joseph Schultz designed the kitchen so that diners are able to see where their food is prepared and he also shares his culinary skills through periodic cooking classes.

The decor of this unique restaurant is simple, so that the emphasis is on presenting the most diverse menu of Near to Far East Asian cuisines anywhere, with entrees appealing to a wide variety of tastes. India Joze serves lunch, dinner and Sunday Brunch. Monday, Tuesday and Wednesday, belly dancing or flamenco entertainment sometimes accompanies the Middle Eastern menu. Thursday and Friday, East Indian dishes are served, and on Saturday and Sunday, the cuisine of Indonesia. Specials are offered in addition to the regular menu offerings, available every evening, which include chicken, calamari and other seafood, lamb, beef, pork and vegetarian dishes. There is an extensive list of selected wines, served at the wine bar or at your table. Diners are invited to enjoy the outdoor patio lunch, dinner and Sunday Brunch.

If the skillful preparation and spices give the main dishes their reputation at India Joze, it is the restaurant's own bakery which earns accolades for its extravagant desserts. Truffles, tortes and pies make your meal an international festival with a flourish.

And don't forget, The International Calamari Festival, now in its eighth year, is presented for the entire month of August.

PEARL ALLEY BISTRO
110 Pearl Alley
Santa Cruz, CA 95060
Tel. (408) 429-8070
Hrs: Tue. - Fri.   Lunch   11:30 a.m. - 2:30 p.m.
     Tue. - Sat.   Dinner   5:30 p.m. - 10:00 p.m.

Tucked away on a narrow back street, the Pearl Alley Bistro is a walk-up famed for its wines and a menu which changes daily. An old mahogany bar greets visitors, and paintings on the walls are changed monthly.

Finding Pearl Alley could be half the fun of dining here. Locate Pacific Garden Mall between Walnut and Lincoln streets. Then get on the Cedar street side of the mall, and should should spot Pearl Alley. It is a short walk up to the bar, where over twenty wines are featured by the glass and two hundred are on the list. Food varies with the whims of Marilyn Strayer, the co-owner and chef. It could be a new recipe in the vogue in California, or an old favorite from southern Europe. Meals are topped off with desserts from Marilyn's kitchen and a selection of coffees.

The atmosphere of Pearl Alley Bistro is unique, a place for local artists to show their works, local musicians to entertain, and Eric and Marilyn Strayer to share their knowledge of fine food and drink.

SEA CLOUD, Santa Cruz Municipal Wharf, Santa Cruz, California. Enjoy dining on the wharf, with a view of the beach and Monterey Bay.

SHADOW BROOK RESTAURANT
1750 Wharf Road
Santa Cruz, CA 95010
Tel: (408) 475-1511
Hrs: Mon. - Fri.   Lunch   11:00 a.m. - 2:30 p.m.
                   Dinner   5:00 p.m. - 10:30 p.m.
    Sat. - Sun.   Brunch   10:00 a.m. - 2:00 p.m.

This enchanting chalet style structure, tucked into a steep hillside overlooking Soquel Creek, is in the picturesque village of Capitola-by-the-Sea on the northern Shore of California's Monterey Bay. Originally a log cabin built in the 1920s, and a restaurant since 1947, Shadowbrook is one of the most beautiful and romantic dining places on the West Coast.

Shadowbrook, accessed by cable car and garden paths, offers a menu, wine list and exceptional service for an unforgettable dining experience. Specialities of the house include prime rib, steaks and fresh seafood. Also, all the breads, pastries and desserts are made from scratch in the kitchen. The popular weekend brunch features the traditional egg dishes and a variety of imaginative light entrees along with their famous home-baked orange rolls and blueberry blintzes. Enjoy your meals in one of the elegant dining rooms or out on the picturesque patio areas.

Shadowbrook is well known for banquet facilities that can accommodate group events such as weddings, business meetings and parties. The well informed staff will assist you in planning the menu. Try the Shadowbrook and enjoy some of the finest food and unmatched atmosphere in the area.

Sport

STAGNARO FISHING TRIPS, 55-C Santa Cruz Wharf, Santa Cruz, California. Charters are available daily to fish for tuna, salmon, cod, or whatever's in season.

CITY TOUR OF SANTA CRUZ

a.m.	Modern Life	Best deco	Santa/Ant
a.m.	Possibilities Unlimited	Best variety	Santa/Ant
p.m.	Pearl Alley	Best lunch	Santa/Ant
p.m.	Harbor Deli	Best deli	Santa/Deli
p.m.	Beach Boardwalk	Best amusement	Santa/Att
After the Boardwalk, try dinner and drinks at any of these restaurants:			
p.m.	Shadow Brook	Best prime rib	Santa/Rest
p.m.	Crow's Nest	Best dine & dance	Santa/Rest
p.m.	Casablanca	Best shellfish	Santa/Rest
p.m.	India Joze	Best India/Indone	Santa/Rest

Soquel

Restaurants

RISTORANTE ITALIANO
4616 Soquel Drive
Soquel, CA 95073
Tel. (408) 462-6991
Hrs: Mon. - Fri.   Lunch   11:30 a.m. - 2:00 p.m.
          Sun. - Thu.   Dinner   5:00 p.m. - 9:30 p.m.
          Fri. - Sat.   Dinner   5:00 p.m. - 10:00 p.m.

A favorite stop for local clientele for over six years, Ristorante Italiano serves up traditional Italian cooking at the skilled hands of owners John and Julie Clymer. The finest ingredients reminiscent of old Italy are combined in each individually prepared order to give each customer a mouth watering, savory experience.

Appetizers that top the menu include steamed mussels, marinated calamari and deep fried shrimp. Traditional Italian dishes are available including fresh pasta that includes choice of soup or salad and warmed Italian bread. The house speciality is Cioppino which is a delightful seafood combination of fresh clams, mussels, fish, prawns and crab steeped in their own Marinara sauce, served only on weekends.

639

From light fare to full entrees Ristorante Italiano will satisfy your Italian itch. Bring the kids too; there's a menu selection for them also. Stop in at this "Best Choice" in Italian dining and tell John and Julie hello.

SALMON POACHER
3035 Main Street
Soquel, CA 95073
Tel: (408) 476-1556
Hrs: Wed. - Sun. 5:30 p.m. - 9:30 p.m.

"Poacher" is a word that can be taken two ways. One - a person who trespasses to catch fish or game illegally. Two - someone who cooks eggs, fish or fruits in a hot liquid that is maintained under the boiling point. Fortunately, the Salmon Poacher is a restaurant falling under the latter definition. And, it's something they do well.

John Kenneth, the chef/owner of Salmon Poacher, has been in the restaurant business over fifteen years. He specializes in only the freshest and top quality ingredients, personally selected on a daily basis. Start off with the Oysters Rockefeller and a special sauteed Monterey Bay prawn appetizer that is beyond comparison. Each dinner comes with crisp salad and soup, such as clam chowder. One of the specialities to move onto is fresh tuna marinated in apple juice, soy sauce, garlic and ginger. Mmmm! Another one is sole stuffed with crab and shrimp, cooked to perfection and very tasty.

And then, it's time for dessert. Choose from fresh cranberry and ginger sorbet to poached pears in a strawberry sauce with coconut and French vanilla ice cream. Oh, and the heart attack cake with vanilla custard sauce, will top off any evening. The Salmon Poacher, although not partaking in illegal activities, is sinfully delicious.

Watsonville

If Santa Cruz is for tourists, and it is, Watsonville is for farmers. The flat and fertile fields get about twenty one inches of rainfall each year, and most farms have access to irrigation which brings in high value crops in the moderate climate. About 25,000 people live inside the city, several thousand more in farms and small communities in the surrounding area.

The town was created in 1852, part of the Rancho Bolsa del Pajaro. Judge John H. Watson and D. S. Gregory laid out the lots. When the Southern Pacific Railroad came to the coast from Gilroy in 1871 farmers had access to national markets, although they waited years for the branch line to arrive at this growing town. Top crops today are strawberries, cut flowers and apples.

Perhaps one-third of California's apple production comes from orchards in the Watsonville area.

Watsonville has a plaza that was once the scene of Sunday horse races on the main street, and bear and bull fights on the square. A small cannon in the plaza was fired by the steamship Oregon when she sailed through the Golden Gate in 1850 with word that California was part of the Union.

Attractions

Old houses of Watsonville abound, along with some beautiful buildings on the plaza. The Watsonville Chamber of Commerce, 444 Main Street, has a pamphlet for a walking and driving tour of the area which includes over twenty historic buildings.

Sunset Beach State Park, west of town, 201 Sunset Beach Road, has a ninety space campground which is so much in demand during summer months that reservations must be made through the Ticketron system. From October through Memorial Day spaces go on a first-come, first served basis. Look for the pilings at the beach, they mark the piers which were a busy port at the turn of the century before the railroad shifted freight patterns. Call 772-1266 for park information.

Pajaro Valley Historical Museum, 261 East Beach Street, traces the valley's roots from a rancho to the present. Open Tuesday through Thursday, 11:00 a.m. to 3:00 p.m. Call 722-0305 for appointments at other times.

Pajaro Dunes State Park is under development near the mouth of the river. Several native plants are being restarted on the rolling dunes.

For more information, contact the **Watsonville Area Chamber of Commerce,** 444 Main Street, Watsonville CA 95076. Telephone 724-3849.

641

SHASTA COUNTY

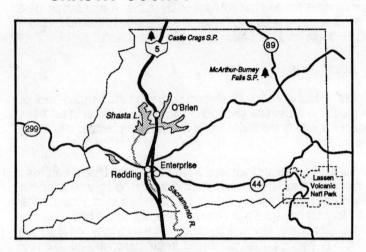

This county at the head of the Sacramento Valley boasts two major reservoirs, a National Recreation Area, and a National Park. Shasta County is named after the towering mountain which is actually in the next county to the north, Siskiyou. Its 3,786 square miles are home to 116,000 people, almost half of them living in the sprawling city of Redding next to I-5. The western boundary is in the rugged coast range mountains, the eastern in the farthest-south reaches of the Cascade mountain range. Cottonwood Creek from the coast range and Digger Creek from the Cascades make the south boundary and the offset from a surveyor's parallel is the north county line just below Dunsmuir on I-5.

Pierson B. Reading, holder of an 1843 land grant, developed the country and blazed the trail which gold miners later followed to Weaverville in the coastal mountains. Summers are hot here. Cattle dominate agriculture, timber and tourists sustain the rest of the economy, and Redding itself has grown rapidly in recent years as the largest retail trade center in the upper valley.

NATIONAL PARK

Mount Lassen, the celebrated volcano which began eruptions in May 1914 is on the eastern edge of a 106,000 acre **Mt. Lassen Volcanic National**

642

Park which is mostly a wilderness of cinder cones and forest. This is the southernmost peak in the Cascade Mountain chain which extends north in to British Columbia. Highway 36 leads to the park from Mineral and reaches a winter sport area just below the celebrated Sulphur Works springs. Highway 44 gives a northern park entrance at Manzanita Lake. From late spring until winter, the connecting highway is open, taking autos to within two-miles of the top of the volcano.

Several camping sites are on the roads, and 150 miles of hiking trails crisscross the back country. Mud slides unleashed by the eruptions left scars on the mountain's flanks which can be reached on foot. The 10,457 foot high peak is climbed by thousands of people every summer, and a park ranger is on duty each afternoon explaining the geology from a perch above the small caldera.

For information, contact **Lassen Volcanic National Park**, Mineral CA 96063. Telephone (916) 595-4444.

ATTRACTIONS

Fort Crook Museum, Fall River Mills, has displays of pioneer life and a collection of Indian artifacts. Open daily from May 1 through November 15, 1:00 p.m. to 4:00 p.m. Telephone (916) 336-5110.

The forested area between Mounts Lassen and Shasta is called **Burney Basin**, sight of extensive forests with scattered resorts and famed for hunting and fishing. Burney Falls is a scenic attraction within a state park near the community of Burney. Lava caves, ice caves and volcanic cones are among the sights elsewhere in the basin. Contact the **Burney Basin Chamber of Commerce**, Box 36, Burney CA 96013 for a list of resorts. Telephone 335-2111.

Shasta State Historic Park, on Highway 299 six miles west of Redding, is the old gold mining town which began life as Reading Springs with a strike made in 1848. Brick and adobe buildings deteriorated until the place was made a state park in 1950. Open daily 10:00 a.m. to 5:00 p.m. Telephone 468-2382.

Whiskeytown and **Shasta Lake National Recreation Areas** are both within the county. Eight recreation sites and an historic area are on the shores of **Whiskeytown Reservoir** west of Redding, where power boating, water skiing and camping are popular. An Indian rancheria is preserved, waterworks and an old gold mine are restored, and an old hotel is on display.

Shasta Lake, a giant impoundment beside I-5 north of Redding, has 370 miles of shoreline and dozens of recreation opportunities.

Limestones of **Shasta Caverns** can be seen on private tours from O'Brien, and commercial marinas will rent vessels from fishing skiffs to luxurious house boats. Nine resorts offer lakeside cabins. The dam, completed just before World War II, towers 602 feet above the Sacramento River, regulating an annual flow of 6.2 million acre feet of water.

Castle Crags State Park, off I-5 south of Dunsmuir, includes two miles of Sacramento River above the Lake Shasta still water and dramatic rock formations which can be reached by hiking to the granite spires polished by glacial ice. Camping and picnicking are available. Campsites are reserved through the Ticketron system. Telephone 235-2684.

For more information, contact the **Tourist Information Center**, 1250 Parkview Avenue, Redding CA 96001. Telephone (916) 225-4100.

O'Brien

Attraction

LAKE SHASTA CAVERNS
P.O. Box 801
O'Brien, CA 96070
Tel. (916) 238-2341
Hrs: Mon. - Sun. From 8:00 a.m.
Special tours available by appointment.

Billed as the West's newest natural wonder, Lake Shasta Caverns is really three adventures in one! Your first fun-filled experience is a fifteen minute cruise through beautiful scenery on the crystal blue waters of Lake Shasta. A specially-equipped bus careens 840 feet up to the stunning caves where you can learn geology, history and enjoy the fascinating interior.

The informative guides will not only give you a background of the caves, but an explanation of the geological formation from the Cryptozoic Eon to present day. Some of the amazing formations are stalactites and stalagmites, helicites, sculptures and crystals in various colors and shapes. Fossil specimens found on the site have helped scientists track the evolution of the caves, the existence and, in some cases, the extinction of several dozen forms of life.

For a day of fun, education and entertainment touring the magical caves be sure to visit this "Best Choice" attraction - Lake Shasta Caverns.

Redding

This busy city of the north valley had a slow start after it was replotted by B.B. Redding, land agent for the Central Pacific Railroad in 1872. The state legislature made it clear that while the developer's name was on the town, the place was to honor Pierson B. Reading, the county pioneer.

Milling of forest products and retail trade for ranchers in the livestock business dominated early history. In recent decades, small manufacturing and a booming tourist traffic swelled retail trade, and annexations pushed out city limits to take in the suburban subdivisions which make up most of the new housing.

Indian artifacts indicate residence on the town site 4,000 years ago. Until the federal government began construction of Shasta Dam in the 1930s, the area remained lightly populated. The massive dam opened the way for a cement industry and a tourist trade to the area.

Attractions

Carter House Science Museum, 1701 Del Rio Drive, features rotating displays of interest to hobbyists and families, and offers natural history programs. Open Wednesday through Sunday, 10:00 a.m. to 4:00 p.m. Telephone (916) 244-0622.

Old City Hall Gallery, 1126 Parkview Avenue, is operated by the non-profit North Valley Art League for display of local works and classes. Open Wednesday through Sunday, 11:00 a.m. to 4:00 p.m. Telephone 243-1023.

Redding Museum and Art Center, 1911 Del Rio Drive, has exhibits prepared by the county historical society, native American art and gallery shows which change monthly. A natural science museum is open Wednesday, Friday and weekends, the main gallery and museum is open Tuesday through Sunday, 10:00 a.m. to 5:00 p.m. during the summer. Winter hours are restricted. Call 244-0622 for off-season schedules.

Waterworks Park, on Highway 299 just west of I-5, has three waterslides, offers innertube rides, and has water play areas for toddlers. Call 246-9550 for hours.

Redding residential areas represent several architectural styles. Three **self-guiding tours**, including commercial and residential buildings, are organized by the city **Convention and Visitor Bureau**. Write them at 777 Auditorium Drive, Redding CA 96001 for copies of the tour brochure.

For more information, contact the **Tourist Information Center**, 1250 Parkview Avenue, Redding CA 96001. Telephone (916) 225-4100.

Accommodation

RED LION MOTOR INN
1830 Hilltop Drive
Redding, CA 96002
Tel. (916) 221-8700
Visa, MasterCard, AMEX, Diner's Club and Discover
cards are accepted.

A convenient stop while traveling I-5 through northern California is the Red Lion Motor Inn. The architecture and decor of natural wood and warm colors was designed to blend with the rugged beauty of the area.

195 beautifully appointed rooms with oversized beds provide a spacious area to relax after a day on the road. Individually controlled air conditioning, color TV and direct dial phones are standard luxuries. Amenities including a courtyard with a swimming pool, wading pool, jacuzzi and putting green beckon to those seeking recreational outlets. Cocktail service is available at the pool and room service, as well as airport transportation are among the ways the friendly staff will pamper you. For a fun-filled evening, start with happy hour then enjoy live entertainment and dancing.

The elegant dining room serves delicious food ranging from oysters Rockefeller as an appetizer to Brie soup, Caesar salad or crab and shrimp Louie. Some of the superb entrees, charmingly presented, include salmon a la Max, halibut Bombay sauteed in butter with macadamia nuts, veal Oscar, prime rib, filet mignon or even an individual rack of lamb. After dinner, succumb to your desire for a pastry, cheesecake, German chocolate cake or Haagen-Dazs ice cream.

For superior room accommodations, luxurious amenities and professional friendly service your "Best Choice" in Redding is the Red Lion Motor Inn.

SHASTA INN
2180 Hilltop Drive
Redding, CA 96002
Tel. (916) 221-8200
Visa, MasterCard, AMEX and Bank America cards are
accepted.

"You're Inn for a Wonderful Time" at Shasta Inn. The spirit of these accommodations is friendly, professional and fun. Located in modern, beautifully appointed and spacious buildings, Shasta Inn has amenities for the business or leisure traveler.

Rooms range from doubles to kings and executive studios to luxurious suites - with complimentary champagne. Complete room service, color TV, individual temperature control and direct dial telephones are provided and, most rooms have private balconies or patios. Available for your relaxation are a swimming pool and jacuzzi surrounded by cool, lush gardens. A fitness center, Michelles, offers classes and equipment to keep in shape, even on the road. Excellent convention facilities will assure smooth running, successful business meetings with podiums, stages, sound systems, and more available for your convenience.

Special weekly events, such as fashion shows on Wednesdays and Monday Night Football gatherings with happy hour prices and complimentary hors d' oeuvres are featured. Choose from entrees such as, steak Diane, Tounedas or Chateaubriand Jardinere in the elegant dining room. For dancing, the lounge has a variety of artist performing jazz to light rock nightly.

Part of the spirit of this "Best Choice" hotel is that everything is done "Just for You." Stop in and enjoy being pampered by the staff of the Shasta Inn.

Art

THE COTTAGE GALLERY
North Valley Art League
1126 Parkview Avenue
Redding, CA 96001
Tel.   (916) 243-1023
Hrs: Wed. - Sun. 11:00 a.m. - 4:00 p.m.

The North Valley Art League began in October of 1980 with a formal purpose, "To bring together men and women interested in Fine Arts and the cultural development of our community." This organization is dedicated to

647

providing a place to show and sell the members' current works of art, holding workshops, demonstrations and juried shows."

Located in a park-like setting with lush lawns, shade trees and picnic tables is The Cottage Gallery, the workplace for this group of dedicated artists. The cottage is warm and cozy, a perfect place for displaying the ever expanding exhibits of acrylics, oils, pastels, watercolors, graphics, sculpture, china painting and photography. Some of the activities held are classes, individual workshops, contests, picnics and a show by a specific artist each month.

This "Best Choice" gallery will inspire artists and delight viewers with the quality and selection shown.

Museum

REDDING MUSEUM AND ART CENTER
P.O. Box 427
Redding, CA 96099
Tel. (916) 225-4155
Hrs: Summer   Tue. - Sun.   10:00 a.m. - 5:00 p.m.
       Winter   Tue. - Sun.   12:00 noon - 5:00 p.m.
                   Saturday   10:00 a.m. - 5:00 p.m.

One of the thrills of traveling is the interesting history you can learn from places such as the Redding Museum and Art Center. The staff of the museum strives to preserve, display and learn from artifacts in order to pass along intriguing details to its patrons. Three main themes of exhibits are maintained at the center, located in beautiful Caldwell Park.

Art - Two galleries feature monthly exhibits that mirror the range of media and style of contemporary art.

History - Displays change once a year and focus on industry, lifestyles and fashion of days gone by in Shasta County.

Ethnography - Features Pre-Columbian and Native American artifacts, such as collections of California Native American baskets.

Another goal of the center is to provide educational and entertaining programs for the community. Some of the programs are: Children's Lawn Festival, Annual Regional Art Competition, Arts and Crafts Faire, lectures and films. Be sure to take time to explore the museum and the surrounding park at this "Best Choice" center in Redding.

CARTER HOUSE SCIENCE MUSEUM
In Caldwell Park
P. O. Box 185
Redding, CA 96099
Tel.   (916) 225-4125
Hrs: Tue. - Sun. 10:00 a.m. - 5:00 p.m.
Visa and MasterCard are accepted.

"Dedicated to the understanding, appreciation and enjoyment of the regional environment - a museum committed to the natural pleasure of learning." This is the goal and the spirit of Carter House Science Museum.

Some of the activities and exhibits that are sponsored by Carter House are live animals, nature walks, films and displays of flora native to the area. A Zoomobile with programs on birds, mammals, reptiles and amphibians, as well as tours of the area providing knowledge and hands-on experience for students. Art contests, science and fungus fairs encourage local residents to become more involved with the museum and nature.   In the Coggins Greenhouse/Solarium you can explore the plant exhibits, and learn more about solar energy.

The staff and volunteers at this "Best Choice" - Carter House Science Museum have created a fun, exciting place to learn about and experience nature.

Redding, in addition to its commercial importance, is one of the springboards into the Whiskeytown-Shasta Recreation Area. The longer you stay, the better it looks.

TOUR OF REDDING			
a.m.	Redding Museum	Best history	Red/Mus
a.m.	Cottage Gallery	Best fine arts	Red/Art
p.m.	Redwood	Best lunch	Red/Rest
p.m.	A Bit of Country	Best country gifts	Redwood/Gift
p.m.	Carter Museum	Best nat. history	Red/Mus
p.m.	Red Lion	Best dine & dance	Red/Acc

SIERRA COUNTY

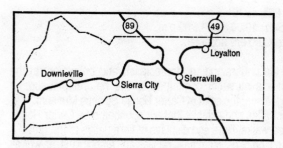

When a 141-pound nugget was found at Sierra City in 1869, this little county at the north end of the Mother Lode, had a place in history books but it has always been mostly a place for a transient population. About 3,100 people live in the county today, perhaps one third of them in the sprawling city of Loyalton and only 400 in the unincorporated Downieville which is the county seat.

There are 959 square miles in the county, with the headwaters of the Yuba River and rugged Sierra mountains on the west of the summit and a 5,000 foot high plateau of grazing and hay land called Sierra Valley on the east side with timbered hills surrounding it.

Sierra Buttes, a jumble of granite rising above lakes carved by glaciers, gave the county its name. Major William Downie led a party of thirteen to settle at the forks of the Yuba and Downie Rivers. Ten of the men were blacks who had been sailors. Their camp was one of the first black settlements in California. Mining played a brief but spectacular part in the county's history and the population has never been as high as it was before the turn of the century. Now timber and livestock drive the economy, along with the forage produced in the 100-square miles of the Sierra Valley's hay fields.

ATTRACTIONS

Sierra City, on Highway 49, is between the Yuba's North Fork and the spectacular Sierra Buttes. Hard rock miners tunneled here following quartz veins long after the placer deposits were scarified by hydraulic washing which laid the river rock into spoils piles. Twenty historic buildings remain and this is a gateway to fishing and hiking in the back country.

Kentucky Mine Museum, just east of Sierra City on Highway 49, is a restored hard rock mine which includes a working stamp mill. Open Memorial Day to Labor Day Wednesday through Sunday, 10:00 a.m. to 5:00 p.m. with

650

stamp mill tours several times each day. Open weekends only in September and October and closed the rest of the year.

Loyalton, on the eastern plateau, was named in 1863 to show support of the Union in the Civil War. The town incorporated in 1901 under prohibitionist leadership with city limits covering 50 square miles--only Los Angles had a larger area at the time--to keep out saloons. A more modest city of 27 square miles was approved in 1935, and this remains the only legal city in the county. Several old buildings are located here.

Yuba Pass, the 6,701 foot crossing memorialized in a Bret Harte story of the Duchess and John Oakhurst, is now a winter ski area called **Yuba Ski Land.** Nearby lakes are famed for their trout and are dotted with resorts. Among them, seven miles north of pass is **Gold Lake,** which several hundred hopefuls came to in 1850 following stories of the banks being covered with nuggets. They didn't find any so the adventurous pushed on to discover the Plumas County deposits.

Downieville has a setting which charms visitors discovering the old town in a small basin with mountains rising all around it. At one time the entire Yuba River was diverted to flumes here so miners could work the the streambed. The town with its crooked streets remains much as it was when miners began drifting away in the mid 1860s. While many buildings are here, the original courthouse was lost to fire in 1947 along with the landmark St. Charles Hotel.

Downieville Museum, on Main Street in the 1852 Chinese store and gambling house, reopened in the summer of 1987 with volunteers. An extensive collection of Civil War guns is on display along with records of mining companies. An outdoor display of mining equipment is next to the pizza parlor. Open Memorial Day to Labor Day, 10:00 a.m. to 5:00 p.m. The unheated building is closed in the winter months.

Tahoe National Forest has twenty-five campgrounds in the county, many of them at scenic mountain lakes.

For information, including walking tour maps of many old towns and mines, contact the **Sierra County Commission for Tourism and Economic Development,** Box 473, Downieville CA 95936. Telephone (916)289-3122.

SIKIYOU COUNTY

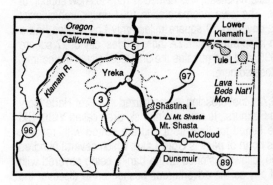

One of California's best kept secrets, Siskiyou County sprawls along its northern border with Oregon, the giant volcanic cone of Mt. Shasta on its eas-tern flanks and the scenic Marble and Salmon Mountains on the west. With 6,312 square miles, Siskiyou is a giant among the state's fifty-eight counties yet is has just a few more than 42,500 residents. Much of the county is national forest and public domain of the federal government, including a vast wilderness which extends into Trinity County to the south. The U.S. Forest Service and county government are the largest employers in the county.

Siskiyou takes its name from the Chinook jargon word for a bob-tailed horse. It was given in 1828 to the pass where I-5 now snakes into Oregon. Trappers of Alexander McLeod, chief factor of Hudson Bay Company, bestowed the name after McLeod's bob-tailed race horse died in a storm. The same trapper's route today brings highway and rail travelers by landmarks of the Siskiyous. Most of the county's population is either in this I-5 corridor, on farm land to the east which is part of the Klamath Basin, or in the interior Scott Valley with its ranches and towns left over from gold mining days. A few people live along the Klamath River where Highway 96 serves Happy Camp and other remote timber communities before winding through one of the really unsettled parts of California.

Valley floors have little winter snow, but huge packs can build on the mountains. Mount Shasta, with two commercial ski areas under development, had its previous ski bowl wiped out by an avalanche in a heavy snow year. Rainfall is eighty inches a year at the town of Mt. Shasta, just 10 inches at the Tulelake agricultural station on the far side of the mountain.

ATTRACTIONS

Mt. Shasta is one of the most-climbed peaks in the Cascade Mountains, usually a two-day effort to reach its crest 14,161 feet above sea level. The Ski

652

Shasta office in Mt. Shasta has information. In addition to the winter sports area on the south of the mountain, a cross-country ski park is on national forest land to the west. Both operate from late November through March in normal snow years.

At **Sission Hatchery,** One Old Stage Road, Mt. Shasta, is an exhibit on skiing at the mountain, the fire which wiped out the first town built here, and displays on logging. Open 10:00 a.m. to 5:00 p.m. Monday through Saturday during the summer. Winter hours are 11:30 a.m. to 3:30 p.m. Monday through Saturday plus Sunday afternoons from 1:00 to 3:30 p.m. Call 926-5508.

Mt. Shasta is home of **P&M Cedar Co.,** one of the world's largest makers of pencils. Cedar logs are purchased in a wide area, trucked here for milling at a special plant and then completed with lead and paint into the finished product--pencils.

College of the Siskiyous, at Weed, has a seismograph station in the student union building. Several sensors are placed around the flanks of Mt. Shasta by the U.S. Geologic Survey to record the frequent tremors of the slumbering volcano. Open daily. North of Weed, mounds of earth blown out by a giant eruption of Mt. Shasta can be seen from Highway 97 and I-5.

Fort Jones, site of a frontier post from 1852 to 1858, is in Scott Valley and had 544 residents at last count. The **Doll Museum** at the **Garrision Residence** on Carlock Street has over 6,000 dolls in residence. Call 486-2382 for an appointment.

There is a **town museum** at 11913 Main Street, which includes Indian and pioneer artifacts and outside is **Rain Rock,** which figures in local folklore. Open Memorial Day to the end of September from 10:00 a.m. to 4:00 p.m. Monday through Saturday.

Etna, at the far end of Scotts Valley where the road starts over the Salmon Mountains, was first settled in 1853. Several small businesses serve travelers and residents of the hills. A community of Greek Orthodox monks maintain a monastery two miles down the Salmon Mountain Road, and welcomes visitors to their small chapel which looks as if it were transported from Europe.

Happy Camp was the end of the line for years when miners and loggers traveled down the Klamath River. It was not until 1919 that the road downstream was opened and it still gets little travel. Several Indian people making their home away from the down-river Hoopa and Klamath River reservations have tribal headquarters here. Resorts serve fishermen drawn to the salmon and steelhead runs on the river. Active gold mining continues in the mountains, although the massive open-pit Norada Grey Eagle diggings, which reopened in the 1970s, are again idle.

Klamath National Forest has over 1,200 miles of foot trails. Forest headquarters at 1312 Failane Road, Yreka, have detailed maps and will provide information to persons heading for the back country. Some areas require permits. Call 842-6131 for information, or check ranger stations at Etna, Fort Jones, Oak Knoll, and Happy Camp.

The age of simple spas in the mountains lives on at **Stewart Mineral Springs Resort**, 2222 Stewart Springs Road, off I-5 just north of Weed. The hot tub is warmed by nature, part of the same geothermal system which is beneath other parts of the Mt. Shasta volcanic area. Telephone 938-2222.

For information contact the **Yreka Chamber of Commerce**, 1000 South Main Street, Yreka CA 96097. Telephone (916) 842-3779.

Mt. Shasta

Art

THE ART CENTER
315 Chestnut
Mount Shasta, CA 96096
Tel. (916) 2297
Hrs: Mon. - Sat.   9:30 a.m. - 5:15 p.m.
Mastercard and Visa are accepted.

Stretching to the heavens with it's snow covered peaks, Mount Shasta is a tremendous sight to behold. It's a work of art that can be admired for hours on end. Well, when in Mount Shasta, there's another attraction that is sure to capture your attention. The Art Center, set so appropriately in the presence of one of nature's most beautiful creations, is that captivating place.
The Art Center specializes in catering to everyone. There, you are able to choose from a large selection of giftables such as brass animals, pottery, crystal figurines, jewelry, Christmas decorations, stained glass, night lights, prints, posters, paintings and assorted greeting cards. For the beginner or

professional, The Art Center carries a full line of art supplies. Paints, brushes, cleaners, canvasses, frames, art classes, art books and even paint by numbers for children are included in the inventory.

Owner Dianne Martin is quite an artist herself. In her shop, she displays her own works alongside the paintings and photographs of several other local artists. When you pick out that favorite print or poster, Dianne, using her expertise, will frame it for your home or office. Come by and visit The Art Center, a delightful shop set in the shadow of a magnificent work of art.

(See special invitation in the Appendix.)

Delicatessen

MT. EDDY BAGEL BAKERY AND CAFE
105 East Alma Street
Mount Shasta, CA 96067
Tel.   (916) 926-2800
Hrs: Mon. - Fri.   7:30 a.m. - 3:00 p.m.
       Saturday   8:00 a.m. - 2:00 p.m.
       Closed Sunday.

Five years ago Linda Powers and Steven Mitchell were going door-to-door selling bagels and teaching people in Mount Shasta about bagels. Today, they own Mt. Eddy Bagel and Bakery Cafe, a shop where people from all over come to them to learn about and enjoy their fascinating bagel success.

The atmosphere at this bakery is informative and friendly, with it's clientele being as broad in range as is their menu. Most of the food they serve is vegetarian, but as Linda said, "In a small town we try to please everyone." They specialize in foods that are good for you. Here, you won't find pre made food or chemicals in any of the baked goods. They even make all their bagels by hand! Some of the favorites include the Mt. Eddy sandwich - cream cheese, avocado, tomato and sprouts, the pizza bagel - cheese, olives and pepperoni and then there's the bagel dog - tomato, sprouts and melted cheese. If you enjoy coffee and pastries, they've got several terrific choices.

When you're in the area, stop and see Linda and Steven. They would love for you to sit and enjoy their wonderful system and taste a true handmade bagel. Mt. Eddy Bagel Bakery and Cafe is a proven success that you're sure to enjoy.

(See special invitation in the Appendix.)

Gift

MY FAVORITE THINGS
321 North Mt. Shasta Boulevard
Mt. Shasta, CA 96067
Tel. (916) 926-6084
Hrs: Mon. - Sat.   10:00 a.m. - 5:00 p.m.
Closed on Mondays during Jan. thru May

This gift store is the kind you look for and never find. Special, unusual, fun collectables may be found along with decorative items for your home. Owner Janet Forrest has quite a few years experience in selling crafts and her displays and quality merchandise shows this fact.

My Favorite Things has post cards, handmade gifts, braided rugs, candleholders and hand-dipped candles, David Winter cottages, soaps, toys and a wide array of kitchen items and much, much more.

For quality merchandise, very friendly service and gifts that are cherishables, drop into My Favorite Things.

Restaurant

BELLISSIMO
204 A West Lake Street
Mt. Shasta, CA 96067
Tel. (916) 926-4461
Hrs.   Mon. - Thu.   9:00 a.m. - 9:00 p.m.
       Fri. - Sun.   9:00 a.m. - 10:00 p.m.

One of the nicest cafes you will visit anywhere from San Francisco to Seattle is Bellissimo's, which means "most beautiful." Owners John Jones and Michele Maggiora have created a restaurant where the food and the atmosphere live up to its name. The decor is light and cheerful with colors that give you a feeling of energy and an appreciation of the finer joys of life.

Bellissimo's menu combines the cuisine of Northern Italy, France and California. The menu changes often to provide fresh seasonal food which is both healthful and visually beautiful.   Fresh seafoods, imported pasta, homemade pizzettas, Cajun style chicken breast, Caesar salad and chicken sesame salad are but a few examples of what may be featured. Bellissimo's is also known for their Blue Ribbon desserts; chocolate mousse, excellent cheesecake and homemade fruit tarts, as well as a complete espresso, wine and beer bar.

656

"Relax and enjoy yourself while we prepare all of your food to order. We use the finest ingredients available. Celebrate with us the joys of good food and good eating," says the menu. Cafe Bellissimo is a "Best Choice" for breakfast, lunch and dinner in the beautiful community of Mt. Shasta.

MICHAEL'S RESTAURANT
313 Mount Shasta Boulevard
Mount Shasta, CA 96067
Tel.   (916) 926-5288
Hrs: Tue. - Sat.   11:00 a.m. - 9:00 p.m.
MasterCard, Visa and AMEX are accepted.

Michael's Restaurant has a beautiful view of majestic Mt. Shasta and a large variety of tempting menu choices. Imagine the delicious aromas rising from the well prepared meals, well, this and much more awaits you at Michael's.

The owners, Michael and Lynn Kobseff, take pride in giving you excellent service and the highest quality food at prices you can afford. Their many years of restaurant experience is expressed by the mouth watering selections featured in the menu. Luncheoners might wish to try a wide variety of sandwiches, soups, salads, pasta and chicken. For dinner, choose from such entrees as veal, chicken, steak, seafood or pasta.

Of course, any meal would be incomplete without one of Michael's tempting desserts. The Chocolate Moussecake, White Chocolate Moussecake and the New York style cheesecakes are just a few of the exquisite choices offered at this restaurant. Michael's, an establishment to visit when a terrific ambiance is just as important to a successful evening as is gourmet food.

Smith River

Restaurant

SHIP ASHORE RESORT
12370 Highway 101 North
Smith River, CA 95567
Tel. (707) 487- 3141
Visa, MasterCard, Diner's Club, AMEX and Discover cards.

Located where the Smith River meets the sea, Ship Ashore is an all-year resort featuring a motel, beach cottages, mobile home park, camper trailer facilities, dining and cocktails, gift shop and boat rentals and guide service. The resort lies fourteen miles south of Brookings, Oregon and

seventeen miles north of Crescent City, California. Combining the romance of
the sea, the majesty of the Redwoods, and the thrill of water sports, Ship
Ashore offers a unique blend of beauty and activities.

The resort features a rustic thirty-five unit (with fifteen more to be
ready in August, 1987) motel complete with a magnificent view of the Pacific
and several units have kitchens. There are accommodations for 300 travel
trailers and mobile homes for a long term, temporary or overnight basis, a
large recreation hall and a full time park manager and recreation director on
duty.

Ship Ashore is noted for its salmon, steelhead and trout as well as all-
year ocean fishing. The mild climate makes it ideal for boating, swimming,
hiking, berry picking, driftwood gathering, rock and mineral hunting and
breathtaking scenery abounds. For a day, a week or a lifetime, visit Ship
Ashore!

SHIP ASHORE RESORT
12370 Highway 101 N
Smith River, CA 95567
Tel. (707) 487- 3141

Located where the Smith River meets the sea, Ship Ashore is an all year
resort featuring a motel, beach cottages, mobile home park, camper trailer
facilities, dining and cocktails, sports and gift shops and boat rentals and
guide service. The resort lies fourteen miles south of Brookings, Oregon and
seventeen miles north of Crescent City, California. Combining the romance of
the sea, the majesty of the Redwoods, and the thrill of water sports, Ship
Ashore offers a unique blend of beauty and activities.

The resort features a rustic thirty-two unit motel complete with a
magnificent view of the Pacific and several units have kitchens. There are
accommodations for 300 travel trailers and mobile homes for a long term,
temporary or overnight basis, a large recreation hall and a full time park
manager and recreation director are on duty.

Ship Ashore is noted for its salmon, steelhead and trout as well as all
year ocean fishing. The mild climate makes it ideal for boating, swimming,
hiking, berry picking, driftwood gathering, rock and mineral hunting and
breathtaking scenery abounds. For a day, a week or a lifetime, visit Ship
Ashore!

Weed

Accommodation

Y RESTAURANT AND MOTEL
90 North Weed Boulevard
Weed, CA 96094
Tel. (916) 938-4481
Hrs: Summer: 6:00 a.m. - 10:30 p.m.
      Winter: 6:30 a.m. - 8:30 p.m.

Featuring breakfast, lunch and dinner, the Y Restaurant has one of the largest menus north of Sacramento. Completely owner operated, the restaurant was originally established over forty years ago out of a home and additions were added later.

The decor features some very nice painting, copies and originals, and there is a small gift shop on the premises. Open 364 days a year, there is a great deal of repeat business, and the Y's lounge is a nice quiet place to relax and enjoy a drink before dinner. The motel has twenty-two rooms, color T.V., telephones and varied sized beds to choose from.

Stop in for a meal at the Y Restaurant and peruse the extensive menu. You'll discover so many things to try you just might have to stay over and eat again the next day! (Do you suppose that's why they built the motel Martha?)!

Yreka

Some 6,700 people now live in the county seat of Siskiyou County. Gold was discovered here in 1851, the same year as southern Oregon gold strikes, and with miners already traveling the California-Oregon trail there were about 2,000 residents by 1852 when the county was created. The legislature also set by law that "Shasta Butte City" be the county seat and that it be called Yreka. The name comes from a pronunciation of the Wintun Indian name for the mountain. Most experts say the spelling used today evolved by mistake. Yreka officially incorporated as a city in 1857.

Fire swept much of the original town in 1871 and many brick buildings in the business district date from that time. Another natural disaster, a flood, washed away most of the Chinese colony which came here and contributed to construction of lengthy canals to bring water to mines.

Attractions

Yreka and Western Railroad operates **excursion trains** from here to Montague during summer months. Tickets and schedules are available at the Yreka Chamber of Commerce offices.

Over seventy-five homes from the nineteenth century remain in Yreka. The **historic district** on Third Street is included in the National Register of Historic places. Walking **tour guides,** with maps, are available at several locations in downtown. West Miner Street includes the old business district.

There's a sampling of raw native gold on display in the entrance to the **Siskiyou County Courthouse,** 311 Fourth Street. Call (916) 842-4531 for information.

Siskiyou County Museum, 910 South Main Street, has a large collection of artifacts and exhibits showing the region's past. One area is devoted to the Mt. Shasta climbs, including a party which took a horse to the top. Open Monday through Saturday 9:00 a.m. through 5:00 p.m., and Sunday afternoons 1:00 p.m. to 5:00 p.m. June 1 through September 1. Winters, closed each Monday. Call 842-3836.

For information contact the **Yreka Chamber of Commerce,** 1000 South Main Street, Yreka CA 96097. Telephone (916) 842-3779.

Accommodation

MINER'S INN, 122 East Miner Street, Yreka, California. Warm and friendly, nice, clean accommodations.

Antique

JAMES PLACE
216 3rd Street
Yreka, CA 96097
Tel. (916) 842-5454
Hrs: Mon. - Sat. 9:30 a.m. - 5:00 p.m.
Mastercard and Visa are accepted.

A pioneer family once saved twenty-four dollars to purchase a stove for their kitchen. Taking over a year to save this money was no easy task, but it was worth the sacrifice. They obtained a quality stove that would serve them in the years to come. Now, it's an antique and still retains the same quality. By visiting James Place, you can see a stove just like this and much more.

James Place, owned and operated by Mary James, is the largest single owner antique shop in the Pacific Northwest. Mary and her husband travel from the West Coast to England in pursuit of interesting items for the shop. They have just about anything you might be looking for, such as Folk art, vintage clothing, miniatures, silver, Oriental items, glass and pottery of all types and hard to find Victorian, Maxfield and Parrish prints. Also, there are great country items including wicker, quilts, stoneware, Majolica, early baskets and much more.

The shop is so large that it would take an entire day to see everything. They offer a layaway plan with no interest or carrying charges for your convenience. Come and visit James Place and see the quality the past has to offer.

Apparel

COWBOY COUNTRY
300 S Broadway
Yreka, CA 96097
Tel. (916) 842-2370
Hrs: Mon. - Sat. 10:00 a.m. - 5:30 p.m.
Visa and MasterCard are accepted.

Reigning your horse right, you bear down on the fleeing calf. Dust fills the air making it hard to breath as you swing the lasso around the calf's neck, pulling it to an abrupt halt. Leaping off the horse, you run to the roped animal, tie it off expertly and throw your hands in the air. Another prize won. Can you imagine someone performing this feat in a pair of slacks and necktie? You're right, you've got to have the proper clothing, and Cowboy Country is the place to go.

Whether you're participating in a rodeo or going to a fancy party with a country theme, Cowboy Country fills your clothing needs. They carry over 400 pairs of traditional and exotic boots including some in shark, ostrich, elephant and bullhide skin. For the young cowboy or cowgirl, there's "Grandma Grabbers" starting in size five and a half. other accessories carried are belt buckles, hats, tack, jeans and anything else needed to create a real outdoors wardrobe.

A bull can't go into a china shop for good reason. Likewise, a person can't enter a rodeo ring in a three piece suit or high heels. Saddle up Trigger and ride into Cowboy Country. You'll leave with the clothing that'll allow you to break any bronco.

Delicatessen

MINER STREET DELI
319 W Miner Street
Yreka, CA 96097
Tel. (916) 842-1854
Hrs: Mon. - Fri.   7:00 a.m. - 3:00 p.m.
     Saturday   6:30 a.m. - 12:30 p.m.

What happens when three cattle rancher's wives and a school teacher go into the delicatessen business? Well, it happened two years ago and Miner Street Deli opened it's doors as a result. It's a deli that has raised the value of a visit to the boom town of Yreka.

At Miner Street Deli, old fashioned service comes home. They specialize in homemade soups and homemade noodles, such as chicken noodle, Navy bean, vegetable beef, cream of broccoli, cream of potato and other soups that are sure to tantalize your tastebuds. Breakfast is served until 10:30 a.m. weekdays and until 12:30 p.m. on Saturday. Of course, they have all the other traditional delicatessen foods. On the walls are hand painted murals by a Russian immigrant dating back to the early 1900's, giving this deli an ambiance that can't be found elsewhere.

For special events, Miner Street Deli offers full catering service, hot or cold in all of Siskiyou county. They are also famous for their wedding cakes and receptions, sometimes delivering as far as Southern California. It's an unlikely combination, three cattle rancher's wives and a schoolteacher, a combination that has created a "Best Choice. Visit Miner Street Deli and enjoy the fine food and service that have made them what they are.

NATURE'S KITCHEN
412 S Main Street
Yreka, CA 96097
Tel. (916) 842-1136
Hrs: Mon. - Fri.   8:00 a.m. - 4:00 p.m.
     Saturday   9:00 a.m. - 3:00 p.m.

Walking the streets of Yreka, your stomach starts to grumble, a sure sign that it's time to eat. Okay, where? You're not really in the mood for an extravagant meal. That takes too long and there's so much more to see today. How about a deli? Sure, the food's good and if you want, you can take it to go. Look, up ahead, Natures Kitchen. What a coincidence.

Nature's Kitchen is a truly unique deli serving the highest quality food. All the bread is made daily from flour ground in the store. As the name implies, all the foods in the deli are natural with an emphasis on health foods. Some of the baked items include bagels, bran muffins, whole wheat cinnamon rolls and croissants. There's a terrific selection of hot and cold sandwiches, such as avocado, cream cheese on raisin, reuben and the vegie burger. For salad lovers, they've got house salad, taco salad, fruit salad and many more. If you're looking for more than a salad, the daily specials, ranging from tostadas to pizza, are deliciously filling.

The atmosphere and decor of Nature's Kitchen give you the feeling you've walked into the Garden of Eden. The plants abound in this healthy ambiance. Mmmm! Nature's Kitchen is an unexpected pleasure during any visit to Yreka.

(See special invitation in the Appendix.)

Gift

BONANZA GIFT GALLERY
312 W Miner Street
Yreka, CA 96097
Tel.   (916)   842-5131
Hrs: May - Sept.
        Mon. - Fri.   9:00 a.m. - 5:30 p.m.
        Saturday   9:00 a.m. - 5:00 p.m.
     Oct. - April
        Mon. - Fri.   9:30 a.m. - 5:30 p.m.
        Saturday   9:30 a.m. - 5:00 p.m.
MasterCard and Visa are accepted.

International travelers are well known for their assortment of strange, but fascinating odds and ends that have been acquired throughout their journeys. They are terrific conversation pieces and, at times, those without such pieces wish they could own something like that. Well, you can after one visit to Bonanza Gift Gallery in Yreka.

The owners of Bonanza Gift Gallery have done all the leg work for you by obtaining many items from all over the world during their travels. They have tapestries from Peru, shell boxes and jewelry from Africa, furniture from the Philippines, hand blown crystal from Korea, pottery from Brazil and many other items from as many countries. Also featured in this Gift Gallery, are enchanting works by Jay Young, a renowned local nature artist whose creations are structured to evoke a much earlier world.

Bonanza Gift Gallery is a shop steeped in culture and momentos of far away places. It's an exotic shopping experience that you're sure to enjoy. Stop by and obtain that conversation piece for yourself or a friend, without having to fly around the world.

(See special invitation in the Appendix.)

PATCH WORKS
321 W Miner Street
Yreka, CA 96097
Tel.   (916)   842-5544
Hrs: Mon. - Fri.   9:30 a.m. - 5:30 p.m.
          Saturday   9:30 a.m. - 5:00 p.m.
Visa, MasterCard and AMEX are accepted.

Patch Works is a shop offering gift items and yarns for knitting, crochet, cross stitch or needlepoint. They display a variety of baskets, coffee mugs, dolls, plush toys, crystal and porcelain giftables. The shop is located in the Nationally Registered Historic District. Gifts have been sold there for 130 years.

For the needlework enthusiast, the Patch Works offers lessons or help. They specialize in yarns by Brunswick, Unger, Brown Sheep and some specialty yarns. Their needlepoint yarn is Paternayan, the embroidery and cross stitch materials are from D.M.C.

The shop owners are particularly proud of their selection of fresh coffee beans. They include the several imports from Columbia, Sumatra, Kona, Java, Mexico, as well as flavored coffees such as Golden Pecan, Irish Cream, Kahlua, Chocolate Orange, Swiss Chocolate Almond and French Vanilla. Their decaffienated coffees are treated with the Swiss Water Process. It's worth your time to stop and sample the coffee and meet the friendly, down home folk at this "Best Choice" shop - Patch Works.

Restaurant

BOSTON SHAFT
1821 Fort Jones Road
Yreka, CA 96097
Tel.   (916)   842-5768
Hrs: Lunch
        Mon. - Fri.   11:00 a.m. - 2:30 p.m.
    Dinner
        Mon. - Thu.   5:00 p.m. - 9:30 p.m.
        Fri. - Sat.   5:00 p.m. - 10:00 p.m.

Interstate 5 is a long stretch of road with many travelers. When first starting on your journey, every mile is exciting, but then, after a while, the miles start to drag. Monotony sets in and the only goal in your mind is the eventual destination. It's times like this when it's nice to pull over to a place, get a good meal, relax a little and then hit the road with renewed enthusiasm. Boston Shaft restaurant in Yreka provides for this kind of stop that travelers so desperately need.

At Boston Shaft, warm decor and excellent food await you. The restaurant is owned by Max and Erich Schuler, who put their thirty years of experience into making your stay a memorable one. Their chefs are European trained and you'll find that special touch in the menu which consists of something for everyone, from veal Oscar to juicy hamburgers. Another of the features of this fine restaurant, is the weekend entertainment. For the country in you, the Cabin Room hosts a Country and Western band. If you'd rather listen to Top Forties, there is a wonderful band downstairs every weekend.

The Boston Shaft is conveniently located off Interstate 5 at the South Yreka exit. The decor, atmosphere and delicious food make this restaurant a "Best Choice" that is sure to pep up any driver.

(See special invitation in the Appendix.)

GRANDMA'S HOUSE RESTAURANT
123 E Central Street
Yreka, CA 96097
Tel.   (916) 842-5300
Hrs: Winter   Mon.-Sun.   6:00 a.m. - 9:00 p.m.
       Summer   Mon.-Sun.   6:00 a.m. - 10:00 p.m.
MasterCard and Visa are accepted.

It's a strange phenomenon that once a woman becomes a grandmother her cooking is suddenly raised a notch in the opinions of others. What is this matriarchal secret? It may never be fully known. However, it is known that Grandma's House lives up to the finest expectations of those seeking the answer to this mystery.

At Grandma's House, in business for over ten years, you can dine in an old fashioned atmosphere of Tiffany lamps and beautiful stained glass. Not only is the ambiance old fashioned, but so is the food. The buttermilk pancakes are Grandma's original recipe brought from Nebraska via covered wagon in the early 1920's. Biscuits and gravy, deli sandwiches and a terrific chicken dinner are only a few features that Grandma's has to offer. There's also a great salad bar with over ten types of already prepared salads from which to choose.

The restaurant also has a gift shop featuring glassware, lovely handcrafted items, coffee mugs, stuffed animals, books and much more. Grandma's House is indeed an old fashioned delight that will make you walk away wondering if the matriarchal mystery will ever be solved.

MING'S RESTAURANT
210 W Miner Street
Yreka, CA 96097
Tel.   (916) 842-1287
Hrs: Mon. - Fri.   11:30 a.m. - 11:00 p.m.
       Sat. - Sun.   12:00 noon - 11:00 p.m.

The first Chinese restaurant in Northern California opened in 1921 in historic downtown Yreka. Today, although remodeled, the building still carries on the tradition of fine Chinese cuisine in the form of Ming's Restaurant.

Neil Loo, the owner of Ming's, has been in the restaurant business since 1966. Making use of this valuable experience, Neil sets rigid standards for his restaurant, resulting in excellent food and a hearty selection. For lunch, you can choose from the buffet which features eight daily changing varieties or try the Szcechwan and Chengtu style dishes. One of the most popular dinner dishes is Chow Yuk, an entree of vegetables, shrimp, pork and chicken. Ming's also has traditional American steaks and seafood including Mahi Mahi, lobster, chicken

Miami and their fabulous barbecue spare ribs. There's even an exotic cocktail menu that is sure to tempt your tastebuds.

The next time you're in Yreka enjoying the historical sites, be sure to make Ming's Restaurant one of your stops. Here, you can assuage both your love for history and your desire for excellent cuisine.

NATURE'S KITCHEN
Bakery, Cafe, Natural Food Store
412 S Main Street
Yreka, CA 96097
Tel.   (916) 842-1136
Hrs: Mon. - Fri.   7:00 a.m. - 4:00 p.m.
       Saturday   8:00 a.m. - 3:00 p.m.
       Sunday   8:00 a.m. - 1:00 p.m.

Walking the streets of Yreka, your stomach starts to grumble, a sure sign that it's time to eat. Okay, where? You're not really in the mood for an extravagant meal. That takes too long and there's so much more to see today. How about a local cafe? Sure, the food's good and if you want, you can take it to go. Look, up ahead, Natures Kitchen. What a coincidence.

Nature's Kitchen is a truly unique cafe serving the highest quality food. All the bread is made daily from flour ground in the store. As the name implies, all the foods in the cafe are natural with an emphasis on health foods. Some of the baked items include bagels, bran muffins, whole wheat cinnamon rolls and croissants. Start your day off with a terrific breakfast or drop in a lunch time, there's a terrific selection of hot and cold sandwiches, such as avocado, cream cheese on raisin, reuben and the vegie burger. For salad lovers, they've got house salad, taco salad, fruit salad and many more. If you're looking for more than a salad, the daily specials, ranging from tostadas to pizza, are deliciously filling.

The atmosphere and decor of Nature's Kitchen give you the feeling you've walked into the Garden of Eden. The plants abound in this healthy ambiance. Mmmm! Nature's Kitchen is an unexpected pleasure during any visit to Yreka.

(See special invitation in the Appendix.)

YREKA BAKERY & CAFE
322 West Miner
Yreka, CA 96097
Tel. (916) 842-2440
Hrs: Mon. - Sat.   7:00 a.m. - 2:30 p.m.
        Sunday   8:00 a.m. - 2:00 p.m.

There is a lot of interesting history in Yreka and this bakery is in the local history books. It's a palindrome.

Barbara Mitchell, the owner, has created a relaxing, homey atmosphere within this cafe. A local art display and wilderness photography by Richard Silva decorate the walls. Hanging plants, bright sunshine and a warm, crackling fire in the wood stove add to your comfort.

All the food items here are made from scratch. The eggs Benedict are a specialty of the house, or try the French toast almondine with pure maple syrup or orange cinnamon syrup. Create your own omelet and have your favorite ingredients added.

Every day Barbara has a special dinner. On Monday it's barbecued chicken and homemade beans; Tuesday features Italian manicotti, which are pasta shells filled with fresh ricotta and Parmesan cheese, seasoned with basil and nutmeg, add sausage and ground beef, dress with a mellow marinara sauce and slices of melted mozzerella. *Buon appetite*. Wednesday there's a Mexican enchilada plate with freshly made salsa; on Thursday its Greek Moussaka; Friday your palate travels to France for Coquelle St. Jacques, which are succulent bites of scallops, fresh mushrooms and green onions sauteed in a creamed sherry sauce and then topped with Parmesan cheese and lightly broiled. *Salut*.

To complement your meals there's fresh ground coffee or a tea list that is longer than most restaurant's wine list. Homemade pies and pastries are presented for the grand finale to your meal.

Oh yes, back to palindrome...it's when the word spelled backwards is another word spelled frontwards. Think about it...anyway, it seems the local history to this area is that the town originally did not have a name...it did have a bakery though. So, one day a miner was cogitating on a name for the town, happened to spell bakery backwards, couldn't pronounce it, so he dropped the "B" and, YREKA was named. Cute, huh?

The Yreka Bakery & Cafe, any way you spell it, a "Best Choice" for homestyle food and fun.

Sport

DON'S SPORTING GOODS
321 W Miner Street
Yreka, CA 96097
Tel.   (916) 842-5152
Hrs: Mon. - Fri.   8:00 a.m. - 6:00 p.m.
           Saturday   8:00 a.m. - 5:30 p.m.
MasterCard and Visa are accepted.

Goodness, what a day it's been! You've been fishing and caught a whopper. Then, there was that game of softball where you hit three home runs. And then,...wait, what's that noise? Oh no, it's the alarm clock. You dreamt the whole thing. Well, before you get too disappointed, go visit Don's Sporting Goods to get the equipment needed to make your dream a reality.

Don's Sporting Goods is owned and operated by Drake and Cara Davis, pride themselves on the uniqueness of their shop. There's a coffee bar where you can enjoy fresh coffee and donuts while you feast your eyes on the third largest elk recorded in Oregon. Many other animals are mounted including deer, geese, bear, antelope, Bighorn sheep and even two deer with their horns locked in battle. Whether you're an amateur or a professionally minded sportsman, you'll find Don's carries a full line of sporting goods, such as hunting accessories, athletic equipment, fishing tackle, camping gear and much more.

It's easy to dream about great sporting feats while sitting in the armchair, but it's quite a different subject when it comes to performing them. Wake up and come down to Don's Sporting Goods for a dream come true.

(See special invitation in the Appendix.)

TOUR OF YREKA

a.m.	Yreka Bakery	Best breakfast	Yre/Rest
a.m.	Grandma House	Best pancakes	Yre/Rest
a.m.	Don's	Best sport goods	Yre/Sport
a.m.	Bonanza Gift	Best collectibles	Yre/Gift
a.m.	Cowboy Country	Best clothes	Yre/App
Take your choice of a family deli lunch:			
p.m.	Miner Street	Best soup	Yre/Deli
p.m.	Nature's Kitchen	Best bread	Yre/Deli
Then resume your tour:			
p.m.	Patch Works	Best knitcrafts	Yre/Need
p.m.	James Place	Best antique	Yre/Ant
Top your day with a top of the line dinner at:			
p.m.	Boston Shaft	Best full menu	Yre/Rest
p.m.	Ming's Dynasty	Best Szcechwan	Yre/Rest

SOLANO COUNTY

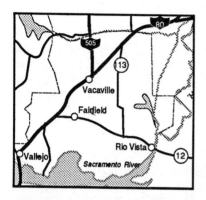

The northern arm of San Francisco Bay, and the Sacramento river which empties into it, form major boun-daries for this 834 square mile county. About 236,000 people live here and the military plays a major role in the local economy with the massive Mare Island Naval Shipyard at Vallejo, and Travis Air Force Base on the outskirts of the county seat of Fairfield, Benicia and Rio Vista both provided U.S. Army logistical support until recent years and a Navy mothball fleet swings on the mooring buoys of Suisun Bay.

Sem Yeto, chief of the Patwin Indian tribe, was given the name Francisco Solano by Franciscan missionaries. That name went with the country as huge ranchos developed, including one of the largest ever, the 284,000 acre El Sobrante in the north county. Solano is one of the original twenty seven counties formed after statehood. Benicia in the Carquinez Straits was picked for a major naval anchorage by early military surveyors. A location close to the Contra Costa plants turning out explosives for gold miners made the port convenient for loading warships with ammunition. Army resupply of troops fighting in the Pacific went through the arsenal, and small boats for army use were serviced upstream at the Rio Vista Depot.

The coming of the California Pacific Railroad created Vacaville as an important produce shipping point. Today, with trucks the major transportation means and I-80 and a short link to I-5, Vacaville continues that role as processor and shipper for the western reaches of the rich Sacramento Valley.

ATTRACTIONS

Lake Solano County Park, Highway 128 west of Winters, provides water recreation on a small scale. It links with the giant Lake Berryessa reservoir, part of the California Water Project, which has a resort and several boat launching ramps.

Benicia

With a pleasant little bay at its door step, and two interstate highway bridges nearby over the Carquinez Strait, Benicia is enjoying a resurgence these days. About 19,000 people live here, many of them returning to the Victorian houses being restored near the waterfront.

This is another of the many towns founded by General Mariano Vallejo, the Mexican officer who saw Northern California through days of the Bear Republic into statehood. Vallejo deeded the town site in 1846. By 1849 it was a busy way point to the mines, a deep water port which missed the congestion of San Francisco. It became state capital for a time after the legislature tired of San Jose.

Attractions

In downtown Benicia is the **original capitol building**, restored in 1956-57. The original was put up in three months time to be ready for the legislative session opening in January, 1853. The Greek temple architecture was originally supported by columns fashioned from ship's masts.

The **Benicia Arsenal**, around the bay a bit from town, was put to military use in 1849. This was a major ammunition supply point for warships

The first **Presbyterian Church** in California was located at First and K streets, now the Municipal Park. Across the street were a Catholic seminary moved here from Monterey in 1854, and the house of the Episcopal bishop of Northern California.

The **Yuba Manufacturing complex**, 670 East H Street, contains several shops. Among them is Yuba Arts, a group of three glass studios. Show rooms are open Monday through Friday from 10:00 a.m. to 4:00 p.m. Telephone (707) 745-1463.

For more information, contact the **Benicia Chamber of Commerce**, Box 185, Benicia, CA 94510. Telephone (707) 745-2120.

Fairfield

The Suisun River, a long arm reaching northward from Suisun Bay and the Carquinez Straits, determined where this community would be located. Josiah Wing picked the head of navigation for his embarcadero of 1850, and it

672

became Suisun City, but the larger Fairfield community soon dominated. There was a flour mill in 1854, and the town was platted in 1856, named after Fairfield, Connecticut, where developer Robert Waterman grew up. The county seat moved here from Benicia in 1858.

Travis Air Force Base is part of Fairfield, and with 14,000 air force and civilian personnel, it is the largest employer in the county. Started in 1942 as one of many West Coast air fields, it was later named for Robert F. Travis, the base commander who died in a 1950 airplane crash.

Attractions

Six miles south of Fairfield on the old highway (U.S. 40) on the right hand side of the road is a **bronze statue of Francisco Solano**, the Indian chief after whom the county is named. It is near the site of the large adobe Solano built on a land grant arranged for him by the Spanish.

For information contact the **Fairfield Chamber of Commerce**, 1111 Webster Street, Fairfield CA 94533. Telephone (707) 425-4625.

Candy

THE HERMAN GOELITZ CANDY COMPANY
2400 North Watney Way
Fairfield, CA 94533
Tel. (707) 428-2800

Send your sweet tooth to candy heaven by visiting the candy wonderland of the Herman Goelitz Candy Company, one of the largest manufacturer of gourmet confections in the United States. Experience a 113-year legacy of quality candy-making, including the infamous "Jelly Belly" jelly bean, President Reagan's favorite.

Throughout the Goelitz family's candy-making history, their goal of making the best quality piece of candy on the market, regardless of cost, has been the secret of their phenomenal success. Their insistence on the highest possible standards can be verified by tantilizing your taste buds on such delectable morsels as jelly beans, Dutch mints™, both chocolate and licorice bridge mix, jordan almonds, boston baked beans, French peanuts and a host of others. The huge automated plant, including a computerized kitchen, is a remarkable sight to see, and the beautiful retail store features everything Goelitz makes - and samples, too!

Become part of candy-making history at this "Best Choice" for superb gourmet confections. Sample the goodies and take the tour, (by reservations only, miniumum groups of ten, no children under six years of age) but be sure and ask about the amazing "Jelly Belly" jelly bean story!

Vacaville

About 48,000 now live in this crossroads agricultural center which has grown rapidly in the 1980s. Incorporated in 1892 with about 1,500 population, Vacaville remained a small fruit and nut trade center for the next sixty years. Irrigation delivered through projects completed in 1957, boosted fruit production to levels few thought possible.

Government remains a significant employer here, with Travis Air Force Base near by, and California's Medical Facility where incoming prisoners are classified before assignment to state prisons scattered throughout the state.

Attractions

The Nut Tree, a popular stop for travelers, is at the junction of I-80 and I-505, the link northward to I-5. Started in 1921, the place has grown to a large plaza with train rides, entertainment and large gift shop. Open twenty-four hours, daily.

For information contact the **Vacaville Chamber of Commerce**, 400 East Monte Vista Avenue, Vacaville CA 95688. Telephone (707) 448-6424.

Restaurant

NUT TREE
From Sacramento   I-80 and Monte Vista Avenue
From San Francisco I-80 and Nut Tree Road
Vacaville, CA 95696
Tel.   (707) 448-6411
          (707) 448-1818 Restaurant reservations.
          (707) 448-1818 Coffee Tree Restaurant.
Hrs.   Store   Mon. - Sun.   7:00 a.m. - 9:30 p.m.
Nut Tree Rest.   Mon. - Sun.   7:00 a.m. - 9:00 p.m.
Coffee Tree Rest.   Mon. - Sun.   5:30 a.m. - 12:00 mid
Open everyday except Christmas, extended hours in Summer.
Visa, MasterCard and AMEX are accepted.

In 1851, Josiah Allison went west in search of gold, but like so many others, he soon discovered that the promise of instant wealth was elusive at best. The real treasure he found was the climate and soil of Northern California. Josiah's niece, Sally Fox, gave him a black walnut that she had found while traveling along the Gila River. The tree that sprang from Sally's walnut was cherished, not only by the pioneer family, but also for its welcome shade given to many a traveler of the hot Sacramento Valley. From this modest beginning grew what is now Nut Tree, California.

Over the years, originally starting with a fruit stand, many facilities have been added. The Nut Tree Restaurant features homemade bread, fresh fruits and vegetables and marvelous "Western Cuisine." In 1952, the Toy Shop was built and in 1955, the Nut Tree Railroad was extended to meet flyers at the airport. For the convenience of travelers along I-80, the Coffee Tree coffee shop was added across from the original site. For your enjoyment there is an Ice Cream Pavillion, a Sandwich Garden and the Good Time Barbeque which features outdoor dinner dances every Friday night from July through mid September. Throughout October there is The Pumpkin Patch and Great Scaregrow Contest.

If you are a road weary traveler looking for a good meal, be sure to stop and enjoy the fare at this restaurant. The Nut Tree was the forerunner of what is now called "California Cuisine." The menu has been built upon their own homegrown, fresh fruits and vegetables, all the bakery and dessert offering are made from scratch. The emphasis at the Nut Tree is on providing a place to relax and enjoy the quality of the food and the entertainment. Convenient access from I-80, and plenty of parking make this an easy, fun stop on your travels.

Vallejo

Industry throbs through this north bay city of 87,000 located at the mouth of the Napa River. The Mare Island Naval Ship Yard, located by itself on the river's west bank, does major ship repairs and overhauls submarines. It is the city's largest employer.

The city, which has some restored Victorian and Georgian homes, was laid out by Mariano Vallejo in 1850, the first full year of California state hood. It served as an interim capital for the state while the offices in Benicia were decided on and built. Vallejo called the place Eureka on his plat, but the Californians decided the town should honor the general and made Vallejo the official name in March, 1851.

675

Solano County

Attractions

Marine World Africa USA, 1000 Fairgrounds Drive, relocated to new quarters on the north side of Vallejo recently. The theme park has several aquarium exhibits, performing whales and dolphins. Open Daily. Telephone (707) 643-ORCA.

For information, contact the **Vallejo Chamber of Commerce,** 2 Florida Street, Vallejo CA 94590. Telephone (707) 644-5551.

676

SONOMA COUNTY

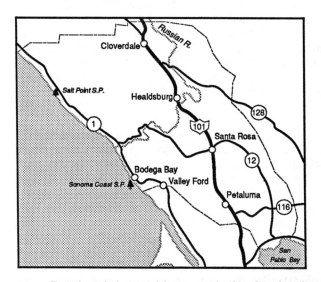

Fog-shrouded coastal bays, sandy river beaches beneath towering redwood forests, apple orchards marching over hills to meet pastures green with feed for dairy cattle, and dry hills with neat vineyards and dark-green oak trees set the scene for this 1,579 square mile county. It rises from the north shore of San Francisco Bay. People, in the fast-growing metropolis of Santa Rosa, tell the story of dramatic growth. Amid the pastoral setting steeped in history is a spreading regional center with over 100,000 residents, now buzzing with light manufacturing and large office complexes.

Russians came ashore in 1812 at Fort Ross to make the first major settlement of Europeans on the West Coast. For twenty years they resupplied their ships in the Alaskan fur trade with produce and livestock grown on the coastal plateau. Spanish padres setting their chain of missions to the Indians put up their last adobe at Sonoma in 1823, a reaction to the Russian presence. Twenty-three years later in the peaceful square of this little town Americans declared their Bear Flag Republic, took prisoner Mariano Vallejo and then enlisted the wealthy land-owner's support in a movement which led to statehood. Jack London wrote stories from a cabin overlooking the vineyards of Glenn Ellen. Luther Burbank conducted his botanical research on four acres which were at the outskirts of Santa Rosa. Count Agoston Haraszthy brought

677

his cuttings of European grapes to the Sonoma Valley after having little success with plantings made in 1852 in San Mateo County, giving birth to California's wine industry which had been little more than vintage for the Franciscan up to that time.

The land upon which events took place is as diverse as the happenings. Rolling down from the north, the Russian River drains a huge basin of the coast range before reaching Sonoma County and turning west through a corridor of redwood timberland to reach the Pacific Ocean at Jenner. Over the hills which sop up the coastal moisture is the Santa Rosa Valley that drains into the Petaluma River and San Pablo Bay, the north arm of San Francisco Bay. Another ridge of hills, protecting even more the final valley, shelter the Sonoma Creek drainage where many of the vineyards bask in near ideal growing conditions.

Geologically, the county has reminders of a volcanic heritage. Much of Santa Rosa's downtown is new construction replacing buildings cracked by a major earthquake three decades ago. Rogers-Healdsburg fault runs from north to south in the most populous part of the county. At the fault's northern end is the edge of the steaming Geysers Geothermal Field with twenty electric power turbines whirring away driven by nature's super-heated water. Where creeks and unlined irrigation ditches wander across the flatter lands, erosion has cut stream-beds far below the surface and deposited soil in sometimes swampy deltas where both Petaluma River and Sonoma Creek spill into San Pablo Bay.

Even with extensive storage reservoirs in upstream reaches, the Russian River retains a potential for flooding. Water from the Eel River basin is now diverted to the Russian River to sustain irrigation and summer flows which in years past sometimes saw the stream dried to puddles at Healdsburg. Santa Rosa itself has a network of reservoirs to store water for municipal use and take the edge off flashy storm runoffs in urban areas.

The Santa Rosa Valley's agriculture is varied, with most of its produce going to market within the bay area. Milk production is near the top of annual reports on source of farm income. Poultry remains strong, although the now bustling city of Petaluma has long since stopped promoting itself as chicken capital of the world. Gravenstein apples from Sebastopol orchards head for the fresh fruit market, while other fruit crops are dried in processing facilities located in the Russian River Valley. Sonoma Valley wine grapes, like high quality grapes grown elsewhere in the county, are likely to be crushed by vintners at local vineyards rather than sold to other wineries.

For all of the commercial and agricultural activity, Sonoma County is also a top destination for tourists. Bodega Bay. an historic small port at the south county line, anchors a chain of county-owned beaches extending north to the mouth of the Russian River. Several resorts, including the exclusive

Bohemian Grove, are located on the sun-drenched Russian River where redwood trees provide shade for instant cooling. Major motor raceways are at Sears Point and Cotati. The wineries are more accessible than many in the Napa Valley to the east. And, in Sonoma County, history is preserved from the quaint square and old mission of Sonoma to the replica of the Russian's Fort Ross.

ATTRACTIONS

The wineries of Sonoma County are a major attraction. The Winegrowers of California, through their **Wine Institute**, 165 Post Street, San Francisco, CA 94108 produce a special winery travel guide. Telephone (4l5) 986-0878.

Jack London State Historic Park is at the little town of Glenn Ellen on a hill rising above the vineyards. Included in the near 800-acre park is a house which burned under construction in 1912 that the author left uncompleted at the time of his death. His widow Charmain's home of native stone, built in 1919, holds London's manuscripts and other memorabilia. Park open daily 8:00 a.m. to sunset, the museum in Charmain's house open 10:00 a.m. to 5:00 p.m. Telephone 938-5216.

High above Kenwood, on the ridge dividing the Napa and Sonoma Valleys, is **Sugarloaf Ridge State Park**. One of the county's regional parks, Hood, connects to the north. Camping, hiking and nature trails are available with sweeping views to San Francisco Bay and into the valleys. Call 833-5712.

The regional **Hood Park** is only opened on weekends, from 8:00 a.m. to sunset. Reach Sugarloaf Ridge on the twisting Adobe Canyon Road off of Highway 12. To drive to Hood Park, use Los Alamos Road to reach a fee parking lot.

The days of Spanish land grants come alive at **Petaluma Adobe State Historical Park,** four miles east of Petaluma on Old Redwood Highway. Gen. Vallejo's old fort and home has replica and restorations of 1830-era furnishings. Early crafts are shown, live animals kept, and several special events staged each year. Open daily 10:00 a.m. to 5:00 p.m. except for holidays. Call 762-4871.

Petaluma itself is worth a look when you find the old downtown and residential areas after entering through modern urban sprawl. A walking tour and several tours of manufacturing plants are available by contacting the

Petaluma Chamber of Commerce, 314 Western Avenue, Petaluma CA 94952. Telephone 762-2785.

Petaluma Historical Library and Museum, 20 Fourth Street, Petaluma, is open Monday through Saturday from 11:00 a.m. to 4:00 p.m. Telephone 778-4398.

The lower **Russian River Valley** around Healdsburg was once a major orchard area. Now grapes are taking over the acreage and there are fifty wineries within a short drive from the center of town. A city beach on the Russian River has canoe rentals and is a popular swimming spot. On Highway 101. Contact the **Healdsburg Chamber of Commerce**, 217 Healdsburg Avenue, Healdsburg CA 95448. Telephone 433-6935.

Healdsburg Museum, 132 Matheson Street, Healdsburg, is open Monday through Friday from 12:00 noon to 5:00 p.m. and Saturday from 1:00 p.m. to 4:00 p.m. Telephone 431-3325.

Trowbridge Recreation, Inc., 20 Healdsburg Avenue in Healdsburg, operates a canoe pickup and delivery service for those planning multi-day paddle trips on the Russian River. Service April through October. Call Telephone 433-7247.

Geyserville on Highway 101 in the northern county is another winery center. This is an access point to the remote **Geysers Geothermal area** located on Geysers Road to the east. A viewpoint and interpretive material at one producing geothermal well gives history of the massive area which is partly in Lake County. Take Highway 128 either from north of Geyserville or from Alexander Valley Road out of Healdsburg, then follow the winding Geysers Road into the foothills, a fifteen mile trip. Geysers Road loops around to join Highway 101 at Cloverdale, a small farming community.

The **Isaac E. Shaw House**, 215 North Cloverdale Boulevard, Cloverdale, is a restored home turned into a local museum of the north county. Open Tuesday through Friday from 10:00 a.m. to 3:00 p.m., or by appointment. Call 894-2067.

Sebastopol, on Highway 12 west of Santa Rosa, is in the heart of the county's Gravenstein apple orchards. Downtown buildings have a flavor of the 1920s, and a Buddhist Temple on Highway 116 attracts the curious as well as the faithful. Contact the **Sebastopol Chamber of Commerce**, 265 South Main Street, Sebastopol CA 95472. Telephone 823-3032.

Carriage Charter, 3325 Gravenstein Highway North, Sebastopol, operates a horse-drawn tours of the farms and vineyards. Daily, except Saturday. Tours are by reservation. Call 800-448-0888.

Bodega Bay, a small commercial and sportsfishing harbor on the coast just five miles north of the county line, has a rich history. Coastguardsmen now watch where smugglers were once supposed to have operated. The bay is named after Juan Francisco de la Bodega y Cuadra, who sailed the schooner Sonora beneath the headlands in October 1775. Bodega's cross, fashioned from a pole and the stave from a cask, was on the head when an English naturalist came ashore in 1793. The site is now permanently marked.

Bodega Head State Park is still under construction. Several other parks and boat launching sites are nearby. Telephone 865-2391 for information on campgrounds and park facilities. The **University of California Marine Laboratory** is open for tours each Friday at 2:00 p.m.

Duncan Mills, a small town on Highway 116 five miles from the mouth of Russian River, features several restored buildings from the 1880s. A **museum** is in the old railroad depot. Several commercial recreation attractions are here. This is the district headquarters for California State Parks' coastal area, and the offices have extensive information for visitors.

Armstrong Grove State Recreation Area, on Armstrong Woods Road two miles north of Guerneville, is a 752 acre basin of redwood trees tucked between the hills. Hiking paths lead into the larger **Austin Creek Recreation Area** to the north where 4,236 acres are set aside for primitive camping and horse back riding. Call 869-2015. There is no potable water in Austin Creek.

Fort Ross, on Highway 1 north of Jenner, is restored to the way it looked shortly after Russians set up farming here in 1812. Exhibits tell the story of growing food for the sea-going fur traders who had suffered scurvy from ship's food while in the Alaskan trade. Some living history exhibits act out early days at Fort Ross. Open daily, 10:00 a.m. to 4:30 p.m. Telephone 847-3286.

Bodega Bay

Accommodation

BODEGA BAY LODGE BEST WESTERN
Coast Highway #1
Bodega Bay, CA 94923
Tel.   (707) 875-3525
       (800) 368-2468
All major credit cards accepted.

Located sixty-eight miles north of San Fransico on the spectacular Sonoma Coast, is Bodega Bay. This place is well known for many things including the site for the filming of Alfred Hitchcock's movie "The Birds." It's also the home to Bodega Bay Lodge, a beautiful accommodation located in an unspoiled coastal region overlooking the Doran Park beaches and bird filled marshes.

This lodge bids you welcome as you check into your room with a private balcony permitting sweeping views of the bay and magnificent, pink sunsets. All the rooms are accentuated with fireplaces, wicker and oak furnishings and blossoming plants. Relax, sheltered from the crashing surf while enjoying the whirlpool spa and swimming pool just a few steps from your room. There are many local features for entertainment including deep sea fishing, whale watching, golfing, hiking and many others. For meals, The Bodega Bay has it's own food service, as well as a terrific local restaurant guide.

If you're looking for place for meeting or seminars, the lodge has professional meeting facilities designed to complement the tranquility of the coastal setting. Whatever the need, Bodega Bay Lodge is sure to satisfy. Oh, "The Birds" are friendly now.

THE INN AT THE TIDES
800 Coast Highway
Bodega Bay, CA 94923
Tel. (707) 875-2751
AMEX, Mastercard and Visa are accepted.

Americans are famous for their vacations, a specified time of the year to get away from the hustle and bustle of everyday life. It's a very important subject in the lives of many, requiring much thought as to where the vacation is to be spent. This is why many go to The Inn at the Tides in Bodega Bay for an enjoyable getaway.

The Inn at the Tides is an enclave of luxuriously appointed guest lodges, only sixty-five miles north of San Fransisco. All accommodations have bay views and most with fireplaces, skylights and vaulted ceilings. Guest services include complimentary firewood delivery, laundry facilities, room service, health spa with indoor/outdoor swimming pool and daily Continental breakfast with newspaper. For dining, The Bay View Room and Lounge is a fine restaurant featuring California Continental cuisine, with adjoining lounge and bar.

If your visit is business oriented, there's over 2,400 square feet of meeting/function space located in two separate areas with fireplaces, skylights and bay views. Whether you go for business or a vacation, at The Inn at the Tides you will not want for comfort and service. However high your expectations, The Inn at the Tide's accommodations will live up to them.

Santa Rosa

By annexation and new residential construction, Santa Rosa seems to keep growing at a rate far exceeding most California cities. The 1987 population of more than 100,000 compares with a 1983 estimate of 88,000 residents. Since early times, this has been a crossroads. Highway 101 is a freeway from far north of here and for the fifty-two miles to San Francisco. Highway 12 gives east-west travelers a much slower passage through agricultural areas of the county, linking the coast with Napa.

Retail trade continues to be significant in the local economy, but health care and the electronics industries have taken significant positions in recent years. Hewlett Packard has almost 3,100 people working at plants here that produce computers. Most of Sonoma County government's 3.100 employees also live in Santa Rosa, the county seat.

The city's name comes from two Spanish grants, Rancho Cabeza de Santa Rosa and Rancho Llano de Santa Rosa, both held by relatives of Mariano Vallejo. Near the corner of Hartley Drive and Franquette Avenue, on property owned by the Diocese of Santa Rosa, is the one remaining building from the ranch owned by Vallejo's widowed mother-in-law who moved here sometime after 1837.

Santa Rosa's civic center, and the adjoining covered shopping mall, have a modern look to them which tells a story of massive urban renewal carried out since the 1950s. A major earthquake brought condemnation of many large buildings, providing the impetus for the redevelopment work. The city now has thirty six parks within its limits, plus playgrounds at twenty-nine schools.

683

Attractions

Annadel State Park, on Annadel Drive East, is a near 5,000 acre collection of hiking, biking and horse trails around a small lake. This is a favorite area for bird watchers. Open daily, one hour before sunrise to one hour after sunset. Telephone 539-3911.

The old **First Baptist Church,** relocated to Ellis Street near Juilliard Park, is said to be build from lumber milled from a single redwood street. Originally built in 1873, the church was erected on B Street between Fifth and Sixth. It is now the **Ripley Memorial Museum.** Work of Robert Ripley, the cartoonist who wrote "Believe it or Not," is on display. Open from May 16 through August 31, daily from 11:00 a.m. to 4:00 p.m. The remainder of the year open Thursday through Monday only, same hours. Telephone 528-5233.

Sonoma County Museum, 425 Seventh Street, is in the old post office building. Open Wednesday through Sunday, 11:00 a.m. to 4:00 p.m. Telephone 579-1500.

Right next to the civic center is **Luther Burbank Park,** on Sonoma Avenue. Many of the hybrids the famed botanist developed on his farm at the city's borders are now on display in the gardens which are open daily. Burbank's home, part of the park, is open by appointment. Telephone 576-5115.

Codding Museum of Natural History, 557 Summerfield Road, features plants and creatures of the north bay and coast range. Open Tuesday through Thursday, and Saturday and Sunday, 1:00 p.m. to 5:00 p.m. Telephone 539-0556.

For further information, contact the **Santa Rosa Chamber of Commerce,** 637 First Street, Santa Rosa CA 95404. Telephone 545-1414.

Sonoma

This was flat country, drained by a meandering creek which snaked eight miles to San Pablo Bay, when the Franciscan fathers were told to move north and check the possible advance of the Russian Fort Ross colony. The valley of Sonoma Creek is about five miles wide, and seventeen miles long. It was in 1823 that Jose Altimira brought his Indian neophytes and began construction of the last of the California missions. When Mexicans ordered secularization of mission property in 1834, Mariano Vallejo was on hand, the leader of the pueblo, or town, of Sonoma which was chartered in 1835. The old mission was deeded to the state in 1903, and is now cornerstone of an historic state park.

The Mexican garrison figured in the 1846 Bear Flag revolt when a group of thirty-three men surprised Vallejo here, and took possession of the fortified town. In the center of the plaza is a bronze statue commemorating the revolt, which was a prelude to California's statehood. Vallejo, who had many properties in Northern California, stayed on despite two months' captivity at the hands of the Bear Flaggers, and his home is part of the park.

Victorian mansions and brightly-painted commercial buildings restored to their early-day styles attract thousands of visitors to Sonoma. The places are all within easy walking distance. Vineyards surround the town. On the south side is the massive Sonoma State Hospital where nearly 2,000 people care for patients. About 7,000 people live in Sonoma itself. The smaller communities of Boyes Hot Springs, Glen Ellen and others have at least that many residents.

Attractions

Depot Park Historical Museum, 285 West First, supplements the state historic park's interpretation of Sonoma's history. Open Wednesday through Sunday, from 1:00 p.m. to 4:30 p.m. Telephone 938-5389.

In an area with many wineries, the **Buena Vista**, one mile northeast of town on Old Winery Road, stands out. This is where California's commercial wine production began after research by an Hungarian count. The casks for aging the fermented wine are in cool caves dug into the hillside. A museum and tasting room are on the grounds. Open daily.

General Mariano Vallejo lived many places in Northern California, but the gothic house here at Spain and Third Street is his last home. Part of **Sonoma State Historic Park,** the big house has a museum next to it, gardens and the cottage in which Napoleon Vallejo once lived. Open daily 10:00 a.m. to 5:00 p.m. Call 938-1578.

Two blocks away, on First Street, also part of the park, are the last Franciscan Mission established in California, an old hotel which dates to Mexican times, the barracks which figured in the Bear Flag revolt of 1846, and the site of Gen. Vallejo's first home in Sonoma.

685

Sonoma Cheese Factory is on the plaza. The family-operated plant, home of Sonoma Jack cheeses, has branched into the deli business in recent year, catering to picnickers and those strolling the plaza. Telephone 996-1931.

The former spa town of **Boyes Hot Springs** is just west of Sonoma on Highway 12. A twenty-two acre **Bouverie Wildflower Preserve** draws visitors in the early spring. Several shops and restaurants are clustered in the town center where the mineral springs used to attract long-term visitors.

For information, contact the **Sonoma Valley Chamber of Commerce**, 453 First Street East, Sonoma CA 95476. Telephone 996-1090.

Valley Ford

Accommodation

SONOMA COAST VILLA AND RESTAURANT
Coast Highway One
Valley Ford, CA 94972
Tel.   (707)   876-3225

On the pleasant route of Coastal Highway One, only two miles north of Valley Ford and in sight of the small village of Bodega Bay, lies Sonoma Coast Villa and Restaurant. Situated in the heart of gently sloping hillsides, the villa captures the tranquility of the surrounding area. It's an elegant retreat for a small number of guests desirous of experiencing the simple grace of country living.

Six well appointed, double occupancy suites are arranged around a crystal clear swimming pool. All are complete with fireplace, telephone and state of the art satellite television. They each have direct access to an indoor jacuzzi. The dining and social rooms all offer comfortable antique furnishings and 19th century sculptures and prints. The food is a major part of the attractions at Sonoma Coast Villa and Restaurant. The concept of freshness is meticulously maintained with Sonoma fresh produce, fresh country goose and duckling, fresh seafood in season and freshly prepared desserts and pastries.

Sonoma Coast Villa and Restaurant, an experience that is not rivalled elsewhere. Stop by and create lasting memories of time well spent.

TEHAMA COUNTY

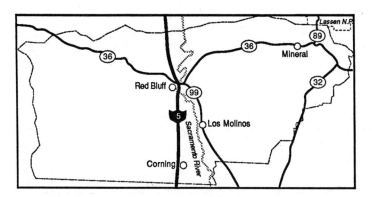

From foothills to the coast range to foothills of the Sierras, Tehama County spreads itself across the Sacramento Valley's upper reaches, enclosing 2,953 square miles of rolling hills and flat flood plains of the Sacramento River. The population is concentrated along the river corridor, which is also the route of modern I-5. Spanish explorers followed the same route northward as early as 1821, and two notables in area history, John Bidwell and Peter Lassen came here in 1843--chasing some horse thieves. Lassen later asked the Mexican government for the first land grant in what became Tehama County in 1856. By that time he had left for the east side of the Sierras and a home which later was the basis for naming Lassen County.

This is a country of hot, dry summers. About twenty-two inches of rain fall in the winter months on the valley floor, with the hill areas on both sides of the vast valley getting fifty inches in the same time. Irrigation from the state water project has changed the nature of agriculture here from its old base of cattle and sheep to more cultivated crops and orchards. Corning, in the south county, styles itself the "olive capital" of the state. Red Bluff, the largest city in this county of 39,000 people, remains with the livestock tradition and is home to a regional auction yard that draws producers from as far away as Oregon.

ATTRACTIONS

The **Sacramento River** and **Black Butte Reservoir** provide dispersed water sport areas and are popular for fishing. Boat launching ramps are scattered along the river.

Woodson Bridge State Recreation Area, six miles east of Corning on South Avenue, is a regional park at the river. Developed campsites are available, and the whole park is shaded by giant cottonwood trees which take the edge off summer heat. Call 839-2112.

Vina, a small community eighteen miles south of Red Bluff where Deer Creek flows into the Sacramento River from the east, is the site of **Lassen's Rancho Bosquejo** where a trading post was set up and hundreds of Indians made camp. A town, Benton City, was started here and a Masonic lodge chartered in May 1848. A monument beside Highway 99 just north of Deer Creek recalls California's first Masonic lodge. Leland Stanford, the railroad builder and politician, later bought much of the Lassen rancho as part of his 55,000 acre Vina Ranch which in 1885 had the largest vineyard in the world. It was later given to the Stanford University endowment. The **New Clairvaux Trappist Monastery** is on a corner of the grant, and welcomes visitors.

Tehama, which is an Indian name, also belongs to the first town that really was established -- **Benton City** floundered because its inhabitants went off to seek gold. Located on the Sacramento's west bank twelve miles south of Red Bluff, Tehama was the ferry crossing for a road between Marysville and the gold mines at Shasta. It's importance was brief after founding in 1849 because in 1850 a river steamer began calling at Red Bluff. The first county courthouse is here, now used as a Masonic lodge.

Tuscan Springs, nine miles east of Red Bluff near the headwaters of Little Salt Creek, was site of the first discovery of **borax** in California. The find was too small for commercial development, but this place became a health resort and its mineral waters were bottled and sold. The buildings burned in 1912 and the springs remain.

Mill Creek Recreation Area, on the Sacramento just north of Los Molinos, includes the **Mill Creek National Fish Culture Station**, where replacement fish are grown to replace miles of spawning gravels flooded by the several upstream water projects on the river.

688

For information, contact the **Red Bluff-Tehama County Chamber of Commerce**, Box 850, Red Bluff CA 96080. Telephone (916) 527-6220.

Red Bluff

This is the head of navigation on the Sacramento River, 246 miles upstream from Suisun Bay where the stream mixes with the San Joaquin River and enters San Francisco Bay. The Orient, a steamboat, first reached the landing at William B. Ide's Rancho de la Barranca Colorada in 1850. Named in Spanish for the fifty foot high cliff with a reddish color to its sands, the ranch and town were quickly shortened to Red Bluff. The modern town has 9,500 residents, and remains oriented to the river which now has its flows controlled by Shasta Dam. For many years the Sacramento was prone to flooding which dictated placement of the main town and railroad tracks which are now operated by the Southern Pacific on the bluffs above the river.

Red Bluff continues as a transportation cross roads with Highway 36 providing east-west connections from Nevada to the coast, and I-5 from the north and south. A few old buildings facing the river mark the once-busy shipping offices where cargo from wagons and pack train was directed to river boats.

Attractions

The William B. Ide Adobe State Historic Park, two miles north of Red Bluff on Adobe Road, is a delightful riverside area shaded by giant oak trees. A museum tells of the Red Bluff pioneer who commanded troops of the 1846 Bear Flag Revolt. An Indian village was here, and a pioneer ferry crossing. Open all year from 8:00 a.m. to 5:00 p.m. Telephone (916) 527-5927.

At 135 Main Street is a home built for the widow of **John Brown, the abolitionist** who staged a pre-Civil War battle at Harper's Ferry in Virginia. When Mrs. Brown came west in 1864, Californians raised money to provide for her and three children. She moved to Humboldt County in 1870. The house is a private dwelling and has been remodeled.

The **Kelly Griggs House Museum**, 311 Washington Street, is a restored Victorian home containing an art gallery and some artifacts owned by Ishi, an Indian whose story charmed thousands of readers. Open Thursday through Sunday, 2:00 p.m. to 5:00 p.m.

For information, contact the **Red Bluff-Tehama County Chamber of Commerce**, Box 850, Red Bluff CA 96080. Telephone (916) 527-6220.

TRINITY COUNTY

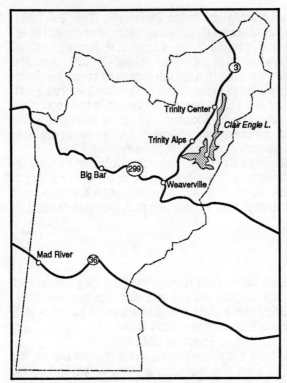

Mountainous Trinity County is the headwaters for several streams which run to the ocean. Heavy winter snowfall and rapid runoff make these mountains a source for some serious downstream floods, and the site of numerous storage reservoirs. Its 3,190 square miles are bounded on the east by the crest of the first mountains rising from the Sacramento Valley. The north line follows the crest of mountains dividing the Klamath River from the Trinity River basin. On the west, the county shares boundaries with coastal Humboldt County.

A scant 12,500 people live here. The county was named by Shasta County pioneer Pierson B. Reading, who thought the Trinity River flowed into Trinidad Bay on the Humboldt Coast. Actually the Trinity is the major tributary of the Klamath River which heads in Oregon. Two gold mining towns on the Trinity and its tributaries, Douglas City and Weaverville, have rich histories. Isolated Hayfork, in a valley with about the only land flat enough for farming, is the county's other community of size. There are less than 2,000 acres of croplands and orchards in the entire county.

690

Part of the Yolla Bolly Wilderness area is in the far southern corner, and much of the north county is in the beautiful Salmon-Trinity Alps Wilderness area. Trinity Lake, a major and controversial reservoir, provides 145 miles of shoreline for recreational use. A tunnel, completed in 1964, carries these coast range waters to the Sacramento River at Keswick.

While timber and livestock are the basic parts of the local economy, mining still remains a viable source of income for some residents. The area draws many visitors for its hunting and fishing, and backpackers bound for the wilderness portions of the national forest. A vast portion of the county remains in federal ownership.

ATTRACTIONS

Trinity and **Lewiston Lakes** are popular with fishermen. The cool waters of the smaller Lewiston Lake, where water is staged for the tunnel under the mountains, makes it unpopular for swimming, but a hit with fishermen seeking trophy trout up to twenty-five pounds. Several resorts and campgrounds are along the lakes, and Trinity Center is a shopping center for the area, and for people going into the wilderness.

Scott's Museum, Trinity Center, has photographs of old mining and logging, exhibits on the U.S. Forest Service role and gold rush settlements. Open May 1 to November 30, daily from 10:00 a.m. to 5:00 p.m. Telephone (916) 623-5211.

Trinity Alps are an alpine area of granite peaks and green meadows dotted with small lakes. Both short day hikes and extended trips with outfitters are available to explore this wilderness area. Packers include Six Pak Packers, Box 301; and Trinity Outfitters, inc., Box 1973; both Weaverville.

Contact the **Shasta Trinity National Forest Weaverville Ranger Station** for information on both the lakes and back-country camping. Telephone (916) 623-2121.

In the south county mountains, some of California's best bear hunting is reported. **Hayfork**, the second largest community in the county, provides a headquarters from which to explore the back-country and arrange for guide service. Contact the **Hayfork Ranger Station**, (916) 628-5227 for information on the south county.

Burnt Ranch, on the lower Trinity River, is an old settlement which took its name from remains of a building destroyed by Indians. This is a famed orchard region, although quite a small one. Salmon and steelhead fishing are popular on this reach of the river.

For information, contact the **Trinity County Chamber of Commerce**, 317 Main Street, Weaverville CA 96093. Telephone 623--6101.

Weaverville

The feeling of the old west is in this community of 6,000 people living under the shade of locust trees in small frame cottages, many protected from the road with white-painted picket fences. The livery stable became a garage, the newspaper still has offices here where publishing began in 1856, and the Chinese Joss House carries on a tradition even though the population of 2,000 Chinese recorded in 1852 has dwindled to a handful who still worship here.

The first gold discoveries were made in 1848, and this was a collection of tents for a long time afterward. Prospector John Weaver built his cabin here in 1850, and gave his name to the town, which became the seat of Trinity County the same year. The courthouse built in 1856 as a saloon remains in use, and like other downtown buildings of the era it has a special architectural flavor. One mark of the town are exterior wrought-iron spiral stair-cases to reach some second story balconies on three buildings which had separate owners for the ground and upper stories.

Attractions

Five-cent Gulch, one mile east of town on East Weaver Road, was the site of the famed Chinese Tong War of 1854. Mining has since changed the topography, but collections in the **J.J. Jackson Museum** include weapons salvaged from the battlefield of 600 combatants.

The Jackson Museum, in Trinity County Historical Park, also has Indian displays and fossils unearthed by miners. Open May 1 through November 30 from 10:00 a.m. to 5:00 p.m. Telephone 623-5211.

Big Ben's Doll Museum, in the business district, includes a gift shop and over 1,000 dolls. Open April through December, from 10:00 a.m. to 6:00 p.m. Telephone 623-6383.

Weaverville **Joss House State Historic Park,** is on Highway 299. This is the oldest Chinese temple in California, including some objects brought from the homeland in 1854 and moved into this building built in 1874 after a fire. Open daily 10:00 a.m. to 5:00 p.m. Telephone 623-5284.

For information, contact the **Trinity County Chamber of Commerce,** 317 Main Street, Weaverville CA 96093. Telephone 623--6101.

YOLO COUNTY

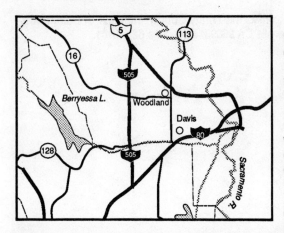

With the Sacramento River for its eastern boundary, the Coast Range foothills for its western limits, Yolo is a vast plain. It is bounded on the south by Putah Creek, which rises in the coast range and drains to the Sacramento. The cities of Winters and Davis are on the creek, almost in neighboring Solano County. Woodland, the county seat, is eleven miles north of Davis. The north boundary, shared with Colusa county, is a few miles north of the town of Dunnigan.

The name Yolo is said to be a mispronunciation of the Indian word meaning tule or rush, and the area's big Indian settlement was translated, by the Spanish, as Pueblo del Tule. Others think the name may come from a chief known as Yodo. Farming dominates the area economy, and the University of California's primary agricultural institution is at Davis, with vast experimental farms on both sides of Putah Creek.

Davis

This city of 40,000 is flat, its streets tree-lined and its homes among the first in California subject to solar access ordinances for use of winter sun to provide energy-saving heat. Bike paths abound, and residents tout themselves as the "bicycle capital" of California.

Davis began with a settlement and freight depot where the California Pacific Railroad crossed Putah Creek. The University of California with an enrollment of 20,000 students, is by far the county's largest employer in modern times.

694

Attractions

The University of California's campus is filled with interesting buildings. There are three art galleries, in the Memorial Union, Gorman Museum and the Art Building. Call 752-1920 for campus information.

Pence Gallery, 212 D Street, features works of local artists. Open Tuesday through Saturday from 12:00 noon to 4:00 p.m. Closed during summer months. Telephone 758-3370.

For information, contact the **Davis Chamber of Commerce,** 228 B Street, Davis CA 95616. Telephone (916) 756-5170.

Accommodation

HOTEL EL RANCHO DAVIS
4120 Chiles Road
Davis, CA 95616
Tel.   (916)   756-2200
         (800)   952-5566

The El Rancho Hotel and Conference Center in Davis, while smaller than the Sacramento El Rancho, is equally as beautiful. It is newly remodeled and offers everything anyone could want, whether for a family vacation or a conference.

There are eighty-five rooms and suites available and each suite features refrigerators and microwave ovens. There is fine dining in Tandem's bar and Grill which offers a varied and extensive menu of deliciously prepared cuisine. There is dancing and live entertainment in the evening and a Sunday champagne brunch. The resort has beautifully landscaped grounds with a swimming pool. Tennis court privileges are available just a few feet away at the Davis Tennis Club.

The El Rancho Hotel is located near the University of California, Davis, and is adjacent to I-80. There are also extensive conference facilities available here. This is a good choice for a relaxing vacation or an enjoyable conference in charming surroundings.

695

PARTRIDGE INN
521 1st Street
Davis, CA 95616
Tel: (916) 753-1211
AMEX, MasterCard and Visa are accepted.

The Partridge Inn is a fine old home from the early days of Davis. Built in 1912, this beautifully appointed California mansion reflects a special family atmosphere, offering the traveler pleasing accommodations. It's a place for those who wish to enjoy the charm of a by gone era.

This large two story house is located close to shops and restaurants. Each room offers pleasant views and comfortable surroundings where you can relax. The day begins with a generous Continental breakfast of juice, fresh pastries and a specially roasted cup of coffee or tea. In the evening, guests gather for wine or sherry and lively conversation. Bicycles are available for guest use when touring the area. You may come and go as you wish. Returning to the Inn at the end of your day's outings is like stepping into another world.

The ambiance of the Inn is casual elegance, yet always private and intimate. At The Partridge Inn you will experience the quiet charm and warm hospitality of a delightful country inn, a place to create lasting memories.

Apparel

THE CHILDREN'S CORNER
206 E Street
Davis, CA 95616
Tel: (916) 756-0200

Children, growing like bean sprouts, are always needing new clothing. But the difficult part is that there aren't too many shops specializing in just children's apparel. That's why when you find a place like Children's Corner, you thank your lucky stars, because you realize it's a veritable treasure trove.

When you first enter Children's corner you will be surprised and pleased by the friendly greeting you receive from the knowledgeable staff. But that is only the tip of the iceberg for this shop. The invaluable staff apart, they've got literally hundreds of clothing items to choose from for your child. You'll find racks and racks of dresses, shirts, sweaters, T-shirts, and shorts. For winter wear, they carry mittens and knitted caps to keep your little one warm on cold days. The Children's Corner even has items for toddlers, such as Zoo Shoes with velcro closures under the faces of assorted animals.

For accessories, this store carries backpacks, hats, shoes, belts, ties, socks and much, much more. Just about anything a child and parent could want is to be found. The next time you notice you child's head extending above the previous notch on the wall, it's probably time to visit Children's Corner, the answer-all to the clothing needs of children.

TARIKA
406 2nd Street
Davis, CA 95616
Tel: (916)   753-2262
Hrs: Mon. - Sat.   10:00 a.m. - 6:00 p.m.
            Thursday until 9:00 p.m.
MasterCard and Visa are accepted.
And,
1804 "J" Street
Sacramento, CA 95814

Three of the basic needs for survival are food, shelter and clothing. In all three categories we can find luxuries, but nowhere is there a clothing store like Tarika, offering exquisitely fine women's clothing, accessories and consummate service.

Tarika's wardrobe consultants help clients select the best colors and styles most suited to their personality and lifestyle. Many clients come in seeking in-depth advice on how to make the most of what they have. Tarika displays it's clothing according to the seasonal harmony theory, an organized system that works. The ambiance is soothing, helpful and rewarding, making shopping there a pleasurable experience. This shop has a very special touch that women from all over the state seek out and enjoy.

So, if you are looking for more out of clothing than simple survival needs, go to Tarika apparel shop and enjoy the luxury of clothiers who care.

Art

THE ARTERY
207 G Street
Davis, CA 95616
Tel: (916) 758-8330
Hrs: Mon. - Sat.   10:00 a.m. - 5:30 p.m.
            Sunday   12:00 noon - 5:00 p.m.

Art is a free flow form of expression, one that circulates and feeds humanities aesthetical values. An artery is much the same thing, however, on a more objective level. It's appropriate that art and arteries share the same root because they are both mediums of circulation. At The Artery you can view one aspect of this all important function.

Local and regional artists exhibit and sell some of the state's finest crafts and fine art, exotic woods, porcelain, Raku, Majolica and stoneware pottery, jewelry made of gold, silver, glass, copper or brass, wearable art in woven, knitted and painted silk designs. The work represents the finest of it's kind available, with many of the artists enjoying national recognition. An adjoining gallery features monthly shows of the work of artists-members.

The Artery came into being as a cooperative and has grown into a renowned haven for artists and lovers of beautiful things. The friendly atmosphere allows customers to browse through the shop for hours on end. Come and see this circulation of art; a medium in where beauty flows freely, nourishing the more subtle senses.

Camera

JEFF'S CAMERA AND FRAMES
420 2nd Street
Davis, CA 95616
Tel: (916) 758-5333
Hrs: Mon. - Wed.   9:00 a.m. - 6:00 p.m.
      Thursday   9:00 a.m. - 8:00 p.m.
      Friday   9:00 a.m. - 6:00 p.m.
      Saturday   10:00 a.m. - 5:00 p.m.
All major credit cards are accepted.

Did you know the first camera was invented in the early 1500's? It was aptly named the Camera Obscura and is credited to the Italian Artist Leonardo Da Vinci. Of course, it didn't actually snap a photo; it just formed an image on a nearby wall that acted as a sketching aid for artists. At Jeff's Camera and Frames you can learn facts like this and much more.

Jeff's Camera and Frames is one of the most complete photographic emporiums in Northern California. It has anything you need to take and develop great photographs. Some of the items carried are a large selection of photography books, a forest of camera stands, camera and lens carriers, filters, batteries, hot shoe adapters, cable releases, flash brackets and much more. Jeff's features film by Kodak, AGFA and Fuji. The store is also well stocked with dark room and studio supplies. Pentax, Nikon, Canon, Leica and Hasselblad are all carried by Jeff's. You'll also find lenses made by Sigma, Tarmon and Tonika.

Jeff's has a first rate repair department. If it can be fixed, it will be at this shop. Cameras and other related equipment sure have developed since the days of Da Vinci and there's nothing obscure about Jeff's Camera and Frames.

Delicatessen

AGGIE LIQUOR AND DELI
606 Covell Boulevard
Davis, CA 95616
Tel. (916) 753-5900
Hrs.   Mon. - Thur.   9:00 a.m. - 11:00 p.m.
      Fri. - Sat.   9:00 a.m. - 12:00 midnight
      Sunday   10:00 a.m. - 10:00 p.m.
Visa and Mastercard are accepted.
Additional locations:
757 Russell Boulevard - (916) 753-4900
511 L Street - (916) 753-4441

Whether you are in the mood for great deli food or perhaps in need of picnic or party supplies, Aggie Liquor and Deli is definitely the place to visit in Davis. The emphasis is on service and a selection of merchandise secondly only to the largest of liquor marts.

Owner Dennis Younglove is particularly proud of his vast assortment of wines. Rightfully so, at any given time, there are as many as 500 different labels. Although most are from Northern California, Dennis does stock a good many imported vintages.   In addition, the stores feature an incomparable variety of domestic and imported beers, stouts and ales, including such brands as Guiness, Bass, Ayinger and Samuel Smith. Aggie's also has a large choice of grain spirits, some that are often hard to find like aquavit, Chambord, Pernod and a number of fine single malt scotches.

Other available items include cookies, crackers, chips, dips, soft drinks and juices, gift baskets and more. There are even box lunches and large or small party trays heaped with fresh meats, cheeses, relishes, vegetables, fruits and breads. Aggie Liquor and Deli - a "Best Choice" for good times.

Game

THE GAME PRESERVE
222 "D" Street, #4
Davis, CA 95616
Tel: (916) 753-GAME
Hrs: Mon. - Sat. 11:00 a.m. - 5:00 p.m.
MasterCard and Visa are accepted.

Three...tap, tap, tap...pick the up card...go directly to jail! Do not pass Go. Do not collect $200. Recognize this set up? It's from the game Monopoly. The Game Preserve once sponsored a game of Monopoly that used huge foam dice on a board as big as a city block. Roll your dice, make your move, and enter The Game Preserve.

Once inside, you'll find all types of board games including the entire luxurious Ravensburger line from West Germany, chess, role-playing games and many, many others. If you like puzzles, they've got a slew of 'em. One is six feet long, they also have manipulative varieties, such as those invented by Professor Erno Rubik. Of course, The Game Preserve also carries other gaming accessories, including darts and all kinds of playing cards. Always seeking community support, they sponsor championships and many other game related functions.

The types of games sold here provide for healthy, stimulating recreation, allowing people to interact with each other. For the whole family, The Game Preserve is a veritable Community Chest just waiting to be opened.

Pizza

WOODSTOCK'S PIZZA PARLOR
219 G Street
Davis, CA 95616
Tel.   (916)   757-2525
Hrs: Sun. - Thu.   11:30 a.m. - 1:00 a.m.
        Fri. - Sat.   11:30 a.m. - 2:00 a.m.

Here at last! The newest of six Woodstock's Pizza Parlors has come to Davis and follows in the footsteps of its alma mater from Corvallis, Oregon where the tradition began, and on down into other college towns in California. Pizza here is made the old fashioned way, with hand rolled crust in a choice of wheat or white, freshly prepared each morning.

You can see the pizza dough being spun up into the air, it's quite a show! There is a wide selection of tasty toppings, a salad bar and beverages available. Woodstock's Special features a choice of any five toppings, or you can matriculate up to the Club U. Special, consisting of sausage, pepperoni, extra cheese, mushrooms, onion and green pepper. You can also create your own "special" choosing from sixteen fresh toppings.

This two story, red and white tiled brick building has a decor of basic wood tones most befitting a pizza parlor. But the most important thing here is the pizza...a most brilliant and scholarly pie!

Stationery

CAROUSEL STATIONERY
706 2nd Street
Davis, CA 95616
Tel: (916) 753-5202
Hrs: Mon. - Wed.   9:00 a.m. - 6:00 p.m.
     Thursday   9:00 a.m. - 8:00 p.m.
     Mon. - Sat.   9:00 a.m. - 6:00 p.m.
MasterCard and Visa are accepted.

It's time to sit down and write all those letters that have been put off for too long. There's about six of them to write, but it's got to be done. All you have to work with is that ugly tablet paper with blue lines, you forgot to pack paper. Yuk! Guess it's time to visit Carousel Stationery.

Your writing needs and more are taken care of at Carousel Stationery. It's a shop of service oriented atmosphere where you'll find a complete line of Hallmark items including cards, wrapping paper, napkins, bags and party items. In fact, there's something by Hallmark for virtually any occasion. They also carry office and business supplies such as file cabinets, desk chairs, catalog cases and large walnut or sandlewood colored desks. You can even choose from several gift items. Wild animal candles, porcelain, ceramic figurines, coffee mugs and stuffed animals, to mention a few.

So, the next time you decide to catch up on your writing, business needs or gift shopping, remember Carousel Stationery. It's a place where you can get everything you need to accomplish your goals with a measure of style.

Davis, a fun, young town centered around the University of California, is certainly worth exploring. Touring the town on a bike will not only easily lead you to these businesses, but maybe help you find other undiscovered best choice attractions.

INTRO TO DAVIS TOUR			
a.m.	U of C Tour	Best bike/walk	Dav/Att
a.m.	The Artery	Best gallery	Dav/Art
a.m.	Jeff's	Best photo shop	Dav/Camp
p.m.	Aggie Liquor	Best deli	Dav/Deli
p.m.	Tarika	Best fashion	Dav/App
p.m.	Game Preserve	Best game	Dav/Game
p.m.	Carousel Stationery	Best cards	Dav/Stationery

Woodland

Food processing and farm suppliers provide much of the employment in Woodland. The town was first settled in 1853, and a major Indian village was at the mouth of Cache Creek where it flows into the Sacramento. Woodland is far back from the river, where modern engineers have designated the Yolo Bypass to handle flood waters. Water from the creek irrigated farm land here as early as 1856.

The two-story Yolo County courthouse with Corinthian columns in front, stands on a town square between Second and Third streets. About 31,000 people live here now.

For information, contact the Woodland Chamber of Commerce, telephone (916)662-7327.

RENO/LAKE TAHOE AREA

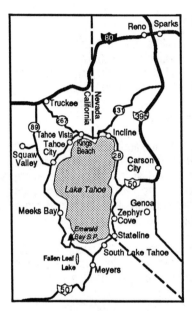

Genoa

The first permanent settlement in Nevada was called Mormon Station. It now is named Genoa. Established, in 1850, around a trading post the Mormon emigrés from Salt Lake City had founded.

In 1859 Nevada's first territorial legislature met at Genoa for a nine day session at which they drafted a declaration seeking to separate this territory from Utah Territory. Congress, recognizing the value of the famed Comstock Lode and its role in financing the Union's efforts in the Civil War, established the Territory of Nevada in 1861.

Attractions

Genoa retains the flavor of olf Nevada. There's a **museum** and a **park** commenorating these early pioneers. On Foothill Road off Highway 207. Telephone (702) 782-2940.

Genoa Courthouse Museum, Main Street, contains antique farm implements, a railroad display, Indian artifacts, needlework, and basketry and a replica of an old school room and kitchen.

Morman Station Historic State Monument, off I-395 on SR 57, is a restored log stockade and trading post. A museum is open for touring.

Resort

WALLEY'S HOT SPRINGS RESORT
2001 Foothill Road (P.O. Box 26)
Genoa, NV 89411
Tel. (702) 782-8155 or (702) 883-6556
Hrs: Spa   Sun. - Thu.   8:00 a.m. - 10:00 p.m.
             Fri. - Sat.   8:00 a.m. - 11:00 p.m.
      Restaurant Wed. - Sat.   11:30 a.m. - 3:00 p.m.
             Dinner   5:30 p.m. - 10:00 p.m.
             Sunday   10:00 a.m. - 3:00 p.m.
AMEX, Visa and MasterCard are accepted.

Ever feel like getting away from it all for fun and relaxation? You can't do it any better than at Walley's Hot Springs Resort, where you'll feel like the rest of the world is light years away. Nestled at the base of the Sierra Nevada Mountains' eastern side, is one of the West's first health spas (established in 1862) featuring famous mineral baths that has turned into a first-class, all-inclusive resort that allows you to be as active or inactive as you wish.

The hot mineral spas, still the chief attraction of the beautiful "oasis," feature six flow-through spas, ranging in temperature from ninety-eight degrees to 104 degrees. To the spas, add a large, sparkling-blue fresh water swimming pool with surrounding decks from which you can look out upon the unspoiled Carson Valley and the majestic Sierras. Walley's fitness center, including the pools and complete weight and workout facilities, are all available to the public for a low daily fee. However, the best way to fully enjoy this splendid resort is to reserve one of the comfortable, well-appointed guest cottages for a few days, or even a week. With only five such cottages available, make sure you make reservations in advance. Bring along a hearty appetite because Walley's features one of the finest restaurants you'll find anywhere. The Zephyr restaurant, multi-leveled so guests can enjoy the sweeping view of the valley and nearby mountains, offers a menu highlighted by tempting fresh seafood and perfectly-aged beef entrees, not to mention the breast of chicken Chardonnay with its plump and tender chicken breast sauteed with fresh mushrooms in a Chardonnay cream sauce - if you happen to be in the mood for something a little different. A perfect meal always includes a delightful dessert, so if you can possibly let the treasure-laden bakery cart pass by, check the menu for coffee crunch ice cream pie, hot fudge sundaes, crepes Suzette or the favorite chocolate decadence, a brownie shell filled with chocolate ice cream and topped with meringue and bittersweet hot fudge.

Adjoining the restaurant is the nicely-furnished bar, the Old Stone Room from the original restaurant.

Walley's Hot Springs Resort has been pampering guests with a special and relaxing brand of elegance for over 125 years. Bring your swimming suits, exercise outfits, tennis rackets, jogging and hiking shoes; but most of all, be sure to bring a desire to totally relax and enjoy the "Best Choice" quiet, gentle pace you'll find at Walley's.

Incline Village

Accommodation

HYATT LAKE TAHOE
Incline Village
Country Club Drive and Lakeshore Boulevard
Incline Village, NV 89450
Tel. (702) 831-1111
Visa, MasterCard, Diner's Club, Carte Blanche, AMEX and Discover cards are accepted.

A year-round playground for the entire family amid the majestic high Sierras, towering pines, crystal clear waters and hushed snowfall . . . this is Hyatt Lake Tahoe at Incline Village. Nestled on Tahoe's north shore with its own private 500 feet of beach front, its exquisitely appointed rooms and the amenities you expect from the name Hyatt, this year-round resort offers it all.

The 460 spacious rooms overlooking Lake Tahoe and the Sierra Mountains, the forty-eight elegant suites (some with fireplaces), and the special touch of the Regency Club on the hotel's tenth and eleventh floors offers something for all travelers. Experience dining to suit your every mood - from casual buffets at Alpine Jacks, to the elegance of Hugos Rotisserie with its panoramic lake view or The Pines nestled in an intimate setting of wood, brass, and etched glass. Relax with a generous cocktail and enjoy the nightly entertainment in the Sugar Pine Lounge. Enjoy swimming, water skiing, fishing and boating on the pristine lake waters, golf on your choice of two eighteen-hole Robert Trent Jones golf courses, or take advantage of the nearby forty-two tennis courts, ten indoor racquet ball courts, outdoor swimming pool, health spa, and an eighteen station exercise course through the pine forest adjacent to the hotel. Or you may prefer horseback riding, bicycling, and hiking in the surrounding countryside. Winter sports enthusiasts can select from six nearby major ski areas, including Squaw Valley, while indoor sports buffs can frolic in a twenty-four-hour-a-day full casino. Children have their own video game room and all ages can enjoy a visit to the Ponderosa Ranch of Bonanza fame.

Yes, it's all here! Elegance and informality, active sports and quiet moments in nature's grandeur. Come and capture the spirit at Hyatt Lake Tahoe, a "Best Choice" for a year-round family resort experience.

Gift

THE POTLATCH SHOP
324 Ski Way
Incline Village, NV 89450
Tel. (702) 831-2485
Hrs: Mon. - Sun. 10:00 a.m. - 5:30 p.m.
Visa, Mastercard, AMEX, Carte Blanche and personal checks are accepted.

Treasure is rare, valuable, and beautiful and treasures are what's found at the Potlatch Shop at Incline Village. Rare placer gold nuggets, fresh water pearls and diamonds are displayed along with sculptures by Oscar Johnson, clay figurines by Stan Langtrauit, and paintings by Anthony Sinclair. Oscar Johnson creates scenes of birds in their natural habitat from redwood and driftwood and Sinclairs paintings and prints capture the drama and beauty of native American life.

Established in 1970, the Potlatch Shop is a veritable treasure house of antique and contemporary artifacts including some of the most beautiful crystal, jewelry, hand blown glass, and brass works available anywhere. Rare gifts include antique P.O. Boxes made into banks and Scheibe snack trays which are not only beautiful to the eye but are useful in the home. Their large contemporary jewelry collection features the work of local artists each with their own style and vision.

To the Native Americans, a Potlatch gathering revolved around an exchange of valuables and gifts, and at the Potlatch Shop you can find that perfect treasure to exchange with a friend or for your own lasting enrichment.

Sport

SKI INCLINE
P.O. Drawer AI
Incline Village, NV 89450
Tel. (702) 832-1177
Hrs: Nov. - Apr. Mon. - Sun. 8:00 a.m. - 4:00 p.m.
Visa, MasterCard and AMEX are accepted.

You'll find more than "just a lift ticket" at Ski Incline, a scenic and innovative ski resort offering superior service on the slopes and off. This popular family resort isn't afraid of change, as evidenced by the incredible nine and one-half million dollar expansion project embarked upon as the result of years of analyzing the needs of skiers and non-skiers alike - all to make your stay at Ski Incline a memorable one.

By the beginning of the 1987/88 ski season, Ski Incline will offer twice as much terrain, will increase the vertical access by 1,800 feet and a new quad chairlift will be available. Ski terrain at Ski Incline is often coined "comfortably challenging" for all levels of skiers with forty percent ideal for intermediate skiers, thirty percent to encourage beginners and thirty percent to challenge the more advanced. The area's wind-protected, sunny slopes are a perfect hideaway for comfort-seeking skiers. When it comes to snow conditions, the resort's innovative snow management techniques continually set the standards for ski areas across the nation. Families searching for an economical approach to skiing, without sacrificing quality, should take advantage of Ski Incline's reduced family rates. This popular destination resort has all the amenities from mountain-top restaurants overlooking the lake, to a newly remodeled full-facility base lodge with a contemporary interior design and a novel apres-ski bar complete with gaming activity. Enjoy a leisurely, scenic drive to Ski Incline or fly into Reno Cannon International Airport where you can arrange for a "skierized" rental car to take advantage of the variety of ski resorts and the many apres-ski activities. Visitors staying at Ski Incline can take advantage of Ski Incline's free shuttle system which operates throughout town, throughout the day. Plus, many of Lake Tahoe's casinos offer twenty-four-hour shuttle service to and from the tables.

Experience a "Best Choice" winter wonderland that combines superb skiing, exciting ski-related activities, first-class service and accommodations and breathtaking scenery. You deserve more than "just a lift ticket." So capture it all at Ski Incline!

Reno/Lake Tahoe Area

Restaurant

SCHWEIZER HAUS
120 Country Club Drive #61
Incline Village, NV 89450
Tel. (702) 831-4694
Hrs: Wed. - Mon.   Dinner   5:30 p.m. - 9:30 p.m.
          Wed.-Mon   Lunch   11:30 a.m. - 2:30 p.m.
Visa, MasterCard, AMEX, Diner's Club, Carte Blanche are
accepted.

The traditional food of the Swiss Alps is now the famous food of the Sierra Nevada at the warm and cozy Schweizer Haus in Incline Village.
Schweizer Haus owners, Master Chef Eugene Schweizer and his wife Inge, have transplanted a bit of their native Germany to the pines of Lake Tahoe. They feature only the finest in milk fed veal specialities along with traditional Swiss entrees such as wiener schnitzel, gesehnetzeltes, piccata, rahmschnitzel, and cordon bleu. All dishes are made fresh to order from scratch. Local favorites include homemade "spaetzle" (noodles), sauerbraten and apple strudel fresh from Eugene's kitchen. For over ten years, the Schweizer's have delighted the discriminating palates with the three ingredients that to them are most important for a fine restaurant; good food, good sauces, and "gemutlichkeit" (good atmosphere).
The fabulous food complemented by the cozy decor make Schweizer Haus a must stop for the best in European mountain traditions in a beautiful American mountain setting.

STEVEN LAKE TAHOE
341 Ski Way
Incline Village, NV 89450
Tel. (702) 832-0222
Hrs: Mon. - Sat.   Lunch   11:30 a.m. - 4:00 p.m.
          Mon. - Sat.   Dinner   6:00 p.m. -10:00 p.m.
          Sunday   Brunch   10:00 a.m. - 4:30 p.m.
          Sunday   Dinner   6:00 p.m. - 9:00 p.m.
Visa, Mastercard, AMEX, Diners Club are accepted.

Named one of the twenty best restaurants in Nevada and with a most spectacular view of Lake Tahoe from every table are two compelling reasons for treating yourself to an elegant evening at Steven Lake Tahoe. The beauty and romance of the mahogany and brass interior decor, silver tableware, fresh flowers, candles, and linen table cloths make the excellence of the food seem that much better.

Begin your meal with glorious appetizers of salmon, escargot, or Cajun shrimp. Full dinners all begin with liver pate, soup or salad, and feature their own homemade pasta. Mesquite grilled chicken, veal, and sirloin steak are popular, delicious entrees; or order lighter fare such as soups, salads, and appetizers a la carte in the cafe . A full wine list complement the generous dinners prepared by chef Evehado Rubio whose repertoire is described as creative American with strong Mexican and European influences.

At Steven Lake Tahoe, owner Bill Frost has created a place of beauty and charm against a backdrop of the awesome natural beauty of Lake Tahoe.

WILD BERRIES RESTAURANT
120 Country Club Drive # 20
Incline Village, NV 89450
Tel. (702) 831-2000
Hrs: Mon.-Sat. 6:00 p.m. - 10:30 p.m.
Visa, Mastercard, AMEX, and personal checks are accepted.

Pheasant with blueberries, roast duck with raspberries, or veal medallions with wild mushrooms served in the warmth and comfort of a French country inn. Sound good? Add the best in California and French cuisine and viola, the menu and ambiance of Wild Berries Restaurant at Incline Village.

Owner Jean Du Fau, Manager pat Mc Carthy and Master Chef Jerry Reten Skaggs invite you to healthy, exciting food prepared in a French manner with fantastic sauces and complemented with majestic desserts. Rare delicacies of lamb, swordfish, tuna, venison, sea bass, or lobster are carefully prepared to order and served by a courteous and attentive staff. An award wining wine selection (Award for Excellence 1985, 1986, 1987 from *Wine Spectator* magazine) of over 100 vintage wines ranging from the 1950's to the 1980's are offered to enhance your evening. Completing the romantic setting are pink linen tablecloths, fresh flowers, fine china, and silver tableware.

The Wild Berries Restaurant is the "Best Choice" in Incline Village for French fine food, fine wine, and fine times.

Kings Beach

Art Gallery

LAKESIDE GALLERY AND GIFTS
8636 North Lake Boulevard
Kings Beach, CA 95719
Tel. (916) 546-3135
Hrs: Mon. - Sat. 10:00 a.m. - 5:00 p.m.

The scene is almost complete. All that remains is a couple of touches from the brush, now poised above the paints. Just the right shade here and a little bit of accent there and *Voila!* What used to be a plain white canvas is now the beautiful scene of a misty forest. Sounds thrilling doesn't it? You too can participate in this kind of excitement at Lakeside Gallery & Gifts.

This gallery, featuring internationally renowned instructors, teaches both the young and old, the experienced and unexperienced. All the needed materials can either be rented, or purchased on the premises. In addition to the painting classes, there are many other services including oil painting, water colors, reproductions, phots, pottery, jewelry, custom and ready-made frames and special two and three day workshops. The building housing this gallery is, in itself, quite a masterpiece, being fifty years old and an original of Kings Beach.

For visitors and residents alike, Lakeside Gallery & Gifts is the place to go for instruction in the arts, art services or just to have a great time admiring beautiful scenes. The canvas is set and the brush is ready. All that is required is you.

Restaurant

CHEZ VILLARET
8504 N Lake Tahoe Boulevard
Kings Beach, CA 95731
Tel. (916) 541-7868
Hrs: Lunch Mon. - Sun. 11:30 a.m. - 2:30 p.m.
 Dinner 6:00 p.m. - 11:00 p.m.
Visa, MasterCard and AMEX accepted.

Lake Tahoe is a vacationer's paradise. It's popular attractions include skiing, fishing, gambling, camping and sailing. But did you know that there is

710

also gourmet dining? That's right, and for the past eleven years Chez Villaret has been building a reputation as the culinary beacon of Lake Tahoe.

Chez Villaret is a French provincial restaurant with white table linen, candles and soft music that creates an intimate dining experience. The chef, trained at The Culinary Academy of Emile Gryson in Brussels, prepares a combination of classic and Nouvelle cuisine that reflects his happy and inventive nature. Only the finest, hand picked produce is incorporated into the four seasonal menus, as well as the daily specials. When ordering the wine for dinner, you may find yourself taking a little more than the expected amount of time, there are 250 selections, both domestic and imported!

The Chez Villaret is a quiet, gracious restaurant with a consistency of excellence. So, whether you're camping or visiting the casinos, don't forget the "Best Choice" for dining in Lake Tahoe is Chez Villaret.

JASON'S SALOON
8338 N Lake Boulevard
Kings Beach, CA 95719
Tel. (916) 546-3315
Hrs: Mon. - Sun. 11:00 a.m. - 10:00 p.m.

You're camping in Tahoe and it's time for dinner. Since you decided to rough it you'll have to build the fire to prepare the food. Oh no, it just started raining. No fire now. However, planning for this, you enter the tent to break out the canned goods, only to find that you forgot to pack them! Your stomach growls as you remember the "Best Choice" guide in the car. Flipping through the pages looking for a good restaurant you find Jason's Saloon and read all about it.

Jason's Saloon has a menu that includes anything from a quick snack or casual lunch, to a delicious yet leisurely dinner. Steaks, ribs, chicken, seafood and thirty-one varieties of large hamburgers are all included. There's a terrific salad bar with homemade croutons, your choice of dressing and their own special cheese bread spread thickly with three kinds of cheese, whipped butter and seasonings! You can warm up with their Late Watch Warmer, a drink in the tradition of Scandanavian sailors made with three types of hot wine mulled in sugars, almonds, raisins and cinnamon sticks.

The many desserts offered are just what it takes to top off a good meal. A well rounded restaurant, Jason's Saloon is sure to make any patron happy. Roughing it isn't going camping, it's not eating at Jason's Saloon.

711

Lake Tahoe

Lake Tahoe is the largest alpine lake in North America and, with a maximum depth of 1,648 feet, is the second deepest, exceeded only by Oregon's Crater Lake. Tahoe is a Washoe Indian word meaning "big water." The Tahoe Basin and Lake Tahoe's seventy-one miles of shoreline are surrounded by Sierra Nevada mountain peaks, some of which exceed 9,000 feet. The lake, itself, has an elevation of about 6,100 feet. Small towns, tourist facilities, state parks, historic and scenic viewpoints, beaches and national forest lands rim the lake along highway US 50, Nevada State Highway 28 and California State Highway 89.

The Lake Tahoe Basin had been home to the Washoe Indians for hundreds of years before the John Fremont Expedition 'discovered' the lake in 1844. Five years later, with the California Gold Rush entering its peak, Fremont's route, part of which followed near the south shore of Lake Tahoe and over several mountain passes, became one of the era's major trails for gold miners coming from the east to the gold fields in California's Sierra foothills.

The Washoe Indians were further imposed upon with the discovery of silver on Virginia City's Comstock Lode in 1859. The Silver Boom brought tens of thousands of miners out of California and into the Lake Tahoe Basin. During the next thirty years while the rich silver veins were being mined, the basin was virtually stripped of timber which was used for buildings, shaft supports and fuel.

Around 1862 Mark Twain set out by foot from Carson City to Lake Tahoe. Over mountains "a thousand miles high" he plodded until he reached his goal. There he wrote that the lake "must surely be the fairest picture the whole earth affords." More than one hundred and twenty-five years later Lake Tahoe is still one of nature's most treasured prizes on our planet.

The silver and the timber ran out about the same time. By the early 1900s, the basin was quiet and left to restore itself. Except for a few resorts and the construction of US 50, which followed the old miner route between Placerville, California and Carson City, Nevada, the area saw little activity until after World War II. Then, a younger and wealthier America began to cast about for areas in which to play. Its eyes fell upon what Nevada's tourist and gaming industries were creating at a revitalized Lake Tahoe and the basin soon became one of America's prime four season vacation spots. As an "interstate navigable waterway" Lake Tahoe is protected by the U.S. Coast Guard and is rumored to be the most desirable Coast Guard duty station in the world.

The year-round resort area of the North Shore of Lake Tahoe is bound to capture your heart. Its spell-binding experiences are only about a two hour drive from Sacramento on US 50 and three and a half hour trip from San

Francisco via Interstate 80. You can anticipate some of the lake's finest dining on the north shore area and accommodations which range from modest cabins to pampering hotel suites. Fully equipped condos can be rented by the day or week.

One of the Reno/Tahoe area's prime attractions are its fish rich streams and lakes, where good quantities of trout and kokanee are taken each season. Forest service lands offer ample opportunities for game bird and big game hunting. Warm weather water sports include boating, sailing, windsurfing and scuba diving. Many of the major resorts have tennis courts and there are five golf courses in the Reno-Sparks area, two designed by Robert Trent Jones. You can pick from seven more golf course in the North Lake Tahoe area. An additional attraction on the Nevada side of Lake Tahoe is the "quick marriage industry." Story book chapels dot the lake's perimeter and you can rent an assortment of hideaway cottages for an idyllic honeymoon.

The downhill ski season usually runs from November through May at most of the ski resorts around Lake Tahoe. Though the basin is graced with about 300 days of sunshine a year it frequently receives as much as 200 inches of snow a year, with the surrounding high Sierra getting anywhere from 300 to 500 inches of snow. This excellent snow pack supports nineteen major ski resorts around the Reno/Tahoe area. Heavenly Valley, the largest ski resort in North America, Squaw Valley, which helped put the Tahoe area on the map when it hosted the 1960 Winter Olympics, and Alpine Meadows are part of Tahoe's unsurpassed concentration of ski facilities. Day time winter temperature highs on the slopes range from twenty-five to a comfortable forty-five degrees. There are also many areas designated for cross country skiing and snowmobiling.

Lake Tahoe's only outlet is the Truckee River, which flows out of the ake near Tahoe City in California on the lake's northwest shore. Joggers and bicyclists are welcome along the river and around the small man-made lakes scattered throughout the area. The Truckee River is stocked with bass, rainbow trout, bluegill and catfish.

Attractions

Without a doubt the view from **Incline Village** on Crystal Bay is one of the most spectacular in The West. Located near the California - Nevada state line on the north shore, this vibrant community among lakeshore pines overlooks the stunning blue, snow-fed waters of Lake Tahoe. For the visitor, Incline has much to offer. It has Sand Harbor, a favorite spot for picnics, boating or sunbathing, three golf courses, ski runs, marinas, tennis courts and nearby nature trails. The nightlife of Reno is a scenic hour's drive away. For more information, call the Incline Village Chamber at (702) 831-4440.

Also at Incline Village is the **Ponderosa Ranch**, the location for much of the filming of the long-running "Bonanza" television series. The ranch is one of the lake's most popular attractions. In addition to guided tours of the grounds, there are hayrides, exhibits, outdoor barbeques and horseback riding. The Ponderosa is open from May until October, depending upon the weather, daily from 10:00 a.m. to 6:00 p.m. during the summer, and from 10:00 a.m. until 5:00 p.m. in the spring and fall. The admission fee is five dollars for adults and four dollars for children. For details call (702) 831-0691.

For a close-up look at Lake Tahoe you have a choice of a variety of lake cruises. You can choose from a stylish old sternwheeler, an authentic paddlewheeler or a shore-hugging cruise boat. The **M.S. Dixie** leaves from Zephyr Cove, the **Tahoe Queen** offers tours from South Lake Tahoe and the **Sunrunner** tours out of North Lake Tahoe. These passenger cruises offer romance, legends and adventure complete with dining, drinking and live music. For more information call the M.S. Dixie at (702) 588-3508 or 882-0786. For the Tahoe Queen call Lake Tahoe Cruises at (916) 541-3364. Details about the Sunrunner can be obtained by calling North Tahoe Cruises at (916) 583-0141.

Ehrman Mansion, D. L. Bliss State Park. Open July through September. An outstanding example of turn-of-the-century architecture. It was one of the filming locations for the movie "Godfather II." Located in Tahoma, California. Telephone (916) 525-7232.

Heavenly Valley Tram offers a beautiful, panoramic view of Lake Tahoe. Open both winter and summer. Telephone 544-6263.

Emerald Bay State Park is one of the world's most photographed spots; beautiful vistas of the lake and mountains offer many choices for your honing photography skills. This is also the site of Tahoe's only island, **Fanette Island**. There are excellent viewpoints at Bayview and Emerald Bay lookout.

Mark Twain cut his literary teeth on **Virginia City**, one of the gaudiest, headiest boom towns of the Old West, and wrote "The first twenty-six graves in Virginia city were occupied by murdered men." Born of the Comstock Silver Strike of 1859, Virginia City flourished for twenty years before the rich ore veins began to wane. At one time, 30,000 miners, shopkeepers and other industrious types from all over the world inhabited the rocky slopes of this raucous community perched on the flank of Mt. Davidson. Today, over one a half million visitors pour through annually to get a taste of its atmosphere. Sam Clemens changed his name to Mark Twain while beginning his writing career with the local *Territorial Enterprise* newspaper.

Miraculously, the town looks much the same as it did in the late 1800s, from the wobbly saloons built on stilts to the well-trodden boardwalks of the main street. There are over 750 miles of tunnels underneath Virginia City. The honeycombs of "square-set timbers" that made mining this rich lode possible are the ones that underpin the city and keep it stable on its mountainous site. Visitors are able to stroll through old mansions, quaint shops and tour mines, churches and museums.

To get to Virginia City from Incline Village, take state highway 431 northeast, cross US 395, then take state highway 341 to Virginia City.

South Lake Tahoe

The **South Lake Tahoe Area** of eastern El Dorado County contains outdoor recreation opportunities and a myriad of services to accommodate the needs of any traveler.
The city of **South Lake Tahoe** is on US 50, about two miles from the California - Nevada state line. It is the largest city on the Tahoe lakeshore and serves as a springboard to four season fun.
To help travelers get more out of their trip through the Tahoe area, the **South Lake Tahoe Chamber of Commerce** staffs a **visitor information center**. Stop by the center at 3066 US Highway 50, or call the chamber at (916) 541-5255.

Accommodations

TAHOE BEACH AND SKI CLUB
3601 Highway 50
South Lake Tahoe, CA 95705
Tel: (916) 541-6220

It's time to go to Tahoe, a vacationers paradise. Everything's ready except for the lodging arrangements. That's the only problem. There are so

715

many hotels, but which one do you choose? The answer is quite simple. Choose the resort of a lifetime, Tahoe Beach and Ski Club.

Tahoe Beach and Ski Club is a full service lakefront hotel located in the heart of Tahoe's excitement. Tennis, windsurfing, skiing and sailboating are all readily available, as well as 400 feet of sandy private beach. During the ski season, a private shuttle will whisk you away to Heavenly Valley, America's largest ski area. There's also convention facilities, retail shops and car rentals at this resort. For relaxation, the Club features a pool and hot tub close to the beach.

Only a few steps from the resort you'll find superb dining at Hodges Restaurant featuring fresh seafood, poultry, choice steaks and much more. Now that the dilemma of a place to lodge has been taken care of, you can rest easy knowing you can make reservations at Tahoe Beach and Ski Club.

Restaurants

CHEZ VILLARET
900 Emerald Bay Road
South Lake Tahoe, CA 95731
Tel: (916) 541-7868
Hrs: Mon. - Sun. Dinner   6:00 p.m. - 11:00 p.m.
AMEX, Mastercard, Diner's Club and Visa are accepted.

Lake Tahoe is a vacationer's paradise. It's popular attractions include skiing, fishing, gambling, camping and sailing. But did you know that there is also gourmet dining? That's right, and for the past thirteen years Chez Villaret has been building a reputation as the culinary beacon of Lake Tahoe.

Chez Villaret is a French provincial restaurant with white table linen, candles and soft music that creates an intimate dining experience. The chef, trained at The Culinary Academy of Emile Gryson in Brussels, prepares a combination of classic and Nouvelle cuisine that reflects his happy and inventive nature. Only the finest, hand picked produce is incorporated into the four seasonal menus, as well as the daily specials. When ordering the wine for dinner, you may find yourself taking a little more than the expected amount of time, there are 250 selections, both domestic and imported!

The Chez Villaret is a quiet, gracious restaurant with a consistency of excellence. So, whether you're camping or visiting the casinos, don't forget the "Best Choice" for dining in Lake Tahoe is Chez Villaret.

716

THE FRESH KETCH
2435 Venice Drive
P. O. Box 10500
South Lake Tahoe, CA 95731
Tel: (916) 541-5683
Hrs: Mon. - Sun. 11:30 a.m. - 1:30 a.m.
AMEX, Mastercard and Visa are accepted.

Overlooking the Tahoe Keys Marina, The Fresh Ketch is the South Shore's only waterfront restaurant. Playing host to many visitors every year, this restaurant offers a chance for an exquisite dining experience along with a tremendous view of Lake Tahoe.

The establishment's owners, Steve Hing, seems to have uncovered the right formula for a successful resort town restaurant. Soft beige walls, textured fabrics, Koa Wood tables, cane backed chairs and an abundance of well manicured plants create an elegant ambiance suitable for fine dining. Living up to it's name, The Fresh Ketch features over fifteen combinations of fresh fish, all sauteed or charbroiled to your satisfaction. For your libation pleasure, they carry more than fifty beers from all over the world and a complete bar with Cappacino machine.

For dessert, you'll want to try the Kimo's Hula pie, a chocolate cookie crust with macademia nut ice cream, Hershey's fudge and real whipped cream. Mmmm, what a way to finish dinner! Steve attributes their success to two things, community involvement and personal image, in addition to the view and superb food. You're always welcome to arrive in jeans and tennis shoes for a relaxed time, efficient servce and an elegant meal. At The Fresh Ketch, they go out of their way to give you a total dining experience.

Reno

It is no wonder Reno calls itself "The Biggest Little City in the World." The "open town" atmosphere of stage shows, twenty-four hour gaming activities and bright neon lights belies the fact that Reno is also an important distribution and merchandising center as well as home to the University of Nevada in Reno. In fact, Reno is a residential city of over 100,000 people who enjoy the benefits of living in this lively enclave tucked amid phenomenal recreation areas.

Though Reno was named for Union General Jesse Lee Reno, around 1868, this colorful town has been known as "Fuller's Folly," "Lake's Crossing" and "End of the Track." Because of its strategic location in relation to mining

717

camps and the Truckee River, Reno became a valuable distribution point. Supplies for booming Virginia City and its miners poured through town, first overland by wagon and then by railroad. Sparks was officially founded in 1903 and developed as a railroad center.

Gambling, first licensed in 1879, was outlawed in 1910. For many years successive laws made gambling legal, then illegal, until it was fully legalized in 1931. It was after this time that Reno reached its own "bonanza." In addition to its importance as a tourist destination, Reno today is the cultural center of Northern Nevada. Reno has become legend not only for gaming, but for its museums, fine and performing arts, higher education and easy access to a myriad of outdoor adventure activities. The area's excellent system of state and federal highways, which includes interstate 80 and US 395, helps ensure the ski areas and other tourist facilities are accessible year-round.

To maintain its environmental and economic integrity, Reno has successfully encouraged only select industries to move into the Reno/Tahoe area, industries which are relatively non-polluting and do not require large amounts of water. Within sight of Reno's downtown strip are green city parks, high desert trails, snowcapped Sierra peaks and the clear Truckee River. The Truckee, Lake Tahoe's only outlet, bisects the cities of Reno and Sparks, and nourishes lush greenery in riverside parks. Canada geese, ducks and other waterfowl make brief stops in the Truckee Meadows' streams and lakes during their seasonal migration.

The high country location of Reno provides a moderate year-round climate with very little humidity. The area has four distinct seasons, sunshine nearly 300 days a year, and the majority of precipitation falls during the winter as snow. Average temperatures range from a low of fifteen to twenty degrees in January to a high of ninety or so in July.

For information about Reno, call the Reno-Sparks Convention and Visitors Authority at (800) 367-7366. While in Reno call the Convention Center at 827-7600. A helpful brochure to order from that office is "The Reno/Tahoe Travel Planner."

Attractions

If you are interested in space travel, alien beings or secrets of the universe, then the **Fleischmann Planetarium** is just the place to tickle your imagination. Located at the north end of the University of Nevada campus in Reno on US Highway 395, the planetarium offers daily films and star shows on all sorts of space phenomena. Scheduled telescope viewing is also offered. For information and schedules call (702) 784-4811.

718

The **Harolds Club Gun Collection and Museum** offers a unique collection of rare firearms including Colts, Winchesters, Remingtons, a Gattling Gun and other exotic and prototype firearms. The museum also contains many fine restored music machines, which are played for your entertainment. Daily hours are from 10:00 a.m. to 10:00 p.m. For more information call (800) 648-5032 or (702) 329-0881.

Described as a "great American treasure," the collection at the **William F. Harrah Automobile Museum** consists of hundreds of antique, classic, vintage and special interest automobile displays. The museum is three and a half miles east of downtown Reno on East Second Street, which is also known as Glendale Road. There you will also be treated to fashions of yesteryear, a research library, snack bar and gift shop. The museum is open from 9:30 a.m. to 5:30 p.m. every day except Christmas. Admission is $6.50 for adults and $3.50 for children between six and fifteen years old. For more information call (702) 355-3500. Free bus transportation to the museum is available from most Reno and Sparks hotels.

Before there was a Reno there was Lake's Crossing, a one-man ferry service over the Truckee River operated by Myron Lake. A century ago Lake built a splendid Victorian home in the Truckee Meadows near the future site of Reno. That house can be visited today at the Reno-Sparks Convention Center grounds on South Virginia Street. Now restored, **Lake Mansion** is a treasure of early American and Nevada history. Admission is free and the hours are from between 8:00 a.m. and 5:00 p.m. For more information call (702) 827-7605.

The **Wilbur D. May Museum and Arboretum** houses hundreds of items collected by Wilbur D. May, late department store magnate, pilot, adventurer, world traveler and big game hunter of the 1920s and '30s. May's adventure-gleaned relics include a trophy room with the mounted heads of more than eighty animals, collected during the days when big game hunting was a pastime of the rich and famous, plus intriguing art objects and curios. The adjoining arboretum is divided into sections representative of the varied vegetation in North Nevada, from an alpine area to a song bird garden. The museum is at Rancho San Rafeal Regional Park, 1502 Washington Street. Summer hours are 10:00 a.m. to 5:00 p.m. Wednesday through Saturday. Guided tours are available. There is a one dollar admission charge for adults and fifty cents for children. For information call (702) 785-5961.

719

Reno/Lake Tahoe Area

Phase One of the ambitious new attraction known as the **Great Basin Adventure** will feature a children's petting zoo. Future plans call for development of five acres of family-oriented educational fun features in Rancho San Farael Regional Park, close to downtown Reno. For information call (702) 785-5961.

For the uninitiated, that first step into the world of a casino can be intimidating, if not costly. Before you take the plunge you can get your feet wet by taking a gaming tour at the **Reno/Tahoe Gaming Academy**. There you will learn the rules to various games, betting techniques and other tips. Then, the tour moves to a local casino for a behind-the-scenes view of the real thing. The academy is at 135 North Sierra Street in downtown Reno. Tours begin 12:30 p.m. and 2:00 p.m. Monday through Friday and cost five dollars per person. For more information and to make reservations call (702) 348-7403.

The work of Dot-So-La-Lee, who has been called the finest weaver of Native American baskets in the country, is among the featured articles of the **Nevada Historical Museum and Library**. Dot-So-La-Lee, a Washoe Indian, lived during the turn-of-the-century; her baskets are a record of how the Washoe viewed and lived life. The museum includes many other Indian artifacts and relics of Nevada history, as well as mining antiques and historical research facilities. The museum is open 10:00 a.m. to 5:00 p.m. Wednesday through Sunday. Admission is free. For more information call (702) 789-0190.

If you find yourself wondering what "that unusual building is" while in downtown Reno, it is probably Reno's 1,400 seat **Pioneer Theater Auditorium**. The magnificent geodesic dome, which is within walking distance of Reno's downtown strip area, is home to dozens of fine musical and theatrical productions throughout the year. For schedule and ticket information call (702) 786-5105.

Black Bart, Johnny Ringo and Billy the Kid are a few of the desperados who will try to stare you down from the walls of Pick Hobson's Riverside Hotel in downtown Reno. The trio is part of the **Pick Hobson's Riverside Gunfighters Art Collection** of famous gunfighters and outlaws. Created by artist Lea McCarty, the display is open twenty-four hours a day and has been acclaimed by historians and art critics throughout The West. Call (702) 786-4400 for details.

Located at 549 Court Street in Reno is the **Sierra Nevada Museum of Art**. Its collection focuses on art of the Great Basin region as well as other

720

aspects of nineteenth and twentieth century American art. The works of many noted artists are shown on a rotating basis and include a wide-ranging selection of paintings, drawing, prints, sculptures, decorative arts and Native American baskets. The museum is an easy walk from downtown Reno via Arlington Avenue. It is open Tuesday through Friday from 10:00 a.m. to 4:00 p.m., weekends from 12:00 noon to 4:00 p.m. and is closed Mondays. For more information call (702) 329-3333.

Some say it was the Colt .45 that made The West. A Nevadan might tell you it was the slot machine. The first three-reeler slot machine, the Liberty Bell of 1898, along with scores of other early slots, are part of the historic slot machine collection at the **Liberty Belle Saloon.** Located at 4250 South Virginia Street, antique buffs and gamblers will be fascinated by its unusual and amusing relics. The collection is open daily from 11:00 a.m. to 11:00 p.m.

Take a break from the Reno excitement and relax by tranquil **Virginia Lake.** This shaded lake is a bird refuge where you will see many species of resident and migrating ducks and other birds. A fitness station, one-mile walking/jogging path, picnic area and playground are available. During August there are band concerts each Wednesday from 7:00 p.m. to 9:00 p.m. To get to the lake take South Virgin Street to West Plumb Lane, then turn on Lakeside Drive.

Pyramid Lake is a germ of a spot (I mean gem of a spot) surrounded by the soft brown and red sandstone mountains of the Pyramid Lake Indian Reservation. While visiting here you may be able to sense why the Paiute Indians revere the lake as a sacred place of power. Upon the lake are rock islands and steam periodically escapes from rock domes and spires. In addition to its scenery, Pyramid Lake is famous for its fishing, especially for cutthroat trout. The last vestige of a mammoth lake that once cover most of Nevada, Pyramid is also the home of the prehistoric cui-ui fish and one of only two pelican rookeries in the country. Water skiing is allowed on the lake and campgrounds are available on shore.

The lake is thirty-two miles north of Reno on state highway 455. Nine miles north of Sutcliffe, a small lakeshore town, is Warrior Point, which has plenty of shoreline visitor facilities.

Washoe Lake State Park offers majestic views of the Sierra Nevada. There are also equestrian trails, sailing, fishing, camping and exploration of the park's sand dune ecosystem. The park is about twenty miles south of Reno. To get there take US 395 and turn at the Washoe Lake Recreation Area turnoff at Little Washoe Lake.

If not for the Comstock Silver Strike, **Carson City** might have become just another footnote in the long history of Nevada ghost towns rather than the state capital. Because of the silver strike, and the fact the Union needed money to fight the Civil War, Congress authorized the hasty construction of the Carson Mint. Until it ceased operations in 1893, the mint coined approximately fifty million dollars in silver and gold. The old mint was housed in an impressive two-story sandstone building which now functions as the **Nevada State Museum**. Inside are relics from the early mining days, a full-scale model of a mine, Indian artifacts, antique gaming equipment, guns and other memorabilia.

The museum is in downtown Carson City on North Carson Street across from The Nugget. It is open daily from 8:30 a.m. to 4:30 p.m. There is a fifty cent admission charge for those eighteen and older. For more information call the museum at (702) 885-4810.

If you like railroad nostalgia combined with history of the Old West, the **Nevada State Railroad Museum** can put you on the right track. A branch of the Nevada State Museum, it includes twenty-two pieces of railroad stock, including four locomotives. Located at the southern end of Carson City in a large green steel shed, it is on U.S. Highway 395 at Fairview Drive. The museum is open from 8:30 a.m. to 4:30 p.m. Friday through Sunday and holidays, from Memorial Day through October 31st. For details call (702) 885-5168.

The **Stewart Indian Museum** is on the scenic grounds of what was Nevada's only non-reservation boarding school for Native Americans, who came from all over the country from many different tribes. The museum has a fine rotating exhibit of rare E.S. Curtis American Indian photogravures. Indian artwork and jewelry is available for purchase in the museum's trading post. Located three miles south of Carson City at 5366 Snyder Avenue, just before the Lake Tahoe/US 50 turnoff, the museum is open every day from 9:00 a.m. to 4:00 p.m. For more information call (702) 882-1808.

A fulsome way to acquaint yourself with Reno:

RENO CULTURE TOUR			
a.m.	W.D. May Museum	Best arboretum	Reno/Att
a.m.	Antique Collective	Best antiques	Reno/Ant
LUNCH			
p.m.	Historical Museum	Best Am. history	Reno/Att
p.m.	Gaming Academy	Best bet training	Reno/Att
DINNERTIME/PLAYTIME			
p.m.	Planetarium	Best starlight	Reno/Att
Then, to pamper yourself, try a day, a weekend or longer at...			
a.m.	Walley's	Best spa	Genoa/Rest

Accommodations

BALLYS-RENO, 2500 East Second Street, Reno, Nevada. Formerly the MGM Grand Hotel. World's largest casino. Seven distinctive dining facilities.

CIRCUS CIRCUS HOTEL/CASINO
500 North Sierra Street
Reno, NV 89513
Tel. (702) 329-0711
Visa, MasterCard, AMEX and Diner's Club are accepted.

Big time adventure in "Big Top" style is what you'll find at Circus Circus Hotel/Casino, long renowned as "Reno's greatest showplace," and the only family-oriented gaming resort in Reno. A stupendous experience for all, Circus Circus has everything for the young through adult seeking fun and excitement.

The key to Circus Circus' commitment to family entertainment is the spectacular array of captivating circus acts found under the Big Top. Daily from 11:30 a.m. to midnight, see outstanding circus stars perform in the world's largest permanent circus. World renowned aerialists execute astounding feats high above the dazzling kaleidoscope of color and light, trained animals bring crowds to exhilarating cheers and whimsical clowns delight guests of all ages with their special magic. Saunter through a spectacular midway surrounding the performing arena, resplendent with a dazzling assortment of your favorite midway games and high-tech video

723

adventures and alive with the vibrant squeals and laughter of the young and young at heart. Amid the glitter, games, circus fun and excitement is superb dining including three outstanding restaurants to suit every taste and every budget - from the giant Circus Buffet to the delightful Three Ring Coffee Shop to the comfort of the Hickory Pit Steak House. Relax in downtown Reno's largest hotel, featuring 1,625 beautiful rooms, all complete with individual climate control, color television and spacious living. Ride the one-of-a-kind monorail Sky Shuttle which ferries guests between Circus Circus' two hotel towers. Park safely in a 2,000 space covered self-parking building or enjoy twenty-four-hour valet parking.

Within the adult-oriented environment of Reno exists a world where children of all ages are made to feel as welcome as their parents. For "Best Choice" in fun, entertainment and excitement the whole family can enjoy, head for big time adventure under the Big Top of Circus Circus!

COLONIAL MOTOR INN AND CASINO, 250 North Arlington Avenue, and COLONIAL MOTOR INN, 232 West Street, Reno, Nevada. Known locally as a small, friendly business catering to the local trade, the casino appeals to those overwhelmed by the size, noise, and crowds of the major casinos. Between the two inns, there are 268 rooms. Many area residents consider the Inn's prime rib the best in town! Lots of repeat customers attest to this spot being a find.

COMSTOCK HOTEL AND CASINO, 200 West Second Street, Reno, Nevada. Deluxe guest rooms, fine restaurants and bustling casino. Old west decor.

ELDORADO HOTEL AND CASINO
4th and Virginia Streets
Reno, NV 89501
Tel. (702) 786-5700
(800) 648-5966

With 411 luxurious rooms, a sparkling swimming pool, convention center and an action packed casino with lively cabaret shows, the Eldorado Hotel is everything a leading hotel and casino should be and more.

General Manager Donald Cotano and his family are active in all stages of this fine operation. This involvement shows in the quality of the food and service in their restaurants:

La Strada - Outstanding Northern Italian cuisine from homemade pasta to delicious veal, chicken and seafood. The setting depicts Old Italy and is highlighted by "The Grape Lady", a magnificent, award winning stained glass art piece.

    <u>Vintage Restaurant</u> - Located on the Mezzanine level, this is a favorite for steaks, prime rib and seafood in a warm, intimate atmosphere.

    <u>Mardi Gras Coffee Shop</u> - In addition to a wide variety of tempting items, savory Chinese food is also available.

    <u>The Market Place Buffet -</u> Succulent prime rib served nightly. Breakfast, lunch and dinner, choose from a large variety of taste tempting items.

    <u>The Deli</u> - On the main casino floor, this is the place for superior "fast food."

    No matter which of the restaurants you sample, try the house wine. These special, premium house wines are produced by the Carano Vineyards.

FITZGERALDS, 255 North Virginia Street, Reno, Nevada. Sixteen floor hotel with casino with varied dining facilities. Center of downtown Reno.

PEPPERMILL HOTEL CASINO
2707 South Virginia Street
Reno, NV 89502
Tel. (702) 826-3121

    If "big is better" you better not miss Reno's Peppermill Hotel Casino with its more than 600-room inn, 15,000 square foot convention center, 20,000 square foot casino, magnificent continental restaurants and large gourmet buffet restaurant. Enjoy Reno in style with an experience you will savor for years to come.

    Discover why the Peppermill's expanded buffet restaurant is famous throughout the West, featuring continental cuisine with a Polynesian touch added to the menu and decor. Although miles from the ocean, you'll feel as though you are feasting aboard a magnificent luxury liner. The Peppermill's latest restaurant is Le Moulin, "The Mill," and is Nevada's newest and brightest star on the fine dining scene. Experience service that is first-class in every way, from masterful tableside preparation by skilled and specially-trained captains to pleasant and knowledgeable wine sommeliers to assist you in finding the perfect wine from the more than 300 selections on the wine list. Dine in a uniquely entertaining, warm, casual and contemporary atmosphere. The entire complex has a special style and feeling and everyone in the casino can enjoy the entertaining sights and sounds coming from the open cabaret stage. Enjoy friendly, professional service from a staff dedicated to make your stay in Reno a memorable one.

When you arrive in Reno, look for the world's largest fiber optic sign high atop the Peppermill's tower. Then, prepare yourself to enjoy your stay in Reno in a "big" way.

PIONEER INN HOTEL/CASINO
221 South Virginia Street
Reno, NV 89501
Tel. (702) 329-9781
      (800) 648-5468
Visa, Mastercard and AMEX are accepted.

Folksy atmosphere, friendly service and an unhurried pace describe the action at the Pioneer Inn Hotel/Casino in Reno. Five minutes from the downtown glitter, the Pioneer Inn boasts 252 well-appointed rooms, three fine restaurants, swimming pool, gift shop, beauty shop, nightly entertainment, and a full size and lively casino.

Dining is a pleasure and convenient at either the Iron Sword for full dinners, Pepe's Cantina for Mexican food, or the Deli for snacks and light meals. Steaks, prime rib, and seafood are the main attractions at the Iron Sword located right next to the casino. Pepe's serves Mexican fare, carefully made, attractively presented, and masterfully served. At any of the restaurants at the Pioneer the food is consistently good and the prices are always excellent.

For over twenty years, the Pioneer Inn Hotel/Casino has thrived on its reputation of genuine Western hospitality and in Reno it's still the best best in town.

THE RENO HILTON, 255 North Sierra Street, Reno Vevada. Large two story casino, 600 rooms and suites, Continental cuisine, Mobil 4-Star rating.

The nights, lights and highlights of Reno combine to create some of the finest glitter, glamor and entertainment in the world. The following hotels, in addition to their restaurants, casinos and floor shows, all offer something unique. This tour can help you find it.

THE WHEELING & DEALING IN RENO TOUR			
p.m.	Pioneer Inn	Best western	Reno/Acc
p.m.	Peppermill	Best design	Reno/Acc
a.m.	Circus Circus	Best entertainment	Reno/Acc
a.m.	Harrah's	Best service	Stateline/Acc

Antique

THE ANTIQUE COLLECTIVE
400 Mill Street
Reno, NV 89502
Tel. (702) 322-3989
Hrs: Tue. - Sat.   10:00 a.m. - 6:00 p.m.
          Sunday   12:00 noon - 5:00 p.m.

An antique heaven for antique lovers: that's what you have at the Antique Collective, Reno's unique collection of fifteen shops, each with it's own particular area of specialization. Join owner Carol Harland who, with her participating dealers, present a large and varied array of antiques and collectibles just certain to stimulate your desire and interest.

Browse through well represented periods including Victorian, Early American and increasingly popular and valuable 1920-30 memorabilia. Antique buffs will enjoy discovering selections of elegant china, fine glass, and beautiful furniture pieces from all periods. With so many dealers displaying their particular specialties, you may just stumble across that elusive item you've been diligently searching for. Roam to your heart's content through specialty areas such as pottery and porcelain, pressed glass, Depression glass, jewelry, art deco, pictures for hanging, needlework, basketry, tinwear, and woodenware. Let Carol and all the fine people at The Antique Collective help you find that unique treasure.

Leave behind the hustle and bustle of Virginia Street and stroll a few blocks to Mill Street. Treat yourself to the peaceful, pleasant atmosphere of The Antique Collective and lose yourself in antique heaven. "Best Choice" for antique lovers. They never had it so good!

Restaurant

CHEZ BERNARD
432 East 4th
Reno, NV 89512
Tel. (702) 323-6262
Hrs: Wed. - Mon. 6:00 p.m.
Bar opens at 5:00 p.m.
Closed Tuesdays.
Visa, Mastercard and AMEX are accepted.

Chez Bernard is that intimate little restaurant to take someone special, to celebrate something special, or to enjoy an especially fine gourmet dinner.

Stepping into the subdued elegance of Chez Bernard is like entering another world. Within a couple of minutes, the atmosphere of peace and comfort will soothe and relax the most anxious spirit. This gem of a restaurant is owned and operated by Monsieur and Madam Bernard Rault. The Raults are master French restauranteurs and welcome their guests in the finest French restaurant traditions. Recommended specialties are Cordon Bleu, Piquante, Piccata, Scallopini, and veal Francais all prepared with the most tender Wisconsin milk-fed veal. Two tasty entrees prepared at your table are flamed steak Diane and New York pepper steak. As in the best French restaurants, the wine list is excellent and extensive. To complete the dining experience Bernard suggests one of their desserts prepared en flambe at your table.

Few towns actually possess a "great little French restaurant", but one of those towns is Reno and the restaurant is Chez Bernard.

FAMOUS MURPHY'S
3127 South Virginia Street
Reno, NV 89509
Tel. (702) 827-4111
Hrs: Mon. - Sun. 11:00 a.m. - 4:00 a.m.
Visa, MasterCard, Diner's Club, Carte Blanche and AMEX accepted.

Famous Murphy's is named after all the Murphys, famous and infamous, who made their reputations during Nevada's colorful mining era.

Owner Michael Wiltshire, himself a well known Reno restauranteur, opened Famous Murphy's on St. Patrick's Day 1987 promising great food, friendly service, and good times. Judging by Famous Murphy's popularity, Mike has kept his word. The menu is American with emphasis on steak, seafood and pasta. Fun and food are found on all three levels of the establishment with an oyster bar and lounge downstairs, a classy restaurant in the middle and a piano bar upstairs. Specialties in the restaurants are "Murphs' Surph and Turph", steak and seafood combinations. Two seafood happy hours (11:00 a.m. -6:00 p.m. and 1:00-4:00 a.m.) in the oyster bar offer great treats at super prices.

Famous Murphy's is fast becoming one of Reno's most popular night spots and even though Nevada has had many famous Murphys in its history, Mike intends to make his Famous Murphy's the most famous Murphy of all.

THE GLORY HOLE, 4201 West Fourth Street, Reno, Nevada. With its heavy beams and plank walls, The Glory Hole transports you back to mining days. Popular with locals, the restaurant provides a bar and excellent meals in intimate, comfortable, surroundings. It's about two miles west of Reno and accepts major credit cards.

LA PINATA RESTAURANT AND CANTINA, 1575 Vassar Street, Town & Country Center, Reno, Nevada. Mexican menu, weekday buffet, full bar.

LIBERTY BELLE SALOON AND RESTAURANT
4250 S Virginia Street
Reno, NV 89502
Tel. (702) 825-1776
Hrs. Mon. - Sat. 11:00 a.m. - 11:00 p.m.
         Sunday   4:00 p.m. - 10:00 p.m.
Mastercard and Visa are accepted. Reservations for seven or more are accepted.

When you step into the Liberty Belle Saloon and Restaurant, you are taking a giant step back in time. By the time you reach the bar on the right, or the dining room on the left, you have already passed one of the main reasons for Reno's existence. By the front door is the original Fey Liberty Belle slot machine, the machine that started a billion dollar industry. You see, the Liberty Belle is owned and operated by Marshall and Frank Fey, the grandson's of Charles Fey who devised the three reel Liberty Belle, a device that grew to be so popular that it's name became synonymous with the term "slot machine." Today, the restaurant houses one of the most extensive collections of historical slot machines in the country. Be sure to browse through then when you come for lunch or dinner.

The decor of the Liberty Belle is of the old west and the food is simply wonderful. Just some of the tempting entrees are juicy, well aged steaks, crab legs, lobster tails, barbeque ribs, prime rib and more. Entrees are served with a tossed green salad or crisp spinach salad, a baked potato and oven baked beans or rice if you prefer, a basket of hot bread, dessert and coffee or tea. Liberty Belle's prices are moderate and there is a children's menu.

Charlie Fey would be proud of his grandsons because the quality and ambience create a "Best Choice" you will enjoy.

LOUIS' BASQUE CORNER
301 East Fourth Street (at Evans)
Reno, NV 89512
Tel. (702) 323-7203
Hrs: Lunch   Mon. - Sat. 11:00 a.m - 2:00 p.m.
         Dinner   Mon. - Sat. From 6:00 p.m.
Visa, MasterCard, AMEX and Diner's Club are accepted.

Can dining be worth celebrating? It can at Louis' where mealtime is an event or, better yet, a celebration. Louis' is a Reno "institution" and owners Louis and Lorraine Errequible are like the city's adopted godparents. Why? They are loved by many and respected by all because of their attitude: they say they have no customers, only friends and guests. You'll find yourself a part of this large, but special group shortly upon entering the restaurant.

Relax and enjoy being served at long tables by friendly waitresses wearing authentic Basque costumes. The food is absolutely delicious and plentiful, usually served in six or seven courses accompanied by the customary glass of wine. For his friends, Louis recommends LePoulet Basquaise, a delightful mouth-watering chicken dish that everyone loves. Or try other traditional Basque specialties such as lamb, oxtail, tripe and beef tongue which are all popular at Louis' Basque Corner. And what makes Basque food so different and special? The spices. "It's all in the seasoning" says Louis. At lunch or dinnertime, you'll find ranchers, doctors, truckers, lawyers, and entertainers all sitting down together. These are friends of the Errequibles and in the age-old Basque tradition, there's always room at the table for a few more.

If you miss Louis' Basque Corner during your stay in Reno, you're missing out on something that's very special. Just three blocks from downtown, near the historic Western Pacific building, you'll find a "Best Choice" age-old Basque event taking place. Have a seat and join in the celebration!

MARIE CALLENDER'S RESTAURANT, 3255 South Virginia Street, Reno, Nevada. Both a restaurant and a saloon, and there's more than just pies!! Enjoy gourmet pizza, exotic tropical drinks, and late-hour desserts.

O.G.'S CLASSIC CUISINE
442 Flint Street
Reno, NV 89501
Tel. (702) 329-1173

Hrs:			
Mon. - Sat.	Lunch		11:30 a.m. - 3:00 p.m.
Mon. - Sat.	Dinner		5:00 p.m. -11:00 p.m.
Sunday			5:00 p.m. -10:00 p.m.
Sunday	Brunch		10:00 a.m. - 3:00 p.m.

Visa, Mastercard and AMEX are accepted.

Hidden amidst the glitz and good natured glamor of Reno's dining scene stands a historic monument to an other era, an era of elegance, class and good taste. Housed in historic Hardy House a nationally registered Victorian landmark, O.G.'s Classic Cuisine offers lunches and dinners, "in the casual yet elegant atmosphere of Reno's only Victorian restaurant", to quote owner Red Pruett.

The food can be described as graceful American featuring roast chicken Dakota, steak Diane, and flame broiled rack of spring lamb. Specials here are really special since they are masterfully prepared and modestly priced. Lunches feature lighter fare such as egg and seafood specialties, the lobster and crab-meat pie are a must. An authentic Victorian bar offers favorite libations which can be enjoyed, weather permitting, in a cozy private courtyard.

In the mathematics of good dining O.G.'s = "Best Choice" in Reno for American food.

PASQUALES PASTA FRESCA RISTORANTE
300 A East Plumb Lane (Park Lane Mall)
Reno, NV 89502
Tel. (702) 826-9018
Hrs: Mon. - Thu.   11:30 a.m.- 10:00 p.m.
      Fri. - Sat.   11:30 a.m. - 11:00 p.m.
      Sunday   11:30 a.m. - 9:00 p.m.
Visa and MasterCard are accepted.

The talk of Reno these days is the secret to the amazing appeal and success of Archie Granata's sensational Italian experience known as Pasquale's Pasta Fresca Ristorante. Study the clues yourself and see if you can discover the secret.

Some say it's Archie's famous fifty-ton, aged oak fueled oven that can exceed 1,000 degrees. They say this high heat and direct cooking on natural stone surfaces is the secret to perfect pizza crust. Others say the secret is Archie's stickler for details when it comes to quality, service, affordable prices, and customer satisfaction and his insistence that everything be done in a first-class manner. It could be the polite, competent service from attractive hostesses who Archie insists must have "naturally good personalities." Or perhaps it's the menu which includes a full description of all the tantalizing pastas and sauces to make ordering easier for dinner guests. It could be the irresistible aroma and taste of the spaghetti, rigatoni, lasagna and other tasty pasta delicacies or maybe the hot, delicious soup or fresh garden salad. Then again, it might be the best garlic bread you'll ever taste - so good that customers on the bar side often order a basket with their favorite beverage. Speaking of beverages, the secret possibly could be found in Pasquale's outstanding array of house brands proudly displayed above a handsome bar, or maybe it's the sixteen-tap cruvinet which allows you to enjoy fine premium wines on an affordable per-glass basis. It may be the Italian coffee drinks or specially blended delights such as a brandy Alexander, grasshopper, or golden

732

Cadillac, all made with real, creamy ice cream. Some have even suggested the secret was the open and spacious rooms that were carefully designed to provide a warm, intimate feeling. The raised round tables with high stools for two or four persons are ideal for close conversation while larger table groupings invite a "let's all join in" atmosphere.

One thing is for certain. You must personally experience these clues if you hope to solve the mystery. Long after the sights and sounds of Reno fade from your memory, the thoughts of the good food and fun time you had at Pasquale's Pasta Fresca Ristorante will remain with you. Enjoy Reno's "Best Choice" for Italian dining and test your skill at solving the mystery.

PIMPAREL LA TABLE FRANCAISE, 3065 West Fourth Street, Reno, Nevada. A total French dining experience and impeccable service has earned the Pimparel family's restaurant a four-star rating for the past eight years in the Mobil Guide. Full course dinners, fine wines, and subtle elegance distinguish this spot, reminiscent of a French country inn.

RAPSCALLION SEAFOOD HOUSE AND BAR
1555 South Wells Avenue
Reno, NV 89502
Tel. (702) 323-1211

Hrs:	Lunch	Mon. - Fri.	11:30 a.m. - 5:00 p.m.
	Dinner	Sun. - Thur.	5:30 p.m - 10:30 p.m.
		Fri. - Sat.	5:30 p.m. -11:00 p.m.
	Sunday Brunch		10:00 a.m. - 2:00 p.m.

Reservations advised.

Dining at the Rapscallion Seafood House and Bar proves you don't have to be within the sound of crashing waves or the smell of salt air to enjoy fresh seafood at its finest. The Rapscallion has fresh fish flown in daily from throughout the world, so you can count on finding twenty-five to thirty varieties on the menu, which is printed daily.

From Ahi to Yellowtail, the expert chefs at Rapscallion know how to prepare each variety to perfection. Superb steaks, lamb, Provimi veal and a delightful dish called Joe's Special with ground beef, eggs, spinach, mushrooms, wine and seasonings also grace the menu. The luncheon and brunch menu feature such delicacies as omelettes and crepes filled with shrimp and crab, eggs Benedict, Rainbow trout and Petrale sole sauteed with mushrooms and butter. Fresh, hot hors d' oeuvres are served in the bar during what the Rapscallion so aptly defines as the "ungnarly hours" from 4:30 p.m. to 6:30 p.m.

Owner John Leonudakis and his outstanding staff take pride in presenting an adventure in fine dining with high quality meals, service and value.

RIVOLI
221 W 2nd Street
Reno, NV 89501
Tel. (702) 784-9792
Hrs: Tue. - Sat. 6:00 p.m. - 10:00 p.m.
Closed Sunday and Monday

This place is so good its dangerous to even mention it. Rivoli is fine dining, unusual entertainment, and personal involvement all rolled into one.

Pier Perotti, the owner, is a classically trained tenor, and, when the mood strikes him, he will spontaneously begin singing classical opera. Often, he is joined by other professional singers in the room and soon the restaurant is aglow in bravura selections from *Carmen* and other masterpieces. This beautiful music serves as a backdrop for a dinner of the finest Italian cuisine, the veal Saltimbocca and veal Cordon Bleu are especially good, prepared by Pier's excellent staff. Be sure and sip one of Rivoli's personally selected vintage wines. Pier, himself a classical treasure, will probably sit down at your table to visit and insure that your evening is the best it can be.

When in Reno, go to Rivoli's for one of those truly memorable experiences; and share with your loved ones this delightful classical secret.

RESTAURANTS YOU CAN BET ON			
a.m.	Famous Murphy's	Best new eats	Reno/Rest
a.m.	El Dorado	Best restaurant	Reno/Rest
p.m.	Liberty Belle	Best full menu	Reno/Rest
p.m.	Louis'	Best Basque	Reno/Rest
p.m.	O.G.'s Classic	Best Victorian	Reno/Rest
p.m.	Pasquales	Best pizza/pasta	Reno/Rest
p.m.	Rapscallion	Best seafood	Reno/Rest
p.m.	Rivoli	Best Saltimbocca	Reno/Rest
p.m.	Chez Bernard	Best French	Reno/Rest

Stateline

Accommodation

HARRAH'S LAKE TAHOE HOTEL/CASINO
Highway 50 P.O. Box 8
Stateline, NV 89449
Tel. (702) 588-6611
      (800) 648-3773
Visa, Mastercard, and AMEX are accepted.

Here's what others say about Harrah's Lake Tahoe, "Outstanding commitment to service, quality and consistent overall excellence distinguishes Harrah's Lake Tahoe among the finest properties in America", so states Allen E. Murray, Chairman and Chief Executive Officer of Mobil Corporation. He goes on to say, "we are proud to honor Harrah's Lake Tahoe with the 1987 Mobil Travel Guide Five-Star Award as representative of America's best". "Five Diamond properties are renowned for superior service to their guests," states James B. Creal, AAA President, while awarding Harrah's Lake Tahoe the coveted AAA Five Diamond rating for 1987. And in the words of Harrah's Lake Tahoe Senior Vice President,Ron Lenczycki, "we devote a great deal of time, energy, and expense to insure that our hotel has the finest amenities imaginable, but the real battle is won through superior service. If you don't have superior service, your amenities don't mean a thing. We are fortunate to have amassed a staff that concerns itself with providing the best possible service day-in, day-out".

A beautiful structure, Harrah's Lake Tahoe is an eighteen story, 540-room gem of a hotel which reflects the natural beauty of Lake Tahoe. Inside the color scheme is gold, yellow, rust, and green which depict the changing seasons of the year. Every room contains two complete bathrooms each with its own TV and phone, remote control TV in the living area, focused bedside reading lights, adjustable heating and air conditioning, and angled windows for a spectacular view of both lake and mountains. Two rooftop restaurants, the elegant Summit - famous for its award winning continental cuisine and the extravagant Forest Buffet, highlight an array of dining facilities in the hotel. Other amenities include twenty-four hour room service, a heated indoor swimming pool, complete health club, supervised video arcade for youngsters, ice-cream parlor, and a mini shopping mall.

To top it all off Harrah's Lake Tahoe presents nightly big name entertainment in the legendary South Shore Room and Stateline Cabaret, and,

735

of course, a 70,000 square-foot casino means an abundance of casino action and with over 2,250 slot machines, the largest collection of slots in the world.

The odds are that you'll agree Harrah's Lake Tahoe is a sure winner at Lake Tahoe.

HARVEY'S RESORT
P. O. Box 128
Stateline, NV 89449
Tel. (702) 588-2411

Harvey's Resort Hotel-Casino is loaded with fun inside and out. Resting smack in the middle of one of this country's most fabulous recreation areas, you're within an incredible range of activities, from fishing and water sports to golf and skiing. Inside this towering Lake Tahoe accommodation is a pulse quickening casino, outstanding dining facilities and a children's arcade.

The Seafood Grotto in Harvey's serves up to six fresh Catch of the Day selections, and invites sport fishermen in the area to bring in their catches and have the fish prepared to order. Or, enjoy superb dining in the Sage Room Steak House, the area's first and finest gourmet restaurant. The Top of the Wheel offers a spectacular view, exotic cocktails and a menu featuring island specialties and Continental cuisine. And for a change of pace, the South Shore's best south-of-the-border cuisine is served at El Vaquero.

Awarded the Mobil Four Star and AAA Four Diamond ratings, Harvey's offers relaxing luxury in 197 rooms and suites where valet and room service are available around the clock. At Harvey's Resort, the fun just never stops!

SACRAMENTO COUNTY

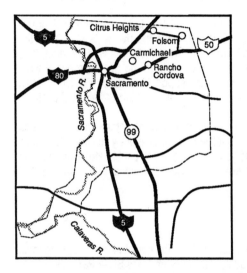

Take one sunny spot at the confluence of two major rivers. Add some of the world's richest farm land, and mix well with tradition steeped in the lore of the gold rush and big government. You now have the makings of country where fortunes are made, political foundations laid, and outdoor activities played. And that's Sacramento County.

Located on Interstate 5 and in the upper central valley, Sacramento county contains flat farm lands and rolling hills and lies between the coastal mountain range to the west, and the Sierra foothills to the east. From the city itself, it's a mere one and half hour drive to Lake Tahoe and the ski areas, about the same distance to San Francisco. Two of the state's largest rivers merge here: The Sacramento River, flowing from the north where it is fed by the snows of Mount Shasta, and the American River, which enters the region from the east. Just as the rivers provided riverboat service to the 49ers, it provides the state with a major inland shipping port in Sacramento.

Together with the mild climate, these two rivers offer a host of year-round recreational opportunities. Hundreds of miles of waterways lie in the course of the American and Sacramento rivers. Thousands enjoy cruising on the deck of a chartered river boat, piloting a house boat, or just plain rafting, swimming, or fishing. Quiet wooded nature trails abound along their shores.

Long before the land and its special features brought white men, the Maidu Indians hunted and fished here. Spanish explorer Gabriel Moraga led an expedition through here in 1808. In 1823 Jedediah Smith led a small band of trappers along the American River in search of a pass through the Sierras. Among the first settlers was Captain John Sutter, a Swiss immigrant who received a Mexican Land grant at the confluence of the two rivers. There he built a fort, and operated a thriving flower and lumber business. That is, until

737

gold was discovered at Sutter's sawmill 50 miles to the east. His workers him in search of their own fortunes, leaving him behind to deal with the thousands of transient miners that came through the area, as well as the squatters who seized much of his land. His debts became overwhelming and was forced to sell his fort.

In 1860, Sacramento was the end of line for for the Pony Express. Thousands of river boats chugged up and down the rivers. And in 1869 the transcontinental railroad linked Sacramento and California with the east, thus insuring that this land would play a major role in the development of what would become the nation's richest and most populous state. Ronald Reagan may not be the last politician to emerge from the Golden State's capital city to take on Washington D.C.

Today Sacramento county, which includes the communities of Rancho Cordova, Elk Grove and Folsom, is a blend of contemporary cosmopolitan living, with well-preserved touches of its past, as seen in cobble stone streets and wooden sidewalks of Sacramento's Old Sacramento and Folsom's Sutter Street.

ATTRACTIONS

Created by a dam completed in 1955, **Folsom Lake** is easily the most popular recreation site in the county. The **Folsom Lake State Park** offers year round camping, swimming and boating. Both boat and sail board rentals are available at the lake. For more information, contact the park headquarters at (916) 988-0205, or drop in at the ranger station at Folsom-Auburn Road and Folsom Dam Road.

Rafting is popular almost everywhere on the river. One of the most popular for experienced rafters, or those accompanied by a guide, is the six hour trip from Coloma, to Folsom Lake State Park. For information on raft rentals and guide service, call   322-3327.

The **American River Parkway**, a 23- mile stretch of land along the American river from Nimbus Dam to downtown **Sacramento's Discovery Park**, is like few public parks in this country. As rafters paddle down the river, you can peddle its length on the paved bike path, or seek quiet solitude among the wooded nature trails, or even take a dip when the mood strikes. The parkway offers something for just about anyone.

For a not-so-quiet time, try the **Prairie City Off-Highway Park**. These 835 acres accommodate the needs of off-road motorcyclists and four-wheel drive enthusiasts.   It boasts motocross tracks and mini bike areas for youngsters, as well as a dirt auto cross track. The park is six miles south of the intersection of U.S. Highway 50 and Prairie City Road.

Now a park, **The Gibson Ranch,** possesses a colorful history dating back to the 1870's . It retains is ranch character with displays of early farm equipment. Visitors are welcome to feed the domestic animals. But it's also a country park for picnicking, camping, swimming, fishing, or sun bathing. The eight acre pond is stocked with a variety of fish. The complex includes five miles of equestrian trails. You'll find Gibson Ranch at the northern end of the county, at Elverta Road and Watt Avenue 366-2061.

Rancho Seco Park offers fishing from a lake stocked with large mouth bass and catfish. Its also a place for cycling, hiking, sailing, and horseback riding. It includes more than 400 acres of shaded picnic areas, a beach,. During summer concessions provide food, beer and soft drinks. From Sacramento, take U.S. 99 south, then east on Twin Cities Road.

Live animals, naturalist talks, and self-guided nature trails are highlights of the **Ancil Hoffman Park,** 3700 Tarshes Drive, Carmicheal. A good place to enjoy American River.

Silver Wings Aviation Museum, at Mather Air Force Base, Rancho Cordova, 364-2908, features military and civilian aircraft from World War I, as well as displays on California aviation history.

Cal Expo, just north of the city, is the site of the state's 133-year-old fair. The fair is held annually for the eighteen days before Labor Day.

If giant turbines turn you on, you'll like the dam and power house tour at **Folsom Dam.** Built in the 1950's at a cost of $60 million it provides a good share of northern California's power needs. The cracks in the marble control panel is testament to the area's most active geological feature: earthquakes. The dam is open weekdays 9:30 a.m. to 5:00 p.m., noon to 5:00 p.m. weekends. For information on tours, contact the Bureau of Reclamation at (916) 988-1707.

Sacramento County

Carmichael

Delicatessen

THE WORLD OF CHEESE
6434 Fair Oaks Boulevard
Carmichael, CA 95608
Tel. (916) 485-1064
Hrs: Mon. - Thu. & Sat.   10:00 a.m. - 6:00 p.m.
       Friday   10:00 a.m. - 8:00 p.m.
       Sunday   12:00 noon - 4:00 p.m.
Visa and MasterCard accepted.

Looking straight into the camera you hear the photographer say, "Cheese." So, following his prompt, you say the word, and a beautiful smile develops on your face. The flash goes off, you blink, and it's a wrap. Photographers have used the cheese trick for ages. Some people say that it works because when formulating the word one automatically smiles, but others know that just thinking about cheese makes them happy. Well, if just thinking about cheese makes these people happy, they'll fall in love with The World of Cheese.

The World of Cheese is a beautiful shop that is virtually peerless in Sacramento. The walls are adorned with colorful photographs, fine art prints and needlework, all revolving around the theme of cheese. As far as the cheese itself is concerned, well, they have over one hundred varieties including Farmhouse cheddar, Brie de Meaux, Roquefort, Parmesan Reggiano, Fontina Val D'aosta and English Shropshire. Also, many related products are carried, such as fondue sets, cheese boards, wine selections and many books about cheeses.

The World of Cheese offers vacuum pack services for gifts, camping and picnicking. If you think you might like a particular cheese, but aren't sure, ask for a taste test. Wow! It's a cheese lover's heaven. Come on in and see what everyone's smiling about.

Citrus Heights

What began as a farming and ranching community in 1850's has become the 85,000 population residential and commercial center of Citrus Heights. Located 14 miles north east of Sacramento, this unincorporated community boasts good schools, extensive park system and great shopping. The Sunrise Recreation and Park District operates a network of twenty-three recreational sites. At press time residents were working to get their community incorporated as a city.

Citrus Heights might be best known for its Sunrise Mall. With more than 100 shops, this is one of the largest fully enclosed regional malls in the state. Across the road from Sunrise Mall is Birdcage Walk, another shopping center known for its tree-lined walkways and well-tended flower planters.

Attractions

When it rains in **Rusch Park**, 7801 Auburn Boulevard, you can head for cover on an old covered bridge that spans the creek. These tree-shaded forty-nine acres included a swimming pool, four tennis courts, picnic areas, a crafts center and a botanical garden. For information contact the park district at (916) 725-1588.

San Juan Park, 5509 Mariposa Avenue, is fifteen acres and includes no less than three soccer fields, as well as tennis courts, picnic grounds and restroom facilities.

The 25 acres at the **C-Bar-C Park**, 5509 Mariposa Avenue , features three softball fields, a Little League baseball field, restroom and concession facilities.

Madera Park, at 8046 Wonder Street, is sixteen acres of picnic, tennis and softball facilities, including a large multiple use field.

Restaurant

CAFE CAPRI
7600 Fair Oaks Boulevard
Carmichael, CA 95608
Tel. (916) 971-9600
Hrs: Mon. - Fri. Lunch 11:30 a.m. - 2:30 p.m.
Mon. - Sat. Dinner 6:00 p.m. - 11:00 p.m.
Banquet facilities are available.

European countries are well known for their exotic gourmet dishes and lavish nightly entertainment. Greece is one such country in Europe that plays favorite to tourists every year. Walking through the streets of Athens, one can smell the delicious aromas wafting from it's many restaurants, and hear the laughs and music emanating from the numerous nightclubs in the area. Wouldn't it be nice to find that combination here? Well, Cafe Capri in Carmichael is just that.

Sophisticated surroundings and exotic European cuisine are featured in this one-of-a-kind restaurant. The owner, a native-born Greek and restauranteur since 1971, acts as your gracious host. There are many succulent meals to choose from including scampi Flambé, veal, rack of lamb, Coq Au Vin, Italian pasta, Greek chicken, just to mention a few. For entertainment, there is a piano bar that plays your favorite music while you move to it on the dance floor.

Cafe Capri is a night club and restaurant fashioned after European hot spots that is sure to provide an exemplary evening out. The saying "Beware of Greeks bearing gifts" may have been true back in the days of Homer, but today it is certainly outdated because Cafe Capri is a jewel of Greek origin that everyone can enjoy.

Restaurant

SCOOP'S CREAMERY & GRILL
7910 Antelope Road
Citrus Heights, CA 95610
Tel. (916) 726-SCOP
Hrs: Mon. - Thu.   11:00 a.m. - 11:00 p.m.
       Fri. - Sat.   11:00 a.m. - 12:00 midnight
       Sunday   11:00 a.m. - 11:00 p.m.

Remember those old fashioned ice cream parlors that used to serve the greatest hamburgers and the most delicious ice cream? Well, that's exactly what Scoop's Creamery & Grill offers, old fashioned delights in contemporary times.

At Scoop's Creamery & Grill they manufacture their own ice cream. And what ice cream! Enjoy such delectables as Scoop's hot fudge sundae, mounds of vanilla ice cream over a whole sliced banana, dripping with Scoop's homemade hot fudge; the Black Gold, chocolate sauce and caramel over a mountain of cream praline ice cream; and The Super Scoop, super large quantities of vanilla, chocolate and strawberry ice cream, loaded with bananas, marshmallow, whipped cream, nuts and cherries. Topped with chocolate, pineapple, strawberry and caramel sauce, it's a sundae fit for a titan!

But like the ice cream parlors of old, Scoop's Creamery & Grill offers much more than delicious ice cream. Tempting hamburgers, sandwiches, corn dogs and hot dogs are all included on the diverse menu. A place for old and young alike, Scoop's features a fifteen percent discount for senior citizens, as well as a super party package for ten or more children. Ahhh, old fashioned treats at their best. Visit Scoop's Creamery & Grill for an experience of past courtesies in modern times.

Elk Grove

Just a few miles south of Sacramento on Highway 99 is Elk Grove, named for the Sacramento Valley Elk who used to favor a stand of oak trees there. Its 16,000 residents live in a are that grew around two hotels built in the 1800's to serve travelers on their way to Stockton. When the Central Pacific Railroad arrived in 1868, the town grew into the thriving community. Although fires have taken their toll over the years, several of the original buildings remain on Main Street. Elk Grove has applied for federal recognition as a registered historic district.

A 1978 attempt to incorporate as a city failed. But recently some of the citizens are beginning a new effort for incorporation as much of the land just outside of Elk Grove is scheduled for major residential and commercial development. Among them is the projected 10,000-member community of Laguna Creek to the west.

Attractions

One of the most used parks by Sacramento area residents is **Elk Grove Park**. Established in 1902, this county park features 125 acres that include a lake stocked for fishing. Other facilities include, a pavilion for group activities, twelve ball fields, a horse arena, swimming pool and bath house. Summer activities include regional softball tournaments and swimming lessons.

Folsom

Twenty five miles east of Sacramento and along the American River is the town "where the West came and stayed." But don't let Folsom's well preserved historic exterior fool you. It's a place where high tech has come and is likely to stay. In recent years several high tech companies have opened plants, finding the living and working easier than the silicon valley.

Having played strong roles in the development of the gold rush, the Pony Express and area electrification, Folsom does have a history every bit as rich as its historic district on Sutter Street would suggest. Today Folsom has 16,000 residents. At the current growth rate, the community is expected to be about 40,000 residents strong by 1990.

A good way to experience Folsom's historic past is to follow the Seven Mile Tour. For maps and details stop in at the Historical Society Museum.

Attractions

Housed in the reconstructed Wells Fargo Assay Office, 823 Sutter Street, is the **Historical Society Museum**. The building, originally constructed in 1860, was the financial center of Northern California. It was also the terminal for the Pony Express and several stage lines. The museum is open Wednesday through Sunday 11:00 a.m. to 4:00 p.m. For information call (916) 985-2707.

Sutter Street was restored to its gold rush splendor in the 1960's. The street is known for its dozen or so art galleries and craft shops that feature hand-made jewelry and pottery. The Candy Store Gallery is considered one of the greatest contemporary art galleries in the region.

The **Folsom Depot** is restored to its hey day appearance. It once served as a terminal for the first train operating west of the Rockies, the Sacramento Valley Railroad. That was in 1856, before completion of the transcontinental railroad. On the grounds you'll find an old miner's shack, a blacksmith shop, and old railroad cars on display. The offices of the city's chamber of commerce are here

Smokey the Bear was the **Folsom Zoo's** first and most famous resident. Smokey died in 1984, but the legacy of the bear cub who survived a forest fire to become fire prevention's mascot lives on at the "misfit zoo." Here a three-legged coyote and a blind bald eagle live in comfort to tell of man's impact on nature. Also featured is a one of the largest wolf packs in captivity. These canines enjoy a large natural enclosure. Admission is free. Zoo hours are 10:00 a.m. to 4:15 p.m. Tuesday through Sunday. For tour or other information call 355-7200.

Folsom City Park is famous for its miniature steam trains. Located on Natoma Street, next to City Hall, picnicking facilities and a variety of recreational activities, including a hike along the riverbank where Indian grinding rocks can be seen. Two miniature steam trains operate at the park, one of which is a replica of the first diamond stack engine to bring passengers from Sacramento to Folsom.

Since 1880 when the granite walls of **Folsom Prison** went up, inmates have been calling it "The End of the World." The subject of a popular Johnny Cash song, Folsom Prison was California's first maximum security prison. Both the prison gift shop and inmate hobby shop are outside of the walls. Gift shop is open daily from 8:00 a.m. - 6:00 p.m.

Restaurant

KEN'S HOP SING PALACE
805 Sutter Street
Folsom, CA 95630
Tel. (916) 985-4133
Hrs: Sun.-Thurs. 11:30 a.m.-9:00 p.m.
      Fri.-Sat.   11:30 a.m -9:30 p.m.

Perhaps the truest compliment for any restaurant can be found in its acceptance by the local folks. Such is the case of Ken's Hop Sing Palace where the local people know they will receive quality food and speedy service is required. Owner Ken Jeong has been greeting his local friends and guests for more than 18 years in the same location. Ken's secret has always been serving quality Chinese and American food at reasonable prices.

Candle-lit tables, friendly food service, and a complete beer and wine list assures you of a pleasant evening. For large groups, the Royal Palm Room accommodates up to 65 for banquets.

North Highlands

Accommodations

THE RODEWAY INN
3425 Orange Grove Avenue
N. Highlands, CA 95660
Tel. (916) 488-4100

The Rodeway Inn is conveniently located off I-880 and Highway 80 at the Watt Avenue exit. As Sacramento is the political and geographical hub of the state, the inn offers the maximum in accessibility to all points of interest and business.

Staying at The Rodeway Inn is having all the comforts of home, in a full service hotel. You can enjoy the luxury of soaking in the sunken tub of the Presidential Suite while sipping wine and munching goodies from their famous Red Apple Restaurant. For your out of town stay, make your way to the Rodeway!

Rancho Cordova

Accommodations

DAY'S INN, 11131 Folsom Boulevard, Rancho Cordova, California. A lovely new hotel with 131 well-appointed guest rooms! Pool, spa, first-run movies in your room, European lobby and cocktail lounge,and a deli/cafe are other amenities.

HOTEL EL RANCHO CORDOVA
10701 Folsom Boulevard
Rancho Cordova, CA 95670
Tel. (916) 635-6711
       (800) 952-5566

Just north of I-50 at Zinfadel and Folsom is the Hotel El Rancho. This hotel is a thirty year old, recently remodeled, landmark in the area. Owner Robert Stahl has used white wicker and forest green fabrics to give the rooms a bright, cheery feeling. Each room has a refrigerator and microwave oven. The rooms on the top floor are spacious; with two settees, a corner table and two armchairs.

Adjoining the hotel is a large cocktail lounge with an atrium for dancing under the stars and a banquet room bordering the swimming pool that will seat 250 people. The dining area is done in brick with bevelled mirrors, etched glass, brass, wainscoting, bamboo and upholstered chairs.

Breakfast in this fine restaurant features five kinds of pancakes; apple, blueberry, banana, buttermilk and buckwheat. Favorite luncheon items include marinated chicken breast, crab and cheese on an English muffin and a Cobb salad. For dinner, choose from the pan-fried trout, veal Parmesan or the vegetable linguini. The prices are modest and the portions generous.

SHERATON SUNRISE HOTEL & TOWERS, 11211 Point East Drive, Rancho Cordova, California. The largest new hotel in the area with over 10,000 square feet of meeting space.   All amenities, two restaurants, lounge, complimentary continental breakfast and afternoon hors d´ oeuvres.

Restaurant

GARBEAU'S DINNER THEATRE
12401 Folsom Boulevard
Rancho Cordova, CA 95670
Tel. (916) 985-6361

Hrs:	Dinner Seating	Wed. - Sat.	6:15 p.m. - 7:30 p.m.
		Sunday	5:30 p.m. - 6:30 p.m.
	Performances	Wed. - Sat.	8:30 p.m.
		Sunday	7:30 p.m

When it's dinner theater you might expect to settle for a little less--a little less theater, a little less food. But Garbeau's gives the best of both fine dining and theater, calling it "gourmet theater."

Garbeau's is probably the only full menu dinner theater in the country. Everywhere else it's three items or a buffet. The quality of the theater is also something special, expect first rate sets, flashy special effects and quickly executed set changes. A staff of five full time designers makes all this possible. Shows change seven times a year, giving theater lovers opportunity to visit over and over.

Garbeau's where you can enjoy full course meals, and full course theater is your "Best Choice" for a completely entertaining evening.

RUDY'S HIDEAWAY, 12303 Folsom Boulevard, Rancho Cordova, California. This family-owned roadhouse has a reputation for the best lobster around, and great steaks, prime rib and seafood.

Sacramento

Elegant neighborhoods of restored Victorian homes and tree-line boulevards, fine art, fine fine music, fine food--all in a city best known at the seat of California's government. The 300,000 residents enjoy a ninety-five square mile twentieth century city that has not forgotten its past. Old Sacramento, is a historic district other cities look to as an example for historic preservation. You might think San Francisco has the honor of claiming the first theater and art museum in the state. But the city by the Golden Gate concedes that honor to Sacramento. Sacramento is host to a world-class Dixieland Jazz Jubilee that brings world class musicians from around the globe to perform every Memorial Day.

Summer weather is dry and on the hot side--upper 80s and 90s. Average annual rainfall is 17 inches. Winter months are notorious for the thick low-laying Tule fog, which keeps day-time temperatures in low 50s and 40s.

Sacramento is a city that truly has its own character, and when it comes to its attractions, many really have class.

Attractions

No doubt the most imposing structure in the city is the **State Capitol building.** The 210 foot high dome easily dominates this this section of the city. Modeled after the nation's Capitol in Washington, D.C., it flourishes with American neo-classic architecture, sporting grand Corinthian columns on the outside and majestic marble mosaic floors on the inside. The building was completed in 1874, and underwent a $70 million restoration between 1975 and 1982. The 40 acres of grounds contain more that 400 varieties of trees and shrubs. The Capitol is open 9:00 a.m. to 5:00 p.m. week days and daily during the summer, 10:00 a.m. to 5:00 p.m. weekends between Labor Day to Memorial Day. For information on tours of the building and grounds: (916) 324-0333.

Old Sacramento is nostalgic world of cobblestone streets, romantic restaurants and quaint shops along the riverfront. Restoration continues along the riverfront between I Street and the Capitol Avenue bridge to create the old wharf. within Old Sacramento's twenty-eight acres are 100 fully-restored 19th century buildings, steam trains, and waterfront attractions, including river boats. It includes several of the attractions listed below. Walking tours are free and available at 10:30 a.m. and 1:30 p.m. For more information on the tours and attractions call 445-4209.

The **California State Historic Railroad Museum,** 125 I Street, is 100,000 square feet, making it the largest museum of this type in the world. It displays twenty-one restored locomotives and cars. The museum hours are 10:00 a.m. to 5:00 p.m. daily. For information, call 448-4466.

If the sound of the steam locomotive give you a thrill, then pull into the **The Central Pacific Passenger Depot,** on Front Street. Its a reconstruction of the depot built in 1876 and depicts the bustling activities of a train station in the 1800's. What's more, during the summer you can answer the call of "all aboard!" and ride a steam train the two miles to Miller Park. The trains operate weekends beginning in May through Labor Day. Depot hours are 10:00 a.m. to 5:00 p.m. daily.

748

The oldest public art museum in the West is the **Crocker Art Museum**, 216 O Street. Since 1873, the Victorian style building has grown and expanded. The original collection of European paintings and drawings were soon expanded to include nineteenth century California paintings, as well as sculpture and oriental art. The museum is open 10:00 a.m. to 5:00 p.m. Wednesday to Sunday, and 2:00 p.m. to 10:00 Tuesday. For further information, call 449-5423.

The first building constructed as a theater in California was the **Old Eagle Theater**, 925 Front St. Today the wooden and canvas structure is home to critically acclaimed professional theater productions. For ticket information, call (916) 446-6761.

Music Circus at 15th and H Streets has brought Broadway-style summer stock theater to Sacramento for nearly forty years. Operating from a gigantic tent, the company features an all musical line-up of plays. Productions run from Memorial Day thru Labor Day. Call 441-3163 for information.

The **Sacramento Theater Company** at 1419 H Street is acknowledged as one of the best theater groups on the West Coast. It is also one of the largest with its own playwright-in-residence and two theaters. Productions are largely mainstream, but you'll find some excellent avant-garde and new work as well. Call 443-6722 for listings.

The **Sacramento Symphony** at the Sacramento Community Center on 14th and L Streets offers, under the direction of its conductor and music director, Carter Nice, some of the world's greatest musical pieces. The setting provides a beautiful environ and near perfect acoustics for this regional symphony. The season runs from September to May. Call for tickets and information at 973-0200.

Opera, well done, is a passion with thousands of Sacramentans. The **Sacramento Opera Association**, at 14th and L Streets, has performances from September thru February. Call 449-5181 for information on performances and tickets.

For up-to-date information on art, entertainment or special events, call the **Sacramento Arts Hotline** at 445-5566.

The **ARCO Arena** is home to the Sacramento Kings, the city's professional basketball franchise. The arena also hosts boxing and bit time wrestling matches, music concerts, the Ice Capes, world-class amateur athletic competitions, and many large community events. Call 922-7362 for up-dated information.

Ronald Reagan once live in the **Historic Governor's Mansion,** and so did a dozen other governors since 1877. Governor Jerry Brown grew up there during the tenure of his father, Pat Brown. Today visitors can tour this 15-room Victorian mansion and marvel at the Italian marble fireplaces, oriental carpets and 14-foot ceilings. Located at 16th and H streets, the mansion is open 10:00 a.m. to 5:00 p.m. daily.

The **Big Four Building,** I Street, is named after for four great railroad barons of California: Leland Stanford, Mark Hopkins, Collins P. Huntington and Charles Crocker. The second floor houses a recreation of the Central Pacific's board room and library. Call 445-4209 for further information.

A must-see is the **Sacramento History Center,** 101 I Street, a reconstruction of the red brick building that housed Sacramento's City Hall and waterworks back in 1854. There are hands-on exhibits using interactive video stations that allow visitors to participate in the history of the region. The History Center is open 10:00 a.m. to 5:00 p.m. 449-2057

The Sacramento's original white settlement is **Sutter's Fort.** Restoration began on the adobe fort in 1891, making it the oldest restored fort in the nation. Its history can be learned through a two-hour self-guided tour that brings the sights and sounds of early California alive. It's located at what is now 27th and L Streets and is open daily from 10:00 a.m. to 5:00 p.m. Telephone 445-4209.

Adjacent to Sutter's Fort is the state's tribute to its very first residents, **The State Indian Museum.** Exhibits include basketry, featherwork and pottery reflecting the cultural and spiritual life styles of native Californians. Museum hours are 10:00 a.m. to 5:00 p.m. daily. Telephone 445-4209.

If you get your fill of history, you can get a load of science and technology at the **Sacramento Science Center and Junior Museum.** It has everything from live animals nature trails, to computers and space-age technology. Visit the stars under the 30-foot dome of the planetarium. Located at 3615 Auburn Boulevard, the center is open 9:30 a.m. to 5 p.m. weekdays, and 12:00 noon to 5:00 p.m. weekends.

Events

The **Sacramento Camellia Festival** honors the flower the Chinese first brought to Sacramento during the gold rush. Events include sailing regattas, a parade, classic cars, a bicycle race. Festival begins in late February with the arrival of visiting ships and continues through March. For information contact the festival association, 917 Seventh Street, Sacramento, 95814. Telephone 442-7673.

The **Sacramento Dixieland Jazz Jubilee** is on of the most popular Old Sacramento events. Held every Memorial Day, the 100 bands draw more than 100,000 people to what has become one of the world's largest jazz festivals.

The **Sacramento Water Festival** is held each July. An action-packed festival guaranteed to thrill and delight all comers. Staged on the Sacramento River, near the quay of picturesque Old Sacramento, the largest attraction is a gritty two-day contest between international-known formula one power boat racers. Those seventeen foot long "tunnel" boats hit speeds upwards of 140 mph. There's also a Floats Parade, a Great Saloon Race, barefoot water-skiing exhibitions, ski jumping and acrobatics, a Yacht Parade and nightly fireworks extravaganzas.

In late September Sacramento hosts **U.S. National Handcar Races** in Old Sacramento. Railroad hand car teams from throughout the nation come here try for the honors of being the fastest.

Accommodations

AUNT ABIGAIL'S BED AND BREAKFAST, 2120 G Street, Sacramento, California. Five bedrooms, breakfast with homemade breads and jams.

BEAR FLAG INN, 2814 "I" Street, Sacramento, California. Four Victorian style bedrooms and breakfast of fresh fruits, yogurt, hot cereal.

BEST WESTERN HARBOR INN
1250 Halyard Drive
Sacramento, CA 95691
Tel: (916) 371-2100
      (800) 528-1234

The people of Best Western are a meticulous lot, only certain establishments can meet the organization's exacting standards of service and quality. Well, the independently owned Harbor Inn passes the muster with flying colors. You can rest assured that your stay will be a friendly and comfortable one.

The Harbor Inn offers many fine touches, such as lithographs by noted artist L. Condenast, non-smoking rooms and rooms specially designed to accommodate handicapped visitors. Deluxe king rooms are equipped with a sofa sleepers and lounge chairs and some have a wet bar or fireplace. Queen deluxe rooms are wonderfully arranged and decorated in a beautiful mauve scheme, all overlooking the pool. Or, you can choose one of the Harbor's spa Double rooms which are quite large and include a small spa tub. For meals, there is a family style restaurant just yards from the lobby.

The Harbor Inn is very conveniently located, being only three minutes west of downtown. It's a perfect lodging for business or pleasure. It's no wonder that this Best Western is also a "Best Choice."

BEST WESTERN PONDEROSA
1100 H Street
Sacramento, CA 95814
Tel. (916) 441-1314
      (800) 528-1234
Major credit cards are accepted.

Only a few blocks from the California State Capitol, the Sacramento Courthouse, city, county and federal offices, the downtown K Street shopping mall, the Crocker Art Gallery and the quaint boardwalks of Old Sacramento, Best Western Ponderosa is very conveniently located. Once unpacked, guests may enjoy a sunny secluded patio area or take a refreshing dip in a solar heated pool. Accommodations may include a king bed, two queen beds or if something special is needed for the children, a comfortable arrangement will be gladly made. Non-smoking rooms are available, all are equipped with electronic locks on the doors, and the decor includes spacious comfortable surroundings complete with original artwork on the walls.

The Inn has exquisite dining, cocktail and banquet facilities and in the mornings, guests may enjoy a complimentary Continental breakfast. An

752

appetizing lunch may include a hearty sandwich such as a Yorkshire broil - English muffin, roast beef, avocado, tomato, cheese and bacon, linguini with clams or breast of chicken teriyaki. The dinner menu offers an excellent selection of entrees such as steak pizzaiola, a New York steak topped with Swiss cheese, flambed in brandy and cooked to perfection with mushrooms, green onions and light tomato sauce or try tender Veal Piccata, sauteed in butter, flambed with brandy and finished in a light lemon and wine sauce peppered with capers.

Best Western Ponderosa has the highest AAA rating and many of the guests return time and time again for the excellent accommodations and outstanding service. So, put aside your cares and relax. Whether you stay for business or for fun, you'll enjoy Best Western Ponderosa.

CLARION HOTEL
700 16th Street
Sacramento, CA 95814
Tel. (916) 444-8000

Prepare to experience the ultimate in fine accommodations at the Clarion Hotel which is located in downtown Sacramento across from the historic Governor's Mansion. Fresh flowers, sparkling fountains, plush towels and unsurpassed elegance greet every guest. Rich woods, green marble and peach fabrics in the lobby continue throughout the hotel and everything has been provided in the 239 guest rooms and suites to ensure first class service without compromise.

Everything about the Clarion evidences commitment. It has the atmosphere of a sophisticated hotel designed for executives and travelers who appreciate quality service, from the chocolates on the pillows every night in the Governor's Court to the individually controlled thermostats in the meeting rooms. The Mansion Court Restaurant features fine California cuisine including fresh fish, poultry, vegetables and salads and all California wines. Popular GUV's lounge is the place to relax and unwind to soft piano music before or after dining. For major sporting events, enjoy the competition on a wide screen television. The outdoor pool is set in a lush landscaped courtyard. Health club facilities, including racquetball are located within one block.

Luxury accommodations include remote control cable TV and a personalized wake up call with coffee and newspaper delivered to the door (if requested). A guest in one of the deluxe "Governor's Court" will receive use of the plush Governor's Club lounge with executive level concierge, complimentary Continental breakfast, evening cocktails, a complete entertainment system, turn down service with chocolate, goodnight cordial and a Clarion bathrobe.

753

The traveler making a stay at the Clarion can expect a level of service unsurpassed in Sacramento!

CONTINENTAL INN
3343 Bradshaw Road
Sacramento, CA 95827
Tel.   (916) 366-1266
       (800) 841-6416

Just south of I-50 at the Bradshaw exit is the Continental Inn. This new 127 room inn has all the amenities you would expect to find in an exclusive hotel.

Shampoo, conditioner, lotion and hairdryers are standard in all the large, contemporary rooms.   Other features include remote control TV, a complimentary movie channel and the ability to select a pay per viewing movie. There is a wet bar and refrigerator in each of the suites and "King Continentals." There are also recreational facilities throughout the premises.

An elegant, three story atrium with a stone fireplace and comfortable seating is available for socializing. There are men's and women's saunas, an exercise facility and an indoor/outdoor pool. The hotel has a 3,000 square foot conference center, a cocktail lounge just off the lobby and a first class family restaurant.

The restaurant is unpretentious; decorated with redwood, river rock and brass. The chef, Patrick Cariddi studied at the Culinary Institute of American in New York. Patrick said, " We use all fresh food as often as possible. We use simple ingredients and take our time to do it right." The restaurant has a casual, cafe appearance, but the large portions make it great value.

Stop by for a visit at the Continental Inn and enjoy the excellent accommodations.

DISCOVERY MOTOR INN
350 Bercut Drive (exit Richards Boulevard off
I-5 or Highway 160)
Sacramento, CA 95814
Tel. (916) 442-6971
Visa, MasterCard, AMEX, Discover, BankAmericard accepted.

Looking for a traveler's paradise? Look no further than the Discovery Motor Inn. What awaits you is a first-class stay at remarkably competitive rates with a host of options.

The inn's 101 rooms, all of which have been freshly redecorated, feature either king or queen-sized beds and plenty of space to relax or (if you must) work. While all of the Discovery Inn's rooms are spacious and comfortable, its suites are fantastic, featuring near acres of floor space, wet bars and small refrigerators. In the morning, enjoy complimentary breakfast in the lobby, and the inn even has an arrangement with the Rusty Duck Restaurant two doors away where each Discovery guest can receive a free cocktail. Outstandingly clean and courteous, the Discovery Motor Inn also offers such amenities as an outdoor pool and hot spa, color television with an in-house movie channel, direct dial phones and complimentary newspapers. Free transportation is provided for any guests planning to attend an event at Sacramento's ARCO Arena, and the inn's shuttle bus goes to both Sacramento Metropolitan and Executive airports. Runners, bicyclists and picnickers will like the fact that the inn is just down the street from the city's Discovery Park, at the confluence of the Sacramento and American Rivers, where you'll find lots of cool grass and shady trees, picnic tables and barbecues, swimming, fishing and the beautiful American River bicycle trail. The park also contains Northern California's only public world-class archery range.

The Discovery Inn, conveniently located adjacent to I-5, no more than two minutes from downtown Old Sacramento and within easy walking distance to no less than five restaurants, is definitely a "Best Choice" for convenience and comfort. You'll feel like you're in traveler's paradise, for sure!

HOTEL EL RANCHO
1029 W Capitol Avenue
Sacramento, CA 95814
Tel.   (916)   371-7631
        (800)   952-5566

The Hotel El Rancho in West Sacramento was built in 1940 and is highly acclaimed for its beautiful architecture and lush landscaping. It is an elegant showplace and one of the first million dollar projects of it's kind. Throughout the years, many famous people have come to the hotel, not to perform, but to relax and be entertained. Among those who have stayed there were Clark Gable, Robert Taylor, Rosalind Russell, and Danny Thomas.

The El Rancho has lost none of its beauty or soothing charm. A refurbishing of the seventeen acre racquet resort was recently completed. It offers 254 guest rooms and suites, fine dining in the El Condor Restaurant and dancing and entertainment at Don Quixote's Windmill Cabaret. There is a racquet and fitness club with complimentary use for hotel guests, as well as tennis and racquetball courts, a swimming pool and spa, sauna, in house masseuse, a weight room, fitness course, exercise classes and a tanning capsule.

The Sacramento El Rancho is located near the intersection of I-5 and I-80 and is only minutes from both downtown and Old Sacramento. There are special weekend packages for two available and special features for business travellers. The remarkably reasonable rates and the truly lovely surroundings make this a good choice for a memorable stay.

RAMADA INN AND CONFERENCE CENTER
1900 Canterbury Road
Sacramento, CA 95815
Tel. (916)   927-3492
       (800)   228-2828

Hundreds of families and Northern California vacationers return time and again to the Sacramento Ramada Inn. It is also a favorite among many frequent business travelers and a growing number of organizations and professionals. The Inn is conveniently located just minutes from both downtown and the city's increasingly vital northeastern business and financial district.

The Ramada Inn and Conference Center offers a quiet, impeccably manicured setting. There are 150 clean, comfortable guest rooms, each with a color television and direct dial phone. The Ramada's restaurant, Howie's Bar & Grill, features a gorgeous interior, remarkable service, a wonderful menu, an oyster bar and the region's finest "happy hour" spread. There is also a large swimming pool and a spa. There are extensive conference facilities available to serve everything from very small to very large groups.

The Ramada offers special low weekend rates and a twenty-five percent senior discount program. The wonderful facilities and gracious hospitality make the Ramada Inn a "Best Choice" for either a family vacation or a business trip.

RED LION INN
2001 Point West Way
Sacramento, CA
Tel. (916)   929-8855

Ask anyone in California's capital city to name the top hotel, and you'll hear a lot of people say "The Red Lion." The Inn boasts 448 units, ranging from the handsome Presidential Suite (which has indeed hosted President Reagan and his wife), complete with jacuzzi and wet bar, to comfortable and tasteful accommodations for the traveling salesperson and tourist. There are two bars with live entertainment, a coffee shop, gift boutique, and an excellent restaurant, Maxi's.Guests can take a dip in one of the two heated swimming pools, or enjoy the amenities of the adjacent new health club facility, with weights, his-and-her saunas, and Nautilus equipment. The Red Lion's meeting rooms can handle small gatherings or conferences of up to 1200 people, with complete banquet facilities. You can expect to enjoy a delicious prime rib at a 400 person banquet, and find the food to be as good as one would expect to be served for an intimate dinner.

Like most fine places, the Red Lion's accommodations book rapidly fills so reservations are advised. If it is fully booked, the Inn's well-known hospitality includes accommodating you, if possible, at the Sacramento Inn, its sister facility across the street.

SIERRA INN
2600 Auburn Boulevard
Sacramento, CA 95021
Tel. (916) 482-4770

Sacramento attracts many visitors every year. Some come to enjoy the historical landmarks, while others make the trip for business reasons. Whatever the occasion, accommodations with all the extras are always in demand. This is why many guests stay at the Sierra Inn, a place where Sacramento welcomes you with style.

At the Sierra Inn, there are over 180 suites and rooms, all beautifully decorated in an air of casual elegance. If you arrived at the airport, this hotel provides free transportation. To make you feel at home, they have many accommodations right at your fingertips including a beauty shop, barber shop, gift shop and room service. You can enjoy the swimming pool and patio on those days when it's time to relax. During the evening, visit the Timber Lounge where some of the best live music Sacramento has to offer is played.

For meals, the Sierra Gardens Restaurant provides for excellent dining at reasonable prices. The Sierra Inn also features 11 banquet and meeting rooms accommodating 10 to 325 people. So, it doesn't matter whether you've come to Sacramento for business or pleasure, because The Sierra Inn caters to both. This hotel has all the extras that will make your stay a pleasurable one.

Restaurants

A SHOT OF CLASS
1020 11th Street
Sacramento, CA 95814
Tel. (916) 447-5340
Hrs: Lunch   Mon. - Fri.   11:00 a.m. - 3:00 p.m.
       Dinner   Mon. - Thu.   5:30 p.m. - 9:00 p.m.
                     Fri. - Sat.   5:30 p.m. - 10:30 p.m.
Visa, MasterCard and AMEX accepted. Reservations are advised.

A Shot of Class is reminiscent of those palatial nightclubs you used to see at the movies.   A fabulous tribute to the era of Art Deco, the restaurant features a high ceiling and an enormous salon accentuated by fine carpets, fluted wall sconces and an occasional flash of chrome. And just like in "Casa Blanca," there's a grand piano that fills the air with melodies. On Friday and Saturday evenings, the restaurant features dancing to a live combo playing music from the 30s and 40s.

Though the varied menu offers such traditional fare as filet mignon and beef Wellington, it's main emphasis is towards an inventive interpretation of California cuisine, a style of cooking based on the imaginative use of spices, light sauces and fresh ingredients. Selections include such dishes as sauteed prawns, finished with Indonesian spices and served with an unexpected variety of raisins, peanuts, coconut and chutney, a chicken breast blackened "Cajun style" and topped with fresh fruit and fresh Swordfish with lime cilantro butter.

Items from the lunch menu include crab cakes prepared "New Orleans style" and topped with red pepper Hollandaise and Calamari Bel Dore, a squid steak with mushrooms, wine and garlic.   A Shot of Class offers banquet facilities and full service catering on or off premise. There is also a charming outdoor dining area on Cathedral Square that has a European flair.   For an excellent meal amidst all the style you deserve, try A Shot of Class. Bogey certainly would have.

A.J. BUMPS SALOON
450 Bercut Drive
Sacramento, CA 95814
Tel. (916) 442-0496

Hrs:	Lunch	Mon. - Fri.	11:00 a.m. - 2:30 p.m.
	Dinner	Mon. - Thu.	5:00 p.m. - 10:00 p.m.
		Fri. - Sat.	5:00 p.m. - 11:00 p.m.
		Sunday	4:00 p.m. - 10:00 p.m.

and,
8055 Freeport Boulevard
Freeport, CA
Tel. (916) 665-2251

Hrs:	Lunch	Mon. - Fri.	11:30 a.m. - 2:00 p.m.
	Dinner	Mon. - Thu.	5:00 p.m. - 10:00 p.m.
		Fri. - Sat.	5:00 p.m. - 11:00 p.m.
		Sunday	4:30 p.m. - 9:30 p.m.

All major credit cards accepted.

History, a truly fascinating subject, is a specialty of A.J. Bumps Saloon. But then, one could say it's the food that's the best. Or perhaps, it's a combination of both. Yes, that's it, a mixture of history and good food makes this unique restaurant one of the most frequented place in Sacramento, as well as Freeport.

When you first enter A.J. Bumps Saloon, you'll be awed at the collection of memorabilia, such as saddles, oil lamps, whiskey jugs, flintlock rifles and old wash tubs hanging on the walls and rafters. There's quite a bit of it, yet it all fits in place and creates a feeling of walking back into the days of the Old West. The food here is just as inspiring. Steaks, lobster, prime rib, chicken, shrimp and ten dinner entrees all named after a person or event from the past are just a few of the menu's items. Each dinner entree includes salad, individual loaves of French bread and a vegetable casserole.

And for that authentic saloon atmosphere, pull a stool up a the bar constructed in 1909, order a Planter's Punch or any other favorite drink and pour over the history that colors the walls. The owners, Tom MacMillan and Terry Osmonson, have really outdone themselves on this one. It's a restaurant that deserves the tip of a hat.

759

Sacramento County

BABE'S BAR AND GRILL
5060 Madison Avenue
Sacramento, CA 95841
Tel. (916) 331-5811
Hrs: Sun. - Thu.   11:00 a.m. - 11:00 p.m.
     Fri. - Sat.   11:00 a.m. - 12:00 midnight

To a true rib lover, there is no better feeling than one of sheer delight that a plate of lip smacking, finger licking ribs brings; add a side of cole slaw and Babe's potato curls and you have the elusive heaven on earth. Voted number one in a *Sacramento Union* readers poll for "great sauce, great taste and just darn good ribs", Babe's serves their meaty racks in an upscale self service restaurant.

Ribs aren't the only mouth watering items to be found at Babe's; a sliced filet marinated in olive oil and garlic, grilled and served on a Babe's bun is euphoric. The bakery produces all of the baked goods ranging from peanut butter pies, cookies and brownies to hot, sticky buns.

Tommy Thomas, owner of Babe's, has a successful philosophy: labor focusing on the product and knowing the customers, "cause they aren't here just to do me a favor." Everything is of the best quality, from the fresh ground beef patties to the full service bar. The result is a restaurant that is a must to explore as a "Best Choice" of Northern California.

BACK DOOR
1112 Firehouse Alley
Sacramento, CA 95814
Tel. (916) 442-5751
Hrs: Mon. - Fri.   11:30 a.m. - 3:00 p.m.
     Saturday   12:00 noon - 2:00 a.m.
     Bar   11:30 a.m. - 2:00 a.m.

Usually, when someone asks directions to the back door, they are greeted with a curious look and possibly a few questions. However, in Sacramento, you'll get a smile as you're told it's midway down cobblestoned Firehouse Alley. The Back Door is a restaurant with a sterling reputation for first class lunches and a low key, comfortable bar.

An enduring favorite of a good many local business people, the Back Door features a no nonsense menu with such tried and true winners as pastrami, club, Monte Cristo and New York steak sandwiches. Also popular, is the selection of incomparable eight ounce choice sirloin hamburgers, such as the Back Door Burger, the Mushroom Burger, the Bacon Burger and the Bleu

Burger. Lighter fares include the chef's salad and shrimp Louie. There's always a daily special to enjoy along with the soups that are second to none.

There's an undeniably honest and friendly air about the Back Door. For that, owner Gail Dick credits her staff, a very real part of the restaurant's attractiveness. Now you can see why, when running for the Back Door, you'll receive no unfriendly stares.

BIBA, 2801 Capitol Avenue, Sacramento, California. Northern Italian cuisine in surroundings of understated elegance.

THE BROILER, 1013 "J" Street, Sacramento, California. The 30-ounce porterhouse here is reputed to be the biggest in town, and their open-face chateaubriand sandwich is a downtown legend. Other specialities include charcoal- broiled fresh fish, prime rib and lobster tail.

BROOKSIDE RESTAURANT, 9819 Horn Road, Sacramento, California. On the site of a historic winery, Brookside does everything well, especially seafood. Enjoy patio dining in warm weather.

BROTHER'S DELICATESSEN & RESTAURANT, 2918 Fulton Avenue, Town and Country Village, Sacramento. Come to Brother's when you crave kosher-style dinners, lox, sandwiches, beer and wine. Breakfast menu includes eggs and bagels.

CAFE RIVER CITY
1340 Howe Avenue
Sacramento, CA 95825
Tel. (916) 920-9709
Hrs: Mon. - Sun. 24 hours.

Good food and good prices -- right here in River City! You can't do better than Cafe River City. If you haven't been around town for awhile, you might remember this place as Eppies. Since the transformation in 1983 it's only become better.

It's amazing that a restaurant that never closes can be this good all the time. The service is efficient, the booths and counters are warm, comfortable and clean. The food is fresh, prepared home style. Chef Danny Avilia has been in the restaurant business since he was fourteen years old.

Breakfast features a variety of omelette, or try potato skins stuffed with bacon, scrambled eggs, green onions and tomatoes. Complement breakfast with fresh squeezed orange or grapefruit juice. Steamed veggies compete with the daily special for lunch time favorite. Come in later for a zucchini Parmesan appetizer, followed by a dinner of mesquite chicken.

Lick your satisfied lips after your meal -- you'll be pleased to know such a great cafe exists right here in River City!

CELESTIN'S FRENCH CARIBBEAN RESTAURANT, 2516 J Street, Sacramento, California. Authentic Caribbean cooking. Delightfully uncommon decor.

THE CHESAPEAKE PUB, 2801 Prospect Park Drive, Sacramento, California. At the Chesapeake, there's a continental cuisine which includes various tasty appetizers, fish-of-the-day, steaks, quiches, and homemade breads and desserts. Dance nightly to DJ tunes!

CHRISTOPHER GREEN
300 Bercut Drive
 At Richards Boulevard and I-5
Sacramento, CA 95814
Tel. (916) 442-6603
Hrs: Mon. - Thu.   6:30 a.m. - 10:00 p.m.
           Friday   6:30 a.m. - 11:00 p.m.
           Saturday   7:00 a.m. - 11:00 p.m.
           Sunday   7:00 a.m. - 10:00 p.m.
Visa, Mastercard and AMEX are accepted.

Some of the best, least known food in this country is "roadfood" - the traveler's dream come true. Comfy places with delicious homemade fare and modest prices near a major highway, can't be beat -- and Christopher Green is a great example of the genre.
Take breakfast, you can try eggs Mornay or "the Woodchuck" - Mornay sauce over toasted sourdough bread, topped with crisp bacon strips or Huevos con Burrito - diced ham, scrambled eggs and fresh salsa wrapped in a warm tortilla and covered with a melted Monterey Jack and cheddar cheese topping or stuffed French toast - sourdough French toast stuffed with sour cream and topped with strawberry preserves, just to name a few of their offerings.
Lunch and dinner are just as delightful. With selections ranging from chicken Cordon Bleu and sauteed giant prawns to New York steak and Cornish game hen, Christopher Green has become increasingly popular as a first class dinner house. They also feature a fine selection of award winning California wines, several children's meals and desserts from banana splits to old fashioned strawberry shortcake. "Roadfood" like this will put "fast food" out of business!

DANILE'S, Town and Country Village at Fulton and Marconi, Sacramento, California. Dessert and gourmet crepes are served in a comfortable French cafe setting. Live music on Wednesdays and Fridays, 6 - 9 p.m.!

EL NOVILLERO, 4216 Franklin Boulevard, Sacramento, California. El Novillero provides a cozy family atmosphere reminiscent of a Mexican villa. Enjoy delicious food, and wine and imported beer.

EL TORITO, 5637 Sunrise Boulevard, Citrus Heights; and 1598 Arden Way, Sacramento, California. El Torito prepares its sauces, meats, hand-rolled enchiladas and chile rellenos fresh daily. A variety of Mexican seafood recipes also tempt you. El Torito is a tradition of quality dining since 1954.

EMMA'S TACO HOUSE, 1617 Sacramento Avenue, Bryte, California. Large Mexican menu with thirty-six combo plates. Casual, beer and wine.

FAT CITY BAR AND CAFE, 1001 Front Street, Old Sacramento, California. A European-like cafe offering a large menu with a bit of everything.

FINNEGAN'S RESTAURANT AND SALOON
3800 Northgate Boulevard
I-80 at Northgate
Sacramento, CA 95834
Tel. (916) 922-8552
Hrs: Mon. - Sun. 7:00 a.m. - 11:00 p.m.

Conveniently located just a fast break away from Arco Arena, Finnegan's Restaurant and Saloon has fast become one of Sacramento's most popular habitats for the true patrons of sports bars & grills.

Finnegan's, home to many Sacramento King's players and fans, has one of the most extensive menus you'll ever see. Whether it's blackened prime rib and scampi or one of their fabulous gourmet hamburgers, even the most discriminating diner will be pleased.

Finnegan's also has one of the best big screen pictures in town, which is supplemented with five monitors throughout both bars and is fed hard to find national and international sports via their satellite dish. If that isn't enough, a high voltage sound system rocks the bar with the latest tunes and videos for nightly dancing Tuesday through Saturday nights, along with drink specials from the bar. Finnegan's also has a festive patio for spring and summer dining, outdoor barbecues and Sunday champagne brunches.

Whether it's a high fashion show, a rowdy Monday night football game or a King's post game dinner 'n drinks, Finnegan's is your fifty yard line seat for great food, fun and entertainment the whole year round!

FIREHOUSE, 1112 Second Street, Old Sacramento, California. An institution among Sacramento's movers and shakers. Courtyard dining during clement weather. Beef Huntington a house specialty.

THE FIRESIDE LOUNGE AND RESTAURANT, 5539 "H" Street, Sacramento, California. The Fireside is a long-established eatery where you'll find reasonably-priced lunches, dinners, and drinks in a congenial atmosphere.

FISH EMPORIUM
2310 Fair Oaks Boulevard
Sacramento, CA 95825
Tel. (916) 923-5757
Hrs: Lunch: Mon. - Sat.   11:00 a.m. - 2:30 p.m.
      Dinner: Mon. - Sun.   5:00 p.m. - 10:00 p.m.
      Brunch: Sunday   10:00 a.m. - 2:00 p.m.

Change and consistency synthesize to create the essence of this exceptional seafood restaurant in the heart of Sacramento's new restaurant row. The owner, Tomas P. Nitopi has been serving superb quality seafood to the discriminating diner since 1978. Originally, "The Fish" was located on J Street. The central dining room was an old 1930s trolley car. When the restaurant moved recently to its attractive new Fair Oaks address, the trolley car came along as well.

Complementing the trolley car is an adjacent dining room, a private meeting room with its separate courtyard, and a comfortable and friendly bar/lounge.

A "Best Choice" when it comes to quality seafood, superior and innovative ambiance, and an extraordinarily friendly service...The Fish Emporium.

764

FRENCHY'S
1030 2nd Street
Sacramento, CA 95814
Tel. (916) 441-2154

Hrs:	Mon. - Thu.	11:00 a.m. - 6:00 p.m.
	Fri. - Sat.	11:00 a.m. - 7:00 p.m.
	Sunday	12:00 noon - 7:00 p.m.

With an oak back bar to rival the finest anywhere, oak tables and chairs, big picture windows and owner Ken Whitcomb's polished baby grand piano, Frenchy's is a gleaming monument to things first rate.

What makes Frenchy's French dip sandwiches so different from most others is that the meat is carved thin from fresh, succulent sirloin of beef, most restaurants use leftovers. Also on the menu is a barbequed beef sandwich made with hearty, tender chunks of beef blended with a zesty Texas style barbeque sauce. On the lighter side, Frenchy's has refreshing shrimp salads and a huge shrimp cocktail. Another item of which Ken is especially proud is his chili beans - a spoon standing winner. The bar, of course, features a full selection of mixed and blended drinks.

A former professional musician, Ken can be found at the piano whenever the mood strikes. Frenchy's makes for a welcome alternative to the plethora of fast food so prevalent these days, a wonderful place wherein to let the world just keep on walking.

FUJI
2422 13th Street
Sacramento, CA 95818
Tel. (916) 446-4135

Hrs:	Lunch	Mon. - Fri.	11:30 a.m. - 10:00 p.m.
	Dinner	Mon. - Fri.	5:00 p.m. - 9:45 p.m.
		Sat. - Sun.	4:30 p.m. - 9:45 p.m.

Open holidays.

If you're looking for a healthy, delicious and pleasant dining experience, take out your kimono and try your fortune at Fuji's. From sushi and tempura to nigiri, gyoza and batayaki, Fuji's caters both to your sense of taste and to your sense of authenticity.

Here you'll find fresh tuna flown in from Hawaii. The sushi chef also presides over a separate sushi bar adjoining the cocktail area off the dining room. Dishes are beautifully displayed and the service is fast and courteous.

The food is complemented by the atmosphere, traditional Japanese screens decorated in warm browns and tans. There are also an abundance of traditional Japanese ceramics and other gift items on display. A "Best Choice" for excellent food at modest prices.

FULTON'S PRIME RIB
900 Second Street
Sacramento, CA 95814
Tel. (916) 444-9641

Hrs:	Lunch	Mon.-Thu.	11:00 a.m. - 3:00 p.m.
	Dinner	Mon. - Thu.	5:00 p.m.-10:00 p.m.
		Friday	5:00 p.m.-11:00 p.m.
		Saturday	4:00 p.m.-11:00 p.m.
		Sunday	12:00 noon -10:00 p.m.

and,
7940 California Ave.
Fair Oaks, CA 95628

During the 1850s, several devastating floods in Sacramento necessitated the raising of the city streets to the second story of most of the city's buildings. Fulton's Prime Rib, when first opened, was built at the original level of Old Sacramento, thus, a portion of the restaurant is below the sidewalk. Referred to as the courtyard level, it offers a view of the city catacombs built by the Chinese. Many fundraisers, promotions, fashion shows, and social functions have been held in Fulton's courtyard.

Owners Bob and Sandra Free have recreated the atmosphere and hospitality of an English-style pub, with serving maids dressed in early English period costumes. Prime Rib and Yorkshire pudding are the house specialties. The house dressing is a cream sherry vinaigrette, with garnishes of grated egg and specially-seasoned croutons. Along with a selection of six to eight other desserts, a freshly baked hot apple pie covered with rum sauce and a generous scoop of vanilla ice cream is served.

Enjoy a fine Napa Valley wine from their extensive wine list, or have a drink in the intimate cocktail lounge. In either location, the soft lights and congenial atmosphere add to a fulfilling dining experience.

GARDEN COURT CAFE
106 L Street
Sacramento, CA 95814
Tel. (916) 441-7630
Hrs: Mon. - Fri.   7:30 a.m. - 3:00 p.m.
         Sat. - Sun.   9:00 a.m. - 3:00 p.m.
Visa, MasterCard and AMEX are accepted.

Like the golden hills that gave it life, Old Sacramento often hides its finest treasures. One of those treasures is the Graden Court Cafe. The place is invisible from the street. Even a glance through the glass door is inconclusive. But go in. The first thing you are likely to notice is the welcoming aroma of homemade food - warm muffins and toast, omelettes and coffee. Then, from somewhere below the high sky-lighted ceiling, comes the sound of water. Decked with greenery, its fountain gurgling away, the Graden Court Cafe is like some secret oasis.

Virtually everything at the cafe is made from scratch. For breakfast you can choose from delicious egg dishes or fresh Danish, croissants and homemade scones with jam and whipped cream. Lunch might be quiche, hot dogs, a roast beef, breast of turkey or corned beef sandwich. The Garden Court is famous for its soups, some of which are - well - unusual. Try a few of these, cream of peanut, tostada, chicken avocado, Canadian cheese, Polish sausage, chilled cantaloupe and one of the cafe's all-time favorites, strawberry.

For desserts - though it may seem that topic's been covered -- the Garden Court is second to none. You'll find delicacies like Kentucky Derby pie, peanut butter cheesecake and Bailey's Irish Cream mousse torte, plus apple-walnut, key lime, shoo-fly and Southern pecan pies.

The Garden Court Cafe is a "Best Choice" you're sure to remember for a long, long time.

THE GOLDEN DRAGON
1115 Front Street
Sacramento, CA 95814
Hrs: Mon. - Fri.   11:00 a.m. - 10:00 p.m.
         Sat. - Sun.   1:00 p.m. - 10:00 p.m.

Down in the basement of 1115 Front Street in historic Old Sacramento is where you'll find the exotic Golden Dragon. Decorated in a lush Oriental motif, the restaurant's charm complements the authentic Cantonese and Mandarin cuisine.

767

From the menu, try the pot stickers and the Kung Bo Sho - slightly breaded prawns mixed with spices and water chestnuts. Unlike many Chinese restaurants, the Golden Dragon serves fantastic liquid libations at the bar or at your table.

A family business, all the family members give personal attention to their regular guests and numerous tourists. Do yourself a favor and hop on the "Orient Express" to the exotic land of the Golden Dragon.

HANA TSUBAKI
5006 J Street
Sacramento, CA 95819
Tel. (916) 456-2849
Hrs: Lunch   Tue. - Fri.   11:30 a.m. - 2:00 p.m.
       Dinner   Tue. - Sat.   5:00 p.m. - 9:00 p.m.
Visa accepted.

Hana Tsubaki has been a Sacramento favorite for nearly a decade. Owned by Katsumi Takashiba and his wife Tsutae, both originally from Hiroshima, the restaurant is famed for its excellent, moderately priced Japanese food.

Hana Tsubaki is traditionally appointed with polished pine wood and rice paper screens. Backlighted screens show the plants behind them in silhouette. Even the carpeting, a subtle combination of forest green, burgundy and mauve, exhibits a poetic artfulness. Hana Tsubaki's menu is large and enticing. Chicken dishes are a favorite here, from yakitori to kara-age. Combination dinners all include crispy vegetable and shrimp tempura together with such delectables as teriyaki, tonkatsu or sashimi.

Naturally, Hana Tsubaki offers warm sake to go along with your meal or you can choose from a variety of beers and wines. Whether you are a connoisseur of Japanese cuisine or a newcomer, Hana Tsubaki is a "Best Choice" you're bound to enjoy.

HARRY'S BAR & GRILL
400 L Street at 4th
Sacramento, CA 95814
Tel. (916) 448-8223
Hrs: Mon. - Sun. 11:00 a.m. - 2:00 p.m.

A favorite of the downtown business crowd and a popular watering hole with many journalists, professionals and others who work in the immediate area, Harry's is one of the classiest spots in Sacramento.

The menu features entrees such as California chicken with avocado and Swiss cheese, chicken crepes with white sauce and fresh veggies, both delicious and sure to please. Hearty, scrumptious soups, sandwiches and salads are also popular, as are the daily specials.

Entertainment, consistently first rate, features bluegrass Monday evenings and Tuesday through Thursday jazz is featured. The place tends to pack 'em in on the weekends, so you might want to get there a little early to enjoy the sounds and dance to rock and roll or the blues.

HOGSHEAD BREWPUB, 114 J Street, Old Sacramento, California. Beer brewed on premises, sandwiches, sausage plates and special dinners.

JAMIE'S BROADWAY GRILLE
427 Broadway
Sacramento, CA 95818
Tel. (916) 442-4044
Hrs: Mon. - Fri. 6:00 a.m. - 10:00 p.m.
Closed Saturday and Sunday except for private parties

Owner/Chef Jamie Bunnell has created an interesting establishment famous for having introduced steak sandwiches with peanut butter on the side, still a tradition at Jamie's. The interior is reminiscent of an Irish pub, complete with an expansive cherry wood bar which originally came round the horn to San Francisco and survived the 1906 earthquake.

Jamie's offers breakfast with extensive selections ranging from eggs to steaks. A specialty is eggs Benedict and Jamie's potatoes are a treat. Lunch selections are numerous and include hamburgers, sandwiches, salads, calamari, and Irish lamb stew, among others. The turkey sandwiches feature fresh turkeys roasted everyday. To complement your meal, they pour one of the best cocktails in town--no computer bar here.

It isn't unusual to find Jamie going from table to table, especially after introducing a new item on the menu to see how everything is being received. The restaurant business was his dream since he was a child; he has used his previous experience and education to create a unique atmosphere offering quality food at economical prices.

JASPER'S
1346 Fulton Avenue
Sacramento, CA 95827
Tel. (916) 487-8500
Hrs: Mon. - Sat. 10:00 a.m. - 12:00 midnight
Sunday 11:00 a.m. - 10:00 p.m.
and,
2946 Bradshaw   1500 West El Camino
Sacramento, CA 95827   Sacramento, CA 95833
Tel. (916) 363-2112   Tel. (916) 648-1600

"Cooked just the way you like 'em," is the theme of Jasper's, a Sacramento burger joint that is fast becoming "the place" to get an old fashioned, home cooked hamburger with all the fixin's. And boy, are you going to love 'em.

A vibrant juke box spins tunes from the fifties and sixties, neon signs shine brightly and a soda fountain counter top off the ambiance of an authentic malt shop at Jasper's. Combining this unique atmosphere with the desire to fill the void for quality hamburgers is the worthy project of a brother and sister team. Robert and Mary Kay Tolleson insist on the best, and this attitude is reflected in the entire Jasper's operation featuring fresh ground beef, garden fresh produce, over thirty domestic and imported beers and many more pluses that make Jasper's an overwhelming favorite.

With so much going for them, what do they do for a following act? They serve breakfast. The Bay Area breakfast Czar, Ed Badger, heads up the early morning assault squad with an enticing menu at the El Camino location. Whether you're on the go or not, you can enjoy a first-class breakfast. Stop by, order up a delicious Jasper's meal, pop in two bits, bop with Elvis and enjoy one of the finest eating establishments in Sacramento. Ahhh, a "Best Choice" to be sure.

KALLIE'S RESTAURANT, 7770 Stockton Boulevard, Sacramento, California. Award winning dinner house with a casual atmosphere. Specialties include beef ribs, scampi, steaks, prime rib and pasta dishes. Cocktail lounge.

LAS BRASAS MESQUITE GRILL, 1309 Fulton Avenue, Sacramento, California. Enjoy Las Brasas's Southwestern Mexican cuisine including fajitas, prawns over charcoal, or mesquite-grilled chicken.

THE LUCKY CAFE
1111 21st Street
Sacramento, CA 95814
Tel. (916) 442-9620
Hrs: Mon. - Fri.   7:00 a.m. -   2:30 p.m.
      Saturday   7:00 a.m. - 12:00 noon

Erick Feil, proprietor of The Lucky Cafe, rises before dawn and gets to work by 4:00 a.m. to prepare for the day. He is quality oriented and offers All American food at prices that are hard to beat. He puts much time and skill into every dish.

Every day Erick makes his own doughnuts, they're ready for early breakfasters, still warm and lightly dusted with cinnamon and sugar. For those who prefer heartier fare, there are buttermilk pancakes, bacon, eggs and hash browns grated directly onto the grill and cooked to perfection. A frequent specialty of the house is the T-bone steak and egg breakfast which arrives on two platters. For lunch, there is fresh roasted turkey with a stuffing that is second to none, or perhaps, chili made from chunks of beef in the true Mexican tradition is served on Tuesdays. There are three different fresh specials created each day and the soup selection changes daily. There are hearty sandwiches and tossed salads to choose from.

Whether it's breakfast or lunch, The Lucky Cafe is a "Best Choice" for delicious, carefully prepared food at very reasonable prices.

MACE'S
501 Pavilion Lane
Sacramento, CA 95825
Tel. (916) 922-0222
Hrs: Lunch   Mon. - Sat.   11:30 a.m. - 5:00 p.m.
      Dinner   Mon. - Thu.   5:00 p.m. - 10:30 p.m.
               Fri. - Sat.   5:00 p.m. - 11:00 p.m.
Lounge   Mon. - Sun.   11:30 a.m. - 2:00 a.m.
      Brunch   Sunday   10:00 a.m. - 3:00 p.m.
      Dinner   Sunday   5:00 p.m. - 10:30 p.m.
Located on Fair Oaks Boulevard near Howe Avenue

The most prestigious "in place" in the greater Sacramento area is Mace's. Any afternoon from 4:00 p.m. - 7:00 p.m. the "movers and shakers" of Sacramento's real estate, politicians, media, attorneys and bankers can be found congregating in this airy, spacious, tasteful lounge. Diners congregate for an exotic dinner from 8:00 p.m. - 10:00 p.m. The dining area expands upon the "airy" theme, with a definite "India" touch. English tables, lush greenery and display cases containing African, South American and Indian artifacts. The overhead fans and small mechanical British soldiers twining them were made on location pattered after similar "punkahs" used in India and Africa. No expense was spared from the Italian marble floor to the rosewood and carpathian elm bur custom built bar, to the glass and brass vaulted enclosure that houses a tremendous selection of domestic, imported exotic wines in the central dining area. There, you'll notice that your dining perspective has been divided into changing views that reflect various activity centers of a bustling British compound - the "embassy house" with its lowered ceiling, wicker work and shutters; the "patio" with its row of canvas topped dining enclosures, the "den" that doubles as their banquet room with its safari trophies and genuine Turkish rugs and tapestries, the "house kitchen" that shows professional pride with every meal prepared.

All dishes are prepared with fresh ingredients. Featuring California cuisine, Mace's fish is flown in fresh daily. The menu also includes a variety of lamb, veal, chicken, beef and pasta. Choose from a wine list of 145 varieties to accompany your meal. Desserts are house made and the coffee is a fresh roasted blend made especially for Mace's. The best Sunday brunch in town is served on the colorful patio or in the dining room. Valet parking is at your disposal, or choose one of the many spaces available.

At Mace's everyone can enjoy a dining experience that is entertaining, comfortable and affordable. Mace's is a "Best Choice" in Sacramento for exquisite decor and an adventure in epicurean delights. From the ibex horns on the doors to the African slate on the floors, Bruce and Gayla Mace delight in bringing you a bit of British adventure and hope that you will find their home as comfortable, as restful, and as interesting as your own.

NICOLE'S, 2815 J Street, Sacramento, California. Nicole's is renowned for their huge selection of omelettes, and also has a good California-style dinner menu.

PARAGARY'S BAR AND OVEN
1401 28th Street at "N" Street
Sacramento, CA 95816
Tel. (916) 457-5737
Hrs: Lunch: Mon. - Fri.   11:20 a.m. -   4:00 p.m.
        Dinner: Mon. - Thu.   4:00 p.m. - 11:00 p.m.
                        Fri. - Sat.   4:00 p.m. - 12:00 mid
                        Sunday   5:00 p.m. - 10:00 p.m.
Visa, MasterCard, AMEX and Diner's Club cards are accepted.
and,
PARAGARY'S BAR AND OVEN
2384 Fair Oaks Boulevard
Sacramento, CA 95825
Tel. (916) 485-7100

Opened five years ago...an instant sensation...Paragary's offers "gourmet pizza." Some may be content to savor the side show pizza parlour where the mechanical animals, birthday song's, and silent movies are the fare; but here, at Paragary's the emphasis is on the pizza.

Take fresh pasta, add homemade pesto, Italian Fontina and Jarlsberg cheeses, a generous dollop of sun-dried tomatoes, sprinkle with Westfallian ham, and choice spices, then add the smoke flavor that comes from baking in a oak-fire, brick oven...that's a "gourmet pizza."

Customers vary in dress from running shorts to tuxedoes. All diehard pizza and Italian food-lovers. Sample the mesquite-grilled chicken with polenta, shitake mushrooms, and herb butter, or the braised rabbit with mustard, pancetta and parsley, and served with roasted new potatoes. You'll find a full bar and an excellent wine list to complement your dining at Paragary's.

POOR VIC'S GLASS TURTLE
2328 Watt Avenue
Sacramento, CA 95825
Tel. (916) 481-6118
Hrs: Mon. - Sun. 10:00 a.m. - 2:00 a.m.

Host Vic Milkulin provides an informal and comfortable setting for lunch or a drink after work. Vic has been a local favorite since 1960 when he owned his first business in Sacramento. Since then he has moved to his present location and opened as Poor Vic's Glass Turtle. He has recently expanded to Roseville and he and partner, William Boys, will franchise their first outlet in

773

Rancho Cordova sometime in 1988, with future sites in south Sacramento and the San Francisco Bay Area.

Lunch is served from 11:30 to 3:00 six days a week. No food is served on Sunday, but libations are served at all times. Poor Vics is reminiscent of the bar on Cheers, the popular television show. The people are friendly and make you feel a part of the neighborhood.

For a reasonably priced lunch of excellent quality, or a friendly, relaxed drink in congenial surroundings, visit Poor Vic's Glass Turtle.

RICK'S DESSERT DINER, 2322 K Street, Sacramento, California. Dessert and gourmet coffee fare in art deco interior.

RICKY'S GRILL
1379 Garden Highway
Sacramento, CA 95833
Tel. (916) 921-5500
Hrs: Mon. - Thur.   11:00 a.m. - 11:00 p.m.
      Friday   11:00 a.m. - midnight
      Saturday   5:00 p.m - midnight
      Sat. - Sun   10:00 a.m. - 3:00 p.m. brunch
      Sunday   5:00 p.m. - 10:00 p.m. dinner

Take a restaurant with a panoramic view of the Sacramento River and its' new marina, a superb menu and kitchen staff, and an ambiance that soothes and carries away all worries with the passing waters--add attention to detail and an outstanding location to make for a very pleasurable dining experience--that's Ricky's Grill.

Owner/chef Ricky DelaCruz and his family have combined these attributes into this fairly recent addition to the Sacramento list of fine and casual dining establishments.

Ricky's epitomizes variety in menu...fresh red snapper filets dabbled with a strawberry beurre blanc sauce and a bottle of Cakebread Cellars Sauvignon Blanc, or, an icy bucket of Chihuahua beers and Ricky's lumpia (specially seasoned fresh ground pork and vegetables, delicately rolled into an egg pastry, deep fried until golden brown and served with a special sweet n' sour sauce). Clad in Ray Ban's and Bermudas, I felt it answered my needs for hedonistic living!

For lunch, regular entrees include their Sacramento River Burger (mesquite grilled on a onion roll) and one of the best steak sandwiches (6 oz. New York marinated in fresh herbs, garlic and butter on sour dough with salad and fries) I've had the pleasure of eating. For dinner, the filet mignon "Kobe style", lamb chops (marinated in fresh basil, rosemary and pure olive oil), and pineapple chicken (boneless chicken breast, sauteed with fresh pineapples, shallots and cream sauce) are definite highlights. The daily specials--usually six to eight--emphasize fresh and seasonal seafood and fish and are innovative.

The desire of the DelaCruz family is to set standards of excellence in freshness, preparation and service. General Manager Mark Norman has assembled a fine staff who are eager to show you why Ricky's Grill on the river is one of Sacramento's finest and one of Northern California's "Best Choices".

RIVER CITY RAVIOLI, 14th and "O" Street, Sacramento, California. River City Ravioli features excellent pasta and ravioli dishes and chicken and steak. There's a solarium, and a full bar.

ROMA'S PIZZERIA, 8491 Folsom Boulevard, Sacramento, California. Stop here when you're craving delicious homemade pizza and Italian cuisine!

ROSEMONT GRILL
3145 Folsom Boulevard
Sacramento, CA 95816
Hrs: Mon. - Fri.   6:30 a.m. - 10:00 p.m.
       Sat. - Sun.   11:00 a.m. - 10:00 p.m.

Rosemont Grill has been a Sacramento tradition since 1914. This is a restaurant that has never changed two elements, a family atmosphere and a full menu.

You will be delighted to find beef, pork, lamb, veal, seafood, soups and salads on the menu. The service is quick and professional and the atmosphere is casual.

Rosemont Grill is one of those rare places that can accommodate anyone, anytime. For early risers, there is a great breakfast, a speedy lunch or a relaxing family meal served in a traditional family setting.

RUSSELL'S
1120 Fulton Avenue
Sacramento, CA 95825
Tel. (916) 971-9113
Hrs: Lunch   Tue. - Fri.   11:00 a.m. - 2:30 p.m.
       Dinner   Tue. - Thu.   5:30 p.m. - 9:00 p.m.
                Fri. - Sat.   5:30 p.m. - 10:00 p.m.
                Sunday   5:00 p.m. - 9:00 p.m.

How would you like to eat at a restaurant that is owned and operated by a well known chef? Russell Mclintock, trained at the Culinary Institute of

America, is the chef and Russell's is the restaurant. Russell has his own column in the California Wine Press, and is currently writing a book that details his methods of cooking. However, the best way to become acquainted with his style is to visit the restaurant where the magic takes place.

Russell's lunch menu is a true delight. You can choose such items as carbonara and shrimp, cannelloni, beautiful salads, an entire list of sandwiches and much more. For dinner, entrees such as veal Saltimbocca, topped with proiscuitto and mozzarella and flamed in Sambucca liqueur and Scampi Jardinaire, a large shrimp sauteed in butter with garden fresh vegetables, garlic, basil, and green peppercorns are only two of the many favorites. There is also the chicken Jacquelyn, a breast of chicken sauteed and finished with artichoke hearts, mushrooms, scallions and olives in a brandy and cream sauce.

As if all this weren't enough, Russell is also the proud creator of over twenty different cheesecakes. the "Ultimate Sin" cheescake is one of Sacramento's favorites. Of course, a diverse list of California wines round out the menu nicely. Well, now that you know all about Russell and his restaurant, stop by and see what this soon-to-be author is writing about.

THE RUSTY DUCK RESTAURANT AND SALOON, 500 Bercut Drive, Sacramento, California. A pleasant, moderately priced restaurant cleverly disguised as a--well--rusty duck hunting lodge. Prime rib, seafood and oyster bar.

TEQUILA WILLY'S, 1212 Howe Avenue, Sacramento, California. Authentic Mexican cuisine prepared fresh daily and a secret recipe for unforgettable Margaritas will lure you back again to this outstanding restaurant.

TOWNHOUSE RESTAURANT
1517 21st Street
Sacramento, CA 95814
Tel. (916) 447-5084
Hrs: Mon. - Fri.   11:00 a.m. - 11:00 p.m.
        Saturday   5:00 p.m. - 11:00 p.m.
        Sunday   10:00 a.m. - 2:30 p.m.
                          4:00 p.m. - 10:00 p.m.

How about some good Mexican food tonight? Oh, only part of the family is in the mood for something spicy. Well, maybe Italian then? That sounds good, but where can you get both of them at the same place? That's easy in Sacramento. Just go to the Townhouse Restaurant.

The Townhouse Restaurant, in business since 1955, has a most diverse menu for both dinner and lunch. The idea of mixing food themes was inspired when owner Jerry Franco made a trip to New Mexico. He visited a French restaurant that also served Mexican food. He brought the idea back to his restaurant, and now serves such dishes as tacos, chili rellenos, burritos, quesadillas and many other Mexican favorites. All the dishes are prepared with health in mind. Lighter food is cooked with less oils and cholesterol.

In addition to the wonderful selection of Mexican entrees, you'll also find traditional foods like veal, chicken and fish. For the Italian in you, they've got plenty of choices including homemade raviolli and the famed garlic steak. The Townhouse Restaurant is a dining establishment the whole family can enjoy. Stop by whenever you want a variety that's going to please everyone.

THE VIRGIN STURGEON
1577 Garden Highway
Sacramento, CA 95833
Tel. (916) 921-2694
Hrs: Summer:

breakfast	Sat.-Sun.	10:00 a.m. 2:00 p.m
lunch	Mon.-Fri.	11:30 a.m. 2:30 p.m
lunch	Sat.-Sun.	12:00 p.m.4:00 p.m
dinner	Mon.-Sun	6:00 p.m.11:00 p.m

Winter:
same except dinner: 5:00 p.m. 10:00 p.m
All major credit cards are accepted.

Smokey Silva used to drop by here on his rounds. Smokey was one of a particular clan of Sacramento River rats whose roots go back nearly as far as the year Jack London, oyster pirate and soon-to-be-hobo, beat upriver from San Francisco Bay. He was a survivor who'd come to the river to get away from the hassles, which is what one ought to come to the river for. Anyway, he liked the place, and that says something about its character. He'd helped to christen The Sturgeon--before the barge it was tacked to sank!

Laurie Patching, the owner hadn't been in business long till it was acclaimed a "instant" success; despite its starboard list and warped railing. Her floating saloon and eatery is famous for its mushroom burgers, cold beer and sunsets that could knock the South Pacific clear out of contention.

Then, of course, it went to the bottom. A survivor herself, Laurie found another barge. During construction of what was to be a real restaurant, a mysterious fire burned the work almost to the waterline. She fought back again and won. The new place is a comforting grotto with plenty of windows, a full bar, inside and outside dining and excellent food.

The menu includes Cuban black beans with rice, succulent cherrystone clams steamed in white wine and garlic butter, and a magnificent sirloin steak sandwich. The writers suggestion is to try the chilled boiled shrimp in the shell, a pint of Moosehead and a riverfront seat.

If you've been down on Broadway you might have noticed The Sturgeon II. Give it a try. The original mushroom burger is served here along with a fine fresh seafood selection. The Hours are the same as The Virgin Sturgeon. It is located at 1704 Broadway, or phone 441-4650.

WULFF'S RESTAURANT
2333 Fair Oaks Boulevard
Sacramento, CA 95825
Tel. (916) 922-8575
Hrs: Lunch   Tue. - Fri.   11:30 a.m. - 2:00 p.m.
      Dinner   Tue. - Thu.   6:00 p.m. - 9:30 p.m.
               Fri. & Sat.   6:00 p.m. - 10:30 p.m.
Visa, MasterCard and AMEX are accepted.

Hidden behind a cleaners on a busy boulevard, Wulff's is a surprise to the first time visitor. Who would expect to discover a French country inn complete with colorful windowboxes in such a location! In spite of the challenging site, Wulff's has continued to tempt lovers of good food to seek it out, and reservations are a must.

Chef Ann Shelton has been with Wulff's since its opening, and in her hands, the simplest dish can be transformed into a tantalizing gem. The menu changes depending on the seasonal availability of ingredients, and in keeping with today's lighter eating, fresh fish and poultry play an important part. Entrees feature such delicacies as flavorful sauteed rabbit, graced with a dark and elegant white wine sauce, or an incomparable seafood mousse, rich with lobster, shrimp and scallops.

A distinguished meal may be topped off with Gateau Chantilly, a light sponge cake filled with whipped cream which floats on a delicate raspberry sauce. One critic has labeled Wulff's desserts as the best in town. There is also a complete bar, and a carefully chosen and fairly priced wine list. Wulff's may be secluded, but the gastronomic delights that await make the effort to get there well worth the search.

YOSEMITE NATIONAL PARK

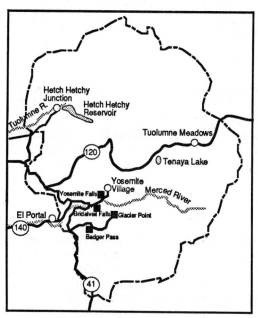

This showcase of California's Sierra Nevada Mountains covers 1,189 square miles, over sixty percent of it in Tuolumne County, the rest in neighboring Mariposa County. Foothills covered with groves of giant sequoia trees give way to granite peaks shaped by prehistoric glaciers which marched from the ridges 13,000 feet above sea level. Yosemite is two parks. One the vast back country open to hikers and pack animal trains, the other the seven-square mile Yosemite Valley, which draws most of the visitors.

The valley and Mariposa Grove with its sequoias was taken from federal lands by act of congress in 1864, and presented in trust to the state of California. High Sierra meadowlands were added as a federal park in 1890 and by 1905 California gave the grant lands back to the fledgling National Park Service, initially a project of the military until formal creation of the park service in 1914.

Yosemite Park and Curry Co., a consolidation of the two major concessionaires made in 1925, runs facilities in the valley on a year around basis. The park service carried out major renovations of facilities in the decade ending in 1966, and the visitor count now approaches three million a year. Within the valley, shuttle bus service is provided to cut down the number of

779

autos clogging the roads. Mariposa Grove, the high country, and the Badger Pass ski area operated in the winter, are accessible by private vehicles.

The geology of Yosemite turns on erosive action over vast periods of time, as glacial ice rode over the top of granite outcroppings, and run-off from the melting snow and ice carved out valleys with drops that now make for spectacular waterfalls. The best time for viewing waterfalls here is the spring and early summer as snow melts in the high country. Sierra summers are warm and dry with some daytime temperatures hitting 100 degrees in the valley at 4,000 feet. January highs are 47 and the lows 25 in the valley floor. Precipitation is concentrated from November through March, often leaving a winter snow depth of two-feet in the valley and ten times that in the mountains.

Three choices of overnight accommodates are offered. Camp sites in the valley floor and for backpackers in the back country are regulated. The park service allocates back-country permits on a first-come and a reservation basis. The park concessionaire handles valley floor facilities. Also offered are cabins and hotels, including the luxurious Ahwahnee at Yosemite Village. Several resorts and motels are located on the highways leading into the park, providing another option for overnight visitors.

Attractions

Yosemite Valley Visitor Center, at the west side of Yosemite Village, provides an orientation to the park's geology, history, and attractions, with frequent presentations in the attached theater. A fascinating Indian exhibit, including living history demonstrations during the summer season, is part of the Visitor Center. The center is open daily.

Glacier Point, reached by driving thirty miles out of the valley south to Chinquapin, then east beyond Badger Pass to a 7,214 foot high cliff, it gives a view of the entire valley plus much of the surrounding country. Several water falls and the classic domed peaks are seen from here, and a foot trail switch-backs its way down 3,000 feet to the valley floor from the parking lot. Open to vehicles May through October.

Half Dome, overlooking the east end of the valley, is reached by an eight-mile trail from **Happy Isle Nature Center** which passes several falls and provides panoramic views. Cables are installed on the slick granite to provide hand-holds for those who go to the top, some 5,000 feet above the valley floor.

El Portal, on Highway 140 west of park boundaries, has a travel exhibit of steam locomotives, old gasoline vehicles and other transportation used to reach the park in times gone by. This community has tourist facilities and the park administrative offices.

Mariposa Grove, on Highway 41 at the south boundary of the park, is filled with weathered sequoias approaching 3,000 years old. To lessen environmental damage, the park service operates a tram inside the grove, with the schedule shown in the park newspaper issued each season. Guided bus tours and tram rides of the valley are available.

Hetch Hetchy Reservoir on Oak Flat Road (use tire chains in the fall and winter) provides a thirty-eight mile drive from the valley through stands of sugar pine and white fir. This tour can be covered easily in two hours.

Tuolumne Meadows is in the High Sierras, surrounded by lofty peaks. The area, about 56 miles from Yosemite Valley, over the Big Oak Flat and Tioga Roads, is an ideal camping place and a good starting point for the avid fisherman, hiker or mountain-climber. Accessible by car from about mid June to mid October. By foot or by horseback take the time to view Waterwheel Falls, Mount Lyell and Lyell Glacier, Lembert Dome, Glen Aulin, Muir Gorge, Soda Springs, Tenaya Lake and other points of interest. Daily bus service is available in the summer.

Walwona Basin provides a recreation area of several square miles that include camping, riding, golf, swimming and tennis facilities. Walwona is 27 miles south of the Yosemite Valley, near Mariposa Grove. Saddle and pack animals are available here, for rental, during the summer months.

Mountain climbing and **cliff scaling** are popular in the park. The National Park Service has a Mountaineering School concession which handles training and guide service. The school also organizes winter cross-country ski tours. Call (209) 372-4405 in the summer, and 372-4611 in winter.

For more information: **National Park Service**, Box 577, Yosemite National Park CA 95389; telephone (209) 372-4461. Yosemite Park and Curry Co., 5410 East Home, Fresno CA 93727, reservation telephone (209) 722-0366. Any Ticketron outlet will handle bookings for Yosemite.

APPENDIX

You are cordially invited to Marina Seafood Grotto, 995 Elizabeth Street, Alviso, CA to receive a complimentary glass of wine with lunch or dinner. Only one per dinner per visit, please.

You are cordially invited to Dressing Up, 1224 Salano Avenue, Berkeley, CA. Receive 20% discount on any jewelry and/or the rental of any costume. Good through April of 1988.

You are cordially invited to Robert Bruce of Berkeley, 2910 Telegraph Avenue, Berkeley, CA to receive a 10% discount on any purchase over $25.

You are cordially invited to Magnum Opus, 2905 College Avenue, Berkeley, CA to receive 10% off any regularly priced purchase.

You are cordially invited to Arinell Pizza, 2109 Shattuck Avenue, Berkeley, to receive a complimentary small drink with any slice of pizza. Valid through April, 1988.

You are cordially invited to Franks Seafood Factory, 3237 Sacramento Street, Berkeley, CA to receive one free order of peach cobbler with purchase of $10 or more.

You are cordially invited to Gertie's Chesapeake Bay Cafe, 1919 Addison Street, Berkeley, CA, to received 10% off of any lunch or Sunday brunch.

You are cordially invited to Larry Blake's Restaurant and Nightclub, 2367 Telegraph Avenue, Berkeley, CA to receive a $1 discount at the door for any night club act.

You are cordially invited to Shattuck Avenue Spats, 1974 Shattuck Avenue, Berkeley, CA to receive one complimentary Fogcutter for a dining party of four or more.

You are cordially invited to Sushi California, 2033 Martin Luther King Way, Berkeley, CA to receive one complimentary bottle of sake with each dinner. Offer good through 1988.

You are cordially invited to The Doll Place, 1202 Broadway, Burlingame, CA to receive a 20% discount off any purchase with this invitation only.

You are cordially invited to Electric Avenue, 1350 Burlingame Avenue, Burlingame, CA to receive a 20% discount off all items except those on sale. Offer ongoing.

You are cordially invited to Serpil's, 1429 Burlingame Avenue, Burlingame, CA for a 10% discount on any item other than those on sale. Offer is ongoing.

You are cordially invited to White Dove Jewelry Exchange, 270 Lorton Avenue, Burlingame, CA, to shop at a 20% discount on jewelry, except those items on sale. Offer is ongoing.

You are cordially invited to The Occasion Place, 275-277 Primrose Road, Burlingame, CA to receive a 10% discount, with the exception of those items on sale. Offer is ongoing.

You are cordially invited to Prestige Fine Wines & Liquors, 1300 Burlingame Avenue, Burlingame, CA for a 20% discount on any case lot, with the exception of those on sale.

You are cordially invited to The Art Emporium, 305 East Campbell Avenue, Campbell, CA to receive a free cup of coffee. Offer ongoing.

You are cordially invited to Chabot Galleries, 132 The Pruneyard, Campbell, CA to receive a 10% discount off of any purchase exceeding $100. Offer ongoing.

You are cordially invited to receive .50 off any Real Polish Dog with this coupon at A & J Polish Deli, 2785 S. Winchester Blvd., Campbell, CA.

You are cordially invited to the Kirkwood Hardware and Gift Shop, 1600 West Cambell Avenue, Campbell, CA to receive 10% off on any purchase of $10.00 or more. Not valid on sale items.

You are cordially invited to Fine Design Jewelers, 880 East Campbell Avenue, Campbell, CA to receive a 20% discount off of any item not on sale. Offer ongoing.

You are cordially invited to The Ship's Chandlery, 1640 West Campbell Avenue, Campbell, CA for a free cup of coffee while enjoying the nautical wares. Offer ongoing.

You are cordially invited to El Lucero, 1875 S Basocom Avenue, Campbell, CA to receive a free margarita with your purchase of lunch or dinner.

Senior citizens are cordially invited to Wheel Away Cycle Center, 402 East Hamilton Avenue, Campbell, CA to receive a 10% discount off all parts and accessories. Offer ongoing.

You are cordially invited to D & J Hobbies and Crafts, 96 San Thomas Aquino Road, Campbell, CA to receive a 10% discount off any item not on sale. Offer good thru 1989.

You are cordially invited to Robin's Nest, 20649 Rustic Drive, Castro Valley, CA to receive a 10% discount with any purchase over $20. Not valid with any other discount.

Your are cordially invited to.Mary' Cookies, 20667 Rustic Drive, Castro Valley, CA .
Buy two cookies and receive your third one free.

You are cordially invited to.Craft Peddler's, 3317 Castro Valley Blvd., Castro Valley, CA.
Receive one free stenciling class.

You are cordially invited to Prior's Esspresso House, 20634 Rustic Drive, Castro Valley, CA. Receive a complimentary glass of wine with purchase of regular lunch. (Valid thru 1988)

You are cordially invited to the Osaka Restaurant, 2650 Monument Boulevard, Concord, CA to receive one free four ounce Sake for party of two or more. Offer good thru April 1988.

You are cordially invited to The Millpond for Sportsmen, 10893 N. Wolfe Road, Cupertino, CA to receive a 10% discount on any purchase.

You are cordially invited to the Old Coast Hotel, 101 North Franklin Street, Fort Bragg, CA for a free dessert with purchase of a full dinner, or a free gift with any purchase of twenty-five dollars or more at the Hot Pepper Jelly Company.

You are cordially invited to Beethovan's Pizza, 1080 D Shell Boulevard, Foster City, CA to receive $3 off any pizza ordered.

You are cordially invited to.J Street Antiques, 120 J Street, Fremont, CA. Receive a 10% discount on any purchase of regularly priced merchandise.

You are cordially invited to My Friends and I, 37521 Niles, Blvd., Fremont, CA.
Receive 10% off any merchandise except sale items.

You are cordially invited to.Les Belles Antiques, 37549 Niles Blvd., Fremont, CA.
Receive a 10% discount on any purchase. (Not valid on sale items.)

You are cordially invited to Mission Delicatessen, 115 Anza Street, Fremont, CA for 10% off any purchase.

You are cordially invited to.The Gift Connection, 3129 Walnut Ave., Fremont, CA.
Receive a free gift upon presentation of this invitation.

You are cordially invited to.Nooks 'N' Crannies, 3964 Washington Blvd., Fremont, CA.
Receive a 20% discount on any purchase of $25 or more. (Not valid on sale merchandise.)

You are cordially invited to.The Alps Restaurant, 5200 Mowry Ave., Fremont, CA.
Receive one free beer with any lunch or dinner.

You are cordially invited to Papillon Restaurant Francais, 37296 Mission Boulvedard, Fremont, CA to receive a complimentary dessert with dinner. Not valid with any other offer.

You are cordially invited to The Gift Carousel, 39199A Farwell Drive, Fremont, CA. Present this invitation to receive a free gift, no purchase necessary. Receive 10% off any purchase.

You are cordially invited to Half Moon Bay, 2400 S. Cabrillo Highway , Half Moon Bay, CA to receive a complimentary bottle of wine upon arrival by mentioning this book when making reservations.

You are cordially invited to B Street Antiques, 1025 B Street, Hayward, California to receive 10% off any purchase you make. Not valid on discounted or sale-priced items.

You are cordially invited to the Cafe Rendezvous, 1060 B Street, Hayward, CA for a free cup of coffee with the purchase of any pastry and/or $3 off the purchase of any two dinners.

You are cordially invited to The Hayward Fishery, 22701 Foothill Boulevard, Hayward, CA or 7400 San Ramon Road, Dublin, CA to receive a complimentary glass of wine with any meal.

You are cordially invited to Clock's, Etc., 3401 Mt. Diablo Road, Lafayette, CA to receive a free gift. Offer good thru May, 1988.

You are cordially invited to Linden Tree, 365 First Street, Los Altos, CA to receive a free book from selected titles.

You are cordially invited to Los Altos Bookstore, 205 State Street, Los Altos, CA to receive a 10% discount on any purchase of $10 or more.

You are cordially invited to T.N. Spice, 271 State Street, Los Altos, CA to receive a ten percent discount on any purchase.

You are cordially invited to Lescaut Jewelry, 220 State Street, Los Altos, CA to receive a 10% discount on any purchase of $75 or more. Not valid on credit card purchases.

You are cordially invited to The Midge Fly Shop, 271 State Street, Los Altos, CA to receive a ten percent discount on purchase of any Alpine or Steffen flyrod.

You are cordially invited to Lin's Toy Cupboard, 237 A Street, Los Altos, CA to receive a 10% discount on any purchase excluding sale items.

You are cordially invited to Mud in Your Eye, 50 University Avenue, Los Gatos, CA to receive 10% off on any purchase.

Bring this invitation to Mimi's Rooftop Cafe, Old Town, 50 University Avenue, Los Gatos , CA to receive a complimentary dessert with purchase of any entree, lunch or dinner.

You are cordially invited to Domaine M. Marion Winery, 300 College Avenue, Los Gatos, California, to receive a free set of coasters and ten percent off any purchase.

You are cordially invited to Nyborg Castle Gifts and Collectibles, 6662 Alhambra Avenue, Martinez, CA to receive 20% off any regular purchase of $25 or more. Not valid on sale merchandise.

You are cordially invited to Karen's Antiques, 712 Santa Cruz Avenue, Menlo Park, CA to receive a 10% discount on any purchase.

You are cordially invited to La Belle France, 705 Santa Cruz, Avenue, Menlo Park CA to receive a 15% discount on any regular purchase.

You are cordially invited to Marlowe's Flowers and Gifts, 200 Serra Way #50, Milpitas, CA to receive a10% discount on cash and carry or local delivery purchases.

You are cordially invited to enjoy two-for-one green fees weekdays, anytime, and weekends after noon. Carts required.
The Tularcitos Golf and Country Club, 1200 County Club Drive, Milpitas, California. Valid through 1988.

You are invited to Edgewater Packing Company, Cannery Row at Prescott, Monterey, CA for one free carousel ride. Offer good through 1988.
You are cordially invited to The Art Center, 315 Chestnut, Mount Shasta, CA to receive a 5% discount off of any item not on sale. Offer good thru 1988.

You are cordially invited to Mt. Eddy Bagel Bakery and Cafe, 105 East Alma Street, Mount Shasta, CA to receive a free bagel with butter or cream cheese. Offer good thru 1988.

You are cordially invited to the Brookside Hotel and Cafe, 5977 Mowry Avenue, Newark, CA for 20% off any purchase at the Brookside Cafe.

You are cordially invited to Nijo Castle, 39888 Balentine Drive, Newark, CA to receive $4.00 off any dinner entree when two dinners are purchased. Not valid with any other offer.

You are cordially invited to.Barelee Haretage, 1431A Grant Ave., Novato, CA to receive 10% off any purchase of $20.00 or more.

You are cordially invited to The Filling Station, 1769 Grant Avenue, Novato, CA to receive a complimentary glass of wine with any meal.

You are cordially invited to Sante Fe Mary's Southwest Grill, 1200 Grant Avenue, Novata, CA to receive $1.00 off entree on bills of $20.00 or more.

You are cordially invited to Me and Mr. C Tees & Sweats, 30 Jack London Square, Oakland, CA to receive some special transfers free with your purchase of a shirt. Offer good through 1988.

You are cordially invited to Cotton Basics, 6052 College Avenue, Oakland, CA to receive 10% off on any purchase (not valid on sale items).

You are cordially invited to Folks' Art, 4164 Piedmont Avenue, Oakland, CA for 20% off all Laurel Burch earrings. Offer good through May 1988.

You are cordially invited to The Crossing Gate, 6128 LaSalle Avenue, Oakland, CA to receive 10% off on any purchase, not valid on credit card purchases.

You are cordially invited to Asta Records, 5488 College Avenue, Oakland, CA to receive 10% off on any purchase of used recodrs or collectors items. Offer good through 1988.

You are cordially invited to the French Quarters Restaurant, 737 Buena Vista Avenue, Oakland, CA to receive a complimentary dessert with your dinner entree. Offer good through May 1988.

You are cordially invited to Teddie's Discount Card and Party, 4009 Piedmont Avenue, Oakland, CA to receive 10% off any purchase of $5.00 or more. Offer good through May 1988.

You are cordially invited to Movie Memories, 165 University Avenue, Palo Alto, CA to receive a $2 discount on any purchase of $10 or more. Offer not valid on books.

You are cordially invited to Blossoms, 199 Stanford Shopping Center, Palo Alto, CA to receive a 50% discount on any purchase excluding holidays, deliveries, and party arrangements.

You are cordially invited to Blatz Folded Ice Cream, 101 California Avenue, Palo Alto, CA to receive one free topping on any size frozen yogurt or one additional mix on any size folded ice cream.

You are cordially invited to Dinah's Shack, 4269 El Camino Real, Palo Alto, CA to receive one free visit to the Smorgasbord with your purchase of an entree.

You are cordially invited to The New Deli, 624 San Pablo Avenue, Pinole, CA to enjoy any meal at a 15% discount. Offer good thru 1988.

You are cordially invited to Sharp Bicycle, 2800 Hilltop Mall Road, Richmond, CA to receive a free water bottle and seat bag with the purchase of any bicycle.

You are cordially invited to the Saving Center, 3438 Watt Avenue, Sacramento, CA and 7143 Greenback Lane, Citrus Heights, CA to receive a free local fishing tips guide. Offer good thru December 31, 1989.

You are cordially invited to the Steinbeck House, 132 Central Avenue, Salinas, CA to receive a free glass of wine with your purchase of a luncheon. Offer good with this invitation only.

You are cordially invited to Deck the Walls, 230 Tanforan Park, San Bruno, CA to receive 15% off on any non-sale purchase.

You are cordially invited to Yarn Crafters, 113 Tanforan Park Shopping Center, San Bruno, CA to receive four D.M.C. floss for $1.00 with this invitation.

You are cordially invited to the Hotel Mark Twain, 345 Taylor Street, San Francisco, CA to facilitate an introduction, the management invites you to present this coupon for a discounted room rate.

You are cordially invited to The King George Hotel, 344 Mason Street, San Francisco, CA to receive one complimentary Continental breakfast with each night's stay.

You are cordially invited to spend the night at The Queen Anne Hotel, 1590 Sutter Street, San Francisco, CA to receive a 10% discount on the room rate.

You are cordially invited to The Clothes Contact at 473 Valencia Street, San Francisco, CA to receive six dollars off your next purchase of four or more pounds of vintage clothing!

You are cordially invited to the Edward II Inn & Carriage House at 3155 Scott Street, San Francisco, CA to enjoy a complimentary glass of wine with each dinner purchased.

You are cordially invited to visit Confetti le Chocolatier, 4 Embarcadero Center, San Francisco, CA where, with a purchase worth $10, they will present you with a complimentary truffle and "make your day."

You are cordially invited to Circle of Friends, 1604 Haight Street, San Francisco, CA mention this book and the owners will present you with a complimentary souvenir of Haight Ashbury.

You are cordially invited to Shades 1645 Market Street in San Francisco, CA where you will receive a 10% discount when you mention this book.

You are cordially invited to The Enchanted Crystal, 1771 Union Street, San Francisco, CA to receive 10% off any purchase with this invitation. Offer good through 1988.

You are cordially invited to India House, 350 Jackson Street, San Francisco, CA where every party of four, or more, will receive a complimentary Pimm's Cup (the original Gin Sling that India House brought to San Francisco in 1947).

Your are cordially invited to Maye's Oyster House, 1233 Polk Street, San Francisco, CA 94109, for a complimentary glass of wine with each dinner purchase.

You are cordially invited to the Radisson Hotel, 1471 North Fourth Street, San Jose, CA to receive 50% off the regular guestroom rates any Friday or Saturday, including holidays. Advance reservations are requested.

You are cordially invited to The Antiquary, 1310 Lincoln Avenue, San Jose, CA to receive 10% discount on any purchase of $20 or more.

You are cordially invited to The Willow Glen Collective, 1349 Lincoln Ave., San Jose, CA to receive 10% dealer discount on everything except new or sale items. Good through 1989.

You are cordially invited to The Crystal Iris Boutique, 227 North First Street, Suite 104, San Jose, CA 95112, for 20% off on any purchase of fine apparel. Not valid with any other offer.

You are cordially invited to Phoenix Books and Espresso Cafe, 17 N San Pedro Street, San Jose, CA to receive a free cup of coffee or espresso with your book purchase.

You are cordially invited to Schurra's Chocolates, 848 The Alameda, San Jose, CA for a 10% discount with any purchase.

You are cordially invited to Su-Elen's Limited, 14 Almaden Plaza, San Jose, CA to receive 10% off any purchase. Not valid on sale items.

You are cordially invited to Anne's Flowers, 955 Lincoln Avenue, San Jose, CA 95126, for one dozen carnations, free with any other purchase.

You are cordially invited to San Jose Florist, 1559 Meridian Avenue, or 1375 Blossom Hill Road, San Jose, CA for a 10% discount on any purchase. Not valid on wire orders.

You are cordially invited to the Candela de Almaden, 5353 Almaden Expressway Unit 53, San Jose, CA 95118 for a 10% discount on any purchase. This offer is limited to one coupon per purchase.

You are cordially invited to Teddy Bear Express, 1337 S Winchester Boulevard, San Jose, CA to receive 20% off on any purchase.

You are cordially invited to Almaden Stained Glass, 4666 Meridian Avenue, San Jose, CA for 10% off on any finished items, supplies or class tuition. This offer does not apply to consignment items, sale items or with other discounts.

You are cordially invited to Glass With Class, 1336 Lincoln Avenue, San Jose, CA to receive a friendly welcome and a10% discount off of any purchase.

You are cordially invited to TJ's Ice Cream, 1375 Blossom Hill Road, San Jose, CA to receive $2 off any cake you can imagine. Not valid with any other offer.

You are cordially invited to Chez Croissant, 51 East San Carlos Street, San Jose, CA 95113, for a complimentary soda with the purchase of any sandwich.

You are cordially invited to dine or dance at D.B. Cooper's, 163 W Santa Clara Street, San Jose, CA 95113, and receive $2 off on the purchase of a t-shirt.

You are cordially invited to Rue de Paris, 19 North Market Street, San Jose, CA for a complimentary aperitif with dinner for each member of your party.

You are cordially invited to Teske's Germania Restaurant, 255 North First Street, San Jose, CA for a complimentary glass of German beer or wine with you dinner purchase.

You are cordially invited to the Black Sheep, 45 Almaden Plaza, San Jose, CA 95118, for 10% off any purchase of needlework or supplies. Not valid on sale items or custom framing.

You are cordially invited to Heidi's Toyland and Peruvian Gifts, 224 El Paseo De Saratoga, San Jose, CA to receive a ten per-cent discount off of any purchase. Offer good with this invitation only.

You are cordially invited to Lynwood Galleries, 360 South Railroad Avenue, San Mateo, CA 94401 for custom framing of your pictures or posters, at 20% off the regular price.

You are cordially invited to Peninsula Art Exchange, 2057 San Mateo Fashion Island, San Mateo, CA for a 10% discount on all framed posters.

You are cordially invited to The Book Store, 132 Third Avenue, San Mateo, CA 94401, for $5 off on any purchase of $25 or more.

You are cordially invited to The Collectors, 140 Hillsdale Mall, San Mateo, CA 94403, for a 10% discount on all but sale items.

You are cordially invited to the Oriental Elegance, 2065 San Mateo Fashion Island, San Mateo, CA 94404, for 10% off on all gift items execept sale items.

You are cordially invited to shop for custom-blown glassware and other gifts at Reflections, 2234-B San Mateo Fashion Island, San Mateo, CA 94404, for a 10% discount on the purchase of any non-sale items.

You are cordially invited to the Prince of Wales Pub at 106 E 25th Street, San Mateo, CA to enjoy the following ongoing offer, with the purchase of two dinners, the Prince will refund to you one half the cost of the least expensive of the two meals purchased.

You are cordially invited to the Clarion Hotel Marin, 1010 Northgat Drive, San Rafael, CA to receive a 20% discount off published room rate. Valid through 1988. (Not applicable with any other discount offer.)

You are cordially invited to a complimentary bottle of champagne, delivered to your room at the Santa Clara Marriott Hotel, 2700 Mission College Boulevard, Santa Clara, CA 95054.

You are cordially invited to Graffiti #2207, 2855 Stevens Creek Boulevard, Santa Clara, CA 95050 to receive a 10% discount on any purchase.

Your are cordially invited to Valley View Inn, Box 66593, Santa Cruz, CA 95066, for a get-a-way vacation. Receive a complimentary bottle of champagne upon arrival with reservations for three or more nights.

You are cordially invited to Fancy Folk, 12241 Saratoga - Sunnyvale Road, Saratoga, CA to receive 20% off any purchase.

You are cordially invited to.Bellamia, 14503 Big Basin Way, Saratoga, CA , to receive one complimentary dessert with any dinner order.

Your are cordially invited to Valley View Inn, Box 66593 Scotts Valley CA 95066, for a get-a-way vacation. Receive a complimentary bottle of champagne upon arrival with reservations for two or more.

You are cordially invited to the Maple Tree Inn, 711 E El Camino Real, Sunnyvale, CA for a 25% discount off regular room rates on any Friday and Saturday. Offer good through 1989.

You are cordially invited to.Kirkish's, 198 S. Murphy Ave., Sunnyvale, CA to receive a 10% discount on any purchase. Not valid on previously discounted or Boy Scout items.

You are cordially invited to J.R. Muggs, 1111 West El Camino, #121, Sunnyvale, CA to receive a free half-pound of coffee beans with your purchase of ten dollars. Offer good thru 1989.

You are cordially invited to the Rusty Scupper, 1235 Oakmead Parkway, Sunnyvale, CA for a complimentary glass of Chardonnay with purchase of an entree.

You are cordially invited to Tiburon Lodge, 1651 Tiburon Boulevard, Tiburon, CA to receive their preferred rate, based upon availability. Bring your copy of "Best Choices" to the desk at check in to take advantage of this offer.

You are cordially invited to the Holiday Inn, 32083 Alvarado-Niles Road, Union City, CA to receive a 10% discount on the normal room rate.

You are cordially invited to Nature's Kitchen, 412 South Main Street, Yreka, CA for a free cup of coffee of tea with your purchase of lunch. Offer good thru 1988.

You are cordially invited to Bonanza Gift Gallery, 312 West Miner Street, Yreka, CA to receive a 10% discount on any item not on sale. Offer good thru 1988.

You are cordially invited to Boston Shaft, 1801 Fort Jones Road, Yreka, CA to receive a free drink of your choice. Offer good thru June 1988.

You are cordially invited to Nature's Kitchen, 412 South Main Street, Yreka, CA for a free cup of coffee of tea with your purchase of lunch. Offer good thru 1988.

You are cordially invited to Don's Sporting Goods, 321 West Miner Street, Yreka, CA to receive a free pair of boot socks with a purchase of Danner or Browning boots. Offer good thru 1988.

INDEX

812

813

ABOUT THE AUTHOR

A Northern California resident since early childhood, Tom Baker has traveled extensively throughout the state. A keen interest in California history and a deep appreciation for its natural wonders makes him an ardent Californian.

Tom is the former editor for the California State Poetry Quarterly, and has published poetry, reviews and interviews in numerous periodicals.

A graduate from the San Jose State University with a B.A. in Speech-Communication, his interest include photography, collecting and outdoor activities.

Tom began with Gable & Gray as manager for the Northern California Best Choices Bay Area Edition. He has since become the General Manager for the state and oversees production of six books currently being compiled.

A LETTER TO THE READER:

The staff of Gable & Gray want to take this time to thank you for purchasing this book. We hope the book contributed substantially to your enjoyment of the area.

In our never ending quest to better our product, we ask you, the visitor, to help us.....if in your travels you encounter a service or business establishment you feel should be a "Best Choice," then please take the time to write us a note.

If your "Best Choice" is interviewed and selected for our next edition, we will ship you one of our books as our way of saying, "Thank You." Simply include the name of the book you choose in your letter.